The Disability Studies Reader

The Disability Studies Reader

EDITED BY

LENNARD J. DAVIS

ROUTLEDGE

New York and London

Published in 1997 by

Routledge
29 West 35th Street
New York, NY 10001

Published in Great Britain in 1997 by

Routledge
11 New Fetter Lane
London EC4P 4EE

Printed in the United States of America
Design: Jack Donner

Library of Congress Cataloging-in-Publication Data

Davis, Lennard J., 1949–
The disability studies reader / Lennard J. Davis
p.   cm.
Includes bibliographical references and index.
ISBN 0–415–91470–1 (hb). — ISBN 0–415–91471–X (pb)
1.   Handicapped.   2. Sociology of Disability.   I. Title.
HV1568.D34   1997
362.4—dc20   96–30187
CIP

Contents

Chapter 3 (pp. 110–22), aproximately 2,945 words) from "Aids and Its Metaphors" in *Illness as Metaphor; AIDS and its Metaphors* by Susan Sontag (Penguin Books, 1989) copyright (c) Susan Sontag, 1988, 1989. Reproduced by permission of Penguin Books Ltd.

Chapter 13 reprinted by permission of Rutgers University Press from *Women With Disabilities*. Michelle Fine and Adrienne Asch, eds. Pp. 13–29. Philadelphia, PA: Temple University Press. Copyright 1988 by Temple University.

Chapter 14 reprinted by permission of Susan Wendell from "Towards a Feminist Theory of Disability" in *Hupatia* 4:2 (Summer 1989), pp. 104–122. Copyright 1989 by Susan Wendell.

Chapters 16, 17 both reprinted by permission of *Radical Teacher Magazine* from Dirksen Bauman and Jennifer Drake,"'Silence Is Not Without a Voice': Including Deaf Culture Within Multicultural Curricula" in *Radical Teacher* 47 (Fall 1995). Copyright 1995 by *Radical Teacher*.

Chapter 19 reprinted by permission of David Hevey from David Hevey, *The Creatures Time Forgot: Photography and Disability Imagery*. New York and London: Routledge. Pp. 53–74. Copyright 1992 by David Hevey.

Chapter 22 reprinted by permission of Nicholas Mirzoeff from *Bodyscape: Art, Modernity and the Ideal Figure*. London and New York: Routledge: pp. 37–57. Copyright 1995 by Nicholas Mirzoeff.

"Excavation" and "Love Poem" copyright 1991 by Kenny Fries. Reprinted by permission of the author.

"I am not One of The" and "Cripple Lullabye" reprinted by permission of Cheryl Marie Wade from *Radical Teacher* 47 (Fall 1995).

"Sex and the Single Gimp" reprinted by permission of Billy Golfus from *Mouth* 5:1 (May/June 1994), pp. 4–10. Copyright 1994 by Billy Golfus.

Acknowledgments

Chapters 1 and 5 reprinted by permission of Lennard J. Davis, *Enforcing Normalcy: Disability, Deafness, and the Body*: pp. 23–72. New York and London: Verso. Copyright 1995 by Verso.

Chapter 4 reprinted by permission of the publisher, from Margaret A. Winzer, *The History of Special Education: From Isolation to Integration* (1993): 6–37. Washington, D.C.: Gallaudet University Press. Copyright 1993 by Gallaudet University.

Chapter 6 reprinted by permission from Johns Hopkins University Press from Douglas Baynton, "A Silent Exile on This Earth: Metaphorical Construction of Deafness in the Nineteenth Century" in *American Quarterly* 44: 2 (June 1992): pp. 216–243. Copyright 1992 by Johns Hopkins University Press.

Chapter 7 reprinted by permission of Carfax Publishing Company, from Harlan Lane, "Constructions of Deafness" in *Disability and Society* 10: 2 (1995): pp. 171–189. Copyright 1995 by Carfax Publishing Company.

Chapter 8 reprinted by permission of the author from Harlan Hahn, "Advertising the Acceptably Employable Image: Disability and Capitalism" in *Policy Studies Journal* 15: 3 (March 1987): pp.551–570. Copyright 1987 by Harlan Hahn.

Chapter 9 reprinted from Ruth Hubbard, *The Politics of Women's Biology*, copyright © 1990 by Rutgers, The State University. Reprinted by permission of Rutgers University Press.

Chapter 10 reprinted with the permission of Simon & Shuster from *Stigma* by Erving Goffman. Copyright © 1963 by Prentice Hall Inc. Renewed 1991.

Chapter 11 reprinted by permission of Plenum Publishinng Corporation from Lerita M. Coleman, "Stigma: An Enigma Demystified" in S. Ainlay, G. Becker, and L. M. Coleman, eds., *A Multidisciplinary View of Stigma*: pp. 211–234. New York: Plenum. Copyright 1986 by Plenum Publishing Corporation.

Chapter 12 reprinted by permission of Farrar, Straus & Giroux, Inc: Excerpts from *Aids and Its Metaphors* by Susan Sontag. Copyright © 1988, 1989 by Susan Sontag.

Introduction

This reader is one of the first devoted to disability studies. But it will not be the last. Disability studies is a field of study whose time has come. For centuries, people with disabilities have been an oppressed and repressed group. People with disabilities have been isolated, incarcerated, observed, written about, operated on, instructed, implanted, regulated, treated, institutionalized, and controlled to a degree probably unequal to that experienced by any other minority group. As fifteen percent of the population, people with disabilities make up the largest physical minority within the United States. One would never know this to be the case by looking at the literature on minorities and discrimination.

Now the impetus to recognize the level of oppression, both overt and by marginalization, is being organized by people with disabilities and other interested parties. The exciting thing about disability studies is that it is both an academic field of inquiry and an area of political activity. The act of assembling a body of knowledge owned by the disability community as opposed to one written about that community by "normals" is part of an ongoing process that includes political actions involving the classroom, the workplace, the courts, the legislature, the media, and so on.

So, this reader appears at the moment that disability, always an actively repressed *memento mori* for the fate of the normal body, gains a new, nonmedicalized, and positive legitimacy both as an academic discipline and as an area of political struggle. As with any new discourse, disability studies must claim space in a contested area, trace its continuities and discontinuities, argue for its existence, and justify its assertions.

To do this, the case must be made clear that studies about disability have not had historically the visibility of studies about race, class, or gender for complex as well as simple reasons. The simple reason is the general pervasiveness of discrimination and prejudice against people with disabilities leading to their marginalization as well as the marginalization of the study of disability. Progressives in and out of academia may pride themselves on being sensitive to race or gender, but they have been "ableist" in dealing with the issue of disability. While race, for example, has become in the past twenty years a more than acceptable modality from which to theorize in the classroom and in print, a discourse, a critique, and a political struggle, disability has continued to be relegated to hospital hall-

ways, physical therapy tables, and remedial classrooms. The civil rights movement, a long history of discussion of the issues around slavery, the attention
demanded by the "problem" of inner cities, and governmental discrimination
have created a consciousness among progressives that legitimizes ethnicity as a
topic for cultural study. It is possible to have a Henry Louis Gates or a bell hooks
in a literature faculty, but it has been virtually impossible to have a person teaching about disability within the humanities. No announcements of jobs in the area
of disability studies yet appear in the professional journals of English, history, or
philosophy. In other words, disability has been seen as eccentric, therapeutically
oriented, out-of-the-mainstream, and certainly not representative of the human
condition—not as race, class, or gender seem representative of that condition.

But, how strange this assumption. What is more representative of the human
condition than the body and its vicissitudes? If the population of people with disabilities is between thirty-five and forty-three million, then this group is the
largest physical minority in the United States. Put another way, there are more
people with disabilities than there are African-Americans or Latinos.[1] But why
have the disabled been rendered more invisible than other groups? Why are not
issues about perception, mobility, accessibility, distribution of bio-resources,
physical space, difference not seen as central to the human condition? Is there
not something to be gained by all people from exploring the ways that the body
in its variations is metaphorized, disbursed, promulgated, commodified,
cathected, and de-cathected, normalized, abnormalized, formed, and deformed?
In other words, is it not time for disability studies to emerge as an aspect of cultural studies, studies in discrimination and oppression, postmodern analyses of
the body and bio-power?

The first assumption that has to be countered in arguing for disability studies
is that the "normal" or "able" person is already fully up to speed on the subject.
My experience is that while most "normals" think they understand the issue of
disability, they in fact do not. When it comes to disability, "normal"[2] people are
quite willing to volunteer solutions, present anecdotes, recall from a vast array
of films instances they take for fact. No one would dare to make such a leap into
Heideggerian philosophy for example or the art of the Renaissance. But disability seems so obvious—a missing limb, blindness, deafness. What could be simpler to understand? One simply has to imagine the loss of the limb, the absent
sense, and one is half-way there. Just the addition of a liberal dose of sympathy
and pity along with a generous acceptance of ramps and voice-synthesized com-
puters allows the average person to speak with knowledge on the subject.

But disability studies, like any other discourse, requires a base of knowledge
and a familiarity with discursive terms and methodologies, as well as, most often,
some personal involvement. The apparent ease of intuitive knowledge is really
another aspect of discrimination against people with disabilities. How could
there be anything complex, intellectually interesting, or politically relevant
about a missing limb or a chronic impairment? Pity or empathy do not lend
themselves to philosophy, philology, or theoretical considerations in general.

But, far from pity or empathy, people working in the field of disability are articulating and theorizing a political, social, and ideological critique. The work contained in this reader, only a sampling of the many articles and books published on the subject, is representative of this growing specialization as it spans the human sciences—literary studies, art history, anthropology, sociology, postcolonial studies, theory, feminist studies, and so on. But be aware: this book is not a collection of articles about how people *feel* about disability; nor is it designed to "sensitize" normal readers to the issue of disability; nor is it a collection of pieces focussing on the theme of disability in literature, film, or television. Rather, this is a reader that places disability in a political, social, and cultural context, that theorizes and historicizes deafness or blindness or disability in similarly complex ways to the way race, class, and gender have been theorized.

It is not as if disability studies has simply appeared out of someone's head at this historical moment. It would be more appropriate to say that disability studies has been in the making for many years, but, like people with disabilities, has only recently recognized itself as a political, discursive entity. Indeed, like the appearance of African-American studies following rapidly on the heels of the civil rights movement, there is a reciprocal connection between political praxis by people with disabilities and the formation of a discursive category of disability studies. That is, there have been people with disabilities throughout history, but it has only been in the last twenty years that one-armed people, quadriplegics, the blind, people with chronic diseases, and so on, have seen themselves as a single, allied, united physical minority.[3] Linked to this political movement, which is detailed in Joseph Shapiro's *No Pity*, David Hevey's *Creatures Time Forgot*, and Oliver Sacks' *Seeing Voices*, among other works, has been the political victory of the passage of the Americans with Disabilities Act (ADA) of 1990, which guarantees the civil rights of people with disabilities.[4]

Disability studies, as did cultural studies, unites a variety of ongoing work. That this work was largely hidden from view is a telling fact. If one looks up "disability" or "disability studies" in a database or library catalogue, one will find slim pickings, particularly if the areas of medical treatment, hospital or institutional management, and out-patient treatment are eliminated. The reason for this dearth of reference is complex. First, there is the historical absence of a discursive category. When I tried to locate a copy of my recent book *Enforcing Normalcy: Disability, Deafness, and the Body* in a university bookstore, I was told to look under "self help." Currently, there is no area in a bookstore where works on disability studies can be placed. This absence of a discursive category was more tellingly revealed at a meeting of the Committee on Academics with Disabilities at the Modern Language Association headquarters. A bibliographer of the *MLA Bibliography* informed the committee that there was almost no way of retrieving articles or books on the cultural history of disability since proper categories did not exist. For example, an article on "crippled saints" could not be searched by computer because the word "crippled" was disallowed by MLA regulations as constituting discriminatory language. The bibliographer therefore filed the article under "saints" thus rendering it unretrievable by anyone with an interest in disability.[5] Further, until now, American Sign Language was listed in the data base as an "invented langugae" along with the language of the Klingons of *Star Trek*. Thanks to the efforts of activists, this categorization will no longer be the case and American sign language will be listed as a legitimate language. This absence of a discursive category is as much as function of discrimination and marginalization as anything else. If one had tried to find the category "composers, female" in music history thirty years ago, there would have been no such category. The category of "African-American literature" would not have existed. In the late 1990s disability studies has been "disappeared." As of 1997, the MLA is redressing this absence in its database.

The absence of categories is only one reason that disability studies has been suppressed. The second reason is the erasure of disability as a category when other "stronger" categories are present. So, unless a writer, artist, or filmmaker is known for his or her disability, as was Beethoven or Helen Keller, they are not thought of as a person with disabilities. Therefore, their work is not included in any canon of cultural production. How outrageous this is can be understood if we made the analogy with the suppression of the gender, color, race, ethnicity, or nationality of a writer. How many people realize that included in the category of people with disabilities are: John Milton, Sir Joshua Reynolds, Alexander Pope, Harriet Martineau, John Keats, George Gordon Byron, Toulouse-Lautrec, James Joyce, Virginia Woolf, James Thurber, Dorothea Lange, José Luis Borges, John Ford, Raoul Walsh, André de Toth, Nicholas Ray, Tay Garnett, William Wyler, Chuck Close, and many others? Moreover, the work of many talented writers, artists, photographers and so on who were disabled have had their work minimalized or suppressed in the same way that people of color or women have experienced. The recovery of this work is only now beginning.[6]

The work of many scholars who have investigated aspects of the body is now being reassembled into the field of disability studies. So for example, Sander Gilman's work on disease, David Rothman on asylums, Erving Goffman on stigma, Leslie Fieldler on freaks, Susan Sontag on the metaphors of illness, Mikhail Bakhtin on the grotesque, followed by postmodern work like Michel Foucault on disease, mental illness, and sexuality, Jacques Derrida on blindness, Kaja Silverman on deformity in film, Judith Butler and Susan Bordo on anorexia—all of these works might not have been seen as existing under the rubric of disability studies, but as the field evolves, it recuperates and includes this earlier work as a retrospectively organized set of originating documents much in the way that structuralism turned back to the work of Saussure or that Marx relied on Hegel.

While this historical reserve of writings on disease, the body, freakishness and so on exists, the work of a newer generation of writers and scholars looks toward feminist, Marxist, postmodern, and cultural studies models for understanding the relation between the body and power. This next generation of writing tends to be created from within the boundaries of disability. While many earlier writers had an anthropological approach, with the weakness and imperial quality of anthropological work, others wrote from the perspective of "having" a disability. That type of work tended to be written so that "normal" people might know what it is like to be blind, crippled, deaf, and so on. The danger of that kind of project is that it is embarked on with the aim of evoking "sympathy" or "understanding." The dialectical relation of power involved in such a transaction ultimately ends up having the writing be *for* the "normal." The inappropriateness of such "sensitizing" work can be seen in works written, for example, to whites explaining what it is like to be black or to men explaining what it is like to be female. Disability studies, for the most part, shuns this unequal power transaction in favor of advocacy, investigation, inquiry, archeology, genealogy, dialectic, and deconstruction. The model of a sovereign subject revealing or reveling in that subjectivity is put into question.

In this anthology, scholars discuss the construction of disability in ancient Greece, in the English Renaissance and Enlightenment, in nineteenth century France, as well as the creation of the concept of "normalcy" in nineteenth and twentieth century Europe and America. This work is reflective of the new historical revisionism allowed by the introduction of the concept of disability into practices of Marxist, feminist, queer, ethnic, postcolonial, and postmodern criticism. Previous work on the body can now be amplified and expanded. In addition, works that theorize disability and Deafness look at the notion of difference as an opportunity to defamiliarize received truths about culture and the body. I have also reprinted some fiction and poetry. This literary work is not here to "sensitize" readers but to explore the richness of experience and creativity offered by the opportunity of disability. The writers are aggressive about their insight, not defensive. They have a constitutive experience of disability and use that knowledge within their aesthetic ability. But these works should not be ghettoized as "disability literature" any more than T. S. Eliot should be used as an example of able-bodied writing.

In assembling this reader, I have selected only some material and some representative impairments, but much more work is being done and needs to be done in this major project of reconceiving history through the lens of disability studies. Many will find their impairments missing. I can only plead limited resources, limited space, and probably limited imagination.

A fair number of articles deal with deafness. The reason for this focus is twofold: 1) personal interest and 2) the rather large body of historical materials on the history of deafness. My apologies to whomever does not find this field of inquiry interesting. This reader is only a beginning, the thin edge of a wedge which will change the normative way we conceive of the world, of literature, of cultural production, of voice, of sight, of language. In its broadest application, disability studies aims to challenge the received in its most simple form—the body—and in its most complex form—the construction of the body. Since we can no longer essentialize the body, we can no longer essentialize its differences, its eccentricities, its transgressions. Perhaps disability studies will lead to some grand unified theory of the body, pulling together the differences implied in gender, nationality, ethnicity, race, and sexual preferences. Then, rather than the marginalized being in the wheelchair or using sign language, the person with disabilities will become the ultimate example, the universal image, the modality through whose knowing the postmodern subject can theorize and act.

NOTES

1. African-Americans make up 11.8 percent of the U. S. population. Latinos comprise 9.5 percent, and Asians are 3.1 percent of the general population (U. S. Census Bureau statistics cited in the *New York Times* (March 25, 1996; A15).

2. I will refrain from putting "normal" in quotation marks henceforth, but I do so as long as readers will recall that I am always using this term with the complex set of ironies and historic specificities the term carries. I will assume, perhaps problematically, an agreement on the fact that not one of us is, or can be, normal, nor can anyone describe what a normal person is.

3. I have deliberately left the Deaf off of this list. (I use the capitalized term to indicate the culturally Deaf, as opposed to the simple fact of physical deafness.) The reason is that many Deaf do not consider themselves people with disabilities but rather members of a linguistic minority. The Deaf argue that their difference is actually a communication difference—they speak sign language—and that their problems do not exist in a Deaf, signing community, whereas a group of legless people will not transcend their motor impairments when they become part of a legless community. The argument is a serious one, and, although I personally feel that the Deaf have much to gain by joining forces with people with disabilities, I honor the Deaf argument in this reader. See Harlan Lane's article "Construction of Deafness" (in this volume).

4. This victory is in some sense a pyrrhic one since the letter of law is easier to manifest than the spirit, and so the number of people with disabilities who are unemployed, for example, remains as high if not higher than before the Act was passed. (*New York Times* October 23, 1994 A: 22) In addition, the Act has no enforcement mechanism or agency, so it relies on individuals bringing lawsuits on their own—a method that for most people with disabilities is not a practical remedy. Most recently, the budget and tax cuts of 1994–96 have sliced dramatically into entitlements for special education, home-care, and many of the other programs that people with disabilities rely on to provide access and support.

5. The MLA is now beginning to redress this problem. Presumably, other databases and catalogues will follow suit.

6. Work that does this recovery includes Nicholas Mirzoeff, *Silent Poetry: Deafness, Sign, and Visual Culture in Modern France*, Martin Nordern, *Cinema of Isolation: A History of Physical Disability in the Movies*, and various articles and books by John S. Schuchman.

part one

Historical Perspectives

1

Constructing Normalcy

The Bell Curve, the Novel, and the Invention
of the Disabled Body in the Nineteenth Century

LENNARD J. DAVIS

If such a thing as a psycho-analysis of today's prototypical culture were possible . . . such an investigation would needs show the sickness proper to the time to consist precisely in normality.

—Theodore Adorno, Minima Moralia

We live in a world of norms. Each of us endeavors to be normal or else deliberately tries to avoid that state. We consider what the average person does, thinks, earns, or consumes. We rank our intelligence, our cholesterol level, our weight, height, sex drive, bodily dimensions along some conceptual line from subnormal to above-average. We consume a minimum daily balance of vitamins and nutrients based on what an average human should consume. Our children are ranked in school and tested to determine where they fit into a normal curve of learning, of intelligence. Doctors measure and weigh them to see if they are above or below average on the height and weight curves. There is probably no area of contemporary life in which some idea of a norm, mean, or average has not been calculated.

To understand the disabled body, one must return to the concept of the norm, the normal body. So much of writing about disability has focused on the disabled person as the object of study, just as the study of race has focused on the person of color. But as with recent scholarship on race, which has turned its attention to whiteness, I would like to focus not so much on the construction of disability as on the construction of normalcy. I do this because the "problem" is not the person with disabilities; the problem is the way that normalcy is constructed to create the "problem" of the disabled person.

A common assumption would be that some concept of the norm must have always existed. After all, people seem to have an inherent desire to compare themselves to others. But the idea of a norm is less a condition of human nature than it is a feature of a certain kind of society. Recent work on the ancient Greeks, on preindustrial Europe, and on tribal peoples, for example, shows that disability was once regarded very differently from the way it is now. As we will see, the social process of disabling arrived with industrialization and with the set of practices and discourses that are linked to late eighteenth- and nineteenth-century notions of nationality, race, gender, criminality, sexual orientation, and so on.

I begin with the rather remarkable fact that the constellation of words describing this concept "normal," "normalcy," "normality," "norm," "average," "abnormal"—all entered the European languages rather late in human history. The word "normal" as "constituting, conforming to, not deviating or different from, the common type or standard, regular, usual" only enters the English language around 1840. (Previously, the word had meant "perpendicular"; the carpenter's square, called a "norm," provided the root meaning.) Likewise, the word "norm," in the modern sense, has only been in use since around 1855, and "normality" and "normalcy" appeared in 1849 and 1857, respectively. If the lexicographical information is relevant, it is possible to date the coming into consciousness in English of an idea of "the norm" over the period 1840–1860.

If we rethink our assumptions about the universality of the concept of the norm, what we might arrive at is the concept that preceded it: that of the "ideal," a word we find dating from the seventeenth century. Without making too simplistic a division in the historical chronotope, one can nevertheless try to imagine a world in which the hegemony of normalcy does not exist. Rather, what we have is the ideal body, as exemplified in the tradition of nude Venuses, for example. This idea presents a mytho-poetic body that is linked to that of the gods (in traditions in which the god's body is visualized). This divine body, then, this ideal body, is not attainable by a human. The notion of an ideal implies that, in this case, the human body as visualized in art or imagination must be composed from the ideal parts of living models. These models individually can never embody the ideal since an ideal, by definition, can never be found in this world. When ideal human bodies occur, they do so in mythology. So Venus or Helen of Troy, for example, would be the embodiment of female physical beauty.

The painting by François-André Vincent *Zeuxis Choosing as Models the Most Beautiful Girls of the Town of Crotona* (1789, Museum de Louvre, Paris) shows the Greek artist, as we are told by Pliny, lining up all the beautiful women of Crotona in order to select in each her ideal feature or body part and combine these into the ideal figure of Aphrodite, herself an ideal of beauty. One young woman provides a face and another her breasts. Classical painting and sculpture tend to idealize the body, evening out any particularity. The central point here is that in a culture with an ideal form of the body, all members of the population are below the ideal. No one young lady of Crotona can be the ideal. By definition, one can never have an ideal body. There is in such societies no demand that populations have bodies that conform to the ideal.

By contrast, the *grotesque* as a visual form was inversely related to the concept of the ideal and its corollary that all bodies are in some sense disabled. In that mode, the grotesque is a signifier of the people, of common life. As Bakhtin, Stallybrass and White, and others have shown, the use of the grotesque had a life-affirming transgressive quality in its inversion of the political hierarchy. However, the grotesque was not equivalent to the disabled, since, for example, it is impossible to think of people with disabilities now being used as architectural decorations as the grotesque were on the façades of cathedrals throughout Europe. The grotesque permeated culture and signified common humanity, whereas the disabled body, a later concept, was formulated as by definition excluded from culture, society, the norm.

If the concept of the norm or average enters European culture, or at least the European languages, only in the nineteenth century, one has to ask what is the cause of this conceptualization? One of the logical places to turn in trying to understand concepts like "norm" and "average" is that branch of knowledge known as statistics. Statistics begins in the early modern period as "political arithmetic'—a use of data for "promotion of sound, well-informed state policy" (Porter 1986, 18). The word *statistik* was first used in 1749 by Gottfried Achenwall, in the context of compiling information about the state. The concept migrated somewhat from the state to the body when Bisset Hawkins defined medical statistics in 1829 as "the application of numbers to illustrate the natural history of health and disease" (cited in Porter, 1986, 24). In France, statistics were mainly used in the area of public health in the early nineteenth century. The connection between the body and industry is tellingly revealed in the fact that the leading members of the first British statistical societies formed in the 1830s and 1840s were industrialists or had close ties to industry (ibid., 32).

It was the French statistician Adolphe Quetelet (1796–1847) who contributed the most to a generalized notion of the normal as an imperative. He noticed that the "law of error," used by astronomers to locate a star by plotting all the sightings and then averaging the errors, could be equally applied to the distribution of human features such as height and weight. He then took a further step of formulating the concept of "l'homme moyen" or the average man. Quetelet maintained that this abstract human was the average of all human attributes in a given country. For the average man, Quetelet wrote in 1835, "all things will occur in conformity with the mean results obtained for a society. If one seeks to establish, in some way, the basis of a social physics, it is he whom one should consider . . ." (cited in ibid., 53). Quetelet's average man was a combination of *l'homme moyen physique* and *l'homme moyen morale*, both a physically average and a morally average construct.

The social implications of this idea are central. In formulating the idea of *l'homme moyen*, Quetelet is also providing a justification for *les classes moyens*. With bourgeois hegemony comes scientific justification for moderation and middle-class ideology. The average man, the body of the man in the middle, becomes the exemplar of the middle way of life. Quetelet was apparently influenced by the philosopher Victor Cousin in developing an analogy between the notion of an average man and the *juste milieu*. This term was associated with Louis Philippe's July monarchy—a concept that melded bourgeois hegemony with the constitutional monarchy and celebrated moderation and middleness (ibid, 101). In England too, the middle class as the middle way or mean had been searching for a scientific justification. The statement in *Robinson Crusoe* in which Robinson's father extols middle-class life as a kind of norm is a good example of this ideology:

the middle Station had the fewest Disasters, and was not expos'd to so many Vicissitudes as the higher or lower Part of Mankind; nay, they were not subjected to so
many Distempers and Uneasiness either of Body or Mind, as those were who, by
vicious Living, Luxury and Extravagancies on one Hand, or by hard Labour, Want
of Necessaries, and mean or insufficient Diet on the other Hand, bring Distempers
upon themselves by the natural consequences of their Way of Living; That the middle
Station of Life was calculated for all kinds of Vertues and all kinds of Enjoyments; that
Peace and Plenty were the Hand-maids of a middle Fortune; that Temperance, Moderation, Quietness, Health, Society, all agreeable Diversions, and all desirable Pleasures, were the Blessings attending the middle Station of Life. (Defoe 1975, 6)

Statements of ideology of this kind saw the bourgeoisie as rationally placed in the
mean position in the great order of things. This ideology can be seen as developing the kind of science that would then justify the notion of a norm.[1]

    With such thinking, the average then becomes paradoxically a kind of ideal,
a position devoutly to be wished. As Quetelet wrote, "an individual who epitomized in himself, at a given time, all the qualities of the average man, would represent at once all the greatness, beauty and goodness of that being" (cited in
Porter 1986, 102). Such an average person might indeed be a literary character
like Robinson Crusoe. Furthermore, one must observe that Quetelet meant this
hegemony of the middle to apply not only to moral qualities but to the body as
well. He wrote: "deviations more or less great from the mean have constituted
[for artists] ugliness in body as well as vice in morals and a state of sickness with
regard to the constitution" (ibid., 103). Here Zeuxis's notion of physical beauty
as an exceptional ideal becomes transformed into beauty as the average.

    Quetelet foresaw a kind of Utopia of the norm associated with progress, just
as Marx foresaw a Utopia of the norm in so far as wealth and production is concerned.

    one of the principal acts of civilization is to compress more and more the limits
    within which the different elements relative to man oscillate. The more that
    enlightenment is propagated, the more will deviations from the mean diminish. . . .
    The perfectibility of the human species is derived as a necessary consequence of all
    our investigations. Defects and monstrosities disappear more and more from the
    body. (ibid., 104)

This concept of the average, as applied to the concept of the human, was used
not only by statisticians but even by the likes of Marx. Marx actually cites
Quetelet's notion of the average man in a discussion of the labor theory of value.
We can see in retrospect that one of the most powerful ideas of Marx—the
notion of labor value or average wages—in many ways is based on the idea of the
worker constructed as an average worker. As Marx writes:

    Any average magnitude, however, is merely the average of a number of separate
    magnitudes all of one kind, but differing as to quantity. In every industry, each

individual labourer, be he Peter or Paul, differs from the average labourer. These individual differences, or "errors" as they are called in mathematics, compensate one another and vanish, whenever a certain minimum number of workmen are employed together. (Marx 1970, 323)

So for Marx one can divide the collective work day of a large number of work- ers and come up with "one day of average social labor" (ibid, 323). As Quetelet had come up with an average man, so Marx postulates an average worker, and from that draws conclusions about the relationship between an average and the extremes of wealth and poverty that are found in society. Thus Marx develops his crucial concept of "abstract labor.'

We tend not to think of progressives like Marx as tied up with a movement led by businessmen, but it is equally true that Marx is unimaginable without a tendency to contemplate average humans and think about their abstract relation to work, wages, and so on. In this sense, Marx is very much in step with the movement of normalizing the body and the individual. In addition, Marxist thought encourages us toward an enforcing of normalcy in the sense that the deviations in society, in terms of the distribution of wealth for example, must be minimized.

The concept of a norm, unlike that of an ideal, implies that the majority of the population must or should somehow be part of the norm. The norm pins down that majority of the population that falls under the arch of the standard bell-shaped curve. This curve, the graph of an exponential function, that was known variously as the astronomer's "error law," the "normal distribution," the "Gaussian density function," or simply "the bell curve," became in its own way a symbol of the tyranny of the norm (see Figure 1). Any bell curve will always have at its extremities those characteristics that deviate from the norm. So, with the concept of the norm comes the concept of deviations or extremes. When we think of bodies, in a society where the concept of the norm is operative, then people with disabilities will be thought of as deviants. This, as we have seen, is in contrast to societies with the concept of an ideal, in which all people have a non-ideal status.[2]

In England, there was an official and unofficial burst of interest in statistics during the 1830s. A statistical office was set up at the Board of Trade in 1832, and the General Register Office was created in 1837 to collect vital statistics. All of this interest in numbers concerning the state was a consequence of the Reform Act of 1832, the Factory Act of 1833, and the Poor Law of 1834. The country was being monitored and the poor were being surveiled. Private groups followed, and in 1833 a statistical section of the British Association for the Advancement of Science was formed in which Quetelet as well as Malthus par- ticipated. In the following year Malthus, Charles Babbage, and others founded the Statistical Society of London. The Royal London Statistical Society was founded in 1835.

The use of statistics began an important movement, and there is a telling con- nection for the purposes of this book between the founders of statistics and their

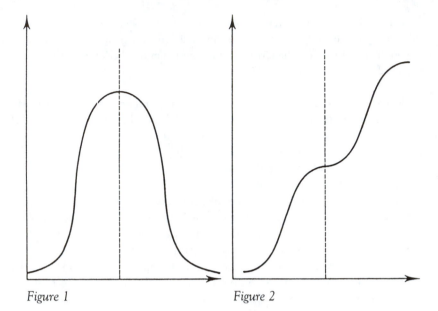

Figure 1   Figure 2

larger intentions. The rather amazing fact is that almost all the early statisticians had one thing in common: they were eugenicists. The same is true of key figures in the movement: Sir Francis Galton, Karl Pearson, and R. A. Fisher.[3] While this coincidence seems almost too striking to be true, we must remember that there is a real connection between figuring the statistical measure of humans and then hoping to improve humans so that deviations from the norm diminish—as someone like Quetelet had suggested. Statistics is bound up with eugenics because the central insight of statistics is the idea that a population can be normed. An important consequence of the idea of the norm is that it divides the total population into standard and nonstandard subpopulations. The next step in conceiving of the population as norm and non-norm is for the state to attempt to norm the nonstandard—the aim of eugenics. Of course such an activity is profoundly paradoxical since the inviolable rule of statistics is that all phenomena will always conform to a bell curve. So norming the non-normal is an activity as problematic as untying the Gordian knot.

MacKenzie asserts that it is not so much that Galton's statistics made possible eugenics but rather that "the needs of eugenics in large part determined the content of Galton's statistical theory" (1981, 52). In any case, a symbiotic relationship exists between statistical science and eugenic concerns. Both bring into society the concept of a norm, particularly a normal body, and thus in effect create the concept of the disabled body.

It is also worth noting the interesting triangulation of eugenicist interests. On the one hand Sir Francis Galton was cousin to Charles Darwin, whose notion of the evolutionary advantage of the fittest lays the foundation for eugenics and also for the idea of a perfectible body undergoing progressive improvement. As one scholar has put it, "Eugenics was in reality applied biology based on the central biological theory of the day, namely the Darwinian theory of evolution" (Farrall 1985, 55). Darwin's ideas serve to place disabled people along the wayside as evolutionary defectives to be surpassed by natural selection. So, eugenics became obsessed with the elimination of "defectives," a category which included the "feebleminded," the deaf, the blind, the physically defective, and so on.

In a related discourse, Galton created the modern system of fingerprinting for personal identification. Galton's interest came out of a desire to show that certain physical traits could be inherited. As he wrote:

> one of the inducements to making these inquiries into personal identification has been to discover independent features suitable for hereditary investigation. . . . it is not improbable, and worth taking pains to inquire whether each person may not carry visibly about his body undeniable evidence of his parentage and near kinships. (cited in MacKenzie 1981, 65)

Fingerprinting was seen as a physical mark of parentage, a kind of serial number written on the body. But further, one can say that the notion of fingerprinting pushes forward the idea that the human body is standardized and contains a serial number, as it were, embedded in its corporeality. (Later technological innovations will reveal this fingerprint to be embedded at the genetic level.) Thus the body has an identity that coincides with its essence and cannot be altered by moral, artistic, or human will. This indelibility of corporeal identity only furthers the mark placed on the body by other physical qualities—intelligence, height, reaction time. By this logic, the person enters into an identical relationship with the body, the body forms the identity, and the identity is unchangeable and indelible as one's place on the normal curve. For our purposes, then, this fingerprinting of the body means that the marks of physical difference become synonymous with the identity of the person.

Finally, Galton is linked to that major figure connected with the discourse of disability in the nineteenth century—Alexander Graham Bell. In 1883, the same year that the term "eugenics" was coined by Galton, Bell delivered his eugenicist speech *Memoir upon the Formation of a Deaf Variety of the Human Race*, warning of the "tendency among deaf-mutes to select deaf-mutes as their partners in marriage" (1969, 19) with the dire consequence that a race of deaf people might be created. This echoing of Dr. Frankenstein's fear that his monster might mate and produce a race of monsters emphasizes the terror with which the "normal" beholds the differently abled.[4] Noting how the various interests come together in Galton, we can see evolution, fingerprinting, and the attempt to control the reproductive rights of the deaf as all pointing to a conception of the body as perfectible but only when subject to the necessary control of the eugenicists. The identity of people becomes defined by irrepressible identificatory physical qualities that can be measured. Deviance from the norm can be identified and indeed criminalized, particularly in the sense that fingerprints came to be associated with identifying deviants who wished to hide their identities.

Galton made significant changes in statistical theory that created the concept of the norm. He took what had been called "error theory," a technique by which astronomers attempted to show that one could locate a star by taking into account the variety of sightings. The sightings, all of which could not be correct, if plotted would fall into a bell curve, with most sightings falling into the center, that is to say, the correct location of the star. The errors would fall to the sides of the bell curve. Galton's contribution to statistics was to change the name of the curve from "the law of frequency of error" or "error curve," the term used by Quetelet, to the "normal distribution" curve (see Figure 1).

The significance of these changes relates directly to Galton's eugenicist interests. In an "error curve" the extremes of the curve are the most mistaken in accuracy. But if one is looking at human traits, then the extremes, particularly what Galton saw as positive extremes—tallness, high intelligence, ambitiousness, strength, fertility—would have to be seen as errors. Rather than "errors" Galton wanted to think of the extremes as distributions of a trait. As MacKenzie notes:

> Thus there was a gradual transition from use of the term "probable error" to the term "standard deviation" (which is free of the implication that a deviation is in any sense an error), and from the term "law of error" to the term "normal distribution." (1981, 59)

But even without the idea of error, Galton still faced the problem that in a normal distribution curve that graphed height, for example, both tallness and shortness would be seen as extremes in a continuum where average stature would be the norm. The problem for Galton was that, given his desire to perfect the human race, or at least its British segment, tallness was preferable to shortness. How could both extremes be considered equally deviant from the norm? So Galton substituted the idea of ranking for the concept of averaging. That is, he changed the way one might look at the curve from one that used the mean to one that used the median—a significant change in thinking eugenically.

If a strait, say intelligence, is considered by its average, then the majority of people would determine what intelligence should be—and intelligence would be defined by the mediocre middle. Galton, wanting to avoid the middling of desired traits, would prefer to think of intelligence in ranked order. Although high intelligence in a normal distribution would simply be an extreme, under a ranked system it would become the highest ranked trait. Galton divided his curve into quartiles, so that he was able to emphasize ranked orders of intelligence, as we would say that someone was in the first quartile in intelligence (low intelligence) or the fourth quartile (high intelligence). Galton's work led directly to current "intelligence quotient" (IQ) and scholastic achievement tests. In fact, Galton revised Gauss's bell curve to show the superiority of the desired trait (for example, high intelligence). He created what he called an "ogive" (see Figure 2), which is arranged in quartiles with an ascending curve that features the desired trait as "higher" than the undesirable deviation. As Stigler notes:

If a hundred individuals' talents were ordered, each could be assigned the numer-
ical value corresponding to its percentile in the curve of "deviations from an average": the middlemost (or median) talent had value 0 (representing mediocrity), an
individual at the upper quartile was assigned the value 1 (representing one probable error above mediocrity), and so on. (1986, 271)

What these revisions by Galton signify is an attempt to redefine the concept
of the "ideal" in relation to the general population. First, the application of the
idea of a norm to the human body creates the idea of deviance or a "deviant"
body. Second, the idea of a norm pushes the normal variation of the body
through a stricter template guiding the way the body "should" be. Third, the
revision of the "normal curve of distribution" into quartiles, ranked in order, and
so on, creates a new kind of "ideal." This statistical ideal is unlike the classical
ideal which contains no imperative to be the ideal. The new ideal of ranked
order is powered by the imperative of the norm, and then is supplemented by the
notion of progress, human perfectibility, and the elimination of deviance, to
create a dominating, hegemonic vision of what the human body should be.

While we tend to associate eugenics with a Nazi-like racial supremacy, it is
important to realize that eugenics was not the trade of a fringe group of right-
wing, fascist maniacs. Rather, it became the common practice of many, if not
most, European and American citizens. When Marx used Quetelet's idea of the
average in his formulation of average wage and abstract labor, socialists as well
as others embraced eugenic claims, seeing in the perfectibility of the human body
a Utopian hope for social improvement. Once people allowed that there were
norms and ranks in human physiology, then the idea that we might want to, for
example, increase the intelligence of humans, or decrease birth defects, did not
seem so farfetched. These ideas were widely influential: in the ensuing years the
leaders of the socialist Fabian Society, including Beatrice and Sidney Webb,
George Bernard Shaw and H. G. Wells, were among the eugenicists (MacKenzie, 1981, 34). The influence of eugenicist ideas persisted well into the twentieth century, so that someone like Emma Goldman could write that unless birth
control was encouraged, the state would "legally encourage the increase of paupers, syphilitics, epileptics, dipsomaniacs, cripples, criminals, and degenerates"
(Kevles 1985, 90).

The problem for people with disabilities was that eugenicists tended to group
together all allegedly "undesirable" traits. So, for example, criminals, the poor,
and people with disabilities might be mentioned in the same breath. Take Karl
Pearson, a leading figure in the eugenics movement, who defined the "unfit" as
follows: "the habitual criminal, the professional tramp, the tuberculous, the
insane, the mentally defective, the alcoholic, the diseased from birth or from
excess" (cited in Kevles 1985, 33). In 1911, Pearson headed the Department of
Applied Statistics, which included the Galton and Biometric Laboratories at
University College in London. This department gathered eugenic information
on the inheritance of physical and mental traits including "scientific, commercial, and legal ability, but also hermaphroditism, hemophilia, cleft palate, hare-

lip, tuberculosis, diabetes, deaf-mutism, polydactyly (more than five fingers) or brachydactyly (stub fingers), insanity, and mental deficiency" (ibid., 38–9). Here again one sees a strange selection of disabilities merged with other types of human variations. All of these deviations from the norm were regarded in the long run as contributing to the disease of the nation. As one official in the Eugenics Record Office asserted:

> the calculus of correlations is the sole rational and effective method for attacking . . . what makes for, and what mars national fitness. . . . The only way to keep a nation strong mentally and physically is to see that each new generation is derived chiefly from the fitter members of the generation before. (ibid., 39–40).

The emphasis on nation and national fitness obviously plays into the metaphor of the body. If individual citizens are not fit, if they do not fit into the nation, then the national body will not be fit. Of course, such arguments are based on a false notion of the body politic—as if a hunchbacked citizenry would make a hunchbacked nation. Nevertheless, the eugenic notion that individual variations would accumulate into a composite national identity was a powerful one. This belief combined with an industrial mentality that saw workers as interchangeable and therefore sought to create a universal worker whose physical characteristics would be uniform, as would the result of their labors—a uniform product.

One of the central foci of eugenics was what was broadly called "feeblemindedness."[5] This term included low intelligence, mental illness, and even "pauperism," since low income was equated with "relative inefficiency" (ibid, 46).[6] Likewise, certain ethnic groups were associated with feeblemindedness and pauperism. Charles Davenport, an American eugenicist, thought that the influx of European immigrants would make the American population "darker in pigmentation, smaller in stature . . . more given to crimes of larceny, assault, murder, rape, and sex-immorality" (cited in ibid., 48). In his research, Davenport scrutinized the records of "prisons, hospitals, almshouses, and institutions for the mentally deficient, the deaf, the blind, and the insane" (ibid., 55).

The loose association between what we would now call disability and criminal activity, mental incompetence, sexual license, and so on established a legacy that people with disabilities are still having trouble living down. This equation was so strong that an American journalist writing in the early twentieth century could celebrate "the inspiring, the wonderful, message of the new heredity" as opposed to the sorrow of bearing children who were "diseased or crippled or depraved" (ibid., 67). The conflation of disability with depravity expressed itself in the formulation "defective class." As the president of the University of Wisconsin declared after World War One, "we know enough about eugenics so that if the knowledge were applied, the defective classes would disappear within a generation" (ibid., 68). And it must be reiterated that the eugenics movement was not stocked with eccentrics. Davenport was funded by Averell Harriman's sister Mary Harriman, as well as John D. Rockefeller, Prime Ministers A. J. Balfour, Neville Chamberlain, and Winston Churchill, President Theodore Roosevelt, H. G. Wells, John Maynard Keynes, and H. J. Laski, among many others, were members of eugenicist organizations. Francis Galton was knighted in 1909 for his work, and in 1910 he received the Copley Medal, the Royal Society's highest honor. A Galton Society met regularly in the American Museum of Natural History in New York City. In 1911 the Oxford University Union moved approval of the main principles behind eugenics by a vote of almost two to one. In Kansas, the 1920 state fair held a contest for "fitter families" based on their eugenic family histories, administered intelligence tests, medical examinations, and venereal disease tests. A brochure for the contest noted about the awards, "this trophy and medal are worth more than livestock sweepstakes. . . . For health is wealth and a sound mind in a sound body is the most priceless of human possessions" (ibid., 62).

In England, bills were introduced in Parliament to control mentally disabled people, and in 1933 the prestigious scientific magazine *Nature* approved the Nazis' proposal of a bill for "the avoidance of inherited diseases in posterity" by sterilizing the disabled. The magazine editorial said "the Bill, as it reads, will command the appreciative attention of all who are interested in the controlled and deliberate improvement of human stock." The list of disabilities for which sterilization would be appropriate were "congenital feeblemindedness, manic depressive insanity, schizophrenia, hereditary epilepsy, hereditary St Vitus's dance, hereditary blindness and deafness, hereditary bodily malformation and habitual alcoholism" (cited in MacKenzie 1981, 44). We have largely forgotten that what Hitler did in developing a hideous policy of eugenics was just to implement the theories of the British and American eugenicists. Hitler's statement in *Mein Kampf* that "the struggle for the daily livelihood [between species] leaves behind, in the ruck, everything that is weak or diseased or wavering" (cited in Blacker 1952, 143) is not qualitatively different from any of the many similar statements we have seen before. And even the conclusions Hitler draws are not very different from those of the likes of Galton, Bell, and others.

> In this matter, the State must assert itself as the trustee of a millennial future. . . . In order to fulfill this duty in a practical manner, the State will have to avail itself of modern medical discoveries. It must proclaim as unfit for procreation all those who are afflicted with some visible hereditary disease or are the carriers of it; and practical measures must be adopted to have such people rendered sterile. (cited in Blacker 1952, 144)

One might want to add here a set of speculations about Sigmund Freud. His work was made especially possible by the idea of the normal. It shows us that sexuality, long relegated to the trash heap of human instincts, was in fact normal and that perversion was simply a displacement of "normal" sexual interest. Dreams which behave in a manner unknown or only exceptionally permissible in normal mental life" (Freud 1977, 297) are seen as actually normal and "the dreams of neurotics do not differ in any important respect from those of normal

people" (ibid., 456). In fact, it is hard to imagine the existence of psychoanalysis without the concept of normalcy. Indeed, one of the core principles behind
psychoanalysis was that we each start out with normal psychosexual development and neurotics become abnormal through a problem in that normal development. As Freud put it: "if the *vita sexualis* is normal, there can be no neurosis"
(ibid., 386). Psychoanalysis can correct that mistake and bring patients back to
their normal selves. Although I cannot go into a close analysis of Freud's work
here, it is instructive to think of the ways in which Freud is producing a eugenics of the mind—creating the concepts of normal sexuality, normal function, and
then contrasting them with the perverse, abnormal, pathological, and even criminal. Indeed, one of the major critiques of Freud's work now centers on his
assumption about what constitutes normal sexuality and sexual development for
women and men.

The first depiction in literature of an attempt to norm an individual member
of the population occurred in the 1850s during the development of the idea of
the normal body. In Flaubert's *Madame Bovary*, Charles Bovary is influenced by
Homais, the self-serving pharmacist, and Emma to perform a trendy operation
that would correct the club foot of Hippolyte, the stableboy of the local inn. This
corrective operation is seen as "new" and related to "progress" (Flaubert 1965,
125). Hippolyte is assailed with reasons why he should alter his foot. He is told,
it "must considerably interfere with the proper performance of your work" (ibid.,
126). And in addition to redefining him in terms of his ability to carry out work,
Homais adds: "Think what would have happened if you had been called into the
army, and had to fight under our national banner!" (ibid., 126). So national
interests and again productivity are emphasized. But Hippolyte has been doing
fine in his job as stableboy; his disability has not interfered with his performance
in the community under traditional standards. In fact, Hippolyte seems to use his
club foot to his advantage, as the narrator notes:

> But on the equine foot, wide indeed as a horse's hoof, with is horny skin, and large
> toes, whose black nails resembled the nails of a horse shoe, the cripple ran about
> like a deer from morn till night. He was constantly to be seen on the Square, jump-
> ing round the carts, thrusting his limping foot forwards. He seemed even stronger
> on that leg than the other. By dint of hard service it had acquired, as it were, moral
> qualities of patience and energy; and when he was given some heavy work to do,
> he would support himself on it in preference to the sound one. (ibid., 126)

Hippolyte's disability is in fact an ability, one which he relies on, and from which
he gets extra horsepower, as it were. But although Hippolyte is more than capable, the operation must be performed to bring him back to the human and away
from the equine, which the first syllable of his name suggests. To have a disability is to be an animal, to be part of the Other.

A newspaper article appears after the operation's apparent initial success,
praising the spirit of progress. The article envisages Hippolyte's welcome back
into the human community.

Everything tends to show that his convalescence will be brief; and who knows if, at our next village festivity we shall not see our good Hippolyte appear in the midst of a bacchic dance, surrounded by a group of gay companions . . . (ibid., 128)

The article goes on to proclaim, "Hasn't the time come to cry out that the blind shall see, the deaf hear, the lame walk?" The imperative is clear: science will eradicate disability. However, by a touch of Flaubertian irony, Hippolyte's leg becomes gangrenous and has to be amputated. The older doctor who performs the operation lectures Charles about his attempt to norm this individual.

This is what you get from listening to the fads from Paris! . . . We are practition-ers; we cure people, and we wouldn't dream of operating on someone who is in per-fect health. Straighten club feet! As if one could straighten club feet indeed! It is as if one wished to make a hunchback straight! (ibid., 131)

While Flaubert's work illustrates some of the points I have been making, it is important that we do no simply think of the novel as merely an example of how an historical development lodges within a particular text. Rather, I think there is a larger claim to be made about novels and norms.

While Flaubert may parody current ideas about normalcy in medicine, there is another sense in which the novel as a form promotes and symbolically pro-duces normative structures. Indeed, the whole focus of *Madame Bovary* is on Emma's abnormality and Flaubert's abhorrence of normal life. If we accept that novels are a social practice that arose as part of the project of middle-class hege-mony,[7] then we can see that the plot and character development of novels tend to pull toward the normative. For example, most characters in nineteenth-cen-tury novels are somewhat ordinary people who are put in abnormal circum-stances, as opposed to the heroic characters who represent the ideal in earlier forms such as the epic.

If disability appears in a novel, it is rarely centrally represented. It is unusual for a main character to be a person with disabilities, although minor characters, like Tiny Tim, can be deformed in ways that arouse pity. In the case of Esther Summerson, who is scarred by smallpox, her scars are made virtually to disappear through the agency of love. On the other hand, as sufficient research has shown, more often than not villains tend to be physically abnormal: scarred, deformed, or mutilated.[8]

I am not saying simply that novels embody the prejudices of society toward people with disabilities. That is clearly a truism. Rather, I am asserting that the very structures on which the novel rests tend to be normative, ideologically emphasizing the universal quality of the central character whose normativity encourages us to identify with him or her.[9] Furthermore, the novel's goal is to reproduce, on some level, the semiologically normative signs surrounding the reader, that paradoxically help the reader to read those signs in the world as well as the text. Thus the middleness of life, the middleness of the material world, the middleness of the normal body, the middleness of a sexually gendered, ethnically middle world is created in symbolic form and then reproduced symbolically. This normativity in narrative will by definition create the abnormal, the Other, the disabled, the native, the colonized subject, and so on.

Even on the level of plot, one can see the implication of eugenic notions of normativity. The parentage of characters in novels plays a crucial role. Rather than being self-creating beings, characters in novels have deep biological debts to their forebears, even if the characters are orphans—or perhaps especially if they are orphans. The great Heliodoric plots of romance, in which lower-class characters are found actually to be noble, take a new turn in the novel. While nobility may be less important, characters nevertheless inherit bourgeois respectability, moral rectitude, and eventually money and position through their genetic connection. In the novelistic world of nature versus nurture, nature almost always wins out. Thus Oliver Twist will naturally bear the banner of bourgeois morality and linguistic normativity, even though he grows up in the workhouse. Oliver will always be normal, even in abnormal circumstances.[10]

A further development in the novel can be seen in Zola's works. Before Zola, for example in the work of Balzac, the author attempted to show how the inherently good character of a protagonist was affected by the material world. Thus we read of the journey of the soul, of everyman or everywoman, through a trying and corrupting world. But Zola's theory of the novel depends on the idea of inherited traits and biological determinism. As Zola wrote in *The Experimental Novel*:

> Determinism dominates everything. It is scientific investigation, it is experimental reasoning, which combats one by one the hypotheses of the idealists, and which replaces purely imaginary novels by novels of observation and experimentation. (1964, 18)

In this view, the author is a kind of scientist watching how humans, with their naturally inherited dispositions, interact with each other. As Zola wrote, his intention in the Rougon-Macquart series was to show how heredity would influence a family "making superhuman efforts but always failing because of its own nature and the influences upon it" (Zola 1993, viii). This series would be a study of the "singular effect of heredity" (ibid.). Zola mentions the work of Darwin and links his own novels to notions of how inherited traits interact in particular environments over time and to generalizations about human behavior:

> And this is what constitutes the experimental novel: to possess a knowledge of the mechanism of the phenomena inherent in man, to show the machinery of his intellectual and sensory manifestations, under the influence of heredity and environment, such as physiology shall give them to us. (Zola 1964, 21)

Clearly stating his debt to science, Zola says that "the experimental novel is a consequence of the scientific evolution of the century" (ibid., 23). The older novel, according to Zola, is composed of imaginary adventures while the new novel is "a report, nothing more" (ibid., 124). In being a report, the new novel rejects idealized characters in favor of the norm.

> These young girls so pure, these young men so loyal, represented to us in certain novels, do not belong to the earth. . . . We tell everything, we do not make a choice, neither do we idealize. (ibid., 127)

Zola's characters belong to "the earth." This commitment constitutes Zola's new realism, one based on the norm, the average, the inherited.

My point is that a disabilities studies consciousness can alter the way we see not just novels that have main characters who are disabled but any novel. In thinking through the issue of disability, I have come to see that almost any literary work will have some reference to the abnormal, to disability, and so on. I would explain this phenomenon as a result of the hegemony of normalcy. This normalcy must constantly be enforced in public venues (like the novel), must always be creating and bolstering its image by processing, comparing, constructing, deconstructing images of normalcy and the abnormal. In fact, once one begins to notice, there really is a rare novel that does not have some characters with disabilities—characters who are lame, tubercular, dying of AIDS, chronically ill, depressed, mentally ill, and so on.

Let me take the example of some novels by Joseph Conrad. I pick Conrad not because he is especially representative, but just because I happen to be teaching a course on Conrad. Although he is not remembered in any sense as a writer on disability, Conrad is a good test case, as it turns out, because he wrote during a period when eugenics had permeated British society and when Freud had begun to write about normal and abnormal psychology. Conrad, too, was somewhat influenced by Zola, particularly in *The Secret Agent*.

The first thing I noticed about Conrad's work is that metaphors of disability abound. Each book has numerous instances of phrases like the following selections from *Lord Jim*:

> a dance of lame, blind, mute thoughts—a whirl of awful cripples. (Conrad 1986, 114)

> [he] comported himself in that clatter as though he had been stone-deaf. (ibid., 183)

> there was nothing of the cripple about him. (ibid., 234)

> Her broken figure hovered in crippled little jumps . . . (ibid., 263)

> he was made blind and deaf and without pity . . . (ibid., 300)

> a blind belief in the righteousness of his will against all mankind . . . (ibid., 317)

> They were erring men whom suffering had made blind to right and wrong. (ibid., 333)

> you dismal cripples, you . . . (ibid., 340)

> unmoved like a deaf man . . . (ibid., 319)

These references are almost like tics, appearing at regular intervals. They tend to focus on deafness, blindness, dumbness, and lameness, and they tend to use these metaphors to represent limitations on normal morals, ethics, and of course language. While it is entirely possible to maintain that these figures of speech are hardly more than mere linguistic convention, I would argue that the very regularity of these occurrences speaks to a reflexive patrolling function in which the author continuously checks and notes instances of normalcy and instances of disability—right down to the linguistic level.

Conrad's emphasis on exotic locations can also be seen as related to the issue of normalcy. Indeed the whole conception of imperialism on which writers like Conrad depend is largely based on notions of race and ethnicity that are intricately tied up with eugenics, statistical proofs of intelligence, ability, and so on. And these in turn are part of the hegemony of normalcy. Conrad's exotic settings are highlighted in his novels for their deviance from European conceptions. The protagonists are skewed from European standards of normal behavior specifically because they have traveled from Europe to, for example, the South Seas or the Belgian Congo. And Conrad focuses on those characters who, because they are influenced by these abnormal environments, lose their "singleness of purpose" (which he frequently defines as an English trait) and on those who do not.

The use of phrenology, too, is linked to the patrolling of normalcy, through the construction of character. So, in *Heart of Darkness* for example, when Marlow is about to leave for Africa a doctor measures the dimensions of his skull to enable him to discern if any quantitative changes subsequently occur as a result of the colonial encounter. So many of the characters in novels are formed from the ableist cultural repertoire of normalized head, face, and body features that characteristically signify personal qualities. Thus in *The Secret Agent*, the corpulent, lazy body of Verloc indicates his moral sleaziness, and Stevie's large ears and head shape are explicitly seen by Ossipon as characteristic of degeneracy and criminality as described in the theories of the nineteenth-century eugenic phrenologist Cesare Lombroso.

Stevie Conrad's most obviously disabled character, is a kind of center or focus of *The Secret Agent*. In a Zolaesque moment of insight, Ossipon sees Stevie's degeneracy as linked to his sister Winnie:

> he gazed scientifically at that woman, the sister of a degenerate, a degenerate herself—of a murdering type. He gazed at her and invoked Lombroso. . . . He gazed scientifically. He gazed at her cheeks, at her nose, at her eyes, at her ears . . . Bad! . . . Fatal! (Conrad 1968, 269)

This eugenic gaze that scrutinizes Winnie and Stevie is really only a recapitulation of the novelistic gaze that sees meaning in normative and nonnormative features. In fact, every member of the Verloc family has something "wrong" with them, including Winnie's mother who has trouble walking on her edematous legs. The moral turpitude and physical grimness of London is embodied in Verloc's inner circle. Michaelis, too, is obese and "wheezed as if deadened and oppressed by the layer of fat on his chest" (ibid., 73). Karl Yundt is toothless, gouty, and walks with a cane. Ossipon is racially abnormal having "crinkly yellow hair . . . a flattened nose and prominent mouth cast in the rough mould of the Negro type . . . [and] almond-shaped eyes [that] leered languidly over high cheek-bones" (ibid., 75)—all features indicating African and Asian qualities, particularly the cunning, opiated glance.

Stevie, the metaphoric central figure and sacrificial victim of the novel, is mentally delayed. His mental slowness becomes a metaphor for his radical inno- cence and childlike revulsion from cruelty. He is also, in his endless drawing of circles, seen as invoking "the symbolism of a mad art attempting the inconceiv- able" (ibid., 76). In this sense, his vision of the world is allied with that of Conrad, who himself could easily be described as embarked on the same project. Stevie is literally taken apart, not only by Ossipon's gaze and by that of the nov- elist, but centrally by the bungled explosion. His fragmented body[11] becomes a kind of symbol of the fragmentation that Conrad emphasizes throughout his opus and that the Professor recommends in his high-tech view of anarchism as based on the power of explosion and conflagration. Stevie becomes sensitized to the exploitation of workers by his encountering a coachman with a prosthetic hook for an arm, whose whipping of his horse causes Stevie anguish. The prosthetic arm appears sinister at first, particularly as a metonymic agent of the action of whipping. But the one-armed man explains: "This ain't an easy world . . . 'Ard on 'osses, but dam' sight 'arder on poor chaps like me." He wheezed just audibly" (ibid., 165). Stevie's radical innocence is most fittingly convinced by the man's appeal to class solidarity, so Stevie ultimately is blown up for the sins of all.

In *Under Western Eyes*, the issue of normalcy is first signaled in the author's Introduction. Conrad apologizes for Razumov's being "slightly abnormal" and explains away this deviation by citing a kind of personal sensitivity as well as a Russian temperament. In addition, Conrad says that although his characters may seem odd, "nobody is exhibited as a monster here" (Conrad 1957, 51). The men- tion of exhibition of monsters immediately alerts us to the issue of nineteenth-cen- tury freak shows and raises the point that by depicting "abnormal" people, the author might see his own work as a kind of display of freaks.[12] Finally, Conrad makes the point that all these "abnormal" characters "are not the product of the exceptional but of the general—of the normality of their place, and time, and race" (ibid., 51). The conjunction of race and normality also alerts us to eugenic aims. What Conrad can be seen as apologizing for is the normalizing (and abnormaliz- ing) role of the novel that must take a group of nationals (Russians) and make them into the abnormal, non-European, nonnormal Other. Interestingly, Conrad refers to anarchists and autocrats both as "imbecile." The use of this word made cur- rent by eugenic testing also shows us how pervasive is the hegemony of normalcy.

Razumov's abnormality is referred to by the narrator, at one point, as being seen by a man looking at a mirror "formulating to himself reassuring excuses for his appearance marked by the taint of some insidious hereditary disease" (ibid., 220). What makes Razumov into the cipher he is to all concerned is his lack of a recognizable identity aside from his being a Russian. So when he arrives in Geneva, Razumov says to Peter Ivanovitch, the radical political philosopher, that he will never be "a mere blind tool" simply to be used (ibid., 231). His refusal to be a "blind tool" ends up, ironically, in Razumov being made deaf by Necator, who deliberately bursts his eardrums with blows to the head. The world becomes for Razumov "perfectly silent—soundless as shadows" (ibid., 339) and "a world of mutes. Silent men, moving, unheard . . ." (ibid., 340). For both Conrad and Razumov, deafness is the end of language, the end of discourse, the ultimate punishment that makes all the rest of the characters appear as if their words were useless anyway. As Necator says, "He shall never be any use as spy on any one. He won't talk, because he will never hear anything in his life—not a thing" (ibid., 341). After Razumov walks into the street and is run over by a car, he is described as "a hopeless cripple, and stone deaf with that" (ibid., 343). He dies from his disabilities, as if life were in fact impossible to survive under those conditions. Miss Haldin, in contrast, gains her meaning in life from these events and says, "my eyes are open at last and my hands are free now" (ibid., 345). These sets of arrangements play an intimate part in the novel and show that disability looms before the writer as a *memento mori*. Normality has to protect itself by looking into the maw of disability and then recovering from that glance.

I am not claiming that this reading of some texts by Conrad is brilliant or definitive. But I do want to show that even in texts that do not appear to be about disability, the issue of normalcy is fully deployed. One can find in almost any novel, I would argue, a kind of surveying of the terrain of the body, an attention to difference—physical, mental, and national. This activity of consolidating the hegemony of normalcy is one that needs more attention, in addition to the kinds of work that have been done in locating the thematics of disability in literature.

What I have tried to show here is that the very term that permeates our contemporary life—the normal—is a configuration that arises in a particular historical moment. It is part of a notion of progress, of industrialization, and of ideological consolidation of the power of the bourgeoisie. The implications of the hegemony of normalcy are profound and extend into the very heart of cultural production. The novel form, that proliferator of ideology, is intricately connected with concepts of the norm. From the typicality of the central character, to the normalizing devices of plot to bring deviant characters back into the norms of society, to the normalizing coda of endings, the nineteenth- and twentieth-century novel promulgates and disburses notions of normalcy and by extension makes of physical differences ideological differences. Characters with disabilities are always marked with ideological meaning, as are moments of disease or accident that transform such characters. One of the tasks for a developing consciousness of disability issues is the attempt, then, to reverse the hegemony of the normal and to institute alternative ways of thinking about the abnormal.

NOTES

1. This thinking obviously is still alive and well. During the U. S. Presidential election of 1994, Newt Gingrich accused President Clinton of being "the enemy of normal Americans." When asked at a later date to clarify what he meant, he said his meaning was that "normal" meant "middle class." (*New York Times*, November 14, 1994, A17)

2. One wants to make sure that Aristotle's idea of the mean is not confused with the norm. The Aristotlean mean is a kind of fictional construct. Aristotle advocates that in choosing between personal traits, one should tend to chose between the extremes. He does not however think of the population as falling generally into that mean. The mean, for Aristotle, is more of heuristic device to assist in moral and ethical choices. In the sense of being a middle term or a middle way, it carries more of a spacial sense than does the term "average" or "norm."

3. This rather remarkable confluence between eugenics and statistics has been pointed out by Donald A. MacKenzie, but I do not believe his observations have had the impact they should.

4. See my *Enforcing Disability* Chapter Six for more on the novel *Frankenstein* and its relation to notions of disability.

5. Many twentieth century prejudices against the learning disabled come from this period. The founder of the intelligence test still in use, Alfred Binet, was a Galton acolyte. The American psychologist Henry H. Goddard used Binet's tests in America and turned the numbers into categories—"idiots" being those whose mental age was one or two, "imbeciles" ranged in mental age from three to seven. Goddard invented the term "moron" (which he took from the Greek for "dull" or "stupid") for those between eight and twelve. Pejorative terms like "moron" or "retarded" have by now found their way into common usage. (Kevles, 78) And even the term "mongoloid idiot" to describe a person with Down's syndrome was used as recently as 1970s not as a pejorative term but in medical texts as a diagnosis. [see Michael Bérubé's fascinating article "Life As We Know It" for more on this phenomenon of labelling.]

6. If this argument sounds strangely familiar, it is being repeated and promulgated in the neo-conservative book *The Bell Curve* which claims that poverty and intelligence are linked through inherited characteristics.

7. This assumption is based on my previous works—*Factual Fictions: Origins of the English Novel* and *Resisting Novels: Fiction and Ideology*—as well as the cumulative body of writing about the relationship between capitalism, material life, culture, and fiction. The work of Raymond Wiliams, Terry Eagleton, Nancy Armstrong, Mary Poovey, John Bender, Michael McKeon, and others points in similar directions.

8. The issue of people with disabilities in literature is a well-documented one and is one I want generally to avoid in this work. Excellent books abound on the subject, including Alan Gartner and Tom Joe, eds.,*Images of the Disabled, Disabling Images* (New York: Praeger,1987) and the work of Deborah Kent including "In Search of a Heroine: Images of Women with Disabilities in Fiction and Drama" in Michelle Fine and Adrienne Asch, eds. *Women with Disabilities: Essays in Psychology, Culture, and Politics* (Philadelphia: Temple University Press, 1988).

9. And if the main character has a major disability, then we are encouraged to identify with that character's ability to overcome their disability.

10. The genealogical family line is both hereditary and financial in the bourgeois novel. The role of the family is defined by Jürgen Habermas thus: "as a genealogical link it [the family] guaranteed a continuity of personnel that consisted materially in the accumulation of capital and was anchored in the absence of legal restrictions concerning the inheritance of property." (47) The fact that the biological connectedness and the financial connectedness are conflated in the novel only furthers the point that normality is an enforced condition that upholds the totality of the bourgeois system.

11. I deal with the Lacanian idea of the *corps morcelé* in Chapter 6 of *Enforcing Normalcy*. In that section I show the relation between the fragmented body and the response to disability. Here, let me just say that Stevie's turning into a fragmented body makes

sense given the fear "normal" observers have that if they allow a concept of disability to associate with their bodies, they will lose control of their normalcy and their bodies will fall apart.

12. See Chapter 4 of *Enforcing Normalcy* for more on the relation of freak shows to nationalism, colonialism, and disability. See also Rosemarie Garland Thompson's *Freakery: Cultural Spectacles of the Extraordinary Body* (New York: NYU Press, 1996).

WORKS CITED

Bell, Alexander Graham. 1969. *Memoir upon the Formation of a Deaf Variety of the Human Race*. Washington, DC: Alexander Graham Bell Association for the Deaf.

Blacker, C. P. 1952. *Eugenics: Galton and After*. Cambridge, Mass.: Harvard University Press.

Conrad, Joseph. 1924. "An Outpost of Progress." In *Tales of Unrest*. Garden City: Doubleday, Page & Company.

———. 1990 [1968]. *The Secret Agent*. London: Penguin.

———. 1989 [1957]. *Under Western Eyes*. London: Penguin.

———. 1924. *Youth*. Garden City: Doubleday, Page, & Company.

———. 1986. *Lord Jim*. London: Penguin.

Defoe, Daniel. 1975. *Robinson Crusoe*. New York: Norton.

Farrall, Lyndsay Andrew. 1985. *The Origin and Growth of the English Eugenics Movement 1865–1925*. New York: Garland.

Flaubert, Gustave. 1965. *Madam Bovary*. Trans. Paul de Man. New York: Norton.

Freud, Sigmund. 1977. *Introductory Lectures on Psychoanalysis*. Trans. James Strachey. New York: Norton.

Kevles, Daniel J. 1985. *In the Name of Eugenics: Genetics and the Uses of Human* Heredity. New York: Alfred A. Knopf.

MacKenzie, Donald. A. 1981. *Statistics in Britain, 1865–1930*. Edinburgh: Edinburgh University Press.

Marx, Karl. 1970. *Capital*. Vol. 1. Trans. Samuel Moore and

Porter, Theodore M. 1986. *The Rise of Statistical Thinking 1820–1900*. Princeton: Princeton University Press.

Stallybass, Peter and Allon White. 1987. *The Politics of Transgression*. Ithaca, NY: Cornell University Press.

Stigler, Stephen M. 1986. *The History of Statistics: The Measurement of Uncertainty before 1900*. Cambridge, Mass.: Harvard University Press.

Zola, Emile. 1964. *The Experimental Novel and Other Essays*. Trans Belle M. Sherman. New York: Haskel House.

———. 1993. *The Masterpiece*. Trans. Thomas Walton. London: Oxford University Press.

ABBREVIATIONS

DAGW   M. Grmek, *Diseases in the Ancient Greek World* (Baltimore, 1989).

FGrH   F. Jacoby, Die Fragmente der griechischen Historiker (Leiden, 1923–).

GG   F. Van Straten, "Gifts for the Gods," *Faith Hope and Worship* (Leiden, 1981).

LCL   Loeb Classical Library.

PCG   R. Kassel and C. Austin, *Poetae Comici Graeci* (Berlin, 1983).

PMG   D. L. Page, *Poetae Melici Graecae* (Oxford, 1967).

SEG   *Supplementurn Epigraphicum Graecum*.

WMH   H. Lane, *When the Mind Hears* (New York, 1985).

2

Deaf and Dumb in
Ancient Greece[1]

MARTHA L. EDWARDS

Just as the nature of traditional scholarship rendered women in the ancient world inconsequential and invisible—save a few, remarkable ladies—people with disabilities have been all but invisible, save a handful of blind prophets. Beyond simply cataloguing disabled people, one must ask what constituted "ability" and "disability" for any given culture. At the heart of disability studies is a recognition that disability is a cultural construction; that is, that "'disability' has no inherent meaning."[2] It is not appropriate to investigate the phenomenon of disability in ancient societies from the perspective of a medical model,[3] whereby people are deemed inherently able-bodied or disabled according to medical definition and categorization. Rather, if disability is viewed as "relational and not inherent in the individual,"[4] the risk is much lower of contaminating the ancient evidence with modern cultural assumptions. The Greeks perceived deafness as an intellectual impairment because of the difficulty in verbal communication that accompanies deafness. The obsolete expression "deaf and dumb" is an apt description of the way in which a deaf person was perceived in ancient Greece.

The surviving ancient Greek material that mentions or depicts deafness is meager. While it does not allow a reconstruction of everyday life for deaf and hearing-impaired people, it does allow an investigation into the environment in which deaf people lived. This discussion of deafness in the ancient Greek world begins with a survey of the etiology of deafness, which suggests that the causes of deafness in the modern world existed in the ancient world. An examination of the term "deaf" (κωφός) reveals both that the term was flexible in its range of meanings, and that deafness was inextricably intertwined in Greek thought with an impairment of verbal communication. Next, I discuss the Greek medical understanding of deafness, as well as medical and nonmedical treatments for deafness in terms of how they illuminate Greek attitudes toward deaf people. Finally, while attitudinal subtleties are lost, we can determine broad cultural assumptions that shaped the realities of hearing-impaired people.

The only significant instance of a deaf person's appearance in the surviving Greek literature is Herodotus' tale (1.34; 1.38; 1.85) of Croesus' anonymous deaf son.[5] Herodotus tells us that Croesus, the king of Lydia and richest man in the world, had two sons. Atys, the elder, was brave and skilled, but died as a youth. The other son, whose name we never learn, was worthless to Croesus because he was deaf and mute. When Croesus has failed at his plans to conquer the Persians and is about to die at the hands of his captors, his son regains his voice at the last minute in order to save his father from the pyre.[6] One deaf boy is hardly representative of the portion of the population that was hearing-impaired, as the following etiological survey will show.

In the United States today, there are about twenty-two million hearing-impaired people; of these, two million are profoundly deaf (unable to hear anything) or severely deaf (unable to hear much).[7] Hearing impairment results from three major factors that are not necessarily exclusive: environmental, hereditary, and old age.

Environmental causes include noise-induced, accidental, toxic, and viral. Noise-induced deafness is primarily a phenomenon of the modern industrial world, though stonemasons, for example, may have been subject to hearing-loss in the ancient world.[8] Permanent deafness resulting from toxicity is also a phenomenon of the modern world.[9] Deafness from accident, such as a blow to the ear, must have resulted from time to time.[10] Viruses, too, were very much part of the ancient world. Of the six main viruses that can cause deafness today—chickenpox, common cold viruses, influenza, measles, mumps, and poliomyelitis—there is evidence for five in ancient Greece.[11] There is also evidence for the presence of bacterial meningitis, whose classic complication is hearing loss.[12] In modern, developed countries, preventative medicine reduces the incidence and severity of these viruses, but in the ancient world, as in third-world countries today, these viruses must have taken their toll.[13]

There is no reason to rule out hereditary deafness in the ancient world, and there is some conjectural evidence for the results of in-breeding, although not specifically for deafness.[14] Plutarch (*Moralia* 616 b) and Strabo (*Geography* 10.5.9), for example, observe the prevalence of premature baldness on Myconos. It is not surprising that island communities would have their own genetic peculiarities. Genetic phenomena such as the present-day prevalence of female muteness on Amorgos and Donussa would have been common in ancient Greece.[15] In addition to inbreeding, other hereditary factors would have produced deafness. Some families simply have a genetic background that favors deafness.[16] Furthermore, a chromosomal aberration can produce deafness, with or without a hereditary factor.[17]

Hearing loss is expected in elderly people in the modern world. Today, almost thirty percent of people sixty-five to seventy-four years old and almost fifty percent of those seventy to seventy-nine years old have some hearing loss; in other words, one third of those over sixty-five years old have clinically abnormal hearing.[18] Fewer people, of course, attained old age in the ancient world.[19] There is no reason to suppose that hearing loss would be less a part of old age in the ancient world than it is today;[20] if the incidence was similar, one Greek in three, sixty-five years or older, would have suffered some degree of hearing loss.

Finally, in addition to the three factors above, any condition that manifested in muteness would not have been differentiated from deafness.[21] Muteness can result from faulty information processing brought on by forms of autism, learning disabilities, and mental illness.[22]

Although Herodotus' fanciful tale of two sons and a kingdom does not represent the proportion of deaf people in the ancient world, it is useful in that it coincidentally illustrates two important ancient Greek assumptions about deaf people. First, and crucial to our understanding of the Greek concept of deafness: deafness went hand-in-hand with muteness. The Lydian boy's deafness was the sole reason for his worthlessness not because he could not hear, but because he could not speak.[23] In this case, the word "deaf" (κωφός) encompassed both conditions; a deaf person was voiceless by nature, mute in the sense that the sea or the earth is mute, "stone deaf."[24]

The second and related assumption seen in Herodotus' tale is that muteness indicated diminished worth. Croesus' deaf son was incapacitated (διέφθαρτο)[25] by his condition (Herodotus, 1.34), and it could not be clearer that the sole reason for the boy's uselessness was his deaf-muteness alone; in all other respects, he was acceptable τὰ μὲν ἄλλα ἐπιεικής, ἄφωος δέ) (Herodotus, 1.85).[26] Croesus literally discounts his deaf son (οὐκ εἶναί μοι λογίζομαι) (Herodotus, 1.38).[27] A deaf male child was perhaps as "worthless" as a girl. Deafness certainly indicated worthlessness in the political sphere; this was so taken for granted that Herodotus uses it as a literary device: when Croesus' son finds his voice, Herodotus has created the irony that Croesus gained an heir when he lost his kingship.[28]

A survey of the use of the word "deaf" (κωφός) shows that the term had a much wider range of meaning than the English term. Deafness and speechlessness were intertwined from the earliest appearance of the word "deaf" (κωφός), and the term does not always refer to a person's speech or hearing. In the *Iliad* (11.390), the term describes the bluntness of a weapon; the silence of an unbroken wave (14.16); and the muteness of the earth (24.54). This basic use of the word continues through the Archaic poets; for example, Alcman refers to a mute (κωφόν) wave.[29]

Even when the term describes deafness as a human characteristic, it implies a range of conditions that include an overall inability to communicate verbally. The first surviving use of "deaf" (κωφός) that probably describes human beings appears in Aeschylus (*Libation Bearers* 881), though "My cry is to the deaf" (κωφοῖς) could refer to anything that does not, or cannot, hear. There is a similar use (*Seven Against Thebes* 202) when Eteocles asks the chorus of Theban women if he speaks to the deaf (κωφῇ).

The term unmistakably refers to a specific human sensory condition in the Hippocratic Corpus, and it appears abundantly there.[30] It is in the Hippocratic Corpus, too, that the term first refers to a class of people.[31] There are two references to deaf people as a distinct group,[32] although most of the references are to deafness as a temporary condition, a symptom of another condition, or a diagnostic tool. Hippocratic writers rarely mention permanent deafness, as opposed to the temporary conditions such as "night deafness" that frequently accompanies other ailments.[33] Deafness is mentioned in passing as a possible complication for the mother during childbirth, and muteness as a potential problem in the case of female hysteria.[34] The author of *Internal Affections* (18.24) warns that deafness may result from a botched cauterization of one of the main veins in the body.[35] In short, throughout the Hippocratic Corpus, deafness is seen more as a valuable diagnostic tool than as a physical infirmity in itself.[36]

There is not much surviving mention of medical treatment for deafness in the Classical period. Hippocratic theory becomes Hellenistic practice in the writings of Celsus, who lived about six centuries after the earliest Hippocratic writers. In Celsus' writings, we see specific medical treatments for hearing impairment that are based on Hippocratic theory.[37] For example, there is a connection throughout the Hippocratic Corpus between bilious bowels and deafness.[38] Celsus (2.8.19) takes this connection another step in his recommendation to balance the humors by producing a bilious stool. Other remedies for ear ailments and dull hearing include shaving the head, if the head is considered too heavy (6.7.7 b), and flushing the ear with various juices (6.7.8 a).[39] Some of the more drastic treatments suggest to the modern reader that hearing impairments might have been aggravated or even caused by medical treatment, such as when a probe with turpentine-soaked wool is inserted into the ear canal and twisted around (6.7.9 a).[40]

While the surviving medical literature of the Classical period does not include treatments for deafness, we do find reports of cures for deafness in the nonmedical literature. For example, psychological trauma instantly restored Croesus' son's capacity to speak (Herodotus, 1.85),[41] and a fourth century B.C. inscription at Epidaurus testifies to a spontaneous cure of muteness (ἄφωνος).[42]

Deafness is not a common ailment among the surviving testimonies of Asclepiadic cures, but the paucity of written remains does not necessarily indicate that the Greeks did not seek cures for it. Because it is an abstract characteristic, deafness is not easily depicted, and, like headache, is difficult to interpret in representation.[43] Clay representations of human ears were prominent among the offerings of body parts at the healing temples, and many survive. They may or may not represent thank offerings or pleas for cures of deafness.[44] The ear was, obviously, connected with hearing and thus communication and—in ancient thought—intelligence. By extension, the ear was for Aristotle (*History of Animals* 1.11.492 a) also indicative of personality.[45] Similarly, Athenaeus (12.516 b) tells us that when Midas became deaf (κεκωφημένον) through his stupidity, he received the ears of an ass to match his "dumbness."

Because deafness and muteness were intertwined, models of mouths or complete heads are just as likely as ears to have represented deafness.[46] But the ear was, certainly, the most obvious channel of hearing, listening, and understanding, and this is why it was important to have the ear of the god from whom one sought a favor. If one's prayer was heard, it was granted.[47] Having the god's ear was taken literally: some temples included depictions of gods' ears into which the suppliant could speak.[48]

Against this background, it is possible to reconstruct generally some of the realities of deaf people's lives in the ancient Greek world. I will discuss people with mild hearing impairments, followed by those people who were more severely deaf but who still spoke, and, finally, people who were prelingually deaf.

People with partial hearing loss outnumber people with severe or profound deafness in the modern world, and there is no reason to think that the situation would be different in the ancient world. Partial loss of hearing, because of the difficulty in verbal communication it brought on, implied partial loss of wit. Perhaps Aristophanes (*Knights* 43) used a hearing impairment as a comic vehicle: Demosthenes describes his master as a bit hard of hearing (ὑπόκωφων), quick-tempered, and country-minded.[49] As in the modern world, old people were expected to become slightly deaf (ὑπόκωφος). Slight deafness was the "old man's forfeit," along with a decrease in sight, wit, and memory (Xenophon, *Memorabilia* 4.7.8).[50] Old men and deafness were so intertwined that it is difficult to separate deafness from old age as the butt of the joke in Attic comedy.[51] Aristophanes' Acharnian men (*Acharnians* 681) contrast the city's brash and forensically skilled youth with their own deafness. The deafness here is literal but it reveals layers of symbolism in the conflict of generations. A diminished ability to communicate by speech accompanies hearing loss; the assumption of faulty thought accompanies this diminished ability to communicate easily; the picture of dull-witted old age results.[52]

What this picture of diminished intellect meant in the everyday life of someone with a mild hearing impairment is impossible to determine in any detail. Hard-of-hearing old men, though portrayed comically, are never portrayed—at least in the surviving material—as "worthless." In fact, an important measure of a Greek man's worth was his participation in the army or, at Athens, in the navy. Old men were not excluded from the hoplite forces. All citizens, regardless of age or physical fitness, were included in the military.[53] Of these old men, a significant proportion—upwards of thirty percent, we have noted—must have been hearing-impaired. This could have worked to their advantage in the noisy confusion of Greek combat, where panic could quickly scatter the phalanx.[54]

As scant as the information is for deaf and hearing-impaired men, there is even less information about women.[55] An epigram from the first century A. D. describes a very deaf old woman (δύσκωφον γραῖαν) who, when asked to bring cheeses (τυφούς) brings grains of wheat (πυρούς) instead.[56] While the epigram, on its own, tells us little about deaf women, it does further illustrate the perceived connection between deafness and impaired communication.[57]

The degree of one's hearing loss never appears to be an important issue; what mattered to the Greeks was one's ability to speak.[58] Even profoundly deaf people who learn spoken language before losing their hearing do not necessarily lose their capacity to speak. When Pseudo-Aristotle (*Problems* 14.962 b) asks why deaf people talk through their noses, he refers to people who remember how to speak, but who do not remember how to regulate their voices.[59] Being able to speak intelligibly, even if imperfectly, separated the "dumb" from those who merely had variations of speech, though the philosophical line was thin.[60] Pseudo-Aristotle (*Problems* 10.40.895 a) compares speech disorders with muteness: he asks why man is the only animal that stammers, and asks in answer if it is because only man suffers from muteness (ἔνεον) and stammering is a form of muteness. The ancient literature is full of references to people who lisped, stuttered, stammered, or mumbled. Their speech was ridiculed (Plutarch, *Demosthenes* 4.4) or admired (Plutarch, *Alcibiades* 1.4), but there is nothing to indicate the degree of derision seen in the story of Croesus' son.[61]

Some deaf people did not learn spoken language. About one in 1000 people in the world today are congenitally deaf[62] and there is no reason to believe that the proportion was much different in the ancient world.[63] In the absence of modern educational methods, one must hear spoken language in order to learn to speak it.[64] People in the ancient world who became deaf *in utero* or before learning to speak were necessarily mute.[65]

Of course, prelingually deaf people who could not talk communicated in other ways;[66] speech is only part of the method by which even people with full hearing transmit information.[67] Deaf children who are not taught a signed language naturally learn a system of gestures.[68] An example from the modern world demonstrates how this might have played out in daily life in ancient Greece. Harlan Lane observed families in Burundi, Africa, where many deaf people are without the means to learn true signed language.[69] A mother describes gestural communication with her profoundly deaf daughter:

> She uses little gestures with me that I understand, that her sisters and brothers understand. . . . We don't have conversations, because that's impossible with a deaf person, but when I want her to go fetch water, I can take the jug that she always uses, show it to her, and point my finger in the direction of the well, and she knows that I need some water.[70]

While all language involves gesture,[71] a system of gestures does not necessarily comprise a language.[72] Conditions for a true, signed language would have been present only in areas in which deaf people interacted.[73] Furthermore, any such area would have to include adults who could teach sign language, and an ongoing need to use the language.[74] Highly populated urban areas such as Athens and, especially, island communities that had a high incidence of deafness due to genetics may have included generations of deaf people who used sign language.[75]

There is no proof of the presence, or the absence, of ancient Greek sign language.[76] Someone signing language looks like someone gesturing.[77] The handful of references to the gestures used by deaf people[78] is inconclusive. A Greek would not have differentiated between gestured communication and true sign language, or cared much, probably, that there was a difference.

People who had learned writing before becoming deaf would have been able to use the written word to communicate. Such people would not have been common. Writing was not available to the average person in Greece,[79] and the vast population of the ancient world was not merely illiterate, but rather, nonliterate.[80] In the case of deaf children, the written word as a means of communication would have been limited to the rare family that included both parents who had mastered fluency of writing and reading[81] and deaf children.[82] Written characters were not the only media by which people who could not talk could transmit information. In the folk tale of the sisters Procne and Philomela, in which Procne's husband, Tereus, cuts out Philomela's tongue in order to prevent her from telling anyone that he raped her, Philomela weaves scenes into her tapestry that depict her story.[83]

In any case, people who did not speak Greek and who, for whatever reason, had to rely on gestured communication, were not admired.[84] Furthermore, the inability to speak went beyond a simple barrier in communication. Aristotle (*History of Animals* 4.9.536 b) observed that all people born deaf (κωφοί) are also mute (ἔνεοι).[85] By mute, Aristotle refers to an inability to express language, not an inability to form sounds.[86] Aristotle (*History of Animals* 4.9.536 b) observes that animals make noise; human beings speak, and though people who are born deaf have a voice, they cannot talk. For the Greeks, as for people of all pre-Enlightenment cultures, speech, language, and reason were intertwined.[87] Because the conditions (inability to hear) and symptoms (inability to speak) of deafness were indistinct, Herodotus could use "deaf" (κωφός) and "speechless" (ἄφωνος; ἔνεος) interchangeably.[88] As Herodotus' audience took for granted, deafness was synonymous with "dumbness" in its full range of meanings. Language was the hallmark of human achievement, so muteness went beyond a physical condition. An inability to speak went hand-in-hand with an inability to reason, hand-in-hand with stupidity.[89] Plato (*Theaetetus* 206 d) has Socrates say that anyone can show what he thinks about anything, unless he is speechless or deaf from birth (ἐνεὸς ἢ κωφὸς ἀπ' ἀρχῆς). The proverb recorded by Plutarch (*Moralia* 512 d) that only the oracle can understand the deaf (κωφοῦ) further highlights the difficulty faced by people unable to communicate verbally.

That muteness was seen as a grave affliction can be traced with three literary examples from the seventh century through the first century B.C. Hesiod (*Theogony* 793–98) describes the punishment for perfidious gods as a sort of temporary death, in which the god must lie for a year without breath, without voice (ἄναυδος). In the chilling final scene of the *Alcestis*, the woman whom Heracles offers to Admetus is not dead yet not quite alive, Alcestis yet not quite Alcestis.[90] The emblem of this liminal state is her muteness (ἄναυδος) (Euripides, *Alcestis* 1143). Finally, Diodorus (4.24.4–5), in his account of Heracles' travels, reports that the punishment for the young men who failed to carry out sacred rites in honor of Iolaüs was that they were struck mute (ἀφώνους), and thus, he writes, resemble dead men (τετελευτηκόσιν).

Deafness was indeed a curse, sometimes literally. The word "deaf" (κωφός) appears in the surviving Greek inscriptions almost exclusively as a curse, and a powerful one. Deprivation of hearing, because it meant a deprivation of verbal communication and perceived intelligence, meant separation from the political and intellectual arena. A curse of deafness was appropriate not only for one's political opponents, whose speech could harm, but also for anyone who had too much power.[91] Aristophanes (*Clouds* 1320) provides a comedic example of this curse when the chorus teases Strepsiades, saying that he will wish his son, soon to be diabolically forensically skilled, were mute (ἄφωνον).[92]

It is crucial to consider that concerns surrounding speech and intelligence were different for the literate elite than they were for the bulk of the population, but that it is the literate elite on whom we must rely for almost all our information about deafness. The elite valued the very skills—such as fluency in communication—that they thought deaf people lacked. On one hand, Herodotus' Greek audience knew that Croesus' son could never become king. On the other hand, the deaf child of a farmer or shepherd, even if considered utterly stupid and incapable of political activity, could certainly carry out any number of tasks. Aristotle and his circle had the luxury to despise lack of eloquence, but the average peasant would be far less concerned with his child's forensic skills.

In summary, we are confined to learning about deafness in the ancient Greek world through the filter of the literary elite. In other words, the closest we can observe everyday life for deaf people is through a partial reconstruction of attitudes toward deaf people. Deafness was perceived not as a physical handicap but as an impairment of reasoning and basic intelligence. Life in Greece for anyone who did not speak must have been frustrating, at best. While the consequences of deafness are synonymous with exile or death in the literature, it is important to remember that more people in the Greek world were interested in farming than rhetoric. While ineligibility in political and intellectual arenas may have been a hardship, the hardship is magnified out of proportion in the surviving material. Furthermore, we must be cautious about our own filter of interpretation. We should not leap to conclusions about constructions of intellectual ability and disability in the ancient world any faster than about physical ability and disability.

NOTES

1. This essay is based on a chapter of my Ph. D. thesis, "Physical Disability in the Ancient Greek World." The essay also developed from my presentation of "Croesus' Other Son: Ancient Greek Attitudes to Deafness" at the meeting of the Classical Association of the Midwest and South, Omaha, 22 April 1995. Many people contributed to this essay. Alan Boegehold and Robert Garland kindly provided me with their work before publication. Roberta Cullen, Lorna Sopçak, and Ross Willits have read and commented on many drafts, as have Lois Bragg and Anthony Hogan. Three anonymous readers associated with Gary Kiger and the Society for Disability Studies offered much helpful criticism and advice. Lennard Davis, too, has been generous and gracious. I appreciate Jenny Singleton's correspondence and suggestions. I also thank Thomas Kelly, my thesis advisor.
2. Gary Kiger et al., "Introduction," *Disability Studies: Definitions and Diversity*, ed. G. Kiger et al. (Salem, Oregon, 1994), 1.
3. Beth Haller ("Rethinking Models of Media Representation of Disability," *Disability Studies Quarterly* 15 [1995]: 29–30) includes a succinct summary of various categories by which the media have represented disability, including the medical model.
4. Kiger et al., "Introduction," *Disability Studies*, 1.

5. Pliny (*Natural History* 35.7.21) relates the story of Quintus Pedius, "born dumb" (*natura mutus esset*), who, on the advice of the orator Messala and with the approval of Augustus, had lessons in painting and was making good progress when he died. Danielle Gourevitch, "Un enfant muet de naissance s'exprime par le dessin: à propos d'un cas rapporté par Pline l'Ancien," *L'Evolution psychiatrique* 56 [1991]: 889–93 discusses this short passage fully, and compares the Latin *mutus* with the various Greek terms for muteness.

6. Herodotus' tale (1.34; 1.38; 1.85), and see Warren Dawson, "Herodotus as Medical Writer," *Bulletin of the Institute of Classical Studies* 33 (1986): 87–96.

7. Nanci Scheetz, *Orientation to Deafness* (Boston, 1993), 203. Aram Gloring and Jean Roberts ("Hearing Levels of Adults by Age and Sex," *Vital and Health Statistics* 11th ser., 11 [1965]: 16) define a person with a severe hearing impairment as anyone who has trouble understanding loud or even amplified speech.

8. Karl Kryter (*The Effects of Noise on Man* [Orlando, 1985], 220) states that people working around noise have always suffered deafness. Still, the noise to which he refers throughout his study is industrial noise.

9. Jiri Prazma ("Ototoxicity of Aminoglycoside Antibiotics," *Pharmacology of Hearing*, ed. R. D. Brown and E. A. Daigneault [New York, 1981], 153–95) discusses cochlear destruction caused by the AmAn drugs, the best-known of which include the streptomycin antibiotics. In antiquity, wormseed, chenopodium oil, and cinchona alkaloids could cause temporary deafness. Calvin Wells (*Bones, Bodies and Disease* [London, 1964], 111–13) discusses paleotoxicology in terms of the difficulty of identification; for example, mineral poisons remain in the tissues and are easily identified, but may have come from the soil, after death.

10. Guido Majno (*The Healing Hand: Man and Wound in the Ancient World* [Cambridge, Mass., 1975], 171–75) discusses various injuries that resulted from boxing in fourth- and third-century Greece, including the "cauliflower ear." He points out (174) that Aristophanes invented the term "ear-breaker" (κάταξις) for a boxer. A type of accident in which the ears themselves are injured is seen in an account by Plutarch (*Moralia* 470 e) of men whose noses and ears were mutilated (περικοπτομένους) as they were digging through Mt. Athos. While this tale is fantastic, designed to show an example of Xerxes' hybris in cutting through Mt. Athos, the detail of injured ears is believable.

11. Grmek (*DAGW*, 334–37) sees evidence for chickenpox, the common cold virus, and mumps. He sees evidence for the possibility of the influenza virus and poliomyelitis. He does not believe that the measles virus existed. Srboljub Živanović (*Ancient Diseases: The Elements of Paleopathology* [New York, 1982], 86, 108) finds possible skeletal evidence for poliomyelitis.

12. Grmek (*DAGW*, 122, 123, 131) discusses meningitis in ancient Greece.

13. Of course, these viruses must have taken their toll not only by causing deafness, but also by killing the victim. Mustafa Abdalla Salih ("Childhood Acute Bacterial Meningitis in the Sudan: An Epidemiological, Clinical and Laboratory Study," *Scandinavian Journal of Infectious Diseases* suppl. 66 [1990]) studied meningitis in a developing area (the Sudan), and reports (76) that both the mortality and the frequency of long-term complications, including hearing loss, was much higher than in developed countries. Among survivors in the Sudan, twenty-two percent had hearing loss (7). Antibiotics (20, 26) and vaccination (27) are the main factors responsible for diminishing the impact of the disease in developed countries.

14. Ancient writers were aware of hereditary physical disability, even if they did not

recognize the underlying genetics. The Hippocratic author of *The Sacred Disease* (3) observes phlegmatic children from phlegmatic parents, bilious children from bilious parents, and so on. Aristotle (*History of Animals* 9(7).585 b) cites lame children born of lame parents; blind children produced by blind parents. Because he does not understand the genetics, he also cites (*Generation of Animals* 1.17.721 b) acquired characteristics, such as scars and brands.

15. Robert Sallares, *The Ecology of the Ancient Greek World* (Ithaca, 1991), 235. Sallares (460) mentions other ancient ecological peculiarities of Myconos. Nora Groce (*Everyone Here Spoke Sign Language: Hereditary Deafness on Martha's Vineyard* [Cambridge, Mass., 1985]) gives a modern account of island communities with a high proportions of people who are deaf—twenty-five percent of the inhabitants in the mid-nineteenth century—as a result of inbreeding. The discussion (40–43) on inbreeding is especially useful.

16. Ha-Sheng Li, "Genetic Influences on Susceptibility of the Auditory System to Aging and Environmental Factors," *Scandinavian Audiology* 21 suppl. 36 (1992): 7.

17. M. Michael Cohen and Robert J. Gorlin ("Epidemiology, Etiology, and Genetic Patterns," *Hereditary Hearing Loss and Its Syndromes*, ed. R. Gorlin et al. [New York, 1995], 9–21) discuss the varieties of genetic deafness in the modern world, listing hereditary factors, acquired factors, and unknown factors as about equal as causes of genetic hearing loss (9). These subcategories of genetic deafness in the ancient world are impossible to determine.

18. Gerhard Salomon, "Hearing Problems and the Elderly," *Danish Medical Bulletin* 33 suppl. 3 (1986): 4.

19. Grmek (*DAGW*, 103) gives 41.7 years as the average age of adults at the moment of death in Greece during Classical times. Here he follows J. Lawrence Angel, "The Length of Life in Ancient Greece," *Journal of Gerontology* 2 (1947): 20. Angel points out (23) that the data are scanty, especially for very old people. Mogens Herman Hansen (*Demography and Democracy* [Herning, Denmark, 1986], 12) calculates that in the fourth century, of all males in Attica eighteen to eighty years and older, 11.9 percent were fifty to sixty-nine years old; 8.7 percent were sixty to eighty years and older. M. I. Finley ("The Elderly in Classical Antiquity," *Greece and Rome* 28 [1981]: 157) contrasts these figures with the projection that by the end of the twentieth century, people sixty years of age and older will comprise twenty percent of the population in Great Britain.

20. The cumulative effect of noise pollution might be responsible for some hearing loss in the elderly that would not have been present in the ancient world. Ha-Sheng Li ("Genetic Influences on Susceptibility of the Auditory System to Aging and Environmental Factors," *Scandinavian Audiology* 21 suppl. 36 [1992]: 8) states that the etiology of deafness through aging is not well understood. Sava Soucek and Leslie Michaels (*Hearing loss in the Elderly: Audiometric, Electrophysiological and Histopathological Aspects* (London, 1990)) conclude (103) that hearing loss is innate to old age.

21. Even in the twentieth century this is the case. Donna Williams (*Somebody Somewhere: Breaking Free From the World of Autism* [New York, 1994], 50) explains, in her account of her own autism, that she was "meaning-deaf," but, like many autistic children, was thought to be sound-deaf.

22. An example of muteness as a result of autism can be seen in Josh Greenfeld's account of his son, *A Child Called Noah* (New York, 1972).

23. W. Pötscher ("Der stumme Sohn der Kroisos," *Zeitschrift für klinische Psychologie und*

Psychotherapie 20 [1974]: 368) argues that Croesus' son was not deaf at all, pointing out that, in order to finally speak, he must have been able to hear all along. He suggests that Herodotus used "deaf" (κωφός) as an interchangeable word for "mute."

24. "Stone deaf" is not an exclusively modern concept, though in the ancient world it was perhaps more literal. A girl's first or second century A.D. grave stele from Smyrna (*Inschriften von Smyrna* I.549, ed. G. Petzl [Bonn, 1982]) refers to the deaf stones (Κωφαὶ . . . πέτραι) of the tomb.

25. It is interesting that Herodotus (1.166 and elsewhere) uses this same term for ships that are damaged so as to be utterly useless.

26. Xenophon (*Cyropaedia* 7.2.20) repeats the assessment.

27. The parallels between discounting a "defective" child and discounting a female child are provocative, and call to mind families who named only male children in census reports, as mentioned by Sarah Pomeroy ("Infanticide in Hellenistic Greece," *Images of Women in Antiquity*, ed. A. Cameron and A. Kuhrt [Detroit, 1993], 208).

28. J. A. S. Evans, *Herodotus: Explorer of the Past* (Princeton, 1991), 49.

29. Frag. 14 c *PMG*.

30. There are sixty-nine instances of the forms of κωφός in the Hippocratic Corpus.

31. Lane (*WMH*, 93) points out that about ten centuries later, deaf people appeared as a legal class for the first time, in the Code of Justinian, 3.20.7; 6.22.10.

32. The class of people who are severely deaf (δύσκωφοι) is mentioned in *Coan Foreknowledge* (193.1) in connection with symptoms they might have; specifically, if their hands tremble, their tongue is paralyzed, and they have torpor, it is a bad sign. Deaf people who are deaf from birth (οἱ κωφοί οἱ ἐκ γενεῆς) are presented to illustrate nonfunctional vocal chords in *Fleshes* (18.8). Danielle Gourevitch ("L'aphonie hippocratique," *Formes de pensée dans la Collection hippocratique*, ed. F. Lasserre and P. Mudry [Geneva, 1983], 302) points out that muteness (ἄφωος) appears in the Hippocratic Corpus as a symptom rather than a condition in itself, and that while the Hippocratics recognized that there were different degrees and typed of muteness, the aim of the practitioners was objective reporting, not analysis. She further points out (303–05), that the meaning of the two common terms for muteness (ἄφωνος and ἀναυδής) shifts from author to author and even within the Hippocratic Corpus.

33. This sort of passing deafness is seen especially frequently throughout *Epidemics*; e.g., 1.3.13(3).5, 15, 16; 1.3.13(5).26; 1.3.13(10).4, and so on. In the writings of Galen, there are twenty-five instances of the term "deaf" (κωφός); four in Pseudo-Galen. Of these, almost all are referrals to the temporary deafness of the Hippocratic Corpus (e.g., 17a.528.5; 17a.530.2; 17a.530.7; 17a.534.4; 17a.557.16; 17a. 560.10; 17a.585.7; 17a.587.2).

34. Deafness as a result of a misdirected lochial purge: Hippocrates, *On the Affections of Women* 41.30. Muteness as an accompanying symptom of hysteria: *On the Nature of Women* 23.1; *On the Affections of Women* 127.1; 201.13; 203.18. Danielle Gourevitch (*Le Mal d'être femme: la femme et la médecine dans la Rome antique* [Paris, 1984], 113–28) provides a good discussion of female hysteria in general. She also explains (27) that women's bodies were usually traumatically out of balance in the view of medical science, which had as its underpinnings the system of humors; that is, blood, phlegm, black bile, and yellow bile all balanced in the right proportions given the season and topography.

35. A main vein, in Hippocratic thought (*Internal Affections* 18.23–25) travels all the

way from the head to the feet. If it is severed in the area of the head, deafness or blindness results. Lameness results if it is severed in the leg. Muteness, not deafness, is at least in one instance a tangible medical phenomenon: a short passage (*Fleshes* 18.8) on the physiology of speaking and muteness explains that air produces sound as it intersects the throat, moderated by the tongue.

36. Naturally, the term continues as an effective and not uncommon metaphor; for example, Plato (*Republic* 3.18.411 d) warns that the soul of a man who does not partake in the Muse will become weak, deaf (κωφός), and blind.

37. Huldrych Koelbing (*Arzt und Patient in der Antiken Welt* [Munich, 1977], 158) points out that although Celsus worked during the Roman, not Hellenistic, period, his work is more a compilation of Hellenistic scientific writing than a reflection of his own practice.

38. When bowels are bilious, deafness ensues, *Aphorisms* 4.28.1; deafness accompanying a bowel movement full of black matter is fatal after a hemorrhage, *Prorrhetic* 1.129; similar examples: *Prorrhetic* 1.127; *Coan Foreknowledge* 324; 623.

39. In case Celsus' treatment seems quaint, I should note Lane, *WMH*, the first part of which is written as an autobiography of Laurent Clerc, a nineteenth-century deaf man. Clerc submitted to visits to a doctor who injected mysterious liquids into his ears in an attempt to cure his deafness (5).

40. Anthony Hogan, letter to the author, 14 July 1994 points out that the treatment is still successfully used today, as a solution of turpentine is helpful in loosening an impaction of cerumen (earwax), and that the danger lies, then and now, in inserting the probe too far, and perforating the ear drum. I thank Mr. Hogan for his help, his generosity in reading several drafts of this chapter, and for his correspondence. A study undertaken by the Health Services Directorate of Canada (*Acquired Hearing Impairment in the Adult* [Ottawa, 1988], 14) confirms that partial deafness can indeed result from an impaction of earwax.

41. Robert Garland (*The Eye of the Beholder* [Ithaca, 1995], 96–97) sees Croesus' son's spontaneous recovery as a symbol that the son was, after all, worthwhile, and that Croesus' moral blindness toward his son is parallel with his senseless invasion of Persia. I thank Dr. Garland for his generosity in providing me with substantial portions of his manuscript before publication, and for his correspondence, advice, and encouragement. W. Pötscher ("Der stumme Sohn der Kroisos," *Zeitschrift für klinische Psychologie und Psychotherapie* 20 [1974], 367–68) argues that the muteness was psychogenic and not connected with deafness at all.

42. Ludwig and Emma Edelstein (*Asclepius: A Collection and Interpretation of the Testimonies*, 2 vols. [Baltimore, 1945]) have collected and translated much of IG IV^2.951, a stele from the healing site at Epidaurus, both sides of which consist of narrations of various complications and cures. For the translation of this case, see 230–31. This cure is typically miraculous, listed among other cures such as the restoration of a lost eyeball and the disappearance of scars.

43. Mabel Lang (*Cure and Cult in Ancient Corinth: A Guide to the Asklepion* [Princeton, 1977], 15) uses headache as an example of an abstract ailment. This difficulty of representation may explain the lack of reference to deafness or muteness in the surviving papyri; I have yet to see a reference to either. Physical characteristics do appear in the papyri, especially in the private documents, but usually as neutral attributes, such as scars, that identify people. A negative characteristic (e.g., not speaking) would be inefficient identification.

44. Such offerings could also represent thank offerings or pleas for cures of ear infec-

tions. Van Straten (GG, 105–43) catalogues votive offerings representing body parts from the Greek world. Models of ears were found on many sites.

45. Here (*History of Animals* 1.11.492 a) Aristotle associates large, projecting ears with senseless chatter.

46. Van Straten (GG, 110) points out that while there are no surviving examples of mouths, there is testimony for eight examples at the Athenian Asclepion. Sara Aleshire (*The Athenian Asklepion: The People, Their Dedications, and the Inventories* [Amsterdam, 1989], 41) has little to add to Van Straten's findings in her study, published eight years after Van Straten's, on the issue of votive mouths: she refers the reader to Van Straten for the discussion of mouths.

47. H. S. Versnel, "Religious Mentality in Ancient Prayer," *Faith Hope and Worship*, ed. H. S. Versnel (Leiden, 1981), 30.

48. Van Straten, GG, 83. Van Straten points out (144) that he restricted the ears, in his catalogue of body parts, to the ears which were votive offerings, not representations of gods' ears, although it is impossible to be completely sure which is which. The atmosphere and appearance of the Asclepions is just lately being reconstructed. Sara Aleshire (*Asklepios at Athens: Epigraphic and Prosopographic Essays on the Athenian Healing Cults* [Amsterdam, 1991], 46) compares the temples of Asclepius, in contrast to the stark reconstructions of bare buildings, to overcrowded antique stores or museum storerooms.

49. We see another example of comedic deafness in Herodas' mime, in which the slave Kydilla, addressing the slave Pyrrhias as "deaf" (κωφέ) tells him that his mistress is calling him, Mime 5.55. I. C. Cunningham (*Herodas Miamiambi* [Oxford, 1971], 155–56) argues that this term (κωφέ)is not a true vocative. There is nothing to indicate that Pyrrhias was to be taken as a literally deaf character, but the line has a slapstick tone. Cunningham (*LCL* 1993) translates the lines: "Pyrries, you deaf wretch, she is calling you" (Πυρρίης, τάλας, κωφέ, / καλεῖ σε). Similarly, a small fragment of Cratinus' comedy, "Archilochoi," frag. 6 PCG, provides just enough information to confirm that the gag of the deaf man and the blind man interacting existed in the fifth century. The stock gag continues; e.g., the interactions between a blind butler and deaf maid are meant to be comic in the film *Murder by Death*, dir. Robert Moore, Columbia, 1984.

50. Here, the phrase is "diminished hearing" (ἀκούειν ἧττον).

51. M. I. Finley ("The Elderly in Classical Antiquity," *Greece and Rome* 28 [1981]: 156 and passim) discusses the role of the elderly in comedy.

52. Meyer Reinhold ("The Generation Gap in Antiquity," *The Conflict of Generations in Ancient Greece and Rome*, ed. M. Bertman [Amsterdam, 1976], 44) argues that the conflict of generations is particularly a fifth-century phenomenon. Gerhard Salomon ("Hearing Problems and the Elderly," *Danish Medical Bulletin* 33 suppl. 3 [1986]: 12) points out that hearing loss may magnify the traits of senility.

53. Victor Hanson, *The Western Way of War: Infantry Battle in Classical Greece* (New York, 1989), 95.

54. Victor Hanson, *The Western Way of War: Infantry Battle in Classical Greece* (New York, 1989), 95. The panic was not necessarily always noise-induced, but may have been: Hanson (147–50, 152–54) reconstructs the chaos and the noise of battle.

55. Jan Bremmer ("The Old Women of Ancient Greece," *Sexual Asymmetry*, ed. J. Blok and P. Mason [Amsterdam, 1987], 191–215) has assembled the evidence that exists. Silence in a woman was virtuous, and women's speech was, at best, considered less valuable than men's speech (e.g., Nancy Sorkin Rabinowitz, "Female

Speech and Female Sexuality: Euripides' *Hippolytus* as Model," *Helios* 13 [1986]: 127–40), and it is interesting to wonder what attitudes a mute woman might have encountered, given the ideals of feminine silence. Because there is no record of such attitudes, all we can do is wonder.

56. *Greek Anthology* 11.74. "In fact," the narrator says, "she does not comprehend a word I say." This is the only significant instance of a deaf woman that I have found in the Greek material.

57. Henry Kisor (*What's That Pig Outdoors?* [New York, 1990]), throughout his autobiography, dispels the notion that a deaf person can always read lips efficiently.

58. Lane (*WMH*, 93) writes that "those who were deaf only but could speak—who had established their credentials in the eyes of hearing society and knew their oral language—have always been regarded as persons at law." That those who could speak have "always" been seen as worthwhile is probably true, but the earliest documentation, as Lane points out, is not until the Code of Justinian, sixth century A.D.

59. The question of nasal speech comes up in Pseudo-Aristotle, *Problems*, 11.2.899 a; the answer hinges on the relation between deafness and dumbness, followed by a physiological explanation about breath and tongue, mirroring the Hippocratic Corpus, *Fleshes* 8; another connection between deafness and dumbness, followed by an explanation that the nostrils of the deaf are distended because the deaf breathe more violently, 11.4.899 a; and a suggestion that deafness is a congestion in the region of the lungs, 33.14.962 b. Similarly, Galen, 8.267.14–16, describes a condition in which injured throat muscles result in a wounded voice, but specifies that a weak voice, not muteness, results (σμικρόφωνος οὔτε δὲ ἄφωνος).

60. Ironically, Hannah Gershon ("Who Gets to be Called Deaf? Cultural Conflicts Between Deaf Populations," Society for Disability Studies 1994 Annual Meeting, Rockville, 24 June 1994) argued that in deaf culture today, while all audiologically deaf people are "permanent exiles" from the world of sound, late- deafened adults are "immigrants" in deaf culture, who "never lose their hearing accent," while those who grew up without hearing have a solid identity in deaf society.

61. Battus, who according to Herodotus, 4.155–58, was the seventh century B.C. founder of Cyrene, is also a good example: on one hand, his speech disorder—usually taken as a stutter—was part of his identity. On the other hand, his legend involves a full role in the political sphere. O. Masson ("Le nom de Battos, fondateur de Cyrene," *Glotta* 54 [1976]: 84–98) discusses the etymology of the name "Battus."

62. William Stokoe, "Language, Prelanguage, and Sign Language," *Seminars in Speech and Language* 11 (1990), 93.

63. Venetta Lampropoulou ("The History of Deaf Education in Greece," *The Deaf Way*, ed. C. Erting et al. [Washington, D.C., 1995], 240) suggests that deaf babies in Sparta were included among those "with disabilities" and discarded. There is no reason, though, to believe that babies born deaf were subject to infanticide, if only because the deafness would not be detected until later, as Danielle Gourevitch ("Un enfant muet de naissance s'exprime par le dessin: à propos d'un cas rapporté par Pline l'Ancien," *L'Evolution psychiatrique* 56 [1991]: 890) points out. It is possible that a child who was perceived as worthless would have received less than his or her share of necessities and thus eventually would have died, but there is no evidence for or against this.

64. Steven Pinker (*The Language Instinct* [New York, 1994], 37–38) points out that suc-

cessful language acquisition must take place in childhood, and (293) that the likelihood of acquiring spoken language is steadily compromised after the age of six. Franklin Silverman, *Communication for the Speechless* (Boston, 1995), 11.

65.   In extreme cases today, children without language are treated as subhuman, even "wild." "Genie" is a recent case of a "wild child" who, until thirteen years old, had been raised in near-isolation, not deaf but language-deprived. Her portrait illustrates the severe consequences of the intertwined lack of language and socialization: Genie "was unsocialized, primitive, hardly human." Susan Curtiss, *Genie: A Psycholinguistic Study of a Modern-Day 'Wiled Child'* (New York, 1977), 9. Russ Rymer (Genie: An Abused Child Flight From Silence [New York, 1993]) discusses several other cases of mute children, including (205) a deaf woman misdiagnosed as mentally retarded, who grew up in the backwoods and was deprived of language until she was in her thirties. It is interesting that satyrs—subhuman inhabitants of the wilds—are vaguely associated with muteness. Silens, too, are intriguing in this context. Guy Michael Hedreen (*Silens in Attic Black-figure Vase-painting: Myth and Performance* [Ann Arbor, 1992], 1) describes silens, the mythical horse-man hybrids who are related to satyrs, but who bear more resemblance to humans than do satyrs. Plutarch (*Sulla* 27.2) relates the tale of Sulla's discovery of a Greek satyr; Sulla was unable to force it to do more than grunt. The satyr Silenus was supposed to possess unlimited wisdom but, at least according to Vergil (*Ecologues* 6.13) had to be forced to speak. One wonders about the lost Sophoclean *Deaf Satyrs*, frags. 362–63, but with only two surviving partial lines to accompany the title, one can only wonder. A. C. Pearson (ed., *The Fragments of Sophocles*, 3 vols. [Cambridge, England, 1917], 2:31) suggests that "the κωφοί" were 'blockheads',", and discusses other scholars' theories on the content of the play.

66.   Carol Padden (review of *A Man Without Words*, by Susan Schaller, *American Journal of Psychology* 105 [1992]: 652–53) writes that the "wild children" such as Victor and Genie lacked not just language, but also the ability to take part in life's social rhythm.

67.   Alan L. Boegehold ("Some Modern Gestures in Ancient Greek Literature," *Transactions of the Greek Humanistic Society 1* [forthcoming]: 2–3) encourages scholars of ancient Greek to pay attention not only to the written words but also to the implied gestures. I thank Dr. Boegehold for providing me with this essay before publication. Boegehold provides a specific example in "A Signifying Gesture: Euripides, *Iphigeneia Taurica*, 965–66, *American Journal of Archaeology* 93 (1989), 81–83, in which he argues that the gesture made by Athena, suggested by the word ὠλένι, has a specific indication: an equal (thus favorable) conclusion of the sorting of votes in the trial of Orestes.

68.   S. Goldin-Meadow and C. Mylander, "The Development of Morphology Without a Conventional Language Model," *From Gesture to Language in Hearing and Deaf Children*, ed. V. Volterra and C. J. Erting (New York, 1990), 165. Lane (*WMH*, 5) describes "home sign," a system of abbreviated gestures. Steven Pinker (*The Language Instinct* [New York, 1994], 36) cites a situation in Nicaragua in the 1970s in which deaf children pooled their gestures and developed what is now a codified system of gestures. Since it is not based on consistent grammar, this system is "basically pidgin."

69.   Harlan Lane, *The Mask of Benevolence: Disabling the Deaf Community* (New York, 1992), 147.

70.   Harlan Lane, *The Mask of Benevolence: Disabling the Deaf Community* (New York,

1992), 151. Mark Golden (*Children and Childhood in Classical Athens* [Baltimore, 1990], 35–36) discusses the agricultural labor of children—gathering stones from the field, breaking up dirt, tending animals—as a criterion that helps assess their value as an economic unit in the family.

71. William Stokoe ("Seeing Clearly Through Fuzzy Speech," *Sign Language Studies* 82 [1994], 90) argues that all language *is* gesture.

72. William Stokoe, *Semiotics and Human Sign Languages*, Approaches to Semiotics 21 (Paris, 1972), 13. Syntax is the difference between gesture and signed language.

73. Robert E. Johnson and Carol Erting ("Ethnicity and Socialization in a Classroom for Deaf Children," *The Sociolinguistics of the Deaf Community*, ed. C. Lucas [New York, 1989], 43) point out that in America, deafness goes beyond a physical disability to include a set of attitudes and behaviors. They further point out (49) that the shared experience based on a visual culture is one of the elements that creates a community among deaf people. Whether or not a deaf community existed anywhere in the ancient Greek world is impossible to determine, though one imagines that at least in the rural areas of Greece, there were only isolated, deaf individuals. Lane (*WMH*, 112 and passim) cites "signing communities" in eighteenth-century France that, he argues, formed the basis of formal education for the deaf. In any case, it is important to distinguish between early communities of deaf people and the newer deaf community. Petra Rose and Gary Kiger ("Intergroup Relations: Political Action and Identity in the Deaf Community," Society for Disability Studies Annual Meeting, Rockville, Maryland, 23 June 1994) trace the newer, radical element of the deaf community to the Deaf Power movement in the 1970s, in which deaf people "acquired a voice" and recognized themselves as a minority with a cultural heritage.

74. M. C. Da Cunha Pereira and C. De Lemos ("Gesture in Hearing Mother-Deaf Child Interaction," *From Gesture to Language in Hearing and Deaf Children*, ed. V. Volterra and C. J. Erting [New York, 1990], 186) point out that, while deaf children in hearing families develop the skills necessary to learning sign language, a sign language does not materialize on its own, even between deaf peers. Sign language must be taught by someone proficient in it.

75. If in Athens, with the largest population of any Greek polis by far, there were 60,000 citizens ca. 500 B.C., as Chester Starr (*The Economic and Social Growth of Early Greece 800–500 B.C.* [New York, 1977], 152–56) calculates, 600 citizens would have been severely deaf; sixty would have been congenitally deaf. The category of "citizens" includes male residents eligible to vote and does not include women, children, slaves, or foreign residents. If we double the population figure of 60,000 to include women, and double it again to include two children for each family, we still have only 240 congenitally deaf people up and down Attica, with no particular reason that they would be aware of each other's presence, especially given the lack of public schools. In a smaller community such as the island of Melos, with its fifth-century population of about 1,250 citizens, as Eberhard Ruschenbusch ("Tribut und Bürgerzahl im ersten athenischen Seebund," *Zeitschrift für Papyrologie und Epigraphik* 53 [1983]: 145) estimates, one or two citizens would be congenitally deaf, and about five people altogether. On one hand, these figures do not account for the possibility that, as noted earlier, the diseases that leave people deaf in the modern world may have killed people in the ancient world. On the other hand, they do not take into account genetic phenomena that might have increased the prevalence of deafness in island communities.

76. But William Stokoe ("Discovering a Neglected Language," *Sign Language Studies*

85 [1994]: 377) believes that sign language has a long history, documented or not: "In my opinion," he writes, "if the ancestor of sign language is ever found, it will turn out to be the first human, most likely a woman, who realized that gestures not only meant whatever two or more people agreed on that they meant, because they may also connect meanings—they may be words or sentences, depending on how one looks at them."

77. As William Stokoe (Language, Prelanguage, and Sign Language," *Seminars in Speech and Language* 11 [1990]: 94) points out.

78. Xenophon (*Anabasis* 4.5.33) describes soldiers with a language barrier using gestures as if mute (ἐνειοῖς). Ctesias (*FGrH* 688 F 45) refers to using signs like "the deaf and speechless" (κωφοὶ καὶ ἄλαλοι). Plato (*Cratylus* 422 d-e) too, has Socrates suggest communication by gesture, "as mute men" (ἐνεοί).

79. William Harris, *Ancient Literacy* (Cambridge, Mass., 1989), 67.

80. Rosalind Thomas (*Literacy and Orality in Ancient Greece* [Cambridge, England, 1992], 2–4) discusses the extent of nonliteracy. Eric Havelock (*Origins of Western Literacy* [Toronto, 1976], 7) drives the point home by pointing out that Pindar and Plato were nearly nonliterate.

81. Eric Havelock (*Origins of Western Literacy* [Toronto, 1976], 46–47) traces the ancient development of reading fluency (possible only when the components of the alphabet have no independent meaning at all). He argues (21) that scriptoral literacy only appeared at the beginning of the fourth century B.C.

82. Mark Golden (*Children and Childhood in Classical Athens* [Baltimore, 1990], 62–65) discusses children's education, of which reading and writing was a component (62). Golden (73–74) discusses the education of girls, which was conducted at home. While there is no evidence one way or the other, it is doubtful that a congenitally-deaf child would be thought to be capable of receiving more than rudimentary instruction, let alone formal education.

83. The tale is recorded in various sources, including the fragments of Sophocles' lost play *Tereus* (frags. 581–95, A. C. Pearson, ed., *The Fragments of Sophocles* [Cambridge, Mass., 1917]); Apollodorus, 3.14.8; Pausanias, 1.41.8–9. Only in Apollodorus' version does Philomela weave written characters (γράμματα), as opposed to images, into her robe.

84. For example, Clytemnestra, in Aeschylus, *Agamemnon* 1060–1061, commands an unresponsive Cassandra, "Speak not, but make with your barbarian hand some sign" (σὺ δ᾽ ἀντὶ φωνῆς φράζε καρθάνω χερί). Similarly, the Phrygian messenger in Euripides, *Orestes* (1369–526), both foreign and terrified, delivers his barely coherent report by pantomime, to the impatience and disgust of his audience.

85. Pseudo-Aristotle (*Problems* 898 b) asks why those who suffer any defect from birth mostly have bad hearing, and asks in answer if it is because hearing and voice arise from the same source; he also observes (*Problems* 33.1.961 b) that men become deaf and dumb (ἔνεοι καὶ κωφοί) at the same time. This observation is echoed by Pliny(*Natural History* 10.88.192).

86. Babies who are born deaf, after all, still cry. Carol Padden and Tom Humphries (*Deaf in America* [Cambridge, Mass., 1988], 91) point out that "a widespread misconception among hearing people is that Deaf people live in a world without sound," and that the metaphor of silence "is clumsy and inadequate as a way of explaining what Deaf people know and do" (109).

87. Yves Violé O'Neill, *Speech and Speech Disorders in Western Thought Before 1600* (Westport, 1980), 3–11.

88. For example, Herodotus (1.34) uses "deaf" (κωφός) and "speechless" (ἄφωνος)(1.85) interchangeably to refer to Croesus' son. It is interesting to note that modern Greek combines the term for deaf (κωφός) and mute (ἄλαλος) into one word for "deaf-mute" (κωφάλαλος). I have not found this compound term in the ancient Greek vocabulary.

89. Harlan Lane (*The Mask of Benevolence: Disabling the Deaf Community* [New York, 1992], 147) points out that this misperception still exists today.

90. There are of course many possible interpretations. D. L. Drew ("Euripides' *Alcestis*," *American Journal of Philology* 52 [1931]: 295–319) argues that this is the corpse of Alcestis. Whether the figure on stage was meant to be seen as alive, dead, or something in between, Drew points out (313) that even if only three speaking actors were available, her continued silence was not necessary from a technical standpoint. Charles Segal (*Art, Gender, and Communication in* Alcestis, Hippolytus, *and* Hecuba [Durham, 1993], 49) writes that Alcestis' final silence has associations with death.

91. John Gager (*Curse Tablets and Binding Spells From the Ancient World* [New York, 1992], 116–50) discusses curses and binding spells in the courtroom. While many of the curses he cites give only the bare information, such as the names of the people to be cursed, others specifically request speechlessness, such as a tablet from the Piraeus (date unknown), in which a woman's tongue is cursed to be bound, made of lead, *and* stabbed (159–60). Nonpolitical curses: SEG 35.214, 216, 218, 220–23. These are A. D. third-century defixiones, discussed by David Jordan ("Defixiones From a Well Near the Southwest Corner of the Athenian Agora," *Hesperia* 54 [1985]: 105–255) as curses on individual athletes. The typical curse: "may he be deaf (κωφός); speechless (ἄλαλος); mindless (ἄνους)," and so on. Although the surviving examples of curses mentioning κωφός are late, Gager (5) shows that defixiones did exist as early as the fifth century B.C. Generally, the earlier the curse tablet, the simpler the spell; the earliest often include only the name of the victim.

92. This is reminiscent of the wisdom that the priestess at the Delphic oracle gives Croesus: it is better, she says, that his son remain mute, Herodotus (1.85).

REFERENCES

Primary Sources

Aeschylus. sixth/fifth centuries B.C. 1973 [1922]. Trans. H. Smyth. Loeb Classical Library. Vol. 1. Cambridge: Harvard University Press. 2 vols.

———. sixth/fifth centuries B.C. 1983 [1926]. Trans. H. Smyth. Loeb Classical Library. Vol. 2. Cambridge: Harvard University Press. 2 vols.

Apollodorus. second century B.C. 1976 [1921]. Trans. G. Frazer. Loeb Classical Library. Cambridge: Harvard University Press. 2 vols.

Aristophanes. fifth century B.C. 1982 [1924]. Trans. B. B. Rogers. Loeb Classical Library. Vol. 2. Cambridge: Harvard University Press. 3 vols.

Aristotle. fourth century B.C. 1979 [1965]. Trans. A. L. Peck. Loeb Classical Library. Cambridge: Harvard University Press. 23 vols.

———. fourth century B.C. 1991. Trans. D. M. Balme. Loeb Classical Library. Vol. 11. Cambridge: Harvard University Press. 23 vols.

———. fourth century B.C. 1979 [1942]. Trans. A. L. Peck. Loeb Classical Library. Vol. 13. Cambridge: Harvard University Press. 23 vols.

———. fourth century B.C. 1970 [1926]. Trans. W. S. Hett. Loeb Classical Library. Vol. 15. Cambridge: Harvard University Press. 23 vols.

———. fourth century B. C. 1983 [1937]. Trans. W. S. Hett. Loeb Classical Library. Vol. 15. Cambridge: Harvard University Press. 23 vols.

Athenaeus. second century A. D. 1980 [1937]. *Deipnosophistae.* Trans. C. B. Gulick. Loeb Classical Library. Vol. 6. Cambridge: Harvard University Press. 7 vols.

Celsus. first century B. C. 1971 [1935]. *De Medecina.* Trans. W. G. Spencer. Loeb Classical Library Vol. 1. Cambridge: Harvard University Press. 3 vols.

———. first century B. C. 1961 [1938]. *De Medecina.* Trans. W. G. Spencer. Loeb Classical Library. Vol. 2. Cambridge: Harvard University Press. 3 vols.

Diodorus Siculus. first century B. C. 1961 [1935]. Trans. C. H. Oldfather. Loeb Classical Library. Vol. 2. Cambridge: Harvard University Press. 12 vols.

Edelstein, Emma and Ludwig Edelstein. 1945. *Asclepius: A Collection and Interpretation of the Testimonies.* Vol 1. Baltimore: Johns Hopkins Press. 2 vols.

Euripides. fifth century B. C. 1987. *Alcestis.* A. M. Dale, ed. Oxford: Clarendon Press.

———. fifth century B. C. 1978. *Orestes.* G. Murray, ed. 2nd ed. Vol. 2. Oxford: Clarendon Press. 3 vols.

Galen. second century A. D. 1821–33. *Medicorum Graecorum.* C. G. Kühn, ed. 20 vols. Leipzig: Knobloch.

Gager, John. 1992. *Curse Tablets and Binding Spells from the Ancient World.* New York: Oxford University Press.

The Greek Anthology. 1979. Trans. W. R. Paton. Vol.4. Loeb Classical Library. Cambridge: Harvard University Press. 5 vols.

Herodas. third century B. C. 1971. *Herodas Miamiambi.* I. C. Cunningham, ed. Oxford: Clarendon Press.

Herodas. third century B. C. 1993. *Mimes.* In *Theophrastus,* Characters; *Herodas,* Mimes; *Cercidas and the Choliambic Poets.* Ed. and trans. I. C. Cunningham. Loeb Classical Library. Cambridge: Harvard University Press.

Herodotus. fifth century B. C. 1981–90 [1920–25]. Trans. A. D. Godley. Loeb Classical Library. Cambridge: Harvard University Press. 4 vols.

Hesiod. ca. seventh century B. C. 1990. Friedrich Solmson, ed. 3rd ed. Oxford: Clarendon Press.

Hippocrates. ca. sixth through fourth centuries B. C. 1839–1861. *Oeuvres complètes d'Hippocrate.* É. Littré, ed. Paris: Ballière. 10 vols.

Homer. ca. eighth century B. C. 1988–93 [1924–25]. *Iliad.* Trans. A. T. Murray. Loeb Classical Library. Cambridge: Harvard University Press. 2 vols.

Jacoby, Felix. 1958. *Die Fragmente der griechischen Historiker.* 3:C. Leiden: E. J. Brill.

Jordan, David. 1985. "Defixiones From a Well Near the Southwest Corner of the Athenian Agora." *Hesperia* 54: 105–255.

Kassel, R. and C. Austin. 1983. *Poetae Comici Graeci.* Vol. 4. Berlin: Walter de Gruyter. 7 vols.

Page, D. L. 1967. *Poetae Melici Graecae.* Oxford: Clarendon Press.

Pausanias. second century A. D. 1977–79 [1918–33]. Trans W. H. S. Jones. Loeb Classical Library. Cambridge: Harvard University Press. 4 Vols.

Pearson, A. C. 1917. *The Fragments of Sophocles.* Vol. 2. Cambridge: Cambridge University Press. 3 vols.

———. *The Fragments of Sophocles.* 1917. Vol. 3. Cambridge: Cambridge University Press, 1917. 3 vols.

Petzl, Georg. 1982. *Die Inschriften von Smyrna.* Inschriften Griechischer Stadte Aus Kleinasien 23. Bonn: Rudolf Habelt.

Plato. fifth/fourth centuries B. C. 1977 [1926]. Trans. H. N. Fowler. Vol. 4. Loeb Classical Library. Cambridge: Harvard University Press. 12 vols.

———. fifth/fourth centuries B.C. 1977 [1927]. Trans. H. N. Fowler. Vol. 5. Loeb Clas-
    sical Library. Cambridge: Harvard University Press. 12 vols.
———. fifth/fourth centuries B.C. 1977 [1921]. Trans. H. N. Fowler. Vol. 7. Loeb Clas-
    sical Library. Cambridge: Harvard University Press. 12 vols.
Pleket, H. W. and R. S. Stroud, eds. 1988. Vol. 35. *Supplementum Epigraphicum Graecum*.
    Amsterdam: J. C. Gieben.
Pliny. first century A.D. 1983 [1940]. *Natural History*. Trans. H. Rackham. Vol. 3. Loeb
    Classical Library. Cambridge: Harvard University Press. 10 vols.
———. first century A.D. 1971 [1962]. *Natural History*. Trans. D. E. Eichholz. Vol. 10.
    Loeb Classical Library. Cambridge: Harvard University Press. 10 vols.
Plutarch. first/second centuries A.D. 1968 [1916]. *Lives*. Trans. B. Perrin. Vol. 4. Loeb
    Classical Library. Cambridge: Harvard University Press. 11 vols.
———. first/second centuries A.D. 1971 [1919]. *Lives*. Trans. B. Perrin. Vol. 7. Loeb Clas-
    sical Library. Cambridge: Harvard University Press. 11 vols.
———. first/second centuries A.D. 1936. *Moralia*. Trans. F. C. Babbit. Vol. 5. Loeb Clas-
    sical Library. Cambridge: Harvard University Press. 15 vols.
Strabo. first century B.C./first century A.D. 1928. *Geography*. Trans. H. L. Jones. Vol. 5.
    Loeb Classical Library. Cambridge: Harvard University Press. 8 vols.
Vergil. first century B.C. 1978 [1916]. Trans. H. R. Fairclaugh. Loeb Classical Library. Vol.
    1. Cambridge: Harvard University Press. 2 vols.
Xenophon. fifth/fourth centuries B.C. 1983 [1914]. Trans. W. Miller. Loeb Classical
    Library. Vol. 4. Cambridge: Harvard University Press. 7 vols.
———. fifth/fourth centuries B.C. 1979 [1923]. Trans. O. J. Todd. Loeb Classical Library.
    Vol. 5. Cambridge: Harvard University Press. 7 vols.

Secondary Material: Ancient Topics

Aleshire, Sara. 1991. *Asklepios at Athens: Epigraphic and Prosopographic Essays on the Athen-
    ian Healing Cults*. Amsterdam: J. C. Gieben.
———. 1989. *The Athenian Asklepion: The People, Their Dedications, and the Inventories*.
    Amsterdam: J. C. Gieben.
Angel, J. Lawrence. 1947. "The Length of Life in Ancient Greece." *Journal of Gerontol-
    ogy* 2: 18–24.
Boegehold, Alan. Forthcoming. "Some Modern Gestures in Ancient Greek Literature."
    Transactions of the Greek Humanistic Society 1.
———. 1989. "A Signifying Gesture: Euripides, *Iphageneia Taurica* 965–66." *American
    Journal of Archaeology* 93: 81–83.
Bremmer, Jan. 1987. "The Old Women of Ancient Greece." *Sexual Asymmetry: Studies
    in Ancient Society*. Ed. J. Blok and P. Mason. Amsterdam: J. C. Gieben. 191–215.
Burford, Alison. 1993. *Land and Labor in the Greek World*. Baltimore: Johns Hopkins Uni-
    versity Press.
Dawson, Warren R. 1986. "Herodotus as a Medical Writer." *Bulletin of the Institute of Clas-
    sical Studies* 33: 87–96.
Drew, D. L. 1931. "Euripides' *Alcestis*." *American Journal of Philology* 52: 295–319.
Evans, J. A. S. 1991. *Herodotus: Explorer of the Past*. Princeton: Princeton University
    Press.
Finley, M. I. 1981. "The Elderly in Classical Antiquity." *Greece and Rome* 28: 156–71.
Garland, Robert. 1995. *The Eye of the Beholder: Deformity and Disability in the Graeco-
    Roman World*. Ithaca: Cornell University Press.
Golden, Mark. 1990. *Children and Childhood in Classical Athens*. Baltimore: Johns Hopkins
    University Press.

Gourevitch, Danielle. 1983. "L'aphonie hippocratique." *Formes de pensée dans la Collection hippocratique*. Ed. F. Lasserre and P. Mudry. Geneva: Librairie Droz: 297–305.

———. 1991. "Un enfant muet de naissance s'exprime par le dessin: à propos d'un cas rapporté par Pline l'Ancien." *L'Evolution psychiatrique* 56: 889–93.

———. 1984. *Le Mal d'être femme: la femme et la médecine dans la Rome antique*. Paris: Société d'edition "Les Belles Lettres."

Grmek, Mirko. 1989. *Diseases in the Ancient Greek World*. Trans. M. Muellner. Baltimore: Johns Hopkins University Press.

Hansen, Mogens Herman. 1985. *Demography and Democracy: The Number of Athenian Citizens in the Fourth Century B.C.* Herning, Denmark: Systime.

Hanson, Victor Davis. 1989. *The Western Way of War: Infantry Battle in Classical Greece*. New York: Knopf.

Harris, William. 1989. *Ancient Literacy*. Cambridge: Harvard University Press.

Havelock, Eric. 1976. *Origins of Western Literacy*. Toronto: Ontario Institute for Studies in Education.

Hedreen, Guy Michael. 1992. *Silens in Attic Black-figure Vase-painting: Myth and Performance*. Ann Arbor: University of Michigan Press.

Koelbing, Huldrych. 1977. *Arzt und Patient in der Antiken Welt*. Munich: Artemis.

Lang, Mabel. 1977. *Cure and Cult in Ancient Corinth: A Guide to the Asklepion*. Princeton: American School of Classical Studies at Athens.

Majno, Guido. 1975. *The Healing Hand: Man and Wound in the Ancient World*. Cambridge: Harvard University Press.

Masson O. 1976. "Le nom de Battos, fondateur de Cyrene," *Glotta* 54: 84–98.

O'Neill, Yves Violé. 1980. *Speech and Speech Disorders in Western Thought Before 1600*. Westport: Greenwood Press.

Pötscher, W. 1974. "Der stumme Sohn der Kroisos." *Zeitschrift für klinische Psychologie und Psychotherapie* 20: 367–68.

Pomeroy, Sarah. 1993. "Infanticide in Hellenistic Greece." *Images of Women in Antiquity*. Ed. A. Cameron and A. Kuhrt. 2nd ed. Detroit: Wayne State University Press. 207–22.

Rabinowitz, Nancy Sorkin. 1986."Female Speech and Female Sexuality: Euripides' *Hippolytus* as Model." *Helios* 13: 127- 40.

Reinhold, Meyer. 1976. "The Generation Gap in Antiquity." *The Conflict of Generations in Ancient Greece and Rome*. Ed. S. Bertman. Amsterdam: Grüner. 15–54.

Ruschenbusch, Eberhard. 1983. "Tribut und Bürgerzahl im ersten athenischen Seebund." *Zeitschrift für Papyrologie und Epigraphik* 53: 125–48.

Sallares, Robert. 1991. *The Ecology of the Ancient Greek World*. Ithaca: Cornell University Press.

Segal, Charles. 1993. *Art, Gender, and Communication in Alcestis, Hippolytus, and Hecuba*. Durham: Duke University Press.

Starr, Chester. 1977. *The Economic and Social Growth of Early Greece 800—500 B.C.* New York: Oxford University Press.

Thomas, Rosalind. 1992. *Literacy and Orality in Ancient Greece*. Cambridge: Cambridge University Press.

Van Straten, F. T. 1981. "Gifts for the Gods." *Faith Hope and Worship*. Ed. H. S. Versnel. Leiden: E. J. Brill. 65–151.

Versnel, H. S. 1981. "Religious Mentality in Ancient Prayer." *Faith Hope and Worship*. Ed. H. S. Versnel. Leiden E. J. Brill. 1–64.

Wells, Calvin. 1964. *Bones, Bodies and Disease: Evidence of Disease and Abnormality in Early Man*. Ancient Peoples and Places 37. Bristol: Western Printing Services.

Živanović, Srboljub. 1982. *Ancient Diseases: The Elements of Paleopathology*. Trans. L. Edwards. New York: Pica Press, 1982.

Secondary Material: Modern Topics

Canadian Task Force of the Health Services Directorate. 1988. *Acquired Hearing Impairment of the Adult*. Ottawa: Minister of National Health and Welfare.

Cohen, M. Michael and Robert J. Gorlin. 1995. "Epidemiology, Etiology, and Genetic Patterns." *Hereditary Hearing Loss and Its Syndromes*. Ed. R. Gorlin, H. Toriello and M. Cohen. Oxford Monographs on Medical Genetics 28. New York: Oxford University Press. 9–21.

Curtiss, Susan. 1977. *Genie: A Psycholinguistic Study of a Modern Day "Wild Child."* New York: Academic Press.

Gershon, Hannah. 1994. "Who Gets to be Called 'Deaf'? Cultural Conflict Between Deaf Populations." Society for Disability Studies Annual Meeting. Rockville, 24 June.

Gloring, Aram and Jean Roberts. 1965. "Hearing Levels of Adults by Age and Sex." *Vital and Health Statistics* Ser. 11, 11: 1–34.

Goldin-Meadow, S. and C. Mylander. 1990. "The Development of Morphology Without a Conventional Language Model." *From Gesture to Language in Hearing and Deaf Children*. Ed. V. Volterra and C. J. Erting. New York: Springer-Verlag. 165–77.

Greenfeld, Josh. 1972. *A Child Called Noah*. New York: Washington Square Press.

Groce, Nora. 1985. *Everyone Here Spoke Sign Language: Hereditary Deafness on Martha's Vineyard*. Cambridge: Harvard University Press.

Haller, Beth. 1995. "Rethinking Models of Media Representation of Disability." *Disability Studies Quarterly* 15: 29–30.

Hogan, Anthony. 1984. Letter to the Author. 14 July.

Itard, Jean Marc Gaspard. 1962. *The Wild Boy of Aveyron (L'enfant sauvage)*. Trans. G. and M. Humphrey. New York: Meredith.

Johnson, Robert E. and Carol Erting. 1989. "Ethnicity and Socialization in a Classroom for Deaf Children." *The Sociolinguistics of the Deaf Community*. Ed. C. Lucas. New York: Academic Press. 41–83.

Kiger, Gary, Stephen Hey and J. Gary Linn. 1994. "Introduction." *Disability Studies: Definitions and Diversity*. Ed. G. Kiger, S. Hey, and J. G. Linn. Salem, Oregon: Society for Disability Studies and Willamette University. 1–4.

Kisor, Henry. 1990. *What's That Pig Outdoors? A Memoir of Deafness*. New York: Penguin Books.

Kryter, Karl. 1985. *The Effects of Noise on Man*. 2nd ed. Orlando: Academic Press.

Lampropoulou, Venetta. 1995. "The History of Deaf Education in Greece." *The Deaf Way: Perspectives from the International Conference on Deaf Culture*. Ed. C. J. Erting, R. C. Johnson, D. L. Smith, and B. D. Snider. Washington, D. C.: Gallaudet University Press. 239–49.

Lane, Harlan. 1992. *The Mask of Benevolence: Disabling the Deaf Community*. New York: Knopf.

———. 1985. *When the Mind Hears: A History of the Deaf*. New York: Random House.

———. and Richard Pillard. 1978. *The Wild Boy of Burundi: A Study of an Outcast Child*. New York: Random House.

Li, Ha-Sheng. 1992. "Genetic Influence on Susceptibility of the Auditory System to Aging and Environmental Factors." *Scandinavian Audiology* 21, Supplement 36: 1–39.

Mohay, H. 1990. "The Interaction of Gesture and Speech in the Language Development of Two Profoundly Deaf Children." *From Gesture to Language in Hearing and Deaf Children*. Ed. V. Volterra and C. J. Erting. New York: Springer-Verlag. 187–204.

Murder By Death. 1984. Directed by Robert Moore. Columbia.

Padden, Carol and Tom Humphries. 1988. *Deaf in America: Voices from a Culture*. Cambridge: Harvard University Press.

Padden, Carol. 1992. Review of *A Man Without Words*, by Susan Schaller. *American Journal of Psychology* 105: 648–53.

Pereira Da Cunha, M. C. and C. De Lemos. 1990. "Gesture in Hearing Mother—Deaf Child Interaction." *From Gesture to Language in Hearing and Deaf Children*. Ed. V. Volterra and C. J. Erting. New York: Springer-Verlag. 178–86.

Pinker, Steven. 1994. *The Language Instinct: How the Mind Creates Language*. New York: William Morrow and Company.

Prazma, Jiri. 1981. "Ototoxicity of Aminoglycoside Antibiotics." *Pharmacology of Hearing: Experimental and Clinical Bases*. Ed. R. D. Brown and E. A. Daigneault. New York: John Wiley.

Rose, Petra and Gary Kiger. 1994. "Intergroup Relations: Political Action and Identity in the Deaf Community." Society for Disability Studies Annual Meeting. Rockville, 23 June.

Rymer, Russ. 1993. *Genie: An Abused Child's Flight From Silence*. New York: Harper Collins.

Salih, Mustafa Abdalla. 1990."Childhood Acute Bacterial Meningitis in the Sudan: An Epidemiological, Clinical and Laboratory Study." *Scandinavian Journal of Infectious Diseases* Supplement 66: 1–103.

Salomon, Gerhard. 1986. "Hearing Problems and the Elderly." *Danish Medical Bulletin Special Supplement Series on Gerontology* 33, Supplement 3: 1–17.

Scheetz, Nanci. 1993. *Orientation to Deafness*. Boston: Allyn and Bacon.

Silverman, Franklin. 1995. *Communication for the Speechless: An Introduction to Nonvocal Communication Systems for the Severely Handicapped*. 3rd ed. Boston: Allyn and Bacon.

Soucek, Sava and Leslie Michaels. 1990. *Hearing Loss in the Elderly: Audiometric, Electrophysiological and Histopathological Aspects*. London: Springer-Verlag.

Stokoe, William. 1994. "Discovering a Neglected Language." *Sign Language Studies* 85: 377–82.

———. 1990. "Language, Prelanguage, and Sign Language." *Seminars in Speech and Language* 11: 92–99.

———. 1994. "Seeing Clearly Through Fuzzy Speech." *Sign Language Studies* 82: 85–91.

———. 1972. *Semiotics and Human Sign Languages*. Approaches to Semiotics 21. Paris: Mouton.

Williams, Donna. 1994. *Somebody Somewhere: Breaking Free From the World of Autism*. New York: Times Books.

ABBREVIATIONS

DAGW   M. Grmek, *Diseases in the Ancient Greek World* (Baltimore, 1989).

FGrH   F. Jacoby, Die Fragmente der griechischen Historiker (Leiden, 1923-).

GG   F. Van Straten, "Gifts for the Gods," *Faith Hope and Worship* (Leiden, 1981).

LCL   Loeb Classical Library.

PCG   R. Kassel and C. Austin, *Poetae Comici Graeci* (Berlin, 1983).

PMG   D. L. Page, *Poetae Melici Graecae* (Oxford, 1967).

SEG   *Supplementum Epigraphicum Graecum*.

WMH   H. Lane, *When the Mind Hears* (New York, 1985).

3

Spoken Daggers, Deaf Ears, and Silent Mouths

Fantasies of Deafness in Early Modern England

JENNIFER L. NELSON AND BRADLEY S. BERENS

In the relentlessly aural world of early modern England—a world in which people regularly enjoyed listening to four-hour sermons—civilization was only possible through *spoken* language. Thomas Wilson, in *The Arte Of Rhetorique*, explains this distinction by way of a revision of the book of Genesis. "After the fall of our first father," Wilson argues, God

> Still tendering his own workmanship, stirred up his faithful and elect, to persuade with reason, all men to society. And gave his appointed ministers knowledge both to see the natures of men, and also granted them the gift of utterance, that they might with ease win folk at their will, and frame them by reason to all good order.
>
> And therefore, whereas men lived Brutishly in open fields, having neither house to shroud them in, nor attire to clothe their backs, nor yet any regard to seek their best avail: these appointed of God called them together by utterance of speech, and persuaded them what was good, what was bad, and what was gainful for mankind. And although at first, the rude could hardly learne, and either for strangeness of the thing, would not gladly receive the offer, or else for lack of knowledge could not perceive the goodness: yet being somewhat drawn and delighted with the pleasantness of reason, and the sweetness of utterance: after a certain space, they became through nurture and good advisement, of wild, sober: of cruel, gentle: of fools, wise: and of beasts, men. Such force hath the tongue, and such is the power of eloquence and reason, that most men are forced even to yield in that, which most standeth against their will. (Wilson, 18–19)

Eloquence is, for Thomas Wilson, the constituting force of humanity. But while it is assuredly the "sweetness" of the speaker's utterance that draws in the rude and ignorant, the transformation "forced" by this eloquence presupposes an audience that has the ability to hear. In early modern England, the members of an already existing civilization identify themselves and are recognized (by others) as civilized by the ability to speak, but the potential to become civilized—to be colonized by the civilized world—requires hearing.

It should come as no surprise, then, that in early modern England there are virtually no fully realized representations of deaf people: this fact only stands to reason if to be human at this time means to be hearing. Strangely, however, while there are almost no representations of deaf people, there are abundant representations of deaf ears.[2] These representations take two general, and related, forms—one the inverted reflection of the other. In the first, early modern deafness is an empowering, temporary and voluntary condition in which a god, ruler, or social superior temporarily turns off her or his sense of hearing in the face of an anxious speaker. The mirror image of such a moment of empowering deafness is a perilous act of audition: the anxiety shifts from the person impotently addressing the deaf to a powerful hearing person striving to escape the world's pestilent voices. In this essay, we seek to explore the relationship between early modern culture's highly selective appropriation of deafness and its inability to acknowledge the humanity of the deaf. Neither the appropriation nor the lack of acknowledgment are exclusively literary. Deafness is metaphorized and the deaf themselves are reduced to metaphor in a process that is played out in sermons, royal proclamations, and a rogue pamphlet, as well as in plays and poems. The virtual absence of the physically deaf ends in the eighteenth century. Literary and cultural representations of the deaf generally begin to occur with the realization—largely during the mid-seventeenth century—that the deaf are actually educable in English, the majority language of their country, and as a result, become "representable" within that majority language.

It is important to understand what we mean by "deaf," because in the Renaissance, as it does today, the word carried two meanings that bleed into each other—one is biological, the other is social. Corbaccio in Jonson's *Volpone* has trouble hearing, but he can hear—he is still a member of an aural world. Likewise, Shakespeare's Julius Caesar asks Antony to walk on his right side when they talk because his left ear is "deaf" (1. 2. 213). Caesar's is the "somdeel deef" of Chaucer's Wife of Bath. However, this partial inability to hear is *not* the topic of this essay. Rather, early modern deafness is more "the adder's sense" of Shakespeare's sonnet #112, in which the speaker's ears are "to critic and to flatterer stopped." This is a common biblical allusion to Psalm 58—the adder who completely "stoppeth her ear . . . will not hearken to the voice of charmers."[1] Shakespeare's adder does not simply refuse to listen; instead, the adder deliberately becomes incapable of hearing. This important distinction reveals deafness to be an exertion of power that, for the person possessing the adder's sense, effectively reduces the speaker's words to nothing, or in the sonnet's final couplet: "You are so strongly in my purpose bred/ That all the world besides methinks are dead."[2] Shakespeare's Sonnet #112 is not about adders; the speaker mentions the adder's sense in passing to reveal the exclusionary power of the speaker's love. Generally, early modern representations of deafness do not manifest themselves on the broad levels of theme, plot, or character; instead, they occur closer to the smaller levels of individual sentences, clauses, or phrases, particularly in Shakespeare. As in the sonnet, most representations of early modern deafness are passing references, except for those in the work of Thomas Traherne, who uses the themes of silence and deafness at length. What makes these representations important is the consistency with which the appropriation of deafness connects to the exercise of power.

Deafness functions as a locus of power: writers and their characters during this time attempt to appropriate this condition in order to assert control over others. Deafness, when temporary, is not a disability *per se*; of course the term is in itself negative, and draws upon a perceived physical problem, but the effect of this condition is to empower the person who chooses not to hear. The epitome of power and control invested in temporary deafness frequently occurs in the context of gods, the divine, or rulers. In this conception of deafness, the god or ruler, isolated from traffic with the common matters of men, possesses impenetrable ears. In Sir Walter Ralegh's "As you came from the holy land" we learn of Cupid:

> Know that love is a careless child
> And forgets promise past,
> He is blind, he is deaf when he list
> And in faith never fast. (Sylvester, 335)

While he is *always* blind, Cupid is only deaf "when he list"—when he chooses to be so.[3] Cupid's ability to be faithless seems to be a product of his assumed deafness: "And in faith never fast" follows hard upon the assertion of Cupid's deafness. Ralegh links the instability of the love god's fidelity to the uncertainty, on the part of his audience, as to whether Cupid has heard the voice of his supplicant. Similarly, in Shakespeare's *Troilus and Cressida*, Cassandra tells Hector that "the gods are deaf to hot and peevish vows" (5. 3. 16). To righteous vows only, it is implied, the gods listen. In Sonnet 29, Shakespeare's speaker cannot "trouble deaf heaven" with his "bootless cries." This is a selective deafness on the part of the gods attributed to them by their mortal inferiors. Attribution is constitutive of the certainty with which anxious speakers presume the gods to be voluntarily deaf: empowering deafness can only be perceived as successful by a second person or group of people. A completely successful first-person statement of voluntary deafness (unless it were to be made by a god) is a contradiction in terms, for to become voluntarily deaf is to remove oneself completely from conversational circulation.

When it suits them, powerful humans (usually rulers, but always powerful) also assume deafness, yet, although still empowering, representations of humanly assumed deafness are usually more tentative than similar representations of the gods. In *Richard II*, John of Gaunt fruitlessly hopes that his deathbed exhortation to the king will make Richard change his ways: "My death's sad tale may yet undeaf his ear" (2. 1. 16). With an identical lack of response on the part of her hearer, Lavinia in *Titus Andronicus* begs Tamora to "Be not obdurate, open thy deaf ears" (2. 3. 160). In these two examples, the voluntarily deaf ruler must face a pleading interlocutor and reassert his deafness. Unlike the gods, the self-deafened ruler is not totally separated from other people. Similarly in *Romeo and Juliet*, after banishing Romeo, Prince Escalus' announcement that he will be "deaf to pleading and excuses" (3. 1. 192) is less than totally convincing at the same moment the statement demonstrates that Escalus possesses the highest status in Verona.[4] This rare first person assertion of empowering deafness deconstructs itself in the act of its own speaking, for to make the statement is paradoxically to engage in conversation even while denying that engagement. The ambivalence of human-assumed deafness—in which the assumption of deafness asserts power and status at the same moment that it shows that power and status being challenged—is also demonstrated in Sidney's *Arcadia.* When Pyrocles tells the story of an attempted seduction by Queen Andromana (through the auspices of her ministers) of both he and his cousin Musidorus, we learn that she had "that scutcheon of her desires supported by certain badly-diligent ministers, who often cloyed our ears with her praises, and would needs teach us a way of felicity by seeking her favor. But . . . she found that we were as deaf to them as dumb to her" (Sidney, 347–348). The morally superior princes can be selectively deaf to the wicked Andromana, but she still keeps them imprisoned.

The last example from the *Arcadia* contrasts nicely with the tribune Murellus' characterization of the Roman Commoners in *Julius Caesar*: "you blocks! you stones! you worse than senseless things!" (1. 1. 35). When an *aristocrat* is deaf, the assumption of deafness is an maneuver of some kind: with plebeians the same phenomenon is considered mere senselessness. A corollary to this is that when the plebeians themselves do voluntarily assume deafness, like those higher on the socioeconomic ladder, they are denounced for their presumption. In Thomas Harman's 1566 rogue pamphlet "A Caveat For Common Cursitors" we learn about one specific kind of rogue, the dummerer:

> These dummerers are lewd and most subtle people. The most part of these are Welshmen, and will never speak unless they have extreme punishment, but will gape, and, with a marvelous force, will hold down their tongues doubled, groaning for your charity and holding up their hands full piteously, so that with their deep dissimulation they get very much.

Harman relates how he helped a skeptical surgeon to expose one such rogue:

> The Surgeon made him gape, and we could see but half a tongue. I required the Surgeon to put his finger in his mouth, and to pull out his tongue, and so he did, notwithstanding he held strongly a pretty while. At the length he plucked out the same, to the great admiration of many that stood by. Yet when we saw his tongue, he would neither speak nor yet could hear. Quoth I to the Surgeon, "Knit two of his fingers together, and thrust a stick between them, and rub the same up and down a little while, and for my life he speaketh by and by." "Sir," quoth this Surgeon, "I pray you let me practice another way." I was well contented to see the same. He had him into a house, and tied a halter about the wrists of his hands, and hoisted him up over a beam, and there did let him hang a good while. At length for very pain, he required for God's sake to let him down. *So he that was both deaf and dumb could in short time both hear and speak.* (Kinney, 132–33, emphasis added)

The dummerer's mock disability will not be tolerated by his social superiors. In successful examples of temporary deafness, the deafness is known by all to be voluntary; in contrast, the dummerer in the example tries to pass himself off as truly deaf and therefore deserving of pity. Like the truly deaf, who are seen as less than human, the dummerer's apparent lack of certain senses does not qualify as legitimately empowering. The surgeons, under suspicion of pretense, take the dummerer seriously enough to torture him for it. From the dummerer we learn, then, that the fantasy of deafness is not just widespread among the powerful, but also that it is an option that the powerful restrict exclusively to themselves: the common folk are not allowed the pretense of deafness.

The anxiety of the speaker addressing his superior is not always that he or she will not be heard—sometimes the reverse is true when the deafness of the ruler is *solicited* by a speaker who fears offending his sovereign. In *Richard II*, before Thomas Mowbray accuses Bolingbroke—the king's cousin—of treason he begs his sovereign to

> turn away his face,
> And bid his ears a little while be deaf,
> Till I have told this slander of his blood. (1. 1. 111–13)

Once again, empowering deafness, or in this case its potential, is attributed to the powerful by the less powerful. We do not know if the holder of the success-fully deafened ear is anxious, for the temporarily deaf person has used this so-called disability to opt out of contact with the rest of the world. The hearing speakers perceive this deafness to be a successful strategy of the powerful. This is Michel de Certeau's sense of the word "strategy," in which the strategist isolates him or herself from a situation in order to manage it more effectively. In *The Practice of Everyday Life*, de Certeau uses the strategist's distance and sepa-ration to distinguish strategy from tactics:

> I call a *strategy* the calculation (or manipulation) of power relationships that becomes possible as soon as a subject with will and power (a business, an army, a city, a scientific institution) can be isolated. It postulates a *place* that can be delim-ited as its *own* and serve as the base from which relations with an *exteriority* com-posed of targets or threats (customers or competitors, enemies, the country surrounding the city, objectives and objects of research, etc.) can be managed. As in management, every "strategic" rationalization seeks first of all to distinguish its "own" place, that is, the place of its own power and will, from an "environment." A Cartesian attitude, if you wish: it is an effort to delimit one's own place in a world bewitched by the invisible powers of the Other. (De Certeau, 35–36)

It is important to emphasize the role of both position and perception in this appli-cation of de Certeau's strategy: the elective and temporary quality of divine deaf-ness makes it seem strategic to the supplicant afflicted with hearing, but the hearing supplicant can never be sure if this strategy is being practiced by his addressee. This mystification of the movements of power causes the anxiety of the hearing who do not know if their words even exist to the gods. Certainly, Mowbray does not *really* think that King Richard is superhumanly able to turn off his hearing; instead, Mowbray metaphorizes deafness to illustrate the difference in status between himself and his audience, as well as to express his fear that what he says might prove dangerous to himself because it slanders Bolingbroke, the cousin of the king. When Mowbray asks Richard to become deaf, he attributes to his king a divine power and mystique. As flattery, this is appropriate to a king, like Richard, who insists stridently on his divine right, maintaining that he is "the deputy elected by the Lord" (3. 2. 57). Richard's arrogance in presuming that he really is like the gods leads to his deposition and eventual death, but the falseness of his power changes neither the perception nor the anxiety of Mowbray.

From the viewpoint of the anxious speaker, the deafened ruler, isolated from traffic with the common matters of men, possesses impenetrable ears, or rather, ears which can only be penetrated at the absolute discretion of the ruler who hears selectively. Furthermore, the speaker will never know—or at least, will never officially know—if his words have indeed penetrated the ears of the ruler, if they have been heard.[5] Empowering deafness is perceived by the speaker to be a successful strategy on the part of the ruler; when the point of view being expressed shifts from the anxious speaker to the potentially deaf auditor—in other words, when empowering deafness is no longer being attributed but attempted—we move from the apparent comforts of deafness to the perils of hearing. In contrast to strategically empowering deafness, the dangers of hearing, which we call "perilous audition," function in a way more akin to de Certeau's idea of a tactic: "a calculus which cannot count on a 'proper' (a spatial or institutional localization), nor thus on a borderline distinguishing the other as a visible totality" (de Certeau, xix). A tactic is a maneuver from within a situation. In chess, the player uses strategy; if the player, however, were suddenly —like Alice—to find herself a Queen on the chessboard, she would only be able to employ tactics. Tactics are fundamentally improvisational and reactionary; unlike strategy, tactics are forced to depend on time:

> Tactics are procedures that gain validity in relation to the pertinence they lend to time—to the circumstances which the precise instant of an intervention transforms into a favorable situation, to the rapidity of the movements that change the organization of a space, to the relations among successive moments in an action, to the possible intersections of durations and heterogeneous rhythms, etc. In this respect, the difference [between strategies and tactics] corresponds to two historical options regarding action and security (options that moreover have more to do with constraints than with possibilities): strategies pin their hopes on the resistance that the *establishment of a place* offers to the erosion of time; tactics on a clever *utilization of time*, of the opportunities it presents and also of the play that it introduces into the foundations of power. (De Certeau, 39)

The reason that the fantasy of empowering deafness changes into a tactic is because the attempted assumption of deafness inevitably fails. Empowering deafness and perilous audition are two sides of the same coin: when we look at the coin with the eyes of the auditor, as opposed to the anxious speaker, we understand that the auditor has never actually been aloof, isolated and safe, regardless of the convictions of the anxious speaker. Instead, when the auditor attempts to become deaf in response to an unwelcome voice he finds that he cannot do so.

In *The Tempest*, when Prospero feels that his daughter Miranda is inattentive to her own biography, Miranda reassures him: "your tale, sir, would cure deafness" (1. 2. 106). Miranda's statement succeeds in comforting her father, in assuring him that she is listening to his tale. But ironically what is locally reassuring is globally threatening: the possibility that deafness can be cured by piercing words comforts no ruler in early modern England. A notable example of this is Ferdinand of *The Duchess of Malfi*. When the Duchess tells her brother that "a scandalous report is spread/touching mine honor," Ferdinand's response is as hopeful as it is unsuccessful, "[L]et me be ever deaf to it" (3. 1. 48). Ferdinand's inability to be deaf to anything concerning his sister's chastity finally results in her death, that of her family, and his own.

From the perspective of the unwilling auditor, the early modern ear is acutely vulnerable: Hamlet's father is killed by poison through the ear. When the young Prince goes to confront his mother in the closet scene he says that he will "speak daggers to her, but use none" (3. 2. 396); when hearing his tale, Gertrude agrees that her son's words "like daggers enter in my ears" (3. 4. 95). A handful of years later in *Othello*, when Brabantio learns that his daughter Desdemona was indeed "half the wooer" in her courtship with the Moor, he cries "who knew the heart could be pierced through the ear!" (1. 3. 176, 219).[6] By the time Milton writes *Paradise Lost*, the stakes associated with hearing are even higher. The angels patrolling Eden find Satan

> Squat like a toad, close at the ear of Eve;
> Assaying by his devilish art to reach
> The organs of her fancy, and with them forge
> Illusions as he list . . .[7]

For Milton, the fall of man is inextricably linked to hearing, but, paradoxically, hearing is also necessary to hear the voice of God.[8] In *Genesis*, God also accuses Adam of listening to his wife's voice, and thus the ear and the voice are the instruments of man's downfall—first Eve, then Adam in a chain reaction that leads to their expulsion from Eden.

The dangers associated with hearing in Renaissance England were not imaginary, not solely the creation of poets and dramatists. In December of 1620, James issued "A Proclamation Against excess of Lavish and Licentious Speech of matters of State" in which loyal subjects were not only required "not to give attention, or any manner of applause or entertainment to" treasonous discourse, but also to report to the Privy Council "respective to the place where such speeches shall be used, within the space of four and twenty hours, under pain of imprisonment" and the King's "high displeasure" (Larkin and Hughes, 495–96). This paradox exponentially increases the anxiety surrounding hearing: the loyal subject must not pay attention to treasonous discourse, but at the same time must pay enough attention to the discourse in order to understand it, recognize its treasonable register, and report it to the authorities.

This paradox creates a condition significantly more complex than a mere fear of hearing something negative. An Elizabethan example of the simpler situation (written long before the Jacobean "Proclamation Against excesse . . . ") is John Donne's *Satire 4* ("Well; I May Now Receive, And Die").[9] Listening unwillingly to a libelous court gossip, Donne's persona (the speaker) is overwhelmed with prospective feelings of guilt:

> I more amazed than Circe's prisoners, when
> They felt themselves turn beasts, felt myself then
> Becoming traitor, and methought I saw
> One of our giant Statutes ope his jaw
> To suck me in; for hearing him, I found
> That as burnt venomed lechers do grow sound
> By giving others their sores, I might grow
> Guilty, and he free. (129–36)

Annabel Patterson deftly describes this anxiety as "not only fear but a subtle form of guilt by association" (Patterson, 101).[10] There is, however, no obligation upon the speaker to do anything in the face of the gossip's libel. The speaker chooses "to pay a fine to 'scape his torturing" (line 142) and flees home. After James's 1620 Proclamation, Donne's speaker would be in a far more uncomfortable position: obligated to report the libel, yet culpable for having listened in the first place.

The perfect example of this paradox-driven anxiety comes not from Donne's poetry, but from a sermon he preached in front of King Charles in 1627. Donne's central text was Mark 4:24—"Take heed what you hear."

Take heed that you hear them whom God hath appointed to speak to you; But, when you come abroad, take heed *what* you hear; for, certainly, the Devil doth not cast in more snares at the eye of man, than at the ear. Our Savior Christ proposes it as some remedy against a mischief, that if *the eye* offend thee, thou mayst pull it out, and if thy *hand or foot offend thee*, thou mayst cut it off and thou art safe from that offense. But he does not name nor mention the *ear*: for, if the ear betray thee, though thou do cut it off, yet thou art open to that way of treason still, still thou canst hear. Where one man libels with the tongue, or hand, a hundred libel with the ear; One man speaks, or writes, but a hundred applaud and countenance a calumny. Therefore *sepi aures tuas spinis*, as the Vulgate reads that place, hedge thine ears with thorns; that he that would whisper a calumny in thine ear, against another man, may be pricked with those thorns, that is, may discern from thee, that he is not welcome to thee, and so forbear; or if he will press upon thee, those thorns may prick thee, and warn thee that there is an uncharitable office done which thou shouldst not countenance.

Neither only may thy charity towards another be violated by such a whisperer, but thine own safety endangered; And therefore *Take heed what you hear*. (Simpson and Porter, 7. 393–95)

For Dr. Donne, hearing is inescapably dangerous, and deafness—the only escape from the dangers of hearing—an unattainable fantasy. Therefore defenses must be erected—"hedge thine ears with thorns"—in order to set up a boundary between the independent self and the outside world. The perils of hearing drive one to depend on self-reliance and personal judgment, rather than external influences. If true voluntary deafness were entirely and easily achievable, the need for censorship and active screening would not exist: it would reduce the dangers of hearing to nothing.

Understanding the dangers of hearing in early modern England can help to make sense finally of the absurd Morose in Jonson's *Epicoene; or, The Silent Woman*. Locked in a house which he has insulated with quilts and having forbidden his servant to speak, Morose labors to save his ears "the discord of sound."[11] The absurdity of Morose's desire is not that he wishes to embrace silence. This is a common desire, the strength of which only increases as we move through the Commonwealth and into the Restoration. Morose's desire is absurd because he wants to turn the fantasy of deafness inside-out: rather than becoming deaf, plugging his ears, or extricating himself from noisy London, Morose wishes to escape the paradox of hearing by reducing the entire world around him to silence.

But with all these images of temporarily deaf ears, and pervasive anxieties about hearing the wrong thing, the question that remains is: why were there virtually no representations of real deaf people? While there are many instances of deafness in early modern England, these fantasies involve deafness only in hearing characters who have something to gain by a temporary escape from perilous audition. Deafness is generally an appropriated quality at that time, but there is one significant exception—Abessa in Book I of Spenser's *Faerie Queene*. When Una approaches Abessa, she

> . . . to her gan call
> To weet, if dwelling place were nigh at hand;
> But the rude wench her answer'd nought at all,
> *She could not hear, nor speak, nor understand;*
> Till seeing by her side the Lion stand,
> Will suddaine fear her pitcher down she threw,
> And fled away : for never in that land
> Fair of fair Lady she before did view,
> And that dread Lions look her cast in deadly hue.[12]

Abessa is not putting on a performance; she is *actually*, not voluntarily, deaf. However, Abessa is the exception that proves the rule, as she is completely outside the culture and outside the sphere of divine salvation. She cannot hear the true will of God and allegorically represents the Catholic Church in opposition to Una, who represents the true Anglican church. Abessa cannot perceive spiritual truth, and her impairments place her outside the realm of redemption.[13] She is perhaps the only physically deaf character in English literature prior to 1720 when Daniel Defoe published his novel about a deaf seer, Duncan Campbell.[14] What Abessa shows us is that only hearing people—those who already belong to the mainstream, "normal" world—can enjoy the privileges pertaining to deafness.

A brief return to *Epicoene* will clarify Abessa's situation. By trying to create a world where he can drown out other voices, Morose attempts to find a refuge in a silent world where he can hear only his own voice, but he does this only because he can already hear other voices. Silence, as in Morose's case or in elective deafness, is salvation only for the hearing; consequently, for Abessa, neither her muteness nor her deafness is a refuge, and she is irrevocably outside salvation. In Abessa's case, her silence entails deafness, and neither is elective. Nonelective deafness and silence are thus in opposition to a conscientious silence conducive to meditation and communion with God, or an active screening out of undesirable sounds and voices. Silence operates in much the same way as the fantasy of deafness: one can only benefit from silence if one is hearing and can selectively ignore the world or choose not to speak; voluntary silence is an act of will and desire. Since, as we first saw in Wilson's *Arte Of Rhetorique*, eloquence and oratory are constitutive of humanity, only from within humanity can the conditions of deafness and its corollary, silence, be beneficial.

In the foregoing pages, the many examples of empowering deafness and perilous audition have generally concerned public interactions. From Thomas Mowbray flattering his king to the dummerer's begging, the fantasies of deafness that we have hitherto discussed concern jockeying for social leverage. With Abessa, we see for the first time that there are spiritual as well as secular consequences to deafness. Spenser condemns Abessa for her nonelective deafness; however, by implication there are potential advantages for an elective spiritual deafness. In his famous study *The Poetry of Meditation*, Louis L. Martz has described the widespread growth of a continental meditative tradition in sixteenth and seventeenth century England. "Meditation," according to Martz,

> thus comes to be regarded . . . as an exercise essential for the ordinary conduct of "good life" and almost indispensable as preparation for the achievement of the highest mystical experience. . . . (16)

In the works of Thomas Traherne, the attributes of deafness—but, once again, only elective deafness—are conducive to such mystical experience. For Traherne, to be deaf is to move inward more easily, away from problematic voices and penetrable ears, and towards a reliance on the self in its solitary purity.

In "Dumnesse," Traherne suggests that a person is best able to achieve divinity through deafness and silence. These qualities enable one to take in God's works in preparation for a later invasion by breaths that carry the poisonous voices of others. Only by being mute first can one shore oneself up in the face of the evils of the outside world that are carried on verbal symbols:

> Sure Man was born to Meditat on Things,
> And to Contemplat the Eternal Springs
> Of God and Nature, Glory, Bliss and Pleasure;
> That Life and Love might be his Heavnly Treasure:
> And therfore Speechless made at first, that he
> Might in himself profoundly Busied be:
> And not vent out, before he hath t'ane in
> Those Antidots that guard his Soul from Sin. (1–8)

To be "speechless" is a necessary preparation for later salvation; in such a way "Man" can contemplate the wisdom and glory of God in nature. From this comes a reliance on the self: "in himself profoundly Busied be." With such a strong foundation anchored in the mute self, rather than business outside, come the "Antidots" that will help when one must finally "vent out" or speak. Deafness, allied with "Dumnesse," is necessary for the development of a divine character:

> Wise Nature made him Deaf too, that he might
> Not be disturbd, wile he doth take Delight
> In inward Things, nor be depravd with Tongues
> Nor Injurd by the Errors and the Wrongs
> That Mortal words convey. For Sin and Death
> Are most infused by accursed Breath
> That flowing from Corrupted Intrails, bear
> Those hidden Plagues that Souls alone may fear (9–16).

Human speech carries within itself a potentially corrupting influence on the soul, akin to a "Plague" or sickness. A preemptive deafness is one way to forestall this mental disease, at least until the soul is fortified to withstand the onslaught of the voice breathing out from the "Corrupted Intrails."

The narrator in the poem goes on to discuss how he himself was in this "Blessed Case" (line 17): "before / There any Mixture was . . . " (28) with external voices, before the "Living Vehicle of Wind / Could breath into me their infected Mind" (25–26). He rhapsodizes about how he was within a "World of Light" (31) where nothing addressed him but "the fair Face / Of heav'n and Earth, before my self could speak . . . " (18–19). He notes that God's "Work . . . did in me lurk" (37–38), and that this work was comprised of seeing "all Creatures full of Deities" (40) with "Cleerer Eys" (39). Silence, solitude and inwardness are all required in order to protect onself from later assault by the world:

> To reign in Silence, and to Sing alone
> To see, love, Covet, hav, Enjoy and Prais, in one:
> To Prize and to be ravishd: to be true,
> Sincere and Single in a Blessed View
> Of all his Gifts. . . . (49–53)

The human qualities of hearing and speaking, then, are combative; the previously silent and deaf body is a fortress against invasive thought carried by the tongue and ears. Prior to this invasion, everything is represented as divine and natural:

> Thus was I pent within
> A Fort, Impregnable to any Sin:
> Till the Avenues being Open laid,
> Whole legions Enterd, and the Forts Betrayd.
> Before which time a Pulpit in my Mind,
> A Temple, and a Teacher I did find,
> With a large Text to comment on. No Ear,
> But Eys them selvs were all the Hearers there.
> And evry Stone, and Evry Star a Tongue,
> And evry Gale of Wind a Curious Song.
> The Heavens were an Orakle, and spake
> Divinity: the Earth did undertake
> The office of a Priest; and I being Dum
> (Nothing besides was dum;) All things did com
> With Voices and Instructions; but when I
> Had gaind a Tongue, their Power began to die.
> Mine Ears let other Noises in, not theirs;
> A Nois Disturbing all my Songs and Prayers. (53–70)

When the outer world finally does enter, it is a rape or a ravishment with the "Avenues being Open laid" and "Whole Legions enterd, and the Forts Betrayd" (55–56). For Traherne, the internal world is pure and virginal: before the voice invades and takes effect, the life of the mind inside is similar to one spent behind a pulpit. Sins are effectively blocked out before one learns to pay attention to the outer world's voices. Even though silence and observation of nature are exemplary here, as opposed to outside voices, vision is nevertheless rewritten as speech and hearing. That is, "No Ear, / But Eys them selvs were all the Hearers there" (59–60). This is a circular movement that starts with "No Ear" and circles around back to "Hearers." In such a way, the eye can stand in for the ear and vision becomes hearing. Even vision, "Eys," has at its heart speech, the governing framework of society. The ultimately voluntary nature of this portrayal of silence is revealed by its rhetorical description. This double reading of silence and deafness continues, as every stone and star has "a Tongue" and "every Gale of Wind a Curious Song." Speech inheres within silence, as the "Heavens were an Orakle, and spake / Divinity." When the narrator finally "gaind a Tongue" he becomes unable to hear the divine tongues of nature: they are drowned out by the clamor of "other Noises."

Similarly, in "Silence" Traherne intimates that silence is akin to a prelapsarian state, and that words may corrupt it:

> A quiet Silent Person may possess
> All that is Great or High in Blessedness.
> The Inward Work is the Supreme: for all
> The other were occasiond by the Fall. (1–4)[15]

Voluntary silence enables a person to be as one with God and blessedness; the rest of the poem describes at length an Eden-like state of being, the making of the perfect internal world. To be perfectly within oneself is to be within God:

> A vast and Infinit Capacitie,
> Did make my Bosom like the Deitie,
> In Whose Mysterious and Celestial Mind
> All Ages and all Worlds together shind.
> Who tho he nothing said did always reign,
> And in Himself Eternitie contain.
> The World was more in me, then I in it.
> The King of Glory in my Soul did sit.
> And to Himself in me he always gave,
> All that he takes Delight to see me have.
> For so my Spirit was an Endless Sphere,
> Like God himself, and Heaven and Earth was there. (75–86)

Traherne focuses on creating a world of one's own rather than on trying to change the surrounding world: "The Second Century" further exemplifies Traherne's project of mental, internal world-making:

> For God hath made you able to Create Worlds in your own mind, which are more Precious unto Him than those which HE Created: And to Give and offer up the World unto Him, which is very Delightfull in flowing from Him, but much more in returning to Him. Besides all which in its own Nature also a Thought of the World, or the World in a Thought is more Excellent than the World, because it is Spiritual and Nearer Unto GOD. *The Material World is Deaf and feeleth Nothing.* But this Spiritual World tho it be Invisible hath all Dimensions, and is a Divine and Living Being, the Voluntary Act of an Obedient Soul. (Traherne 1.102, emphasis added)

The implication is that an interior world of one's own creation is more valuable than that which is already created. To feel and recognize spirituality is to have a soul, whereas the body and material world are "Deaf" to the spirit. But by extension of this logic, people who are born deaf and mute are stuck within the physical body because they are subject to that silent condition involuntarily. Actual physical deafness and muteness do not come from the inward, glorious soul, but from the weak body.

By the time Traherne began writing the *Centuries* in the late 1650s, an unprecedented and sudden burst of interest in the education of the deaf was already well underway. It is tempting to see Traherne's writings as a product of the new work in deaf education; it is even more tempting to consider the partial recognition of the humanity of deaf people (and the fact of any attempt to educate them entails such a partial recognition) as the result of the new meditative tradition (articulated by Martz). In such an alluring causal trajectory, a meditative withdrawal from the world into silence would lead to an acknowledgment that those already residing in silence were human after all; from this acknowledgment would come an interest in educating the deaf, from which Traherne builds his sentimental conviction that the physical characteristics of an elective deafness facilitate a higher spirituality. For two reasons, we do *not* assert such a causal relationship between the literary appropriations of deafness in early modern England and the rise of deaf education in the 1640s.

First and most obviously, the lack of direct historical evidence makes such a claim difficult. To take Traherne as one example, there is very little known of his life or his influence (Bush, 147): his poems and the *Centuries* were not even published until the late nineteenth century, making it impossible to trace direct lines between his poems and any other cultural artifact. Similarly, the rise of deaf education cannot be attributed to any one factor: a lot besides poetry was happening in England in the 1640s. Moreover, since continental education of the deaf had a significant head start on the English (as early as the mid sixteenth century in Spain), the influence of European treatises on deaf education would have to be taken into account.[16]

The second and more important reason that we do not articulate a causal link between literary appropriations of deafness and deaf education is that the narrative suggested by this link exaggerates the recognition of the deaf by early modern English culture out of its proper proportion. Such a reading would be a tale of progress, in which the cultural appropriation of deafness by the hearing evolves into a recognition of the deaf as human with its attendant attempt to educate them, and hearing society comes out looking pretty good. We reject this story. Instead of an evolution in which hearing society comes to accept the deaf on the deaf people's own terms, we see a continuum in which the way the deaf were being educated by the hearing replays the literary appropriation of deafness. Rather than emphasize the cultural evolution that deaf education might suggest, we prefer to point out the continuity of hearing values imposed upon and shaping the deaf. Deaf education is not the result of a sudden recognition of a heterogeneous deaf subjectivity by hearing society but another appropriation of the deaf condition by the hearing.

Before the 1640s, education to "cure" deafness was generally thought impossible.[17] New interest in deaf education does not result in literary representations of deaf characters, or any representation of a deaf subjectivity; rather, there are only curious glances at the actual condition of deafness and discussions of how to deal with it. Even with the later Trahernian spiritual emphasis on silence, the deaf are still seen as lacking a defining human trait, and are excluded from society and from full recognition as people with a language of their own—sign language. This exclusion is structurally similar to the English perception of savages as being "without language" because they do not speak English. The deaf epitomize the world of silence, but ironically, this is not a comfortable idea for the hearing in early modern England because the deaf are not already participants in hearing culture. They are partially recognizable at this time as human only because it was discovered that they have the ability to learn to communicate in English. This attitude, however, is not limited to early modern England: it was, and remains, common to most Western societies.[18] In early modern England, silence is only comfortable when it is a refuge, not a pathological condition.

When silence and deafness are treated as actual physical conditions in mainstream literature, these conditions are viewed as pathological and as needing to be cured if at all possible: for the English, this cure is what deaf education means. In 1641, John Wilkins in his book, *Mercury*, recognizes that the deaf can converse through gestures much as people speak: "And it is a strange thing to behold, what dialogues of gestures there will pass betwixt such as are born both Deafe and Dumb; who are able by this means alone, to answer and reply unto one another as directly as if they had the benefit of Speech" (Wilkins, 60). However, rather than recognize this communication as a language unto itself that is not derived from English, Wilkins proposes that the deaf be instructed in the English language. Wilkins thinks that it is a miserable thing for a rational soul to be imprisoned in a body born deaf. He proposes that the deaf should initially learn by writing the names of things—in English, of course—and then move on to other skills necessary for communication with the hearing world.

Sir Kenelm Digby exemplifies this conviction that deaf education must invariably involve assimilation. Digby wrote two treatises on the body and the soul in which he briefly discusses the phenomenon of how a deaf man—a Spanish Prince—"could discern sounds with his eyes" (Digby, 318–19). One sense, according to Digby, can stand in for another; this easy substitution is another example of the colonizing nature of the hearing recognition of the deaf. Digby memorializes this deaf and dumb prince as a person because he can understand speech with his eyes—that is, he can use his eyes to learn to speak and understand the speech of others. Digby goes on to discuss the deaf man's progress in speech and lip-reading, observing how nature serves to sharpen other senses when one is absent. He notes that odors may be tasted, light may be felt, and of course, sound may be seen (Digby, 319–21). One sense may, for Digby, at least functionally stand in for another in order to complete a person otherwise seen as defective. Digby's focus is not on the individuality of the prince, or on the heterogeneity of the prince's perceptions of the world; rather, Digby is only concerned with how an individual can make up for a perceived lack in order to fit in better with hearing society.

Like Digby, John Bulwer's *Philocophus: Or, The Deafe and Dumbe Mans Friend* (1648) examines the potential use of one sense to make up for the socially inhibiting lack of another sense.[19] Bulwer discusses the possibility that the deaf may be enabled, "with an observant Eie, to Heare what any man Speaks by the moving of his lips . . . to Heare the sound of words with his Eie, & thence learne to Speake with his Tongue" (title page). Bulwer uses the character of Philocophus to address indirectly those "who as yet can neither heare or speake" (a1v–a2r). "As yet" means that later they will be able to "heare or speake" through writing, speech, and lip-reading, once his book has done the good he intends it to. He also implicitly addresses the hearing reader when he says that the contents of his book should be "communicated unto them that can, and have acquaintance, or alliance with any whom it may concerne" (a2r).

Bulwer initially applauds the deaf for their fortitude, despite the attitude of some ". . . who understand not the mystery of your condition, looke upon you as *misprisions* in nature; yet to me who have studied your perfections, and well observed the strange recompences Nature affords you, I behold nothing in you but what may be a just object of admiration!" (a2v). He adds:

> What though you cannot express your mindes in those verball contrivances of mans invention; yet you want not *speech*, who have your *whole Body*, for a *Tongue*, having a language more naturall and significant, which is common to you with us, to wit *gesture*, the generall and *universall language of Humane nature*. . . . (a3v–a4r)

Bulwer then proceeds to discuss how speech has more "life and efficacy" (a4r) when joined with gestures; gesture, as the "universall language of Humane nature," is what the deaf have in common with hearing people. Bulwer seizes on gesture as the lowest common denominator for humanity. In his *Chirologia* and *Chironomia*, he writes at great length on the subject of how the hands put a "glosse upon the inward motion" (quoted in Agnew, 91); Bulwer argues that gestures can supplement religious rhetoric and speech. This notion validates gesture as a means of conveying and enhancing emotions; however, Bulwer also sees gesture as the "viceregent of the Tongue" (Agnew, 90). Bulwer's admiration of gesture—albeit in connection with speech or some sort of analog to speech—is clear from his later comments on the use of signs as the gateway to "Lip Grammar" and possibly to speech. Gesture, for Bulwer, is a fascinating subject and leads to his speculations on its importance for the connections between the body and the mind; yet the universality of gesture that he perceives fails to validate gesture as an entity legitimately separate from speech.

In discussing the effect of the chirological pictures of his alphabet on a deaf person, Bulwer says that he cannot improve on the natural language of the deaf:

> A worthy Friend of yours who had observed you not onely to be affected but seemingly edified upon the sight of the Alphabets of my *Chirologia* or naturall language

of the hand which hee had presented you with, to an endeavour of accommodating them more to your life; I was enforced ingeniously to confesse, I could not
improve them to any considerable advantage for you; since you already can
express your selves so truely by signes, from a habit you have gotten by using
always signes, as wee doe speech: nature also recompencing your want of speech,
in the invention of signes to expresse your conceptions. . . . (*Philocophus*, a4r-a4v)

Bulwer proceeds to reveal his own linguistic bias while applauding the deaf for
their creativity:

Yet a while after having well observed by your multiplying signes and gestures, that
you earnestly desired to unfold your lips to an *orall elocution*; seeming as if you
accounted your *dumbenesse* to be your greatest *unhappinesse*; in tender pitty of your
case, I began to cast about which way as a *Motist* [one skilled in depicting or
describing movement] to be serviceable unto you, by supplying a medium of
greater Discipline, whereby you might arrive nearer unto the intimate essences of
things, by apprehension whereof your intellect might gaine somewhat a more
proper perfection. . . . (a4v)

Bulwer thinks that, even though they possess their own manual language, the
deaf want to speak; he pities this, and proceeds to consider how he might
enable the deaf person's apprehension of "the intimate essences of things."
Bulwer reveals his conviction that the deaf are imperfect when he says that he
might develop the deaf intellect to a "*more proper* perfection." As a result, Bulwer
considers setting up a school for the "deafe and dumb" for the "enlarging of your
Charter, and to bring you into a neerer incorporation of society and communion
with us. . ." (a6r); however, he reveals that people were amused by his planned
school and did not take his intentions seriously (a5v). On the goals of this
school, Bulwer is clear:

I here commend unto you the *Accommodations* this Art holds out, wishing you all
in good time a happy *metamsychosis* or *transmigration* of your senses, that so at least
by way of *Anagram* you may enjoy them all: That learning first to write the *Images
of words*, and to understand the conveyances of a *visible and permanent Speech*; from
that H and A.B.C you may proceed unto a Lip Grammar, which may inable you
to *heare with your eye and thence learn to speak with your tongue*. . . . (a6r–a6v)

The end results of sign language at his projected school are to be "visible and permanent speech" and a "Lip Grammar," and possibly speech. The "tongue" is the
ultimate goal of this progression from signs to speech.

Bulwer's imagined school that would teach the deaf to communicate with the
hearing world returns us to the subject of linguistic colonialism, or the imposition of another, foreign, language onto others. We borrow the idea of "linguistic colonialism" from Stephen Greenblatt, who—in his essay "Learning to
Curse: Aspects of Linguistic Colonialism in the Sixteenth Century"—uses the

term to describe the attitude of English writers towards the New World. Greenblatt's account begins with Samuel Daniel's *Musophilus*, in which Daniel makes clear that he considers the English language to be "the best glorie" that "shal be sent" to the "unknowing nations" of the New World. By means of this best glory, the English will redeem the savages:

> Daniel does not consider the spread of English a conquest but rather a gift of inestimable value. He hasn't the slightest sense that the natives might be reluctant to abandon their own tongue; for him, the Occident is "yet unformed," its nations "unknowing." . . . This illusion that the inhabitants of the New World are essentially without a culture of their own is both early and remarkably persistent, even in the face of overwhelming contradictory evidence. (Greenblatt, 16–17)

Words—and specifically English words—are priceless cargo for the redemption of savages by the English. Even as Wilkins and others recognize the existence of religious gestures and the sign language of the deaf, they still operate from within the colonizing project of educating the deaf through the framework of the speech or the written representation of speech. Later in his essay, Greenblatt relates early modern linguistic colonialism to the work of the anthropologist Clifford Geertz: "If anything, *The Tempest* seems closer in spirit to the attitude of the present-day inhabitants of Java who . . . quite flatly say, 'To be human is to be Javanese'" (Greenblatt, 26; Geertz, 52). Of course, the irony is that the people vulnerable to colonization also take themselves to be representative of humanity as well.

In mid-seventeenth century England, the explosion in writings about the education of the Deaf[20] through the English language shows that involuntary silence is unacceptable; silence can only be accepted after actual knowledge of the "language of hearing culture." Similarly, to the hearing inhabitants of early modern England, to be human is to be hearing. Against this background, the Deaf are not fully accepted as they are, with a language of their own: only with the possibility of writing the English language onto them, of linguistically colonizing the Deaf, is there recognition in mainstream forms of literature. Prior to this, the Deaf are generally dropped from literary history, except tangentially insofar as the conditions of physical deafness and silence are abstracted into the temporary and elective realm for the attempted empowerment of the hearing.

Representation of the Deaf within mainstream literature is a Catch-22: we can only "know" them through these writings (beginning in the mid-seventeenth century), yet writing about the Deaf and educating them through the English language "shapes" them for consumption by a hearing audience.[21] We cannot know them *as Deaf* because their deafness is distorted into something that mirrors the hearing world and its dominant language. Anything else, such as sign language, is glossed over and rejected. The hearing impose their subjectivity onto the Deaf in the act of inscription, and therefore the Deaf are always rewritten as lacking, soulless, or primitive. As such, the deaf are viewed as problematically other within this aural frame of reference. The colonialism of the

English language, masquerading as education, is Daniel's "best glory," and the recognition of deaf people within written media merely leads to an expectation of conformity. There is no Deaf subjectivity whatsoever in early modern English literature, even though educators of the deaf begin to write about them as people and not just as conditions to be appropriated. These inclusions of the Deaf and their characteristics in literary and educational history can ultimately be seen as fantasies that say more about the hearing and what it means to be hearing than as true representations of the deaf. The Deaf are silenced, not silent in the Trahernian sense. In the Renaissance, as today, we are a long way from a world in which silenced "voices" can be . . . heard.

NOTES

1. All Shakespearean citations are to *The Riverside Shakespeare*; all Biblical quotations are taken from the *King James Bible*.
2. This couplet is a famous interpretive crux, and we have adopted the most common emendation. The original fourteenth line from the 1609 Quarto is "That all the world besides me thinks y'are dead." The fullest discussion of this crux is contained in Stephen Booth's edition of the Sonnets (Booth, 362–72). For the sake of our argument, however, the adder's sense, or senses (since, as Booth points out, the subject carries a plural verb [364]), the ability of the adder to stop "others' voices" (10) through voluntary deafness, remains the same regardless of the sonnet's last line.
3. Ralegh does not mention how Cupid's blindness relates to his empowering deafness, but Ben Jonson's "My Picture Left In Scotland" (Donaldson, 324) explores similar territory. The poem begins, "I now think Love is rather deaf than blind" and argues that the poet's "mountain belly" and "rocky face" have deafened his beloved to his eloquence. Here, deafness is a product not of blindness but vision: the poem ends with "her eyes have stopped her ears."
4. Friar Lawrence later bears out this sense of the Prince's deafness as less assured than Escalus would have his audience think: in 3. 3., Lawrence argues with a suicidal Romeo, banished to Mantua, to suffer banishment quietly until the friar and the Montagues can

> find a time
> To blaze your marriage, reconcile your friends,
> Beg pardon of the Prince, and call thee back
> With twenty hundred thousand times more joy
> Than thou went'st forth in lamentation. (150–54)

5. The operation of this strategic empowering deafness seems particularly appropriate for the longest reign of the era: Queen Elizabeth's body was—at least officially—perceived to be as distant and impenetrable as her ears. In a paper presented to the Shakespeare Association in 1988, the late Joel Fineman made a similar association between Elizabeth's ears and her sexuality, although his account has to do with Renaissance phallogocentrism and not with deafness. Fineman drew particular and fascinating attention to the Rainbow Portrait of Elizabeth in which the queen wears a gown adorned with both eyes and ears: "the painting places an exceptionally pornographic ear over Queen Elizabeth's genitals, in the crease formed where the two folds of her dress fold over on each other, at the wrinkled conclusion of the arc projected by the dildo-like rainbow clasped so imperially by the Virgin Queen. . . . In reproduction, the vulva-like quality of the ear is perhaps not so readily apparent, but, enlarged and in florid color, the erotic quality of the

image is really quite striking . . ." (Fineman, 228). The rainbow held by Elizabeth graphically represents her ultimate and total control of access to the ears which surround her. Two classic accounts of the imagery surrounding Elizabeth's reign can be found in Yates (1975) and Strong (1977).

6. In this latter line, "ear" is the Q1 reading; the Folio read "eares." For the purposes of our argument, however, the sense of the line is the same regardless.

7. Book IV, lines 800–804; (Orgel and Goldberg).

8. See also the foregoing passage quoted from Wilson's *Arte Of Rhetorique.*

9. According to A. J. Smith (editor of the Penguin edition of Donne's poems), "The Satires were probably written over the period 1593 to 1598" (Donne, 469).

10. Patterson discusses both Donne's *Satire 4* and the 1627 Sermon (of which we discuss a different section below) in her *Censorship and Interpretation: The Conditions of Writing and Reading in Early Modern England.* Her discussion is related to, but distinct from, our topic. In a new introduction to the 1984 paperback re-release of her book, Patterson neatly encapsulates her subject: "I argue throughout this book that the unstable but unavoidable relationship between writers and the holders of power was creative of a set of conventions that both sides partially understood and could partly articulate: conventions as to how far a writer could go in explicit address to the contentious issues of his day, and how, if he did *not* choose the confrontational approach, he could encode his opinions so that nobody would be *required* to make an example of him." (Patterson, 12). Patterson's argument is explicitly oriented towards performance and the way limitations both constrict and enable literary production. In contrast, we orient our subject towards audience reception, and the ways in which voluntary deafness, by eliminating the audience, also eliminates the problems of reception so clearly revealed in the two works by Donne we discuss. Voluntary deafness precludes the need for censorship because it reduces the speaker's potentially dangerous words to nothing.

11. 2. 1. 3 (Fraser and Rabkin).

12. Book I, canto iii, stanza 11; the italics are ours (Spenser).

13. According to A. C. Hamilton, "Abessa's deafness, muteness, and intellectual blindness also associate her with various New Testament figures whose sensory deficiencies declare their need for the grace that roots out sin and enables perception of spiritual truth. Yet Christ heals these biblical figures, and the Samaritan woman of John 4 gradually recognizes that she has met the Messiah. In contrast, Abessa flees from terror of Una, whose beauty manifests Christ's alluring grace, and her lion, here a symbol of Christ's awesome justice manifested in earthly executors of his will. . . .

    "Abessa's name also suggests 'abess.' As head of the parodic religious house that harbors Corceca and Kirkrapine, she reflects the majkor charges such as licentiousness and ignorance that Protestants brought against monks" (Hamilton, 3).

14. Deaf characters such as Campbell suddenly break into various forms of literature in the eighteenth century with realization that deaf people are actually educable in reading and writing. Duncan Campbell has a whole book to himself; however, there are innumerable digressions on the supernatural and the history of the education of the deaf up to Defoe's time. Very little of the book is actually about Campbell: as a result, it can be argued that Campbell is marginalized, even as a "main character," as the book primarily seems to be an opportunity for Defoe simultaneously to discourse on the supernatural and to advertise his brother-in-law, Dr. Wallis, as an educator of the deaf (Lane, *When The Mind Hears*, 105). Campbell is an appropriate trope for the supernatural: he is on the edge of the text, both literally and figuratively, and as such he is still generally unknowable to society—much

like the supernatural. He is on the edge of society in that he cannot hear, even though he can write. Thus deaf characters after Defoe's novel begin to have a fictional, if tentative and unstable, presence in *literature* as well as in academic tomes on the education of the deaf.

15. In the case of each Traherne poem, we have chosen to quote from the longer, quarto version rather than the abbreviated Folio version (Traherne, 2, 40–51).

16. For a thorough history of deafness and deaf education, see Harlan Lane's *The Deaf Experience: Classics in Language and Education.*

17. Until the mid-sixteenth century in Spain, and the early-to-mid seventeenth century in England (Lane, *Deaf Experience*).

18. It was not until the mid–1960s in America that sign language was linguistically recognized as a language in its own right, rather than as a language deriving from a spoken one. In this scenario, the ultimate goal of the deaf signer would be to learn to speak. For a cogent history of this recognition, see Wolkomir.

19. John Bulwer wrote three books concerning the deaf, yet never educated them; he was a noted plagiarist who got a great deal of mileage out of a subject that was, for him, an intellectual exercise, not a practical one. See Lane's *When the Mind Hears* for a brief mention and indictment of Bulwer. Lane ignores Bulwer, other than this, because he did not practice what he preached. However, we must note that because Bulwer wrote so much, his work is most likely what people read, rather than those who actually did educate the deaf but did not write so prolifically.

20. "Deaf" with a capital "D" indicates a culture or community, whereas "deaf" with a lowercase "d" indicates the physical or physiological phenomenon. Padden and Humphries cogently articulate the reason for this:

Following a convention proposed by James Woodward (1972) , we use the lowercase *deaf* when referring to the audiological condition of not hearing, and the uppercase *Deaf* when referring to a particular group of deaf people who share a language—American Sign Language (ASL)—and a culture. The members of this group reside in the United States and Canada, have inherited their sign language, use it as a primary means of communication among themselves, and hold a set of beliefs about themselves and their connection to the larger society. We distinguish them from, for example, those who find themselves losing their hearing because of illness, trauma or age; although these people share the condition of not hearing, they do not have access to the knowledge, beliefs, and practices that make up the culture of Deaf people (Padden and Humphries, 2).

As we do not discuss Deaf culture until later in the essay—since the suppression and appropriation of Deaf identity is our topic—the use of Deaf (with a capital "D") is not yet appropriate.

21. The same attitude evinced by Bulwer and others is still dominant in deaf education today; see Harlan Lane's *The Mask of Benevolence: Disabling the Deaf Community.*

WORKS CITED

Agnew, Jean-Christophe. 1986. *Worlds Apart: The Market and the Theater in Anglo-American Thought, 1550–1750.* Cambridge: Cambridge University Press.
Booth, Stephen, ed. 1977. *Shakespeare's Sonnets.* New Haven: Yale University Press.
Bulwer, John. 1648. *Philocophus: Or, The Deafe and Dumbe Mans Friend.* London
Bulwer, John. 1974 [1644]. *Chirologia: or the Natural Language of the Hand & Chironomia: or the Art of Manual Rhetoric. Landmarks in Rhetoric and Public Address.* Carbondale: Southern Illinois University Press.

Bush, Douglas. 1945. *English Literature In The Earlier Seventeenth Century: 1600–1660*. Vol. V of *The Oxford History of English Literature*. New York: Oxford University Press.

De Certeau, Michel. 1984. *The Practice of Everyday Life*. Trans. Steven Rendall. Berkeley: University of California Press.

Digby, Sir Kenelm. 1644. *Of Bodies, and of Mans Souls. To Discover the Immortality of Reasonable Souls. With two discourses Of the Powder of Sympathy, and Of the Vegetation of Plants*. London.

Donaldson, Ian, ed. 1985. *Ben Jonson*. The Oxford Authors. Oxford: Oxford University Press.

Donne, John. 1986. *The Complete English Poems*. Ed. A. J. Smith. New York: Penguin Classics.

Fineman, Joel. 1991. "Shakespeare's Ear." *The Subjectivity Effect in Western Literary Tradition: Essays Toward the Release of Shakespeare's Will*. Cambridge, Massachusetts: The MIT Press. 22–231.

Fraser, Russell A., and Norman Rabkin, eds. 1976. *Drama of the English Renaissance II: The Stuart Period*. New York: MacMillan.

Geertz, Clifford. 1973. *The Interpretation of Cultures*. New York: Basic Books.

Greenblatt, Stephen. 1990. "Learning To Curse: Aspects of Linguistic Colonialism in the Sixteenth Century." *Learning To Curse: Essays in Early Modern Culture*. New York: Routledge. 16–39.

Hamilton, A. C., ed. 1990. *The Spenser Encyclopedia*. Toronto and Buffalo: University of Toronto Press.

Kinney, Arthur, ed. 1990. *Rogues, Vagabonds & Sturdy Beggars*. Amherst: University of Massachusetts Press.

Lane, Harlan. 1992. *The Mask of Benevolence: Disabling the Deaf Community*. New York: Knopf.

Lane, Harlan. 1984. *When the Mind Hears*. New York: Random House.

Lane, Harlan, ed. 1984. *The Deaf Experience: Classics in Language and Education*. Franklin Philip, trans. Cambridge, Mass.: Harvard University Press.

Larkin, James F., and Paul L. Hughes, eds. 1973. *Stuart Royal Proclamations*. Oxford: Clarendon Press. 2 vols.

Martz, Louis L. 1962. *The Poetry Of Meditation*. 2nd, *rev*. ed. New Haven: Yale University Press.

Orgel, Stephen, and Jonathan Goldberg, eds. 1990. *John Milton*. The Oxford Authors. Oxford: Oxford University Press.

Padden, Carol, and Tom Humphries. 1988. *Deaf in America: Voices from a Culture*. Cambridge, Mass.: Harvard University Press.

Patterson, Annabel. 1984. *Censorship and Interpretation: The Conditions of Writing and Reading in Early Modern England, With a New Introduction*. Madison: University of Wisconsin Press.

Sidney, Sir Philip. *The Countess of Pembroke's Arcadia*. 1977. Harmondsworth: Penguin Classics. The "New" Arcadia.

Simpson, Evelyn M., and George R. Porter, eds. 1962. *The Sermons of John Donne*. Berkeley: University of California Press.

Spenser, Edmund. 1977. *The Faerie Queene*. London: Longman.

Sylvester, Richard, ed. 1983. *The Anchor Anthology of Sixteenth-Century Verse*. Gloucester, Mass.: Peter Smith.

Traherne, Thomas. 1958. *Centuries, Poems, and Thanksgivings*. Oxford: The Clarendon Press. 2 vols.

Webster, John. 1974 [1623]. *The Duchess of Malfi*. *The Revels Plays*. Manchester: Manchester University Press.

Wilkins, John. 1984 [1707]. *Mercury: Or The Secret And Swift Messenger; Shewing how a Man may with Privacy and Speed communicate his Thoughts to a Friend at any distance (1707)*. *Foundations of Semiotics*. Amsterdam: John Benjamins Publishing Company. Facsimile of the third ed. First ed. published 1641. Third ed. published 1707.

Wilson, Thomas. 1982. *Arte Of Rhetorique*. *The Renaissance Imagination*. New York & London: Garland Publishing.

Wolkomir, Richard. 1992. "American Sign Language: "It's not mouth stuff—it's brain stuff." *Smithsonian Magazine* 23 July: 31–32.

Disability and Society
Before the Eighteenth Century

Dread and Despair

MARGARET A. WINZER

The treatment the members of any society extend to the exceptional persons in their midst cannot be understood or evaluated in a vacuum. We must know, first, something about the physical and social conditions confronting all people in a society. Our exploration, then, of the fate of disabled persons in the premodern societies of the Middle East and Europe begins with an overview of daily life in these cultures.

The vast distances of time and differences between our conditions and those of the far past so cloud our perceptions of the lives of our ancestors that it is difficult to visualize daily life in earlier societies. However, it is not so difficult to imagine that poverty, dirt, disease, and vermin were constant accompaniments to the daily round. Life for most people before the rise of modern medicine and public health was difficult and short. As late as the year 1800 the population of Europe reached only 150 million; half of the population were aged below twenty-one years, and the average life expectancy was only about thirty-five years (Mahendra, 1985).

Plague, disease, and malnutrition decimated the ranks of the great as well as the common. Women faced the continual peril of childbirth; until well into the nineteenth century, most females were perpetually in a state of pregnancy. Women spent their adult life, in addition to their other duties, in bearing, rearing and, all too often, burying their children. The male population was periodically decimated by war, at home or abroad. Besides the miseries of almost constant war, early societies suffered the incursions of great hordes of raiders, political and social chaos, and the dreadful affliction of inescapable, mysterious, and deadly diseases. People suffered not only from the evil effects of diseases now vanquished such as small pox and typhus but also from the results of unsophisticated medical treatment and ubiquitous dental decay.

Social conditions also were very unlike our own. Illiteracy flourished among all classes. Although schools have been an integral part of society for centuries, probably emerging with the first literate city states of Mesopotamia, the ethical imperative to provide universal education for all children is a relatively recent phenomenon. Today the education of children is linked with the age of the child, but young people in earlier times lived lives we would consider adult. It was not until the seventeenth century that children were thought worthy of a teacher's attention and not until the middle decades of the nineteenth century that the acquisition of literacy skills constituted a principal developmental task for children between the ages of six and twelve.

Imperatives for universal schooling were closely tied to concerns for children as a separate and important part of society. Until a society recognized the child as an active, feeling person who had a value independent of any other purpose and saw childhood as a discrete stage of development, not merely miniature adulthood, special facilities for the care and training of children would not be made available. Indeed, until fairly recently in recorded history, children were not even considered legally to be persons: they had no rights and were usually considered the property of their parents.

In premodern western societies infant mortality was high. Even in the mid-eighteenth century less than half the children born were expected to reach adulthood. Those who did survive infancy had little to look forward to. There were no special nurseries, no playgrounds, certainly no special toys. Children's books appeared as early as the fifteenth century, but until the beginning of the nineteenth, they were instructive or moralistic, not intended for the pleasure of the child. For most children, growing up was a haphazard experience, and among poorer classes even very young children were expected to contribute economically to the family.

In such a social setting, where general hardship was the norm and dependent persons, children included, were not viewed as problems for social solution, the status of exceptional children and adults was radically different from what it is today. In the thousands of years of human existence before 1800, life for most exceptional people appears to have been a series of unmitigated hardships. The great majority of disabled persons had no occupation, no source of income, limited social interaction, and little religious comfort. Conspicuously abnormal persons were surrounded by superstition, myth, and fatalism—especially fatalism. Their lives were severely limited by widely held beliefs and superstitions that justified the pervasive prejudice and callous treatment. Individuals seen as different were destroyed, exorcised, ignored, exiled, exploited—or set apart because some were even considered divine (Hewett, 1974).

THE INVISIBLE MINORITY: THE PREVALENCE OF DISABILITY

It is difficult even to estimate the true numbers of people with disabilities in any early society. Confined by the uncertainty of historic data and the paucity of records, we can only guess at prevalence, although the most easily supported assumption is that disabling conditions were noticeably more prominent than they are today. Plague, pestilence, and poverty—all precursors of major and minor disabling conditions—were the constant companions of humans in their trek through history.

Moreover, scattered evidence in early writings supports the notion that disabling conditions were widespread and that disabled people have been present from the earliest times. Beginning with Homer, Greek and Roman writers portrayed a very wide range of human behavior, including instances so unusual as to be considered abnormal and requiring some special explanation. The ancients regarded history as a genre of storytelling and not as a careful record of fact; nevertheless, such historical writings as Herodotus' portrayal of a deaf prince (Herodotus, 1954, book 2) or Suetonius' references to disabled people in Imperial Rome (Suetonius, [A. D. 120] 1957) offer glimpses into the past. Later, after storytelling and history diverged, the authors of fictional stories continued to incorporate exceptional persons into their tales. The roles they assigned to disabled characters likewise offer important insights into the prevailing social attitudes about exceptionality down through the years (see Box 1–1).

Legal mandates are more telling: legislators did not enact laws to control the orderly but to sanction divisive elements and others who were the focus of concern. Fragments remaining from the writings of the great jurists of the ancient world imply that careful consideration was directed toward the disabled population (Gaw, 1906, 1907; Hodgson, [1952] 1973).

The widespread occurrence of debilitating physical and mental conditions in premodern times probably resulted from a combination of factors. The absence of modern prenatal care and enlightened medical assistance, combined with poor maternal nutrition, meant that many infants did not survive or were born with physical or mental anomalies. Epidemics, plagues, and fevers periodically decimated the population, leaving survivors with a range of disabling, conditions. For example, scarlet fever got its modern name in 1685, but it is one of the oldest known diseases. It was common in the pre-Christian era and may have been responsible for many of the deaf, blind, insane, and mentally retarded cases mentioned in ancient writings (MVD, 1925). The problems of unchecked virulent fevers and other illnesses were compounded by unsanitary conditions and the primitive state of medical knowledge. Limited mobility and consequent inbreeding ensured the passage of inherited conditions from one generation to the next; at the same time, the movement of troops in the constant wars that beset the ancient and medieval world spread many epidemics.

Fascinating conjunctions of epidemics or plagues and the resurgence of laws designed to control or eliminate the disabled population occur from time to time, but the evidence for a cause-and-effect connection remains too slim to support more than bare surmise. We could speculate, for example, that the plague that ravaged Athens in the fourth century B.C. led Plato to suggest that only the mental and physical elite be allowed to marry and procreate and Aristotle to advocate infanticide laws. Or that the great plague named for the Emperor Justinian prompted that monarch's jurists to direct minute attention to the status of disabled people in society.

No doubt throughout premodern history the disabled population formed a small though resilient minority—a minority always exposed to the prejudices of the majority, not only because they could not partake of normal life, but also

Box 1–1
LITERARY SOURCES

Disability per se has rarely been the central subject of literature because it is not a universal concern. But literature offers some insight into the status of exceptional people in the past. It is not possible to know if in any instance literature reflected or molded prevailing attitudes toward the disabled; it does, however, give us some insight into the opinions concerning special people that were held by a society. When exceptional or disabled people do appear in literature and other artistic works, they are usually rendered as stereotypes, appearing to be either more or less than human (see Biklen, 1986; Brulle and Mihail, 1991; D. Kent, 1986; Kriegel, 1986).

Literary and artistic works show disability by means of a number of common images—disabled persons are portrayed as criminals or monsters or as people who are suicidal, maladjusted, or sexually deviant (Brulle and Mihail, 1991; Klobas, 1985; Longmore, 1985). Disabled people are often seen as suffering punishment for doing evil; they are portrayed as embittered by their fate, or as resentful of non-disabled people, whom they seek to destroy (Longmore, 1985). Such images reinforce negative stereotypes and foster common prejudices.

Traditionally, certain disabled groups appealed more to writers' imaginations, sometimes as part of a general societal concern. Insanity, madness, possession, seen as manifestations of divine punishment, form a common literary theme (Byrd, 1974). It may be no coincidence that the literature of the sixteenth and early seventeenth centuries—the time of the Spanish Inquisition, the witch hunts, and the establishment of the great lunatic hospitals—is so rich with portrayals of distraught and insane characters. Hamlet, Lear, Timon, and Ophelia, for example, all wear the mask of madness (Rosen, 1968). But Shakespeare's characters are simply among some of the best known of a whole gallery of characters to be found in such diverse contemporary sources as the plays of John Fletcher, John Webster, John Ford, Ben Jonson, and works by other Elizabethan and Jacobean writers (Rosen, 1968).

Shakespeare's Richard III serves as the prototype of the deformed villain whose outward manifestations illustrate his inward malignity (Fiedler, 1982). This villain emerges again and again, especially in Victorian literature. He is seen in the peg-legged sea captains Ahab and Long John Silver created by Herman Melville and Robert Louis Stevenson, in Victor Hugo's hunchback, and in the sinister Quilp who pursues Little Nell throughout Charles Dickens's *Old Curiosity Shop* (Fiedler, 1982).

In literature deaf persons often had their place in comedies; the blind, often in tragedies. In the early eighteenth century Daniel Defoe presented *The History of the Life and Surprising Adventures of Mr. Duncan Campbell* ([1720] 1903), a sensitive portrait of a deaf fortune teller in London and the first popular examination of the problems of the deaf person (Defoe 1903). Other writers treated deaf people with less kindness; some, like Oliver Goldsmith, made them fools, buffoons, and the butt of jokes. Blind individuals fared somewhat better in literature. From the time of Homer, blind persons have generally been portrayed in sympathetic terms; the arts abound with blind poets, storytellers and musicians, and literature presents blind heroes for our contemplation.

Truly mentally retarded individuals rarely appear in pre-Victorian literature—the fools of Shakespeare and his contemporaries were comics who were anything but foolish. Dickens paints gentle portraits of—retarded and slower functioning characters; there is Little Dorritt's friend Maggy, forever a ten-year-old because of a childhood fever; Barnaby Rudge, a young man unable to cope with the complexities of emerging industrial society; and David Copperfield's droll friend Mr. Dick. John Steinbeck adopted the theme with Lennie Small in *Of Mice and Men.*

Charles Dickens was deeply concerned with heroes oppressed by the unfortunate circumstances of their environment. The master of pathos, Dickens awakens strong sentimental responses with characters such as Tiny Tim. Most poignant are Dickens's characterizations of vagrant and delinquent children. No sadder character exists than Jo, the vagrant crossing sweeper in *Bleak House.*

Dickens's Artful Dodger and his gang of small thieves were of the ilk that drew the attention of reformers in the latter half of the nineteenth century. But the foundling child, the epitome of poverty, emerged as a common figure in literature a century earlier. Henry Fielding's *The History of Tom Jones: A Foundling* (1749), for example, proved enormously popular. In *The Expedition of Humphry Clinker* (1771) Tobias Smollett developed the theme of reconciliation between an old man and his illegitimate son (Ramsland, 1989).

From the first, the movies have made dramatic statements about society's negative reactions to people who were different. Charles Chaplin's wonderful *City Lights* (1930) tells the story of a tramp and a blind woman; *Johnny Belinda* (1948) is about a deaf girl; and *The Miracle Worker* (1962) portrays the relationship of Helen Keller and her brilliant teacher, Anne Sullivan (see Michal-Smith, 1987).

because they represented evil or were seen as public threats. Being different drew cruel and callous reactions from society, yet the penalties society inflicted—legal sanctions, church expulsion, starvation, exile, or even death—were too unevenly administered to exterminate all persons with disabilities.

The concept of exceptionality throughout history has not been static. The paucity of information we have on prevalence is compounded by the pervasive lack of clarity in the differentiations among disabling conditions and by difficulties in determining just who constituted the disabled population. Individuals who challenged the political, social, or value systems of some earlier societies were apt to be judged mad, insane, heretical, or blasphemous and so were destined to be subjected to harsh sanctions. How many political and religious nonconformists were confused in the public mind with the genuinely disabled population is unknown.

Our ability to assess the scope of the problem in earlier societies is further obscured by the lack of a consistent, sound means of discriminating between people who had physical disabilities (i.e., were crippled, dwarfed, epileptic, or deaf) and those who were intellectually impaired or mentally ill. All were considered to form one, all-encompassing category. The lack of clear definitions means that the history of disability tends to focus on particular disabilities, those that were more clearly distinguished from the others. Until the close of the eighteenth century those who fell under the broad, elastic categories labeled as insane or blind or deaf and dumb commanded most notice.

Madness particularly attracted attention, although "idiocy" (mental retardation) as a discrete and separate condition was rarely mentioned (Mahendra, 1985).[1] The etiology and character of deafness eluded early physicians and philosophers; the condition was usually attributed to super natural causes. Blindness was more clearly conceptualized, and blind persons throughout the centuries generally attracted more humane treatment than did those suffering other conditions. History records how some blind persons, estranged from their families and rejected by society, became bards, wandering from court to court, singing "strains divine." The tradition is reflected in many legends; for example, Ossian, the son of the Caledonian king Fingal, was just such a heroic figure of the third century. After losing his sight in a battle, he is said to have wandered about the countryside playing a harp and singing songs of battle and freedom (Farrell, 1956b).

Given the social and occupational requisites for survival in early societies, some groups that we so assiduously label and classify today were not even recognized as the logical or deserving recipients of social or legal concern. Before the advent of widespread literacy, when pushing the plow was more important than pushing the pen, mildly intellectually disabled people—those labeled to day as learning disabled and those at the upper end of the spectrum of mental retardation, for example—would simply have merged into the general populace. In early times it seems probably that only the grossest examples of mental defect would have been considered remarkable (Penrose, [1949] 1966). However, those far down the continuum, affected perhaps with multiple disabilities or medically fragile conditions, could not have been expected to survive.

THE MANAGEMENT OF DISABLING CONDITIONS IN ANTIQUITY
Prehistoric and Egyptian Practices

Preagricultural societies could provide little aid and minimal solace to disabled persons; high survival rates are unlikely. Severely impaired individuals would have been incapable of enduring the hardships of nature, unlikely to have been able to detect and ward off enemies, and unable to hunt or forage for food. Moreover, as noncontributing members of the group, they would have constituted an economic hazard.

Archeological findings indicate that aberrant behavior was treated by shamans, priests, or magicians. The shaman or witch doctor, with his skill in invoking help from the spirit world, probably served as the physical and mental healer, and shamanic law was as real to early civilizations as that of today's medicine is to us. Paleontologists, working with remnants of the Stone Age and later, hypothesize that bits of bone, teeth of animals, and vertebrae of snakes found in amulet bags were thought to contain magic force that shamans used to ease their patients (Schmidt, 1936). Cave dwellers treated sufferers by chipping holes in their skulls in order to allow the possessing demons to escape (Apter and Conoley, 1984; Harms, 1976). Hebrew writings indicate that in that society bizarre behavior was interpreted as evidence of the invasion of the body by evil spirits. Terrible exorcism rites were performed by priests, who sometimes succeeded in ridding the people of possession only by killing them (Apter and Conoley, 1984).

After about 10,000 B.C. humanity began a gradual, remarkable transformation: the revolution was the introduction of farming, which began in the Middle East and from there spread over most of Europe. Hunting and food gathering began to give way to agriculture in the areas that constitute present-day Syria, Iran, Iraq, and Turkey. Eventually, in the warm and fertile lands between the great rivers Tigris and Euphrates in present-day Iran the Sumerians built the world's first hill towns of mud and brick and created the essential foundation of civilization—the literate city state.

Up to this point in history humans had only been figures on the landscape. Following game, a single family needed many miles of land over which to roam in search of food; but for sowing crops and raising livestock a few dozens of acres were enough, and food could be stored. Now, as humans began to dominate and change their environment, shaping it to their own purposes, they moved on from nomadic hunting to agriculture, symbolic reasoning, verbal communication, and life in ever larger groups. Towns and cities began to emerge.

With the advent of agriculture and urbanization, opportunities for disabled persons, at least for mere survival, seem to have increased. The ancient Egyptians were the first to document an interest in disabilities and disabled individuals. The Egyptian Ebers papyrus (1550 B.C.), which is probably based on even earlier writing (Feldman, 1970) woven around Imhotep, the Egyptian physician (3000 B.C.), contains a collection of ancient recipes, sober advice, and magic for physicians covering many human ailments, from abortion to tumors. The papyrus contains oblique references to mental retardation and specific discussions of epilepsy, as well as the first known reference to deafness (Moores, 1987).

Given the amount of water-borne blindness and other visually impairing conditions prevalent in Egypt even today, it is not surprising that physicians of ancient Egypt directed much attention to blindness. Early manuscripts described trachoma and gave prescriptions for its cure. To the accompaniment of incantations, a solution of copper, myrrh, and cyprus seeds as well as other ingredients was applied to the patient's eyes with a goose quill (Farrell, 1956b).

The Egyptians were concerned not only with the study of causes and cures of disabilities but with the personal and social well-being of afflicted individuals. At Karmah the priests trained blind persons in music, art, and massage; they participated in religious ceremonies, and in some periods blind persons represented the largest portion of poets and musicians (Moores, 1987). Mentally retarded and other disabled children may have been protected by the followers of Osiris, the most revered of all Egyptian gods (Harms, 1976; Scheerenberger, 1982). Deaf persons garnered less regard: "There is no use wasting words upon the dumb," succinctly commented one early Egyptian (De Land, 1931, p. 7).

Infanticide, the Family, and the State

Ancient medicine seems to have made very little of the life of the newborn, and many early societies practiced infanticide. The Greeks and Romans shared the notion that a vital state arises from the innate strength of its citizens, and they enacted laws designed to weed out early those who could not contribute. "As to the exposure and rearing of children," said Aristotle in his *Politics*, "let there be a law that no deformed child shall live." In a similar vein Hippocrates found it natural to raise the question, "Which children should be raised?" Later Soranus (early second century A. D.) defined the art of child rearing as that of recognizing "the newborns that are worth bringing up" (Etienne, 1976, p. 131).

To the Greeks, children were the property not of their parents, but of the commonwealth. In Sparta, under the laws of Lycurgus, newborn babies were routinely brought before the elders to be examined for their fitness for citizenship. Those seen as being physically capable of developing into warriors were formally adopted by the state, although they were left in the charge of their mothers until age seven. Infants found to be idiotic, blind, or otherwise disabled were exposed to the elements in a gorge in the Taygetus Mountains, thrown into the River Eurotes, or abandoned in the wilderness. Following Solon's laws, Athenians killed their weak children outright or placed them in clay vessels and left them to die by the wayside (French, 1932; Pritchard, 1963). Similar customs, repellent to us for their astounding cruelty, were found in other Mediterranean and European cultures. In Carthage, for example, blind children were burned on a slow fire as a sacrifice to the sun (Bowen, 1847).

Cicero intimated that Rome readily adopted the Greek attitude toward handicapped infants (Barr, [1904b] 1913), although the Romans looked to the family, rather than the state, as the basic unit of socialization (Despert, 1970). The ancient Roman legal code, the Law of the Twelve Tables, dating from the fifth century B.C., was essentially a codification into statutory law of existing customs, reflecting the preponderantly agricultural character of the Roman community (see Steinberg, 1982). Following mandates detailed in the Tables, the family was regarded as sacred; all descendants were subject to the authority of the male head of the human family, the *paterfamilias*. He, as the sole family member considered as a Roman citizen with full legal rights, possessed the power of life and death over family members. As child rearing was the responsibility of the family rather than the state, the father, with his absolute power in the family, had the right to reject a child at birth (de Mause, 1974), to kill, mutilate, exile, or sell his children, or to divorce a wife on any grounds. Any child under three who might someday become a burden on society was thrown into the Tiber by the father. Infants were also left to die in the sewers that ran through the streets of ancient Rome.

Despite the existence of such practices, there are indications of a reluctance to resort to infanticide in ancient times. Early sources contain references to sickly or deformed children and illegitimate sons—the ones who could have been exposed and were not (Bell and Harper, 1977). Greece and Rome began to place restrictions on infanticide; some cities began to limit the right of the parents to kill their newborns; some required that the approval of five neighbors be obtained before infants could be killed; and others halted the infanticide of first-born males. Thebes outlawed infanticide altogether (de Mause, 1981).

By the time of the Empire (from about 30 B. C.) the rural character of Rome had altered, and strict adherence to the Twelve Tables relaxed. The inflexible authority of the *paterfamilias* was gradually reduced; he no longer had absolute authority over his wife and could not exile his children. Now, unwanted infants were sometimes placed at the base of the Columna Lactaria, and the state provided wet nurses to feed and save the children found there (Scheerenberger, 1982, 1983). In the second century A. D. the *paterfamilias* was deprived of the right to expose his children; by the third century child exposure was the equivalent of murder, although it was not until the fourth century that male parents finally lost all power of death over members of the family. Edward Gibbon (1952) surmises that great numbers of infants who might have been exposed by their parents were rescued and then baptized, educated, and maintained by the early Christians. By the fourth century the Emperor Constantine offered financial assistance to families who might otherwise have abandoned or killed their new-born children (Gibbon, 1952).

Disabled children who survived these Draconian measures—and there appear to have been many, possibly the result of parental solicitude, undetected congenital conditions, or postnatal handicaps—were tolerated if they were of economic or social value. In Rome many blind boys were trained to become beggars or were sold as rowers; blind girls became prostitutes (French, 1932). Mentally retarded people were sold as slaves, taken for beggars, or sometimes deliberately maimed to add to their value as objects of charity. Some disabled people served Rome as amusements or diversions; a wealthy family occasionally kept a mentally retarded person as a fool for the amusement of the household and its guests (Kanner, 1964). Seneca, sometime tutor of Nero, speaks of a blind imbecile (*fatua*) who belonged to his wife (Barr, 1904b). By the second century

Roman tastes led to greater popularity for disabled people as a source of house-hold amusement. A special market was established where a buyer might pur-chase legless, armless, or three-eyed men, giants, dwarfs, or hermaphrodites (Durant, 1944).

Aversion and distaste characterized the general attitudes of Romans toward disabled persons. Suetonius, premier gossip of the doings of Imperial Rome, con-fided that the Emperor Augustus "loathed people who were dwarfish or in any way deformed, regarding them as freaks of nature and bringers of bad luck" (Sue-tonius, [A. D. 120?] 1957, p. 100). It must then be assumed that Augustus avoided the stage performances of the well-born Lycius, a dwarf less than two feet tall with a tremendous voice. Yet, in deference to the will of Julius Caesar, Augustus assumed responsibility for the education of deaf Quintus Pedius; the lad was taught painting, the first recorded evidence of the education of a deaf person (H. P. Peet, 1851).

Medical Treatment

Throughout history, the medical aspects of disabilities have been paramount; other concerns relating to disability have been secondary, where they have been considered at all. What Harlan Lane (1991) and Steven Gelb (1989) refer to as the "medicalization" of special education can be traced back to the Greeks and beyond. Medical investigation typically preceded attempts at education; cer-tainly, no formal training facilities for disabled people were available until the mid-eighteenth century, though attempts to treat medically were widespread long before that. Typically, the causes of a condition have garnered far more attention than its impact.

In the eyes of the Greeks and Romans three categories of disability warranted attention—insanity, deafness, and blindness. Of these, madness (joined as it was with mental retardation and epilepsy) assumed the gravest proportions in the opinion of physicians, philosophers, and the general population.

Hippocrates (460–377 B. C.?), who founded one of the great medical schools on the island of Cos, illuminated the path that later physicians would follow. In the treatment of disabilities Hippocrates adopted accounts of medical techniques from ancient Egypt. He attempted to treat a variety of disabling conditions— visual impairment, deafness, epilepsy, and mental retardation—and, in doing so, largely discounted older conceptions of etiology.

For many centuries humans believed that there was a pantheon of gods who lived on mountains or in trees or wherever, and that the afflictions of disabled persons were a visitation of divine or demonic origin (Hodgson, [1952] 1973; H. P. Peet, 1851; Zinsser, 1935). It was widely supposed that disabilities were in the charge of invisible superhuman entities who behaved unpredictably. Early humans deeply believed that the power to cause physical and mental derange-ment was carried by the gods, who inflicted disability as a punishment upon those who incurred their anger. If the gods were not to blame, then a malignant being who disliked humanity was seen as responsible for evil and unhappiness.

With the rise of Christianity came the belief in the Devil, or Satan, as the prime suspect in disabling conditions. Although early Christianity saw itself as having vanquished a pantheon of gods, piety now conceived the notion of punishment or vengeance from a Divine Master in retaliation for the sins of the affected individual or the parents. Rampant superstition, for example, placed deaf individuals "under the special curse of God" (Stone, 1869, p. 97). Madness signified divine punishment, and blindness was "one of those instruments by which a mysterious Providence has chosen to afflict man" (Dunscombe, 1836, p. 96). Many disabled persons were viewed as polluted, creatures of evil omen, dangerous to the community and to themselves. They were shunned by all who did not wish to be defiled or corrupted, or who had any regard for the safety of their own body and soul. Yet physicians, beginning with Hippocrates, inveighed against the notion that evil spirits and demons caused mental derangement and other disabling conditions (Rosen, 1968).

Hippocrates stressed physiological diagnosis but still retained a nodding acquaintance with the supernatural. He practiced a "rational supernaturalism" (Edelstein, 1937); he assumed that the mystical origins of mental and physical anomalies were less important than causes explainable through observation and diagnosis. Hippocratic medicine was based on knowledge obtained by butchering animals and examining battle wounds, not by examining the human body. Wounds rising from external causes were studied in terms of cause and effect; symptoms without a wound were variously attributed to a common physiological cause, to the spirits, or to the gods.

Fundamental to Hippocratic medicine were the four humors (fluids)—blood, lymph, yellow bile, and black bile—of which the ancients deemed blood to be the most important. Each humor was endowed with a basic quality, such as heat, cold, dryness, and moistness, from which arose certain traits and conditions. A sanguinous person, for example was thought to be subject to inflammatory diseases but could sustain much blood letting; a choleric person was thought to be one who acted hastily and rashly. Disease developed when internal or external factors produced an excess of one of the humors or when an imbalance of these basic qualities acted on organs to produce deleterious effects.

To Hippocrates, mental abnormality was a disease, or a symptom of one, caused in the same way as diseases of the body (Rosen, 1968). madness was produced by excess of a humor. When present in abundance and under certain conditions, black bile was thought to be a particularly potent cause of various forms of mental illness, especially the condition called melancholia (Rosen, 1968).

Misunderstandings about the nature and causes of sensory impairments prevailed, partly because of reluctance to dissect the human body and to indulge in self-study and partly because of the difficulties in studying the ear, the eye, and the brain resulting from their inaccessibility and extreme delicacy. Blindness, both in its manifestations and its consequences, was more clearly conceptualized than deafness. When dealing with hearing loss, the ancients considered only the middle and outer ear; Hippocrates attempted no more than the treatment of otitis media (middle ear infection) (Hodgson, [1952] 1973).

In the time of Augustus and Tiberius Caesar (the first half of the first century

A. D.), the medical knowledge of the world was collected and probably amplified by Aulus Cornelius Celsus (25 B. C.–A. D. 50) in *De Medicina* (Hodgson,
1973). Census described how he followed the prescriptions of his great predecessors, especially Hippocrates (Rosen, 1968), although he diverged from Hippocratic dictums in treatment regimes. For insanity, Hippocrates prescribed
rest, useful work, and understanding companionships. In contrast, Celsus prescribed a wide variety of animal, vegetable, and mineral substances. Probably the
most widely used was hellebore, which, given the numerous references in the
nonmedical literature, may have been used in antiquity much as aspirin is today
(Rosen, 1968). The violently purgative effect of hellebore was employed in the
standard treatment of insanity (Rosen, 1968). Celsus recommended black hellebore for depression and, if the patient was "hilarious," white hellebore
(Bromberg, 1975). If herbs and medication failed, then Celsus approved correction by blows, stripes, and chains (Beck, 1811).

The primitive state of anatomical knowledge led Celsus to prescribe for ear
problems cures and agents that could only have aggravated the damage to an ear
drum already subject to chronic otitis media. For example, for ears with pus he
recommended that the sufferer "pour in box-thorn juice by itself . . . or leek juice
with honey . . . or the juice of sweet pomegranate warmed in its rind, to which
a little myrrh is added . . . to wash out the ear with diluted wine, through an ear
syringe, and then pour in dry wine mixed with rose-oil, to which a little oxide
has been added" (Hodgson, [1952] 1973, p. 64). For those dull of hearing
because of age, Celsus suggested "hot oil poured in, or verdigris mixed with
honey wine," and for other hearing problems "oil in which worms have been
boiled" (Hodgson, [1952] 1973, p. 64).

Of all the physicians who thronged toward Rome, Galen (A. D. 130–200) was
one of the most influential. He extended the humoral theory of Hippocrates into
a body of medical writing that influenced medical progress until the Renaissance
(Bromberg, 1975). Galen maintained the Hippocratic stance that rejected
supernatural explanations of mental disorder and viewed the condition in essentially physiological terms (Rosen, 1968). He held conventional attitudes toward
deafness, assuming a common cerebral origin for speech and hearing (Hodgson,
1973). In treating deaf persons, Galen and later physicians often performed an
operation "to cure their dumbness by an operation on the ligament of the
tongue" (De Land, 1931), a procedure that persisted well into the twentieth
century.

PHILOSOPHICAL SPECULATION

In the ancient world philosophy and medicine were closely intertwined: medical
prescriptions and philosophical assumptions about disabling conditions mirrored
each other, to be echoed in legal mandates. In searching out the effects of sensory deprivation, Aristotle (384–322 B. C.) concluded, in essence, that if one of
the faculties is lost, some knowledge must also inevitably be lost. Of the three
senses of smell, hearing, and sight, he noted that sight was the most valuable as
far as the necessities of life were concerned but that hearing was more important

in the development of the intellect. Aristotle viewed blindness as the more seri-ous handicap but less debilitating intellectually than deafness; he assumed that those blind from birth were more intelligent than those born deaf. With his con-tention that, of all the senses, hearing contributed most to intelligence and knowledge, Aristotle was led to characterize deaf individuals as "senseless and incapable of reason," and "no better than the animals of the forest and unteach-able" (McGann, 1888, p. 9).

Deafness baffled Hippocrates—he understood the mechanism of speech but assumed a common cerebral origin for speech and hearing (H. P. Peet, 1851), and he finally surmised that there was something supernatural about deafness (Hodg-son, [1952] 1973). Aristotle viewed speech as an instinct, not as a skill acquired by imitation, and also saw speech and hearing as arising from a common site. "Men that are born deaf," he stated in *Historia Animalium*, iv. 9, "are in all cases dumb; they can make vocal noises but they cannot speak" (Aristotle, 1910).

With his pronouncements on the status and intelligence of deaf people, Aris-totle determined their fate for nearly two thousand years. In the domains of sci-ence and philosophy Aristotle's statements were accepted without reservation by the medical scholars; what the Scriptures were to theology, his work became to science and philosophy (H. C. Barnard, 1922). Hence, Aristotle's notion that speech was divine and his teaching that nothing can exist in the human mind that has not been received through the senses (Smith and Ross, 1910) pro-foundly affected the way deaf people were perceived in society as recently as the eighteenth century. Coupled with this was Hippocrates' establishment of an inti-mate relation between the nerves of speech and hearing, which further exacer-bated the plight of deaf individuals. They were treated as not only deaf but as dumb, owing to some defect of the brain, some incapacity of the vocal organs, or to possession by some diabolical spirit (see Ferrari, 1906). On the other hand, Aristotle attributed to blind people equal intellects with the sighted; that, com-bined with the overt nature of visual impairment, explains why they were accorded marginally more humane treatment.

LEGAL MANDATES

A march through the centuries shows that disabled people were always the object of social concern, but whether community attention was a boon or a lia-bility depended on many different factors. No two societies viewed their disabled populations in precisely the same way.

Hebraic law contains some of the first known provisions for the disabled, founded on the biblical question, "Or who maketh the dumb or deaf, or the seeing or the blind? Have not I, the Lord?" (Exodus 4: 10 ff.). Under structures outlined in the Talmud and Midrash, blind and deaf persons, widows, orphans, and the needy were all treated with special consideration; this rabbinical law was in turn based on certain key passages in Hebrew scripture (Deuteronomy 24: 17–18 and 26: 18; Leviticus 19: 9–10, 14, and 23: 22, for example). The Old Testament enjoined: "Thou shalt not curse the deaf nor put a stumbling block before the blind" (Leviticus 19: 14) and cursed those "that maketh the blind to

wander out of the path." Benign protection under Hebraic law was later reiterated by Maimonides of Moses ben Maimon in the twelfth century and by Shul-
han Aruch in the sixteenth (Hodgson, [1952] 1973).

The Greeks sought medical answers to disabilities, but Greek law took little
account of the disabled; it was left to the legal minds of Rome to wrestle with
the social problems of disabled children and adults. The Roman jurists were not
concerned with the nature and cause of disabilities; their sole concern was to
ascertain the fact of unsoundness of mind or body and its consequences for the
performance of acts judged before the law. This focus led them to create a legal
framework characterized by institutions such as guardianships that provided a
pattern for later legal developments affecting exceptional persons (see Gaw,
1906, 1907; Hodgson, [1952] 1973).

When confronting mental illness, Roman law took madness into account
chiefly to protect property and the members of the community. Under Roman law
mental defectives (*mente capti*) were designated as deficient in intellect and provided with guardians. Roman law recognized that those who were born deaf but
were capable of speech were persons at law and proficient to discharge legal oblig-
ations; those deaf from birth without speech, however, were considered incapable
and were classed with madmen and infants, unable to perform any legal act on
their own behalf (Gaw, 1906). The law was based on the belief that deaf persons
who could not speak had not been deprived of their rights; rather, they had been
relieved of the responsibilities of citizenship they could not meet (Gaw, 1906).

In 533 the Roman emperor Justinian (d. 565) commanded that a revised collection of the statute laws be compiled. Scholars brought together many scraps
of ancient laws and edicts and finally compiled a fifty-volume rendering of judi-
cial interpretations, the *Corpus Juris Civilis*, which contained the *Digest* as well
as a four-volume handbook of civil law, the *Institutes*. Justinian did not make
many changes in the law regarding disabled individuals (Gaw, 1907) but simply
codified the ancient edicts that encompassed mental defectives (*mente capti,
fatui*), the deaf, the dumb, and those subject to incurable malady (*cura debilium*).

The Code of Justinian classified disabled persons in infinite detail, allowing
or denying rights and responsibilities to the different grades of impairment.
Under Justinian's law, for example, lunatics and idiots were considered incapable
of contracting marriage. The consent of an insane father was not necessary for
the marriage of his children, and a person with an insane descendant was permitted to name substitute persons as heirs. There were five classes of deafness,
ranging from those who were deaf but could speak to those totally without hearing and without speech (Gaw, 1906).

Although only two manuscripts of the original *Corpus* survived, we do know
that Justinian's laws were merged with the codes of the Germanic invaders to
form the basis of the law in most European countries. Thanks in part to the uniformity supplied by Justinian, the status of disabled individuals did not alter
materially in those countries where the civil law prevailed from the time of Justinian in the sixth century to the mid-eighteenth.

DISABILITY AND THE RISE OF CHRISTIANITY
The Early Christian Era

Beginning in the third century great hordes of ravaging barbarians invaded the Roman Empire. In 410 Alaric and his Visigoths sacked Rome and humiliated the imperial city when its proud senators refused to pay the landless barbarians protection money. With the fall of Rome, those parts of western Europe that had developed urban centers retreated to an agrarian form of society, and systems of feudalism arose. Education, culture, and learning now were relegated to a far less elevated status.

From the death throes of Rome arose a new religion that rapidly overwhelmed paganism and its many cults. In three short centuries Christianity grew from the creed of a tiny handful of believers to become the official religion of most of the Western world. Constantine, the first of the Holy Roman Emperors, legitimized Christianity, declaring it to be the official religion of the Roman Empire in 312. For many centuries to come, civil and religious affairs in Europe were to be inextricably mingled.

The fall of Rome ushered in long centuries of disaster in Europe—social turbulence, plague, warfare, hunger, and famine threatened the lives of the entire population. Life for most people was short; less than half the population survived to maturity (Mahendra, 1985). Cruelty at the hands of humans and hardship at the vicissitudes of nature were commonplace. In a period when disaster periodically threatened the survival of the fit, disabled persons must have fared badly. Little if any aid was proffered on their behalf, and even then, solace was granted only a few.

Monasticism proved to be singularly suited to the needs of the chaotic age that followed the collapse of the Roman Empire. By the fourth century strict cloistering was prevalent, as monastic life attracted increasing numbers of men and women who strove for moral perfection through asceticism. By the sixth and seventh centuries monks and nuns had become the principal agents of civilization; in fact, throughout the Middle Ages little work that was rooted in learning and enlightenment was produced outside the cloisters.

The cloistering of disabled persons seemed a natural outgrowth of the monastic impulse, and, in the context of these dark times, it proved advantageous, as it protected them from the dangers confronting them in the general society. A hospice for the blind was established in the fourth century in Caesarea in Cappadocia (in present-day Turkey). As the centuries passed, hospices—many offering facilities for other special groups—gradually spread across Europe.

For example, in the fifth century Saint Lymnaeus built special cottages adjoining his hermitage at Syr in Syria where he taught blind persons to sing pious songs and they, in turn, accepted alms from those who were moved by their singing. Saint Herre (d. 565) was born in a tiny village in Brittany. Tradition presents him as a sightless, barefooted man who, led by a white dog, wandered throughout the countryside teaching children. Apparently, Herre later formed a small monastery in Brittany that became a shrine for blind musicians (Farrell,

1956b). Saint Bertrand, bishop of Le Mans in France, founded an institution for the blind in the seventh century (see Farrell, 1956b; French, 1932).

Cloistering was not restricted to blind persons. Saint Basil, bishop of Caesarea in A. D. 370, gathered all types of disabled people into the monastic institutions that he controlled. Each group had separate quarters, but all engaged in common work and worship. Legend holds that during the same century Nicholas, the bishop of Myra, a town in present-day southern Turkey, provided dowries for poor girls and cared for idiots and imbeciles (Barr, [1904b] 1913). For his contributions, Saint Nicholas became the patron saint of the mentally retarded and of pawn brokers, although we remember him as Santa Claus. And the Belgian village of Gheel is famous for its unique system of caring for the mentally ill. Here was located an infirmary and a church centered on the shrine of Saint Dympna. Retarded children were given work in the fields and in the household under the guidance of country folk and the spirit of the saint (Bromberg, 1975; Scheerenberger, 1982).

Even more rare in the early Christian era than isolated attempts to provide care for disabled persons are any indications of attempted cures. Although most references to cures are permeated by an aura of magic, some may well point to what were valid educational attempts posing as miracles. In 504, for example, Saint Severinus "healed Eululius, Bishop of Nevers, who has for some time been deaf and dumb" (De Land, 1931, p. 13). Saint John of Beverly in England was said to have "cured a dumme man with blessing him" (Porter, 1847), the reason that Saint John later became patron saint of the deaf (see Bede, 1849). The life and miracles of Saint Louis, attributed to Guillaume Pathos, confessor of Queen Margaret of Provence, and composed in 1302 or 1303, contains the story of an eight-year-old boy who had never heard or spoken but who regained his hearing at the tomb of Saint Louis (P. B Fay, 1923). Saint Elizabeth of Hungary was reported to have cured a boy's deafness and dumbness, and Saint Claire is credited with the cure of one Sister Christine (De Land, 1931; H. P. Peet, 1851).

Accounts of treatment in this period point to the influence of the church. Nevertheless, the early Christian church, a potent and stern overseer of people's lives, proved to be equivocal in its attitudes toward those with disabling conditions. The early Christians aspired to create a spiritual revolution rather than a series of coherent social changes. As they preached the spiritual equality of all and diligently promised the kingdom of heaven to the meek in spirit, the hierarchy marked for heavenly attainment systematically omitted certain groups.

Saint Augustine of Numidia, bishop of Hippo in the late fourth century and early fifth century, for example, exalted marriage and formulated the basic Christian attitude that marriage provides a lawful channel for the relief of lust, results in the procreation of children, and establishes a Christian atmosphere for their rearing. However, Augustine renounced any claims of disabled people for participation in the covenant of the Lord. He may have interpreted Paul's charge to "comfort the feeble-minded" as applicable to those unfortunates weak in intellect, not weak in faith (Barr, [1904b] 1913, p. 25), but he interpreted the

Pauline dictum "Faith comes by hearing" to mean that "those who are born deaf are incapable of ever exercising the Christian faith, for they cannot hear the Word, and they cannot read the Word" (OSD, 1895, p. 12). Augustine's declarations effectively denied church membership to deaf persons; they were restricted from the celebration of mass, disallowed the sacrament of communion, and generally excluded because they were unable to express their sins. Until the twelfth century an express dispensation of the pope was necessary to authorize the marriage of a deaf person (H. P. Peet, 1851).

Augustine further paved a troubled route for other disabled groups when his opinions on miraculous healing were accepted by the Council of Toledo in the fifth century. The church fathers avowed that "demonic seizures can be cured only by miracles, whereas diseases . . . can also be overcome by human medical effort" (Veith, 1965). With this ruling, epilepsy and other nervous disorders ceased to be primarily viewed as bodily diseases in the Hippocratic convention, but instead fell totally within the purview of the church.

The Medieval Mind and Disability

By the mid-eleventh century a more settled world began to emerge from the troubled feudal society of Europe. Populations were growing, nomadic invaders had finally been repelled, commerce was expanding, and the cities were reviving after their long neglect. The church led in establishing the new tone of society; the Gregorian Revolution of the late eleventh century built on a revived papacy and focused on basic church reforms that eventually led to new centralized institutions. Secular society was quick to follow the lead of the church.

On might assume that when ecclesiastical thought more closely concerned itself with the social and political conditions of society, more help for disabled persons would develop. But those concerned with the creation of a whole society operating on moral principles ignored the exceptional or questioned their capacity for spiritual achievement and social responsibility. Church law discriminated against disabled individuals, and the conventions of secular society subjected them to unjust laws and treatment. The early legal code of nearly every European country imposed strict civil disabilities on disabled people—they were deprived of rights of inheritance, forbidden to testify in a court of justice, and not allowed to make a deed, contract, note, or will (see Gaw, 1906).

With both crown and church disinclined to defend them and indeed often arrayed against them, disabled persons drew small regard and little compassion from the people around them. In the thirteenth century when Henry III of England found his small daughter, Catherine, to be deaf, Matthew Paris, a contemporary historian, described the child as "dumb, and fit for nothing, though possessing great beauty" (De Land, 1931, p. 14). Often disabled persons became the butts of crude humor, as we see in the 1425 tale of four blind men. Encased in full armor and armed with clubs, the men were placed in a square with a large hog, a prize going to the one who could kill the animal (French, 1932). People were likely to interpret the behavior of mentally retarded persons as evil and their mutterings as conversations with the Devil. In sixteenth-century Hamburg, in Germany, for example, mentally retarded individuals were confined in a tower in the city wall, appropriately named the Idiot's Cage (Burdett, 1891).

Most disabled persons in medieval Europe seem to have led an insecure and precarious existence; only a scattered few were granted aid. There is no evidence of public support, but under the aegis of the church hospices to care for exceptional persons did develop, though painfully slowly. In the thirteenth century three hundred French knights captured by the Moslems had their eyes put out. After Louis IX ransomed them, he established the Hospice des Quinz-Vingts to care for the blinded soldiers. Inmates were provided an allowance from the privy purse provided they made soup for the poor. Illiterates and paupers were taken in but provided little training. This establishment later played a role in setting the direction of the education of the blind as well as establishing the pattern for future institutions for blind children and adults (see Farrell, 1956b; French, 1932).

Throughout medieval times varied attitudes to mentally retarded persons are evident. Some observers interpreted the mutterings of mentally retarded persons with dialogues with the devils, but others held them to be mysteriously connected with the unknown and their talk as evidence of divine inspiration (Barr, [1904b] 1913; Burdett, 1891). In some societies a house into which an imbecile was born was considered blessed by God (Barr, 1904b). And yet exploitation and ridicule was common. Following the tradition of the Romans, some lords granted mentally retarded people the freedom of their castles to serve as household fools. Pope Leo X was said to have retained a number of mentally retarded dwarfs to serve as entertainment (Hibbert, 1975).

As the Middle ages drew to a close, the feudal order slowly gave way to political absolutism and the national state, and new urban social groups arose. Plagues and the disruptions of social change and urbanization created a pervasive pessimism; discontent within the monolithic church mounted. There developed a widespread sense that all of Christendom was sick, and the world seemed to be falling apart. A new order, the outlines of which could be seen but dimly, was struggling to emerge.

The medieval Christian commonwealth, fashioned and guided by the church of Rome, was wracked by dissension, hatred, and violence. Abuses within the church led many to a desire to return it to its original state, to lend it new life, a process begun as early as 1095 when Pope Urban II called the First Crusade. A little later, in 1150, the church embraced the doctrine of original sin (Durant, 1950, p. 820), which meant that from then on Christians viewed themselves and all humans as inherently evil, saved only by the grace of the good God.

Medieval life was further disrupted in the fourteenth century by the appearance of the Black Death, also called the pestilence of the Great Mortality. Beginning in Central Asia, the plague spread outward to reach the heart of Europe around 1348. This was not the first or only plague to attack Europe, but it was one of the most virulent. It is estimated that between 1347 and 1351 in the whole of Europe, 25 million persons, as much as one-third of the population, were lost (see Slack, 1985; Zinsser, 1935).

In the face of devastating plague, humans stood helpless and terrified, trapped by a peril against which they had no defense. Responses to the crisis were often extreme. In the early days of the Black Death, mental derangement was obvious in the behavior of those belonging to the sects of flagellants and of those in some parts of central Europe who were caught up in the dancing manias. All who were deranged, whether as a consequence of the disease itself or of the terror it inspired, were prime candidates for the witch hunters who were just beginning to fan out on their grisly search across he Continent. Many believed that the sins of Adam, cast upon his children, was what brought death and dissension to life. With so much evil in the world, apocalyptic thinkers predicted that God would destroy the world and substitute a new one for the old. The final struggle of Armageddon would be between the hosts of Christ and the hosts of the Antichrist.

Belief in the power of the Devil grew, and his might appeared capable of overthrowing the church and with it, all existing order (Rosen, 1968). As awareness of the Devil and his powers was carried to new and terrifying heights, the search for the Antichrist assumed dreadful proportions. By the late thirteenth century conceptions of Armageddon, of pervasive evil, and of social chaos slowly fused into the intertwined threads of the Inquisition and the prevailing stereotypes about heretics.

As dissension within the church and disruption everywhere assumed alarming proportions, society and the church increasingly proclaimed heresy to be rampant. People believed that the extermination of the agents of the Antichrist was a prerequisite for the salvation of all humanity, and a popular movement arose as church, state, and indeed all of European society demanded the suppression of heresy. Medieval churchmen invented a grotesque ideology, which came to be massively embodied in the Inquisition, of an evil unity between heresy, sorcery, and witchcraft. It was the belief of the church that heretics were the authors, the patrons, and the objects of witchcraft. Hence, the witch hunts grew out of the hunt for heretics, just as the witch trials evolved out of the trials for heresy (Rosen, 1968).[2]

By 1484 Pope Innocent VIII declared open war on witches. Then in 1487 two Dominicans, the chief inquisitors for Germany, a center of intense witch hunting, produced the notorious *Malleus Maleficarum* [The hammer of witches], which provided intimate details of the habits and characteristics of witches. It served as well as a manual of procedures and theory for witchcraft trials. By the time Martin Luther posted his ninety-five theses to a church door in Wittenburg (1517), Europe already possessed excellent descriptions of witches, and all Europe seemed to swarm with them (Rosen, 1968). Many believed that a preternatural dominion of the earth was exercised by old women and widows, and by any person who was unusual, different, deviant, or, no doubt, disabled.

Until the eighteenth-century Enlightenment, European civilization was haunted by the idea of witches. Witch hunting was prosecuted with vigor; for almost three centuries Europe and its overseas colonies were the sites of organized witch hunts. The hunts and the trials led to the deaths of hundreds of thousands of people by burning, hanging, drowning, or other methods. The full count of victims of the witchcraft mania cannot be calculated; the likeliest guess is that the total number of trials exceeded 100,000 and the number of executions was below this number (Monter, 1977). Witchcraft became the most important capital crime for women in early modern Europe; perhaps 80 percent of the accused were women.[3]

How many disabled persons were accused or perished is unknown; that they were implicated seems beyond question. Much earlier, Saint Augustine had included madness and epilepsy within the domain of the religious authorities. Now the *Malleus* prescribed measures to differentiate witches from normal persons: "If the patient can be relieved by no drugs, but rather, seems to be aggravated by them, then the disease is caused by the devil" (quoted by Alexander and Selesnick, 1966, p. 68). One treatise on exorcism asserted that symptoms of possession were obvious in those feigning to be mad, or those who became deaf, dumb, insane, or blind (Bromberg, 1975). Another expert enumerated the signs that indicated possession and included diseases that doctors could not diagnose and treat (Bromberg, 1975). With many disabling conditions such as deafness, mental retardation, insanity, and epilepsy already linked by tradition to the supernatural and unamenable to medieval medical treatment, the consequences for disabled individuals of assertions like these from the authorities must have been devastating. Take a case reported by Ambroise Paré, a medical surgeon who treated a young nobleman who suffered "convulsions that involved different parts of his body such as the left arm, or the right, or on occasion only a single finger, one loin or both, or his spine, and then his whole body would become so suddenly convulsed and disturbed that four servants would have difficulty in keeping him in bed" (quoted in Bromberg, 1975, p. 48). It was discovered that the Devil, forced to reveal himself by means of religious exorcism, caused this malady. Many of the people put to death for witchcraft were likely not possessed by satanic spirits at all, but instead may have been the victims of neurological or emotional disorders (D. H. Tuke, 1882).

Mentally ill persons were turned over to the clergy and the secular powers, who combined to punish the "agents of the devil" by burning them at the stake or otherwise disposing of them. Mentally retarded people may have also fallen into the witch hunters' net. Scheerenberger (1982) states that during the Inquisition some mentally retarded individuals were executed, either because they were perceived as being the offsprings of witches or because their own behavior seemed bizarre or threatening.

John Calvin preached that mentally retarded persons are possessed by Satan; Martin Luther was of the opinion that a mentally retarded child is merely a mass of flesh (*massa carnis*) with no soul (Kanner, 1964). Luther further subscribed to the belief that the Devil is the father of idiots; he denounced the mentally handicapped as "filled with Satan" (Barr, [1904b] 1913, p. 26) and even suggested that one child be taken to the nearest river and drowned (Kanner, 1964).

It is also possible that disabled people or the parents of disabled children would attribute a disorder to witchcraft as a last resort, when prayers or medicines had failed and exorcism seemed the last hope of a cure. Sawyer (1989) points out that witchcraft lies at the intersection of the biological, existential, and social worlds of the infirm. Of all the afflictions attributed to witchcraft, none was more common among adults than disturbances of the mind; the next largest category among children and adults was lameness with a chronic wasting away of the body or limbs that boded permanent disability and probable death (Sawyer, 1989). When the onset of a disorder was sudden and unexpected, or when naturalistic medicine offered little or no relief, then witchcraft might well have seemed an unavoidable alternative.

The response to witch hunting included dismay and disagreement from many quarters throughout the course of its unhappy history, and it must not be assumed that the ideas embodied in the *Malleus* received universal assent (Teall, 1962). However, it was not until the late seventeenth century that the light of reason began to drive the long prevalent beliefs in witchcraft underground.

DISABILITY IN A MORE HUMANISTIC WORLD

The witchcraft mania, indeed, many forms of superstition, actually began to sub-side in the liberal atmosphere of the Renaissance, which brought about new knowledge in medicine and psychiatry, and, in all fields of learning, as well as unprecedented activity in exploration and colonization. Philosophers in the six-teenth and seventeenth centuries scrutinized the old shibboleths and fostered an increased skepticism. Adventurous thinkers, those of a liberal turn of mind and novel ideas, spoke against witch hunts and their trappings.

For example, Gironimo Cardano, an Italian physician of the sixteenth cen-tury (see Box 1–2), not only railed against witch hunting but proposed some of the earliest known measures for special education. Witchcraft as a crime gradu-ally faded from the European scene. In England, for example, the penal laws against witchcraft were repealed in 1736. As witch hunts became less frequent and the very existence of witches came into question more often and more openly, the safety of disabled people increased, and their lives became somewhat less precarious.

The experience of disabled people in medieval times was not a tale of unmit-igated hardship, deprivation, isolation, and gruesome witch hunts. Even as some fanatics pursued the swarms of witches they imagined were polluting daily and ecclesiastical life, others, following more humanistic impulses, pursued ideas more in tune with emerging Renaissance thought.

Primarily an Italian experience, the Renaissance began in the fourteenth cen-tury and reached its height in the fifteenth and sixteenth centuries. With the movement arose a new interest in humanistic principles, individuality, learning, and the secular arts. Humanism in art led to a more intense focus on the human body and so to the development of more sophisticated surgery and medical prac-tices. The age-old fear of dissecting the human body subsided, and the fields of anatomy and physiology enjoyed a period of vigorous development. The ear, for example, one of the smallest and most complex organs of the body, was exam-ined and its basic mechanisms traced. Two Italian anatomists made important discoveries about the structure of the ear: Gabriello Fallopio (1523–1562)

BOX 1–2
GIRONIMO CARDANO (1501–1576)

New philosophies wrought by the many social and intellectual changes of the Renaissance began to burn away the mists of superstition and fear and to lead away from the medieval reliance on supernatural explanations for any phenomenon. One of the liveliest speculative thinkers of the Renaissance was Gironimo Cardano (in English, Jerome Cardan), the illegitimate son of a lawyer who rose to become the rector of Padua University, the leading medical facility in Europe. A genius, a physician by profession, a mathematician by natural taste and talent, Cardano is sometimes described as the first psychiatrist. He railed against the obscenities of the witch hunts; as early as 1550 he described those called vulgarly *stigae* as miserable, beggarly old women, and attributed their unusual or aberrant behavior to poverty, hunger, and hardship.

When one of his sons was found to have defective hearing, Cardano was drawn into philosophical speculation about the potentialities of disabled individuals and methods for their education. He disregarded Aristotelian imperatives and, adopting principles that would characterize the empirical psychology of John Locke a century later, was probably the first to see the true relationship among the senses. He believed that the instruction of the sensorily handicapped was possible (Monroe, 1926) and surmised that it would be successful through the use of alternative stimuli.

It would be possible, assumed Cardano, to teach the blind by means of feeling, and so he devised a sort of Braille code. He also held that "the instruction of the deaf is difficult, but it is possible" and further reasoned that "writing is associated with speech, and speech with thought," so therefore "written characters and ideas may be connected without the intervention of sound" (quoted by Monroe, 1926, p. 257). Although Cardano elaborated a sort of raised print code for the use of deaf people, he did not essay a practical application of his theories. Nevertheless, his statements mark a turning point in attitudes toward sensorily deprived persons (see Hodgson, [1952] 1973).

---

described the bony labyrinth of the ear, and Bartolommeo Eustachio (1524?–1574) identified the tensor tympani muscle and the Eustachian tube (Hodgson, [1952] 1973). Others added to the understanding of the ear: Costanzo Varoli identified the stapedius muscle in 1570, and Aquapendente described the function of middle ear muscles in 1598.

At the same time, the invention of printing resulted in a wider dissemination of knowledge and a surge in the spread of literacy. More books were produced during the half-century after Johann Gutenberg's press began operating in the 1450s than were likely to have issued from all the scriptoria of Europe and the Roman Empire since the first years A.D. Literacy grew rapidly (Bromberg, 1975). Moreover, the availability of reading materials motivated efforts to understand the mechanics of the visual system and to seek ways of improving sight for reading. Legend claims that eye glasses were invented by Saint Jerome (340?–420), perhaps because Jerome was the most notable student of Didymus (308–395), the blind scholar of Alexandria. Whoever the inventor may have been, spectacles began to appear in Italy in the fourteenth century and were in common use by the sixteenth.

The State of Medicine

Medieval society was not a medical desert; it was replete with empirics or quacks, divines, parsons, and magicians, as well as responsible physicians. From the thirteenth century on, these practitioners created a mixture of the rational and the unreasoned in a body of medical literature that described an enormously wide range of disabling conditions and their cures. A science of medicine merged slowly, although Renaissance anatomy, physiology and medicine continued to draw from the notions of Hippocrates, Celsus, and Galen, often grafting onto these occasional bizarre notions taken from religion and demonology to construct its understanding of the etiology and treatment of disease. Anatomy and physiology were not exact sciences, and the treatments proposed for epilepsy, madness, and sensory impairments often amounted to nothing more than incantations, spells, and witches' brews, in short, little more than quackery.

Bromberg (1975) offers insight into Renaissance medicine with a glance at the table of contents of one medical treatise, Karl F. Paullini's *Flagellum salutis* [From sickness arises health] (1698). Paullini dealt with "the usefullness of voluntary beatings in many diseases of the head; Beatings in meloncholia; in frenzy; in paralysis; in epilepsy; in facial expression of feebleminded; in hardness of hearing; in toothache; in dumbness; hysterical crying; in nymphomania" (original punctuation, quoted by Bromberg, 1975, p. 53).

Epilepsy particularly was subject to a wide range of treatments. The condition drew considerable attention from Hippocrates, Celsus, and Galen, and during the Middle Ages its importance is testified to by is inclusion in nearly every medical treatise concerning children (see Zilboorg and Henry, 1941). Considered a particularly virulent manifestation of madness, epilepsy was long thought to abate under the influence of blood, the most important bodily humor. The Romans lined their epileptics up at the Forum to drink the supposedly curative blood of slain gladiators. Cures of the Middle Ages were little more appealing. One involved the consumption of "the brain of a mountain goat drawn through a golden ring." In another, the afflicted person could ingest "the gall still warm from a dog who should have been killed the moment the epileptic fell in the fit" (D. H. Tuke, 1882, p. 8). The Scots suggested that the sacrifice of a live cock would benefit epileptics, probably with the passage of the evil spirit from the afflicted person to the cock. To carry out the cure it was suggested: "On the spot where the patient falls, the black cock is buried alive, along with a lock of the patient's hair and some parings of his nails" (D. H. Tuke, 1882, pp. 20–21).

For those manifesting "idiocy and folly" the cure consisted of putting ". . . into ale cassia, and lupins, bishopwort, alexander, githfife, fieldmore, and holy water, then let him drink" (D. H. Tuke, 1882, p. 4). For "mad and furious men" one treatment echoed Celsus–the black hellebore of the Christmas rose "purgeth all melancholy humors" (D. H. Tuke, 1882, p. 31).

Attempts during the Middle Ages and Renaissance to alleviate hearing problems were varied. One treatment forced deaf persons to shout so loudly that blood flowed from their mouths, in order to awaken their latent hearing (Hiedsiek, 1898). In other treatments, the occipital bone was struck hard enough to fracture it, in the hope that the blow might shake something loose (Hodgson, [1952] 1973). Sufferers from earaches were advised to drop the juice of a baked onion in the affected ear or to plug the ear with lint saturated with laudanum (Kile, 1916). Or they could take "Earth Wormes and fry them with Goose-grese, and drop a little thereof warme into the Deafe or, pained eares" ("Cures," 1926, p. 393). Cases of infection were treated with a white-hot iron applied to the mastoid, or the burning of a cottony material in contact with the skin from the back of the neck around to the chin in order to draw off the pus and "feculent humours" (Hodgson, [1952] 1973; "On attempted," 1851, p. 244).

More benign cures, if not more effective ones, began to appear in British periodicals in the seventeenth century. Jean Paul Siegel (1969) relates the story of a reader of the British Apollo who observed that normally he had to speak as loud as he was able in order to communicate with his deaf friend. But when riding in a coach with him on stone, the friend could hear distinctly every word he said. Apollo explained: "we shall impute the Cause of this Gentlemen's Deafness to a vitiation or laxity of the Drum of the Ear. Now, by the Impulse of the continu'd and more Vehement Sound, This Thin Membrane or Drum is Enforc'd to its due Extension, and is thereby in some measure Enabled to Perform its Proper Office" (quoted in Seigel, 1969, p. 102).

Institutionalization

Antiquity had no institutions for the care of disabled or indigent persons, and the early Christian era saw only scattered hospices and asylums established across Europe beginning in the fourth century. Public institutionalization for health problems developed between the sixth and thirteenth centuries when leprosy became a major health concern. Leprosariums multiplied—there were perhaps as many as 19,000 throughout the Christian world (Foucault, 1965).

As the leprosy epidemic in Europe began to subside at the beginning of the seventeenth century, many of these institutions were converted, especially to the needs of those who were considered insane. Early medieval society made no effort to conceal the insane and mental defectives from public view. They were a visible part of everyday society, and, by and large, community attitudes toward these individuals were a compound of fear and contempt, mingled to a lesser extent with an element of compassion (Rosen, 1968). Insane persons occupied a special place in society; they were seen as outcasts characterized by disorder and incoherence, particularly the most dangerous among them, namely, the frenzied, the angry, the threatening, and the maniacal (Doermer, [1969] 1981).

Though many outcasts wandered freely through the squalor and cruelty of the late Middle Ages, society eventually reached the point where it could no longer tolerate the potential dangers posed by the insane. Converted leprosariums became the focal points of a complex of institutions, variously termed mad-houses, bedlams, or lunatic hospitals. Rarely were these places named *asylums*— this gentler term was generally reserved for places of protection, retreat, and shelter, which little resembled the realities of seventeenth-century madhouses. It was not until the late eighteenth century that the word *asylum* was used to describe a hospital for lunatics.

Institutions do not exist in a vacuum, nor do they arise without precedent. The practice of confining mad people and other exceptional persons that became widespread in mid-seventeenth century constituted a response to both their higher visibility in society and the perceived need for society to protect itself against the harm that the deviant, the defective, or the dependent person might incur. Witch hunters had not managed to exterminate all of society's troubling elements; now alternative methods were sought, and the confined congregate institution seemed a logical solution. Unlike the monasteries and hospices that arose to save disabled persons from a vile world, the institutions that developed from the early seventeenth century served to protect society from the physically, intellectually, and socially deviant and dependent persons in its midst.

The early lunatic hospitals housed many more people than just those who were mentally ill; about 10 percent of the inmates, on the average, were labeled as insane. The lunatic hospitals also incarcerated heretics, social dissidents, and others who threatened the established order without actually committing any crimes. Beggars and vagabonds; those without property, jobs, or trades; political gadflies and heretics; prostitutes; libertines, syphilitics, and alcoholics; idiots and eccentrics; rejected wives, deflowered daughters, and spendthrift sons—could all be incarcerated and thus rendered harmless and virtually invisible (Doermer, [1969] 1981).

In London the Hospital of St. Mary of Bethlehem, first established in 1247, arose again in 1676 from the ashes of the Great Fire (Byrd, 1974) to become a major lunatic hospital. The name quickly degenerated into the nickname "Bedlam," which eventually became a generic designation for any lunatic hospital and has come to mean any noisy chaos.

Similar centers were established in Paris in 1630 under the tutelage of Saint Vincent de Paul (1581–1660). Cardinal Richelieu had begun to turn the ancient chateau of St. Lazare into a military hospital but ceded the property to Vincent de Paul, who gathered there the homeless, the outcast, and the feeble in mind and body. Bicêtre, as the institution soon came to be called, rapidly assumed the character of a congregate institution (large, multicelled) with entrance criteria based solely on need. Vincent de Paul also obtained the property known as Salpêtrière, which the government later managed as a house for beggars. By the eighteenth century Salpêtrière had become the women's lunatic hospital, Bicêtre the men's (see Ireland, 1877).

Callous treatment was the hallmark of all early lunatic hospitals. In England prescriptions for "the curing of Mad people" were based on "their reverence or standing in awe of such as they think their Tormentors." It was believed that "Furious Mad-men are sooner, and more certainly cured by punishments, and hard usage, in a straight room, than by Physick or Medicines." Hence, overseers were advised to "Let the diet be slender and not delicate, their clothing coarse, their beds hard, and their handling severe and rigid" (quoted by Doermer, [1969] 1981 p. 26).

Whether to raise funds, to illustrate the potential rationality of the disabled, or simply to titillate a curious public, those whose responsibility was to care for exceptional people exhibited them to the public in a variety of contexts, a practice that persisted until the close of the nineteenth century. Indeed, the exhibiting of deviance and disability in their various forms for money can be traced to the first lunatic hospitals, where inmates were shown as caged monsters to a paying populace (Doermer, [1969] 1981). City folk, searching entertainment, flocked to see the lunatics and their antics. For a few pennies' admission, Londoners could visit Bedlam on a Sunday and promenade past cells arrayed like a circus sideshow (Byrd, 1974). So popular were the lunatic exhibitions that contemporary accounts from London, Paris, and various German cities tell how they vied for audiences with animal acts (Doermer, [1969] 1981).

EDUCATIONAL ADVANCES

The gathering humanistic and philosophical spirit of the Renaissance flowered into genuine educational attempts that, though nascent and primitive, demonstrated that disabled persons could learn and achieve. Some of the major principles that were to guide special education were established during the late Renaissance period. It was deaf persons who were first granted consideration in educational contexts, followed by blind, and, much more tardily, mentally retarded people. Closely linked to this progression was the philosophical precept that underlay special education at its founding. Teachers, writers, and philosophers based their interventions on the belief that discovering the manner in which deaf persons learned, especially the way in which they acquired language, would provide a key to the history of thought and of humankind in general.

The Beginnings in Spain

However, it was Spain, not Renaissance Italy, that spawned the first authenticated special educational efforts, and it was fiscal considerations, not philosophy, that provided the immediate motive for this first attempt. From the Benedictine monastery of San Salvador, near Burgos in northern Spain, comes the earliest evidence of formal and systematic instruction of any disabled individuals. A strong trait of hereditary deafness haunted Spain's ruling families. Under laws of inheritance that harked back to the Justinian legal codes, deaf boys could not claim their inheritance if they could not speak. Thus, the laws of inheritance that affected great estates became the educational spur for the establishment of the means to educate the deaf sons of Spanish aristocrats.

Pedro Ponce de León (1520–1584), a Benedictine monk, employing methods of his own devising, assumed the instruction of the scions of some of Spain's wealthiest families. Detailed descriptions of Ponce's methods are not available, but his own testimony and that of his pupils and impartial observers indicates that the lads learned to speak with facility. Apparently, Ponce "instructed the boys in writing, then pointed out the objects signified by the written characters, and finally exercised them in the repetition of the vocal organs of the utterances which corresponded to the characters" (OSD, 1884, p. 10). In a legal document of 1578 Ponce detailed the advances of the boys under his tutelage:

> I have had for my pupils, who were deaf and dumb from birth, sons of great lords and notable people, whom I have taught to speak, read, write and reckon; to pray, and assist at mass, to know the doctrines of Christianity, and to know how to confess themselves by speech; some of them also learn Latin, and some both Latin and Greek, and to understand the Italian language; and one was ordained, and held office and emolument in the Church, and performed the services of the Canonic Hours; and he also, and some others, arrived at a knowledge of natural philosophy and astrology; and another succeeded to an estate and marquisate, and entered the army, and in addition to his other attainments, as has been related, was skilled in the use of all kinds of arms, and was especially an excellent rider. And besides all this, some were great historians of Spanish, and foreign history; and, above all, they were versed in the doctrine, Politics and Discipline from which Aristotle excluded them. (Quoted in Mathison, 1906, p. 416)

To observers steeped in ancient prejudices, Ponce's achievements seemed miraculous, but his own reports hold a great deal of colorful exaggeration. Moreover, as Susan Plann (1991) argues, Ponce's work was less of an "astounding cognitive leap" than an astute application of the sign language he and his brother Benedictine monks used daily. Ponce's great achievements may not have been teaching speech and language to the deaf boys but more his recognition that disability did not hinder learning and his use of alternative stimuli, in this case, sign language. Most importantly, perhaps, Ponce de Leon was the first successful special educator, and 1578 the year in which special education truly began.

The Constable of Castile had a deaf younger brother, so it is not surprising that the constable's secretary, a former soldier named Jean Pablo Bonet (1579–1629), continued the work, assisted by Ramirez de Carrion. Whereas Ponce used conventional signs but not fingerspelling or speechreading, Bonet added a manual component, employing a methodology that incorporated a hand alphabet, signs, writing, speech, and a stress on lipreading, which, he claimed, could not be taught but only acquired through concentrated attention (Lane, 1976). To stimulate and teach speech, Bonet suggested the use of a flexible leather tongue to imitate the positions of the living tongue (Seguin, 1876).

In 1620 Bonet published the first practical treatise on the art of teaching the deaf, his *Simplification of the Letters of the Alphabet, and a Method of Teaching Deaf Mutes to Speak* (see H. P. Peet, 1850). Bonet's work did not appear in English until 1890; only coincidence and good luck sent a version to London by a circuitous route in 1644.

The British Pioneers

Sir Kenelm Digby, son of one of the Gunpowder Plot conspirators, visited Spain with the Prince of Wales, later Charles I, in 1623 and met one of Bonet's pupils, Luis de Valesco. In exile in Paris in 1644, Digby wrote *Treatise on the Nature of Bodies*, in which he recounted the unprecedented accomplishments in Spain with the deaf (see Digby, 1665, 1827). Through his close correspondence with John Wallis on philosophical subjects, Digby presented the Spanish accomplishments to a small British audience avidly searching for new lines of philosophical inquiry. Over the following half-century Bonet's work guided and inspired a quintet of British works on the nature of language, the elements of speech, and practical methodologies for teaching deaf persons.

In seventeenth-century England philosophical inquiry rather than pragmatic considerations underlay early designs for intervention with disabled individuals. Philosophers, avidly probing the origin and development of language, recruited deaf people as objects of study. Blind people were also studied. The philosophers wished to discover whether a person who had never seen could, if sight were suddenly restored, recognize through vision what had previously been learned by touch.

The Royal Society of London, an organization of thinkers and scientists, gained a royal charter in 1662 with an informal mandate to find "histories of phenomena," the universal and natural "history of things."

Paralleling the quest for a universal history was a desire for a universal language, frequently marked by a demand for a dictionary of words to provide accuracy and precision to the language. Calls for a universal language, first heard in the mid-seventeenth century, echoed again and again across the next three hundred years, always to the ultimate advantage of deaf persons. For example, the search was continued in the next century by such redoubtable characters as John Cleland, who wrote the immortal (or immoral) *Fanny Hill* to finance his elusive search. And as we shall see, in the nineteenth century Alexander Melville Bell's quest for a universal alphabet altered the education of deaf children for nearly a hundred years.

With their strong emphasis on language, it is little wonder that members of the Royal Society issued so many studies of deafness; examples are those undertaken by William Holder, George Dalgarno, John Bulwer, and John Wallis. Their purpose was to learn from deaf persons the secret of what people were like before language, what their ideas were before being filtered and shaped by conversation. These philosopher-scientists elucidated their work with deaf children and adults in philosophical papers written for the society: Wallis's *De loquela* (1653) and "A Letter to Robert Boyle Esq." ([1670] n.d.); William Holder's *Elements of Speech* ([1699] 1967); George Dalgarno's *Didascalocophus* ([1680] 1971); and George Sibscota's *Deaf and Dumb Man's Discourse* ([1670] 1967). These were chiefly philosophical treatises concerning the nature of language that contained elaborate analyses of the different elements of speech. The teaching of deaf people was used to illustrate the new theories that were beginning to take hold. Some, depending on the bent of the author, stressed the acquisition of artificial speech

(Mathison, 1906). The reports of these pioneers thus hold interest today chiefly as early instances of educational efforts; they did not represent advances in the comprehension of the psychology of deafness. Most of the members of the Royal Society interested in deafness were dilettantes who had little or no insight into the epistemological and psychological complexities of deafness (Siegel, 1969). In concert with notions prevalent since the days of Hippocrates, they viewed deaf people as curiosities and were more often concerned with speculations of the physiological causes and cures for deafness than with the psychological, social, and educational applications of their findings.

John Wallis (1616–1703), a professor of geometry at Oxford and one of the founding members of the Royal Society, was the most influential British authority on deafness in the seventeenth and eighteenth centuries (Hoolihan, 1985). As an internationally respected mathematician, a prolific author, a correspondent with some of the best minds in Europe, and one of the greatest of Newton's English precursors (Hoolihan, 1985), Wallis's reputation in his own and later ages was such that he exerted a profound influence on the nascent field of special education.

Wallis's *Grammatica linguae anglicanae. Cui praefigur, De loquela sive sonorumm formastione, tractacus grammaticophysicus* was a grammar of the English language for non-English speakers printed at Oxford in 1653 and written in Latin. Prefaced to the *Grammatica* was a treatise of particular importance to the education of deaf persons. Wallis's "De loquela" [On speech] described the organs of speech and the nature of voice; it also presented a detailed analysis of the phonetic elements of English pronunciation, which was useful, according to the author, to foreigners and deaf people.

When Wallis assumed the instruction of twenty-five-year-old Daniel Whalley in 1661, "De loquela" served as the basis for his teaching. Wallis attempted to make Whalley understand the structural elements of language, that is, "to teach him to understand the significance of words and their relations" (OSD, 1884, p. 11). Wallis relied on instruction in written language, and then he used some method of signs for speech, most likely a hand alphabet designed by his friend and contemporary George Dalgarno (1626–1687), which Wallis appropriated without credit (*AADD*, 1850). To stimulate speech, Wallis showed Whalley how the organs of speech moved for specific sounds so that the student "may, by art, pronounce those sounds, which others do by custome" (Wallis, [1670] n.d., p. 1089). So proficient did Whalley become that John Wallis presented him before the Royal Society to demonstrate his speech ability, which he did, "though not elegantly, yet so as to be understood" (OSD, 1884, p. 11).

William Holder (1616–1698), musician, clergyman, fellow of Royal Society, and brother-in-law of Christopher Wren, also taught deaf students through the use of a finger alphabet and stylized signs. George Dalgarno (1626–1687), brought to deaf education original conceptions that anticipated some of the methods that are used even today (see Dalgarno, 1971). Sensing that language development required early intervention, Dalgarno suggested that mothers and nurses could make "successful addresses" to the dumb child if "the mother or nurse had but as nimble a hand as they usually have a tongue" (quoted by A. G. Bell, 1884b, p. 32).

Unlike Holder, Wallis, and Dalgarno who instructed individual deaf persons, John Bulwer was a theorist who pointed out safe routes for other teachers to follow. Bulwer preceded Wallis by producing in 1648 the first English work in deafness, *Philocophus* [The deaf man's friend], which he dedicated to Sir Edward Gosticke, a deaf gentleman who knew signs and fingerspelling but who wanted to learn to speak. In 1654 John Bulwer published a companion volume, *Chirologia, or, the naturall Language of the Hand* ([1654] 1975). Bulwer's stress was not in the acquisition of artificial speech but in finding means to overcome, or at least accommodate to, the impairment of deafness. Rejecting the Hippocratic dictum that there existed a common site in the brain for hearing and speech, Bulwer argued that "the truth is they speak not, because they cannot hear" (quoted by Farrell, 1956a, p. 6). And, as Bonet had done earlier, Bulwer emphasized the value of lipreading: "a Man Born Deaf and dumbe," he stated, "may be taught to Heare the sound of words with the Eie" (Bulwer, 1648, preface).

Even more startling was Bulwer's petition for "an academy for the mute," possibly the first time that anyone had suggested special schooling for a disabled group. But the ramparts of entrenched superstition were yet unassailable, as Bulwer "soon perceived by falling into discourse with some rationall men." The design, he wrote, appeared "so paradoxicall, prodigious and Hyperbolicall, that it did rather amuse them than satisfie their understandings" (quoted by J. C. Gordon, ed., 1892b, p. xx), it being the prevailing opinion that "original deafness and dumbness is not curable but by miracle" (quoted by Mathison, 1906, p. 414).

As the British philosophers and teachers labored to discover causes and cures for deafness, their efforts touched the lives of very few deaf people. However, in 1720, the year follow publication of *Robinson Crusoe*, Daniel Defoe made the hero of one of his tales a deaf man. *The Life and Adventures of Mr. Duncan Campbell* was based on a real person, a deaf seer who had captivated London society. In this first popular exposé of the problems of deaf people, Defoe pointed out that "a great many more believe it impossible for persons born deaf and dumb to write and read" (Defoe, [1720] 1903, p. 43), a myth he punctured by interweaving the pedagogy of John Wallis with his tale of Duncan Campbell.

Henry Baker (1698–1774), naturalist and a fellow of the Royal Society, read Defoe's book (and married his daughter, Sophia) and thus learned about the methods of Dr. Wallis there enumerated. Baker's interest in deafness and its implications originally developed when he visited a relative who had a deaf daughter. Jane Forester was Baker's first pupil. After succeeding with her, he became a visiting teacher; he had no school, but lived with his pupils (Oxley, 1930). Baker was very secretive, so much so that he extracted securities for as much as £100 from pupils not to disclose his methods. He took only those pupils with whom success was assured and, as the work soon became his sole livelihood, Baker is remembered more as the first professional teacher of deaf persons than for any methodological or psychological insights.

Oral Methodologies

Almost since its inception the education of deaf people has been marred by divisive controversy concerning the most appropriate modes of communications. One school, that of the manualists, views deafness as a human difference, deserving its own unique language that would circumvent the major deficits of hearing impairment. The opposing faction, the oralists, sees deafness as a handicap that can, and should, be overcome if deaf people will assume normal positions in society. Although the controversy regarding communication methods reached its most divisive pitch in late-nineteenth-century North America, the seeds of the debate were unwittingly sown by the pioneers of the seventeenth century.

As the British teachers all employed methodologies reliant on finger alphabets, possibly combined with stylized sign languages, a contrasting pedagogy arose in Europe. John Conrad Amman and Franciscus Mercurius endeavored to maintain the primacy of spoken language; they "made the essence to consist of the artificial restoration and use of the voice" (Mathison, 1906, p. 420).

John Conrad Amman (1669–1724), a Swiss doctor of medicine who emigrated to the Netherlands, was fascinated by the problem of language development, especially what he saw as its mystical and divine origin: "the Voice," he cried, "Is an Emanation from that very Spirit, which God breathed into Man's nostrils, when He created him a living soul" (Amman, [1694] 1972, p. 6). Echoing Aristotelian imperatives, Amman held that speech was a mysterious gift of God and the only means for the expression of language, which led him to develop an extravagant estimate of the importance of oral language and of is absolute necessity in the cultivation of the intellect (Rae, 1848c). Amman asserted that speech that "is performed by signs and Gestures" is "base and deficient" (Amman, [1694] 1972, preface), and he bemoaned the "miserable . . . condition of those deaf individuals compelled to employ such modes" (Amman, [1694] 1972, p. 4).

Beginning with Baker and Amman, it became characteristic of those who were developing methods to impart speech to deaf persons to guard their pedagogy closely; it was equally characteristic of manual promoters to share their methods with all comers. Amman cloaked his methods in secrecy and, although he published two influential books, *Surdus loquens* The talking deaf man] (1694) and *Dissertatio de loquela* (1700), they revealed much of his philosophy but merely a taste of his pedagogy (Amman, [1694] 1972, [1700] 1873). As Édward Seguin (1876a) pointed out, Amman's books fail to delineate how he "developed the minds and hearts of his pupils" or even how he applied speech to other teaching. All we known is that Amman encouraged perfect articulation through the use of touch and a mirror, teaching the vowels first, and insisted that his pupils be "neither too young nor too stupid" (Amman, 1873). Nevertheless, Amman's philosophy, with its extravagant estimate of the importance of speech, introduced a line of reasoning that was fundamental to the formulation of oral methods of deaf instruction and that, from the first, exerted a leading influence in Germany (E. A. Fay, 1874).

Franciscus Mercurius, the Baron van Helmont (1614?–1699), a Belgian chemist and oculist, produced less impact on the developing field of the education of deaf persons; in fact, the peculiar bent he adopted is more curious than valuable. Van Helmont believed in a metaphysical origin of language and theorized that Hebrew was the natural language of humanity. He demonstrated how the shape and character of each letter of the alphabet in Hebrew conformed to the position of the organs of speech when making the sound (Bender, 1970; E. A. Fay, 1875). In pursuit of his firm conviction that the Hebrew tongue was superior to all other languages, van Helmont instructed deaf students in Hebrew (*AADD*, 1875, p. 172). Their progress in language is unknown. Van Helmont was also interested in the insane and recommended submersion in water as the cure, but again, the patients' progress toward rationality is unknown.

The establishment of the Royal Society and the speculations of its members, the early attempts to unravel the mysteries of the human body and the senses, and the first attempts to instruct the deaf, all signaled a new, emergent attitude toward exceptionality. In the age of enlightenment to come, new hope for all forms of exceptionality would flourish.

NOTES

1. On the perceptions of and treatment for mental illness in antiquity, see Gill (1985).
2. The witch hunts in their various manifestations have received intense attention from scholars. Herein, my concern is with but one facet, the implications for disabled people. On the witch hunts in general see Anglo (1977); Estes (1984); Mac-Farlane (1970); E. Midelfort (1968); H. C. Midelfort (1982); Monter (1972, 1977); Thomas (1971); Trevor-Roper (1969).
3. On the gender bias of the witch hunters, see Quaife (1987).

WORKS CITED

AADD see *American Annals of the Deaf and Dumb.*

Alexander, F. G. and S. T. Selesnick 1966. *The history of psychiatry: An evaluation of psychiatric thought and practice from prehistoric times to the present.* New York: Harper and Row.

American Annals of the Deaf and Dumb. 1850, 1875

Amman, J. C. [1694] 1972. *Surdus loquens* [The talking deaf man]. Amsterdam. Rpt. edited by R. C. Alston. English Linguistics Series, 1500–1800, no. 357. Menston, England: Scholar Press.

———, [1700 Apter, S. J and J. C. Conoley. 1984. *Childhood behavior disorders and emotional disturbance.* Englewood Cliffs, N. J.: Prentice-Hall.

Aristotle n.d. *Politics*, trans. B. Jewett. New York: Carleton House.

———, 1910. Historia Animalium. In J. A . Smith and W. D. Ross, trans. *The works of Aristotle.* vol. 4: *Historia animalium.* Oxford: Clarendon Press.

Barnard, H. C. 1922. *The French tradition in education: Ramus to Mme. Necker de Saussure.* Cambridge: Oxford University Press.

Barr. [1904b] 1913 *Mental defectives: Their history, treatment, and training.* Philadelphia: Blakiston.

Beck, T. R. 1811. *An inaugural dissertation on insanity.* New York: J. Seymour.

Bede, the Venerable. 1849. *Ecclesiastical history of England, also the Anglo-Saxon chronicle*, edited by J. A. Giles. London: H. B. Bohm.

Bell, A. G. 1884b. Deafness in white cats. *Science* 3: 170–172

Bell, R. Q., and L. V. Harper. 1977. *Child effects on adults*. Lincoln: University of Nebraska Press.

Bender, R. E. 1970. *The conquest of deafness: A history of the long struggle to make normal living possible for those handicapped by lack of normal hearing*. Cleveland: Press of Case Western Reserve.

Biklen, D. 1986. Framed: Journalism's treatment of disability. *Social Policy*, Winter, pp. 45–51.

Bowen, B. B. 1847. *Blind man's offering*. 4th Edition. New York: Author.

Bromberg, W. 1975. *From shaman to psychotherapist: A history of the treatment of mental illness*. Chicago: Henry Regnery.

Brulle, A. R. and T. Mihail. 1991. The dark side. Paper presented at the International Conference on Special Education. Milwaukee. May.

Burdett, H. 1891. *Hospitals and asylums of the world*. London: J. and A. Churchill.

Byrd, M. 1974. *Visits to Bedlam: Madness and literature in the eighteenth century*. Columbia: University of South Carolina Press.

Cures for deafness. 1926. *Volta Review* 28: 392–393.

Dalgarno, G. 1971. [1680] 1971. *Didascolocophus. (The deaf and dumb man's tutor*. Oxford: Timo. Halton. Rpt. English Linguistic Series, 1500–1800. no. 286. Menston, England: Scholar Press. Also *American Annals of the Deaf and Dumb* 9 (1859): 14–64.

Defoe, D. [1720] 1903. The history of the life and surprising adventures of Mr. Duncan Campbell. In *The works of Daniel Defoe*, vol. 4. New York: George D. Sproul.

De Land, F. 1931. *The story of lip reading*. Washington. D. C.: Alexander Graham Bell Association for the Deaf.

de Mause, L. 1981. The fetal origins of history. *Journal of the History of Ideas* 30: 413–22.

Despert, J. L. 1970. *The emotionally disturbed child: An inquiry into family patterns*. New York: Anchor Books.

Digby, K. 1665. *The nature of bodies*. London: John Williams.

Doermer, K. [1969] 1981. *Madmen and the bourgeoisie*. Basil Blackwell.

Dunscombe, C. 1836. *Report upon the subject of education made to the Parliament of Upper Canada 25 February 1836.* . . Upper Canada: M. C. Reynolds.

Durant, W. 1944. *Caesar and Christ*. New York: Simon and Schuster.

Etienne, R. 1976. Ancient medical conscience and the life of children. *Journal of Psychohistory* 4: 131–161.

Farrell, G. 1956b. *The story of blindness*. Cambridge: Harvard University Press.

Fay, E. A. 1874. Notices of publication: Review of J. C. Amman's A dissertation on speech. *American Annals of the Deaf and Dumb* 19: 31–34.

Fay, P. B., 1923. A miracle of the 13th century. *American Annals of the Deaf* 68: 121–22

Feldman, H. 1970. *A history of audiology*. New York: Columbia University.

Ferrari, G. 1906. The deaf in antiquity. *American Annals of the Deaf* 51: 469–70.

Fiedler, L. 1982. Pity and Fear

Foucault, M. 1965. *Madness and civilization: A history of insanity in the age of reason*. New York: Pantheon.

French, R. S. 1932. *From Homer to Helen Keller: A social and educational study of the blind*. New York: American Foundation for the Blind.

Gaw, A. 1906. The development of the legal status of the deaf. *American Annals of the Deaf* 51: 269–75, 401–23.

108 MARGARET A. WINZER

————, 1907. The development of the legal status of the deaf. *American Annals of the Deaf* 52: 1–12, 167–83, 229–45.

Gelb, S. A. 1989. "Not simply bad and incorrigible": Science, morality and intellectual deficiency. *History of Education Quarterly* 29: 359–80.

Gibbon, E. [1776] 1952. *The decline and fall of the Roman Empire*. Abridged ed. Edited by D. A. Saunders. London: Penguin.

Gordon, J. C. 1892. The new departure at Kendall Green. *American Annals of the Deaf* 37: 121–27.

Harms, E. 1976. The historical aspect of child psychiatry. In J. R. Jenlins and E. Harms, eds. *Understanding disturbed children*. Seattle: Special Child Publications.

Herodotus. 1954. *The histories*. New York: Penguin.

Hewett, F. 1974. *Education of exceptional learners*. Boston: Allyn and Bacon.

Hibbert, C. 1975. *The house of Medici*. New York: William Morrow.

Hiedsiek, J. 1898. Hearing deaf mutes, 3. *American Annals of the Deaf* 43: 283.

Hodgson, K. [1952] 1973. *The deaf and their problems: A study in special education*. London: Watts. Facsimile ed., Ann Arbor: University Microfilms.

Hoolihan, C. 1985. Too little too soon: The literature of deaf education in 17th century Britain (part 2). *Volta Review* 86: 28–44.

Ireland, W. 1877. *On idiocy an imbecility*. London: J. and A. Churchill.

Kanner, L. 1964. *A history of the care and study of the mentally retarded*. Springfield, Ill.: Thomas.

Kent, D. 1986. Disabled women, portraits in fiction and drama. In A. Gartner and T. Joe, eds. *Images of the disabled/disabling images*. New York: Praeger.

Kile, B. C. 1916. The menace of suppurating ears. *Volta Review* 18: 403.

Klobas, L. 1985. TV's concept of people with disabilities: Here's lookin' at you. *Disability Rag*. January-February, pp. 2–6.

Kriegel, L. 1986. The cripple in literature. In A. Gartner and T. Joe, eds. *Images of the disabled/disabling images*. New York: Praeger.

Lane, H. 1976. *The wild boy of Aveyron*. Cambridge: Harvard University Press.

————, 1991. Keynote address. Presented at the First International Conference on the History of Deafness, Washington, D. C., June.

Longmore, P. K. 1985. Screening stereotypes: Images of disabled people. *Social Policy* 16: 31–37.

Mahendra, B. 1985. Subnormality revisited in early nineteenth century France. *Journal of Mental Deficiency Research* 29: 391–401.

Mathison, R. 1906. Historical sketch of the origin and progress of deaf-mute education. In *Ontario, Department of Education Annual Report*, pp. 413–35. Toronto: L. K. Cameron.

Michal-Smith, H. 1987. Presidential address 1987: Hollywood's portrayal of disability. *Mental Retardation* 25: 259–66.

Monroe, P. 1926. *A cyclopedia of education* 2: 257–65. New York: Macmillan.

Monter, E. W. 1977. Pedestal and stake: Courtly love and witchcraft. In R. Bridenthal and C. Koonz, eds., *Becoming visible: Women in European history*. pp 119–36. Boston: Houghton Mifflin.

Moores, D. 1987. *Educating the deaf: Philosophy, principles, and practices* 3rd ed. Boston: Houghton Mifflin.

M. V. D. 1925. Routing an ancient enemy. *Volta Review* 27: 81–85.

On attempted cures of deafness. 1851. *American Annals of the Deaf and Dumb* 3: 244–50.

OSD. 1895. Ontario Institution for the Education and Instruction of the Deaf and Dumb [name varies]. *Annual Reports* [title varies]. Toronto: Government Printer.

Oxley, S. 1930. Some new sidelights on Henry Baker. *American Annals of the Deaf* 75: 6–8.

Peet, H. P. 1851. Memoir on the origin and early history of the art of instructing the deaf and dumb. *American Annals of the Deaf and Dumb* 3: 129–60.

Penrose, L. S. [1949] 1966. *The biology of mental defects.* London: Sidgwick and Jackson.

Plann, S. 1991. Fray Pedro Ponce de Leon: Myth and reality. Paper presented at the First International Conference on the History of Deafness, Washington, D. C., June.

Porter, S. 1847. Review of The historie of the Church of England, compiled by Venerable Bede, Englishman. book 5, part 2. London, 1622, Thomas Stapleton (trans). In *American Annals of the Deaf and Dumb* 1: 33–34.

Pritchard, D. G. 1963. *Education and the handicapped.* London: Routledge and Kegan Paul.

Rae, L. 1848c. Historical sketch of the instruction of the deaf and dumb before the time of de l'E'pée. *American Annals of the Deaf and Dumb* 1: 197–208.

Ramsland, J. 1989. The foundling hospital in eighteenth century London: Social, cultural, and educational perspectives. Paper presented at the Australian and New Zealand History of Education Conference. Newcastle, July.

Rosen, M. G. Clark and M. Kivitz. 1976. *The history of mental retardation.* Baltimore: University Park Press.

Sawyer, R. C. 1989. "Strangely handled in all her lyms": Witchcraft and healing in Jacobean England. *Journal of Social History* 22: 461–86.

Scheerenberger, R. C. 1982. Treatment from ancient times to the present. In P. Cegelka and H. Prehm, eds. Mental retardation: From categories to people, pp. 44–75. Columbus, Ohio: Merrill.

Schmidt, R. R. 1936. *The dawn of the human mind,* trans. R. A. MacAlister. London: Sidgwick and Jackson.

Seguin, E. 1876. Education of the deaf and mute. In *Commissioners of the United States, Reports to the International Exhibition held in Vienna, 1873, volume 2.* Washington, D. C.: Government Printing Office.

Siegel, M. 1939. *Population, race and eugenics.* Hamilton, Ont.: author.

Slack, P. 1985. *The impact of the plague in Tudor and Stuart England.* London: Routledge and Kegan Paul.

Smith, J. A. and W. D. Ross, eds. 1910. *The works of Aristotle.* Oxford: Clarendon Press.

Steinberg, M. 1982. The Twelve Tables and their origins: An eighteenth-century debate. *Journal of the History of Ideas* 43: 379–96.

Stone, C. 1869. Address upon the history and methods of deaf mute instruction. *American Annals of the Deaf and Dumb* 14: 95- 121.

Suetonius [A. D. 120] 1957. *The twelve Caesars.* Translated by R. Graves. London: Penguin.

Teall, J. L. 1962. Witchcraft and Calvinism in Elizabethan England: Divine power and human agency. *Journal of the History of Ideas* 23: 21–36.

Tuke, D. H. [1882] 1968. *Chapters in the history of the insane in the British Isles.* Amsterdam: E. J. Bonset.

Vieth, I. 1965. *Hysteria, the history of a disease.* Chicago: University of Chicago Press.

Zilboorg, G. and G. W. Henry. 1941. *History of medical psychology.* New York: Norton.

Zinsser, H. 1985. *Rats, lice and history.* New York: Bantam.

5

Universalizing Marginality

How Europe Became Deaf in the Eighteenth Century

LENNARD J. DAVIS

> This [sign] language is so natural to mankind that despite the help we get from spoken languages to express our thoughts and all their nuances, we still make frequent use of it, especially when we are moved by some passion, and we leave off using the cold and measured tone prescribed by our institutional training, to bring us closer to the tone of nature.
>
> —*Synthetic Essay on the Origin and Formation of Languages*,
> (author unknown, 1774)

The point of this essay is that deafness, far from being an epiphenomenon of eighteenth-century cultural interests, was perhaps one of its central areas of concern. I want to make a claim for the centrality of what might seem to be extremely marginal. Further, I want to make the somewhat preposterous suggestion that Europe became deaf during the eighteenth century. I hope to show how cultural deafness became one of the hallmarks of early modern ideas about public symbol and information production, and how the deaf person became an icon for complex intersections of subject, class position, and the body.

My claim to the centrality of deafness needs to be broken down into separate smaller claims. The first of these is that deafness becomes of interest to European culture in the eighteenth century; the second, related claim is that this interest is the reciprocal reaction to, or perhaps the cause of, deafness becoming visible for the first time as an articulation in a set of discursive practices.

Michel Foucault in his classic *Madness and Civilization* shows how madhouses replaced leper colonies as the dominant confining institution in Europe at the close of the Middle Ages. This switch from the confinement of defects of the body to the confinement of defects of the mind signals a switch to an age of Reason and, by extension, madness, from an age that focused on the superficial disease of the body. Thus madness became visible, and the treatment of madness became a discourse. I shall argue in a similar vein that deafness became visible in the Enlightenment and thus became the subject of a discourse of treatment by professionals while ironically also becoming symbolic of an aspect of the Enlightenment subject itself.

Before the late seventeenth and early eighteenth centuries, the deaf were not constructed as a group. There is almost no historical or literary record of the deaf as such. We may rarely read of a deaf person, but there is no significant discourse constructed around deafness. The reason for this discursive nonexistence is that, then as now, most deaf people were born to hearing families, and therefore were isolated in their deafness. Without a sense of group solidarity and without a social category of disability, they were mainly seen as isolated deviations from a norm, as we now might consider, for example, people who are missing an arm. For these deaf, there were no schools, no teachers, no discourse, in effect, no deafness.

Likewise, the deaf themselves could not constitute themselves as a subgroup, as might other outsiders such as Jews, subalterns, even women, because they remained isolated from each other and were thus without a shared, complex language. The only deaf people who fully attained sociability were found in urban areas or in families or groupings of hereditary deafness. Here the use of sign language, as it developed over time, allowed the deaf to consider themselves a group and to communicate with each other.[1]

Of course, while deafness did not "exist" before the eighteenth century, a number of authors had written about deafness. There are references to deafness in the Old and New Testaments and in writings by Aristotle, Augustine, Descartes, and others. But something qualitatively different happens during the eighteenth century. Consider that up to the beginning of the century no deaf schools had ever existed in England, on the European continent, or anywhere else for that matter. According to one writer, "it was not until the middle of the eighteenth century that Britain and Europe turned to the education and training of their disabled populations." By the end of the century deaf schools had been established in the cities of Amsterdam, Paris, Vienna, Karlsruhe, Prague, Munich, Waitzen, Fresing, Lenz, Rome, Naples, Malta, Goningen, Tarente, Madrid, and Zurich, and in Portugal, Poland, Denmark, and Sweden. By 1789 a dozen schools had been founded in Europe and by 1822 there were sixty. Clearly, these data amount to something more than a statistical blip. The beginning of what we know call "special education" started with deafness, so that "by the close of the eighteenth century, special education was accepted as a branch of education, albeit a minor enterprise" (Winzer 1993, 39).

Of course, one might conclude that deafness itself was not so much the central phenomenon as was education. But there had consistently been hospices for the blind in Europe since the third century.[2] The blind were historically regarded as objects of charity, if not veneration for their alleged "second sight." The most famous institution for the blind was the Hospice de Quinze-Vingts founded in Paris by Louis IX in 1260, where it still exists. Quinze-Vingts was established to care for three hundred knights captured and blinded during the Crusades. While it is true that systematic education for the blind began only in the eighteenth century with the founding of the Institution des Enfants Aveugles in Paris in 1784, the blind had been constituted as a group long before that point. William Paulson argues that the development of education for the blind in turn involved a desacralization of the blind and an accompanying medicalization of the disability. Deafness as a phenomenon engaged the intellectual moment of this period in a way that blindness and other disabilities did not. Deafness, after all, was about language, about the essential human quality of verbal communication. While Diderot wrote on both the blind and the deaf, he saw blindness as posing a fundamental question about the nature of perception, whereas deafness was more fundamentally about the existence and function of language. Citing Diderot, Paulson says (1987, 48):

> What the blind man lacks is *denomination*, the ability to name visible objects, to put signs and referents together. Yet without that ability he is able to manipulate the signs as well as anyone else, creating an illusion of reference that is broken only when one remembers that he is blind.

The relation to language is therefore not as vexed for the blind as it is for those who are deaf.[3]

An indication of how special a place the deaf held in the eighteenth-century imagination can be seen in the remarkable success of Jean Nicolas Bouilly's play about the Abbé de l'Epée, the founder of the first deaf school. This theatrical piece had over one hundred performances in Paris at the end of the eighteenth century, making it the second-greatest dramatic success of the era, surpassed only by Beaumarchais's *Marriage of Figaro*.[4]

The seventeenth and eighteenth centuries saw the first major publications of books relating to deafness. Among the early works published in Europe were a medical treatise by a German physician, Solomon Alberti's *Discourse on Deafness and Speechlessness* (1591); G. Bonifacio's treatise *Of The Art of Signs* (1616); and Juan Pablo Bonet's *A Method of Teaching Deaf Mutes to Speak* (1620). In England, the first books published were John Bulwer's *Philocophus* [The Deaf Man's Friend] (1648) and later his *Chirologia, or the Natural Language of the Hand* (1654). Bulwer was a member of the Royal Society, as were a number o the early writers on deafness. George Delgarno's *Art of Communication* (1680); John Wallis's *De loquela* (1653); "A Letter to Robert Boyle Esq." (1670); and William Holder's *Elements of Speech* (1699) were all products of Royal Society members. George Sibscota's *Deaf and Dumb Man's Discourse* (1670) and Johan Ammon's *Surdus Loquens* [The Talking Deaf Man] (1694) were other works published in the latter part of the seventeenth century. The eighteenth century witnessed Ammon's *Dissertatio de loquela* (1700); Daniel Defoe's *Duncan Campbell* (1720); the Abbé de l'Epée's *Instruction of Deaf and Dumb by Means of Methodical Signs* (1776); J. L. F. Arnoldi's *Practical Instructions for Teaching Deaf-Mute Persons to Speak and Write* (1777); and R. A. Sicard's *Theory of Signs* (1782), among others.

Starting in 1771 in Paris, the Abbé de l'Epée held public displays of the ability of deaf students every Tuesday and Friday morning from 7 a.m. until noon, but the crowds increased so dramatically that he had to add another session in the evening. In 1772 printed programs warned that "because the assembly hall can only hold one hundred people, spectators are kindly requested not to remain more than two hours" (Lane 1984b, 47). It is hard to imagine this kind of devo-

tion to a cause that was in effect marginal. In 1794 Sicard held performances
once a month for Parisians, in addition to special demonstrations for the various emperors of Europe, the pope, and even a command performance before the
British parliament. These monthly sessions began at noon and ended at 4 p.m.,
with three to four hundred spectators assembled. Deaf people were asked abstract
questions through interpreters, like "Why is baptism called the portal of the
sacraments?" Deaf students replied in written French as well as in Latin, Italian,
Spanish, German, and English. These public demonstrations were attended by
many French intellectuals, including Condillac, the philosopher Lord Monboddo, the papal nuncio, the statesman John Quincy Adams, and many others
(ibid., 46–7). On a tour of the Hebrides in 1773, Dr. Johnson made a special stop
to visit the deaf school run by Thomas Braidwood.

What I am trying to demonstrate is that deafness was for the eighteenth century an area of cultural fascination and a compelling focus for philosophical
reflection. The question is, why?

Some answers may be obvious. As Harlan Lane points out in his *Wild Boy of
Aveyron*, philosophers of this period were obsessed with trying to define what
made humans human. Aristotle's classic and elegant definition included upright
gait, human appearance, and language. The investigation of "savages," orang-
utans, wild children, and the deaf allowed "scientific" observation as to what
"natural man" might be like. Rosseau, Herder, Condillac, Monboddo, Locke and
others argued over how language began, how reason and thought intertwined
into the human essence. The wild child and the deaf person provided living
examples of the mind untouched by civilization. Here questions such as the following could be put: Are there thoughts prior to language? Can a being be human
without language? Condillac, in his *Treatise on Sensations*, imagined a statue
brought to life in stages, illustrating the development of human from animal.
How appropriate that Sicard at one of his pubic events found a prelingual deaf
child and presented him before a crowd saying, "I have been waiting to introduce
you to a new subject, almost an infant, a little savage, a block of unchiseled
marble or rather a statue, yet to be animated and endowed with intellect" (Lane
1984b, 34). Sicard went on to give the child his very first lessons in language
before the eyes of the crowd, who were conscious of seeing the new natural man
sought by explorers and now by philosophers. Such theatrical displays employed
a controlling gaze which allowed the audience to observe the primitive emerge
into language—and into deafness.

The irony, of course, is that deafness, while an area of cultural fascination, had
to be contained and controlled, as it still is, by the very hearing world that was fascinated by it.[5] The panopticon created by Sicard put the deaf on display but did
not allow the deaf to control their own display except by the deviousness of subaltern strategies. We can hear the somewhat sadistic probing by the hearing world
and the competent but defiant response of Jean Massieu at one of these sessions.

"What is a sense?" Massieu was asked.
"An idea-carrier," he answered.

"What is hearing?" asked some people trying to disconcert him
"Hearing is auricular sight."
"What is gratitude?" asked the abbé Sicard.
"Gratitude is the memory of the heart," Massieu answered him.
"What is God?"
"The necessary Being—the sun of eternity."
"What is eternity?" someone asked.
"A day without yesterday or tomorrow," Massieu immediately replied.
(Lane 1984a, 78–9)

In response to being at the focal point of the clinical gaze, Massieu develops an almost aerobic response to these difficult mental exertions. His deafness is anatomized by examining his language abilities, a procedure for which he creates strategies of compliance.

These types of examinations and philosophical disquisitions help us to place deafness as an emergent, constructed category. Yet I would suggest that philosophical and even medical curiosity are only epiphenomenons of another condition that brought deafness to cultural attention. The wild child/deaf person scenario is based on the idea that deaf people are without a language, unless they learn either to write or to speak the language of the hearing majority. Dr. Johnson called deafness "one of the most desperate human calamities" for that reason. Johnson voices one view of deafness as a limit to sociability, social intercourse, education, and, indeed, humanity and reason. But there is another and more powerful view of deafness woven into eighteenth-century culture. This view sees the deaf person as someone who reasons, feels, thinks, and uses language just as hearing people do, only the language used is different from that of the linguistic majority. The language is in fact the language of texts, of writing, of novels.

In *Duncan Campbell*, Daniel Defoe embodies this idea of the deaf man as textual master. Duncan Campbell is not merely equal to hearing people but is portrayed as a hyperbolically superior being, a godlike man of great intelligence, handsome looks, and supernatural powers. Far from being perceived as disabled, he is seen as enabled with the gift of second sight which allows him to write a person's name and foretell his or her future at first meeting. Although in actuality Campbell was a fraud, the fact that Defoe regards him as deaf allows us to learn something about attitudes toward the deaf, if not about Defoe's attitude to fact and fiction.[6] What is interesting about Defoe's account is that it rests on the assumption that Campbell has his own integral language. Defoe quotes extensively from John Wallis, who had published a book on educating the deaf (though he seems simply to have plagiarized the method from George Delgarno) and was, interestingly, Defoe's brother-in-law.[7] According to Defoe, Wallis had written:

> It will be convenient all along to have pen, ink, and paper, ready at hand, to write down in a word what you signify to him by signs, and cause him to write, or show how to write what he signifies by signs, which way of signifying their mind by signs

deaf persons are often very good at: and we must endeavor to learn their language, if I may so call it, in order to teach them ours, by showing what words answer to their signs. (Defoe 1974, 31)

Wallis, and by extension Defoe, acknowledges that the deaf have their own pre-existing language and that language is mediated for the hearing world through writing and textuality. In Defoe's novel, when Duncan meets an old hearing friend, the author comments, "Here the reader must understand they discoursed on their fingers, and wrote by turns" (ibid., 164).

In addition to making the point that the deaf possess a language, many writers, including Wallis, emphasize a connection between deafness and writing. For Defoe, writing seems the natural way for a deaf person to communicate, as natural as sign language. Defoe names other famous deaf people, including Sir John Gawdy, Sir Thomas Knotcliff, Sir Henry Lydall, and Mr. Richard Lyns of Oxford who "were all of this number, and yet men eminent in their several capacities, for understanding many authors, and expressing themselves in writing with wonderful facility" (ibid., 32). here, being deaf leads naturally to writing. This correlation is made clearly by trope when Duncan must tell a beautiful young woman that she will be disfigured by smallpox and then die: ". . . he begged to be excused, and that his pen might remain as dumb and silent as his tongue on that affair." The metonymy of pen and tongue again connects writing to deafness. This link is made more explicit when Duncan "tells" a long story to a group of friars by writing it down:

so taking up another piece of paper, Fathers, said he, shall I entertain you with a story of what passed upon this head, between two religious fathers, as all of you are, and a prince of Germany. . . . The story is somewhat long, but very much to the purpose and entertaining; I remember it perfectly by heart, and if you will have patience while I am writing it, I do not doubt but that I shall not only satisfy you, but please you and oblige you with the relation. (ibid., 131)

In this moment, Duncan acts as a novelist, translating experiential reality into textual signs, and his deafness melts away into a matrix of writing. It is no coincidence, then, that one of Duncan's favorite activities is walking in graveyards "one would imagine he takes delight to stalk along by himself on that dumb silent ground, where the characters of the persons are only to be known, as his own meaning is, by writing and inscriptions on the marble" (ibid., 154). The character of the dead and the ground, considered "dumb" and "silent," is given language in the graphic trace on the tombstones, and Duncan can read them as can any novel reader who, of course, must get at character through decoding a cluster of signs.

What I am saying is that given a written text, there is little difference between a hearing person and a deaf one in the reading or writing process. The deaf can read and write—they only have to translate from sign language to the signs of written language. This point of connection, which may be thought fanciful, was recognized by at least one eighteenth-century reader, who wrote to the *Spectator* (No. 474, 3 September 1712) seeking the whereabouts of Duncan Campbell:

> now hearing you are a dumb man too, I thought you might correspond and be able to tell me something.

This reader sees the narrative persona of "the *Spectator*" as "dumb" specifically because he cannot speak except through writing! Authors are mute *because* of typography.

Writing is in effect sign language, a language of mute signs. Sicard emphasized this connection when he said "written language . . . alone can replace speech" (Lane 1984b, 37). Saboureux de Fontenay, a deaf man writing in 1764, describes finger spelling as a language in which "the hand is used like a pen" (Lane 1984a, 26), and the Abbé l'Epée described sign language as a type of "writing in the air" (cited in Mirzoeff 1992, 581). Rousseau acknowledges that both writing and gesture are forms of sign language virtually equal to speech. He says if humans could not speak:

> We would have been able to establish societies little different from those we have, or such as would have been better able to achieve their goals. We would have been able to institute laws, to choose leaders, to invent arts, to establish commerce, and to do, in a word, almost as many things as we do with the help of speech. (1966, 9)

Rousseau's theory is echoed in a statement attributed to the Abbé Sicard:

> May there not exist in some corner of the world an entire people of deaf-mutes? Well suppose these individuals were so degraded, do you think that they would remain without communication and without intelligence? They would have, without any manner of doubt, a language of signs, and possibly more rich than our own; it would be, certainly unequivocal, always the faithful portrait of the affections of the soul; and then what should hinder them from being civilized? Why should they not have laws, a government, a police, very probably less involved in obscurity than our own? (cited in Kitto 1852, 107)

Herder, too, acknowledges that speech is not necessary for language, and he notes that "the savage, the hermit living alone in the forest, would have had to invent language for himself . . . without the help of a mouth and without the presence of a society" (1966, 118). Diderot in his *Letter on the Deaf and Dumb* says that speech itself is just a representation of the state of the soul: "Ah sir, how much our apprehension is modified by the signs we use! And how cold a copy is even the most vivid speech of what takes place within us" (1966, 34). All of these philosophers point to the notion that any sign system can be language.

So intertwined were the issues of writing and language with the issue of deafness that they seemed inseparable. Tellingly, Sicard's career was deeply interwoven with textual language. In 1795 he was appointed to the section on grammar in the French Institute, which later became the French Academy. He helped lay he groundwork for the academy's dictionary of the French language and was also a member of the Grammatical Society. Another dictionary maker, Dr. Johnson, is described by Boswell during a visit to Braidwell's school for the deaf in a "circumstance . . . which was truly characteristic of our great Lexicographer. "Pray," said he, "Can they pronounce any *long words?*" Mr. Braidwood informed him they could. Upon which Dr. Johnson wrote one of his *sesquipedalia verba*, which was pronounced by the scholars, and he was satisfied" (Boswell 1936, 389). Johnson saw his visit to the deaf as, among other things, an opportunity for a lexicographical exhibition.

Why then was deafness such an area of focused activity and philosophical reflection in Europe during the eighteenth century? Why the obsessive connection between deafness and writing? We need to recall that it was during this period that reading became consolidated as an activity. J. Paul Hunter points to data suggesting that "literacy in the English-speaking world grew rapidly between 1600 and 1800 so that by the latter date a vast majority of adult males could read and write, whereas two centuries earlier only a select minority could do so" (1990, 65). Debates ensued during the period as to whether written or spoken language was the primary form of linguistic communication. David Bartine details the transition from an oral culture to a culture of silent reading in his *Early English Reading Theory: Origins of Current Debates*. These debates imagine the possibility that written language was the primary form of linguistic enterprise. Benjamin Smart, for example, "asserted more emphatically than his predecessors that writing is the original and primary language for all forms of reading. Even for an oral reader the nature of written language is the *first* consideration" (Bartine 1989, 133). If this is the case, then the deaf are living examples of the ideology of the written text at work. As Oliver Sacks notes (1989, 6, note 13):

> The congenitally deaf, it should be added, may have the richest appreciation of (say) written English, of Shakespeare, even though it does not "speak" to them in an auditory way. It speaks to them, one must suppose, in an entirely visual way— they do not hear, they *see*, the "voice" of the words.

As if chosen by Roland Barthes, the deaf experience the text at the degree zero of writing, as a text first and foremost. That is, to be deaf is to experience the written text in its most readerly incarnation. The text would not then be transformed into an auditory translation but would be seen as language itself. It is probably no coincidence that John Kitto, who wrote an autobiography about becoming deaf called *Lost Senses*, ends his opening chapter with a history of his reading. Kitto has to apologize for his emphasis on reading by saying, "These facts, although they may seem at first to bear more upon my literary biography than upon my deafness, which is my proper theme, are necessarily introduced here" (1852, 18–19). The fact is that Kitto more or less intuitively senses a connection between deafness and textuality.

This point can also be turned around. Because the eighteenth century was a period in which readers on a large scale first began to experience reality through texts,[8] they may be said to have had a different relation to reality and to texts. Part of that difference has to do with the fact that in order to become readers, people in the eighteenth century had to become deaf, at least culturally so. That is, to read requires muteness and attention to nonverbal signs. Writing and reading became the dominant forms of using sign language, the language of printed signs, and thus hearing readers and deaf readers could merge as those who see the voice of the words. Elizabeth Eisenstein points out that the political world changed through the advent of print. "Printed materials encouraged silent adherence to causes whose advocates could not be located in any one parish and who addressed an invisible public from afar" (1968, 42). The very nature of political assent, through the silent decoding of reading, became a newly "deafened" process that did not require adherents to gather in a public place, that did not rely on a vocal response to a rallying cry. As the hearing person became deaf, the deaf person became the totemic representation of the new reading public.

One can see this attention to deafness as part of a general transition from a society that based its cultural production on performances to one that focused its cultural attention on texts. In a text-based society, the physical presence of an auditor or an audience is no longer necessary, as it would be in a world based on performances. The cultural narrowness of a society in which spoken language is paramount expands to include all users of language, spoken or not.[9]

This point may seem strange, but the fact that you are reading this essay without my physical presence proves that it is irrelevant whether or not you are deaf, at least insofar as receiving and understanding my meaning are concerned. Further, if you consider that most of the knowledge you have about academic discursive matters is almost entirely derived from nonhearing knowledge acquisition, then you can understand the import of this widespread shift from performance to text-based knowledge.[10] As Foucault and others have noticed, knowledge *per se* since the classical period is embedded in discursive structures, and for the past three hundred years such discursive forms are mainly recorded in texts, making up the ensemble that constitute the archive.

In opposition to this archival knowledge, the eighteenth century's fascination with conversation can be seen as a kind of cultural nostalgia for a form that was in the process of becoming anachronistic.[11] It is of course most telling that such accounts of conversation, particularly the obsessive compiling of Johnson's conversation by Boswell and the splenetic compendium of conversational abuse by Swift in his *Polite Conversation*, are themselves only known in their typographic incarnation. The deaf then, seen as readers and writers *par excellence*, as fellow creatures who existed first and foremost in semiology, were the first totemic citizens in the new age of textuality.

Yet, as with any good totem, the deaf person was both universalized and marginalized, held up as an object of admiration and patronized as an object of pity. Like contemporary African-Americans and Chicanos, who are celebrated in an area of putative multiculturality and made visible as such by the media, but who are in reality reviled and oppressed by an economic system that relies on their impoverishment, so the deaf in the eighteenth century had this polysemous interpretation imposed on them. Their subject positions were, in this sense, overdetermined. Here the issue of class comes into syncretic combination with the issues of otherness and of disability. As is still the case, unless a deaf person happened to be born into a wealthy or noble family, he or she would occupy the lowest economic rungs of society. In families in which deafness is hereditary, that economic position will be passed along to the next generation as well. So the majority of deaf in the eighteenth century had jobs as menial workers. They may therefore be described as necessarily part of a working class, and their disability is made complex and multifaceted by its connection with issues of class, as well as linguistic domination.

The testimony of Pierre Desloges, a student of the Abbé de l'Epée, may illustrate some of the themes I have been describing in this essay. Fittingly, most of what we know about Desloges comes from a pamphlet he wrote in 1779 entitled *Observations d'un sourd et muet sur "Un Cours élémentaire d'éducation des sourds et muets' publié en 1779 par M. l'abbé Deschamps*.[12] His marginality, like that of the majority of deaf people in his moment, is universalized through print, which articulates him as part of an official discursive practice, removing him from the marginality of the streets. He becomes a representation of a group, yet, as Ernesto Laclau and Chantal Mouffe point out, "every relation of representation is founded on a fiction: that of the presence at a certain level of something which is absent from it" (Laclau and Mouffe 1989, 119). In this sense, what is absent from any account by Desloges is the physical presence of his deafness. Ironically, that feature of his existence is under erasure because of the very existence of print and Desloges's writerly existence.[13]

These are the facts of his life presented by the writer. Desloges was born in 1747 in the town of Le Grand-Pressigny in the Loire valley. After an attack of childhood smallpox, he became deaf and mute. His education ended with his disability, but he had acquired some skills in reading and writing. At the age of twenty-one he went to Paris and took up the trades of bookbinding and paper-hanging. Only at the age of twenty-seven did he learn the sign language used by the Paris deaf community.

The first significant aspect of his pamphlet is its very existence. Had there not been an interest in deafness, it is hard to imagine that an obscure paperhanger in Paris could have been launched into print. Moreover, his purpose in writing is not mainly autobiographical but rather an attempt to defend deaf education based on sign language, as practiced by the Abbé de l'Epée, against the attack made by Deschamps, who in turn was influenced by the first "oralist," Jacob Pereire. That a publisher was willing to print a commentary on this debate indicates the cultural relevance of the subject.

Desloges's marginality is signaled initially by the hearing editor, who first highlights the dubious status of the work by insisting on its not being a fiction. By now, such assertions of factuality only serve to fictionalize a work.[14] Further, the editor stresses that the writing is authentic:

> [I] corrected the young man's quite faulty spelling. I pruned some repetitions and
> softened a few words that could have given offense. Aside from these minor
> emendations, the essay is entirely the work of the deaf Desloges. (Lane 1984a, 29)

These words immediately contextualize the otherness of Desloges, who must
be linguistically sanitized and standardized. His deafness is seen as a mark of difference that separates him from normal readers whose spelling does not have to
be corrected and whose usage will not offend. Yet, at the same time, the entrance
of the deaf consciousness into the realm of the textual is celebrated: "I felt the
chief interest of this essay would come from its author, that perhaps for the first
time a deaf-mute had the honor of being published" (ibid., 29). This doubleness
of attitude toward Desloges's marginality will play out in much more complex
ways, as I will show.

Desloges begins his essay constructing a subject position from his own marginality. He notes immediately that he is of the lower classes, saying, "My line
of work obliges me to go into many homes." He adds that "the whole of my sub-
sistence comes from my daily work, while my writing must be done during the
time I have for sleeping" (ibid., 30). He is speaking both as a deaf man and, in
some sense more tellingly, as a working man. His writing is seen as occupying a
time other than that which a man of letters devotes to it; writing time is in fact
stolen from a very full workday. Although there certainly was a tradition of working-class characters in fiction, it was much rarer to have an actual member of
that class appear in print. The otherness of Desloges's deafness permits the class
element to be overridden and permitted through the gate of print. Body always
effaces class in the sphere of bourgeois narrative, as in Richardson's novel
Pamela's body erases her class lines.

Desloges is writing out of a profound marginalization. His contact with the
hearing world is based on misunderstanding; through writing, that is, using the
non-hearing text, he is hoping to eliminate such miscommunication: "I am
invariably questioned about the deaf. But most often the questions are laughable
as they are absurd; they merely prove that almost everyone has gotten the falsest
possible ideas about us" (ibid., 30). Here too we see that he is not simply questioned about being deaf, but about "the deaf," a clear indication that the category of deafness has emerged as an area of cultural curiosity. Furthermore, he
notes that he is writing this work to correct the public's errors, particularly "the
last straw" (ibid., 30) of misunderstanding accomplished by Deschamps's book
against the use of sign language as an instructional medium. One of the advantages of a text-based society is that individual voices and minority opinions can
be more easily heard, if they are permitted access, and Desloges recognizes this
empowerment provided by print. In the same way that print culture was involved
in the development of nationalism,[15] print also created some version of solidarity for marginalized groups. So Desloges can write:

> As would Frenchman seeing his language disparaged by a German who knew at
> most a few words of French, I too felt obliged to defend my own language from the
> false charges leveled against it by Deschamps. (ibid., 30)

Here we can see that perhaps some aspect of the emergence of the deaf is linked to their defining themselves as a linguistic subgroup. Like races, nationalities, ethnic groups, and nations, their redefinition as a political entity is linked to larger issues about the growth of nationalism in the eighteenth and nineteenth centuries.

Like other writers translating from a foreign language, Desloges will have problems explaining the subtleties of his own language. He can write in French, but to try to convey the sense of sign language may be an insurmountable problem. A single sign "made in the twinkling of an eye would require entire pages" to describe, and such detail would "soon become boring to the delicate ears accustomed to the winsome sounds of speech." Desloges is looking across a cultural divide between speech and sign language. The fact that Desloges sees this transaction as audible rather than textual, referring to the reader's "ears" rather than eyes as the recipient of his text, points to a curious structuring of languages. Sign language for Desloges is actually a text, but one performed rather than printed. Speech is a "winsome sound," more ethereal and less text-based, less semiological than sign. At the same time, the performative nature of sign gives it "so much strength and energy" that it can only lose its muscular verve when translated into written language. Here we see the mediating role of sign language as a middle term between speech and writing.

For Desloges, spoken language has a double impossibility. Most deaf people are mute only because they cannot hear, but Desloges has an additional impairment he attributes to smallpox but which is clearly part of a larger neurological problem. When he developed smallpox at seven years of age, he remained ill for two years with complications that caused him to lose all his teeth and develop a strokelike dysfunction of his lips, so that they "became so slack that I can close them only with great effort or the assistance of my hand. . . . One can reproduce my speech fairly accurately by trying to speak with the mouth open, without closing lips or teeth" (ibid., 31). This double impossibility, both deaf and physiologically mute, makes speech seem quite arbitrary to Desloges. He feels acutely that spoken language is privileged over textual language. This privileging of one sense over another is not natural, as Rousseau argued, but arbitrary. As Desloges writes, sign language is the "most natural means for leading the deaf to an understanding of languages, nature having given them this language to substitute for the other languages of which they are deprived." Some of the cognitive dissonance one experiences in reading Desloges's work may arise from the fact that he is writing about his deafness and mutism in the most logical, coherent, and elegant language. The arbitrary privileging of hearing language over nonspoken language, and the consequent marginalization of those who do not participate in that linguistic majority, emerges as a fact of power.

Desloges gains the strength to overcome this linguistic domination by chance when he is twenty-seven years old. At this point, he gains the power of sign language—a power linked to seeing himself as belonging to an oppressed group, the deaf. Before this period, "for as long as I was living apart from other deaf people, my only resource for self-expression was writing or my poor pronunciation" (ibid.,

32). But it is only through contact with the other deaf people in Paris, who are themselves working class, that Desloges finds power in his marginal status. Fatefully, he meets a deaf, "illiterate" Italian servant who teaches him signing. The fact that the man is described as illiterate makes us realize how strong the association between letters and literacy is. This servant was certainly "literate" in sign language, but that kind of literacy is discounted, even by Desloges.

At this point in the book, frustratingly Desloges abruptly announces, "I think this is enough about me and that a longer treatment of such a minor subject would try my readers' patience" (ibid.). One can speculate that Desloges's entrance into sign language leads him to the subject of the Abbé de l'Epée, in whose defense he spends the rest of the book. Truly marginalizing himself, confining his own story to the margins of the text, Desloges only exists insofar as he is a successful example of a teaching method. But, like subalterns and slaves, Desloges is able to exist by tactics of submission that are in fact defensive. He does, after all, narrate his own life, and present a textual representation of his language and therefore of himself.

Without mentioning his own life story again, Desloges inserts his deaf existence and working-class perspective into the text. He attacks indirectly the power of the hearing world over the deaf when he notes that "deaf people who are abandoned in asylums or isolated somewhere in the provinces" (ibid., 16) do not learn sign language. When deaf people are united, as they are in major urban areas like Paris, they can organize linguistic power. He gives himself as an example of someone whose signs had been "unordered and unconnected" before coming into contact with "deaf people more highly educated" than himself. When this synergistic meeting occurs, language happens through the regulation of a subaltern community.

This critical mass of deaf people is uniquely both deaf and underclass. In Desloges' tones, one can hear a will to power that perhaps reflects republican sentiments of the time.

> There are congenitally deaf people, Parisian laborers, who are illiterate and who have never attended the abbé de l'Epée's lessons, who have been found so well instructed about their religion, simply by means of signs, that they have been judged worthy of admittance to the holy sacraments, even those of the eucharist and marriage [which had been previously denied to the deaf]. No event—in Paris, in France, or in the four corners of the world—lies outside the scope of our discussion. We express ourselves on all subjects with as much order, precision, and rapidity as if we enjoyed the faculty of speech and hearing. (ibid., 36)

The matter of class and the matter of deafness merge into a kind of empowerment founded on community and communication. In fact, Desloges makes the argument that deafness and sign actually reconfigure the Deaf into the category of people with special abilities: ". . . our ideas concentrated in ourselves, so to speak, necessarily incline us toward reflectiveness and meditation" (ibid., 37). That is, ideas seem not to need a semiology; the deaf experience ideas in themselves. To bolster this point further, Desloges echoes Hobbes's lament that modern languages have fallen away from original ideas when he says that sign language is "a faithful image of the object expressed." The metonymic nature of sign anchors the deaf to the signified rather than the signifier. As such, sign can better express emotions and sentiments, and Desloges goes so far as to claim that "no other language is more appropriate for conveying great and strong emotion" (ibid.). But the romantic aspirations for sign language as a physical form of poetry are balanced by an Enlightenment concern for rationality. Desloges thus claims that sign is more efficient than speech: "The phrase *le mos [sic] qui vient* contains four words; nevertheless I use only two signs for it, one for the month and one for the future" (ibid., 38).

Sign language, as a language of the underclass, is replete with class markers. In Desloges's words: ". . . when necessity or expressive clarity demands, we always mention the social class of the person we are speaking about or wish to introduce" (ibid., 41). To designate a close acquaintance one needs only three signs: gender, then class, then profession. In designating nobility, there are signs for upper and lower nobility, which are followed by occupation, coat of arms, or livery. Manufacturers are distinguished from tradesmen "for the deaf have the good sense not to confuse these two occupations." The sensitivity of the deaf as constituting a marginalized underclass is reflected in their minute gradations of class. So the sign for tradesman is made as follows: "with the thumb and index finger, we take the hem of a garment or some other object and present it the way a tradesman offers his merchandise; we then make the movement for counting money with our hands, and cross our arms like someone resting." This gestural rebus combines the ideas of capital, trade, money, and leisure, painting the very essence of the bourgeois cash nexus. The same subtlety of class analysis is included in the sign for "working" that applies to "manufacturers, artisans, and laborers." But an additional sign is added to indicate who is doing the supervising and who is doing the obeying. "We raise the index finger and lower it in a commanding way—that is the sign common to all supervisors" (ibid., 41). The same sign distinguishes a shopkeeper from a street vender.

The point here is that sign language renders visible in linguistic form the nuances of class power. This language is most universally a language of the laboring classes. It contains within its very structure the strategies and tactics of conformity and transgressivity typical of a subaltern group. Yet at the same time sign language offers, by virtue of its marginality, a kind of universality, as Desloges notes:

> several famous scholars have worn themselves out in the vain search for the elements of a universal language as a point of unification for all the people of the world. How did they fail to perceive that it had already been discovered, that it existed naturally as sign language?

Citing Condillac and Court de Gébelin, who praised sign language as a kind of universal language, Desloges goes on to observe:

I cannot understand how a language like sign language—the richest in expressions, the most energetic, the most incalculably advantageous in its universal intelligibility—is still so neglected and that only the deaf speak it. (ibid., 45–6)

The fact that Desloges would even consider recommending that sign language be used by the hearing world indicates the very great extent to which universal language schemes, and the notion of internationality, were a part of the revolutionary period at the end of the eighteenth century. Yet his idea is not so wild. In many ways, sign language provides us with a language that opens many doors. In one sense, critically, its existence as a third term mediating between text and speech opens the possibility for mediating that theoretically troubling divide. The age-old and currently lively debates between those who see literature as primarily a text and those who see it primarily as an expression of the body, of reality, can perhaps find a complex intersection by admitting the "literature" of sign language into the discussion.

But precisely because sign language will never actually become a universal language, we must stop and consider how truly hegemonic and controlling a concept is the notion of writing and speech as a "hearing" phenomenon. The argument I have tried to make is that the deafness of textuality is one of the best-kept secrets of the Enlightenment and beyond. It is not so much that convention has ruled here, but that there has been an active suppression of the insights I have proposed in this essay. After all, the body is political. Its form and function have been the site of powerful control and management. An able body is the body of a citizen; deformed, deafened, amputated, obese, female, perverse, crippled, maimed, blinded bodies do not make up the body politic. Utterances must all be able ones produced by conformed, ideal forms of humanity. In effect, there cannot be a complete analysis of early modern, modern and postmodern culture without bringing the disabled body and the disabled utterance into line.

NOTES

1. So deafness did not "exist" before the eighteenth century for two reasons. First, the isolated deaf person was simply seen as an aberration in his or her town or family. He or she was first and foremost a non-person. However, the deaf person in an extended group of deaf might not be thought of as deaf since that person was part of a functioning system. For example, Nora Ellen Groce's book *Everyone Here Spoke Sign Language: Hereditary Deafness on Martha's Vineyard* describes how an inherited trait brought to the island in 1633 resulted in the deafness of a substantial minority of people living on Martha's Vineyard. Because the minority made up a substantial number, the deaf were actually not visible as deaf. One resident responded to the author's question about what the hearing thought of the deaf by saying, "Oh, they didn't think anything of them, they were just like everyone else," and went on to describe to the author's amazement how everyone on Martha's Vineyard spoke sign language.
2. The radical difference between the blind and the deaf goes back to antiquity. The Egyptians, for example, used the blind as musicians, artists, and masseuses. There is documentation to show that priests at Karmah trained the blind for these pur-

poses, but of the deaf, it was written "There is no use wasting words upon the dumb." (Winzer, 13) Aristotle set the tone for much of Western treatment of the deaf versus the blind. He said that the deaf were "senseless and incapable of reason," and "no better than the animals of the forest and unteachable," while the blind were thought of as having equal intellect with the sighted. (Winzer, 18) Saint Augustine added to the denigration of the deaf by denying them membership in the Church, when he interpreted the statement of Saint Paul, "Faith comes by hearing" to mean that those without hearing can never have faith. Until the 12th century a deaf person's marriage within the Church was only possible through papal dispensation. (Winzer, 22)

3.   It is telling, too, that the language of the deaf, sign, was an indigenous language that arose spontaneously where groups of deaf people formed a community. The language taught in deaf schools was more or less a standardization of that autochthonous language. Braille, by contrast, was a system invented by a seeing man, Charles Barbier, who had invented this form of writing during wartime to enable messages to be read at night without the use of light, which would betray position to the enemy. In 1830, Barbier brought the system to the Institution des Enfans Aveugles in Paris, where a blind student, Louis Braille developed and pro-mulgated Barbier's plan. In this sense, deaf language is a special issue, whereas Braille is actually a system not exclusively "blind" in its applications.

4.   Nicholas Mirzoeff points out in his article "Body Talk: Deafness, Sign and Visual Language in the Ancien Régime" that there was a long-standing tradition in French theater of portraying deaf characters. Mirzoeff points out the appearance of Le Sourd as early as the sixteenth century. But as he also notes, "these 'deaf' char-acters normally spoke and often were pretending to be deaf in order to deceive others in pursuit of a love affair." (570) So we can assume that these depictions were not of the Deaf per se but of comic imitators of deafness.

5.   See Harlan Lane, *The Mask of Benevolence: Disabling the Deaf Community* and my review of it in *The Nation* (July 6, 1992).

6.   The fact that Duncan Campbell was a huckster who only pretended to be deaf and who made his money by duping people, has little bearing on the attitudes toward the deaf that Defoe espouses. Defoe is always a writer whose ambivalence to fact and fiction only makes his work more interesting to a modern reader. For more on this ambivalence, see my *Factual Fictions: Origins of the English Novel*, 154–173.

7.   The family story goes a bit deeper. Defoe's daughter Sophia married Henry Baker (1698–1774), who learned about the methods of Wallis from reading *Duncan Campbell*. Baker then went on to educate the deaf daughter of a relative, one Jane Forester. After succeeding with her, Baker became a teacher of the deaf as his sole livelihood, and thus became the first professional teacher of the deaf.

8.   See Joseph Allen Boone, *Tradition Counter Tradition: Love and the Form of Fiction* and Nancy Armstrong, *Desire and Domestic Fiction: A Political History of the Novel* along with my *Resisting Novels: Fiction and Ideology* for examples of this shift to tex-tual forms of assimilating ideology.

9.   Martin Jay, in his *Downcast Eyes: The Denigration of Vision in Twentieth-Century French Thought* details a general historical trend that conceives of the Middle Ages as biased toward hearing or touch, and the enlightenment as favoring sight. For example, Roland Barthes in *Sade, Fourier, Loyola* wrote concerning Ignatius Loyola that "in the Middle Ages, historians tell us, the most refined sense, the perceptive sense, *par excellence*, the one that established the richest contact with the world

was hearing: sight came in only third, after touch. Then we have a reversal: the eye becomes the prime organ of perception (Baroque, art of the thing seen, attests to it)." (46) But Jay questions this simplifying tendency on the part of writers like Barthes, although Jay does end up affirming that something happens in European culture to the question of vision. One of the areas he pinpoints is the separation of the visual and the textual—what he calls "the secular autonomization of the visual as a realm unto itself." (44) This point fits well into the idea that the eighteenth-century text, though requiring vision, is actually more about the issue of hearing. The vision of reading, then, is not necessarily the vision of seeing. Indeed, the vision of reading is in effect one that is more about incorporating hearing language through the eyes than it is about seeing objects.

10. Further technological advances like those provided by computer networks, fiber optics, and other advanced forms of communications have completely shifted the ground from spoken language to semiological representations. As electronic mail, computer bulletin boards, and other computer-based forums for communication develop, we will find ourselves less and less reliant on spoken language. Computer literacy has already become a valuable, if not indispensable, skill in many areas of culture. This poses new problems for the blind, who can use much of computer technology to their advantage, but are stymied by software that uses icons, for example, in its operation.

11. See Leland Warren, "Turning Reality Round Together: Guides to Conversation in Eighteenth-Century England," *Eighteenth Century Life*, new ser., Vol. VIII (May 1983), 65–87.

12. I cite all further quotes of Desologes' text from Harlan Lane, *The Deaf Experience*.

13. In a sense, Jacques Derrida deals with a similar phenomenon in his book *Memoirs of the Blind*. Derrida says of the work of Antoine Coypel and others who draw the blind, "the operation of drawing would have something to do with blindness, would in some way regard blindness. . . . Every time a draftsman lets himself be fascinated by the blind, every time he makes the blind a *theme* of his drawing, he projects, dreams, or hallucinates a figure of a draftsman, or sometimes, more precisely, some draftswoman." (2) Drawing blindness involves blindness in the process of drawing and points to the blindness in drawing as well as the sightedness in the concept of blindness. In a similar vein, writing from the deaf point of view reveals the deafness in writing, while concealing the deafness of the writer.

14. See my *Factual Fictions: Origins of the English Novel*, 11–24 for a discussion of this notion of denial as a hallmark of fictional ambivalence.

WORKS CITED

Bartine, David. 1989. *Early English Reading Theory: Origins of Current Debates.*(Columbia, SC: University of South Carolina Press).

Boswell, James. 1936. *Boswell's Journal of a Tour to the Hebrides*. New York: The Literary Guild Inc.

Davis, Lennard. 1983. *Factual Fictions: Origins of the English Novel*. New York: Columbia University Press. Rpt. University of Pennsylvania Press, 1997.

Defoe, Daniel. 1974 [1720]. *The History and Life and Adventures of Mr. Duncan Campbell*. New York: AMS Press.

Diderot, Denis. 1996. *Letter on the Deaf and Dumb* in *Diderot's Selected Writings*. Ed. Lester G. Crocker. Trans. Derrick Coltman. New York: Macmillan.

Eisenstein, Elizabeth. 1986. "Some Conjectures about the Impact of Printing on Western Society and Thought: A Preliminary Report." *Journal of Modern History* 40: 1 (March): 1–56. Foucault, Michel. 1965. *Madness and Civilization*. Trans. Richard Howard. New York: Random House.

Herder, Johann Gottfried. 1966. "Essay on the Origin of Language." In *On the Origin of Language: Two Essays by Jean-Jacques Rousseau and Johan Gottfried Herder*. Trans. John H. Moran and Alexander Gode. New York: Unger.

Hunter, J. Paul. 1990. *Before Novels: The Cultural Contexts of Eighteenth Century English Fiction*. New York: Norton.

Kitto, John. 1862 [1845]. *The Lost Senses: Deafness and Blindness*. New York: Robert Carter. Laclau, Ernesto and Chantal Mouffe. 1989 [1985]. *Hegemony and Socialist Strategy*. New York and London: Verso.

Lane, Harlan, ed. 1984. *The Deaf Experience: Classics in Language and Education*. Trans. Franklin Philip. Cambridge, Mass.: Harvard University Press.

———. 1992. *The Mask of Benevolence: Disabling the Deaf Community*. New York: Knopf.

———. 1984b. *When the Mind Hears: A History of the Deaf*. New York: Random House.

Paulson, William R. 1987. *Enlightenment, Romanticism. and the Blind in France*. Princeton: Princeton University Press. 1987.

Sacks, Oliver. 1989. *Seeing Voices: A Journey into the World of the Deaf*. New York: HarperCollins.

Winzer, Margret A. 1993. *The History of Special Education: From Isolation to Integration*. Washington, D. C.: Gallaudet University Press.

6

"A Silent Exile on This Earth"

*The Metaphorical Construction of Deafness
in the Nineteenth Century*

DOUGLAS BAYNTON

Deafness is a cultural construction as well as a physical phenomenon. The difference between the hearing and the deaf is typically construed as simply a matter of audiology. For most hearing people, this is the common sense of the matter—the difference between the deaf and the hearing is that the deaf cannot hear. The result is that the relationship between the deaf and the hearing appears solely as a natural one. The meanings of "hearing" and "deaf" are not transparent, however. As with gender, age, race, and other such categories, physical difference is involved, but physical differences do not carry inherent meanings. They must be interpreted and cannot be apprehended apart from a culturally created web of meaning. The meaning of deafness is contested, although most hearing and many deaf people are not aware that it is contested, and it changes over time. It has, that is to say, a history.[1]

The meaning of deafness changed during the course of the nineteenth century for educators of the deaf, and the kind of education deaf people received changed along with it. Until the 1860s, deafness was most often described as an affliction that isolated the individual from the Christian community. Its tragedy was that deaf people lived beyond the reach of the gospel. After the 1860s, deafness was redefined as a condition that isolated people from the national community. Deaf people were cut off from the English-speaking American culture, and *that* was the tragedy. The remedies proffered for each of these kinds of isolation were dramatically different. During the early and middle decades of the nineteenth century, sign language was a widely used and respected language among educators at schools for the deaf. By the end of the century it was widely condemned and banished from many classrooms. In short, sign language was compatible with the former construction of deafness, but not with the latter.

Schools for deaf people were first established in the United States by Evangelical Protestant reformers during the Second Great Awakening. They learned sign language, much as other missionaries of the time learned Native American or African languages, and organized schools where deaf people could be brought together and given a Christian education. The first school, the American Asylum for the Deaf and Dumb at Hartford, Connecticut, was founded in 1817 by the Reverend Thomas H. Gallaudet, with a young deaf man from Paris, Laurent Clerc, as his head teacher.

With the creation of this residential school, and the others which soon followed, the deaf in the United States may be said to have become the Deaf; that is, hearing-impaired individuals became a cultural and linguistic community.[2] To be sure, wherever sufficient numbers of deaf people have congregated, a distinctive community has come into existence—we know of one such community in eighteenth-century Paris.[3] These early schools, however, gathered together larger numbers of deaf people than ever before, most of them in adolescence, placed them in a communal living situation, and taught them formally not only about the world but also about themselves. Those from small towns and the countryside—the majority—met other deaf people for the first time and learned, also for the first time, how to communicate beyond the level of pantomime and gesture. They encountered the surprising knowledge that they had a history and an identity shared by many others. Embracing a common language and common experience, they began to create an American deaf community.[4]

Beginning in the 1860s and continuing into the twentieth century, another group of reformers sought to unmake that community and culture. Central to that project was a campaign to eliminate the use of sign language in the classroom (referred to in the nineteenth century as the philosophy of "manualism") and replace it with the *exclusive* use of lip-reading and speech (known as "oralism"). Residential schools for the deaf had been manualist from their beginnings, conducting their classes in sign language, finger-spelling, and written English. Lessons in speech and lip-reading were added to curriculums in most schools for the deaf by the latter decades of the century, but this was not the crux of the issue for those who called themselves oralists. They were opposed to the use of sign language in any form, for any purpose.[5]

Afraid that deaf people were isolated from the life of the nation, and comparing the deaf community to communities of immigrants, oralists charged that the use of sign language encouraged deaf people to associate principally with each other and to avoid the hard work of learning to communicate with people who were *speaking* English. All deaf people, they thought, should be able to learn to communicate orally. They believed that a purely oral education would lead to greater assimilation, which they believed to be a goal of the highest importance.

The larger goals of the oralist movement were not achieved—the deaf community was not unmade, and sign language continued to be used within it. Most deaf people rejected the oralist philosophy, and maintained an alternative vision of what being deaf meant for them. The deaf community did not, however, control the schools, and the campaign to eliminate sign language from the classroom was largely successful. By the turn of the century, nearly 40 percent of American deaf students were taught without the use of sign language, and over half were so taught in at least some of their classes.[6] The number of children taught entirely without sign language was nearly 80 percent by the end of World War I, and oralism remained orthodox until the 1970s.[7]

Why did educators of the deaf take this road? While this widespread and rapid shift away from the use of sign language has been well documented and described, it has yet to be adequately explained. Oralists at the turn of the century, looking back upon the ascendance of their cause and the demise of manualism, explained it in terms of the march of progress.[8] Improved techniques and knowledge made the use of sign language no longer necessary, they believed. This remained the dominant view in the field until the efficacy of purely oral education began to be questioned in the 1960s and 1970s. Since most recent research and practice supports an eclectic approach that includes the use of sign language—and since, as one recent writer said with only slight exaggeration, the "Old Orthodoxy of oral-or-nothing paternalism has died a richly deserved death"—the progress model has become rather less tenable.[9]

Most deaf adults and their organizations in the nineteenth century strenuously opposed the elimination of sign language from the classroom.[10] At the Convention of American Instructors of the Deaf in 1890, an angry deaf member pointed out that "Chinese women bind their babies' feet to make them small; the Flathead Indians bind their babies' heads to make them flat." Those who prohibit sign language in the schools, he declared, "are denying the deaf their free mental growth . . . and are in the same class of criminals."[11]

Scholars today in the new and still very small field of deaf history have, in general, agreed with this assessment, and have been uniformly critical of oralism. Oralists, it has been argued, were in many cases woefully ignorant of deafness. Their faith in oralism was based more upon wishful thinking than evidence, and they were often taken in by charlatans and quacks.[12] Others, such as Alexander Graham Bell, were more knowledgeable but motivated by eugenicist fears that intermarriage among the deaf, encouraged by separate schools and the use of sign language, would lead to the "formation of a deaf variety of the human race." Bell's prestige, leadership skills, and dedication to the cause gave a tremendous boost to oralism.[13] Opponents of sign language believed that its use discouraged the learning of oral communication skills; hearing parents, eager to believe their deaf children could learn to function like hearing people, supported its proscription. State legislators were persuaded by claims that oral education would be less expensive.[14] Finally, "on the face of it, people are quite afraid of human diversity. . . . [This] fear of diversity leads majorities to oppress minorities"; the suppression of sign language by an intolerant majority.[15]

The question of why schools adopted and continued to practice manualism for over half a century has been given less attention. Manualism has seemed less in need of explanation than oralism; since it is closer to current practice, the manualist philosophy of the nineteenth century has simply come to seem more sensible. With oralism now widely rejected, the focus has been upon explaining how and why such a philosophy gained ascendance.[16] Why manualism took root so readily in the first half of the nineteenth century and why attempts to establish oral schools were unsuccessful until the decades after the Civil War are questions that have not been adequately addressed. Rather than treating manualism as merely sensible and oralism as an unfortunate aberration, seeing both as embedded in historically created constructions of deafness can illuminate them as well as the reform eras of which they were a part.

Manualism and oralism were expressions of two very different reform eras in American history. Manualism was a product of the Evangelical, romantic reform movements of the antebellum years, which emphasized moral regeneration and salvation. Reformers of this period usually traced social evils to the weaknesses of individuals and believed that the reformation of society would come about only through the moral reform of its members. The primary responsibility of the Evangelical reformer, then, was to educate and convert individuals. The Christian nation they sought, and the millennial hopes they nurtured, came with each success one step closer to fruition.

Oralism was the product of a much changed reform atmosphere after the Civil War. While Protestantism continued to be an important ingredient, the emphasis shifted from the reform of the individual to, among other things, the creation of national unity and social order through homogeneity of language and culture. Much reform of the time, oralism included, reflected widespread fears of unchecked immigration and expanding, multiethnic cities. Deaf people in both eras served as convenient, and not always willing, projection screens for the anxieties of their times. The history of deaf education is as much, or more, about concerns over national identity and selfhood as it is about pedagogical technique or theory.

Oralists and manualists have generally been portrayed as standing on opposite sides of an ideological fault line. While in many ways accurate, this formulation obscures fundamental similarities between them. Both created images of deaf people as outsiders. Implicit in these images was the message that deaf people depended upon hearing people to rescue them from their exile. And both based their methods of education upon the images they created. Where they differed was in their definition of the "outsider," and of what constituted "inside" and "outside." For the manualists, the Christian community was the measure, while for the oralists it was an American nation defined in the secular terms of language and culture. Deafness, constructed as a condition that excluded people from the community, was defined and redefined according to what their hearing educators saw as the essential community.

The manualist image of deafness can be seen in the pages of what was in 1847 a remarkable new journal. Published by the American Asylum for the Deaf and Dumb and proclaiming itself the first of its kind in the English language, the *American Annals of the Deaf and Dumb* was intended to be not only a journal of education but also a "treasury of information upon all questions and subjects related, either immediately or remotely, to the deaf and dumb." The editors noted that not only did "the deaf and dumb constitute a distinct and, in some respect, strongly marked class of human beings," they also "have a history peculiar to themselves . . . sustaining relations, of more or less interest, to the general history of the human race." The implication of this, and of the editors' suggestion of such topics for investigation as the "social and political condition in ancient times" of the deaf, and "a careful exposition of the philosophy of the language of signs," was that deaf people were not so much handicapped *individuals* as they were a collectivity, a people—albeit, as we shall see, an inferior one, and one in need of missionary guidance.[17]

In "The Natural Language of Signs," Gallaudet wrote that there was "scarcely a more interesting sight than a bright, cheerful deaf-mute, of one or two years of age" in the midst of its hearing family. "The strangeness of his condition, from the first moment of their discovering it, has attracted their curiosity. They wonder at it." Gallaudet and others of his generation also wondered at the deaf. The source of their wonderment, and of the "greatest delight" for the family, was the child's efforts "to convey his thoughts and emotions . . . by those various expressions of countenance, and descriptive signs and gestures, which his own spontaneous feelings lead him to employ." For Gallaudet, "substantial good has come out of apparent evil," for this family would now have the privilege of learning "a novel, highly poetical, and singular descriptive language, adapted as well to spiritual as to material objects."[18]

Gallaudet praised the beauty of sign language, the "picture-like delineation, pantomimic spirit, variety, and grace . . . the transparent beaming forth of the soul . . . that merely oral language does not possess." Not only should the language of signs not be denied to the deaf, but it should also be given as a gift to the hearing as well, in order to "supply the deficiencies of our oral intercourse [and] perfect the communion of one soul with another." Superior to spoken language in its beauty and emotional expressiveness, sign language brought "kindred souls into a much more close and conscious communion than . . . speech can possibly do."[19]

Such a language was ideal for alleviating what Gallaudet saw as the overriding problem facing deaf people: they lived beyond the reach of the gospel. They knew nothing of God and the promise of salvation, nor had they a firm basis for the development of a moral sense. An essential part of education was learning "the necessity and the mode of controlling, directing, and at times subduing" the passions. Gallaudet emphasized the need to develop the conscience, to explain vice and virtue, to employ both hope and fear and "the sanctions of religion" in order to create a moral human being.[20]

The "moral influence" with which Gallaudet was concerned, however, could not "be brought to bear . . . without language, and a language intelligible to such a mind." Learning to speak and read lips was a "long and laborious process, even in the comparatively few cases of complete success." Communication between student and teacher, furthermore, was not sufficient. A language was needed with which "the deaf-mute can intelligibly conduct his private devotions, and join in social religious exercises with his fellow pupils."[21]

For Gallaudet, then, to educate was to impart moral and religious knowledge. Such teaching was not primarily directed to the mind through abstractions— rather, "the heart is the principle thing which we must aim to reach"; oral language may better communicate abstraction, he believed, but "the heart claims as its peculiar and appropriate language that of the eye and countenance, of the attitudes, movements, and gestures of the body."[22] Gallaudet described the progress of the student with the use of sign language:

> Every day he is improving in this language; and this medium of moral influence is rapidly enlarging. His mind becomes more and more enlightened; his conscience

more and more easily addressed; his heart more and more prepared to be accessible to the simple truths and precepts of the Word of God.[23]

The interdependence of the mind, the heart, and the conscience, of both knowledge and morality, run through these teachers' writings. Morality, and the self-discipline it required, depended upon a knowledge of God's existence as well as a heartfelt conviction that the soul was immortal and that the promise of its salvation was real. What was more, the proper development of the moral nature not only depended upon knowledge but in its turn also stimulated the higher faculties to yet greater learning.[24]

As David Walker Howe has recently pointed out, achieving inner self-discipline was important for Evangelicals not just for the sake of self-control, but for the liberation of the self as well. Liberation and control were seen by antebellum Evangelicals as "two sides of the same redemptive process." Evangelicals, according to Howe, "were typically concerned to redeem people who were not functioning as free moral agents: slaves, criminals, the insane, alcoholics, children."[25] The contributors to the *Annals* in its first year clearly placed deaf people in this same category: outsiders to the Christian community. Teachers at the Asylum at Hartford, "preeminently a Christian institution" dedicated to teaching those "truths which are received in common by all evangelical denominations," bemoaned the fact that "in this Christian land" there were still deaf people living "in utter seclusion from the direct influences of the gospel."[26] These deaf people "might almost as well have been born in benighted Asia, as in this land of light," and were "little short of a community of heathen at our very doors."[27]

Throughout this first year of the journal, images of imprisonment, darkness, blankness, and isolation were repeatedly used to describe the condition of deaf people without education. These metaphors were interconnected, as was made plain by the descriptions of the uninstructed deaf by the Reverend Collins Stone, a teacher at the Hartford school: "scarcely a ray of intellectual or moral light ever dawns upon his solitude"; "his mind is a perfect blank"; if "he dies unblessed by education, he dies in this utter moral darkness"; we must "open the doors of his prison, and let in upon him the light of truth," for the terrible fact is that "even in the midst of Christian society, he must grope his way in darkness and gloom . . . unless some kind hand penetrates his solitude."[28]

The image of the animal appeared frequently as well. Stone wrote that the uneducated deaf were reduced "to the level of mere animal life" because the "great facts and truths relating to God and a future state" are unknown to them. What "makes us differ from the animals and things around us" is the possession of a soul and an understanding of what that possession means. Without this understanding, deaf people were capable of nothing higher than "mere animal enjoyment."[29] With the use of sign language, however as J. A. Ayres believed, "it will be seen at once that the deaf-mute is restored to his position in the human family, from which his loss had well-nigh excluded him."[30]

Writer after writer used the same or similar metaphors, with the same emphasis upon the knowledge of God and the immortality of the soul as that which distinguishes the human from the nonhuman. The Reverend Luzerne Ray, speculating upon the "Thoughts of the deaf and Dumb before Instruction," asked the reader to imagine a child born with no senses, to imagine that "the animal life of this infant is preserved, and that he grows up to be, in outward appearance at least, a man." Ray asked, "can we properly say that here would be any mind at all? . . . [C]ould there be any conscious self-existence or self-activity of a soul imprisoned within such a body?" He concluded that to answer in the affirmative would be to succumb to "the lowest form of materialism." While no such person had ever existed, uneducated deaf people living "in a state of isolation the most complete that is ever seen among men" came close.[31] Henry B. Camp, writing on the "Claims of the Deaf and Dumb upon Public Sympathy and Aid," lamented the "darkness and solitude" of the person who lives in a "condition but little superior to that of the brute creation," with "no key to unlock the prison of his own mind."[32]

For the manualists, then, the "real calamity for the deaf-mute" was "not that his ear is closed to the cheerful tones of the human voice"; and it was "not that all the treasures of literature and science, of philosophy and history . . . are to him as though they were not"; the calamity was that "the light of divine truth never shines upon his path."[33] The darkness, the emptiness, the solitude, were all of a particular kind: uneducated deaf people were cut off from the Christian community and its message.

A peculiar duality that runs throughout their writings illuminates the meaning of deafness for these teachers. Deafness was an affliction, they believed, but they called it a blessing as well. One explained that the only unusual aspect of educating deaf people on moral and religious matters was that they had "a *simplicity* of mental character and an *ignorance* of the world, highly favorable to the entrance and dominion of this highest and best motive of action" (emphasis added). The properly educated deaf person, he believed, will exhibit "a pleasing combination of strength and simplicity." The strength would come from proper education, but the simplicity was inherent in the deafness; it "flows naturally from that comparative isolation of the mind which prevents its being formed too much on the model of others."[34]

Another writer touched on the same duality when explaining the "beautiful compensation" for deafness:

> Deprived of many blessings, he is also shut out from many temptations, and it is rare indeed that the claims of religion and the reasonings of morality fail to secure the ready assent both of his heart and his understanding.[35]

Deaf people were thought to have a great moral advantage in that they have been left relatively unscathed by a corrupt world. They are innocent, rather than living in darkness, and their deafness is an asylum rather than a prison. Deafness, then, confers both the benefit of innocence and the burden of ignorance: two sides of the same coin. It is a positive good if temporary and discovered by the right people but an evil if neglected and left uncultivated. The difference

between virginity and barrenness (whether of women or of land) is analogous—
the first is a blessed state, the second a calamity. The deaf are blessed if virginal,
innocent, and fertile, but would be accursed if left forever in that state. They
would then be barren. Innocence holds within it the germ of knowledge and salvation. Ignorance is only darkness.

The dark side was expressed in a poem by a former student at the Hartford
school, published in the *Annals*:

> I moved—a silent exile on this earth;
> As in his dreary cell one doomed for life,
> My tongue is mute, and closed ear heedeth not;
>
> Deep silence over all, and all seems lifeless;
> The orators exciting strains the crowd
> Enraptur'd hear, while meteor-like his wit
> Illuminates the dark abyss of mind—
> Alone, left in the dark—*I hear them not.*
>
> The balmy words of God's own messenger
> Excite to love, and troubled spirits sooth—
> Religion's dew-drops bright—*I feel them not.*[36]

But some months later, a poem entitled "The Children of Silence" was published in response "to show that there are times and circumstances," in the
editor's words, "when not to be able to hear must be accounted a blessing rather
than a misfortune":

> Not for your ears the bitter word
> Escapes the lips once filled with love;
> The serpent speaking through the dove,
> Oh Blessed! ye have never heard.
> Your minds by mercy here are sealed
> From half the sin in man revealed.[37]

The use of "silent" and "silence" in these poems embodies the contradictions
in the innocence and ignorance metaphor. It was (and is) a common description
of the world of deafness, and at first glance would seem a common sense description as well. Deaf people use it as well as hearing people. In the nineteenth century, for example, journals by and for the deaf had such titles as the *Silent Worker*
and *Silent World*. Today there are newspapers such as the *Silent News*, and clubs
with such names as the Chicago Silent Dramatic Club.

"Silence" is not a straightforward or unproblematic description of the experience of a deaf person, however. First, few deaf people hear nothing. Most have
hearing losses which are not uniform across the entire range of pitch—they will
hear low sounds better than high ones, or vice versa. Sounds will often be quite

distorted, but heard nevertheless. And second, for those who do not hear, what does the word silence signify? Unless they once heard and *became* deaf, the word is meaningless as a description of their experience. (Even for those who once heard, as the experience of sound recedes further into the past, so too does the significance of silence diminish.) Silence is experienced by the hearing as an absence of sound. For those who have never heard, deafness is not an absence. To be deaf is *not* to not hear for most profoundly deaf people, but a social relation—that is, a relation with other human beings, those called "hearing" and those called "deaf." What the deaf person sees in these other people is not the presence or absence of hearing, not their soundfulness or their silence, but their mode of communication—they sign, or they move their lips. That is why deaf people in the nineteenth century typically referred to themselves not as deaf people but as "mutes." That is why the sign still used today that is translated as "hearing person" is made next to the mouth, not the ear, and literally means "speaking person."

Silence is a metaphor rather than a simple description of the experience of most deaf people.[38] Deafness is a relationship, not a state, and the use of the "silence" metaphor is one indication of how the relationship is dominated by the hearing. Hearing is defined as the universal, and deafness, therefore, as an absence, as an emptiness. Silence can represent innocence and fertility, and silence can represent darkness and barrenness. In both cases it is empty. In both cases it needs to be filled. Images such as these—images of light and dark, of solitude and society, of animal and human—construct a world in which deaf people lack what hearing people alone can provide.

The absence which defined deaf people was framed as a place in which the deaf lived: a darkness within which they could not escape, a blankness and ignorance which denied them humanity. But of course the converse was also true: the problem was not only that the deaf could not see *out* but also that the hearing could not see *in*. The minds of deaf people represented impenetrable dark spaces within Christian society—or better, *without* Christian society—of which the hearing had little knowledge. Sign language was the light that could illuminate the darkness.

In 1899, the *Association Review* was established as the journal of the American Association to Promote the Teaching of Speech to the Deaf, the first president of which was Alexander Graham Bell. In the introduction to the first issue, the editor Frank Booth was able to state confidently that "the spirit prevalent in our schools is one entirely favorable to speech for the deaf, and to more and better speech teaching so soon as more favorable conditions may warrant and permit."[39] Indeed, with 55 percent of their teachers now speech teachers (as compared with 24 percent in 1886, the first year for which we have figures), the acquisition of speech was rapidly becoming the preeminent aim in the education of the deaf.[40]

The times were not only favorable to speech but quite hostile to sign language. Nearly 40 percent of American deaf students now sat in classrooms from which sign language had been banished. Within twenty years it would be 80 percent.[41] Deaf teachers were rarely hired by the schools anymore and made up less than 20 percent of the teaching corps, down from more than twice that number in the 1850s and 1860s.[42] Those who remained were increasingly confined to teaching industrial education courses, to which students who were "oral failures" were relegated. The new teacher training school established in 1891 at Gallaudet College, a liberal arts college primarily for deaf students, itself refused, as a matter of policy, to train deaf teachers.[43] Booth himself would forbid the use of sign language at the Nebraska school when he became its superintendent in 1911. "That language is not now used in the school-room," he wrote to Olaf Hanson, president of the National Association of the Deaf, "and I hope to do away with its use outside of the school-room."[44]

Booth was certainly correct that the "spirit now prevalent" was much changed. The *American Annals of the Deaf* at the turn of the century reflected the changed climate as well. Educational philosophy had shifted ground so dramatically that unabashed manualism had nearly disappeared from its pages, with the majority of opinion ranging between oralism and what was called the "combined system." The definition of the latter varied widely. In some cases it mean supplementing speech with fingerspelling but forbidding sign language; in others, speech alone was used in the classroom, with sign language permitted outside; in many cases it meant using speech with all young students and resorting later to sign language only with older "oral failures." To Edward M. Gallaudet, son of Thomas and first president of Gallaudet College, the combined system meant preserving sign language but using it in the classroom "as little as possible." He defended his tiny remnant of his father's world in an article bearing the plaintive title "Must the Sign-Language Go?"[45]

The new aversion to sign language had many causes, but a profound change in the images and meanings of deafness during the second half of the nineteenth century was fundamental. The opening article of the first issue of the *Association Review* is revealing. Reprinted from an address delivered before a meeting of the Association by John M. Tyler (president of Amherst College), "The Teacher and the State" was concerned with what teachers could do about two related national problems: the new immigration and the decline in law and order. There was a "struggle between rival civilizations" within America. "Shall her standards and aims, in one word her civilization, be those of old New England, or shall they be Canadian or Irish, or somewhat better or worse than any of these?" The burden rested upon the teachers, for "'Waterloo was won at Rugby' [and] it was the German schoolmaster who triumphed at Sedan." Furthermore, teachers could no longer focus on "purely intellectual training," for "[t]he material which we are trying to fashion has changed; the children are no longer of the former blood, stock, and training." Teachers must make up for the new immigrants' deficiencies as parents, he warned: "the emergency remains and we must meet it as best we can." If they do not, the "uncontrolled child grows into the lawless youth and the anarchistic adult."[46]

Tyler's speech was not directly about deaf people, but it must have resonated with his audience of educators of the deaf. Metaphors of deafness by the turn of the century were no longer ones of spiritual darkness but instead conjured images of foreign enclaves within American society. Articles about deaf people in the *Association Review* might just as well have been about immigrant communities, with metaphors of foreignness at work on several levels. First there was the problem of what was not commonly referred to as "the foreign language of signs."[47] Educators worried that if deaf people "are to exercise intelligently the rights of citizenship, then they must be made people of our language."[48] They insisted that "the English language must be made the vernacular of the deaf if they are not to become a class unto themselves—foreigners among their own countrymen."[49] Oralism was about much more than just speech and lip-reading. It was part of a larger argument about language and the maintenance of a national community.

The image of foreignness was not confined to the pages of the *Association Review*. A parent wrote to the superintendent of the Illinois Institution in 1898, requesting information about methods of deaf education. The answer she received was that there were two: "the English language method," and the method in which "the English language is considered a foreign language," taught through "translation from the indefinite and crude sign language."[50]

"Sign language is an evil," avowed a teacher from the Pennsylvania Institution for Deaf-Mutes, one of the first state schools to adopt the oralist philosophy, in an 1892 article in the *Silent Educator*. The mastery of English was not, by itself, the point, he argued. Sign language made deaf people "a kind of foreigners in tongue," and this was so whether or not they also mastered English. Deaf people who signed could not be full members of the English-speaking American community; they were, instead, "a sign making people who have studied English so as to carry on business relations with those who do not understand signs." Using another language was the offense, for "English is a jealous mistress. She brooks no rival. She was born to conquer and to spread all over the world. She has no equal."[51]

This was an extreme example of a usually more subtle nationalism expressed by opponents of sign language. Most oralists did not exhibit open xenophobia, insist upon Anglo-Saxon superiority, nor advocate one worldwide language. Most emphasized their belief that sign language isolated deaf people and made the deaf person an outsider who was "not an Englishman, a German, a Frenchman, or a member of any other nationality, but, intellectually, a man without a country."[52] They were convinced and deeply troubled by the conviction that signing deaf people existed apart and isolated from the life of the nation. An earlier generation of educators had believed that sign language liberated deaf people from their confinement, but for oralists it was the instrument of their imprisonment.

Even some hearing educators who had long supported sign language had begun to criticize what they termed the "clannishness" of deaf people. In 1873, Edward M. Gallaudet had condemned the conventions, associations and newspapers of deaf people, as well as their intermarriage, for discouraging the intercourse of the deaf "with their race and the world." It was injurious to the best interests of the deaf when they came to consider themselves "members of society with interests apart from the mass, . . . a 'community,' with its leaders and rulers, its associations and organs, and its channels of communication." Gallaudet's concerns were similar to those of the oralists, except that sign language was, he thought, still necessary—a "necessary evil." It could not be relinquished, he argued, because few people profoundly deaf from an early age could become proficient enough at oral communication for a full education or participation in religious services.[53] Oralists escalated the charge of "clannishness" to "foreignness," however, a term with more ominous connotations.

This was a metaphor of great significance for Americans of the late nineteenth century. References to deaf people as foreigners coincided with the greatest influx of immigrants in U. S. history. The new immigrants were concentrated in urban areas, and no major city was without its quilt pattern of immigrant communities. Many came from eastern and southern Europe, bringing with them cultural beliefs and habits that native-born Americans often regarded as peculiar, inferior, or even dangerous. As Frederick E. Hoxie has noted in his study of the Indian Assimilation movement (a movement contemporaneous with and sharing many characteristics with the oralist movement), in the late nineteenth century "growing social diversity and shrinking social space threatened many Americans' sense of national identity."[54] Nativism, never far from the surface of American life, resurged with calls for immigration restriction, limits on the employment of foreigners, and the proscription of languages other than English in the schools. To say that sign language made deaf people appear foreign was to make a telling point for these educators. That foreignness should be avoided at all costs was generally expressed as a self-evident truth.

"Foreignness" had two related meanings. As with the manualists' metaphor of darkness, this was a metaphor with two centers. Looking from the outside in, the metaphor suggested a space within American society that was mysterious to outsiders, into which hearing Americans could see only obscurely if at all. As such it posed vague threats of deviance from the majority culture. Looking from the inside out—that is, empathizing with what the oralists imagined to be the experience of deaf people—it seemed a place in which deaf people became trapped, from which they could not escape without assistance. "Foreignness" was both a threat and a plight. The deaf community, as one of a host of insular and alien-appearing communities, was seen as harmful to both the well-being of the nation and to its own members.

For many hearing people, what they saw looking in from the outside was troubling. Journals and magazines such as the *Silent World* and the *Deaf-Mute Journal*, written and printed by deaf people for a deaf audience, were thriving in every state. Deaf adults across the country were actively involved in local clubs, school alumnae associations, and state and national organizations. They attended churches together where sign language was used. The great majority found both their friends and their spouses within the deaf community. According to the research of Bell, the rate of intermarriage was at least 80 percent, a fact that caused him great alarm.[55]

The two chief interests of Bell's life, eugenics and deaf education, came together over this issue. In a paper published by the National Academy of Sciences in 1884, Bell warned that a "great calamity" for the nation was imminent due to the high rate of intermarriage among the deaf: the "formation of a deaf variety of the human race." The proliferation of deaf clubs, associations, and periodicals, with their tendency to "foster class-feeling among the deaf," were ominous developments. Already, he warned, "a special language adapted for the use of such a race" was in existence, "a language as different from English as French or German or Russian."[56]

While other oralists would call for legislation to "prevent the marriage of persons who are liable to transmit defects to their offspring," Bell believed such legislation would be difficult to enforce.[57] His solution was this: *(1) Determine the causes that promote intermarriages among the deaf and dumb; and (2) remove them"* [emphasis his]. Bell identified two principal causes: "segregation for the purposes of education, and the use, as a means of communication, of a language which is different from that of the people." Indeed, he wrote, "if we desired to create a deaf variety of the race . . . we could not invent more complete or more efficient methods than those."[58]

Bell's fears were unfounded. His findings, published in the year of Gregor Mendel's death and before the latter's research on genetic transmission had become known, were based upon a faulty understanding of genetics. Others soon countered his empirical evidence as well; most deafness was not heritable, and marriages between deaf people produced on average no greater number of deaf offspring than mixed marriages of deaf and hearing partners.[59] But the image of an insular, inbred, and proliferating deaf community, with its own "foreign" language and culture, became a potent weapon for the oralist cause. Bell was to become one of the most prominent and effective crusaders against both residential schools and sign language.[60]

More often, oralists emphasized the empathetic side of the metaphor. They insisted that their intent was to rescue deaf people from their confinement, not to attack them. Deaf adults, however, actively defended the space from which they were urged to escape and from which deaf children were supposed to be rescued. But just as deaf people resisted the oralist conception of their needs, oralists likewise resisted the portrayal of themselves by deaf leaders as "enemies of the true welfare of the deaf."[61] As did the advocates of Indian and immigrant assimilation, they spoke of themselves as the "friends of the deaf." They tried to project themselves into that mysterious space they saw deaf people inhabiting and to empathize with the experience of deafness.

They were especially concerned that "because a child is deaf he is . . . considered peculiar, with all the unpleasant significance attached to the word."[62] The great failure of deaf education was that "in many cases, this opinion is justified by deaf children who are growing up without being helped . . . to acquire any use of language."[63] ("Language" was frequently used as a synonym for "spoken English.") Peculiarity was spoken of as part of the curse of foreignness, and "to go through life as one of a peculiar class . . . is the sum of human misery. No other human misfortune is comparable to this."[64] This peculiarity of deaf people was not unavoidable, but "solely the result of shutting up deaf children to be educated in sign schools, whence they emerge . . . aliens in their own country!"[65] Cease to educate deaf people with sign language, oralists believed, and they will "cease to be mysterious beings."[66]

Like their contemporaries in other fields of reform, oralists worried that the lives of people were diminished by being a part of such restricted communities as the deaf community; they would not, it was feared, fully share in the life of the nation. The deaf community, like ethnic communities, narrowed the minds and outlooks of its members. "The individual must be one with the race," one wrote in words that could have come from Jane Addams or John Dewey or any number of Progressive reformers, "or he is virtually annihilated"; the chief curse of deafness was "apartness from the life of the world," and it was just this that oralism was designed to remedy.[67] This was the darkness of the manualists redefined for a new world.

Oralists believed sign language was to blame for making deaf people seem foreign, peculiar, and isolated from the nation and claimed it was an inferior language that impoverished the minds of its users. This language of "beauty and grace," in the words of Thomas H. Gallaudet, now was called a wretched makeshift of the language."[68] It was "immeasurably inferior to English" and any "culture dependent upon it must be proportionately inferior."[69] The implication of foreignness, barbarism, was not left unspoken. As one opponent of sign language stated, "if speech is better for hearing people than barbaric signs, it is better for the deaf."[70] In an age when social scientists ranked cultures and languages on The evolutionary scale from savage to civilized, teachers of the deaf came to depict sign language as "characteristic of tribes low in the scale of development."[71] It was in fact identical to the gestures used by "a people of lowest type" found to exist "in the ends of the earth where no gleam of civilization had penetrated."[72] Like the races supposed to be lowest on the evolution scale, sign language was barely human.

For some it was not human at all. The metaphor of animality reappeared in different guise. Benjamin D. Pettingill, a teacher at the Pennsylvania School for the Deaf, noted as early as 1873 that sign language was being "decried, denounced, and ridiculed . . . as a set of monkey-like grimaces and antics."[73] Sarah Porter, a teacher at the Kendall School, in 1894 wrote that the common charge against the use of sign language—"You look like monkeys when you make signs"—would be "hardly worth noticing except for its . . . incessant repetition."[74] A teacher from Scotland complained in 1899 in the pages of the *American Annals of the Deaf* that it was wrong to "impress [deaf people] with the thought that it is apish to talk on the fingers."[75]

Lewis Dudley, a trustee of the first oral school in the nation, the Clarke Institution, implied in 1880 that deaf people who used sign language themselves felt less than human. When he visited a school in which sign language was used, the children looked at him

with a downcast pensive look which seemed to say, "Oh, you have come to see the unfortunate; you have come to see young creatures human in shape, but only half human in attributes; you have come here much as you would go to a menagerie to see something peculiar and strange."[76]

He contrasted the demeanor of these children with that of a young girl he had met who had recently learned to speak: "the radiant face and the beaming eye showed a consciousness of elevation in the scale of being. It was a real elevation."[77] The metaphors of the subhuman and the animal had been used by the manualists to signify ignorance of the soul. To the oralists they came to signify ignorance of spoken language.

Clearly the "real calamity of the deaf-mute" had been redefined. The 1819 annual report of the American Asylum did not ask if most Americans could understand signs, but "does God understand signs?"[78] To this they answered yes and were satisfied. At mid-century the calamity still was "not that his ear is closed to the cheerful tones of the human voice," but that the deaf person might be denied "the light of divine truth."[79] When the manualist generation had spoken of deaf people being "restored to society" and to "human brotherhood," membership in the Christian community was the measure of that restoration.[80] Sign language had made it possible. The isolation of the deaf was a problem that had been solved.

By the turn of the century, however, the problem had returned. Once again educators of the deaf spoke of rescuing the deaf from their "state of almost total isolation from society," "restoring" them to "their proper and rightful place in society,"[81] and once again deaf people lived "outside." They were "outside" because "inside" had been redefined. Whereas manualists had believed that to teach their students "the gospel of Christ, and by it to save their souls, is our great duty," it was now the "grand aim of every teacher of the deaf . . . to put his pupils in possession of the spoken language of their country."[82] The relevant community was no longer the Christian community, but a national community defined in large part by language.

Both manualists and oralists understood deafness in the context of movements for national unity, and their metaphors came from those movements. Evangelical Protestantism brought together a nation no longer unified by the common experience of the Revolution, unsettled by rapid social and economic change, and worried about the effects of the opening of the West upon both the morality and the unity of the nation. In crafting that unity, by creating a common set of experiences for understanding of the world, Evangelicalism emphasized above any other kind of cultural or linguistic homogeneity a common spiritual understanding. When Evangelicals saw dangers in the immigration of the time, it was not foreignness per se that principally concerned them, but Catholicism.[83] That definition of unity was not necessarily more tolerant of difference in general, but it did mean that sign language and the deaf community were not seen as inimical to it.

The movement for national unity at the time of the rise of oralism had a different source. This time it was the multiplicity of immigrant communities crowded into burgeoning industrial cities that seemed to threaten the bonds of nationhood. Two streams converged to make sign language repugnant to many hearing Americans: at the same time that deaf people were creating a deaf community, with its own clubs, associations, and periodicals, American ethnic communities were doing the same to an extent alarming to the majority culture. At the same time that deaf children were attending separate schools in which deaf teachers taught them with both English and sign language, immigrant children were attending parochial schools in which immigrant teachers taught them in both English and their native languages.[84] The convergence was merely fortuitous, but it was not difficult to transfer anxieties from one to the other.

If the fragmentation of American society into distinct and unconnected groups was the fear that drove the oralists, the coalescence of a homogeneous society of equal individuals was the vision that drew them together. For the oralists, as for their contemporaries in other fields of reform—the assimilation of the Indian, the uplifting of the working class, the Americanization of the immigrant—equality was synonymous with sameness. The ideal was achieved when one could "walk into . . . our hearing schools and find the deaf boys working right along with their hearing brothers . . . [where] no difference is felt by the teacher."[85] Just as manualism arose within a larger Evangelical revival, so did oralism partake of the late nineteenth-century quest for national unity through the assimilation of ethnic cultures.[86]

Humans use metaphor and mental imagery to understand things of which they have no direct experience.[87] For people who are not deaf, then, the use of metaphor to understand deafness is inevitable: they can approach it no other way. The problem is that hearing people are in positions to make, on the basis of their metaphors—usually unaware that they *are* metaphors—decisions with profound and lasting effects upon the lives of deaf people. The most persistent images of deafness among hearing people have been ones of isolation and exclusion, and these are images that are consistently rejected by deaf people who see themselves as part of a deaf community and culture. Feelings of isolation may even be less common for members of this tightly knit community than among the general population.[88] The metaphors of deafness—of isolation and foreignness, of animality, of darkness and silence—are projections reflecting the needs and standards of the dominant culture, not the experiences of most deaf people.

The oralists and the manualists appeared to be opposing forces—"old-fashioned" manualists fought bitterly with "progressive" oralists. The deaf community saw a clear difference, siding with the manualists and resisting with all its resources the changes in educational practice that the oralists sought. One reason was that manual schools employed deaf teachers. Oral schools generally did not—deaf people could not teach speech.[89] Furthermore, oralists simply did not believe that the deaf should exist as a social group; to hire deaf teachers would imply that deaf people had something to teach each other, that there was a significant group experience. Manualists seem to have been more egalitarian for this reason. While deaf people taught in manualist schools, however, they generally found positions of authority closed to them. Few became principals or superintendents, and probably no deaf person ever sat on a school governing board.[90] One result was that when the hearing society refashioned its images of deafness and turned toward oralism, the deaf community had limited means of resistance.

Resist it did through that combination of open and subterranean means commonly resorted to by beleaguered minorities. From the beginnings of oralism until its demise in the 1970s, deaf people organized to lobby legislatures and school boards in support of sign language in the schools.[91] Deaf parents passed sign language on to their children, and those children who were deaf and attended schools where sign language was banned surreptitiously taught others. Those unable to learn sign language as children learned it as adults when they found themselves free to associate with whomever they pleased, however they pleased; over 90 percent continued to marry other deaf people and deaf clubs and associations continued to thrive.[92] But their means of resistance within the educational establishment were scant, a legacy at least in part of the paternalism of the manualist educators.

Manualists and oralists had paternalism in common, and much else. Both groups saw deafness through their own cultural biases and sought to reshape deaf people in accordance with them. Both used similar clusters of metaphors to forge images of deaf people as fundamentally flawed, incomplete, isolated and dependent. And both used that imagery to justify not only methods of education, but also the inherent authority of the hearing over the deaf. That did not change.

Still, deaf people sided with the manualists. We do not know exactly how deaf people responded to the images created by either manualists or oralists, to what extent they internalized them, rejected them, or used them for their own purposes. The creation of alternative meanings for deafness by the deaf community has a complex history all its own, one that is still largely unwritten.[93] But while the reception of the Evangelical *message* by deaf people during the manualist years is not yet clear, the Evangelical *medium*—sign language within a sign-using community—was clearly welcomed by most. And whether or not deaf adults accepted the oralist depiction of their community as "foreign" or akin to an immigrant community, most of them clearly rejected the oralist understanding of what those images meant.

Whatever metaphors of deafness manualists may have used, manualism allowed the possibility of alternative constructions of deafness by deaf people themselves. So long as deaf people had their own language and community, they possessed a cultural space in which to create alternative meanings for their lives. Within that space they could resist the meanings that hearing people attached to deafness, adopt them and put them to new uses, or create their own. Oralism, whose ideal was the thoroughly assimilated deaf person, would do away with that alternative. Oralism failed, finally, and sign language survived, because deaf people chose not to relinquish the autonomous cultural space their community gave them.

NOTES

1.   For an example of a radically different construction of deafness than has been typical in the United States, see Nora Groce, *Everyone Here Spoke Sign Language:*

Hereditary Deafness on Martha's Vineyard (Cambridge, Mass., 1985). From the six-teenth to the nineteenth century, an unusually high rate of inherited deafness on Martha's Vineyard combined with premodern village values to produce communities in which deafness was apparently not considered a significant difference at all. The hearing people in these communities were all bilingual in spoken English and a variety of British Sign Language. There were no apparent differences between the social, economic, or political lives of the hearing and the deaf, according to Groce.

2. Within forty years there would be twenty residential schools in the United States; by the turn of the century, more than fifty. See "Tabular Statement of Schools for the Deaf, 1897–98," *American Annals of the Deaf* 43 (Jan. 1898): 46–47 (hereafter cited as *Annals*).

    The use of "deaf" (with a lower case *d*) to refer primarily to an audiological condition of hearing loss, and "Deaf" (with an upper case *D*) to refer to a cultural identity (deaf people, that is, who use American Sign Language, share certain attitudes and beliefs about themselves and their relation to the hearing world, and self-consciously think of themselves as part of a separate Deaf culture) has become standard in the literature on Deaf culture. The distinction, while useful and important, is often difficult in practice to apply to individuals, especially when dealing with historical figures. I have not tried to make the distinction in this paper. See Carol Padden and Tom Humphries, *Deaf in America: Voices from a Culture* (Cambridge, Mass., 1988), 2–6.

3. Pierre Desloges, a deaf Parisian, wrote in 1779 that "matters are completely different for the deaf living in society in a great city like Paris. . . . In intercourse with his fellows he promptly acquires the supposedly difficult art of depicting and expressing all his thoughts. . . . No event—in Paris, in France, or in the four corners of the world—lies outside the scope of our discussion. We express ourselves on all subjects with as much order, precision, and rapidity as if we enjoyed the faculty of speech and hearing." Desloges's short book, *Observations d'un sourd et muet sur "Un Cours elementaire d'education des sourds et muets,"* is translated in Harlan Lane, ed., *The Deaf Experience: Classics in Language and Education*, trans. Franklin Philip (Cambridge, 1984), 36.

4. The best account of the contemporary American Deaf community can be found in Padden and Humphries, *Deaf in America*. For anyone wishing to understand the world of deaf people, this small but rich and insightful book is a fine place to start. For a concise history of the formation of the deaf community in nineteenth-century United States, see John Vickrey Van Cleve and Barry Crouch, *A Place of Their Own: Creating the Deaf Community in America* (Washington, D.C., 1989); see also, Jack Gannon, *Deaf Heritage: A Narrative History of Deaf America* (Silver Spring, Md., 1981), a popular history that was written by a deaf man, published by the National Association of the Deaf, and created primarily for the deaf community.

5. I am using "sign language" here as a generic term referring to any complex means of manual communication. In the nineteenth century, as today, there were (to simplify) two forms of sign language in use: American Sign Language, a natural language that has evolved over the course of American history within the deaf community, having roots in French Sign Language, indigenous sign languages, and a variety of British Sign Language brought to Martha's Vineyard; and signed English (called "methodical signs" in the nineteenth century), of which several varieties exists. These latter are not true languages but manual codes invented for

educational use to represent English manually. Manualists in the nineteenth century at different times used both, and oralists opposed both. See Joseph D. Stedt and Donald F. Moores, "Manual Codes on English and American Sign Language: Historical perspectives and Current Realities," in Harry Borstein, ed., *Manual Communication: Implications for Education* (Washington, D.C., 1990), 1–20; James Woodward, "Historical Bases of American Sign Language," in Patricia Siple, ed., *Understanding Language Through Sign Language Research* (New York, 1978), 333–48.

6. According to Alexander Graham Bell, 23.7 percent "taught wholly by oral methods"; 14.7 percent "taught also by Manual Spelling (no Sign-language)"; 53.1 percent "with whom speech is used [in at least some classes] as a means of instruction." See "Address of the President," *Association Review* 1 (Oct. 1899), 78–79 (in 1910 renamed the *Volta Review*). Bell's figures differ somewhat from those provided by the *American Annals of the Deaf*–see, for example, Edward Allen Fay in "Progress of Speech-Teaching in the United States," *Annals* 60 (Jan. 1915): 115. Bell's method of counting, as he explains in the same issue, is more precise in that he distinguishes between those taught wholly by oral methods and those taught in part orally and in part manually.

7. "Statistics of Speech Teaching in American Schools for the Deaf," *Volta Review* 22 (June 1920): 372.

8. See, for example, J. C. Gordon, "Dr. Gordon's Report," *American Review* 1 (Dec. 1899): 213; Mary McCowen, "Educational and Social Work for the Deaf and Deafened in the Middle West," *Oralism and Auralism* 6 (Jan. 1927): 67.

9. Henry Kisor, *What's That Pig Outdoors? A Memoir of Deafness* (New York, 1990), 259; Kisor was orally educated, never learned sign language, and has been very successful communicating orally all his life. Nevertheless he condemns "the history of oralism, the unrelenting and largely unsuccessful attempt to teach *all* the deaf to speak and read lips without relying on sign language" (9).

    The reintroduction of sign language into the classroom has been even more rapid than its banishment at the turn of the century; it occurred amidst widespread dissatisfaction with oralism—after a series of studies suggested that early use of sign language had no negative effect on speech skills and positive effects on English acquisition as well as social and intellectual development. See Donald F. Moores, *Educating the Deaf: Psychology, Principals and Practices* (Boston, 1987), 10–13. Julia M. Davis and Edward J. Hardick, *Rehabilitative Audiology for Children and Adults* (New York, 1981), 319–25; Mimi WheiPing Lou, "The History of Language Use in the Education of the Deaf in the United States," in Michael Strong, ed., *Language Learning and Deafness* (Cambridge, 1988), 88–94; Leo M. Jacobs, *A Deaf Adult Speaks Out* (Washington, D.C., 1980), 26, 41–50.

10. Van Cleve and Crouch, *A Place of Their Own*, 128–41; Beryl Lieff Benderly, *Dancing Without Music: Deafness in America* (Garden City, N.Y., 1980), 127–29; Harlan Lane, *When the Mind Hears: A History of the Deaf* (New York, 1984), 371–72; Padden and Humphries, *Deaf in America*, 110–12; Oliver Sacks, *Seeing Voices: A Journey into the World of the Deaf* (Berkeley, 1989), 25–28.

11. Quoted in Lane, *When the Mind Hears*, 371

12. Lane, *When the Mind Hears*, 301–2.

13. Richard Winefield, *Never the Twain Shall Meet: Bell, Gallaudet, and the Communications Debate* (Washington, D.C., 1987), 81–96; Van Cleve and Crouch, *A Place of Their Own*, 114–27; Lane, *When the Mind Hears*, 353–61.

14. Van Cleve and Crouch, *A Place of Their Own*, 106–7, 119, 126.

15. Lane, *When the Mind Hears*, xiii, 283–85.

16. Instruction in oral communication is still given in all educational programs for deaf and hearing-impaired children. "Oralism" as a philosophy of education does not mean simply oral instruction, but is rather a philosophy that maintains that all or most deaf children can be taught this way *exclusively*. The current philosophy, known as "Total Communication," and nineteenth-century manualism have in common the use of sign language. But American Sign Language was commonly used in the nineteenth century, while today some form of signed English delivered simultaneously with speech is most common. The integration of deaf pupils into the public schools, with the use of interpreters, is now the norm. The arguments today are not for the most part between oralists and manualists but between the advocates of signed English and American Sign Language, and between mainstreaming and separate residential schooling. See Moores, *Educating the Deaf*, 1–28.

17. Luzerne Ray, "Introductory," *Annals* 1 (Oct. 1847): 4.

18. Thomas H. Gallaudet, "The Natural Language of Signs," *Annals* 1 (Oct. 1847): 55–56.

19. Ibid., 56.

20. Thomas H. Gallaudet, "The Natural Language of Signs—II" *Annals* 1 (Jan. 1848): 82, 88.

21. Ibid., 82–85.

22. Ibid., 88–89. The emphasis on the heart rather than the intellect was of course a commonplace of Second great Awakening Evangelicalism. Reason and knowledge were not, however, seen as opposed to religion, and were also highly valued; see Jean V. Matthews, *Toward a New Society: American Thought and Culture, 1800–1830* (Boston, 1991) 35.

23. Thomas H. Gallaudet, "The Natural Language of Signs—II," 86.

24. Lucius Woodruff, "The Motives to Intellectual Effort on the part of the Young Deaf-Mute," *Annals* 1 (Apr. 1848): 163–65.

25. David Walker Howe, "The Evangelical Movement and Political Culture in the North during the Second Party System," *Journal of American History* 77 (Mar. 1991): 1220.

26. Collins Stone, "The Religious State and Instruction of the Deaf and Dumb," *Annals* 1 (Apr. 1848): 144.

27. Henry B. Camp, "Claims of the Deaf and Dumb Upon Public Sympathy and Aid," *Annals* 1 (July 1848): 213–14.

28. Stone, "The Religious State," 133–34, 137.

29. Ibid., 134–35, 138.

30. J. A. Ayres, "An Inquiry into the Extent to which the Misfortune of Deafness may be Alleviated," *Annals* 1 (July 1848): 223.

31. Luzerne Ray, "Thoughts of the Deaf and Dumb before Instruction," *Annals* 1 (Apr. 1848): 150–51.

32. Camp, "Claims of the Deaf," 210–15. See also Woodruff, "The Motives to Intellectual Effort," 163–65.

33. Stone, "The Religious State," 136–37.

34. Woodruff, "The Motives to Intellectual Effort," 165–66.

35. Ayres, "An Inquiry," 224.

36. John Carlin, "The Mute's Lament," *Annals* 1 (Oct. 1847): 15. Carlin, a successful artist, was well known for his expressions of what today might be termed "self hatred." He was a contradictory individual. Although he married a deaf woman, used sign language, and was an ardent supported of the establishment of Gallaudet College, he claimed to prefer the company of hearing people and expressed con-

tempt for deaf people and sign language. While he did not speak or lipread, he became one of the small minority of deaf adults who supported the oralist movement. Carlin derided proposals for a separatist community of deaf people on the grounds that "it is a well known fact that the majority of them [deaf people] show little decision of purpose in any enterprise whatever." *Annals* 10 (Apr. 1858): 89. See also Lane, *When the Mind Hears*, 245–46, 275–76, 325; Van Cleve and Crouch, *A Place of Their Own*, 66, 76–78.

37.   Anon., *Annals* 1 (July 1848): 209.
38.   Padden and Humphries identify the use of "silence" in reference to deaf people as metaphorical. They explain that sound (to greatly simplify their argument) directly and indirectly plays an important role in the lives of deaf people and has important meanings for them, albeit quite different ones than for the hearing; *Deaf in America*, 91–109.
39.   Frank Booth, "The Association Magazine," *Association Review* 1 (Oct. 1899): 4.
40.   Alexander Graham Bell, "Address of the President," *Association Review* 1 (Oct. 1899): 74–75, 85.
41.   Bell, "Address of the President," 78–79 (see note 6). "Statistics of Speech Teaching in American Schools for the Deaf," 372.
42.   Percentages of deaf teachers by year: 1852–38 percent; 1858–41 percent; 1870–41 percent; 1880–29 percent; 1892–24 percent; 1897–18 percent; 1915–15 percent, compiled from periodic reports of schools for the deaf, published in the *American Annals of the Deaf* during the years indicated, under the heading "Tabular Statement of American Schools for the Deaf."
43.   Winefield, *Never the Twain Shall Meet*, 48.
44.   John Van Cleve, "Nebraska's Oral Law of 1911 and the Deaf Community," *Nebraska History* 65 (Summer 1984): 208.
45.   *Annals* 44 (June 1899): 221–29.
46.   John M. Tyler, "The Teacher and the State," *Association Review* 1 (Oct. 1899): 9, 12–13.
47.   Katherine T. Bingham, "All Along the Line, *Association Review* 2 (Feb. 1900): 27, 29.
48.   Edward C. Rider, "The Annual Report of the Northern New York Institution for the Year Ending September 30, 1898," reprinted in the *Association Review* 1 (Dec. 1899): 214–15.
49.   S. G. Davidson, "The Relation of Language to Mental Development and of Speech to Language Teaching," *Association Review* 1 (Dec. 1899), 132. See also, Alexander Graham Bell, *Proceedings of the Twelfth Convention of American Instructors of the Deaf* (New York, 1890), 181.
50.   Joseph C. Gordon, *The Difference Between the Two Systems of Teaching Deaf-Mute Children the English Language: Extracts from a Letter to a Parent Requesting Information Relative to the Prevailing Methods of Teaching Language to Deaf-Mutes in America* (Washington, D.C., 1898), 1.
51.   J. D. Kirkhuff, "The Sign System Arraigned," *Silent Educator* 3 (Jan. 1892): 88a.
52.   S. G. Davidson, "The Relation of Language Teaching to Mental Development," *National Educational Association: Journal of Proceedings and Addresses of the Thirty-Seventh Annual Meeting* (Washington, D.C., 1898), 1044.
53.   Edward M. Gallaudet, "'Deaf-Mute' Conventions, Associations, and Newspapers," *Annals* 18 (July 1873): 200–206.
54.   Frederick E. Hoxie, *A Final Promise: The Campaign to Assimilate the Indians, 1880–1920* (Lincoln, Neb., 1984), 12.

55. Alexander Graham Bell, *Memoir Upon the Formation of a Deaf Variety of the Human Race* (Washington, D.C., 1884), 194.
56. Bell, *Memoir*, 194, 217–18, 223.
57. Mary S. Garrett, "The State of the Case," *National Educational Association: Journal of Proceedings and Addresses of the Thirty-Ninth Annual Meeting* (Washington, D.C., 1900), 663; Bell, *Memoir*, 221–22.
58. Bell, *Memoir*, 217, 221–23.
59. Edward Allen Fay, "An Inquiry Concerning the Results of Marriages of the Deaf in America," *Annals* 42 (Feb. 1897): 100–102; see also the discussion of this issue in Van Cleve and Crouch, *A Place of Their Own*, 150–52.
60. On the influence of eugenics upon Bell's work in deaf education, see Winefield, *Never the Twain Shall Meet*, 82–96; Lane, *When the Mind Hears*, 353–61; Van Cleve and Crouch, *A Place of Their Own*, 145–52; for a more sympathetic view of Bell's eugenic concerns about deafness, see Robert V. Bruce, *Bell: Alexander Graham Bell and the Conquest of Solitude* (Ithaca, N.Y., 1973), 409–12.
61. Quoted in Padden and Humphries, *Deaf in America*, 36.
62. Helen Taylor, "The Importance of a Right Beginning," *Association Review* 1 (Dec. 1899): 159.
63. Ibid.
64. Bingham, "All Along the Line," 28–29.
65. Ibid. See also, J. C. Gordon, "Dr. Gordon's Report," *Association Review* 1 (Dec. 1899): 204.
66. Gordon, "Dr. Gordon's Report," 213.
67. Bingham, "All Along the Line," 29; see also Emma Garrett, "A Plea that the Deaf 'Mutes' of America May be Taught to Use Their Voices," *Annals* 28 (Jan. 1883): 18.
68. Thomas H. Gallaudet, "The Natural Language of Signs—II," 89; J. D. Kirkhuff, "The Sign System Arraigned," 88a.
69. Davidson, "The Relation of Language," 132.
70. Emma Garrett, "A Plea," 18.
71. Gordon, "Dr. Gordon's Report," 206.
72. Bingham, "All Along the Line," 22.
73. Benjamin D. Pettingill, "The Sign-Language," *Annals* 18 (Jan. 1873), 4.
74. Sara Harvey Porter, "The Suppression of Signs by Force," *Annals* 39 (June 1894): 171. Porter repeated this observation in 1913, when she stated that in the "old primitive fighting days the oralists cried to us, derisively: 'Your children, making signs, look like monkeys!'" In the context it is not clear whether she believed those fighting days were over, or whether she was calling for their end; *Annals* 58 (May 1913): 284.
75. R. W. Dodds, "The Practical Benefits of Methods Compared," *Annals* 44 (Feb. 1899): 124.
76. Lewis J. Dudley, "Address of Mr. Dudley in 1880," *Fifteenth Annual Report of the Clarke Institution for Deaf-Mutes* (Northhampton, Mass., 1882), 7.
77. Ibid.
78. From extracts reprinted in Alexander Graham Bell, "Historical Notes Concerning the Teaching of Speech to the Deaf," *Association Review* (Apr. 1902): 151.
79. Stone, "On the Religious State," 137.
80. Camp, "Claims of the Deaf," 214.
81. Bingham, "All Along the Line," 28; Taylor, "The Importance of a Right Beginning," 158.

82. J. A. Jacobs, "To Save the Souls of His Pupils, the Great Duty of a Teacher of Deaf-Mutes," *Annals* 8 (July 1856): 211; Susanna E. Hull, "The Psychological Method of Teaching Language," *Annals* 43 (Apr. 1898): 190.

83. Donald G. Matthews, "The Second Great Awakening as an Organizing Process, 1780–1830; An Hypothesis," *American Quarterly* 21 (Spring 1969): 23–43; Richard Carwardine, "The Know-Nothing Party, the Protestant Evangelical Community and American National Identity," in *Religion and National Identity*, Stuart Mews, ed. (Oxford, 1982), 449–63.

84. Rivka Shpak Lissak, *Pluralism and Progressives: Hull House and the New Immigrants, 1890–1919* (Chicago, 1989): 50–55.

85. Taylor, "The Importance of a Right beginning," 158. The equation of equality with sameness was a staple of Progressive reform thought; see Lissak, *Pluralism and Progressives*, 153.

86. Lissak, *Pluralism and Progressives*; Hoxie, *A Final Promise*; Joshua A. Fishman, *Language Loyalty in the United States: The Maintenance and Perpetuation of Non-English Mother Tongues by American Ethnic and Religious Groups* (The Hague, 1966).

87. George Lakoff, *Women, Fire, and Dangerous Things: What Categories Reveal about the Mind* (Chicago, 1987), xiv.

88. Leo M. Jacobs, *A Deaf Adult Speaks Out* (Washington, D.C., 1980), 90–100; Jerome D. Schein, *At Home Among Strangers: Exploring the Deaf Community in the United States* (Washington, D.C., 1989), 130; Paul C. Higgins, *Outsiders in a Hearing World: A Sociology of Deafness* (Beverly Hills, 1980), 69–76; James Woodward, "How You Gonna Get to Heaven if You Can't Talk with Jesus: The Educational Establishment vs. the Deaf Community," in *How You Gonna Get to Heaven if You Can't Talk with Jesus: On Depathologizing Deafness* (Silver Spring, Md., 1982), 11.

89. In the first five years of Gallaudet College (1869 to 1874), a liberal arts college exclusively for deaf students, 75 percent of its graduates became teachers at schools for the deaf. From 1894 to 1899, fewer than a third did so. See Edward P. Clarke, "An Analysis of the Schools and Instructors of the Deaf in the United States," *American Annals of the Deaf* 45 (Apr. 1900): 229.

90. Van Cleve and Crouch, *A Place of Their Own*, 128.

91. See W. Earl Hall, "To Speak or Not to Speak: That is the Question Behind the Bitter Deaf-Teaching Battle," *Iowan* 4 (Feb.–Mar. 1956) for a brief description of a battle between the Iowa Association of the Deaf and the Iowa School for the Deaf in the 1950s over this issue. See also Van Cleve, "Nebraska's Oral Law," 195–220; Van Cleve and Crouch, *A Place of Their Own*, 128–41.

92. Padden and Humphries, *Deaf in America*, 5–6; Benderly, *Dancing Without Music*, 218–39; Schein, *At Home Among Strangers*, 72–105, 106, 120.

93. Padden and Humphries, *Deaf in America*, 26–38, 110–21, explore the alternative meanings of deafness created by the deaf community; their focus is on the present, but their brief forays into the historical roots of these meanings are suggestive and insightful.

part two

Politics of Disability

Construction of Deafness

HARLAN LANE

SOCIAL PROBLEMS ARE CONSTRUCTED

It is obvious that our society is beset by numerous social problems. A brief historical perspective on four of them reveals something not so obvious: social problems are constructed in particular cultures, at particular times, in response to the efforts of interested parties.

The social problem of alcoholism evidently consists in this: there is a particular segment of the population that suffers from the use of alcohol; these sufferers need specially trained people to help them—for example alcoholism counselors, psychologists and psychiatrists; they need special facilities such as detoxification centers; and special organizations like AA. This understanding of alcoholism is less than fifty years old. Recall that the Temperance Movement of the last century viewed excessive drinking not as a disease but as an act of will; alcoholics victimized their families and imposed on the rest of society. The movement advocated not treatment but prohibition. Some groups favored prohibition and took the moral high ground; other groups felt justified in breaking the law. Special facilities existed then to house and treat many problem groups—mentally ill people, for example—but not people who drank too much. Only recently has a consensus developed that excessive drinking "is" a disease—a matter of individual suffering more than a political dispute. With this shift in the construction of alcoholism and alcoholics—from victimizers to victims—the evident need was for medical research to alleviate suffering; vast sums of money are now devoted to research on alcoholism, and there is now a large treatment establishment with halfway houses, hospital wards, outpatient clinics, and specialized hospitals (Gusfield, 1982).

The discovery of child abuse dates from the 1950s. Radiologists and pediatricians first decried the evidence they were seeing of parents beating their children. The Children's Bureau and the media took up the cause (it is still very present in TV and the newspapers) and made the public aware of this social problem. In the decade that followed, the states passed laws requiring reports of child abuse and providing penalties. Of course, parents did not start beating their children only in the 1950s. Rather, a social consensus emerged in that decade that a problem existed requiring laws, special welfare workers, and special budgetary provisions. In the last century, the major problems associated with children concerned poverty and child labor—a rather different and much more political construction of the problem of improper treatment of children (Gusfield, 1989).

For a very long time, the dominant construction of homosexuality, like that of alcoholism, was a moral one: men and women were making sinful choices; the problem was "owned" by the church. Later psychiatry gave it a new construction: it "is" an illness they claimed that psychiatrists could treat (Conrad & Schneider, 1980). In the third phase, Gays and Lesbians were presented as a minority group; they ask for the same protection as all other groups that are discriminated against based on the circumstances of their birth, such as blacks and women.

Disability, too, has had moral, medical and now social constructions, as numerous articles in this journal have explicated. The Disability Rights Movement has shifted the construct of disability "off the body and into the interface between people with impairments and socially disabling conditions" (Hevey, 1993, p. 426).

Alcoholism has changed from a moral failure to a disease; child abuse from an economic problem to a criminal one; homosexuality from disease to personal constitution to human rights; disability from tragic flaw to social barriers. Social problems, it seems, are partly what we make of them; they are not just out there "lying in the road to be discovered by passers-by" (Gusfield, 1984, p. 38). The particular way in which society understands alcoholism, disability and so forth determines exactly what these labels mean, how large groups of people are treated, and the problems that they face. Deafness, too, has had many constructions; they differ with time and place. Where there were many deaf people in small communities in the last century, on Martha's Vineyard, for example, as in Henniker, New Hampshire, deafness was apparently not seen as a problem requiring special intervention. Most Americans had quite a different construction of deafness at that time, however: it was an individual affliction that befell family members and had to be accommodated within the family. The great challenge facing Thomas Gallaudet and Laurent Clerc in their efforts to create the first American school for the deaf was to persuade state legislatures and wealthy Americans of quite a different construction which they had learned in Europe: Deafness was not an individual but a social problem, deaf people had to be brought together for their instruction, special "asylums" were needed. Nowadays, two constructions of deafness in particular are dominant and compete for shaping deaf peoples' destinies. The one construes deaf as a category of disability; the other construes deaf as designating a member of a linguistic minority. There is a growing practice of capitalizing Deaf when referring specifically to its second construction, which I will follow hereafter.

DISABILITY VS. LINGUISTIC MINORITY

Numerous organizations are associated with each of the prominent constructions of deafness. In the U. S., National organizations primarily associated with deafness as disability include the A. G. Bell Association (4,500 members), the American Speech-Language-Hearing Association (40,000), the American Association of Late-Deafened Adults (1,300), Self-Help for the Hard of Hearing (13,000), the American Academy of Otolaryngology, Head and Neck Surgery (5,600), and the National Hearing Aid Society (4,000). National organizations associated primarily with the construction of Deaf as a linguistic minority include the National Association of the Deaf (20,000), the Registry of Interpreters for the Deaf (2,700), and the National Fraternal Society of the Deaf (13,000) (Van Cleve, 1987; Burek, 1993).

Each construction has a core client group. No one disputes the claim of the hearing adult become deaf from illness or aging that he or she has a disability and is not a member of Deaf culture. Nor, on the other hand, has any one yet criticized Deaf parents for insisting that their Deaf child has a distinct linguistic and cultural heritage. The struggle between some of the groups adhering to the two constructions persists across the centuries (Lane, 1984) in part because there is no simple criterion for identifying most childhood candidates as clients of the one position or the other. More generally, we can observe that late deafening and moderate hearing loss tend to be associated with the disability construction of deafness while early and profound deafness involve an entire organization of the person's language, culture and thought around vision and tend to be associated with the linguistic minority construction.

In general, we identify children as members of a language minority when their native language is not the language of the majority. Ninety percent of Deaf children, however, have hearing parents who are unable to effectively model the spoken language for most of them. Advocates of the disability construction contend these are hearing-impaired children whose language and culture (though they may have acquired little of either) are in principle those of their parents; advocates of the linguistic minority construction contend that the children's native language, in the sense of primary language, must be manual language and that their life trajectory will bring them fully into the circle of Deaf culture. Two archetypes for these two constructions, disability and linguistic minority, were recently placed side by side before our eyes on the U.S. television program, "Sixty Minutes." On the one hand, seven-year-old Caitlin Parton, representing the unreconstructed disability-as-impairment: presented as a victim of a personal tragedy, utterly disabled in communication by her loss of hearing but enabled by technology, and dedicated professional efforts (yes, we meet the surgeon), to approach normal, for which she yearns, as she herself explains. On the other hand, Roslyn Rosen, then president of the National Association of the Deaf, from a large Deaf family, native speaker of ASL, proud of her status as a member of a linguistic minority, insistent that she experiences life and the world fully and has no desire to be any different (*Sixty Minutes*, 1992).

PROFESSIONAL INFLUENCE OVER CONSTRUCTIONS

Organizations espousing each construction of deafness compete to "own" the children and define their needs. Their very economic survival depends on their success in that competition. Which construction of a social problem prevails is thus no mere academic matter. There is a body of knowledge associated with construction A and a quite different body with construction B; the theories and facts associated with construction A have been studied by the professional people who grapple with the social problem; they are the basis of their specialized training and professional credentials and therefore contribute to their self-esteem; they are used to maintain respect from clients, to obtain federal and state funding, to insure one's standing in a fraternity of like professionals; they legitimate the professional person's daily activities. Professionals examine students on this body of knowledge, give certificates, and insert themselves into the legal and social norms based on their competence in that body of knowledge. Whoever says A is a mistaken construction is of course not welcome. More than that, whoever says A is a construction is not welcome, for that implies that there could be or is another construction, B, say, which is better. What the parties to each construction want is that their construction not be seen as a construction at all; rather, they insist, they merely reflect the way things are in the world (cf. Gusfield, 1984).

These "troubled-persons industries," in the words of sociologist Joseph Gusfield, "bestow benevolence on people defined as in need" (Gusfield, 1989, p. 432). These industries have grown astronomically in recent decades (Albrecht, 1992). The professional services fueled by the disability construction of deafness are provided by some administrators of schools and training programs, experts in counseling and rehabilitation, teachers, interpreters, audiologists, speech therapists, otologists, psychologists, psychiatrists, librarians, researchers, social workers, and hearing aid specialists. All these people and the facilities they command, their clinics, operating rooms, laboratories, classrooms, offices and shops, owe their livelihood or existence to deafness problems. Gusfield cites the story about American missionaries who settled in Hawaii. They went to do good. They stayed and did well (Gusfield, 1989).

The troubled-person professions serve not only their clientele but also themselves, and are actively involved in perpetuating and expanding their activities. Teachers of the Deaf, for example, seek fewer students per teacher and earlier intervention (Johnson et al., 1989). American audiologists have formally proposed testing of the hearing of all American newborns without exception. The self-aggrandizement of the troubled-persons professions when it comes to Deaf people is guided by a genuine belief in their exclusive construction of the social problem and their ability to alleviate it. Some of their promotional methods are readily seen; for example, they employ lobbyists to encourage legislation that requires and pays for their services. Other measures are more subtle; for example, the structural relation between the service provider and the client often has the effect of disempowering the client and maintaining dependency.

LESSONS FROM SERVICES FOR BLIND PEOPLE

The history of services to blind people illustrates some of the pitfalls of the professionalization of a social problem. Workshops for blind people have large budgets, provide good income for sighted managers, and have a national organization to lobby for their interest. Blind people, however, commonly view sheltered workshops as a dead end that involves permanent dependency. The editor of the journal *Braille Monitor* says that "professional" is a swear word among blind people, "a bitter term of mockery and disillusionment" (Vaughan, 1991). A light-house for the blind was raked over the coals in that journal for having one pay scale for blind employees and a higher one for sighted employees performing the same work; moreover, the blind employees were paid below minimum wage (Braille Monitor, 1989). the National Accreditation Council for Agencies Serving the Blind and visually Handicapped (NAC) was disowned by organizations of blind people for its efforts to keep blind people in custodial care, its refusal to hear blind witnesses, and its token representation of blind people on the board; the Council rebutted that it had to consider the needs of agencies and professionals and not just blind people. For decades blind people picketed the NAC annual meetings (Braille Monitor, 1973; Jernigan, 1973; Vaughan, 1991).

A conference convened to define the new specialization of mobility trainer for the blind concluded that it required graduate study to learn this art and that "the teaching of mobility is a task for the sighted rather than a blind individual" (quoted in Vaughan, 1991, p. 209). This approach was naturally challenged by blind consumers. At first, the American Association of Workers with the Blind required normal vision for certification; then this was seen as discriminatory, in violation of section 504 of the Rehabilitation Act of 1973. So the criteria were changed. To enter the training program, the student must be able to assess the collision path of a blind person with obstacles nearly a block away. As it turns out, the functions claimed to be essential to mobility teaching just happen to require normal vision. Needless to say, blind people have been teaching blind people how to get about for centuries (Olson, 1981).

Workers with blind people view blindness as a devastating personal tragedy although blind people themselves commonly do not. Said the president of the National Association of the Blind "We do not regard our lives . . . as tragic or disastrous and no amount of professional jargon or trumped up theory can made us do so" (Jernigan quoted in Olson, 1977, p. 408). As sociologist R. A. Scott explains in his classic monograph, *The Making of Blind Men*, the sighted professionals believe that the blind man's only hope for solving his problems is to submit to their long-term program of psychological services and training. To succeed, the blind man is told, he must change his beliefs about blindness, most of all, his belief that he is basically fine and only needs one or two services. The cooperative client is the one who welcomes all the services provided; the unco-operative client is the one who fails to realize how many and great his needs are—who is in denial. The troubled-persons industries thus stand the normal relation between needs and services on its head: services do not evolve purely to meet needs; clients must recognize that they need the services provided by the professionals. Scott comments that it is easy to be deluded about the reality of these special needs. There are always a few blind clients who can be relied on to endorse these beliefs in the profound need for professional services. These blind individuals have been socialized, perhaps since childhood, to the professional construction of blindness. They confirm that blind people have the needs the agency says they have (Scott, 1981).

So it is with deafness. In much of the world, including the United States, deaf people are largely excluded from the ranks of professionals serving deaf children. In many communities it just happens that to be a teacher of deaf children you must first qualify as a teacher of hearing children, and deaf people are excluded as teachers of hearing children. In other communities, it just happens that to become a teacher of deaf children the candidate who is most capable of communicating with them is disbarred because he or she must pass an examination couched in high register English without an interpreter. And as with services for blind people, many of the professions associated with the disability construction of deafness insist that the plight of the deaf child is truly desperate—so desperate, in fact, that some professionals propose implant surgery followed by rigorous and prolonged speech and hearing therapy. The successful use of a cochlear implant in everyday communication calls on a prior knowledge of spoken language (Staller et al., 1991) that only one child candidate in ten possesses (Allen et al., 1994); this has not, however, deterred professionals from recruiting among the other ninety percent; it is doubtful that the cochlear-implant industry would survive, certainly not flourish, if it sold its services and equipment only to the core clientele for the disability construction.

As with service providers for blind people, the troubled-persons industry associated with deafness seeks total conformity of the client to the underlying construction of deafness as disability. In the words of an audiology textbook: "One is not simply dealing with a handicapped child, one is dealing with a family with a handicap" (Tucker & Nolan, 1984 quoted in Gregory & Hartley, 1991, p. 87). The text goes on to state: "This concept of 'total child' being child plus hearing aids is one which parents may need time to come to terms with and fully accept." The profession wants to intervene in that family's life as early as possible and seeks to provide "a saturation service" (Tucker & Nolan, 1984 quoted in Gregory & Hartley, 1991, p. 97).

The criteria for disability, presented as objective, in fact conform to the interests of the profession (Oliver, 1990). Audiologic criteria decide which children will receive special education, so the audiologist must be consulted. In most countries of the world, audiology and special education are intimately related; the role of special education is to achieve as far as possible what audiology and otology could not do—minimize the child's disability. Writes one audiologist: "Education cannot cure deafness; it can only alleviate its worst effects" (Lynas, 1986, quoted in Gregory & Hartley, 1991, p. 155). Parents generally have little say about the right educational placement for their child; neither are there any functional tests of what the child can understand in different kinds of classrooms. Instead, audiologic criteria prevail, even if they have little predictive value. For example, the academic achievement scores of children classified as severely hearing-impaired are scarcely different from those of children classified as profoundly hearing impaired (Allen, 1986). Research has shown that some children categorized as profoundly hearing impaired can understand words and sentences whereas others do not even detect sound (Osberger et al., 1993). Likewise, Scott states that the official definition of blindness is "based upon a meaningless demarcation among those with severely impaired vision" (Scott, 1981, p. 42).

THE MAKING OF DEAF MEN

The family that has received "saturation services" from the deafness troubled-persons industry will participate in socializing the deaf child to adapt the child's needs to those of the industry. A recent handbook for parents with implanted children states: "Parents should accept a primary role in helping their child adjust to the implant. They must assume responsibility for maintaining the implant device, for ensuring that the child is wearing it properly, and assuring that the auditory speech stimulation occurs in both the home and school" (Tye-Murray, 1992, p. xvi). "The child should wear the implant during all waking hours" (Tye-Murray, 1992, p. 18). Ultimately, the child should see the implant as part of himself, like his ears or hands. The handbook recounts enthusiastically how one implanted schoolchild, told to draw a self portrait, included the speech processor and microphone/transmitter in great detail: "This self-portrait demonstrated the child's positive image of himself and the acceptance of his cochlear implant" (Tye-Murray, 1992, p. 20).

The construction of the deaf child as disabled is legitimized early on by the medical profession and later by the special education and welfare bureaucracy. When the child is sent to a special educational program and obliged to wear cumbersome hearing aids, his or her socialization into the role of disabled person is promoted. In face-to-face encounters with therapists and teachers the child learns to cooperate in promoting a view of himself or herself as disabled. Teachers label large numbers of these deaf children emotionally disturbed or learning disabled (Lane, 1992). Once labeled as "multiply handicapped" in this way, deaf children are treated differently—for example, placed in a less demanding academic program where they learn less, so the label is self-validating. In the end, the troubled-persons industry creates the disabled deaf person.

DEAF AS LINGUISTIC MINORITY

From the vantage point of Deaf culture, deafness is not a disability (Jones & Pullen, 1989). British Deaf leader Paddy Ladd put it this way: "We wish for the recognition of our right to exist as a linguistic minority group . . . Labeling us as disabled demonstrates a failure to understand that we are not disabled in any way within our own community" (Dant & Gregory, 1991, p. 14). U. S. Deaf scholar Tom Humphries concurs: "There is no room within the culture of Deaf people for an ideology that all Deaf people are deficient. It simple does not compute. There is no "handicap" to overcome . . . (Humphries, 1993, p. 14). American Deaf leader MJ Bienvenu asks: "Who benefits when we attempt to work in coalition with disability groups? . . . How can we fight for official recognition of ASL and allow ourselves as "communication disordered" at the same time?" And she concludes: "We are proud of our language, culture and heritage. Disabled we are not!" (Bienvenu, 1989, p. 13).

Nevertheless, many in the disability rights movement, and even some Deaf leaders, have joined professionals in promoting the disability construction of all deafness. To defend this construction, one leading disability advocate, Vic Finkelstein, has advanced the following argument based on the views of the people directly concerned: Minorities that have been discriminated against, like blacks, would refuse an operation to eliminate what sets them apart, but this is not true for disabled people: "every (!) disabled person would welcome such an operation" (*Finkelstein's exclamation point*). And, from this perspective, Deaf people, he maintains, "have more in common with other disability groups than they do with groups based upon race and gender" (Finkelstein, 1991, p. 265). However, in fact, American Deaf people are more like blacks in that most would refuse an operation to eliminate what sets them apart (as Dr. Rosen did on "Sixty Minutes"). One U.S. survey of Deaf adults asked if they would like an implant operation so they could hear; more than eight out of 10 declined (Evans, 1989). When the magazine *Deaf Life* queried its subscribers, 87 percent of respondents said that they did not consider themselves handicapped.

There are other indications that American Deaf culture simply does not have the ambivalence that, according to Abberley, is called for in disability: "Impairment must be identified as a bad thing, insofar as it is an undesirable consequence of a distorted social development, at the same time as it is held to be a positive attribute of the individual who is impaired" (Abberley, 1987, p. 9). American Deaf people (like their counterparts in many other nations) think cultural Deafness is a good thing and would like to see more of it. Expectant Deaf parents, like those in any other language minority, commonly hope to have Deaf children with whom they can share their language, culture and unique experiences. One Deaf mother from Los Angeles recounted to a researcher her reaction when she noticed that her baby did not react to Fourth of July fireworks: "I thought to myself, 'She must be deaf.' I wasn't disappointed; I thought, 'It will be all right. We are both deaf, so we will know what to do' (Becker, 1980, p. 55). Likewise an expectant Deaf mother in Boston told the *Globe*, "I want my daughters to be like me, to be deaf" (Saltus, 1989, p. 27). The Deaf community, writes Paddy Ladd, "regards the birth of each and every deaf child as a precious gift" (quoted in Oliver, 1989, p. 199). Deaf and hearing scholars expressed the same view in a 1991 report to the U.S. National Institutes of Health; research in genetics to improve deaf people's quality of life is certainly important, they said, but must not become, in the hands of hearing people, research on ways of reducing the deaf minority (Padden, 1990).

Finkelstein acknowledges that many Deaf people reject the label "disabled" but he attributes it to the desire of Deaf people to distance themselves from social discrimination. What is missing from the construction of deafness is what lies at the heart of the linguistic minority construction: Deaf culture. Since people with disabilities are themselves engaged in a struggle to change the construction of disability, they surely recognize that disabilities are not "lying there in the road" but are indeed socially constructed. Why is this not applied to Deaf people? Not surprisingly, deafness is constructed differently in Deaf cultures than it is in hearing cultures.

Advocates of the disability construction for all deaf people, use the term "deaf community" to refer to all people with significant hearing impairment, on the model of "the disability community." So the term seems to legitimate the acultural perspective on Deaf people. When Ladd (*supra*) and other advocates of the linguistic minority construction speak of the Deaf community, however, the term refers to a much smaller group with a distinct manual language, culture, and social organization.[1] It is instructive, as American Deaf leader Ben Bahan has suggested, to see how ASL speakers refer to their minority; one term can be glossed as DEAF-WORLD. The claim that one is in the DEAF-WORLD, or that someone else is, is not a claim about hearing status at all; it is an expression of that self-recognition or recognition of others that is defining for all ethnic collectivities (Johnson & Erting, 1989). It is predictive about social behavior (including attitudes, beliefs and values) and language, but not about hearing status. All degrees of hearing can be found among Deaf people (it is a matter of discussion whether some hearing people with Deaf parents are Deaf), and most people who are hearing-impaired are not members of the DEAF-WORLD.

In ASL the sign whose semantic field most overlaps that of the English "disability" can be glossed in English LIMP-BLIND-ETC. I have asked numerous informants to give me examples from that category: they have responded by citing (in literal translation) people in wheelchairs, blind people, mentally retarded people, and people with cerebral palsy, but no informant has ever listed DEAF and all reject it when asked. Another term in use in the Boston area (and elsewhere), which began as a fingerspelled borrowing from English, can be glossed D–A. My informants agree that Deaf is not D–A. The sign M–H–C (roughly, "multiply-handicapped') also has some currency. When I have asked Deaf people here for examples of M–H–C, DEAF-BLIND has never been listed, and when I propose it, it is rejected.

Other important differences between culturally Deaf people and people with disabilities come to light when we consider these groups' priorities. Among the preconditions for equal participation in society by disabled persons, the U.N. *Standard Rules* (1994) list medical care, rehabilitation, and support services such as personal assistance. "Personal assistance services are the new top of the agenda issue for the disability rights movement," one chronicler reports (Shapiro, 1993, p. 251). From my observation, Deaf people do not attach particular importance to medical care, not place any special value on rehabilitation or personal assistance services,[2] not have any particular concern with autonomy and independent living. Instead, the preconditions for Deaf participation are more like those of other language minorities: culturally Deaf people campaign for acceptance of their language and its broader use in the schools, the workplace, and in public events.

Integration, in the classroom, the workforce and the community, "has become a primary goal of today's disability movement" (Shapiro, 1993, p. 144). School integration is anathema to the DEAF-WORLD. Because most Deaf children have hearing parents, they can only acquire full language and socialization in specialized schools, in particular the prized network of residential schools; Deaf children are drowning in the mainstream (Lane, 1992). While advocates for people with disabilities recoil in horror at segregated institutions, evoking images of Willowbrook and worse, the Deaf alumni of residential schools return to their alma mater repeatedly over the years, contribute to their support, send their Deaf children to them, and vigorously protest the efforts of well-meaning but grievously ill-informed members of the disability rights movement to close those schools. These advocates fail to take account of language and culture and therefore of the difference between imposed and elective segregation. Where people with disabilities cherish independence, culturally Deaf people cherish interdependence. People with disabilities may gather for political action; Deaf people traditionally gather primarily for socializing. Deaf people marry Deaf people 90 percent of the time in the U.S. (Schein, 1989).

With the shift in the construction of disability has come an emphasis on the bonds that unite people with disabilities to the rest of society with whom they generally share not only culture but also ranges of capacities and incapacities (cf. Barton, 1993). "We try to make disability fixed and dichotomous," writes Zola, "but it is fluid and continuous" (Zola, 1993, p. 24). More than 20 percent of the noninstitutionalized population of the U.S. has a disability, we are told, and over 7.7 million Americans report that hearing is their primary functional limitation (Dowler & Hirsch, 1994). This universalizing view, according to which most people have some disability at least some of the time, is strikingly at odds with the DEAF-WORLD, small, tightly knit, with its own language and culture, sharply demarcated from the rest of society: there is no slippery slope between Deaf and hearing. "Deaf people are foreigners," wrote an early president of the National Association of the Deaf, "[living] among a people whose language they can never learn" (Hanson, cited in Van Cleve & Crouch, 1989, p. ix).

It is significant that the four student leaders who led the uprising known as the Gallaudet Revolution, were Deaf children of Deaf parents, deeply imbued with a sense of DEAF-WORLD, and natively fluent in ASL. One of them explained to USA Today the significance of the Revolution as it relates to the construction of deafness: "Hearing people sometimes call us handicapped. But most—maybe all deaf people—feel that we're more of an ethnic group because we speak a different language . . . We also have our own culture . . . There's more of an ethnic difference than a handicap difference between us and hearing people" (Hlibok, 1988, p. 11a). The new Deaf president of Gallaudet sought to explain the difference in the underlying construction in these terms: "More people realize now that deafness is a difference, not a deficiency" (Jordan, quoted in Gannon, 1989, p. 173).

So there is no reason to think that Paddy Ladd, Tom Humphries and MJ Bienvenu are being insincere when they claim that Deaf people are not disabled. Quite the contrary: since all are leaders of Deaf communities and are steeped in deaf culture, they advance the construction of deafness that arises from their culture. Mr. Finkelstein could have been tipped off to this very different construction by observing how various groups choose to be labeled: disability groups may find labels such as "disabled" or "motorically-impaired" or "visually handicapped" distasteful and reserve for themselves the right to call someone a "crip," but Deaf culture embraces the label "Deaf" and asks that everyone use it, as in The National Association of the Deaf and The World Federation of the Deaf.

It seems right to speak of "the Deaf" as we speak of "The French" or "The British." It is alien to Deaf culture on two counts to speak of its members as "people with hearing-impairment." First, it is the troubled-persons industry for deafness that invented and promoted the label in English "hearing-impaired" (Ross & Calvert, 1967; Wilson *et al.*, 1974; Castle, 1990). Second, the "people with" construction implies that the trait is incidental rather than defining, but one's culture is never an incidental trait. It seems to be an error in ordinary language to say, "I happen to be Hispanic," or "I happen to be Deaf"; who would you be, after all, if you were you and yet not Hispanic, or not Deaf? But it is acceptable to say, "I happen to have a spinal cord injury."

Deaf cultures do not exist in a vacuum. Deaf Americans embrace many cultural values, attitudes, beliefs and behaviors that are part of the larger American culture and, in some instances, that are part of ethnic minority cultures such as African-American, Hispanic-American, etc. Because hearing people have obliged Deaf people to interact with the larger hearing society in terms of a disability model, that model has left its mark on Deaf culture. In particular, Deaf people frequently have found themselves recipients of unwanted special services provided by hearing people. "In terms of its economic, political and social relations to hearing society, the Deaf minority can be viewed as a colony" (Markowicz & Woodward, 1978, p. 33). As with colonized peoples, some Deaf people have internalized the "other's" (disability) construction of them alongside their own cultural construction (Lane, 1992). For example, they may be active in their Deaf club and yet denigrate skilled use of ASL as "low sign"; "high sign" is a contact variety of ASL that is closer to English-language word order. The Deaf person who uses a variety of ASL marked as English frequently has greater access to wider resources such as education and employment. Knowing when to use which variety is an important part of being Deaf (Johnson & Erting, 1989). Granted that culturally Deaf people must take account of the disability model of deafness, that they sometimes internalize it, and that it leaves its mark on their culture, all this does not legitimize that model—any more than granting that African-Americans had to take account of the construction of the slave as property, sometimes internalized that construction, and found their culture marked by it legitimizes that construction of their ethnic group.

Neither culturally Deaf people nor people with disabilities are a homogeneous group.[3] Many of the differences between the two that I have cited will not apply to particular subgroups or individuals; nevertheless, it should be clear that cultural Deafness involves a constellation of traits quite different from those of any disability group. Faced with these salient differences, those who would argue that Deaf people are "really" disabled, sometimes resort instead to arguing that they are "really not" like linguistic minorities (Fishman, 1982). Certainly there are differences. For example, Deaf people cannot learn English as a second language as easily as other minorities. Second and third generation Deaf children find learning English no easier than their forbears, but second and third generation immigrants to the U. S. frequently learn English before entering school. The language of the DEAF-WORLD is not usually passed on from generation to generation; instead, it is commonly transmitted by peers or associates. Normally, Deaf people are not proficient in this native language until they reach school age. Deaf people are more scattered geographically than many linguistic minorities. The availability of interpreters is even more vital for Deaf people than for many other linguistic minorities because there are so few Deaf lawyers, doctors and accountants, etc. Few Deaf people are in high-status public positions in our society (in contrast with, say, Hispanics), and this has hindered the legitimation of ASL use (Kyle, 1990, 1991; Parratt & Tipping, 1991). However, many, perhaps all, linguistic minorities have significant features that differentiate them: Members of the Chinese-American community are increasingly marrying outside their linguistic minority but this is rare for ASL speakers. Many Native American languages are dying out or have disappeared; this is not true of ASL which is unlikely ever to die out. Spanish-speaking Americans are so diverse a group that it may not be appropriate to speak of the Hispanic community in the U. S. (Wright, 1994). Neither the newer strategy of citing what is special about the ASL-speaking minority nor the older one of minimizing ASL itself hold much promise of discrediting the construction of deafness as linguistic minority.

It is undeniable that culturally Deaf people have great common cause with people with disabilities. Both pay the price of social stigma. Both struggle with the troubled-persons industries for control of their destiny. Both endeavor to promote their construction of their identity in competition with the interested (and generally better funded) efforts of professionals to promote *their* constructions. And Deaf people have special reasons for solidarity with people with hearing impairments; their combined numbers have created services, commissions and laws that the DEAF-WORLD alone probably could not have achieved. Solidarity, yes, but when culturally Deaf people allow their special identity to be subsumed under the construct of disability they set themselves up for wrong solutions and bitter disappointments.

It is because disability advocates think of Deaf children as disabled that they want to close the special schools and absurdly plunge Deaf children into hearing classrooms in a totally exclusionary program called inclusion. It is because government is allowed to proceed with a disability construction of cultural Deafness that the U. S. Office of Bilingual Education and Minority Language Affairs has refused for decades to provide special resources for schools with large numbers of ASL-using children although the law requires it to do so for children using any other non-English language. It is because of the disability construction that court rulings requiring that children who do not speak English receive instruction initially in their best language have not been applied to ASL-using children. It is because of the disability construction that the teachers most able to communicate with Britain's Deaf children are excluded from the profession on the pretext that they have a disqualifying disability. It is because lawmakers have been encouraged to believe by some disability advocates and prominent deaf figures that Deaf people are disabled that, in response to the Gallaudet Revolution, the U. S. Congress passed a law, not recognizing ASL or the DEAF-WORLD as a minority, but a law establishing another institute of *health*, The

National Institute on Deafness and Other Communications Disorders [sic], operated by the deafness troubled persons industry, and sponsoring research to reduce hereditary deafness. It is because of the disability construction that organizations *for* the Deaf (e.g., the Royal National Institute for the Deaf) are vastly better funded by government that organizations *of* the Deaf (e.g., the British Deaf Association).

One would think that people with disabilities might be the first to grasp and sympathize with the claims of Deaf people that they are victims of a mistaken identity. People with disabilities should no more resist the self-construction of culturally Deaf people, than Deaf people should subscribe to a view of people with disabilities as tragic victims of an inherent flaw.

CHANGING TO THE LINGUISTIC MINORITY CONSTRUCTION

Suppose our society were generally to adopt a disability construction of deafness for most late-deafened children and adults and a linguistic minority construction of Deaf people for most others, how would things change? The admirable Open University course, *Issues in Deafness* (1991) prompted these speculations.

(1) Changing the construction changes the legitimate authority concerning the social problem. In many areas, such as schooling, the authority would become Deaf adults, linguists and sociologists, among others. There would be many more service providers from the minority: Deaf teachers, foster and adoptive parents, information officers, social workers, advocates. Non-Deaf service providers would be expected to know the language, history, and culture of the Deaf linguistic minority.

(2) Changing the construction changes how behavior is construed. Deaf people would be expected to use ASL (in the U.S.) and to have interpreters available; poor speech would be seen as inappropriate.

(3) Changing the construction may change the legal status of the social problem group. Most Deaf people would no longer claim disability benefits or services under the present legislation for disabled people. The services to which the Deaf linguistic minority has a right in order to obtain equal treatment under the law would be provided by other legislation and bureaucracies. Deaf people would receive greater protection against employment discrimination under civil rights laws and rulings. Where there are special provisions to assist the education of linguistic minority children, Deaf children would be eligible.

(4) Changing the construction changes the arena where identification and labeling take place. In the disability construction, deafness is medicalized and labeled in the audiologist's clinic. In the construction as linguistic minority, deafness is viewed as a social variety and would be labeled in the peer group.

(5) Changing the construction changes the kinds of intervention. The Deaf child would not be operated on for deafness but brought together with other Deaf children and adults. The disability construction orients hearing parents to the question, what can be done to mitigate my child's impairment? The linguistic minority construction presents them with the challenge of insuring that their child has language and role models from the minority (Hawcroft, 1991).

OBSTACLES TO CHANGE

The obstacles to replacing a disability construction of deafness for much of the concerned population with a linguistic minority construction are daunting. In the first place, people who have little familiarity with deafness find the disability construction self-evident and the minority construction elusive. As I argue in *The Mask of Benevolence* (Lane, 1992), hearing people led to reflect on deafness generally begin by imagining themselves without hearing—which is, of course, to have a disability but not to be Deaf. Legislators can easily grasp the disability construction, not so the linguistic minority construction. The same tendency to uncritically accept the disability model led *Sixty Minutes* to feature a child from among the nine percent of childhood implant candidates who were deafened after learning English rather than from the 91 percent who do not identify with the English-speaking majority (Allen *et al.*, 1994). Not only did the interviewer find the disability construction of deafness easier to grasp but no doubt the producers thought heir millions of viewers would do likewise. Social problems are a favorite theme of the media but they are almost always presented as private troubles—deafness is no exception—because it makes for more entertaining viewing.

The troubled-persons industry associated with deafness—the "audist establishment" (Lane, 1992)—vigorously resists efforts to replace their construction of deafness. Audist policy is that ASL is a kind of primitive prosthesis, a way around the communication impasse caused by deaf peoples' disability. The audists control teacher training programs, university research facilities, the process of peer review for federal grant monies, the presentations made at professional meetings, and publications in professional journals; they control promotion and through promotion, salary. They have privileged access to the media and to lawmaking bodies when deafness is at issue. Although they lack the credibility of Deaf people themselves, they have expert credentials and they are fluent in speaking and writing English so law and policy makers and the media find it easier to consult them.

When a troubled-persons industry recasts social problems as private troubles it can treat, it is protecting its construction by removing the appearance of a social issue on which there might be political disagreement. The World Health Organization, for example, has medicalized and individualized what is social; services are based on an individualized view of disability and are designed by professionals in the disability industry (Oliver, 1991). The U. S. National Institute on Deafness and Other Communications Disorders proclaims in its very title the disability construction of deafness that it seeks to promote. The American Speech-Language Hearing Association, for example, has the power of accrediting graduate programs for training professionals who work with Deaf people; a program that deviated too far from the disability construction could lose its accreditation; without accreditation its students would not be certified; without the promise of certification, no one would enter the training program.

Some of the gravest obstacles to broader acceptance of the linguistic minority model come from members of the minority itself. Many members of the minority were socialized in part by professionals (and parents) to adopt a disabled role. Some Deaf people openly embrace the disability construction and thus undercut the efforts of other Deaf people to discredit it. Worse yet, many opportunities are provided to Deaf people (e.g., access to interpreters) on the condition that they adopt the alien disability construction. This double blind—accept our construction of your life or give up your access to equal citizenship—is a powerful form of oppression. Thus, many members of the DEAF-WORLD endorsed the Americans with Disabilities Act with its provisions for deaf people, all the while believing they are not disabled but lending credence to the claim that they are. In a related double blind, Deaf adults who want to become part of the professions serving Deaf people, find that they must subscribe to audist views of rehabilitation, special education, etc.

Exponents of the linguistic minority construction are at a further disadvantage because there is little built-in cultural transmission of their beliefs. The most persuasive advocates for Deaf children, their parents, must be taught generation after generation the counter-intuitive linguistic minority construction because most are neither Deaf themselves nor did they have Deaf parents.

A further obstacle arising within the DEAF-WORLD to promoting the linguistic minority construction concerns, ironically, the form that much Deaf political activism takes. Ever since the first congresses of Deaf people organized in response to the Congress of Milan in 1880, Deaf leaders have appeared before friendly Deaf audiences to express their outrage—to preach to the converted. Written documents—position papers, articles and proceedings—have similarly been addressed to and read by primarily the DEAF-WORLD. It is entirely natural to prefer audiences with whom one shares language and culture, the more so as Deaf people have rarely been permitted to address audiences comprised of hearing professionals. Admittedly, preaching to the converted has value—it may evoke fresh ideas and it builds solidarity and commitment. Advocates of the disability construction do the same; childhood implant conferences, for example, rigorously exclude the voices of the cautious or frankly opposed.

I hope it may be allowed, however, to someone who has been invited to address numerous Deaf audiences and is exasperated by the slow pace of reform to point out that too much of this is an obstacle to true reform because it requires effort, permits the illusion that significant action has been taken, and yet changes little since Deaf people themselves are not responsible for the spread of the disability construction and have little direct power to change its range of application. What part of the battle is won when a Deaf leader receives a standing ovation from a Deaf audience? In the tradition of Deaf activism during the International Congress on the Education of the Deaf in Manchester in 1985, and during the Gallaudet Revolution, the past year have seen a striking increase in Europe of Deaf groups turning outward and presenting their views to hearing people and the media uninvited, particularly in opposition to cochlear implant surgery on Deaf children (Lane, 1994).

PRODUCING CHANGE

Despite all the obstacles, there are powerful social forces to assist the efforts of the DEAF-WORLD to promote the linguistic minority construction. The body of knowledge developed in linguistics, history, sociology, and anthropology (to mention just four disciplines) concerning Deaf communities has influenced Deaf leadership, bureaucratic decision-making, and legislation. The civil rights movement has given great impetus to the belief that minorities should define themselves and that minority leaders should have a significant say in the conduct of minority affairs. Moreover, the failure of the present predominant disability construction to deliver more able deaf children is a source of professional and public embarrassment and promotes change. Then, too, Deaf children of Deaf parents are frequently insulated against the disability construction to a degree by their early language and cultural acquisition within the DEAF-WORLD. These native ASL-users have important allies in the DEAF-WORLD, among hearing children of Deaf parents, and among disaffected hearing professionals. The Gallaudet Revolution did not change the disability construction on a large scale but it led to inroads against it. Growing numbers of schools, for example, are turning to the linguistic minority construction to guide their planning, curricula, teacher selection and training.

Numerous organizations have committed extensive effort and money to promoting the disability construction. What can the national associations of the Deaf do to promote the linguistic minority construction? Publications like the British Deaf Association *News* or the National Association of the Deaf *Deaf American* are an important step because they provide a forum for national political discussion. However, the discussion has lacked focus. In addition to a forum, such associations need an explicit political agenda and a plan for implementing it. Such an agenda might include, illustratively, building a greater awareness of the difference between hearing-impairment and cultural Deafness; greater acceptance of the national sign language; removal or reduction of language barriers; improving culturally sensitive health care. Nowhere I know of are such agendas made explicit—given priorities, implementation, a time plan. If these were published they could provide the needed focus for the debate. Commentary on the agenda and plan would be invited as well as rebuttals to the commentaries in subsequent issues. Such agendas, plans and debates are buttressed by scholarship. An important resource to develop is a graduate program in public administration or political science focused on the DEAF-WORLD and the promotion of the linguistic minority construction.

NOTES

I acknowledge gratefully helpful discussions with Ben Bahan, and Robert Hoffmeister, Boston University; Alma Bournazian, Northeastern University; Robert E. Johnson, Gallaudet University; Osamu Nagase, United Nations Program on Disability; MJ Bienvenu, the Bicultural Center; and helpful criticism from two unidentified journal reviewers.

1. Padden (1980) makes a distinction between a deaf community, a group of Deaf and hearing individuals who work to achieve certain goals, and a Deaf culture, to which Deaf members of that community belong.

2. In an effort to retain the disability construction of deafness, it has been suggested that sign language interpreters should be viewed as personal assistants. However, the services of these highly trained professionals are frequently not personal but provided to large audiences and they "assist" hearing people as well as, and at the same time as, Deaf people. Nor is interpreting between any other two languages (for example, at the United Nations) considered personal assistance.

3. I am not contending that there is a unitary homogenous DEAF-WORLD. My claims about Deaf culture are best taken as hypotheses for further verification, all the more as I am not a member of the DEAF-WORLD. My means of arriving at cultural principles are the usual ones for an outsider: encounters, ASL language and literature (including stories, legends, anecdotes, poetry, plays, humor, rituals, sign play), magazines and newspaper stories, films, histories, informants, scholarly studies, and the search for principles of coherence. See Stokoe (1994) and Kyle (1990).

REFERENCES

Albrecht, G. L. (1992) *The Disability Business: Rehabilitation in America* (Newbury Park CA, Sage).

Aberley, P. (1987) The concept of oppression and the development of a social theory of disability, *Disability, Handicap and Society*, 2, pp. 5–19.

Allen, T. E. (1986) Patterns of academic achievement among hearing-impaired students: 1974 and 1983, in: A. N. Schildroth & M. A. Karchmer (Eds.) *Deaf Children in America* (San Diego, College-Hill).

Allen, T. E., Rawlings, B. W. & Remington, E. (1994) Demographic and audiologic profiles of deaf children in Texas with cochlear implants, *American Annals of the Deaf*, 138, pp. 260–266.

Barton, L. (1993) The struggle for citizenship: the case of disabled people, *Disability, Handicap and Society*, 8, pp. 235–248.

Becker, G. (1980) *Growing Old in Silence* (Berkeley, University of California Press).

Bienvenu, M. J. (1989) Disability, *The Bicultural Center News*, 13 (April), p. 1.

Braille Monitor (1973) NAC—unfair to the blind, *Braille Monitor*, 2, pp. 127–128.

Braille Monitor (1989) Blind workers claim wages exploitative, *Braille Monitor*, 6, p. 322.

Burek, D. M. (Ed.) (1993) *Encyclopedia of Associations* (Detroit, Gale Research).

Castle, D. (1990) Employment bridges cultures, *Deaf American*, 40, pp. 19–21.

Conrad, P. & Schneider, J. (1980) *Deviance and Medicalization: from Badness to Sickness* (Columbia, OH, Merrill).

Cant, T. & Gregory, S. (1991) Unit 8. The social construction of deafness, in: Open University (Eds.) *Issues in Deafness* (Milton Keynes, Open University).

Dowler, D. L. & Hirsh, A. (1994) Accommodations in the workplace for people who are deaf or hard of hearing, *Technology and Disability*, 3, pp. 15–25.

Evans, J. W. (1989) Thoughts on the psychosocial implications of cochlear implantation in children, in: E. Owens & D. Kessler (Eds.) *Cochlear Implants in Young Deaf Children* (Boston, Little, Brown).

Finkelstein, V. (1991) 'We' are not disabled, 'you' are, in: S. Gregory & G. M. Hartley (Eds.) *Constructing Deafness* (London, Pinter).

Fishman, J. (1982) A critique of six papers on the socialization of the deaf child, in: J. B. Christiansen (Ed.) *Conference highlights: National Research Conference on the Social Aspects of Deafness*, pp. 6–20 (Washington, DC, Gallaudet College).

Gannon, J. (1989) *The Week the World Heard Gallaudet* (Washington, DC, Gallaudet University Press).

Gregory, S. & Hartley, G. M. (Eds.) (1991) *Constructing Deafness* (London, Pinter).

Gusfield, J. (1982) Deviance in the welfare state: the alcoholism profession and the entitlements of stigma, in: M. Lewis (Ed.) *Research in Social Problems and Public Policy*, Vol. 2 (Greenwich, CT, JAI press).

Gusfield, J. (1984) On the side: practical action and social constructivism in social problems theory, in: J. Schneider & J. Kitsuse (Eds.) *Studies in the Sociology of Social Problems* (Rutgers, NJ, Ablex).

Gusfield, J. (1989) Constructing the ownership of social problems: fun and profit in the welfare state, *Social Problems*, 36, pp. 431–441.

Hawcroft, L. (1991) Block 2, unit 7. Whose welfare?, in: Open University (Eds.) *Issues in Deafness* (Milton Keynes, Open University).

Hevey, D. (1993) From self-love to the picket line: strategies for change in disability representation, *Disability, Handicap and Society*, 8, pp. 423–430.

Hlibok, G. (1988) Quoted in *USA Today*, 15 March, p. 11a.

Humphries, T. (1993) Deaf culture and cultures, in: K. M. Christensen & G. L. Delgado (Eds.) *Multicultural Issues in Deafness* (White Plains, NY, Longman).

Jernigan, K. (1973) Partial victory in the NAC battle—and the beat goes on, *Braille Monitor*, January, pp. 1–3.

Johnson, R. E. & Erting, C. (1989) Ethnicity and socialization in a classroom for deaf children, in: C. Lucas (Ed.) *The sociolinguistics of the Deaf Community*, pp. 41–84 (New York, Academic Press).

Johnson, R. E. Liddell, S. K. & Erting, C J. (1989) Unlocking the curriculum: principles for achieving access in deaf education, *Gallaudet Research Institute Working Papers*, 89–3.

Jones, L. & Pullen, G. (1989) 'Inside we are all equal': a European social policy survey of people who are deaf, in: L. Barton (Ed.) *Disability and Dependency* (Bristol, PA, Taylor & Francis/Falmer Press).

Kyle, J. (1990) The Deaf community: culture, custom and tradition, in: S. Prillwitz & T. Vollhaber (Eds.) *Sign Language Research and Application* (Hamburg, Signum).

Kyle, J. (1991) Deaf people and minority groups in the UK, in: S. Gregory & G. M. Hartley (Eds.) *Constructing Deafness* (London, Pinter).

Lane, H. (1984) *When the Mind Hears: a history of the deaf* (New York, Random House).

Lane, H. (1992) *The Mask of Benevolence: disabling the deaf community* (New York, Alfred Knopf).

Lane, H. (1994) The cochlear implant controversy, *World Federation of the Deaf News*, 2–3, pp. 22–28.

Lynas, W. (1986) *Integrating the Handicapped into Ordinary Schools: a study of hearing-impaired pupils* (London, Croom Helm).

Markowicz, H. & Woodward, J. (1978) Language and the maintenance of ethnic boundaries in the deaf community, *Communication and Cognition*, 11, pp. 29–38.

Oliver, M. (1989) Disability and dependency: a creation of industrial societies, in: L. Barton (Ed.) *Disability and Dependency*, pp. 6–22 (Bristol, PA, Taylor & Francis/Falmer Press).

Oliver, M. (1990) *The Politics of Disablement* (New York, St. Martin's Press).

Oliver, M. (1991) Multispecialist and multidisciplinary—a recipe for confusion? 'Too many cooks spoil the broth', *Disability, Handicap & Society*, 6, pp. 65–68.

Olson, C. (1977) Blindness can be reduced to an inconvenience, *Journal of Visual Impairment and Blindness*, 11, pp. 408–409.

Olson, C. (1981) Paper barriers, *Journal of Visual Impairment and Blindness*, 15, pp. 337–339.

Open University (1991) *Issues in Deafness* (Milton Keynes, Open University).

Osberger, M. J., Maso, M. & Sam, L. K. (1993) Speech intelligibility of children with cochlear implants, tactile aids, or hearing aids, *Journal of Speech and Hearing Research*, 36, pp. 186–203.

Padden, C. (1980) The deaf community and the culture of deaf people, in: C. Baker & R. Battison (Eds.) *Sign Language and the Deaf Community: essays in honor of William C. Stokoe*, pp. 89–103 (Silver Spring, MD, National Association of the Deaf).

Padden, C. (Ed.) (1990) *Report of the Working Group on Deaf Community Concerns* (Bethesda, MD, National Institute on Deafness and Other Communication Disorders).

Parratt, D. & Tipping, B. (1991) The state, social work and deafness, in: S. Gregory & G. M. Hartley (Eds.) *Constructing Deafness* (London, Pinter).

Ross, M. & Calvert, D. R. (1967) Semantics of deafness, *Volta Review*, 69, pp. 644–649.

Saltus, R. (1989) Returning to the world of sound, *Boston Globe*, 10 July, pp. 27, 29.

Schein, J. D. (1989) *At Home Among Strangers* (Washington, DC, Gallaudet University Press).

Schneider, J. & Kitsuse, J. (Eds.) (1989) *Studies in the Sociology of Social Problems* (Rutgers, NJ, Ablex).

Scott, R. A. (1981) *The Making of Blind Men* (New Brunswick, NJ, Transaction).

Shapiro, J. P. (1993) *No Pity: people with disabilities forging a new Civil Rights Movement* (New York: Times Books).

Sixty Minutes (1992) Caitlin's story, 8 November.

Staller, S. S., Better, A. L., Brimacombe, J. A., Mecklenburg, D. J. & Arndt, P. (1991) Pediatric performance with the Nucleus 22-channel cochlear implant system, *American Journal of Otology*, 12 (Suppl.), pp. 126–136.

Stokos, W. (1994) An SLS print symposium [on culture]: an introduction, *Sign Language Studies*, 83, pp. 97–102.

Tucker, I. & Nolan, M. (1984) *Educational Audiology* (London, Croom Helm).

Tye-Murray, N. (1992) *Cochlear Implants and Children: a handbook for parents, teachers and speech professionals* (Washington, DC, A. G. Bell Association).

United Nations (1994) *The Standard Rules on the Equalization of Opportunities for Persons with Disabilities* (New York, United Nations).

Van Cleve, J. (Ed.) (1987) *The Gallaudet Encyclopedia of Deaf People and Deafness* (New York, McGraw-Hill).

Vaughan, C. E. (1991) The social basis of conflict between blind people and agents of rehabilitation, *Disability, Handicap & Society*, 6, pp. 203–217.

Wilson, G. B., Ross, M. & Calvert, D. R. (1974) An experimental study of the semantics of deafness, *Volta Review*, 76, pp. 408–414.

Wright, L. (1994) Annals of politics: one drop of blood, *The New Yorker*, 25 July, pp. 46–55.

Zola, I. K. (1993) Disability statistics, what we count and what it tells us, *Journal of Disability Policy Studies*, 4, pp. 9–39.

8

Advertising the Acceptably Employable Image

Disability and Capitalism

HARLAN HAHN

In recent years, there has been a growing interest in the development of alternative approaches to the analysis of disability policy. Much of this trend can be attributed to a significant shift in the definition of disability from a *medical* orientation, which focuses on functional impairments, and an *economic* understanding, which concentrates on vocational limitations, to a *socio-political* perspective, which regards disability as a product of the interaction between individuals and the environment (Hahn, 1982, 1985b). As a result, a new "minority-group" model has arisen to challenge the "functional-limitations" paradigm that has traditionally guided research on disability (Gliedman and Roth, 1980; Hahn, 1985a).

Perhaps even more relevant to this study is the emergence of efforts to relate disability to dominant modes of production. Clearly the process of industrialization under capitalism is a major factor that has contributed to the prevalence of disability (Krause, 1976; Krause, 1982). Moreover, a review by Oliver (1984) represents an important attempt to develop a materialist interpretations of disability. Central to this approach is what Marx termed the "industrial reserve army." As Gough (1979: 25–26) has noted, "The industrial reserve army consists of not only the unemployed but also marginal groups like the disabled, the seasonally employed, those displaced from previous modes of production (like peasants), immigrants from other countries, and . . . housewives." The presence of these groups has tended to defuse the revolutionary potential of the dynamics of a capitalist system by exerting downward pressure on wages, thereby permitting employers to maintain high rates of profit. In addition, people with disabilities and other exploited populations often are compelled to perform routine jobs that are neither readily mechanized nor regarded by capitalists as justifying the payment of prevailing wages. Finally, they are available to fill a void in the labor force in periods of relative prosperity or in war-time when the absence of nondisabled men creates an exceptional demand for other workers.

The concept of the "industrial reserve army" seems to provide an explanation for the depressed economic position of men and women with disabilities. Available estimates indicate that approximately two-thirds of disabled persons in most industrialized nations are unemployed, a level that exceeds the unemployment rate among other deprived and disadvantaged groups (Hahn, 1984). Disabled workers also have been the victims of exploitation in so-called "sheltered workshops" that violate organizational purposes by retaining their most productive employees at sub-standard wages rather than releasing them to the competitive labor market (Nelson, 1971). Furthermore, in World War II, physical exams and other conditions of employment were waived by many corporations to open up jobs for disabled persons, and other members of the industrial reserve, who compiled favorable records of productivity and work performance (Hahn, 1984). During the war, the unemployment rate among disabled adults temporarily declined, only to rise again when these job requirements were reinstated to permit the hiring of returning veterans. Ironically, the issue of providing benefits for disabled citizens, which had never been resolved during the New Deal, finally was settled after the war by the adoption of a definition that equated disability with unemployability, or an inability to engage in "substantial gainful activity" (Erlanger and Roth, 1985). Other research has demonstrated that applications for—and the approval of—disability benefits tend to increase in regions of the country experiencing unemployment and economic adversity (Howards, Brehm, and Nagi, 1980). In addition, Johnson and Lambrinos (1985) found that more than one-third of the wage differential of visibly disabled men and women could be attributed to discrimination.

The examination of disability and the industrial system indicates that the unemployment rate of disabled adults may be traced to broad economic forces rather than to individual impairments and that the existence of persons with disabilities as well as other marginal groups reduces pressures which might otherwise disrupt the operation of capitalism. But these investigations could be pursued without questioning prevalent suppositions about the alleged correlation between disability and a lack of productivity that have formed a keystone of the "functional-limitations" paradigm. There seems to be little doubt that disability has been used as a device for screening out potential employees on application forms and that employers often cannot accurately evaluate the capabilities of disabled job-seekers. And yet an economic interpretation of the oppression of women and men with disabilities might be developed within the context of the "functional-limitations" approach by ascribing their unemployment primarily to bodily deficiencies and the supposedly restricted range of occupational opportunities available to them. Such an analysis can be conducted almost as if discrimination does not occur. While some may contend that legal efforts to end job bias merely control the behavior of capitalists to protect them from severe conflicts that might otherwise result from direct assaults on racism, sexism, and similar forms of inequality in the structure of society, this argument fails to take adequate consideration of the imperative need for extensive changes in the social, institutional, and built environment that are essential to improve the status of disabled people. The major tenets of the "minority-group" model for disability and of the socio-political definition upon which it is based would seem to be indispensable components of further studies of disability and dominant modes of production.

The basic thrust of the "minority-group" model of disability asserts that disabled men and women have been subjected to the same forms of prejudice, discrimination, and segregation imposed upon other oppressed groups which are differentiated from the remainder of the population on the basis of characteristics such as race or ethnicity, gender, and aging. Disabled persons not only have exhibited one of the highest rates of unemployment, welfare dependency, and poverty in the United States; but they also have experienced a more pervasive form of segregation in education, housing, transportation, and public accommodations than the most rigid policies of apartheid enacted by racist governments (Hahn, 1985b). As prior analyses have demonstrated, there is also no intrinsic incompatibility between theories of prejudice or inter-group relations and economic interpretations of oppression (Cox, 1948; Ehrlich, 1973; Hraba, 1979; Banton, 1983). While many of these theories have been strongly influenced by American concepts of pluralism and assimilation, others have recognized that discrimination fundamentally stems from the dynamics of production and the interactions that necessarily emanate from this process. In fact, one analyst has concluded that "economic forces" are "the source of ethnicity itself" (Muga, 1984: 18). The analogy between the experience of persons with disabilities and several theories of the economic origins of discrimination seem to be relatively direct. Clearly, for example, the treatment of disabled workers in many industries and workshops has displayed evidence not only of the exploitation of labor as a dehumanized commodity but also of the tendency by capitalists to use physical characteristics as a basis for creating a cheap and docile group of workers as postulated by the "split labor market theory" (Bonacich, 1979).

There are, however, some differences between the economic experience of people with disabilities and the exploitation of other oppressed minorities. Unlike most disadvantaged groups, disabled adults never had been a significant threat to the jobs of nondisabled workers. To the extent that disabled persons had any legitimized role in an inhospitable environment prior to the advent of industrialization, they were beggars rather than competitive members of the labor force (Stone, 1984). Only in extraordinary circumstances, such as World War II, were disabled men and women allowed to assume jobs in a way that might provoke the economic anxieties of the nondisabled majority.

In addition, while other economically deprived groups possess identifiable characteristics that were once erroneously interpreted as indications of biological inferiority, the functional impairments of disabled individuals often have been viewed as obvious evidence of heir unequal or noncompetitive position. Undoubtedly, the task of unraveling the effects of bodily limitations and prejudice or discrimination in an environment that has not been adapted to the needs or interest of disabled people is a complex undertaking (Hahn, 1985a). And yet this endeavor would be incomplete without an exercise of human imagination providing the vision of an environment—includign businesses and worksites—modified to accommodate citizens with disabilities. The importance of this perspective is indicated by one version of the "minority-group" model of disability which a) begins with the examination of attitudes—instead of impairments—revealing evidence of widespread public aversion and rejection of disabled persons, b) then points out that all aspects of the environment are molded by public policy, and c) concludes with the democratic notion that policies are a reflection of pervasive attitudes and values (Hahn, 1986). From this vantage point, policies shaping the environment that have had a disadvantageous and discriminatory impact on men and women with disabilities cannot be excused as accidental or coincidental. In an environment designed to meet the needs of disabled individuals, traditional assumptions about their capacities and productivity embedded in the "functional-limitations" model of disability probably could no longer be sustained.

The fact that primacy in the "minority-group" paradigm is assigned to the attitudes of perceptions of the nondisabled public rather than to the functional limitations of disabled individuals has important implications for research on the economic sources of prejudice and discrimination. This emphasis is consistent with the view that the major problems associated with disability can be found in the external environment and not in the defects of deficiencies of disabled persons themselves. In addition, this orientation indicates that people with disabilities are subjected to forms of prejudice and segregation similar to the type imposed upon other oppressed groups which have been differentiated from the dominant majority primarily on the basis of physical characteristics that allow this sort of discrimination to occur. Wagley (1968), for example, in his study of Europeans and non-Europeans in the Western Hemisphere during the sixteenth through the nineteenth centuries, noted that the main differences between these groups were founded on ancestry, socio-cultural status, and appearance. Each of these distinctions gradually became less controllable. But the salience and importance of identifiable physical dissimilarities cannot be overlooked, especially perhaps for a group—such as disabled citizens—that is not defined by genealogy, that lacks a well-described cultural tradition, and that includes members in all social classes. In the absence of physical clues that permit the separate treatment of human beings, of course, discrimination against any group would be impossible. Thus efforts to discover the economic origins of prejudice toward women and men with disabilities need to include consideration of the effects of permanence and visibility or labeling (Hahn, 1984). Disabled individuals become the objects of employment and other kinds of discrimination as a result of enduring attitudes that are either immediately obvious or that become known through a process which compels disclosure. As a result, Hahn (1984: 14) has devised a "disability continuum" that posts a correlation between the visibility of disabilities and the amount of discrimination which they might elicit in employment or other areas of society. Although resources have not yet been made available to investigate this hypothesis rigorously, the significance of perceptible physical or behavioral differences between disabled and nondisabled segments of the population cannot be discounted in the study of prejudice and discrimination.

The influences that have relegated people with disabilities to a significant role in the "industrial reserve army" probably can be traced by historical sources that antedate the rise of capitalism. Even a cursory review of attitudes toward disabled persons reveals extensive evidence of antipathy and aversion in earlier eras (Oberman, 1965). In many respects, predominate feelings about disability have seemed to parallel the persistent legacy of perceptions of aliens in distance lands who were imagined as possessing unusual appearances (Renard, 1984). And yet, in searching for a significant part of the explanation for prejudice and discrimination against men and women with disabilities, researchers need look no further than major social and economic trends in capitalist nations such as the United States during the nineteenth and twentieth centuries. In numerous subtle ways, the agents of powerful industrialists in this era implicitly promoted pervasive messages about acceptable forms of human appearance that encouraged consumers to strive relentlessly to approximate these images. Fueled by the quest for expanded markets and higher profits, capitalists were responsible for promulgating a rigorous set of standards concerning physical characteristics that indirectly resulted in the exclusion of oppressed groups from many areas of community life. Although persons with visible physical or other disabilities probably were not significantly affected by these developments, commercial imagery of approved bodily attributes also has had a disadvantageous impact on the social and economic opportunities available to others with personal traits that differ from the norms of the dominant majority. This paper argues that these influences have had an important effect upon entrance to the labor force as well as admission to other social activities. Moreover, as further technological advances in the twentieth century increased the pervasiveness of visual symbols of an ideal appearance, the social and economic power of these images was constantly reinforced by the mass media. Hence, a major source of the historical forces that prevented disabled persons and other oppressed groups from assuming a significant role in the labor market can be found in the dynamics of capitalism itself. While these trends may have been based on widespread fears and prejudices that existed previously, much of their strength and effectiveness in producing circumstances that were especially disadvantageous to disabled people resulted from processes that seemed to be dictated by the logic of a capitalistic economic system.

The purpose of this essay, therefore, is to examine historical patterns in the dynamics of capitalism that contributed to discrimination against people with disabilities by promulgating mass imagery that promoted the exclusion of disabled adults from the labor force and that consigned them to a subordinate position in the social structure. Critical to this investigation is an assessment of the rise of a consumer economy, the role of advertising in promoting images of physical appearance that may have had a major impact on entrance to the labor force as well as other areas of social activity, and the continuous reinforcement of these images by the mass media.

HISTORICAL TRENDS IN THE DYNAMICS OF CAPITALISM

The conditions of daily life that prevailed in western societies before the advent of industrialization might appear to be so different that modern observers have difficulty imagining them. Prior to the nineteenth century, most everyday goods were hand made rather than purchased. The preponderant masses of people generally dressed in the same type of clothing that had been worn for centuries. Home furnishings were simple and individually constructed. In a predominately agrarian society, the family was a crucial economic unit bound together by an unrelenting quest for survival. Although there is unfortunately almost no available information about the role of women and men with disabilities in a preindustrial economy, speculation about their status in these circumstances suggest that they may have encountered both advantages and disadvantages in comparison with subsequent eras. Probably, in a harsh environment that was not adapted to their needs, the life spans of most disabled persons were exceeding short. And yet it is difficult to the escape the impression that, within the economic unit of the home, they may have found a role that contributed in some way to the survival of the family. Evidence of infanticide and genocide against disabled persons was not unknown at this time, but many may have acquired a measure of acceptance and legitimized status as beggars or in other capacities (Finkelstein, 1980). Even the early English Poor Laws recognized the responsibility of communities to provide assistance to disabled individuals who could not work in an unaccommodating environment outside the dreaded workhouses to which some people with disabilities were consigned. These patterns may have contributed to the subsequent confinement and concealment of disabled persons in back rooms or residential institutions; but, in a society where a rigid separation had not yet been made between home and work and where travel was difficult for anyone, citizens with disabilities may not have been exposed to some of the egregious inequities that have subsequently become apparent in highly impersonal and autonomous cultures.

THE EMERGENCY OF A CONSUMER ECONOMY

The rise of industrialism produced extensive changes in the lives of disabled as well as nondisabled people. As factories replaced private dwellings as the primary sites of production, routines and architectural configurations were standardized to suit nondisabled workers. Both the design of worksites and of the products that were manufactures gave virtually no attention to the needs of people with disabilities. As a result, patterns of aversion and avoidance toward disabled persons were embedded in the construction of commodities, landscapes, and buildings that would remain for centuries. In addition, the mechanization of production often resulted in accidents that expanded the ranks of the disabled minority and that prompted a demand by employers for worker's compensation policies to increase the predictability of the relatively slight legal risks of such incidents (Erlanger and Roth, 1985).

Perhaps even more significantly, the growth of mass production eventually spawned an increased emphasis on mass consumption. In a variety of ways, capitalists sought to persuade workers they should spend the wages they were earning in factories on items that they formerly produced themselves. Fashions, which were once the concern of royal courts and elite groups, gradually spread to affect the buying habits of increasing numbers of women and men (Banner, 1983). In urban areas, department stores arose to exhibit a cornucopia of goods in an atmosphere subtly designed to entice consumption; and, for those who remained in rural areas, catalogs presented a dazzling display of the wonders that capitalism had to offer. Ewen (1976: 12) argues that such effort represented a plan by "American industry . . . to produce a cultural apparatus aimed at defusing or neutralizing potential unrest." This thesis has been variously criticized for neglecting the complexity of economic dynamics and resistance to commercial appeals or for assuming that workers were suppressed by sales campaigns directed at other customers (Wolfe, 1978; Benson, 1979; Schudson, 1984: 175–176). And yet, in pointing out that laborers usually lacked the economic resources necessary to purchase the goods that industrialization seemingly proffered them, attention is directed at the most salient and crucial dimension of this process. Industrialists were not merely attempting to sell their products; they were also promoting a vision of satisfaction that could become available to those prepared to reshape themselves. What seems to be missing in most analyses of the growth of consumerism is a realization that the images depicted in these appeals may have been even more important than their content, or the specific product that they were attempting to sell. When other kinds of messages failed, pleas addressed to personal vanity or to the narcissistic feelings of the dominant majority were remarkably successful. As Ewen (1976: 46) notes, the promotion of many commercial products "attempted to focus man's critique against himself—his body had kept him from happiness." There does not seem to be any accurate and available records of the amount of money that consumers increasingly spent on items relating to their personal appearance from the middle of the nineteenth century to the 1930s, but the total undoubtedly was sizeable. Although these trends obviously also had an impact on oppressed groups defined by physical characteristics such as skin color, gender, or aging, they probably had the most pronounced effect on people with visible disabilities.

The social and economic changes fostered by industrialization may have been exacerbated by the accompanying process of urbanization. As workers increasingly moved from farms and rural villages to live near the institutions of mass production, the character of community life appeared to shift perceptibly. Deviant or atypical personal characteristics that may have gradually become familiar in a small community seemed bizarre or disturbing in an urban milieu. Many residents began to strive to mold their appearances in a manner that would enable them to fit into a community of strangers. Much of this effort was expended on the purchase of goods that promised to transform themselves and their bodies into socially acceptable beings. For some, an ethnic or other type of subculture might have allowed them to find the sort of public approval needed to maintain a preferred means of presenting oneself to the outside world. For others who lacked an identified subculture such as disabled persons, the strains imposed by these normative pressures may have been almost unbearable. Ironically, in cities that were supposed to be havens of heterogeneity, influences promoting conformity may have imposed an even more severe burden on visibly disabled men and women than in the rural environs that had flourished prior to the so-called industrial revolution.

THE ROLE OF ADVERTISING

The principal vehicle that projected images of appropriate or acceptable forms of personal appearance to the public in the late nineteenth and early twentieth centuries was, of course, advertising. Emerging in part from a traditional preoccupation with patent medicines and from a legacy that stressed the importance of a healthy body as a major theme in the Victorian era (Haley, 1978), advertising slowly became the leading apologist and proponent of the mass consumption that seemed to be a natural corollary of mass production in a capitalist economic system. As the practitioners of this profession gained increasing sophistication, the focus of their activities represented a growing concentration on physical characteristics. Fox (1984–97), for example, notes that the "most enduring effect of . . . advertising on "the habits and modes of life" involved the discovery of the human body." Surrounded by an environment in which the self seemed to be determined less by individual understandings than by images reflected in the eyes of others, consumers were warned about an almost endless series of bodily imperfections that allegedly required the use of specific products to avoid giving offense in personal interactions at the workplace or elsewhere. As Marchand (1985: 208–217) has pointed out, a dominant motif of advertising in this era was the so-called "parable of the first impression," which played upon the anxieties of urban inhabitants who feared they were constantly being evaluated in a context that provided little time or opportunity for more than fleeting encounters. Perhaps even more importantly, the increasing use of human models in ads was confined almost exclusively to the most attractive and appealing representatives of the WASP majority. In the advertisements of the first half of the twentieth century, readers may search in vain for black Americans, disabled people, or even older adults. Yet, by holding out the illusory promise that the lowest denizens of the working class might resemble at least superficially the image of dominant members of society, the subtle messages of American advertising seemed to smother popular discontent. As Ewen and Ewen (1982: 189) note, "While sweatshop labor dampened the hopes of many who had sought a land of freedom, there were other, provocative elements of urban America that encouraged one to 'dress for success.' Forsaken in the promised land, working people saw mass-produced fashion as one key to the mastery of a new world. The term of that world can be reduced to a single word: *appearance*."

A variety of tactics were utilized to control different segments of the industrial reserve army. For the largest brigade in this corps, a principal instrument of oppression consisted of powerful messages instilling a belief that women should confine their activities to the home, which was no longer a primary unit of production, rather than assuming a prominent role in the work force. It is perhaps no accident or coincidence that a crucial rebirth of the feminist movement in the twentieth century began with an analysis of the portrayal of women in the advertising and other columns of major magazines (Friedan, 1963). For most of this century, women were depicted almost exclusively either in household sur-roundings or as passive recipients of the admiring glances of men (Courtney and Whipple, 1983). Perhaps even more importantly, these images communicated an overwhelming stress on beauty that seemed to provoke severe anxieties about supposed bodily imperfections (Ellis, 1954). Incessant commercial campaigns revolving about standards of personal appearance that relatively few mortals could ever hope to achieve provided capitalists with a two-edge sword. On the one hand, although the behavior of men also was obviously affected by this con-centration on physical characteristics, the tendency of advertisers to focus on women clearly enhanced their capacity to dominate the job decisions and aspi-rations of this portion of the populations. The implicit notion that human appearances falling short of the criteria indicated by pervasive models were somehow inappropriate and unacceptable in the workplace or elsewhere gave these agents of the capitalist system of production an awesome power to manip-ulate the economic life of the entire society. On the other hand, since consumers are preponderantly women, the unceasing encouragement of buyers to strive to fulfill unattainable prototypes of attractiveness also seemed to prod them to spend more than they could afford. But the indirect economic implications of the ubiquitous promotion of idealized male and especially female appearance in advertising and mass communications may have had more effects on the socio-economic position of women and other disadvantaged groups in a capitalist economy than their simple impact on the sale of products. To a greater extent than many observers have been willing to concede, symbols of the allegedly infi-nite perfectibility of the female and the male appearance produced by the seem-ing imperatives of mass production and consumption have played a decisive role in shaping inequalities in the social and economic structure.

Other economically deprived groups have been oppressed by the mass imagery of commercial communications in different ways. As another large division of the industrial reserve army, immigrants became a particular target of advertisers who sought to persuade them that the purchase of commodities was the most assured means of becoming part of the American way of life. Ewen (1976: 43) points out that ads directed at this market often "were geared to make people ashamed of their origins and . . . the habits and practices that betrayed them as alien." Perhaps the most common method utilized by capitalists to perpetuate the subordinate status of oppressed groups, however, was simply to exclude them from their economic appeals. Even though the unusual demand for labor during World War I had prompted many black Americans to migrate from the rural South to the industrial North, they were not recognized in the advertising of this era period as a salient portion of the consuming public. Magazine adver-tisements from the 1920s to the 1960s hardly disclose any glimpse of a model whose skin color differs from the hue of the white majority. Similar observations could be made about other perceptible signs of ethnicity or aging. In fact, it is difficult to escape the impression that, by ignoring these markets, advertisers were at least implicitly declaring their willingness to forego short-run sales in the pursuit of broader objectives such as the promotion of unreachable standards of youth and beauty. These images stimulated the purchasing proclivities of affluent customers in the dominant majority as well as serving other social and economic purposes. Naturally, persons with identifiable disabilities have been conspicuously absent in American advertising. In fact, visibly disabled persons did not appear in advertisements until a few television commercials containing a brief glimpse of individuals using wheelchairs were released in the 1980s (Longmore, 1985). Perhaps a partial explanation for this omission is indicated by an exception to this finding recorded by Fox (1984: 99). An initial draft of an ad prepared for Kotex to promote the use of cellucotton bandages as sanitary pads during menstruation showed a nurse and four soldiers, but it was withdrawn by the agency because they felt that men should not be depicted in an intimate discussion of feminine hygiene. Subsequently, another version containing three nurses and a soldier in a wheelchair was published as the first advertisement for this product in 1921. Apparently, the common difficulty of disabled people in gaining acceptance as human beings even permitted the belief that a male seated in a wheelchair was not really a man. *Advertising and other forms of mass imagery were not merely designed to yield the increased sale of commodities; they also comprised a cultural force with an influence that has permeated all aspects of American life. From this perspective, issues of causation, such as whether advertising simply reflected widespread sentiments about disability or whether it contributed to implanting such feelings, become less critical than the assessment of contexts and effects. Clearly mass communications played a prominent role in molding an environment in which consumers were encouraged, both by the prevalence of certain images and by the comparative absence of other models, to strive relentlessly to satisfy unachievable standards of personal appearance. One of the consequences of this process has been to render people with disabilities, who may differ most noticeably from the normative prescriptions of this imagery, virtually invisible.* Although these patterns might be interpreted as an incidental result of the dynamics of capitalism rather than as the outcome of conscious intentions, their impact on visibly disabled individuals and other oppressed peoples seems undeniable.

These trends were intensified by technological developments that increased the pervasiveness of visual images of acceptable or appropriate appearance in modern society. During the nineteenth century, the display of consumer goods and other symbols of affluence had been appreciably advanced by the invention of chromolithography (Ewen and Ewen, 1982). Significantly, one of the first persons in this era to recognize the power of visual messages was P. T. Barnum (Green, 1980) who, despite his unsavory reputation for exploitation, at least allowed the public to display rather than to suppress its natural curiosity and fascination with people whose physical appearances represented a marked departure from conventional perceptions of the human form (Fiedler, 1978). By contrast, the approach of advertising seemed to discourage the display of unusual bodily characteristics. Subsequently, the expanding presence of still photography and eventually motion pictures and television heightened the overwhelming stress on physical similarities rather than differences. With the exception of "the man in the Hathaway shirt," advertisers continued to spurn even the attention-getting use of perceptible human differences. As mass imagery became overwhelmingly visual and non-verbal, popular preferences about physical characteristics oscillated within an increasingly narrow range. The reification of advertising and other commercial messages solidified a hegemony of acceptable appearance that accentuated conformist instead of heterogeneous cultural propensities. These trends undoubtedly affected employment as well as other areas of social life. They were both a product of economic forces and a profound influence on the operation of a capitalist economy.

The cumulative impact of these developments seems to have played a crucial role in relegating disabled adults and other oppressed minorities to the ranks of the industrial reserve army. Whereas the subjugation of women and immigrants appeared to be directly related to the impetus for mass consumption in a capitalist economy, the social and economic subordination of black Americans, aging citizens, disabled persons, and other groups seemingly was accomplished through subtle and indirect means. Each of these segments of the economy—and as well as affluent white consumers—have had to bear the burden of seemingly impossible standards of physical appearance, but this load has seemed to fall disproportionately on those portions of society that have been traditionally excluded from advertising and other forms of commercial communication. At a time when the economic subservience of people such as disabled and aging workers still is popularly attributed to the restrictions of their functional impairments instead of the constraints of an unaccommodating environment, the barriers that have prevented them from becoming a valuable part of the economic system also can be readily ascribed to their alleged biological inferiority or lack of productivity rather than to stigma and discrimination. *But the ubiquitous power of pervasive images of acceptable physical appearance seems indisputable. Clearly, immunity from these influences has not been extended to employers who make hiring decisions. In fact, many personnel manuals stress the importance of presenting a favorable appearance; and visibly disabled persons often are encouraged to attempt to minimize the prominence of their disabilities on employment applications and interviews.* Even more fundamentally, the standards of appearance promulgated by advertising and mass communications traditionally have guided and shaped personal choices about the kinds of people with whom they wish to associate. These forces undoubtedly have had an impact on preferences about prospective associations in the workplace as well as in other areas of social life. As Powell and Williamson (1985: 38) have found, "Negative media stereotyping of socially disadvantaged groups such as the aged, the poor, women, the disabled, and minorities facilitates control over them by rationalizing their subordination, economic exploitation, and devalued status in the larger society." The statement directs attention not only at the plight that disabled persons share with other members of the industrial reserve army but also at the intrinsic difficulty of establishing rigorous levels of proof to support such a conclusion. Obviously, in appraising the strength of a variable that permeates the atmosphere such as mass imagery of acceptable forms of physical appearance, conventional measures of causality are inappropriate. But the effects of these considerations in determining membership in the work force— or the industrial reserve army—cannot be dismissed or ignored.

The discriminatory impact of visual communications might be considered an inevitable by-product of the connection between mass production and consumption in a capitalist system; but, in many respects, the implicit social and economic consequences of these inundating messages may even have exceeded their specific purpose in stimulating the sale of commodities. In describing advertising as "capitalist realism," Schudson (1984: 233) explains, "Advertisements pick up and represent values already in the culture. But these values, however deep or widespread, are not the only ones people have or aspire to, and the pervasiveness of advertising makes us forget this. Advertising picks up some of the things that people hold dear and represents them to people as all of what they value, assuring them that the sponsor is the patron of common ideals. That is what capitalist realist art, like other pervasive symbolic systems, does." Contrary to popular impressions, the virtually unattainable standards of youth and attractiveness portrayed in mass communications might not be the only forms of human appearance that people find valuable; but the massive omnipresence of these images has nearly eliminated alternative perceptions from public consciousness. These influences undoubtedly have played a decisive role in controlling access to the labor market in the same way that they have shaped other kinds of social or economic participation. The outcome of these forces for many deprived groups, and especially for persons with visible disabilities, has been debilitating.

MEDIA REINFORCEMENT

As visual images of the alleged perfectibility of human appearance were multiplied profusely by movies and television, the representation of physical differences in the media continued to diminish. Without exception, the so-called "stars" of these new commercial productions, who became role models for entire generations, have displayed anatomical characteristics that, while they might shift slightly according to the latest fads, exemplify an appearance that others are encouraged to strive to emulate. In fact, given the prevalence of these ideals, the suggestion that anyone who embodies a significant departure from these normative prescriptions—such as a visibly disabled person—might become a movie or television idol seems almost incongruous and incomprehensible.

Unlike advertising, however, the supposed intrinsically dramatic nature of disability has spawned numerous disabled characters in motion pictures and television programming. While the tendency to use external physical traits as a manifestation of inner qualities has meant that many monstrous or demonic roles are associated with disabled characters, other productions have portrayed disability as a process of adjustment to be accomplished simply by gaining a positive outlook—resulting in hardly any disabled women or men who can be viewed as ordinary human beings (Longmore, 1985). Moreover, in pointing out that disabled adults seldom are depicted in either intimate or job settings, Zola (1985: 9) observes, "the non-family and non-worklife of those with a disability reinforces the notion of their unproductivity in all senses of that word." *The widespread characterization of individuals with disabilities as the passive recipients of medical attention has reaffirmed the prevalent insistence that their functional impair-*

ments must be the central concern of their lives, overshadowing other roles such as participation in the labor force or in personal relationships. By allowing visibly disabled people few opportunities to be seen either as socially acceptable and attractive human beings or as valued employees, the mass media have not disrupted the seemingly indissoluble link between these images that was forged by advertising. These messages provide no means of escaping the impression that both social role models and desirable workers must be nondisabled.

The narcissistic impulse that prompts humans to seek to associate with others who are perceived as resembling themselves undoubtedly has been a powerful influence in molding social and economic behavior. *What seems to be lacking in much prior research on disability and other topics is a conscious recognition of the extent to which human conduct is affected by how other people look.* In the advertising and media images produced by the seemingly inexorable logic of a capitalist system, this imagery has represented a goal that persons can only strive to attain rather than a faithful reproduction of common appearances. The result has been a kind of visual paradigm that gravitates increasingly around idealized standards and that consequently reinforces the exclusion of marginal groups such as visibly disabled adults from the work force as well as from other areas of community life. As the contours of this perceptual range narrow and move away from men and women with visible disabilities, the pernicious ramifications of this sort of discrimination are intensified. The superficiality of these images cannot be allowed to divert attention from the awesome force that they exert on many economic and political choices or decisions. In fact, processes spawned by capitalism have seemed to breed their own form of monstrosity to the severe detriment of disadvantaged portions of society such as people with perceptible disabilities.

SUMMARY AND DISCUSSION

There seems to be little doubt that the mass imagery emanating from advertising and the media has played a major role in perpetuating discrimination against citizens with disabilities as well as other oppressed groups. In assessing the factors that have consigned disabled adults to the ranks of the industrial reserve army in an adaptable environment, public perceptions and attitudes may deserve greater attention than the functional impairment of a disability. Moreover, this type of bias could be at least partially remediated by the rigorous enforcement of anti-discrimination laws to promote impartial treatment for women and men with visible disabilities in employment as well as other public activities. The quest for civil rights need not be considered a bourgeoisie instrument designed to forestall revolution. On the contrary, this goal may be viewed as a necessary historical process in which oppressed groups seek to mitigate the impact of prejudice imposed upon them by the idealized standards of appearance promulgated by the unfolding dynamics of a capitalist system. In fact, the pervasive effects of media images on portions of society which were prevented from meeting these normative prescriptions by physical characteristics such as gender, skin color, ethnicity, aging, or disability might even be interpreted as a significant dimension of the social structure that has inhibited the emergence of class struggle in modern society. For people with visible disabilities, the imagery which promoted their exclusion from common forms of social and economic participation may have been so powerful that they never became a serious threat to the jobs of other workers. And yet the fact that numerous disadvantaged peoples—including women, black Americans, ethnic groups, and aging persons—share the same forms of oppression as visibly disabled citizens seems to employ a potential for coalitions that could yield both a realignment in the structure of society and a corresponding tendency for conflict to reflect class rather than other sorts of divisions.

Standards of acceptable and appropriate personal appearance promoted by the agents of a capitalist economy have vast implications for the study of social and economic behavior. Although these images may seem to comprise an almost indestructible hegemony, analysts must not ignore the unique propensity of human beings to change their feelings about perceptible physical differences at various times. The symbols of beauty that dominate twentieth century America are not the ones which have been seen as desirable or attractive by most societies. In fact, history contains many examples of admired and prized physical attributes that would subsequently be viewed as deviant and bizarre. These trends might indicate that, for people with visible disabilities and other oppressed groups, there may be important values to be derived from honoring and even accentuating their differences—instead of stressing their similarities—in relation to the narcissistic standards of the dominant majority.

REFERENCES

Banner, Lois W. 1980. *American Beauty* (Chicago: University of Chicago Press).

Banton, Michael. 1983. *Racial and Ethnic Competition* (New York: Cambridge University Press).

Benson, Susan Porter. 1979. "Advertising America." *Socialist Review* 9(1): 143–155.

Bonacich, Edna. 1979. "The Past, Present, and Future of Split Labor Market Theory." *Research in Race and Ethnic Relations* 1(1): 17–64.

Courtney, Alice E. and Thomas W. Whipple. 1983. *Sex Stereotyping in Advertising* (Lexington, MA: D. C. Heath and Co.).

Cox, Oliver Cromwell. 1948. *Caste, Class, and Race* (Garden City, NY: Doubleday).

Ehrlich, Howard J. 1973. *The Social Psychology of Prejudice* (New York: John Wiley and Sons).

Ellis, Albert. 1954. *The American Sexual Tragedy* (New York: Twayne Publishers).

Erlanger, Howard S. and William Roth. 1985. "Disability Policy: The Parts and the Whole." *American Behavioral Scientist* 28(3): 319–345.

Ewen, Stuart. 1976. *Captains of Consciousness* (New York: McGraw-Hill Co.).

Ewen, Stuart, and Elizabeth Ewen. 1982. *Channels of Desire* (New York: McGraw-Hill).

Fiedler, Leslie. 1978. *Freaks* (New York: Simon and Schuster).

Finkelstein, Victor. 1980. *Attitudes and Disabled People* (New York: World Rehabilitation Fund).

Fox, Stephen. 1984. *The Mirror Makers* (New York: Random House).

Friedan, Betty. 1963. *The Feminine Mystique* (New York: W. W. Norton).

Gliedman, John and William Roth. 1980. *The Unexpected Minority* (New York: Harcourt, Brace, Jovanovich).

Gough, Ian. 1979. *The Political Economy of the Welfare State* (London Macmillan Press).

Green, Gregory. 1980. "Show-Man." *Journal of Popular Culture* 14(3): 385–393.

Hahn, Harlan. 1982. "Disability and Rehabilitation Policy: Is Paternalistic Neglect Really

Benign?" *Public Administration Review* 42(5): 385–389.

Hahn, Harlan. 1984. *The Issue of Equality: European Perceptions of Employment Policy for Disabled Persons* (New York: World Rehabilitation Fund).

Hahn, Harlan, 1985a. "Disability Policy and the Problem of Discrimination." *American Behavioral Scientist* 28(3): 293–318.

Hahn, Harlan. 1985b. "Toward a Politics of Disability: Definitions, Disciplines, and Policies." *The Social Science Journal* 22(4): 87–105.

Hahn, Harlan. 1985c. "Changing Perceptions of Disability and the Future of Rehabilitation." Pp. 53–64 in Leonard G. Perlman and Gary F. Austin, eds., *Social Influences in Rehabilitation Planning: Blueprint for the Twenty-first Century* (Alexandria, VA: National Rehabilitation Association).

Hahn, Harlan. Forthcoming. "Disability and the Urban Environment: A Perspective on Los Angeles." *Society and Space.*

Haley, Bruce. 1978. *The Healthy Body and Victorian Culture* (Cambridge, MA: Harvard University Press).

Howards, Irving, Henry P. Brehm, and Saad Z. Nagi. 1980. *Disability: From Social Problem to Federal Program* (New York: Praeger Publishers).

Hraba, Joseph. 1979. *American Ethnicity* (Itasca, IL: F. E. Peacock Publishers, Inc.).

Johnson William G. and James Lambrinos. 1985. "Wage Discrimination Against Handicapped Men and Women." *The Journal of Human Resources* 20(2): 264–277.

Krause, Elliott A. 1979. "The Political Sociology of Rehabilitation." Pp. 201–221 in Gary L. Albrecht, ed., *The Sociology of Physical Disability and Rehabilitation* (Pittsburgh, PA: University of Pittsburgh Press).

Longmore, Paul K. 1985. "Screening Stereotypes: Images of Disabled People." *Social Policy* 16(1): 31–37.

Marchand, Roland. 1985. *Advertising the American Dream: Making Way for Modernity, 1920–1940* (Berkeley, CA: University of California Press).

Muga, David. 1984. "Academic Sub-Cultural Theory and the Problematic of Ethnicity: A Tentative Critique." *The Journal of Ethnic Studies* 12(1): 1–52.

Nelson, Nathan. 1971. *Workshops for the Handicapped in the United States* (Springfield, IL: Charles Thomas).

Obermann, C. Esso. 1965. *A History of Vocational Rehabilitation in America* (Minneapolis, MN: T. S. Denison and Co.).

Oliver, Michael. 1984. "Disability into the 1980s: A Review Article." Unpublished paper.

Powell, Lawrence A. and John B. Williamson. 1985. "The Mass Media and the Aged." *Social Policy* 16(1): 38–49.

Renard, Jean-Bruno. 1984. "The Wild Man and the Extraterrestrial: Two Figures of Evolutionist Fantasy." *Diogenes* 127: 63–81.

Schudson, Michael. 1984. *Advertising, The Uneasy Persuasion* (New York: Basic Books).

Stone, Deborah A. 1984. *The Disabled State* (Philadelphia, PA: Temple University Press).

Wagley, Charles. 1968. *The Latin American Tradition* (New York: Columbia University Press).

Wolfe, Rick. 1978. "Economics, Advertising, and Consumer Culture." *Monthly Review* 29(10): 49–55.

Zola, Irving Kenneth. 1985. "Depictions of Disability—Metaphor, Message, and Medium in the Media: A Research and Political Agenda." *The Social Science Journal* 22(4): 5–17.

9

Abortion and Disability

Who Should and Who Should Not Inhabit the World?

RUTH HUBBARD

Political agitation and education during the past few decades have made most people aware of what constitutes discrimination against blacks and other racial and ethnic minorities and against women. And legal and social measures have been enacted to begin to counter such discrimination. Where people with disabilities are concerned, our level of awareness is low, and the measures that exist are enforced haphazardly. Yet people with disabilities and disability-rights advocates have stressed again and again that it is often far easier to cope with the physical aspects of a disability than with the discrimination and oppression they encounter because of it (Asch, 1988; Asch and Fine, 1988). People shun persons who have disabilities and isolate them so they will not have to see them. They fear them as though the disability were contagious. And it is, in the sense that it forces us to face our own vulnerability.

Most of us would be horrified if a scientist offered to develop a test to diagnose skin color prenatally so as to enable racially mixed people (which means essentially everyone who is considered black and many of those considered white in the Americas) to have light-skinned children. And if the scientist explained that because it is difficult to grow up black in America, he or she wanted to spare people suffering because of the color of their skin, we would counter that it is irresponsible to use scientific means to reinforce racial prejudices. Yet we see nothing wrong, and indeed hail as progress, tests that enable us to try to avoid having children who have disabilities or are said to have a tendency to acquire a specific disease or disability later in life.

The scientists and physicians who develop and implement these tests believe they are reducing human suffering. This justification seems more appropriate for speed limits, seat-belt laws, and laws to further occupational safety and health than for tests to avoid the existence of certain kinds of people. When it comes to women or to racial or ethnic groups, we insist that it is discriminatory to judge individuals on the basis of their group affiliation. But we lump people with disabilities as though all disabilities were the same and always devastating and as though all people who have one were alike.

Health and physical prowess are poor criteria of human worth. Many of us know people with a disease or disability whom we value highly and so-called healthy people whom we could readily do without. It is fortunate for human variety and variability that most of us are not called on to make such judgments, much less to implement them.

It is not new for people to view disability as a form of pollution, evidence of sin. Disability has been considered divine punishment or, alternatively, the result of witches' spells. In our scientific and medical era we look to heredity for explanations unless there is an obvious external cause, such as an accident or infectious disease. Nowadays, even if an infection can explain the disability, scientists have begun to suggest that our genes might have made us unusually susceptible to it.

In a sense, hereditary disabilities are contagious because they can be passed from one generation to the next. For this reason, well before there was a science of genetics, scientists proposed eugenic measures to stem the perpetuation of "defects."

THE RISE OF EUGENICS IN BRITAIN AND THE UNITED STATES

Eugenics met its apotheosis under the Nazis, which is why many Germans oppose genetic testing and gene therapy and their use is being hotly debated in the parliament. Germans tend to understand better than people in other countries what can happen when the concern that people with disabilities will become social and economic burdens or that they will lead to a deterioration of the race begins to dictate so-called preventive health policies. They are aware that scientists and physicians were the ones who developed the Nazi policies of "selection and eradication" (*Auslese und Ausmerze*) and who oversaw their execution. What happened under the Nazis has been largely misrepresented and misinterpreted in this country, as well as among Nazi apologists in Germany. To make what happened clearer, I shall briefly review the scientific underpinnings of the Nazi extermination program, which are obscured when these practices are treated as though they were incomprehensible aberrations without historical roots or meaning—a holocaust.

German eugenics, the attempt to improve the German race, or *Volk*, by ridding it of inferior and foreign elements, was based on arguments and policies developed largely in Great Britain and the United States during the latter part of the nineteenth and the beginning of the twentieth centuries. (In what follows I shall not translate the german word *Volk* because it has no English equivalent. The closest is "people," singular, used as a collective noun, as in "the German people *is* patriotic." But "people," singular, does not convey the collectivity of *Volk* because to us "people" means individuals. Therefore, we would ordinarily phrase my example, "the German people *are* patriotic.")

The term *eugenics* is derived from the Greek word for "well born." It was coined in 1883 by Francis Galton, cousin of Charles Darwin, as "a brief word to express the science of improving the stock, which is by no means confined to questions of judicious mating, but which, especially in the case of man [sic], takes cognizance of all the influences that tend in however remote a degree to give the more suitable races or strains of blood a better chance of prevailing speedily over the less suitable than they otherwise would have had" (pp. 24–25). Galton later helped found the English Eugenics Education Society and eventually became its honorary president.

British eugenics counted among its supporters many distinguished biologists and social scientists. Even as late as 1941, while the Nazis were implementing their eugenic extermination program, the distinguished biologist Julian Huxley (1941)—brother of Aldous—opened a semipopular article entitled "The Vital Importance of Eugenics" with the words: "Eugenics is running the usual course of many new ideas. It has ceased to be regarded as a fad, is now receiving serious study, and in the near future, will be regarded as an urgent practical problem." In the article, he argues that it is crucial for society "to ensure that mental defectives [sic] shall not have children" and defines as mentally defective "someone with such a feeble mind that he cannot support himself or look after himself unaided." (Notice the mix of eugenics and economics.) He says that he refuses to enter into the argument over whether such "racial degeneration" should be forestalled by "prohibition of marriage" or "segregation in institutions" combined with "sterilization for those who are at large." He states as fact that most "mental defects" are hereditary and suggests that it would therefore be better if one could "discover how to diagnose the carriers of the defect" who are "apparently normal." "If these could but be detected, and then discouraged *or prevented* from reproducing, mental defects could very speedily be reduced to negligible proportions among our population" (my emphasis). It is shocking that at a time when the Nazi program of eugenic sterilization and euthanasia was in full force across the Channel, Huxley expressed regret that it was "at the moment very difficult to envisage methods for putting even a limited constructive program [of eugenics] into effect" and complained that "that is due as much to difficulties in our present socioeconomic organization as to our ignorance of human heredity, and most of all to the absence of a eugenic sense in the public at large."

The American eugenics movement built on Galton and attained its greatest influence between 1905 and 1935. An underlying concern of the eugenicists is expressed in a statement by Lewis Terman (1924), one of the chief engineers of I. Q. testing: "The fecundity of the family stocks from which our most gifted children come appears to be definitely on the wane. . . . It has been figured that if the present differential birth rate continues 1,000 Harvard graduates will, at the end of 200 years, have but 56 descendants, while in the same period, 1,000 S. Italians will have multiplied to 100,000." To cope with this dire eventuality, eugenics programs had two prongs: "positive eugenics"—encouraging the "fit" (read "well-to-do") to have lots of children—and "negative eugenics"—preventing the "unfit" (defined to include people suffering from so-called insanity, epilepsy, alcoholism, pauperism, criminality, sexual perversion, drug abuse, and especially feeble-mindedness) from having any.

Many distinguished American geneticists supported eugenics, but none was more active in promoting it than Charles Davenport, who, after holding faculty appointments at Harvard and the University of Chicago, in 1904 became director of the "station for the experimental study of evolution," which he persuaded the Carnegie Institution of Washington to set up in Cold Spring Harbor on Long

Island. His goal was to collect large amounts of data on human inheritance and store them in a central office. In 1910, he managed to persuade the heiress to the Harriman railroad fortune to fund the Eugenics Record Office at Cold Spring Harbor, for which he got additional money from John D. Rockefeller, Jr. He appointed Harry W. Laughlin, a Princeton Ph. D., as superintendent and recruited a staff of young graduates from Radcliffe, Vassar, Cornell, Harvard, and other elite institutions as fieldworkers to accumulate interview data about a large number of so-called mental and social defectives. The office and its staff became major resources for promoting the two legislative programs that formed the back-bone of U.S. eugenics: involuntary-sterilization laws and the Immigration Restriction Act of 1924.

The first sterilization law was enacted in Indiana in 1907, and by 1931 some thirty states had compulsory-sterilization laws on their books. Aimed in general at the insane and "feeble-minded" (broadly interpreted to include many recent immigrants and other people who did badly on I. Q. tests because they were func-tionally illiterate or barely spoke English), these laws often extended to so-called sexual perverts, drug fiends, drunkards, epileptics, and "other diseased and degen-erate persons" (Ludmerer, 1972). Although most of these laws were not enforced, by January 1935 some twenty thousand people in the United States had been forcibly sterilized, nearly half of them in California. Indeed, the California law was not repealed until 1980 and eugenic-sterilization laws are still on the books in about twenty states.

The eugenic intent of the Immigration Restriction Act of 1924 was equally explicit. It was designed to decrease the proportion of poor immigrants from southern and eastern Europe so as to give predominance to Americans of British and north European descent. This goal was accomplished by restricting the number of immigrants allowed into the United States from any one country in each calendar year to at most 2 percent of U. S. residents who had been born in that country as listed in the Census of 1890 (so, thirty-four years earlier). The date 1890 was chosen because it established as a baseline the ethnic composition of the U. S. population prior to the major immigrations from eastern and south-ern Europe, which began in the 1890s. Laughlin of the Eugenics Record Office was one of the most important lobbyists and witnesses at the Congressional hear-ings that preceded passage of the Immigration Restriction Act and was appointed "expert eugenical agent" of the House Committee on Immigration and Natu-ralization (Kevles, 1985).

RACIAL HYGIENE IN GERMANY

What was called eugenics in the United States and Britain came to be known as racial hygiene in Germany. It was the response to several related and widely held beliefs: (1) that humane care for people with disabilities would enfeeble the "race" because they would survive to pass their disabilities on to their children; (2) that not just mental and physical diseases and so-called defects, but also poverty, criminality, alcoholism, prostitution, and other social problems were based in biology and inherited; and (3) that genetically inferior people were reproducing faster than superior people and would eventually displace them.

Although these beliefs were not based in fact, they fueled racist thinking and social programs in Britain and the United States as well as in Germany.

German racial hygiene was founded in 1895, some dozen years after Galton's eugenics, by a physician, Alfred Plötz, and was based on much the same analysis of social problems as the British and American eugenics movements were. In 1924, Plötz started the *Archive of Race- and Socio-biology (Archiv für Rassen- und Gesellschaftsbiologie)* and the next year helped found the Society for Racial Hygiene (Gesellschaft für Rassenhygiene). German racial hygiene initially did not concern itself with preventing the admixture of "inferior" races, such as Jews or gypsies, in contrast to the British and American movements where miscegenation with blacks, Asians, Native Americans, and immigrants of almost any sort was one of the major concerns. The recommended means for preventing racial degeneration in Germany, as elsewhere, was sterilization. Around 1930 even some German socialists and communists supported the eugenic sterilization of inmates of psychiatric institutions, although the main impetus came from the Nazis. The active melding of anti-Semitism and racial hygiene in Germany began during World War I and accelerated during the 1920s, partly in response to economic pressures and a scarcity of available positions, which resulted in severe competition for jobs and incomes among scientists and physicians, many of whom were Jews.

Racial hygiene was established as an academic discipline in 1923, when Fritz Lenz, a physician and geneticist, was appointed to the newly created Chair of Racial Hygiene at the University of Munich, a position he kept until 1933, when he moved to the Chair of Racial Hygiene at the University of Berlin. Lenz, Eugen Fischer, and Erwin Baer coauthored the most important textbook on genetics and racial hygiene in German. Published in 1921, it was hailed in a review in the *American Journal of Heredity* in 1928 as "the standard textbook of human genetics" in the world (quoted in Proctor, 1988, p. 58). In 1931, it was translated into English, and the translation was favorably reviewed in Britain and the United States despite its blatant racism, or perhaps because of it. By 1933, eugenics and racial hygiene were being taught in most medical schools in Germany.

Therefore the academic infrastructure was in place when the Nazis came to power and began to build a society that gave biologists, anthropologists, and physicians the opportunity to put their racist and eugenic theories into practice. Looking back on this period, Eugen Fischer, who directed the Kaiser Wilhelm Institute for Anthropology, Human Genetics, and Eugenics in Berlin from 1927 to 1942, wrote in a newspaper article in 1943: "It is special and rare good luck when research of an intrinsically theoretical nature falls into a time when the general world view appreciates and welcomes it and, what is more, when its practical results are immediately accepted as the basis for governmental procedures" (quoted in Müller-Hill, 1984, p. 64; my translation). It is not true, as has sometimes been claimed, that German scientists were perverted by Nazi racism. Robert Proctor (1988) points out that "it was largely medical scientists who *invented* racial hygiene in the first place" (p. 38; original emphasis).

A eugenic-sterilization law, drafted along the lines of a "Model Sterilization Law" published by Laughlin (the superintendent of Davenport's Eugenics Record

Office at Cold Spring Harbor), was being considered in 1932 by the Weimar government. On July 14, 1933, barely six months after Hitler took over, the Nazi government passed its eugenic-sterilization law. This law established genetic health courts (*Erbgesundheitsgerichte*), presided over by a lawyer and two physicians, one of whom was to be an expert on "hereditary pathology" (*Erbpathologie*), whose rulings could be appealed to similarly constituted supreme genetic health courts. However, during the entire Nazi period only about 3 percent of lower-court decisions were reversed. The genetic health courts could order the sterilization of people on grounds that they had a "genetically determined" disease, such as "inborn feeble-mindedness, schizophrenia, manic-depressive insanity, hereditary epilepsy, Huntington's disease, hereditary blindness, hereditary deafness, severe physical malformations, and severe alcoholism" (Müller-Hill, 1984, p. 32; my translation). The law was probably written by Dr. Ernst Rüdin, professor of psychiatry and director of the Kaiser Wilhelm Institute for Genealogy and Demography of the German Research Institute for Psychiatry in Munich. The official commentary and interpretation of the law was published under his name and those of an official of the Ministry of the Interior, also a medical doctor, and of a representative of the Health Ministry in the Department of the Interior who was a doctor of laws. All practicing physicians were sent copies of the law and commentaries describing the acceptable procedures for sterilization and castration.

The intent of the law was eugenic, not punitive. Physicians were expected to report patients and their close relatives to the nearest local health court and were fined if they failed to report someone with a so-called hereditary disease. Although some physicians raised the objection that this requirement invaded the doctor-patient relationship, the health authorities argued that this obligation to notify then was no different from requirements that physicians report the incidence of specific infectious diseases or births and deaths. The eugenic measures were to be regarded as health measures pure and simple. And this is the crucial point: the people who designed these policies and the later policies of euthanasia and mass extermination as well as those who oversaw their execution looked on them as sanitary measures, required in this case to cure not individual patients but the collective—the *Volk*—of threats to its health (Lifton, 1987; Proctor, 1988).

As early as 1934, Professor Otmar von Verschuer, then dean of the University of Frankfurt and director of its Institute for Genetics and Racial Hygiene and later the successor of Fischer as director of the Kaiser Wilhelm Institute for Anthropology, Human Genetics, and Eugenics in Berlin, urged that patients should not be looked on, and treated, as individuals. Rather the patient is but "one part of a much larger whole or unity: of his family, his race, his *Volk*" (quoted in Proctor, 1988, p. 105). Minister of the Interior Wilhelm Frisch estimated that at least half a million Germans had genetic diseases, but some experts thought that the true figure was more like one in five, which would be equivalent to thirteen million. In any event, by 1939 some three to four hundred thousand people had been sterilized, with a mortality of about 0.5 percent (Proctor, 1988, pp. 108–109). After that there were few individual sterilizations. Later, large numbers of people were sterilized in the concentration camps, but that was done without benefit of health courts, as part of the program of human experimentation.

The eugenic-sterilization law of 1933 did not provide for sterilization on racial grounds. Nonetheless, in 1937 about five hundred racially mixed children were sterilized; the children had been fathered by black French colonial troops brought to Europe from Africa after World War I to occupy the Rhineland (the so-called Rheinlandbastarde).

The first racist eugenic measures were passed in 1935. They were the Nürnberg antimiscegenation, or blood-protection laws, which forbade intermarriage or sexual relations between Jews and non-Jews and forbade Jews from employing non-Jews in their homes. The Nürnberg laws also included a "Law for the Protection of the Genetic Health of the German People," which required premarital medical examinations to detect "racial damage" and required people who were judged "damaged" to marry only others like themselves, provided they first submitted to sterilization. The Nürnberg laws were considered health laws, and physicians were enlisted to enforce them. So-called positive eugenics was practiced by encouraging "genetically healthy" German women to have as many children as possible. They were persuaded to do so by means of propaganda, economic incentives, breeding camps, and strict enforcement of the law forbidding abortion except for eugenic reasons (Koonz, 1987).

The next stage in the campaign of "selection and eradication" was opened at the Nazi party congress in 1935, where plans were made for the "destruction of lives not worth living." The phrase was borrowed from the title of a book published much earlier, in 1920, by Alfred Hoche, professor of psychiatry and director of the Psychiatric Clinic at Freiburg, and Rudolf Binding, professor of jurisprudence at the University of Leipzig. In their book, entitled *The Release for Destruction of Lives Not Worth Living* (*Die Freigabe zur Vernichtung lebensunwerten Lebens*), these professors argued for killing "worthless" people, whom they defined as those who are "mentally completely dead" and those who constitute "a foreign body in human society" (quoted in Chorover, 1979, p. 97). At the time the program was initiated, the arguments focused on the money wasted in keeping institutionalized (hence "worthless") people alive, for in the early stages the rationale of the euthanasia campaign was economic as much as eugenic. Therefore the extermination campaign was directed primarily at inmates of state psychiatric hospitals and children living in state institutions for the mentally and physically disabled. Jews were specifically excluded because they were not considered worthy of euthanasia. (Here, too, the Nazis were not alone. In 1942, as the last inmates of German mental hospitals were being finished off, Dr. Foster Kennedy, an American psychiatrist writing in the official publication of the American Psychiatric Association, advocated killing mentally retarded children of five and older (Proctor, 1988). The arguments were phrased in humane terms like these: "Parents who have seen the difficult life of a crippled or feebleminded child must be convinced that though they have the moral obligation to care for the unfortunate creatures, the wider public should not be obliged . . . to assume the enormous costs that long-term institutionalization might entail" (quoted in Proctor, 1988, p. 183). This argument calls to mind the statement by Bentley Glass (1971) about parents not having "a right to burden society with a malformed or a mentally incompetent child."

In Germany, the propaganda was subtle and widespread. For example, Proctor (1988, p. 184) cites practice problems in a high school mathematics text published for the school year 1935–36, in which students were asked to calculate the costs to the Reich of maintaining mentally ill people in various kinds of institutions for different lengths of time and to compare the costs of constructing insane asylums and housing units. How is that for relevance?

Although the euthanasia program was planned in the mid-1930s, it was not implemented until 1939, when wartime dislocation and secrecy made it relatively easy to institute such extreme measures. Two weeks before the invasion of Poland an advisory committee commissioned by Hitler issued a secret report recommending that children born with Down syndrome, microcephaly, and various deformities be registered with the Ministry of the Interior. Euthanasia, like sterilization, was to proceed with the trappings of selection. Therefore physicians were asked to fill out questionnaires about all children in their care up to age three who had any of these kinds of disabilities. The completed questionnaires were sent to three-man committees of medical experts charged with marking each form "plus" or "minus." Although none of these "experts" ever saw the children, those whose forms were marked "plus" were transferred to one of a number of institutions where they were killed. Some of the oldest and most respected hospitals in Germany served as such extermination centers. By 1941 the program was expanded to include older children with disabilities and by 1943, to include healthy Jewish children. Also in 1939, evaluation forms were sent to psychiatric institutions for adults for selection and so-called euthanasia.

By September 1941 over seventy thousand inmates had been killed at some of the most distinguished psychiatric hospitals in Germany, which had been equipped for this purpose with gas chambers, disguised as showers, and with crematoria (Lifton, 1986; Proctor, 1988). (When the mass extermination of Jews and other "undesirables" began shortly thereafter, these gas chambers were shipped east and installed at Auschwitz and other extermination camps.) Most patients were gassed or killed by injection with legal drugs, but a few physicians were reluctant to intervene so actively and let children die of slow starvation and the infectious diseases to which they became susceptible, referring to this as death from "natural" causes. Relatives were notified that their family member had died suddenly of one of a number of infectious diseases and that the body had been cremated for reasons of public health. Nevertheless, rumors began to circulate, and by 1941 hospital killings virtually ceased because of protests, especially from the Church.

There is a direct link between this campaign of "selection and eradication" and the subsequent genocide of Jews, gypsies, communists, homosexuals, and other "undesirables." Early on these people were described as "diseased" and their presence, as an infection or a cancer in the body of the *Volk*. Proctor (1988, p. 194) calls this rationalization "the medicalization of antisemitism." The point is that the Nazi leaders shouted anti-Semitic and racist propaganda from their platforms, but when it came to devising the measures for ridding the Thousand Year Reich of Jews, gypsies, and the other undesirables, the task was shouldered by the

scientists and physicians who had earlier devised the sterilization and euthanasia programs for the mentally or physically disabled. Therefore, nothing came
easier than a medical metaphor: Jews as cancer, Jews as disease. And so the Nazi
extermination program was viewed by its perpetrators as a gigantic program in
sanitation and public health. It started with quarantining the offending organ-
isms in ghettoes and concentration camps and ended with the extermination of
those who did not succumb to the "natural" consequences of the quarantine, such
as the various epidemics and hunger.

Yet a measure of selection was practiced throughout the eradication process:
It was still *Auslese* as well as *Ausmerze*. At every step choices were made of who
could still be used and who had become "worthless." We have read the books and
seen the films that show selections being made as the cattle cars emptied the victims into the concentration camps: to work or to die? That is where Joseph Mengele, an M. D./Ph. D., selected the twins and other unfortunates to use as subjects
for his scientific experiments at Auschwitz, performed in collaboration with Professor von Verschuer, at that time director of the Kaiser Wilhelm Institute for
Anthropology, Human Genetics, and Eugenics in Berlin. And von Verschuer was
not the only distinguished scientist who gratefully accepted the human tissues
and body fluids provided by Mengele. After the war it became fashionable to
characterize the experiments as "bad science," but as Beno Müller-Hill (1984)
emphasizes, nothing about them would be considered "bad" were they done with
mice. What was "bad" was not their scientific content but the fact that they were
being done with "disenfranchised human beings" (p. 97).

PRENATAL TESTING: WHO SHOULD INHABIT THE WORLD?

I want to come back to the present, but I needed to go over this history in order
to put my misgivings and those of some of the Germans who are opposing genetic
testing into the proper perspective. I can phrase the problem best by rephrasing
a question Hannah Arendt asks in the epilogue of her commentary on the trial
of Adolf Eichmann. Who has the "right to determine who should and who
should not inhabit the world?" (1977). That's what it comes down to.

So let me be clear: I am not suggesting that prenatal diagnosis followed by
abortion is similar to euthanasia. Fetuses are not people. And a woman must have
the right to terminate her pregnancy, whatever her reasons. I am also not drawing an analogy between what the Nazis did and what we and others in many of
the industrialized countries are doing now. Because the circumstances are different, different things are being done and for different reasons. But a similar
eugenic ideology underlies what happened then and the techniques now being
developed. So it is important that we understand how what happened then came
about—and not in some faraway culture that is altogether different from ours but
in the heart of Europe, in a country that has produced artists, writers, composers,
philosophers, jurists, scientists, and physicians the equal of any in the Western
world. Given that record, we cannot afford to be complacent.

Scientists and physicians in this and other countries are once more engaged
in developing the means to decide what lives are worth living and who should

and should not inhabit the world. Except that now they provide only the tools, while pregnant women themselves have to make the decisions, euphemistically called choices. No one is forced to do anything. A pregnant woman must merely "choose" whether to terminate a wanted pregnancy because she has been informed that her future child will have a disability (although, as I have said before, usually no one can tell her how severe the disability will be). If she "chooses" not to take the tests or not to terminate a pregnancy despite a positive result, she accepts responsibility for whatever the disability will mean to that child and to her and the rest of her family. In that case, her child, her family, and the rest of society can reproach her for having so-to-speak "caused" that human being's physical pain as well as the social pain he or she experiences because our society does not look kindly on people with disabilities.

There is something terribly wrong with this situation, and although it differs in many ways from what went wrong in Germany, at base are similar principles of selection and eradication. Lest this analogy seem too abstract, let me give a few examples of how the principle of selection and eradication now works in practice.

Think of people who have Huntington's disease; as you may remember they were on the list of people to be sterilized in Germany. Huntington's disease is a degenerative disease of the nervous system and is unusual among hereditary diseases in that it is inherited as what geneticists call a dominant trait. In other words, even people in whom only one of the pair of genes that is involved with regulating the relevant metabolic processes is affected manifest the disease. Most other gene-mediated diseases, such as Tay-Sachs disease or sickle-cell anemia, are so-called recessives: Only people in whom both members of the relevant pair of genes are affected manifest the disease. In the case of recessive diseases, people with only one affected gene are called carriers: They do not have the disease and usually do not even know that they carry a gene for it. To inherit a recessive disease such as sickle-cell anemia, a child must get an affected gene from each of its parents; to inherit a dominant disease, such as Huntington's disease, it is enough is she or he gets an affected gene from either parent.

The symptoms of Huntington's disease usually do not appear until people are in their thirties, forties, or fifties—in other words, after most people who want to have children have already had one or more. Woody Guthrie had Huntington's disease, but he did not become ill until after he had lived a varied and productive life, produced a large legacy of songs, and fathered his children. At present, there is no cure for Huntington's disease, although scientists have been working to find one. However, a test has been developed that makes it possible to establish with fair reliability whether a person or fetus carries the gene for Huntington's disease, provided a sufficient number of people in that family is willing to be tested.

The existence of this test puts people with a family history of Huntington's disease in an outrageous position: Although they themselves are healthy and do not know whether they will get the disease, they must decide whether to be tested, whether to persuade as many of their relatives as possible to do the same, and whether to test their future child prenatally so they can terminate the pregnancy if the test reveals that the fetus has the gene for Huntington's disease. If it does and they decide on abortion, they are as much as saying that a life lived in the knowledge that one will eventually die of Huntington's disease is not worth living. What does that say about their own life and the lives of their family members who now know that they have the gene for Huntington's disease? If the fetus has the gene and they do not abort, they are knowingly wishing a cruel, degenerative disease on their future child. And if they refuse the test, they can be accused of sticking their heads in the sand. This is an obscene "choice" for anyone to have to make!

Some other inherited diseases also do not become evident until later in life, such as retinitis pigmentosa, a degenerative eye disease. People with this disease are born with normal vision, but their eyesight deteriorates, although usually not until midlife, and they may eventually lose their sight. (People with this disease presumably also were slated for sterilization by the Nazis because it is a form of "hereditary blindness.") There are different patterns of inheritance of retinitis pigmentosa, and prenatal diagnosis is becoming available for one of these patterns and being sought for others. What are prospective parents to do when confronted with the "choice" of aborting a pregnancy because their future child may become blind at some time during its life?

Another, rather different, problem arises with regard to the so-called neural-tube defects (NTDs), a group of developmental disorders which, in fact, are not inherited. They include anencephaly (failure to develop a brain) and spina bifida (failure of the spinal column, and sometimes also the overlying tissues, to close properly). babies with anencephaly die before birth or shortly thereafter. The severity of the health problems of children who have spina bifida depends on where along the spinal column the defect is located and can vary from life-threatening to relatively mild. The incidence of NTDs varies geographically and tends to be higher in industrialized than in nonindustrialized areas. Women who carry a fetus with a neural-tube defect have a grater than usual concentration of a specific substance, called alpha-feto-protein, in their blood. A blood test has been developed to detect NTDs prenatally, and California now requires that all pregnant women in the state be offered this test. The women are first counseled about NTDs and about the test and then have to sign a consent or refusal form. If they refuse, that is the end of it. If they consent, they can later refuse to abort the fetus even if the test is positive. This procedure sounds relatively unproblematical, although the requirement to sign a refusal form is coercive. (You cannot walk away; you must say no.) The trouble is that although the test detects virtually all fetuses who have NTDs, it yields a large number of false positive results that suggest that the fetus has a NTD although it does not.

Let us look at some numbers. In California there are about two hundred thousand births a year and the incidence of NTDs is about one per thousand. So, about 200 pregnant women a year carry fetuses with NTDs and 199,800 do not. However, about 5 percent of women test positive on a first test. In other words, if all pregnant women agreed to be tested, 10,000 women would have a positive test, 9,800 of which would be false positives. Those 10,000 women would then have to undergo the stress of worrying as well as further tests in order to determine who among them is in fact carrying a fetus with a NTD. And no test will tell the 200 women whose fetus, in fact, has a NTD how severe their child's health problem will be. All this testing with uncertain results must be offered at this time, when health dollars in California, as elsewhere, have been cut to the bone, and increasing numbers of pregnant women are coming to term with little or no prenatal services of any sort.

The reason I have spelled this problem out in such detail is to make it clear that in many of these situations parents have only the most tenuous basis for making their decisions. Because of the fear of raising a child with a serious disability, many women "choose" to abort a wanted pregnancy if they are told that there is any likelihood whatever that their future child may have a health problem. At times like that we seem to forget that we live in a society in which every day people of all ages are disabled by accidents—at work, on the street, or at home—many of which could be prevented if the necessary money were spent, the necessary precautions taken. What is more, because of the deteriorating economic conditions of poor people and especially women, increasing numbers of babies are born with disabilities that could easily be prevented and are prevented in most other industrialized nations. I question our excessive preoccupation with inherited diseases while callousness and economic mismanagement disable and kill increasing numbers of children and adults.

To say again, I am not arguing against a woman's right to abortion. Women must have that right because it involves a decision about our bodies and about the way we will spend the rest of our lives. But for scientists to argue that they are developing these tests out of concern for the "quality of life" of future children is like the arguments about "lives not worth living." No one can make that kind of decision about someone else. No one these days openly suggests that certain kinds of people be killed; they just should not be born. Yet that involves a process of selection and a decision about what kinds of people should and should not inhabit the world.

German women, who know the history of Nazi eugenics and how genetic counseling centers functioned during the Nazi period, have organized against the new genetic and reproductive technologies (Duelli Klein, Corea, and Hubbard, 1985). They are suspicious of prenatal testing and counseling centers because some of the scientists and physicians working in them are the same people who designed and implemented the eugenics program during the Nazi period. Others are former co-workers or students of these Nazi professors.

Our history is different, but not different enough. Eugenic thinking is part of our heritage and so are eugenic sterilizations. Here they were not carried over to mass exterminations because we live in a democracy with constitutional safeguards. But, as I mentioned before, even in recent times black, Hispanic, and Native-American women have been sterilized against their wills (Rodriguez-Trias, 1982). We do not exalt the body of the people, as a collective, over that of individuals, but we come dangerously close to doing so when we question the "right" of parents to bear a child who has a disability or when we draw unfavorable comparisons between the costs of care for children with disabilities and the costs of prenatal diagnosis and abortion. We come mighty close when we once again let scientists and physicians make judgments about who should and who should not inhabit the world and applaud them when they develop the technologies that let us implement such judgments. Is it in our interest to have to decide not just whether we want to bear a child but what kind of children to bear? If we try to do that we become entirely dependent on the decisions scientists and physicians make about what technologies to develop and what disabilities to "target." Those decisions are usually made on grounds of professional interest, technical feasibility, and economic and eugenic considerations, not out of a regard for the needs of women and children.

PROBLEMS WITH SELECTIVE ABORTION

I want to be explicit about how I think a woman's right to abortion fits into this analysis and about some of the connections I see between what the Nazis did and what is happening now. I repeat: A woman must have the right to abort a fetus, whatever her reasons, precisely because it is a decision about her body and about how she will live her life. But decisions about what kind of baby to bear inevitably are bedeviled by overt and unspoken judgments about which lives are "worth living."

Nazi eugenic practices were fairly coercive. The state decided who should not inhabit the world, and lawyers, physicians, and scientists provided the justifications and means to implement these decisions. In today's liberal democracies the situation is different. Eugenic principles are part of our largely unexamined and unspoken preconceptions about who should and who should not inhabit the world, and scientists and physicians provide the ways to put them into practice. Women are expected to implement the society's eugenic prejudices by "choosing" to have the appropriate tests and "electing" not to initiate or to terminate pregnancies if it looks as though the outcome will offend. And to a considerable extent not initiating or terminating these pregnancies may indeed be what women want to do. But one reason we want to is that society promises much grief to parents of children it deems unfit to inhabit the world. People with disabilities, like the rest of us, need opportunities to act in the world, and sometimes that means that they need special provisions and consideration.

So once more, yes, a woman must have the right to terminate a pregnancy, whatever her reasons, but she must also feel empowered not to terminate it, confident that the society will do what it can to enable here and her child to live fulfilling lives. To the extent that prenatal interventions implement social prejudices against people with disabilities they do not expand our reproductive rights. They constrict them.

Focusing the discussion on individualistic questions, such as every woman's right to bear healthy children (which in some people's minds quickly translates into her duty not to "burden society" with unhealthy ones) or the responsibility of scientists and physicians to develop techniques to make that possible, obscures crucial questions such as: How many women have economic access to these kinds of choices? How many have the educational and cultural background to evaluate the information they can get from physicians critically enough to make an

informed choice? It also obscures questions about a humane society's responsibilities to satisfy the requirements of people with special needs and to offer them
the opportunity to participate as full-fledged members in the culture.

Our present situation connects with the Nazi past in that once again scientists and physicians are making the decisions about what lives to "target" as not
worth living by deciding which tests to develop. Yet if people are to have real
choices, the decisions that determine the context within which we must choose
must not be made in our absence—by professionals, research review panels, or
funding organizations. And the situation is not improved by inserting a new
group of professionals—bioethicists—between the technical professionals and
the public. This public—the women and men who must live in the world that
the scientific/medical/industrial complex constructs—must be able to take part
in the process by which such decisions are made. Until mechanisms exist that
give people a decisive voice in setting the relevant scientific and technical agendas and until scientists and physicians are made accountable to the people
whose lives they change, technical innovations do not constitute new choices.
They merely replace previous social constraints with new ones.

WORKS CITED

Arendt, Hannah. 1977. *Eichmann in Jerusalem: A Report on the Banality of Evil*. New York:
    Penguin.
Asch, Adrienne. 1988. "Reproductive Technology and Disability." In Sherrill Cohen and
    Nadine Taub, eds., *Reproductive Laws for the 1990s*. Clifton, N.J.: Humana Press.
Asch, Adrienne, and Michelle Fine. 1988. "Introduction: Beyond Pedestals." In Michelle
    Fine and Adrienne Asch, eds., *Women with Disabilities*. Philadelphia: Temple Uni-
    versity Press.
Chrorover, Stephan L. 1979. *From Genesis to Genocide*. Cambridge, Mass.: MIT Press.
Duelli Klein, Renate, Gena Corea, and Ruth Hubbard. 1985. "German Women say No
    to Gene and Reproductive Technology: Reflections on a Conference in Bonn,
    West Germany, April 19–21, 1985." *Feminist Forum: Women's Studies International
    Forum* 9(3):I–IV.
Galton, Francis. 1883. *Inquiries into Human Faculty*. London: Macmillan.
Glass, Bentley. 1971. "Science: Endless Horizons or Golden Age?" *Science* 171:23–29.
Kevles, Daniel J. 1985. *In the Name of Eugenics: Genetics and the Uses of Human Hered-
    ity*. New York: Knopf.
Koonz, Claudia. 1987. *Mothers in the Fatherland: Women, the Family and Nazi Politics*. New
    York: St. Martin's Press.
Lifton, Robert J. 1986. *The Nazi Doctors*. New York: Basic Books.
Ludmerer, Kenneth M. 1972. *Genetics and American Society*. Baltimore: Johns Hopkins
    University Press.
Müller-Hill, Benno. 1984. *Tödliche Wissenshaft*. Reinbek, West Germany: Rowohlt.
    (Translation 1988. *Murderous Science*. Oxford: Oxford University Press.)
Proctor, Robert N. 1988. *Racial Hygiene: Medicine and the Nazis*. Cambridge: Harvard Uni-
    versity Press.
Rodriguez-Trias, Helen. 1982. *In Labor: Women and Power in the Birthplace*. New York:
    Norton.
Terman, Lewis M. 1924. "The Conservation of Talent." *School and Society*
    19(483):359–364.

part three

Stigma and Illness

10

Selections from *Stigma*

ERVING GOFFMAN

STIGMA AND SOCIAL IDENTITY

The Greeks, who were apparently strong on visual aids, originated the term *stigma* to refer to bodily signs designed to expose something unusual and bad about the moral status of the signifier. The signs were cut or burnt into the body and advertised that the bearer was a slave, a criminal, or a traitor—a blemished person, ritually polluted, to be avoided, especially in public places. Later, in Christian times, two layers of metaphor were added to the term: the first referred to bodily signs of holy grace that took the form of eruptive blossoms on the skin; the second, a medical allusion to this religious allusion, referred to bodily signs of physical disorder. Today the term is widely used in something like the original literal sense, but is applied more to the disgrace itself than to the bodily evidence of it. Furthermore, shifts have occurred in the kinds of disgrace that arouse concern. Students, however, have made little effort to describe the structural preconditions of stigma, or even to provide a definition of the concept itself. It seems necessary, therefore, to try at the beginning to sketch in some very general assumptions and definitions.

PRELIMINARY CONCEPTIONS

Society establishes the means of categorizing persons and the complement of attributes felt to be ordinary and natural for members of each of these categories. Social settings establish the categories of persons likely to be encountered there. The routines of social intercourse in established settings allow us to deal with anticipated others without special attention or thought. When a stranger comes into our presence, then, first appearances are likely to enable us to anticipate hxs category and attributes, his "social identity"—to use a term that is better than "social status" because personal attributes such as "honesty" are involved, as well as structural ones, like "occupation." We lean on these anticipations that we have, transforming them into normative expectations, into righteously presented demands. Typically, we do not become aware that we have made these demands or aware of what they are until an active question arises as to whether or not they will be fulfilled. It is then that we are likely to realize that all along we had been making certain assumptions as to what the individual before us ought to be. Thus, the demands we make might better be called demands made "in effect" and the character we impute to the individual might better be seen as an imputation made in potential retrospect—a characterization "in effect," a *virtual social* identity. The category and attributes he could in fact be proved to possess will be called his *actual social identity*.

While the stranger is present before us, evidence can arise of his possessing an attribute that makes him different from others in the category of persons available for him to be, and of a less desirable kind—in the extreme, a person who is quite thoroughly bad, or dangerous, or weak. He is thus reduced in our minds from a whole and usual person to a tainted, discounted one. Such an attribute is a stigma, especially when its discrediting effect is very extensive; sometimes it is also called a failing, a shortcoming, a handicap. It constitutes a special discrepancy between virtual and actual social identity. Note that there are other types of discrepancy between virtual and actual social identity, for example the kind that causes us to reclassify an individual from one socially anticipated category to a different but equally well-anticipated one, and the kind that causes us to alter our estimation of the individual upward. Note, too, that not all undesirable attributes are at issue, but only those which are incongruous with our stereotype of what a given type of individual should be.

The term stigma, then, will be used to refer to an attribute that is deeply discrediting, but it should be seen that a language of relationships, not attributes, is really needed. An attribute that stigmatizes one type of possessor can confirm the usualness of another, and therefore is neither creditable nor discreditable as a thing in itself. For example, some jobs in America cause holders without the expected college education to conceal this fact; other jobs, however, can lead the few of their holders who have a higher education to keep this a secret, lest they be marked as failures and outsiders. Similarly, a middle class boy may feel no compunction in being seen going to the library; a professional criminal, however, writes:

> I can remember before now on more than one occasion, for instance, going into a public library near where I was living, and looking over my shoulder a couple of times before I actually went in just to make sure no one who knew me was standing about and seeing me do it.[1]

So, too, an individual who desires to fight for his country may conceal a physical defect, lest his claimed physical status be discredited; later, the same individual, embittered and trying to get out of the army, may succeed in gaining admission to the army hospital, where he would be discredited if discovered in not really having an acute sickness.[2] A stigma, then, is really a special kind of relationship between attribute and stereotype, although I don't propose to continue to say so, in part because there are important attributes that almost everywhere in our society are discrediting.

The term stigma and its synonyms conceal a double perspective: does the stigmatized individual assume his differentness is known about already or is evident on the spot, or does he assume it is neither known about by those present nor immediately perceivable by them? In the first case one deals with the plight of the *discredited*, in the second with that of the *discreditable*. This is an important difference, even though a particular stigmatized individual is likely to have experience with both situations. I will begin with the situation of the discredited and move on to the discreditable but not always separate the two.

Three grossly different types of stigma may be mentioned. First there are abominations of the body—the various physical deformities. Next there are blemishes of individual character perceived as weak will, domineering or unnatural passions, treacherous and rigid beliefs, and dishonesty, these being inferred from a known record of, for example, mental disorder, imprisonment, addiction, alcoholism, homosexuality, unemployment, suicidal attempts, and radical political behavior. Finally there are the tribal stigma of race, nation, and religion, these being stigma that can be transmitted through lineages and equally contaminate all members of a family.[3] In all of these various instances of stigma, however, including those the Greeks had in mind, the same sociological features are found: an individual who might have been received easily in ordinary social intercourse possesses a trait that can obtrude itself upon attention and turn those of us whom he meets away from him, breaking the claim that his other attributes have on us. He possesses a stigma, an undesired differentness from what we had anticipated. We and those who do not depart negatively from the particular expectations at issue I shall call the *normals*.

The attitudes we normals have toward a person with a stigma and the actions we take in regard to him, are well known, since these responses are what benevolent social action is designed to soften and ameliorate. By definition, of course, we believe the person with a stigma is not quite human. On this assumption we exercise varieties of discrimination, through which we effectively, if often unthinkingly, reduce his life chances. We construct a stigma-theory, an ideology to explain his inferiority and account for the danger he represents, sometimes rationalizing an animosity based on other differences, such as those of social class.[4] We use specific stigma terms such as cripple, bastard, moron in our daily discourse as a source of metaphor and imagery, typically without giving thought to the original meaning.[5] We tend to impute a wide range of imperfections on the basis of the original one,[6] and at the same time to impute some desirable but undesired attributes, often of a supernatural cast, such as "sixth sense," or "understanding":[7]

> For some, there may be a hesitancy about touching or steering the blind, while for others, the perceived failure to see may be generalized into a gestalt of disability, so that the individual shouts at the blind as if they were deaf or attempts to lift them as if they were crippled. Those confronting the blind may have a whole range of belief that is anchored in the stereotype. For instance, they think they are subject to unique judgment, assuming the blinded individual draws on special channels of information unavailable to others.[8]

Further, we may perceive his defensive response to his situation as a direct expression of his defect, and then see both defect and response as just retribution for something he or his parents or his tribe did, and hence a justification of the way we treat him.[9]

Now turn from the normal to the person he is normal against. It seems generally true that members of a social category may strongly support a standard of judgment that they and others agree does not directly apply to them. Thus it is that a businessman may demand womanly behavior from females or ascetic behavior from monks, and not construe himself as someone who ought to realize either of these styles of conduct. The distinction is between realizing a norm and merely supporting it. The issue of stigma does not arise here, but only where there is some expectation on all sides that those in a given category should not only support a particular norm but also realize it.

Also, it seems possible for an individual to fail to live up to what we effectively demand of him, and yet be relatively untouched by this failure; insulated by his alienation, protected by identity beliefs of his own, he feels that he is a full-fledged normal human being, and that we are the ones who are not quite human. He bears a stigma but does not seem to be impressed or repentant about doing so. This possibility is celebrated in exemplary tales about Mennonites, Gypsies, shameless scoundrels, and very orthodox Jews.

In America at present, however, separate systems of honor seem to be on the decline. The stigmatized individual tends to hold the same beliefs about identity that we do; this is a pivotal fact. His deepest feelings about what he is may be his sense of being a "normal person," a human being like anyone else, a person, therefore, who deserves a fair chance and a fair break.[10] (Actually, however phrased, he bases his claims not on what he thinks is due *everyone*, but only everyone of a selected social category into which he unquestionably fits, for example, anyone of his age, sex, profession, and so forth.) Yet he may perceive, usually quite correctly, that whatever others profess, they do not really "accept" him and are not ready to make contact with him on "equal grounds."[11] Further, the standards he has incorporated from the wider society equip him to be intimately alive to what others see as his failing, inevitably causing him, if only for moments, to agree that he does indeed fall short of what he really ought to be. Shame becomes a central possibility, arising from the individual's perception of one of his own attributes as being a defiling thing to possess, and one he can readily see himself as not possessing.

The immediate presence of normals is likely to reinforce this split between self-demands and self, but in fact self-hate and self-derogation can also occur when only he and a mirror are about:

When I got up at last . . . and had learned to walk again, one day I took a hand glass and went to a long mirror to look at myself, and I went alone. I didn't want anyone . . . to know how I felt when I saw myself for the first time. But here was no noise, no outcry; I didn't scream with rage when I saw myself. I just felt numb. That person in the mirror *couldn't* be me. I felt inside like a healthy, ordinary, lucky person—oh, not like the one in the mirror! Yet when I turned my face to the mirror there were my own eyes looking back, hot with shame . . . when I did not cry or make any sound, it became impossible that I should speak of it to anyone, and the confusion and the panic of my discovery were locked inside me then and there, to be faced alone, for a very long time to come.[12]

Over and over I forgot what I had seen in the mirror. It could not penetrate into the interior of my mind and become an integral part of me. I felt as if it had nothing to do with me; it was only a disguise. But is was not the kind of disguise which is put on voluntarily by the person who wears it, and which is intended to confuse other people as to one's identity. My disguise had been put on me without my consent or knowledge like the ones in fairy tales, and it was I myself who was confused by it, as to my own identity. I looked in the mirror, and was horror-struck because I did not recognize myself. In the place where I was standing, with that persistent romantic elation in me, as if I were a favored fortunate person to whom everything was possible, I saw a stranger, a little, pitiable, hideous figure, and a face that became, as I stared at it, painful and blushing with shame. It was only a disguise, but it was on me, for life. It was there, it was there, it was real. Everyone of those encounters was like a blow on the head. They left me dazed and dumb and senseless every time, until slowly and stubbornly my robust persistent illusion of well-being and of personal beauty spread all through me again, and I forgot the irrelevant reality and was all unprepared and vulnerable again.[13]

The central feature of the stigmatized individual's situation in life can now be stated. It is a question of what is often, if vaguely, called "acceptance." Those who have dealings with him fail to accord him the respect and regard which the uncontaminated aspects of his social identity have led them to anticipate extending, and have led him to anticipate receiving; he echoes this denial by finding that some of his own attributes warrant it.

How does the stigmatized person respond to his situation? In some cases it will be possible for him to make a direct attempt to correct what he sees as the objective basis of his failing, as when a physically deformed person undergoes plastic surgery, a blind person eye treatment, an illiterate remedial education, a homosexual psychotherapy. (Where such repair is possible, what often results is not the acquisition of fully normal status, but a transformation of self from someone with a particular blemish into someone with a record of having corrected a particular blemish.) Here proneness to "victimization" is to be cited, a result of the stigmatized person's exposure to fraudulent servers selling speech correction, skin lighteners, body stretchers, youth restorers (as in rejuvenation through fertilized egg yolk treatment), cures through faith, and poise in conversation. Whether a practical technique or fraud is involved, the quest, often secret, that results provides a special indication of the extremes to which the stigmatized can be will to go, and hence the painfulness of the situation that leads them to these extremes. One illustration may be cited:

Miss Peck [a pioneer New York social worker for the hard of hearing] said that in the early days the quacks and get-rich-quick medicine men who abounded saw the League [for the hard of hearing] as their happy hunting ground, ideal for the promotion of magnetic head caps, miraculous vibrating machines, artificial eardrums, blowers, inhalers, massagers, magic oils, balsams, and other guaranteed, sure-fire, positive, and permanent cure-alls for incurable deafness. Advertisements for such hokum (until the 1920s when the American Medical Association moved in with an investigation campaign) beset the hard of hearing in the pages of the daily press, even in reputable magazines.[14]

The stigmatized individual can also attempt to correct his condition indirectly by devoting much private effort to the mastery of areas of activity ordinarily felt to be closed on incidental and physical grounds to one with his shortcoming. This is illustrated by the lame person who learns or re-learns to swim, ride, play tennis, or fly an airplane, or the blind person who becomes expert at skiing and mountain climbing.[15] Tortured learning may be associated, of course, with the tortured performance of what is learned, as when an individual, confined to a wheelchair, manages to take to the dance floor with a girl in some kind of mimicry of dancing.[16] Finally, the person with a shameful differentness can break with what is called reality, and obstinately attempt to employ an unconventional interpretation of the character of his social identity.

The stigmatized individual is likely to use his stigma for "secondary gains," as an excuse for ill success that has come his way for other reasons:

> For years the scar, harelip or misshapen nose has been looked on as a handicap, and its importance in the social and emotional adjustment is unconsciously all embracing. It is the "hook" on which the patient has hung all inadequacies, all dissatisfactions, all procrastinations and all unpleasant duties of social life, and he has come to depend on it not only as a reasonable escape from competition but as a protection from social responsibility.
>
> When one removes this factor by surgical repair, the patient is cast adrift from the more or less acceptable emotional protection it has offered and soon he finds, to his surprise and discomfort, that life is not all smooth sailing even for those with unblemished, "ordinary" faces. He is unprepared to cope with this situation without the support of a "handicap," and he may turn to the less simple, but similar, protection of the behavior patterns of neurasthenia, hysterical conversion, hypochondriasis or the acute anxiety states.[17]

He may also see the trials he has suffered as a blessing in disguise, especially because of what it is felt that suffering can teach one about life and people:

> But now, far away from the hospital experience, I can evaluate what I have learned. [A mother permanently disabled by polio writes.] For it wasn't only suffering: it was also learning through suffering. I know my awareness of people has deepened and increased, that those who are close to me can count on me to turn all my mind and heart and attention to their problems. I could not have learned *that* dashing all over a tennis court.[18]

Correspondingly, he can come to re-assess the limitations of normals, as a multiple sclerotic suggests:

> Both healthy minds and healthy bodies may be crippled. The fact that "normal"

people can get around, can see, can hear, doesn't mean that they are seeing or hearing. They can be very blind to the things that spoil their happiness, very deaf to
the pleas of others for kindness; when I think of them I do not feel any more crippled or disabled than they. Perhaps in some way I can be the means of opening
their eyes to the beauties around us: things like a warm handclasp, a voice that is
anxious to cheer, a spring breeze, music to listen to, a friendly nod. These are
important to me, and I like to feel that I can help them.[19]

And a blind writer.

That would lead immediately to the thought that there are many occurrences
which can diminish satisfaction in living far more effectively than blindness, and
that lead would be an entirely healthy one to take. In this light, we can perceive,
for instance, that some inadequacy like the inability to accept human love, which
can effectively diminish satisfaction of living almost to the vanishing point, is far
more a tragedy than blindness. But it is unusual for the man who suffers from such
a malady even to know he has it and self pity is, therefore, impossible for him.[20]

And a cripple:

As life went on, I learned of many, many different kinds of handicap, not only the
physical ones, and I began to realize that the words of the crippled girl in the
extract above [words of bitterness] could just as well have been spoken by young
women who had never needed crutches, women who felt inferior and different
because of ugliness, or inability to bear children, or helplessness in contacting
people, or many other reasons.[21]

The responses of the normal and of the stigmatized that have been considered
so far are ones which can occur over protracted periods of time and in isolation
from current contacts between normals and stigmatized.[22] This book, however,
is specifically concerned with the issue of "mixed contacts"—the moments
when stigmatized and normal are in the same "social situation," that is, in one
another's immediate physical presence, whether in a conversation-like encounter
or in the mere co-presence of an unfocused gathering.

The very anticipation of such contacts can of course lead normals and the
stigmatized to arrange life so as to avoid them. Presumably this will have larger
consequences for the stigmatized, since more arranging will usually be necessary
on their part:

Before her disfigurement [amputation of the distal half of her nose] Mrs. Dover,
who lived with one of her two married daughters, had been an independent, warm
and friendly woman who enjoyed traveling, shopping, and visiting her many relatives. The disfigurement of her face, however, resulted in a definite alteration in her
way of living. The first two or three years she seldom left her daughter's home, pre-

ferring to remain in her room or to sit in the backyard. "I was heartsick," she said; "the door had been shut on my life."[22]

Lacking the salutary feed-back of daily social intercourse with others, the self-isolate can become suspicious, depressed, hostile, anxious, and bewildered. Sullivan's version may be cited:

> The awareness of inferiority means that one is unable to keep out of consciousness the formulation of some chronic feeling of the worst sort of insecurity, and this means that one suffers anxiety and perhaps even something worse, if jealousy is really worse than anxiety. The fear that others can disrespect a person because of something he shows means that he is always insecure in his contact with other people; and this insecurity arises, not from mysterious and somewhat disguised, sources, as a great deal of our anxiety does, but from something which he knows he cannot fix. Now that represents an almost fatal deficiency of the self-system, since the self is unable to disguise or exclude a definite formulation that reads, "I am inferior. Therefore people will dislike me and I cannot be secure with them."[24]

When normals and stigmatized do in fact enter one another's immediate presence, especially when they there attempt to sustain a joint conversational encounter, there occurs one of the primal scenes of sociology; for, in many cases, these moments will be the ones when the causes and effects of stigma must be directly confronted on both sides.

These stigmatized individual may find that he feels unsure of how we normals will identify him and receive him.[25] An illustration may be cited from a student of physical disability:

> Uncertainty of status for the disabled person obtains over a wide range of social interactions in addition to that of employment. The blind, the ill, the deaf, the crippled can never be sure what the attitude of a new acquaintance will be, whether it will be rejective or accepting, until the contact has been made. This is exactly the position of the adolescent, the light-skinned Negro, the second generation immigrant, the socially mobile person and the woman who has entered a predominantly masculine occupation.[26]

This uncertainty arises not merely from the stigmatized individual's not knowing which of several categories he will be placed in, but also, where the placement is favorable, from his knowing that in their hearts the others may be defining him in terms of his stigma:

> And I always feel this with straight people—that whenever they're being nice to me, pleasant to me, all the time really, underneath they're only assessing me as a criminal and nothing else. It's too late for me to be any different now to what I am, but I still feel this keenly, that that's their only approach, and they're quite incapable of accepting me as anything else.[27]

Thus in the stigmatized arises the sense of not knowing what the others present are "really" thinking about him.

Further, during mixed contacts, the stigmatized individual is likely to feel that he is "on,"[28] having to be self-conscious and calculating about the impression he is making, to a degree and in areas of conduct which he assumes others are not.

Also, he is likely to feel that the usual scheme of interpretation for everyday events has been undermined. His minor accomplishments, he feels, may be assessed as signs of remarkable and noteworthy capacities in the circumstances. A professional criminal provides an illustration:

> "You know, it's really amazing you should read books like this, I'm staggered I am. I should've thought you'd read paper-backed thrillers, things with lurid covers, books liked that. And here you are with Claud Cockburn, Hugh Klare, Simone de Beauvoir, and Lawrence Durrell!"
>
> You know, he didn't see this as an insulting remark at all: in fact, I think he thought he was being honest in telling me how mistaken he was. And that's exactly the sort of patronizing you get from straight people if you're a criminal. "Fancy that!" they say. "In some ways you're just like a human being!" I'm not kidding, it makes me want to choke the bleeding life out of them.[29]

A blind person provides another illustration:

> His once most ordinary deeds—walking nonchalantly up the street, locating the peas on his plate, lighting a cigarette—are no longer ordinary. He becomes an unusual person. If he performs them with finesse and assurance they excite the same kind of wonderment inspired by a magician who pulls rabbits out of hats.[30]

At the same time, minor failings or incidental impropriety may, he feels, be interpreted as a direct expression of his stigmatized differentness. Ex-mental patients, for example, are sometimes afraid to engage in sharp interchanges with spouse or employer because of what a show of emotion might be taken as a sign of. Mental defectives face a similar contingency:

> It also happens that if a person of low intellectual ability gets into some sort of trouble the difficult is more or less automatically attributed to "mental defect" whereas if a person of "normal intelligence" gets into a similar difficulty, it is not regarded as symptomatic of anything in particular.[31]

A one-legged girl, recalling her experience with sports, provides other illustrations:

> Whenever I fell, out swarmed the women in droves, clucking and fretting like a bunch of bereft mother hens. It was kind of them, and in retrospect I appreciate their solicitude, but at the time I resented and was greatly embarrassed by their interference. For they assumed that no routine hazard to skating—no stick or

stone—upset my flying wheels. It was a foregone conclusion that *I* fell because I was a poor, helpless cripple.[32]

Not one of them shouted with outrage, "That dangerous wild bronco threw her!"—which, God forgive, he did technically. It was like a horrible ghostly visitation of my old roller-skating days. All the good people lamented in chorus, "That poor, poor girl fell off!"[33]

When the stigmatized person's failing can be perceived by our merely directing attention (typically, visual) to him—when, in short, he is a discredited, not discreditable, person—he is likely to feel that to be present among normals nakedly exposes him to invasions of privacy,[34] experienced most pointedly perhaps when children simply stare at him.[35] This displeasure in being exposed can be increased by the conversations strangers may feel free to strike up with him, conversations in which they express what he takes to be morbid curiosity about his condition, or in which they proffer help that he does not need or want.[36] One might add that there are certain classic formulae for these kinds of conversations: "My dear girl, how did you get your quiggle"; "My great uncle had a quiggle, so I feel I know all about your problem"; "You know I've always said that Quiggles are good family men and look after their own poor"; "Tell me, how do you manage to bathe with a quiggle?" The implication of these overtures is that the stigmatized individual is a person who can be approached by strangers at will, providing only that they are sympathetic to the plight of persons of his kind.

Given what the stigmatized individual may well face upon entering a mixed social situation, he may anticipatorily respond by defensive cowering. This may be illustrated from an early study of some German unemployed during the Depression, the words being those of a 43-year-old mason:

How hard and humiliating it is to bear the name of an unemployed man. When I go out, I cast down my eyes because I feel myself wholly inferior. When I go along the street, it seems to me that I can't be compared with an average citizen, that everybody is pointing at me with his finger. I instinctively avoid meeting anyone. Former acquaintances and friends of better times are no longer so cordial. They greet me indifferently when we meet. They no longer offer me a cigarette and their eyes seem to say, "You are not worth it, you don't work."[37]

A crippled girl provides an illustrative analysis:

When . . . I began to walk out alone in the streets of our town . . . I found then that wherever I had to pass three or four children together on the sidewalk, if I happened to be alone, they would shout at me, . . . Sometimes they even ran after me, shouting and jeering. This was something I didn't know how to face, and it seemed as if I couldn't bear it. . . .

For awhile those encounters in the street filled me with a cold dread of all unknown children . . .

One day I suddenly realized that I had become so self-conscious and afraid of all strange children that, like animals, they knew I was afraid, so that even the mildest and most amiable of them were automatically prompted to derision by my own shrinking and dread.[38]

Instead of cowering, the stigmatized individual may attempt to approach mixed contacts with hostile bravado, but this can induce from others its own set of troublesome reciprocation. It may be added that the stigmatized person sometimes vacillates between cowering and bravado, racing from one to the other, thus demonstrating one central way in which ordinary face-to-face interaction can run wild.

I am suggesting, then, that the stigmatized individual—at least "visibly" stigmatized one—will have special reasons for feeling that mixed social situations make for anxious unanchored interaction. But if this is so, then it is to be suspected that we normals will find these situations shaky too. We will feel that the stigmatized individual is either too aggressive or too shamefaced, and in either case too ready to read unintended meanings into our actions. We ourselves may feel that if we show direct sympathetic concern for his condition, we may be overstepping ourselves; and yet if we actually forget that he has a failing we are likely to make impossible demands of him or unthinkingly slight his fellow-sufferers. Each potential source of discomfort for him when we are with him can become something we sense he is aware of, aware that we are aware of, and even aware of our state of awareness about his awareness; the stage is then set for the infinite regress of mutual consideration that Meadian social psychology tells us how to begin but not how to terminate.

Given what both the stigmatized and we normals introduce into mixed social situations, it is understandable that all will not go smoothly. We are likely to attempt to carry on as though in fact he wholly fitted one of the types of person naturally available to us in the situation, whether this means treating him as someone better than we feel he might be or someone worse than we feel he probably is. If neither of these tacks is possible, then we may try to act as if he were a "non-person," and not present at all as someone of whom ritual notice is to be taken. He, in turn, is likely to go along with these strategies, at least initially.

In consequence, attention is furtively withdrawn from its obligatory targets, and self-consciousness and "other-consciousness" occurs, expressed in the pathology of interaction—uneasiness.[39] As described in the case of the physically handicapped:

Whether the handicap is overtly and tactlessly responded to as such or, as is more commonly the case, no explicit reference is made to it, the underlying condition of heightened, narrowed, awareness causes the interaction to be articulated too exclusively in terms of it. This, as my informants described it, is usually accompanied by one or more of the familiar signs of discomfort and stickiness: the guarded references, the common everyday words suddenly made taboo, the fixed stare elsewhere, the artificial levity, the compulsive loquaciousness, the awkward solemnity.[40]

214   ERVING GOFFMAN

In social situations with an individual known or perceived to have a stigma, we are likely, then, to employ categorizations that do not fit, and we and he are likely to experience uneasiness. Of course, there is often significant movement from this starting point. And since the stigmatized person is likely to be more often faced with these situations than are we, he is likely to become the more adept at managing them.

NOTES

1. T. Parker and R. Allerton, *The Courage of His Convictions* (London: Hutchinson & Co., 1962), p. 109.
2. In this connection see the review by M. Meltzer, "Countermanipulation through Malingering," in A. Biderman and H. Zimmer, eds., *The Manipulation of Human Behavior* (New York: John Wiley & Sons, 1961), pp. 277–304.
3. In recent history, especially in Britain, low class status functioned as an important tribal stigma, the sins of the parents, or at least their millieu, being visited on the child, should the child rise improperly far above his initial station. The management of class stigma is of course a central theme in the English novel.
4. D. Riesman, "Some Observations Concerning Marginality," *Phylon*, Second Quarter, 1951, 122.
5. The case regarding mental patients is represented by T. J. Scheff in a forthcoming paper.
6. In regard to the blind, see E. Henrich and L. Kriegel, eds., *Experiments in Survival* (New York: Associatino for the Aid of Crippled Children, 1961), pp. 152 and 186; and H. Chevigny, *My Eyes Have a Cold Nose* (New Haven, Conn.: Yale University Press, paperbound, 1962), p. 201.
7. In the words of one blind woman, "I was asked to endorse a perfume, presumably because being sightless my sense of smell was super-discriminating." See T. Keitlen (with N. Lobsenz), *Farewell to Fear* (New York: Avon, 1962), p. 10.
8. A. G. Gowman, *The War Blind in American Social Structure* (New York: American Foundation for the Blind, 1957), p. 198.
9. For examples, see Macgregor *et al.*, *op. cit.*, throughout.
10. The notion of "normal human being" may have its source in the medical approach to humanity or in the tendency of large-scale bureaucratic organizations, such as the nation state, to treat all members in some respects as equal. Whatever its origins, it seems to provide the basic imagery through which laymen currently conceive of themselves. Interestingly, a convention seems to have emerged in popular life-story writing where a questionable person proves his claim to normalcy by citing his acquisition of a spouse and children, and, oddly, by attesting to his spending Christmas and Thanksgiving with them.
11. A criminal's view of this nonacceptance is presented in Parker and Allerton, *op. cit.*, pp. 110–111.
12. K. B. Hathaway, *The Little Locksmith* (New York: Coward-McCann, 1943), p. 41, in Wright, *op. cit.*, p. 157.
13. *Ibid.*, pp. 46–47. For general treatments of the self-disliking sentiments, see K. Lewin, *Resolving Social Conflicts*, Part III (New York: Harper & Row, 1948); A. Kardiner and L. Ovesey, *The Mark of Oppression: A Psychological Study of the American Negro* (New York: W. W. Norton & Company, 1951); and E. H. Erikson, *Childhood and Society* (New York: W. W. Norton & Company, 1950).
14. F. Warfield, *Keep Listening* (New York: The Viking Press, 1957), p. 76. See also H.

von Hentig, *The Criminal and His Victim* (New Haven, Conn.: Yale University Press, 1948), p. 101.

15. Keitlen, *op. cit.*, Chap. 12, pp. 117–129 and Chap. 14, pp. 137–149. See also Chevigny, *op. cit.*, pp. 85–86.

16. Henrich and Kriegel, *op. cit.*, p. 49.

17. W. Y. Baker and L. H. Smith, "Facial Disfigurement and Personality," *Journal of the American Medical Association*, CXII (1939), 303. Macgregor *et al.*, *op. cit.*, p. 57ff., provide an illustration of a man who used his big red nose for a crutch.

18. Henrich and Kriegel, *op. cit.*, p. 19.

19. *Ibid.*, p. 35.

20. Chevigny, *op. cit.*, p. 154.

21. F. Carlin, *And Yet We Are Human* (London: Chatto & Windus, 1962), pp. 23–24.

22. For one review, see G. W. Allport, *The Nature of Prejudice* (New York: Anchor Books, 1958).

23. Macgregor *et al.*, *op. cit.*, pp. 91–92.

24. From *Clinical Studies in Psychiatry*, H. S. Perry, M. L. Gawel, and M. Gibbon, eds. (New York: W. W. Norton & Company, 1956), p. 145.

25. R. Barker, "The Social Psychology of Physical Disability," *Journal of Social Issues*, IV (1948), 34, suggests that stigmatized persons "live on a social-psychological frontier," constantly facing new situations. See also Macgregor *et al.*, *op. cit.*, p. 87, where the suggestion is made that the grossly deformed need suffer less doubt about their reception in interaction than the less visibly deformed.

26. Barker, *op. cit.*, p. 33.

27. Parker and Allerton, *op. cit.*, p. III.

28. This special kind of self-consciousness is analyzed in S. Messinger, *et al.*, "Life as Theater: Some Notes on the Dramaturgic Approcah to Social Reality," *Sociometry*, XXV (1962), 98–110.

29. Parker and Allerton, *op. cit.*, p. III.

30. Chevigny, *op. cit.*, p. 140.

31. L. A. Dexter, "A Social Theory of Mental Deficiency," *American Journal of Mental Deficiency*, LXII (1958), 923. For another study of the mental defective as a stigmatized person, see S. E. Perry, "Some Theoretical Problems of Mental Deficiency and Their Action Implications," *Psychiatry*, XVII (1954), 45–73.

32. Baker, *Out on a Limb* (New York: McGraw-Hill Book Company, n.d.), p. 22.

33. *Ibid.*, p. 73.

34. This theme is well treated in R. K. White, B. A. Wright, and T. Dembo, "Studies in Adjustment to Visible Injuries: Evaluation of Curiosity by the Injured," *Journal of Abnormal and Social Psychology*, XLIII (1948), 13–28.

35. For example, Henrich and Kriegel, *op. cit.*, p. 184.

36. See Wright, *op. cit.*, "The Problem of Sympathy," pp. 233–237.

37. S. Zawadski and P. Lazarsfeld, "The Psychological Consequences of Unemployment," *Journal of Social Psychology*, VI (1935), 239.

38. Hathaway, *op. cit.*, pp. 155–157, in S. Richardson, "The Social Psychological Consequences of Handicapping," unpublished paper persented at the 1962 American Sociological Association Convention, Washington, D. C., 7–8.

39. For a general treatment, see E. Goffman, "Alienation from Interaction," *Human Relations*, X (1957), 47–60.

40. F. Davis, "Deviance Disavowal: The Management of Strained Interaction by the Visibly Handicapped," *Social Problems*, IX (1961), 123. See also White, Wright, and Dembo, *op. cit.*, pp. 26–27.

11

Stigma

An Enigma Demystified

LERITA M. COLEMAN

> Nature caused us all to be born equal; if fate is pleased to disturb this plan of the general law, it is our responsibility to correct its caprice, and to repair by our attention the usurpations of the stronger.
>
> —Maurice Blanchot

What is stigma and why does stigma remain? Because stigmas mirror culture and society, they are in constant flux, and therefore the answers to these two questions continue to elude social scientists. Viewing stigma from multiple perspectives exposes its intricate nature and helps us to disentangle its web of complexities and paradoxes. Stigma represents a view of life; a set of personal and social constructs; a set of social relations and social relationships; a form of social reality. Stigma has been a difficult concept to conceptualize because it reflects a property, a process, a form of social categorization, and an affective state.

Two primary questions, then, that we as social scientists have addressed are how and why during certain historical periods. In specific cultures or within particular social groups, some human differences are valued and desired, and other human differences are devalued, feared, or stigmatized. In attempting to answer these questions, I propose another view of stigma, one that takes into account its behavioral, cognitive, and affective components and reveals that stigma is a response to the dilemma of difference.

THE DILEMMA

No two human beings are exactly alike: there are countless ways to differ. Shape, size, skin color, gender, age, cultural background, personality, and years of formal education are just a few of the infinite number of ways in which people can vary. Perceptually, and in actuality, there is greater variation on some of these dimensions than on others. Age and gender, for example, are dimensions with limited and quantifiable ranges; yet they interact exponentially with other physical or social characteristics that have larger continua (e.g., body shape, income, cultural background) to create a vast number of human differences. Goffman states, though, that "stigma is equivalent to an undesired differentness" (see Stafford & Scott). The infinite variety of human attributes suggests that what is undesired or stigmatized is heavily dependent on the social context and to some extent arbitrarily defined. The large number of stigmatizable attributes and several taxonomies of stigmas in the literature offer further evidence of how arbitrary the selection of undesired differences may be (see Ainlay & Crosby; Becker & Arnold; Solomon; Stafford & Scott).

What is most poignant about Goffman's description of stigma is that it suggests that all human differences are potentially stigmatizable. As we move out of one social context where a difference is desired into another context where the difference is undesired, we begin to feel the effects of stigma. This conceptualization of stigma also indicates that those possessing power, the dominant group, can determine which human differences are desired and undesired. In part, stigmas reflect the value judgments of a dominant group.

Many people, however, especially those who have some role in determining the desired and undesired differences of the zeitgeist, often think of stigma only as a property of individuals. They operate under the illusion that stigma exists only for certain segments of the population. But the truth is that any "nonstigmatized" person can easily become "stigmatized." "Nearly everyone at some point in life will experience stigma either temporarily or permanently. . . . Why do we persist in this denial?" (Zola, 1979, p. 454). Given that human differences serve as the basis for stigmas, being or feeling stigmatized is virtually an inescapable fate. Because stigmas differ depending upon the culture and the historical period. It becomes evident that it is mere chance whether a person is born into a nonstigmatized or severely stigmatized group.

Because stigmatization often occurs within the confines of a psychologically constructed or actual social relationship, the experience itself reflects relative comparisons, the contrasting of desired and undesired differences. Assuming that flawless people do not exist, relative comparisons give rise to a feeling of superiority in some contexts (where one possesses a desired trait that another person is lacking) but perhaps a feeling of inferiority in other contexts (where one lacks a desired trait that another person possesses). It is also important to note that it is only when we make comparisons that we can feel different. Stigmatization or feeling stigmatized is a consequence of social comparison. For this reason, stigma represents a continuum of undesired differences that depend upon many factors (e.g., geographical location, culture, life cycle stage) (see Becker & Arnold).

Although some stigmatized conditions appear escapable or may be temporary, some undesired traits have graver social consequences than others. Being a medical resident, being a new professor, being 7 feet tall, having cancer, being black, or being physically disfigured or mentally retarded can all lead to feelings of stigmatization (feeling discredited or devalued in a particular role), but obviously these are not equally stigmatizing conditions. The degree of stigmatization might depend on how undesired the difference is in a particular social group.

Physical abnormalities, for example, may be the most severely stigmatized dif-

ferences because they are physically salient, represent some deficiency or distortion in the bodily form, and in most cases are unalterable. Other physically
salient differences, such as skin color or nationality, are considered very stigmatizing because they also are permanent conditions and cannot be changed. Yet
the stigmatization that one feels as a result of being black or Jewish or Japanese
depends on the social context, specifically social contexts in which one's skin
color or nationality is not a desired one. A white American could feel temporarily stigmatized when visiting Japan due to a difference in height. A black
student could feel stigmatized in a predominantly white university because the
majority of the students are white and white skin is a desired trait. But a black
student in a predominantly black university is not likely to feel the effects of
stigma. Thus, the sense of being stigmatized or having a stigma is inextricably
tied to social context. Of equal importance are the norms in that context that
determine which are desirable and undesirable attributes. Moving from one
social or cultural context to another can change both the definitions and the
consequences of stigma.

Stigma often results in a special kind of downward mobility. Part of the power
of stigmatization lies in the realization that people who are stigmatized or
acquire a stigma lose their place in the social hierarchy. Consequently, most
people want to ensure that they are counted in the nonstigmatized "majority."
This, of course, leads to more stigmatization.

Stigma, then, is also a term that connotes a relationship. It seems that this
relationship is vital to understanding the stigmatizing process. Stigma allows
some individuals to feel superior to others. Superiority and inferiority, however,
are two sides of the same coin. In order for one person to feel superior, there must
be another person who is perceived to be or who actually feels inferior. Stigmatized people are needed in order for the many nonstigmatized people to feel good
about themselves.

On the other hand, there are many stigmatized people who feel inferior and
concede that other persons are superior because they possess certain attributes.
In order for the process to occur (for one person to stigmatize another and have
the stigmatized person feel the effects of stigma), there must be some agreement
that the differentness is inherently undesirable. Moreover, even among stigmatized people, relative comparisons are made, and people are reassured by the fact
that there is someone else who is worse off. The dilemma of difference, therefore, affects both stigmatized and nonstigmatized people.

Some might contend that this is the very old scapegoat argument, and there
is some truth to that contention. But the issues here are more finely intertwined.
If stigma is a social construct, constructed by cultures, by social groups, and by
individuals to designate some human differences as discrediting, then the stigmatization process is indeed a powerful and pernicious social tool. The inferior-
ity/superiority issue is a most interesting way of understanding how and why
people continue to stigmatize.

Some stigmas are more physically salient than others, and some people are
more capable of concealing their stigmas or escaping from the negative social

consequences of being stigmatized. The ideal prototype (e.g., young, white, tall, married, male, with a recent record in sports) that Stafford cites may actually possess traits that would be the source of much scorn and derision in another social context. Yet, by insulating himself in his own community, a man like the one described in the example can ensure that his "differentness" will receive approbation rather than rejection, and he will not be subject to constant and severe stigmatization. This is a common response to stigma among people with some social influence (e.g., artists, academics, millionaires). Often, attributes or behaviors that might otherwise be considered "abnormal" or stigmatized are labeled as "eccentric" among persons of power or influence. The fact that what is perceived as the "ideal" person varies from one social context to another, however, is tied to Martin's notion that people learn ways to stigmatize in each new situation.

In contrast, some categories of stigmatized people (e.g., the physically disabled, members of ethnic groups, poor people) cannot alter their stigmas nor easily disguise them. People, then, feel permanently stigmatized in contexts where their differentness is undesired and in social environments that they cannot easily escape. Hence, power, social influence, and social control play a major role in the stigmatization process.

In summary, stigma stems from differences. By focusing on differences we actively create stigmas because any attribute or difference is potentially stigmatizable. Often we attend to a single different attribute rather than to the large number of similar attributes that any two individuals share. Why people focus on differences and denigrate people on the basis of them is important to understanding how some stigmas originate and persist. By reexamining the historical origins of stigma and the way children develop the propensity to stigmatize, we can see how some differences evolve into stigmas and how the process is linked to the behavioral (social control), affective (fear, dislike), and cognitive (perception of differences, social categorization) components of stigma.

THE ORIGINS OF STIGMA

The phrase *to stigmatize* originally referred to the branding or marking of certain people (e.g., criminals, prostitutes) in order to make them appear different and separate from others (Goffman, 1963). The act of marking people in this way resulted in exile or avoidance. In most cultures, physical marking or branding has declined, but a more cognitive manifestation of stigmatization—social marking—has increased and has become the basis for most stigmas (Jones *et al.*, 1984). Goffman points out, though, that stigma has retained much of its original connotation. People use differences to exile or avoid others. In addition, what is most intriguing about the ontogenesis of the stigma concept is the broadening of its predominant affective responses such as dislike and disgust to include the emotional reaction of fear. Presently, *fear* may be instrumental in the perpetuation of stigma and in maintaining its original social functions. Yet as the developmental literature reveals, fear is not a natural but an acquired response to differences of stigmas.

Sigelman and Singleton offer a number of insightful observations about how children learn to stigmatize. Children develop a natural wariness of strangers as their ability to differentiate familiar from novel objects increases (Sroufe, 1977). Developmental psychologists note that stranger anxiety is a universal phenomenon in infants and appears around the age of seven months. This reaction to differences (e.g., women versus men, children versus adults, blacks versus whites) is an interesting one and, as Sigelman and Singleton point out, may serve as a prototype for stigmatizing. Many children respond in a positive (friendly) or negative (fearful, apprehensive) manner to strangers. Strangers often arouse the interest (Brooks & Lewis, 1976) of children but elicit negative reactions if they intrude on their personal space (Sroufe, 1977). Stranger anxiety tends to fade with age, but when coupled with self-referencing it may create the conditions for a child to learn how to respond to human differences or how to stigmatize.

Self-referencing, or the use of another's interpretation of a situation to form one's own understanding of it, commonly occurs in young children. Infants often look toward caregivers when encountering something different, such as a novel object, person, or event (Feinman, 1982). The response to novel stimuli in an ambiguous situation may depend on the emotional displays of the caregiver; young children have been known to respond positively to situations if their mothers respond reassuringly (Feinman, 1982). Self-referencing is instrumental to understanding the development of stigmatization because it may be through this process that caregivers shape young children's responses to people, especially those who possess physically salient differences (Klinnert, Campos, Sorce, Emde, & Svejda, 1983). We may continue to learn about how to stigmatize from other important figures (e.g., mentors, role models) as we progress through the life cycle. Powerful authority figures may serve as the source of self-referencing behavior in new social contexts (Martin).

Sigelman and Singleton also point out that preschoolers notice differences and tend to establish preferences but do not necessarily stigmatize. Even on meeting other children with physical disabilities, children do not automatically eschew them but may respond to actual physical and behavioral similarities and differences. There is evidence, moreover, indicating that young children are curious about human differences and often stare at novel stimuli (Brooks & Lewis, 1976). Children frequently inquire of their parents or of stigmatized persons about their distinctive physical attributes. In many cases, the affective response of young children is interest rather than fear.

Barbarin offers a poignant example of the difference between interest and fear in his vignette about Myra, a child with cancer. She talks about young children who are honest and direct about her illness, an attitude that does not cause her consternation. What does disturb her, though, are parents who will not permit her to baby-sit with their children for *fear* that she might give them cancer. Thus, interest and curiosity about stigma or human differences may be natural for children, but they must *learn* fear and avoidance as well as which categories or attributes to dislike, *fear*, or stigmatize. Children may learn to stigmatize without ever grasping "why" they do so (Martin), just as adults have beliefs about members of stigmatized groups without ever having met any individuals from the group (Crocker & Lutsky). The predisposition to stigmatize is passed from one generation to the next through social learning (Martin) or socialization (Crocker & Lutsky; Stafford & Scott).

Sigelman and Singleton agree with Martin that social norms subtly impinge upon the information-processing capacities of young children so that negative responses to stigma later become automatic. At some point, the development of social cognition must intersect with the affective responses that parents or adults display toward stigmatized people. Certain negative emotions become attached to social categories (e.g., *all* ex-mental patients are dangerous, *all* blacks are angry or harmful). Although the attitudes (cognitions) about stigma assessed in paper-and-pencil tasks may change in the direction of what is socially acceptable, the affect and behavior of elementary- and secondary-school children as well as adults reflect the early negative affective associations with stigma. The norms about stigma, though, are ambiguous and confusing. They teach young children to avoid or dislike stigmatized people, even though similar behavior in adults is considered socially unacceptable.

STIGMA AS A FORM OF COGNITIVE PROCESSING

The perceptual processing of human differences appears to be universal. Ainlay and Crosby suggest that differences arouse us; they can please or distress us. From a phenomenological perspective, we carry around "recipes" and "typifications" as structures for categorizing and ordering stimuli. Similarly, social psychologists speak of our need to categorize social stimuli in such terms as *schemas* and *stereotypes* (Crocker & Lutsky). These approaches to the perception of human differences indirectly posit that stigmatizing is a natural response, a way to maintain order in a potentially chaotic world of social stimuli. People want to believe that the world is ordered.

Although various approaches to social categorization may explain how people stereotype on the basis of a specific attribute (e.g., skin color, religious beliefs, deafness), they do not explain the next step—the negative imputations. Traditional approaches to sociocognitive processing also do not offer ideas about how people can perceptually move beyond the stereotype, the typification, or stigma to perceive an individual. Studies of stereotyping and stigma regularly reveal that beliefs about the inferiority of a person predominate in the thoughts of the perceiver (Crocker & Lutsky).

Stigma appears to be a special and insidious kind of social categorization or, as Martin explains, a process of generalizing from a single experience. People are treated categorically rather than individually, and in the process are devalued (Ainlay & Crosby; Barbarin; Crocker & Lutsky; Stafford & Scott). In addition, as Crocker and Lutsky point out, coding people in terms of categories (e.g., "X is a redhead") instead of specific attributes ("X has red hair") allows people to feel that stigmatized persons are fundamentally different and establishes greater psychological and social distance.

A discussion of the perceptual basis of stigma inevitably leads back to the notion of master status (Goffman, 1963). Perceptually, stigma becomes the master status, the attribute that colors the perception of the entire person. All other aspects of the person are ignored except those that fit the stereotype associated with the stigma (Kanter, 1979). Stigma as a form of negative stereotyping has a way of neutralizing positive qualities and undermining the identity of stigmatized individuals (Barbarin). This kind of social categorization has also been described by one sociologist as a "discordance with personal attributes" (Davis, 1964). Thus, many stigmatized people are not expected to be intelligent, attractive, or upper class.

Another important issue in the perception of human differences or social cognition is the relative comparisons that are made between and within stigmatized and nonstigmatized groups. Several authors discuss the need for people to accentuate between-group differences and minimize within-group differences as a requisite for group identity (Ainlay & Crosby; Crocker & Lutsky; Sigelman & Singleton). Yet these authors do not explore in depth the reasons for denigrating the attributes of the out-group members and elevating the attributes of one's own group, unless there is some feeling that the out-group could threaten the balance of power. Crocker and Lutsky note, however, that stereotyping is frequently tied to the need for self-enhancement. People with low self-esteem are more likely to identify and maintain negative stereotypes about members of stigmatized groups; such people are more negative in general. This line of reasoning takes us back to viewing stigma as a means of maintaining the status quo through social control. Could it be that stigma as a perceptual tool helps to reinforce the differentiation of the population that in earlier times was deliberately designated by marking? One explanation offered by many theorists is that stereotypes about stigmatized groups help to maintain the exploitation of such groups and preserve the existing societal structure.

Are there special arrangements or special circumstance, Ainlay and Crosby ask, that allow people to notice differences but not denigrate those who have them? On occasion, nonstigmatized people are able to "break through" and to see a stigmatized person as a real, whole person with a variety of attributes, some similar traits and some different from their own (Davis, 1964). Just how frequently and in what ways does this happen?

Ainlay and Crosby suggest that we begin to note differences within a type when we *need* to do so. The example they give about telephones is a good one. We learn differences among types of telephones, appliances, schools, or even groups of people when we need to. Hence stereotyping or stigmatizing is not necessarily automatic; when we want to perceive differences we perceive them, just as we perceive similarities when we *want* to. In some historical instances, society appears to have recognized full human potential when it was required, while ignoring certain devalued traits. When women were needed to occupy traditionally male occupations in the United States during World War II, gender differences were ignored as they have been ignored in other societies when women were needed for combat. Similarly, the U.S. armed forces became racially integrated when there was a need for more soldiers to fight in World War II (Terry, 1984).

Thus, schemas or stereotypes about stigmatized individuals can be modified but only under specific conditions. When stigmatized people have essential information or possess needed expertise, we discover that some of their attributes are not so different, or that they are more similar to us than different. "Cooperative interdependence" stemming from shared goals may change the nature of perceptions and the nature of relationships (Crocker & Lutsky). Future research on stigma and on social perception might continue to investigate the conditions under which people are less likely to stereotype and more likely to respond to individuals rather than categories (cf., Locksley, Borgida, Brekke, & Hepburn, 1980; Locksley, Hepburn & Ortiz, 1982).

THE MEANING OF STIGMA FOR SOCIAL RELATIONS

I have intimated that "stigmatized" and "nonstigmatized" people are tied together in a perpetual inferior/superior relationship. This relationship is key to understanding the meaning of stigma. To conceptualize stigma as a social relationship raises some vital questions about stigma. These questions include (a) when and under what conditions does an attribute become a stigmatized one? (b) can a person experience stigmatization without knowing that a trait is devalued in a specific social context? (c) does a person feel stigmatized even though in a particular social context the attribute is not stigmatized or the stigma is not physically or behaviorally apparent? (d) can a person refuse to be stigmatized or destigmatize an attribute by ignoring the prevailing norms that define it as a stigma?

These questions lead to another one: Would stigma persist if stigmatized people did not feel stigmatized or inferior? Certainly, a national pride did not lessen the persecution of the Jews, nor does it provide freedom for blacks in South Africa. These two examples illustrate how pervasive and powerful the social control aspects of stigma are, empowering the stigmatizer and stripping the stigmatized of power. Yet a personal awakening, a discover that the responsibility for being stigmatized does not lie with oneself, is important. Understanding that the rationale for discrimination and segregation based on stigma lies in the mind of the stigmatizer has led people like Mahatma Gandhi and civil rights activist Rosa Parks to rise above the feeling of stigmatization, to ignore the norms, and to disobey the exiting laws based on stigma. There have been women, elderly adults, gays, disabled people, and many others who at some point realized that their fundamental similarities outweighed and outnumbered their differences. It becomes clear that, in most oppressive situations the primary problem lies with the stigmatizer and not with the stigmatized (Sartre, 1948; Schur, 1980, 1983). Many stigmatized people also begin to understand that the stigmatizer, having established a position of false superiority and consequently the need to maintain it, is enslaved to the concept that stigmatized people are fundamentally inferior. In fact, some stigmatized individuals question the norms about stigma and attempt to change the social environments for their peers.

In contrast, there are some stigmatized persons who accept their devalued status as legitimate. Attempting to "pass" and derogating others like themselves are two ways in which stigmatized people effectively accept the society's negative perceptions of their stigma (Goffman, cited in Gibbons). It is clear, especially from accounts of those who move from a nonstigmatized to a stigmatized role, that stigmatization is difficult to resist if everyone begins to reinforce the inferior status with their behavior. Two of the most common ways in which nonstigmatized people convey a sense of fundamental inferiority to stigmatized people are social rejection or social isolation and lowered expectations.

There are many ways in which people communicate social rejection such as speech, eye contact, and interpersonal distance. The stigmatized role, as conceptualized by the symbolic interactionism approach, is similar to any other role (e.g., professor, doctor) in which we behave according to the role expectations of others and change our identity to be congruent with them. Thus, in the case of stigma, role expectations are often the same as the stereotypes. Some stigmatized people become dependent, passive, helpless, and childlike because that is what is expected of them.

Social rejection or avoidance affects not only the stigmatized individual but everyone who is socially involved, such as family, friends, and relatives (Barbarin). This permanent form of social quarantine forces people to limit their relationships to other stigmatized people and to those for whom the social bond outweighs the stigma, such as family members. In this way, avoidance or social rejection also acts as a form of social control or containment (Edgerton, 1967; Goffman, 1963; Schur, 1983; Scott, 1969). Social rejection is perhaps most difficult for younger children who are banned from most social activities of their peers.

Social exile conveys another message about expectations. Many stigmatized people are not encouraged to develop or grow, to have aspirations or to be successful. Barbarin reports that children with cancer lose friendships and receive special, lenient treatment from teachers. They are not expected to achieve in the same manner as other children. Parents, too, sometimes allow stigmatized children to behave in ways that "normal" children in the same family are not permitted to do. Social exclusion as well as overprotection can lead to decreased performance. Lowered expectations also lead to decreased self-esteem.

The negative identity that ensues becomes a pervasive personality trait and inhibits the stigmatized person from developing other parts of the self. Another detrimental aspect of stigmatization is the practice of treating people, such as the ex-con and ex-mental patient who are attempting to reintegrate themselves into society, as if they still had the stigma. Even the terms we use to describer such persons suggest that role expectations remain the same despite the stigmatized person's efforts to relinquish them. It seems that the paradoxical societal norms that establish a subordinate and dependent position for stigmatized people while ostracizing them for it may stem from the need of nonstigmatized people to maintain a sense of superiority. Their position is supported and reinforced by their perceptions that stigmatized people are fundamentally inferior, passive, helpless, and childlike.

The most pernicious consequence of bearing a stigma is that stigmatized people may develop the same perceptual problems that nonstigmatized people have. They begin to see themselves and their lives through the stigma, or as

Sartre (1948) writes about the Jews, they "allow themselves to be poisoned by the stereotype and live in fear that they will correspond to it" (p. 95). As Gibbons observes, stigmatized individuals sometimes blame their difficulties on the stigmatized trait, rather than confronting the root of their personal difficulties. Thus, normal issues that one encounters in life often act as a barrier to growth for stigmatized people because of the attributional process involved.

The need to maintain one's identity manifests itself in a number of ways, such as the mischievous behavior of the adolescent boy with cancer cited in Barbarin's chapter. "Attaining normalcy within the limits of stigma" (Tracy & Gussow, 1978) seems to be another way of describing the need to establish or recapture one's identity (Weiner, 1975).

Stigma uniquely alters perceptions in other ways, especially with respect to the notion of "normality", and raises other questions about the dilemma of difference. Most people do not want to be perceived as different or "abnormal." Becker and Arnold and Gibbons discuss normalization as attempts to be "not different" and to appear "normal." Such strategies include "passing" or disguising the stigma and acting "normal" by "covering up"—keeping up with the pace of nonstigmatized individuals (Davis, 1964; Gibbons; Goffman, 1963; Weiner, 1975). For stigmatized people, the idea of normality takes on an exaggerated importance. Normality becomes the supreme goal for many stigmatized individuals until they realize that there is no precise definition of normality except what they would be without their stigma. Given the dilemma of difference that stigma reflects, it is not clear whether anyone can ever feel "normal."

Out of this state of social isolation and lowered expectations, though, can arise some positive consequences. Although the process can be fraught with pain and difficulty, stigmatized people who manage to reject the perceptions of themselves as inferior often come away with greater inner strength (Jones et al., 1984). They learn to depend on their own resources and, like the earlier examples of Mahatma Gandhi and Rosa Parks, they begin to question the bases for defining normality. Many stigmatized people regain their identity through redefining normality and realizing that it is acceptable to be who they are (Ablon, 1981; Barbarin; Becker, 1980; Becker & Arnold).

FEAR AND STIGMA

Fear is important to a discussion of how and why stigma persists. In many cultures that do not use the term *stigma*, there is some emotional reaction beyond interest or curiosity to differences such as children who are born with birthmarks, epilepsy, or a caul. Certain physical characteristics or illnesses elicit fear because the etiology of the attribute or disease is unknown, unpredictable, and unexpected (Sontag, 1979). People even have fears about the sexuality of certain stigmatized groups such as persons who are mentally retarded, feeling that if they are allowed to reproduce they will have retarded offspring (Gibbons). It seems that what gives stigma its intensity and reality is fear.

The nature of the fear appears to vary with the type of stigma. For most stigmas stemming from physical or mental problems, including cancer, people experience fear of contagion even though they know that the stigma cannot be developed through contact (see Barbarin). This fear usually stems from not knowing about the etiology of a condition, its predictability, and its course.

The stigmatization of certain racial, ethnic, and gender categories may also be based on fear. This fear, though, cannot stem from contagion because attributes (of skin color, ethnic background, and gender) cannot possibly be transmitted to nonstigmatized people. One explanation for the fear is that people want to avoid "courtesy stigmas" or stigmatization by association (Goffman, 1963). Another explanation underlying this type of fear may be the notion of scarce resources. This is the perception that if certain groups of people are allowed to have a share in all resources, there will not be enough: not enough jobs, not enough land, not enough water, or not enough food. Similar explanations from the deviance literature suggest that people who stigmatize feel threatened and collectively feel that their position of social, economic, and political dominance will be dismantled by members of stigmatized groups (Schur, 1980, 1983). A related explanation is provided by Hughes, who states, "that it may be that those whose positions are insecure and whose hopes for the higher goals are already fading express more violent hostility to new people" (1945, p. 356). This attitude may account for the increased aggression toward members of stigmatized groups during dire economic periods.

Fear affects not only nonstigmatized but stigmatized individuals as well. Many stigmatized people (e.g., ex-cons, mentally retarded adults) who are attempting to "pass" live in fear that their stigmatized attribute will be discovered (Gibbons). These fears are grounded in a realistic assessment of the negative social consequences of stigmatization and reflect the long-term social and psychological damage to individuals resulting from stigma.

At some level, therefore, most people are concerned with stigma because they are fearful of its unpredictable and uncontrollable nature. Stigmatization appears uncontrollable because human differences serve as the basis for stigmas. Therefore, *any* attribute can become a stigma. No one really ever knows when or if he or she will acquire a stigma or when societal norms might change to stigmatize a trait he or she already possesses. To deny this truth by attempting to isolate stigmatized people or escape from stigma is a manifestation of the underlying fear.

The unpredictability of stigma is similar to the unpredictability of death. Both Gibbons and Barbarin note that the development of a stigmatized condition in a loved one or in oneself represents a major breach of trust—a destruction of the belief that life is predictable. In a sense, stigma represents a kind of death—a social death. Nonstigmatized people, through avoidance and social rejection, often treat stigmatized people as if they were invisible, nonexistent, or dead. Many stigmas, in particular childhood cancer, remove the usual disguises of mortality. Such stigmas can act as a symbolic reminder of everyone's inevitable death (see Barbarin's discussion of Ernest Becker's (1973) *The Denial of Death*). These same fears can be applied to the acquisition of other stigmas (e.g., mental illness, physical disabilities) and help to intensify and perpetuate the negative responses to most stigmatized categories. Thus, irrational fears may help stigmatization to be self-perpetuating with little encouragement needed in the form of forced segregation from the political and social structure.

The ultimate answers about why stigma persists may lie in an examination of why people fear differences, fear the future, fear the unknown, and therefore stigmatize that which is different and unknown. An equally important issue to investigate is how stigmatization may be linked to the fear of being different.

CONCLUSION

Stigma is clearly a very complex multidisciplinary issue, with each additional perspective containing another piece of this enigma. A multidisciplinary approach allowed us as social scientists to perceive stigma as a whole; to see from within it rather than to look down upon it. Our joint perspectives have also demonstrated that there are many shared ideas across disciplines, and in many cases only the terminology is different.

Three important aspects of stigma emerge from this multidisciplinary examination and may forecast its future. They are fear, stigma's primary affective component; stereotyping, its primary cognitive component; and social control, its primary behavioral component. The study of the relationship of stigma to fear, stereotyping, and social control may elucidate our understanding of the paradoxes that a multidisciplinary perspective reveals. It may also bring us closer to understanding what stigma really is—not primarily a property of individuals as many have conceptualized it to be but a humanly constructed perception, constantly in flux and legitimizing our negative responses to human differences (Ainlay & Crosby). To further clarify the definition of stigma, one must differentiate between an "undesired differentness" that is likely to lead to feelings of stigmatization and actual forms of stigmatization. *It appears that stigmatization occurs only when the social control component is imposed, or when the undesired differentness leads to some restriction in physical and social mobility and access to opportunities that allow an individual to develop his or her potential. This definition combines the original meaning of stigma with more contemporary connotations and uses.*

In another vein, stigma is a statement about personal and social responsibility. People irrationally feel that, by separating themselves from stigmatized individuals, they may reduce their own risk of acquiring the stigma (Barbarin). By isolating individuals, people feel they can also isolate the problem. If stigma is ignored, the responsibility for its existence and perpetuation can be shifted elsewhere. Making stigmatized people feel responsible for their own stigma allows nonstigmatized people to relinquish the onus for creating or perpetuating the conditions that surround it.

Changing political and economic climates are also important to the stigmatization and destigmatization process. What is economically feasible or politically enhancing for a group in power will partially determine what attributes are stigmatized, or at least how they are stigmatized. As many sociologists have suggested, some people are stigmatized for violating norms, whereas others are stigmatized for being of little economic or political value (Birenbaum & Sagarin, 1976, cited in Stafford & Scott). We should admit that stigma persists as a social problem because it continues to have some of its original social utility as a means of controlling certain segments of the population and ensuring that power is not easily exchanged. Stigma helps to maintain the existing social hierarchy.

One might then ask if there will ever be societies or historical periods without stigma. Some authors hold a positive vision of the future. Gibbons, for example, suggests that as traditionally stigmatized groups become more integrated into the general population, stigmatizing attributes will lose some of their onus. But historical analysis would suggest that new stigmas will replace old ones. Educational programs are probably of only limited help, as learning to stigmatize is a part of early social learning experiences (Martin; Sigelman & Singleton). The social learning of stigma is indeed very different from learning about the concept abstractly in a classroom. School experiences sometimes merely reinforce what children learn about stigmatization from parents and significant others.

From a sociological perspective, the economic, psychological and social benefits of stigma sustain it. Stigmas will disappear when we no longer need to legitimize social exclusion and segregation (Zola, 1979). From the perspective of cognitive psychology, when people find it necessary or beneficial to perceive the fundamental similarities they share with stigmatized people rather than the differences, we will see the beginnings of a real elimination of stigma. This process may have already occurred during some particular historical period or within particular societies. It is certainly an important area for historians, anthropologists, and psychologists to explore.

Although it would seem that the core of the problem lies with the nonstigmatized individuals, stigmatized people also play an important role in the destigmatization process. Stigma contests, or the struggles to determine which attributes are devalued and to what extent they are devalued, involve stigmatized and nonstigmatized individuals alike (Schur, 1980). Stigmatized people, too, have choices as to whether to accept their stigmatized condition and the negative social consequences or continue to fight for more integration into nonstigmatized communities. Their cognitive and affective attitudes toward themselves as individuals and as a group are no small element in shaping societal responses to them. As long as they continue to focus on the negative, affective components of stigma, such as low self-esteem, it is not likely that their devalued status will change. Self-help groups may play an important role in countering this tendency.

There is volition or personal choice. Each stigmatized or nonstigmatized individual can choose to feel superior or inferior, and each individual can make choices about social control and about fear. Sartre (1948) views this as the choice between authenticity or authentic freedom, and inauthenticity or fear of being oneself. Each individual can choose to ignore social norms regarding stigma. Personal beliefs about a situation or circumstance often differ from norms, but people usually follow the social norms anyway, fearing to step beyond conformity to exercise their own personal beliefs about stigma (see Ainlay & Crosby and Stafford & Scott, discussions of personal versus socially shared forms of stigma). Changing human behavior is not as simple as encouraging people to exercise their personal beliefs. As social scientists, we know a number of issues may be involved in the way personal volition interacts with social norms and personal values.

The multidisciplinary approach could be used in a variety of creative ways to study stigma and other social problems. Different models of how stigma has evolved and is perpetuated could be subject to test by a number of social scientists. They could combine their efforts to examine whether stigma evolves in a similar manner in different cultures, or among children of different cultural and social backgrounds, or during different historical periods. The study of stigma encompasses as many factors and dimensions as are represented in a multidisciplinary approach. Some of these factors, dimensions, and the responses they produce are represented in Figure 1. All of the elements are interactive and in constant flux. The effective, cognitive, and behavioral dimensions are subject to the current cultural, historical, political, and economic climates, which are in turn linked to the norms and laws. Although, in Figure 1, the responses of stigmatized and nonstigmatized individuals appear to be separate, we know that they are also interconnected and may produce other responses when considered together. This graphic portrayal of the issues vital to the study of stigma is neither exhaustive nor definitive. It does suggest, however, that a multidimensional model of stigma is needed to understand how these factors, dimensions, and responses co-vary.

We need more cross-disciplinary research from researchers who do not commonly study stigma. For example, a joint project among historians, psychologists, economists, and political scientists might examine the relationship between economic climate, perceptions of scarcity, and stigmatization. Other joint ventures by anthropologists and economists could design research on how much income is lost over a lifetime by members of a stigmatized category (e.g., blind, deaf, overweight), and how this loss adversely affects the GNP and the overall economy. Another example would be work by political scientists and historians or anthropologists to understand the links between the stigmatization of specific attributes and the maintenance of social control and power by certain political groups. Psychologists might team up with novelists or anthropologists to use case studies to understand individual differences or to examine how some stigmatized persons overcome their discredited status. Other studies of the positive consequences of stigma might include a joint investigation by anthropologists and psychologists of cultures that successfully integrate stigmatized individuals into nonstigmatized communities and utilize whatever resources or talents a stigmatized person has to offer (as the shaman is used in many societies) (Halifax, 1979, 1982).

The study of stigma by developmental and social psychologists, sociologists, anthropologists, economists, and historians may also offer new insights into the evolution of sex roles and sex role identity across the life cycle and during changing economic climates. Indeed, linguists, psychologists, and sociologists may be able to chronicle the changes in identity and self-concept of stigmatized and nonstigmatized alike, by studying the way people describe themselves and the language they use in their interactions with stigmatized and nonstigmatized others (Coleman, 1985; Edelsky & Rosengrant, 1981).

The real challenge for social scientists will be to better understand the need to stigmatize; the need for people to reject rather than accept others; the need for people to denigrate rather than uplift others. We need to know more about the relationship between stigma and perceived threat, and how stigma may represent "the kinds of deviance that it seeks out" (Schur, 1980, p. 22). Finally, social scientists need to concentrate on designing an optimal system in which every member of society is permitted to develop one's talents and experience one's full potential regardless of any particular attribute. If such a society were to come about, then perhaps some positive consequences would arise from the dilemma of difference.

REFERENCES

Ablon, J. 1981. "Stigmatized Health Conditions." *Social Science and Medicine*, 15: 5–9.

Ainlay, S. and F. Cosby. 1986. "Stigma, Justice and the Dilemma of Difference." In S. Ainlay, G. Becker, and L. M. Coleman, *The Dilemma of Difference: A Multicultural View of Stigma*, 17–38. New York: Plenum.

Barbarin, O. 1986. "Family Experience of Stigma in Childhood Cancer." In S. Ainlay, G. Becker, and L. M. Coleman, *The Dilemma of Difference: A Multicultural View of Stiqma*. New York: Plenum, 163–184.

Becker, G. 1980. *Growing Old in Silence*. Berkeley: University of California Press.

Becker, G. and R. Arnold. 1986. "Stigma as Social and Cultural Construct." In S. Ainlay, G. Becker, and L. M. Coleman, *The Dilemma of Difference: A Multicultural View of Stigma*. New York. Plenum, 39–58.

Brooks, J. and Lewis, M. 1976. "Infants' responses to strangers: Midget, adult, and child." *Child Development* 47: 323–332.

Coleman, L. 1985. "Language and the evolution of identity and self-concept." In F. Kessel, ed., *The development of languaqe and language researchers: Essays in honor of Roger Brown*. Hillsdale, N. J.: Erlbaum.

Crocker, J. and N. Lutsky. 1986. "Stigma and the Dynamics of Social Cognition." In S. Ainlay, G. Becker, and L. M. Coleman, *The Dilemma of Difference: A Multicultural View of Stigma* New York. Plenum, 95–122.

Davis, F. 1964. "Deviance disavowal: The management of strained interaction by the visibly handicapped." In H. Becker, ed., *The Other Side*. New York: Free Press, 119–138.

Edelsky, C. and Rosengrant, T. 1981. "Interactions with handicapped children: Who's handicapped?" *Sociolinguistic Working Paper 92*. Austin, TX: Southwest Educational Development Laboratory.

Edgerton, R. G. 1967. *The Cloak of Competence: Stigma in the Lives of the Mentally Retarded*. Berkeley: University of California Press.

Feinman, S. 1982. "Social referencing in infancy." Merrill-*Palmer Quarterly* 28: 445–70. Gibbons, F. X. 1986. "Stigma and Interpersonal Relations." In S. Ainlay, G. Becker, and L. M. Coleman, *The Dilemma of Difference: A Multicultural View of Stigma*. New York. Plenum. 123–144.

Goffman. E. 1963. *Stigma: Notes on the Management of Spoiled Identity*. Englewood Cliffs, N. J.: Prentice Hall.

Hallifax, J. 1979. *Shamanic Voices: A Survey of Visionary Narratives*. New York: Dutton.
———. 1982. *Shaman: The Wounded Healer*. London: Thames and Hudson.

Jones. E. E., A. Farina, A. H. Hastof, H. Markus, D. T. Miller, and R. A. Scott, 1984. *Social Stigma: The Psychology of Marked Relationships*. New York: Freeman.

Kanter, R. M. 1979. *Men and Women of the Corporation*. New York: Basic Books.

Klinnert, M. D., J. J. Campos, J. F. Sorce, R. Emde and M. Svejda. 1983. "Emotions as behavior regulators: Social referencing in infancy." In R. Plutchik & H. Kellerman, eds. *Emotion Theory, Research, and Experience. Vol. II. Emotions in Early Development*. New York: Academic Press, 57–88.

Locksley, A., E. Borgida, N. Brekke, and C. Hepburn. 1980. "Sexual stereotypes and social judgment." *Journal of Personality and Social Psychology*, 39: 821–31.

Locksley, A., C. Hepburn, and V. Ortiz. 1982. "Social stereotypes and judgments of individuals: An instance of the base-rate fallacy." *Journal of Experimental Social Psychology*. 18: 23–42.

Martin, L. G. 1986. "Stigma: A Social Learning Perspective." In S. Ainlay, G. Becker, and L. M. Coleman, *The Dilemma of Difference: A Multicultural View of Stigma*. New York. Plenum, 1–16.

Sartre, J. 1948. *Anti-Semite and Jew*. New York: Schocken Books.

Schur, E. 1980. *The Politics Of Deviance: A Sociological Introduction*. Englewood Cliffs, N. J.: Prentice Hall.

———. 1983. *Labeling Women Deviant: Gender, Stigma, and Social Control*. Philadelphia: Temple University Press.

Scott, R., 1969. *The Making of Blind Men*. New York: Russel Sage Foundation.

Sigelman, C. and L. C. Singleton. 1986. "Stigmatization in Childhood: A Survey of Developmental Trends and Issues." In S. Ainlay, G. Becker, and L. M. Coleman, *The Dilemma of Difference: A Multicultural View of Stigma*. New York. Plenum. 185–210.

Solomon, Howard M. 1986. "Stigma and Western Culture: A Historical Approach" In S. Ainlay, G. Becker, and L. M. Coleman, *The Dilemma of Difference: A Multicultural View of Stigma*. New York: Plenum, 59–76.

Sontag, S. 1979. *Illness as metaphor*. New York: Random House.

Sroufe, L. A. 1977. "Wariness of strangers and the study of infant development." *Child Development*, 48: 731–46.

Stafford, M and R. Scott. 1986. "Stigma, Deviance and Social Control: Some Conceptual Issues." In S. Ainlay, G. Becker, and L. M. Coleman, *The Dilemma of Difference: A Multicultural View of Stigma*. New York. Plenum, 77–94.

Terry, W. 1984. *Bloods: An Oral History of the Vietnam War by Black Veterans*. New York: Random House.

Tracy, G. S., and Gussow, Z. 1978. "Self-help health groups: A grass-roots response to a need for services." *Journal of Applied Behavioral Science*: 81–396.

Weiner, C. L., 1975. "The burden of rheumatoid arthritis: Tolerating the uncertainty." *Social Science and Medicine*: 99, 97–104.

Zola, I. Z. 1979. "Helping one another: A speculative history of the self-help movement. *Archive of Physical Medicine and Rehabilitation*: 60, 452.

12

AIDS and Its Metaphors

SUSAN SONTAG

Because of countless metaphoric flourishes that have made cancer synonymous with evil, having cancer has been experienced by many as shameful, therefore something to conceal, and also unjust, a betrayal by one's body. Why me? the cancer patient exclaims bitterly. With AIDS, the shame is linked to an imputation of guilt; and the scandal is not at all obscure. Few wonder, Why me? Most people outside of Sub-Saharan Africa who have AIDS know (or think they know) how they got it. It is not a mysterious affliction that seems to strike at random. Indeed, to get AIDS is precisely to be revealed, in the majority of cases so far, as a member of a certain "risk group," a community of pariahs. The illness flushes out an identity that might have remained hidden from neighbors, jobmates, family, friends. It also confirms an identity and, among the risk group in the United States most affected in the beginning, homosexual men, has been a creator of community as well as an experience that isolates the ill and exposes them to harassment and persecution.

Getting cancer, too, is sometimes understood as the fault of someone who has indulged in "unsafe" behavior—the alcoholic with cancer of the esophagus, the smoker with lung cancer: punishment for living unhealthy lives. (In contrast to those obliged to perform unsafe occupations, like the worker in a petrochemical factory who gets bladder cancer.) More and more linkages are sought between primary organs or systems and specific practices that people are invited to repudiate, as in recent speculation associating colon cancer and breast cancer with diets rich in animal fats. But the unsafe habits associated with cancer, among other illnesses—even heart disease, hitherto little culpabilized, is now largely viewed as the price one pays for excesses of diet and "life-style"—are the result of a weakness of the will or a lack of prudence, or of addiction to legal (albeit very dangerous) chemicals. The unsafe behavior that produces AIDS is judged to be more than just weakness. It is indulgence, delinquency—addictions to chemicals that are illegal and to sex regarded as deviant.

The sexual transmission of this illness, considered by most people as a calamity one brings on oneself, is judged more harshly than other means—

especially since AIDS is understood as a disease not only of sexual excess but of perversity. (I am thinking, of course, of the United States, where people are currently being told that heterosexual transmission is extremely rare, and unlikely—as if Africa did not exist.) An infectious disease whose principal means of transmission is sexual necessarily puts at greater risk those who are sexually more active—and is easy to view as a punishment for that activity. True of syphilis, this is even truer of AIDS, since not just promiscuity but a specific sexual "practice" regarded as unnatural is named as more endangering. Getting the disease through a sexual practice is thought to be more willful, therefore deserves more blame. Addicts who get the illness by sharing contaminated needles are seen as committing (or completing) a kind of inadvertent suicide. Promiscuous homosexual men practicing their vehement sexual customs under the illusory conviction, fostered by medical ideology with its cure-all antibiotics, of the relative innocuousness of all sexually transmitted diseases, could be viewed as dedicated hedonists—though it's now clear that their behavior was no less suicidal. Those like hemophiliacs and blood-transfusion recipients, who cannot by any stretch of the blaming faculty be considered responsible for their illness, may be as ruthlessly ostracized by frightened people, and potentially represent a greater threat because, unlike the already stigmatized, they are not as easy to identify.

Infectious disease to which sexual fault is attached always inspire fears of easy contagion and bizarre fantasies of transmission by nonvenereal means in public places. The removal of doorknobs and the installation of swinging doors on U.S. Navy ships and the disappearance of the metal drinking cups affixed to public water fountains in the United States in the first decades of the century were early consequences of the "discovery" of syphilis's "innocently transmitted infection"; and the warning to generations of middle-class children always to interpose paper between bare bottom and the public toilet seat is another trace of the horror stories about the germs of syphilis being passed to the innocent by the dirty that were rife once and are still widely believed. Every feared epidemic disease, but especially those associated with sexual license, generates a preoccupying distinction between the disease's putative carriers (which usually means just the poor and, in this part of the world, people with darker skins) and those defined—health professionals and other bureaucrats do the defining—as "the general population." AIDS has revived similar phobias and fears of contamination among *this* disease's version of "the general population": white heterosexuals who do not inject themselves with drugs or have sexual relations with those who do. Like syphilis a disease of, or contracted from, dangerous others, AIDS is perceived as afflicting, in greater proportions than syphilis ever did, the already stigmatized. But syphilis was not identified with certain death, death that follows a protracted agony, as cancer was once imagined and AIDS is now held to be.

That AIDS is not a single illness but a syndrome, consisting of a seemingly open-ended list of contributing or "presenting" illnesses which constitute (that is, qualify the patient as having) the disease, makes it more a product of definition or construction than even a very complex, multiform illness like cancer. Indeed, the contention that AIDS is invariably fatal depends partly on what doctors decided to define as AIDS—and keep in reserve as distinct earlier stages of the disease. And this decision rests on a notion no less primitively metaphorical than that of a "full-blown" (or "full-fledged") disease.[1] "Full-blown is the form in which the disease is inevitably fatal. As what is immature is destined to become mature, what buds to become full-blown (fledglings to become full-fledged)—the doctors' botanical or zoological metaphor makes development or evolution into AIDS the norm, the rule. I am not saying that the metaphor creates the clinical conception, but I am arguing that it does much more than just ratify it. It lends support to an interpretation of the clinical evidence which is far from proved or, yet, provable. It is simply too early to conclude, of a disease identified only seven years ago, that infection will always produce something to die from, or even that everybody who has what is defined as AIDS will die of it. (As some medical writers have speculated, the appalling mortality rates could be registering the early, mostly rapid deaths of those most vulnerable to the virus—because of diminished immune competence, because of genetic predisposition, among other possible co-factors—not the ravages of a uniformly fatal infection.) Construing the disease as divided into distinct stages was the necessary way of implementing the metaphor of "full-blown disease." But it also slightly weakened the notion of inevitability suggested by the metaphor. Those sensibly interested in hedging their bets about how uniformly lethal infection would prove could use the standard three-tier classification—HIV infection, AIDS-related complex (ARC), and AIDS—to entertain either of two possibilities or both: the less catastrophic one, that *not* everybody infected would "advance" or "graduate" from HIV infection, and the more catastrophic one, that everybody would.

It is more catastrophic reading of the evidence that for some time has dominated debate about the disease, which means that a change in nomenclature is under way. Influential administrators of the way the disease is understood have decided that there should be no more of the false reassurance that might be had from the use of different acronyms for different stages of the disease. (It could never have been more than minimally reassuring.) Recent proposals for redoing terminology—for instance, to phase out the category of ARC—do not challenge the construction of the disease in stages, but do place additional stress on the *continuity* of the disease process. "Full-blown disease" is viewed as more inevitable now, and that strengthens the fatalism already in place.[2]

From the beginning the construction of the illness had depended on notions that separated one group of people from another—the sick from the well, people with ARC from people with AIDS, them and us—while implying the imminent dissolution of these distinctions. However hedged, the predictions always sounded fatalistic. Thus, the frequent pronouncements by AIDS specialists and public health officials on the chances of those infected with the virus coming down with "full-blown" disease have seemed mostly an exercise in the management of public opinion, dosing out the harrowing news in several steps. Estimates of the percentage expected to show symptoms classifying them as having AIDS within five years, which may be too low—at the time of this writing, the figure is 30 to 35 percent—are invariably followed by the assertion that "most," after which comes "probably all," those infected will eventually become ill. The critical number, then, is not the percentage of people likely to develop AIDS within a relatively short time but the *maximum* interval that could elapse between infection with HIV (described as lifelong and irreversible) and appearance of the first symptoms. As the years add up in which the illness has been tracked, so does the possible number of years between infection and becoming ill, now estimated, seven years into the epidemic, at between ten and fifteen years. This figure, which will presumably continue to be revised upward, does much to maintain the definition of AIDS as an inexorable, invariably fatal disease.

The obvious consequence of believing that all those who "harbor" the virus will eventually come down with the illness is that those who test positive for it are regarded as people-with-AIDS, who just don't have it . . . yet. It is only a matter of time, like any death sentence. Less obviously, such people are often regarded as if they *do* have it. Testing positive for HIV (which usually means having been tested for the presence not of the virus but of antibodies to the virus) is increasingly equated with being ill. Infected *means* ill, from that point forward. "Infected but not ill," that invaluable notion of clinical medicine (the body "harbors" many infections), is being superseded by biomedical concepts which, whatever their scientific justification, amount to reviving the antiscientific logic of defilement, and make infected-but-healthy a contradiction in terms. Being ill in this new sense can have many practical consequences. People are losing their jobs when it is learned that they are HIV-positive (though it is not legal in the United States to fire someone for that reason) and the temptation to conceal a positive finding must be immense. The consequences of testing HIV-positive are even more punitive for those selected populations—there will be more—upon which the government has already made testing mandatory. The U.S. Department of Defense has announced that military personnel discovered to be HIV-positive are being removed "from sensitive, stressful jobs," because of evidence indicating that mere infection with the virus, in the absence of any other symptoms, produces subtle changes in mental abilities in a significant minority of virus carriers. (The evidence cited: lower scores on certain neurological tests given to some who had tested positive, which could reflect mental impairment caused by exposure to the virus, though most doctors think this extremely improbably, or could be caused—as officially acknowledged under questioning—by "the anger, depression, fear, and panic" of people who have just learned that they are HIV-positive.) And, of course, testing positive now makes one ineligible to immigrate everywhere.

In every previous epidemic of an infectious nature, the epidemic is equivalent to the number of tabulated cases. This epidemic is regarded as consisting *now* of that figure plus a calculation about a much larger number of people apparently in good health (seemingly healthy, but doomed) who are infected. The calculations are being made and remade all the time, and pressure is building to identify these people, and to tag them. With the most up-to-date biomedical testing, it is possible to create a new class of lifetime pariahs, the future ill. But the result of this radical expansion of the notion of illness created by the triumph of modern medical scrutiny also seems a throwback to the past, before the era of medical triumphalism, when illnesses were innumerable, mysterious, and the progression from being seriously ill to dying was something normal (not, as now, medicine's lapse or failure, destined to be corrected). AIDS, in which people are understood as ill before they are ill; which produces a seemingly innumerable array of symptom-illnesses; for which there are only palliatives; and which brings to many a social death the precedes the physical one—AIDS reinstates something like a premodern experience of illness, as described in Donne's *Devotions*, in which "every thing that disorders a faculty and the function of that is a sicknesse," which starts when we

> are preafflicted, super-afflicted with these jealousies and suspitions, and apprehensions of Sicknes, before we can cal it a sicknes; we are not sure we are ill; one hand askes the other by the pulse, and our eye asks our own urine, how we do. . . . we are tormented with sicknes, and cannot stay till the torment come. . . .

whose agonizing outreach to every part of the body makes a real cure chimerical, since what "is but an accident, but a symptom of the main disease, is so violent, that the Phisician must attend the cure of that" rather than "the cure of the disease it self," and whose consequence is abandonment:

> As Sicknesse is the greatest misery, so the greatest misery of sicknes is solitude; when the infectiousnes of the disease deterrs them who should assist, from comming; even the Phisician dares scarse come. . . . it is an Outlawry, an Excommunication upon the patient. . . .

In premodern medicine, illness is described as it is experienced intuitively, as a relation of outside and inside: an interior sensation or something to be discerned on the body's surface, by sight (or just below, by listening, palpating), which is confirmed when the interior is opened to viewing (in surgery, in autopsy). Modern—that is, effective—medicine is characterized by far more complex notions of what is to be observed inside the body: not just the disease's results (damaged organs) but its cause (microorganisms), and by a far more intricate typology of illness.

In the older era of artisanal diagnoses, being examined produced an immediate verdict, immediate as the physician's willingness to speak. Now an examination means tests. And being tested introduces a time lapse that, given the unavoidably industrial character of competent medical testing, can stretch out for weeks: an agonizing delay for those who think they are awaiting a death sentence or an acquittal. Many are reluctant to be tested out of dread of the verdict, out of fear of being put on a list that could bring future discrimination or worse, and out of fatalism (what good would it do?). The usefulness of self-examination for the early detection of certain common cancers, much less likely to be fatal if treated before they are very advanced, is now widely understood. Early detection of an illness thought to be inexorable and incurable cannot seem to bring any advantage.

Like other diseases that arouse feelings of shame, AIDS is often a secret, but not from the patient. A cancer diagnosis was frequently concealed from patients by their families; an AIDS diagnosis is at least as often concealed from their families by patients. And as with other grave illnesses regarded as more than just illnesses, many people with AIDS are drawn to whole-body rather than illness-specific treatments, which are thought to be either ineffectual or dangerous. (The disparagement of effective, scientific medicine for offering treatments that are *merely* illness-specific, and likely to be toxic, is a recurrent misconjecture of opinion that regards itself as enlightened.) This disastrous choice is still being made by some people with cancer, an illness that surgery and drugs can often cure. And a predictable mix of superstition and resignation is leading some people with AIDS to refuse antiviral chemotherapy, which, even in the absence of a cure, has proved of some effectiveness (in slowing down the syndrome's progress and in staving off some common presenting illnesses), and instead to seek to heal themselves, often under the auspices of some "alternative medicine" guru. But subjecting an emaciated body to the purification of a macrobiotic diet is about as helpful in treating AIDS as having oneself bled, the "holistic" medical treatment of choice in the era of Donne.

NOTES

1. The standard definition distinguishes between people with the disease or syndrome "fulfilling the criteria for the surveillance definition of AIDS" from a larger number infected with HIV and symptomatic "who do not fulfill the empiric criteria for the full-blown disease. This constellation of signs and symptoms in the context of HIV infection has been termed the AIDS-related complex (ARC)." Then follows the obligatory percentage. "It is estimated that approximately 25 percent of patients with ARC will develop full-blown disease within 3 years." Harrison's *Principles of Internal Medicine*, 11th edition (1987), p. 1394.

    The first major illness known by an acronym, the condition called AIDS does not have, as it were, natural borders. It is an illness whose identity is designed for purposes of investigation and with tabulation and surveillance by medical and other bureaucracies in view. Hence, the unselfconscious equating in the medical textbook of what is empirical with what pertains to surveillance, two notions deriving from quite different models of understanding. (AIDS is what fulfills that which is referred to as either the "criteria for the surveillance definition" or the "empiric criteria": HIV infection plus the presence of one or more diseases included on the roster drown up by the disease's principal administrator of definition in the United States, the federal Centers for Disease Control in Atlanta.) This completely stipulative definition with its metaphor of maturing disease decisively influences how the illness is understood.

2.   The 1988 Presidential Commission on the epidemic recommended "de-emphasizing" the use of the term ARC because it "tends to obscure the life-threatening aspects of this stage of illness." There is some pressure to drop the term AIDS, too. The report by the President Commission pointedly used the acronym HIV for the epidemic itself, as part of a recommended shift from "monitoring disease" to "monitoring infection." Again, one of the reasons given is that the present terminology masks the true gravity of the menace. ("This longstanding concentration on the clinical manifestations of AIDS rather than on all stages of HIV infection [i.e., from initial infection to seroconversion, to an antibody-positive asymptomatic stage, to full-blown AIDS] has had the unintended effect of misleading the public as to the extent of infection in the population. . . .") It does seem likely that the disease will, eventually, be renamed. *This* change in nomenclature would justify officially the policy of including the infected but asymptomatic among the ill.

part four

Gender and Disability

Nurturance, Sexuality and Women With Disabilities

The Example of Women and Literature

ADRIENNE ASCH AND MICHELLE FINE

"Each time I announced I was pregnant, everyone in the family looked shocked, dropped their forks at the dinnertable—not exactly a celebration" (35-year-old, white married woman, mother of two, who contracted polio at age 5).

DISABLED WOMEN AS PARTNERS

The income-earning opportunities of women with disabilities are severely constrained. So, too, are their opportunities to be nurtured and to nurture, to be lovers and be loved, to be mothers if they desire. Women with disabilities are less likely than non-disabled women or disabled men to fulfill roles customarily reserved for their respective sexes. Exempted from the "male"productive role and the "female" nurturing one, having the glory of neither, disabled women are arguably doubly oppressed—or, perhaps, "freer" to be nontraditional. Should they pursue what has been thought nontraditional, however, the decision to work, to be a single mother, to be involved in a lesbian relationship, or to enter politics may be regarded as a default rather than a preference. We recognize that many women have no desire to marry, mother, or be sexual with men, and that marriage and childbearing statistics must not be used to measure "social success." Nonetheless, while many nondisabled and disabled women are choosing nontraditional lifestyles, other disabled women go other routes not by choice alone.

Franklin (1977) reported that disabled women were less likely than non-disabled women to be married, more likely to marry later, and more likely to be divorced. Bowe (1984) and Hanna and Rogovsky (1986) report similar findings from the Current Population Survey's data of the early 1980s. Whereas 60 percent of men with disabilities and women without them are married, only 49 percent of disabled women are married. As with employment and earnings data, actual disparities between disabled and non-disabled women may be greater when the age factor previously cited is taken into account. Seventy percent of non-disabled women are under 44 years of age, 26 percent under age 24. It can be expected that many of these non-disabled younger women who show up in census data as unmarried will at some time marry. These data alone do not reveal how much the presence of a woman's disability affects her choices, chances, or inclinations to marry or be involved in a loving relationship with a woman or a man. That more disabled women are unmarried than non-disabled women might be explained by demographic differences alone: being older they have had more time for their marriages to sour just as have millions of others whose relationships dissolve. Many are widowed, as are women of comparable age with disabilities.

When disabled women are compared with non-disabled women and disabled men on rates of divorce and separation, glaring differences again surface between the situation of disabled women and either comparison group. The New York City Affiliate of the National Council on Alcoholism has documented that 90 percent of women alcoholics versus 10 percent of male alcoholics are left by their spouses (Natl. Council on Alcoholism 1980). Hanna and Rogovsky (1986) analyzed 1985 Current Population Survey data on marital status, dividing a subsample of ever-married but not widowed men and women into three categories: non-disabled, mildly disabled, and severely disabled. They found that of this group, more women than men in all categories were divorced, but that significant differences emerged between "severely disabled women" and other groups. Only 14 percent of men termed "severely disabled" were divorced, but 26 percent of severely disabled women were. While men's rates of separation were 3 percent, 5 percent, and 7 percent for each category of disability status, women's rates of separation were 4 percent, 6 percent, and 11 percent. Thirty-seven percent of "severely disabled" women, as contrasted with 22 percent of "severely disabled" men who were once married, are no longer married, for reasons *other* than death of a spouse.

Anecdote, interview, and autobiography corroborate the census data and the stereotype of the disabled woman as alone. For both men and women whose disabilities occur before marriage, literature reveals considerable apprehension about finding a mate. Hahn (1983b) and Asch and Sacks (1983) reviewed large numbers of published autobiographies and noted how little could be found about intimate relationships; of those who did live with adult partners, nearly all were men.

In personal accounts and interviews reported in Bowe (1981), Brightman (1984), Duffy (1981), Heinrich and Kriegel (1961), Matthews (1983), and Roth (1981), we discover how relatively difficult it is for disabled men or women to find a partner relationship. Nonetheless, many more men than women eventually established relationships they found satisfying. Matthews (1983) found that only five of the forty-five women she interviewed were married, and more than half reported no sexual relationship since becoming disabled. Only half of the seventy-five orthopedically disabled women who responded to Duffy's (1981) questionnaire had ever been married. Bonwich (1985) recounts that twenty-nine of the thirty-six rural, spinal-cord-injured women she interviewed had been romantically involved or married prior to their becoming disabled; of these twenty-nine, fifteen saw the end of these relationships soon after onset of disability. Only one of the more than sixty pieces in Browne, Connors, and

Stern's (1985) collection of disabled women's writing mentions marriage. Although many of the women represented are lesbians, none discusses an ongoing intimate relationship or provides a glimpse of the trials and pleasures of meeting a lover and maintaining a valued partnership.

In conferences of disabled girls and women in which the topic of relationships comes up at all, discussion centers around the difficulty of meeting men who pay them any notice. The only group of disabled adults in which women are *more* likely than men to be married is women who are labeled retarded. Safilios-Rothschild (1977) has suggested that the retarded wife may fit all too well the criteria of the "good wife": one who is docile, passive, loyal, and dependent, not likely to show her husband up.

How can we explain these data? If disability is thought to reinforce the customary female characteristics of passivity, compliance, and good nature, why should women with disabilities frequently be without partners?

A look at the literature on the views of the non-disabled toward persons with disabilities reveals that the attitudes of non-disabled women and men are overwhelmingly negative. Men's attitudes, however, are the more extreme (Siller, Ferguson, Vann, Holland 1976). These researchers found that disabled children and adults were more likely to be rejected as family members than as acquaintances or workmates by both men and women, but rates of rejection were greater for non-disabled men. Hanna and Rogovsky (1986) suggest that the disabled woman may be more negatively viewed by both women and men than the similarly disabled man. In surveying non-disabled college students at an Eastern public university they found that images of "disabled woman," "disabled man," and "woman," differed markedly. When asked how women and men using wheelchairs became disabled, non-disabled students attributed male disability to external situations such as war, work injury, or accident. They attributed female disability to internal causes, such as disease. The authors suggest that attributing disability to disease may foster more negative attitudes because disease stimulates primitive fears of contagion or of the person's inherent moral badness. Thus, the disabled woman may be viewed as more dangerous than a similarly disabled male, more morally suspect, or more deserving of her fate.

When these same students were asked to draw associations for "woman," and "disabled woman," the associations cited for the two could not have been more different. "Woman" drew associations of worker (intelligent, leader, career), of sexuality (soft, lovable, orgasm), of mother or wife (wife, mother, mom, married, childbearer). When asked to associate to "disabled woman," students described her in terms of dependence and impairment (crippled, almost lifeless), of age (gray, old, white hair), of despair (someone to feel sorry for, pity, sorry, lonely, ugly). She was virtually never depicted as wife, mother, or worker by the more than one hundred students questioned.

ATTRACTIVENESS AND NURTURANCE

To understand these phenomena and their consequences for disabled women, we speculate about the implications for disabled women of cultural views of attractiveness and nurturance. First, it is important to note that a pervasive "attractiveness stereotype" enables people to believe that those who are attractive are also "more sensitive, kind, interesting, strong, poised, modest, sociable, outgoing, and exciting, sexually warm and responsive," and will "hold better jobs, have more successful marriages, and happier and more fulfilling lives" (Berscheid and Walster 1972: 46, 74). In short, attractiveness is linked to virtue, to all that is desired, especially by men of women. In the cultural imagination, beauty is linked to goodness and nurturance, the traits more sought after in women both as lovers and as workers. Ample evidence substantiates that perceptions of women's attractiveness influence women's educational and work opportunities (Unger 1985; Unger, Hilderbrand, and Mardor 1982). Unfortunately for the disabled woman, only a few attributes count toward attractiveness in the United States and a woman's bodily integrity is one such requirement (Hahn 1983a; Lakoff and Scherr 1984). Furthermore, a woman's beauty is seen as a reflection of a male partner's social status. As Lakoff and Scherr (1984) note in *Face Value: The Politics of Beauty*: "The message we are give daily by the myriad images of beauty is that women must look a certain way to be loved and admired, to be worth anything" (p. 114).

In a discussion of male notions of attractiveness, these authors note that physical grace and ease are also important in the assessment of what is desirable in women. The woman with a disability, whether apparent or invisible, may display less than the norm or the fantasied ideal of bodily integrity, grace, and ease. The very devices she values for enhancing free movement and communication (braces, crutches, hearing aids, or canes) may repel men seeking the fantasied flawlessness. Even those with "intact" bodies, such as Mary, a woman with a severe perceptual/motor problem stemming from a learning disability, can find themselves deemed clumsy and therefore unattractive. Given that disabled women are found unattractive by college students as well as by clinicians (Hanna and Rogovsky 1986; Unger 1985; Unger, Hilderbrand, and Mardor 1982), and given that men value physical attractiveness in a partner significantly more than women do, it is little wonder that heterosexual women with disabilities are more likely than disabled men to be alone.

The argument of women's attractiveness as a display of male status is not sufficient, however, to explain the underinvolvement of disabled women in intimate relationships with men (and women). To pursue the heterosexual question first and more extensively, it appears that men's unacknowledged needs and dependencies—satisfied often in relationships with women—reduce men's desire to become connected in work or in love with disabled women. Drawing on the writing of Miller (1976), we contend that if a woman's role in heterosexual relationships has been to accommodate a man emotionally while not exposing his vulnerabilities, the disabled woman may be thought unfit. If men desired only the passive, doll-like female of the stereotype, disabled women might do, but the doll must be functional as well as decorative. Feminist theorists such as Hartmann (1981) and Zillah Eisenstein (1984) have argued that the smooth functioning of advanced capitalism requires the illusion, if not the reality, of a heterosexual nuclear home warmed and nurtured by an all-giving and all-comforting woman.

Brownmiller (1984) characterizes nurturance when applied to women as "warmth, tenderness, compassion, sustained emotional involvement in the welfare of others, and a weak or nonexistent competitive drive. Nurturant labor includes child care, spouse care, cooking and feeding, soothing and patching, straightening out disorder and cleaning up dirt, little considerations like sewing a button on a grown man's raincoat, major considerations like nursing relationships and mending rifts, putting the demands of family and others before one's own, and dropping one's work to minister to the sick, the troubled, and the lonely in their time of need" (pp. 221–22). Men may assume incorrectly that a disabled woman could not contribute either physical or emotional housekeeping to a spouse and children. If a woman cannot sew on a button because she cannot use her hands, she may be thought unfit to help with the mending of emotional fences as well.

Disabled persons (men and women) often elicit in non-disabled others powerful existential anxieties about their own helplessness, needs, and dependencies (Hahn 1983a). For a man who may have such emotional residues well-buried, their activism in the present of a disabled woman may stimulate reflexively his rejection of her. Even if a man believed that a particular disabled woman could manage to run her own life and master the details of helping him with his, how could he accept help from an unwhole, "sick" woman? How can she minister to his needs when a disabled woman epitomizes all that is needy herself? Might it be that taking help from such a presumably helpless woman arouses guilt or shame in any man who might consider it? If men can accept emotional sustenance only from women who can provide the maximum in physical caretaking, the woman with limitations may be viewed as inadequate to give the warmth, companionship, and shelter men traditionally expect from their mates. If men fear both their own and another's dependency and intimacy to the extent that Chodorow (1978) and Gilligan (1982) have argued, if disabled persons awaken such feelings, and if men desire women who can satiate their own emotional needs without either publicly acknowledging them or requiring reciprocity, disabled women are likely to be rejected forcefully as lovers/partners.

Disabled women who have partners, especially if they are non-disabled men, are likely to discover that they and their partners are subjected to curiosity, scrutiny, and public misunderstanding. Ubiquitously perceived as a social burden, the disabled woman evokes pity that spreads to her partner. "Whenever my husband and I are shopping and he is pushing my wheelchair, people stop us and say [to him], 'You must be a saint.' What about me? Do you think it's easy to live with him?" The public assumption is that this woman is a burden and her husband is either saintly or a loser himself.

The view of the disabled woman as limited emotionally because she may be limited physically may account for the acknowledged preference of disabled men for non-disabled partners. In their review of the autobiographies of blind women and men, Asch and Sacks (1983) discovered that the men sought sighted wives to complement them; to confer upon them a status of normal, successful, integrated; and to ensure their smooth navigation literally and figuratively through the world. In a study of the coping strategies of disabled scientists, a group that was overwhelmingly male, many reported that one major strategy was acquisition of a woman/wife (Redden, personal communication, 1980). In a *New York Times* article enshrining negative stereotypes about non-disabled women who marry disabled men and the men they marry, Rose (1984) postulated that the disabled man is the perfect outlet for nurturance and competence for non-disabled women who could not fulfill themselves or demonstrate their full capacity in a relationship with a truly competent male. Here, disabled men are perceived as lacking all capacities for self-direction merely because they cannot walk or see; non-disabled women are pictured as dominating their disabled spouses. The reverse situation of a disabled woman with a non-disabled male partner is omitted altogether from the discussion.

Male commitment to narrow conceptions of attractiveness and nurturance also may illuminate the rejection of disabled women as workers. The presumed costs of hiring disabled workers have been refuted elsewhere [Hill et al. 1987; U. S. Dept. of Labor 1982]; the resistance to hiring women with disabilities stems from sources more primitive and unrecognized than either fiscal conservatism or esthetic and existential anxiety (Hahn 1983a). To the extent that women are employed in ways that sustain male domination, the "neutered" disabled woman fails to fill the bill (Rich 1980). We assert that the resistance to employing disabled women derives in part from the unacknowledged forms of heterosexual male privileges sustained in the workplace. Sheehy (1984) reminds us that male judges sometimes have awarded workers' compensation benefits to women with disabilities deemed so unattractive that future employment was highly unlikely!

We contend that men spurn disabled women as workers and partners because they fail to measure up on grounds of appearance or of perceived abilities in physical and emotional caretaking. Although this argument aids understanding of her marginality in the arenas of heterosexual love and male-controlled work, it fails to fully explain the situation of disabled lesbians. We have found no data on the numbers of lesbians with disabilities or on their acceptance by non-disabled lesbians as partners, but comments made by many disabled lesbians indicate that within the community of lesbians the disabled woman is still in search of love. Disabled lesbians have described being dismissed, shunned, or relegated to the status of friend and confidante rather than lover, just as have heterosexual disabled women.

Chodorow (1978) and Gilligan (1982) have much to say about women's capacity for relatedness. At its best, that relational potential renders women well-suited to cooperate, empathize, affiliate, examine the interpersonal dimensions of moral questions, anticipate others' needs—all those qualities current feminists at once struggle against and delight in. Cultivated by the culture to perpetuate male dominance and now seen as the source of women's potential strength for our own and the world's betterment (H. Eisenstein 1983; Miller 1976), these very qualities may be stimulated when a woman confronts a disabled woman as a potential lover. If the dark, problematic side of a capacity for relatedness is a too-ready potential for merger with another, stereotypes about the presumed dependency and neediness of a disabled woman could easily send women scurrying in the other direction. So long as non-disabled women hold the stereotype that the disability rights movement fights against, the thought of a disabled woman as a lover may engender fears of merger, exaggerate lack of boundaries, and spawn fantasies of endless responsibility, of unremitting and unreciprocated care. Until non-disabled men and women recognize that disabled people can can contribute to others' well-being, contemplating "taking on" such a woman as friend or lover will tend to activate such fears.

These arguments admittedly, are speculative, whether or not these dynamics operate in intimate heterosexual or lesbian couples involving a disabled partner remains to be explored. Whether or not heterosexual and lesbian relationships are characterized by similar patterns must be discovered. So, too, must we inquire about interdependence, reciprocity, and gender roles in couples where both partners have disabilities. Although many disabled people shun other disabled people as intimates, not all do. From our interviews, observations at disability conferences, and conversations with scores of women, we suspect that disabled women who marry *after* onset of disability are more likely than similarly disabled men to have a disabled spouse. Becker (1980) reports that 75 percent of deaf women marry deaf men. Because disability, unlike race or ethnicity, has not created natural cultures or communities wherein people customarily look to one another to create intimacy and family, one wonders whether those women whose partners are also disabled consider this a positive choice, a default option, or an irrelevant characteristic. What is crucial is that readers understand that *why* disabled women encounter difficulty in establishing nurturing relations is a significant question and not one with an "obvious answer."

Why disabled women are alone is an important question. That they are has complicated consequences. For example, Kutner and Gray (1985) and Kutner (1985) have specified how the condition of "aloneness" interacts with access to medical care and social support. In their investigations of people with renal failure who used various forms of dialysis, Kutner and Gray learned that maintenance of a home dialysis regimen (which is considered optimal for people with this condition) was substantially affected by marital status. Home dialysis requires a partner ready to assist the user for four to six hours three times a week. As a consequence of gender-stratified aloneness, men are more likely than women to receive home dialysis (and white women are more likely to receive it than black women). Supportive people, of course, need not be spouses, but for those Kutner and Gray surveyed, lack of such a spouse often resulted in less than the best medical care.

When Kutner surveyed 332 Atlanta-area residents with cardiac, kidney, and mobility disabilities regarding their perceptions of social support, she found that married people received help from more sources than did their never-married or formerly-married peers. However, the gap in help received between married and nonmarried was greater for women than for men. As is all too often true, the women getting the least help was the one most likely to need it. She was more likely than an unmarried man to head a household with dependent children and thus to face the combined stresses of single parenthood and disability.

SEXUALITY AND MOTHERHOOD

Often deprived of the chance for long-term intimacy, disabled women also are commonly considered unfit as sexual partners and as mothers. Many women speak angrily of the unavailability of adequate counseling on sexuality, birth control, pregnancy, and childbirth from either gynecologists or rehabilitation professionals. Ignorant of the adverse consequences of some birth control devices for women with particular conditions, many gynecologists prescribe unsafe methods. Safilios-Rothschild (1977) notes that since coronary research has been conducted almost exclusively on men, it has produced data relevant only to men. Women who seek information about resuming sexual activity after a heart attack have been provided with male standards or with no answers at all. So astonishing is it to some physicians that disabled women might be sexual that Galler (1984) reports completely unnecessary abdominal surgery for one woman because no one believed that someone with cerebral palsy could have the symptoms of venereal disease.

One woman with spina bifida described a preadolescent encounter with her gynecologist this way:

"Will I be able to have satisfying sexual relations with a man?"

"Don't worry, honey, your vagina will be tight enough to satisfy any man."

Her satisfaction probably didn't cross his mind.

Motherhood, the institution and experience that perhaps has dominated all cultural conceptions of women—eclipsing even expectations of beauty, softness, or ever-present sexuality—often has been proscribed for a woman with a disability. Many states have had laws forbidding people with histories of epilepsy, mental retardation, and psychiatric disability from marrying. Fears that disabled women would produce children with similar conditions (nearly always groundless since the vast majority of disability is not hereditary) have mingled with convictions that they would harm, deprive, or burden children they attempted to rear. As a result, many medical professionals still urge or coerce women into being sterilized (Finger, 1984; Macklin and Gaylin 1981; U. S. Comm. on Civil Rights (1983). Women in interviews cite recent sessions with gynecologists who urged them not to bother with birth control by saying, "Get your tubes tied. You couldn't take care of a child yourself." Women with diabetes, epilepsy, and spinal cord injuries report difficulty in finding obstetricians or midwives willing to help them through what they view as "high-risk" pregnancies (Asrael 1982; Collins 1983).

Problems in mothering for disabled women are not limited to the medical aspects of reproduction. Regardless of marital status or the disability status of any partners, disabled women report discrimination in adopting, in being permitted to provide foster care, and in winning child custody after divorce. Sadly and perversely, Gold (1985) reports, a 1978 amendment to the California welfare and institutions code intended to prevent discrimination against disabled parents has, in fact, been used to sanction unannounced home visits and the removal of children simply on the grounds that mothers were blind. In 1986 a Colorado social service agency took custody of a 13-month girl, alleging that the underweight child was malnourished because her blind single mother could not feed her properly. Even after two doctors testified that the child, though small, was not malnourished, the social service agency would not permit the child to be returned to her mother (*Braille Monitor* 1986).

Exemption or exclusion from voluntary sexuality and reproduction has not exempted disabled females from sexual abuse and victimization. Perhaps even more than non-disabled women, disabled women confront serious psychological and social problems in ending abusive or exploitative relationships. Galler (1984) and *Disability Rag* (1986) relate instances in which women with cerebral palsy or mental retardation have been ignored by professionals when they report rape. If women without disabilities hesitate to give up abusive relationships because they cannot imagine how they will survive economically, disabled women in abusive homes may feel even more trapped. Melling (1984) discusses the problem of wife abuse in the deaf community, noting a battery of factors that conspire against deaf women standing up for themselves in degrading or even dangerous situations. Even more than the non-disabled girl, a disabled girl is an easy victim of abuse by male relatives. Unfortunately, even personal care attendants employed by the disabled woman are not infrequently reported to abuse the women they have been hired to assist. One counselor of disabled women in a Denver domestic violence project has commented that many disabled women, like their non-disabled counterparts, return to the abusive relationships because "it is the only thing they have had. As bad as it is, for many it is better than living in an institution or going back to their families" (*Disability Rag* 1986: 9–10).

Disabled girls and women, in numbers hard to estimate, are raped at home, in institutions, or on the streets. We know of women whose stay in long-term care institutions or rehabilitation facilities included sterilization with official approval because, they were told, there was danger of molestation in the institution. An inquiry into California's community care facilities for the mentally and physically disabled and for the elderly found that "daily, throughout this state, residents of community care facilities are being sexually abused, beaten, fed spoiled food, forced to live with toilets that don't work" (*New York Times* 1984). We wonder how many of these same women have been sterilized to keep the effects of rape from the public eye. That such exploitation frequently occurs outside of institutions as well is demonstrated by one study conducted by the Seattle Rape Relief Center. The center found that between May 1977 and December 1979, more than three hundred cases of sexual exploitation of physically or mentally disabled women came to its attention (Bellone and Waxman 1983). Extrapolating to the state of Washington, the center estimated that perhaps thirty thousand rapes of such women occur annually.

SELF-ESTEEM, RESISTANCE, AND IDENTITY

If our culture views being female and disabled as "redundant," whereas being male and disabled is a contradiction, we must ponder on the effects of such role definitions and social options on the self-concept of the disabled woman. Some women accommodate societal projections, becoming the dependent creatures their parents, teachers, and others expected. In fact, the psychological literature suggests this response to be the norm. Consider this in relation to findings that disabled girls and women perceive themselves and are perceived by others more

negatively than is the case with disabled boys and men. They report more negative self-images (Weinberg 1976), are viewed in less favorable ways (Miller
1970), and are more likely to be victims of hostility than are disabled men (Titley
and Viney 1969). The Asch and Sacks (1983) analysis of autobiographies of
blind women and men indicated that the women internalized negative messages
much more than did the men, seeing themselves as burdensome, unwanted, and
unlovable, whereas men rarely did.

Weinberg's (1976) self-concept research found that negative self-concept was
less related to one's level of disability than to one's gender—with women reporting more negative feelings than either disabled or non-disabled males. In a
review of the self-esteem literature on disability, Darling (1979) found that—
contrary to predictions of much psychoanalytic and labeling theory discussions—disabled children and adolescents demonstrated levels of self-esteem
not substantially different from those of their non-disabled counterparts.
Nonetheless, she reports, disabled girls evidence lower self-esteem than disabled
boys and either non-disabled girls and boys.

Such findings about self-esteem need to be analyzed. It may be that males
with disabilities can escape some of the trap of the disability role by aspiring to
male characteristics of mastery, competence, and autonomy; disabled women and
girls, however, forsake their gender role if they seek to escape from disability-
imposed dependence by such means. We believe that such role contradictions
can plague the female seeking to affirm her identity in the presence of a disability. Particularly for the disabled girl (and the self-esteem literature generally
concentrates on children and adolescents) becoming socialized in a family and
school unclear about what norms to suggest or what hopes to give her for her
future, self-esteem may be a serious problem.

A look at current discussions of male and female paths of development suggests ideas about the sense of self and of socialization of the disabled girl. Many
of these are elaborated upon by Harris and Wideman in this volume. What happens to a disabled girl growing up in a family where her mother perceives that,
because the daughter is disabled, she is fundamentally different from the mother
and thus is not expected to develop into the kind of woman the mother aspired
to be? Friedman (1980) suggests that a mother's major task is to "hand down the
legacy of womanhood . . . to share it and be an example of it" (p. 90). If the
mother's definition of womanhood is based upon being attractive to and caring
for a mate, she may inculcate in her daughter the belief that disability renders
such a life impossible.

Thus, the disabled girl's best hope may be to turn to the traditionally male
norms of achievement for establishing a sense of herself. Although she may
acquire many skills and psychological resources to assist her in the productive
world, she is not becoming the typical girl and young woman for whom establishing affiliative ties is of paramount importance (Person 1982). Autobiographies of many disabled women emphasize their quest for independence, work,
and escape out of the stereotype of disability as helplessness. As one disabled
woman put it to us: "I was raised to be a non-disabled son." However proud she

may be of her accomplishments, the disabled girl knows she is not becoming like other women. Unless she likes that difference, it may lead to the lowered self-esteem found in psychological studies and in the autobiographical literature (Asch and Sacks 1983).

We have said that her "best" hope is to turn toward male standards of achievement. Like the 15-year-old Maria quoted earlier, however, many disabled girls are sheltered, kept from activities and opportunities where they might manage mastery of skills or acquiring of friends. In such a sad and too-common situation, the disabled girl may have no sense of identity with her mother or other girls and women, and no validation for accomplishments beyond the home. Little wonder, then, that there are trapped and demoralized girls and women.

At the other end of the spectrum are disabled females who resist all the gender-based and disability-based stereotypes and take pride in the identities they forge. Because of or despite their parents, they get an education and a job. They live independently, enjoy sex with men or women, become pregnant and carry to term if they choose, or abort if they prefer. They relish their friendships, intimacies, lovers, activities. Some determine that they will play by the rules of achievement and succeed at meeting standards that are often deemed inaccessible to them. Some accept societal norms of attractiveness and enjoy the challenge of living up to them, disability notwithstanding. Others choose to disregard anything that seems like "passing" (Goffman 1963). Like Sarah in *Children of a Lesser God*, they demand that the world accept them on their terms, whether those terms be insisting upon signing rather than speaking, not covering their burn scars, not wearing clothing to hide parts of their bodies others may see as "ugly" or "deformed," or rejecting prostheses that inhibit and do not help.

Following her mastectomy, Lorde (1980) refused to wear a prosthetic breast: "On the day after the stitches came out . . . I got so furious with the nurse who told me I was bad for the morale of the office because I did not wear a prosthesis. . . ." (p. 52). Diane, a quadri-amputee interviewed by Gelya Frank, refused her prostheses because "I knew it was going on my body. And that would add more sweat, and more asthma, because I would have to work harder with it. So I always saw my body as something that was mine, and something that was free, and I hated anything kind of binding . . ." (Frank 1981:84). Michele, a 17-year-old Hispanic high school student, told us that she wore her prosthetic arms only to her doctor's appointments. They are clumsy, she said, and she could manage to do things much more easily without them; she was perfectly comfortable having people see her short and "deformed" arms.

Having, as a child, incorporated her disability into her identity, Harilyn Rousso (1984) resisted her mother's attempts to make her appear more typical. She explains: "She [her mother] made numerous attempts over the years of my childhood to have me go for physical therapy and to practice walking more 'normally' at home. I vehemently refused all her efforts. She could not understand why I would not walk straight. . . . My disability, with my different walk and talk and my involuntary movements, having been with me all of my life, was part of me, part of my identity. With these disability features, I felt complete and whole. My mother's attempt to change my walk, strange as it may seem, felt like an assault on myself, an incomplete acceptance of all of me, an attempt to make me over" (p. 9).

From these and many other examples, we know that some disabled girls and women flourish in spite of the pressures from family and the distortions and discrimination meted out by society. We need to know much more than we do about what helps some disabled girls and women resist, and we must acknowledge the travails and the victories of these women.

DISABLED WOMEN: IMPLICATIONS
FOR DISABILITY RIGHTS AND FEMINISM

The struggles of feminism and of disability rights have much in common. In order to pursue gender and disability equality, activists have argued for the elimination of laws, institutional structures and practices, and social attitudes that have reduced women or disabled people to one biological characteristic. Although both movements have borrowed and profited from the black civil rights movement, these later movements share the indisputable fact that in some situations biology *does* and *should* count. However, feminism and disability rights advocates insist that instances where biology matters are extremely rare, and such cases can be minimized by changing society to better incorporate all its citizens.

In the writings of such socialist-feminists as Hester Eisenstein (1983, 1985), one discovers a fine understanding of the differences among women. Also present are continued commitment to economic and political freedom as well as to psychological liberation, and a balanced appreciation of women's attributes of nurturance and cooperation that neither glorifies women nor denigrates men. She and others, such as many of the contributors to the Sargent (1981) discussion of the "unhappy marriage" of Marxism and feminism, maintain that women's situation will not and cannot improve substantially until they gain full economic, political, sexual, reproductive, and psychological recognition. Recognition in their terms includes appreciation of both sameness *and* difference, and it entails social transformation in order for diversity to be tolerated and not punished. They understand that some differences, even if culturally created, are acceptable and perhaps even valuable, not only for women but for men and for social and political institutions.

We believe such an analysis can readily incorporate the particular issues of disability rights and of disabled women. That portion of the disability rights movement calling for societal change along with equality of opportunity would also be able to address concerns particular to disabled women. We suggest that progress for disabled people will not be achieved through stress on equality of opportunity alone, no matter how crucial such equality is, and we believe that disability rights theorists and activities can borrow from socialist-feminists who call for societal transformation in addition to equality of opportunity within existing arrangements.

Although we could not now assess the relative contributions of race, sex, or disability discrimination to any one woman's life experience or to that of disabled women in general, we can cite areas of theory and politics in disability rights and feminism that will benefit from specific attention to the concerns of today's disabled women. In thinking about the barriers to disabled women's full social, economic, and political participation, we also seek to recognize which ones are most amenable to work through disability rights activity, which ones through feminism, and which ones through both.

Omolade (1985) and Joseph (1981) have argued that in certain instances black women share more commonalities with black men than they do with white women. To ignore that fact and look to white feminists to embrace all of black women's concerns violates political and psychological reality. The same can be said for women with disabilities—including racial/ethnic minority women with disabilities—who may need to look to feminists, to their ethnic or racial group, and to the disability rights movement for support. One must recall the crucial difference between relations of disabled women and men and relations of women and men of color commented upon earlier: many disabled men reject disabled women as intimates based on their own feelings about nurturance and attractiveness. Black men, however, may be intimate with black women even if sexism persists within family and community relations. While we in no way suggest that disabled women and men should look only to one another for intimacy, that disabled people often reject one another for such intimacy may make genuine political struggle together for all disabled people's rights especially difficult.

Nonetheless, access to transportation, to housing, and to public places is a concern of all disabled people in which disabled women's best hope probably hinges on their joining and broadening the existing disability rights movement. As we have said, independent living for disabled women may raise special problems in the training and supervision of personal care attendants and assistants. Independent living centers will need to pay attention to reports of abuse and domestic violence, perhaps modifying recruitment, training, and supervision of attendants; assisting disabled women with assertiveness training and self-defense classes; and pressuring domestic violence projects and battered women's shelters to reach out to disabled women.

Disabled girls and women confronting the separate, nearly always inferior, special-education and vocational rehabilitation systems must ally themselves with the disability rights movement to improve (or abolish) these bureaucracies that so profoundly affect disabled people's access to knowledge and employment. To make these systems less biased against disabled people—the very people they purport to serve—and less perpetuating of disability stigma and stereotype, disabled women must act in consort with the disability rights movement. Some sectors of that movement are male-dominated and may, without persistent pressure from women, ignore the gender and racial biases pervading these institutions. The mission of compelling regular educational, vocational training, and employment services to properly assist disabled people—thus abolishing or circumscribing the need for special services altogether—is one for the disability rights movement as a whole.

If we can generalize from our interviews, conference participation, and reading of the stories of disabled women, disability dominates gender in discussions about education and employment opportunity, notwithstanding the disparities between disabled women and men noted earlier. Although disabled women may object to being channeled into traditionally female occupations by the vocational rehabilitation system, or to being kept from sports and adventures by parents and schools, they focus on how their disability affects their access to education and jobs. Whether disabilities are apparent or invisible, they focus on fielding the humiliating and non-job-related disability questions of the employment interviewer or the medical examiner, and not on questions about marital status, dependents, or sexual harassment on the job. Perhaps this lack of concern stems from their awareness that they are not viewed as sexual beings, or perhaps from an accurate assessment that their disability obscures everything else about them to the employer or the college admissions officer. (We wonder, though, if 40-year-old disabled men are asked if they live with their parents, as 40-year-old disabled women are asked by men and women who should know better.)

While getting jobs for disabled women may be a disability problem impeded only secondarily by sexism, what happens on the job is as likely to be influenced by gender as by disability. Earnings and benefits for disabled women are far less than for disabled men, and thus disabled women must join with other women workers in struggles for comparable worth, for an end to job segregation by sex, and for an end to tying disability, pension, and Social Security benefits exclusively to earnings. Thus, for disabled women, equal access to education, to jobs, and to economic security depends on work with both disability rights and feminist groups.

The task of broadening the horizons of disabled girls and women awaits feminist commitment to showing disabled women how much they have in common with other women. Disabled women need to know that they are faring less well than disabled men in education and employment, in getting a range of jobs, in receiving the economic security and social support they need, and in their access to sexuality and intimacy. Harilyn Rousso, founder of the pioneer networking Project for Disabled Women and Girls now being replicated throughout the country, comments that many young disabled women look to the most conventional of women's jobs simply to assert their sisterhood with non-disabled women, from whom they otherwise feel separate and different (Rousso 1987). The desire to be "normal" and "like other women" may actually foster disabled women's tolerance of sexism within the specialized service systems they encounter, as well as within disability rights groups and within marriages to disabled men. Disabled women will never fight such sexism until they are enabled to discover their commonalities with non-disabled women.

Women with disabilities have not been "trapped" by many of the social expectations feminists have challenged. They have not been forced to get married or to subordinate paid work to childrearing or housekeeping. Instead, they have been warned by parents that men only "take advantage"; they have been sterilized by force or "choice," rejected by disabled and non-disabled heterosexual and lesbian partners, abandoned by spouses after onset of disability, and thwarted when they seek to mother.

NOTES

Acknowledgements: We would like to thank Richard K. Scotch and Irving Kenneth Zola for comments that have assisted us in developing this chapter, and Janet Francendese and Tina Trudel for thorough reading, suggestions, and wording that have clarified and sharpened our ideas.

1. Since 1982 and the First National Conference on Disabled Women and Girls, the authors have participated in more than twenty conferences in the Northeast and Midwest on disabled women and girls. Many have been sponsored by the Networking Project for Disabled Women and Girls or by the Women and Disability Awareness Project. Others have been held by colleges and universities, state or local offices for the handicapped, independent living centers, feminist groups, disability organizations, professional rehabilitation or service organizations, the National Women's Studies Association, and the Association for Women and Psychology. We have heard the stories of hundreds of women with a range of disabilities, including many whose disabilities occurred before adulthood and others who have discovered its meaning during adulthood. Unless otherwise cited, our examples come from conversations at these conferences, from formal interviews, or from our participation in many meetings with the Women and Disability Awareness Project.

REFERENCES

Alexander, V. 1985. Black women's health concerns. *National Campaign to Restore Abortion funding* (Fall), 8–9.

Asch, A. 1984. The experience of disability: A challenge for psychology. *American Psychologist* 39(5): 529–36.

———. 1986a. Will populism empower disabled people? In *The new populism: The politics of empowerment*, ed. H. C. Boyte and F. Riessman. Philadelphia: Temple University Press.

———. 1986b. Real moral dilemmas. *Christianity and Crisis* 46(10): 237–40.

———. 1986c. On the question of Baby Doe, *Health/PAC Bulletin* 16(6): 6–10.

Asch, A., and L. Sacks. 1983. Lives without, lives within: The autobiographies of blind women and men. *Journal of Visual Impairment and Blindness* 77(6): 242–47.

Asrael, W. 1982. An approach to motherhood for disabled women. *Rehabilitation Literature* 43(7–8): 214–18.

Becker, G. 1980. *Growing old in silence*. Berkeley, Calif.: University of California Press.

Bellone, E., and B. Waxman. 1983. *Sexual assault and women with disabilities: An overview*. Los Angeles: Planned Parenthood. (Monograph.)

Berscheid, E., and E. Walster. 1972. Beauty and the beast. *Psychology Today* (March), 42–46, 74.

Bonwich, E. 1985. Sex role attitudes and role reorganization in spinal cord injured women. In *Women and disability: The double handicap*, ed. M. J. Deegan and N. A. Brooks, New Brunswick, N. J.: Transaction.

Boston Women's Health Book Collective. 1985. *The New Our Bodies, Ourselves*. 2d ed., revised. New York: Simon and Schuster.

Bowe, F. 1980. *Rehabilitating America*. New York: Harper and Row.

———. 1981. *Comeback: Six remarkable people who triumphed over disability*. New York: Harper and Row.

———. 1984. *Disabled women in America*. Washington, D. C.: President's Committee on Employment of the Handicapped.

Braille Monitor. 1986. Legalized kidnapping: State takes child away from blind mother (August-September), 432–35.

Brightman, A. J., ed. 1984. *Ordinary moments: The disabled experience*. Baltimore, Md.: University Park Press.

Broverman, I., S. Vogel, D. Broverman, F. Clarkson, and S. Rosenkrantz. 1972. Sex-role stereotypes: A current appraisal. *Journal of Social Issues* 28: 59–78.

Browne, S., D. Connors, and N. Stern, eds. 1985. *With the power of each breath*. Pittsburgh, Pa.: Cleis Press.

Brownmiller, S. 1984. *Femininity*. New York: Simon and Schuster.

Campling, J., ed. 1981. *Images of ourselves: Disabled women talking*. Boston: Routledge and Kegan Paul.

Chodorow, N. J. 1978. *The reproduction of mothering*. Berkeley, Calif.: University of California Press.

Collins, G. 1983. The success story of a disabled mother. *New York Times*. October 12, cdd1–2.

Cox, S., ed. 1981. *Female psychology: The emerging self*. New York: St. Martin's Press.

Crewe, N., and I. K. Zola, eds. 1983. *Independent living for physically disabled people*. San Francisco: Jossey-Bass.

Darling, R. B. 1979. *Families against society: A study of reactions to children with birth defects*. Beverly Hills, Calif.: Sage.

Davis, F. 1961. Deviance disavowal: The management of strained interaction by the visibly handicapped. *Social Problems* 9: 120–32.

———. 1963. *Passage through crisis: Polio victims and their families*. Bloomington, Inc.: Bobbs-Merrill.

Deegan, M. J., and N. A. Brooks, eds. 1985. *Women and disability: The double handicap*. New Brunswick, N. J.: Transaction.

Disability Rag. 1984. Special issue. June.

———. 1986. Care that kills. 7(6): 9–10.

Duffy, Y. 1981. . . . *All things are possible*. Ann Arbor, Mich.: A. J. Garvin Associates.

Eisenstein, H. 1983. *Contemporary feminist thought*. Boston: G. K. Hall.

Eisenstein, H., and A. Jardine, eds. 1985 (1981). *The future of difference*. New Brunswick, N. J.: Rutgers University Press.

Eisenstein, Z. 1984. *Feminism and sexual equality: Crisis in liberal America*. New York: Monthly Review Press.

Fine, M., and A. Asch. 1981. Disabled women: Sexism without the pedestal. *Journal of Sociology and Social Welfare* 8(2): 233–48.

———. 1982. The question of disability: No easy answers for the women's movement. *Reproductive Rights Newsletter* 4(3): 19–20.

Finger, A. 1983. Disability and reproductive rights. *off our backs* 13(9).

———. 1984. Claiming all of our bodies: Reproductive rights and disabilities. In *Test-tube women: What future for motherhood?* ed. R. Arditti, R. Duelli-Klein, and S. Minden. Boston: Pandora.

Frank, G. 1981. *Venus on wheels: The life history of a congenital amputee*. Unpublished doctoral diss., Anthropology Department, University of California, Los Angeles.

Franklin, P. 1977. Impact of disability on the family structure. *Social Security Bulletin* 40: 3–18.

Freeman, J., ed. 1984. *Women: A feminist perspective*. Palo Alto, Calif.: Mayfield.

Friedman, G. 1980. The mother-daughter bond. *Contemporary Psychoanalysis* 16(1): 90–97.

Funk, R. 1987. Disability rights: From caste to class in the context of civil rights. In *Images of the disabled: Disabling images*, ed. A Gartner and T. Joe. New York: Praeger.

Galler, R. 1984. The myth of the perfect body. In *Pleasure and danger*, ed. C. S. Vance.

Boston: Routledge and Kegan Paul.

Gillespie, P., and A. Fink. 1974. The influence of sexism on the education of handicapped children. *Exceptional Children* 5: 155–62.

Gilligan, C. 1982. *In a different voice: Psychological theory and women's development.* Cambridge, Mass.: Harvard University Press.

Gliedman, J., and W. Roth. 1980. *The unexpected minority: Handicapped children in America.* New York: Harcourt Brace Jovanovich.

Goffman, E. 1963. *Stigma: Notes on the management of spoiled identity.* Englewood Cliffs, N.J.: Prentice-Hall.

Gold, S. 1985. A year of accomplishment: Sharon Gold reports to the blind of California. *Braille Monitor* (November), 629–40.

Haber, L., and McNeil, J. 1983. *Methodological questions in the estimation of disability prevalence.* Available from Population Division, Bureau of the Census. Washington, D. C.: Government Printing Office.

Hahn, H. 1983a. Paternalism and public policy. *Society* (March—April), 36–44.

———. 1983b. "The good parts": Interpersonal relationships in the autobiographies of physically disabled persons. *Wenner-Gren Foundation Working Papers in Anthropology* (December), 1–38.

———. 1987. Civil rights for disabled Americans: The foundations of a political agenda. In *Images of the disabled: Disabling images,* ed. A. Gartner and T. Joe. New York: Praeger.

Hanna, W. J., and B. Rogovsky. 1986. Women and disability: Stigma and "the third factor." Unpublished papers, Department of Family and Community Development, College of Human Ecology, University of Maryland, College Park.

Hannaford, S. 1985. *Living outside inside: A disabled woman's experience: Towards a social and political perspective.* Berkeley, Calif.: Canterbury Press.

Harrison, B. W. 1986. Feminist realism. *Christianity and crisis* 46(10): 233–36.

Hartmann, H. 1981. The unhappy marriage of Marxism and feminism: Towards a more progressive union. In *Women and revolution: A discussion of the unhappy marriage of Marxism and feminism,* ed. L. Sargent. Boston: South End Press.

Heinrich, E., and L. Kriegel. 1961. *Experiments in survival.* New York: Association for the Aid of Crippled Children.

Higgs, P. 1980. *Outsiders in a hearing world.* Beverly Hills, Calif.: Sage.

Hill, N., T. Mehnert, H. Taylor, M. Kagey, S. Leizhenko, et al. 1986. *The ICD survey of disabled Americans: Bringing disabled Americans into the mainstream.* Study no. 854009. New York: International Center for the Disabled.

Hill, N., T. Mehnert, H. Taylor, M. Kagey, S. Leizhenko, et al. 1987. *The ICD survey II: Employing disabled Americans.* Study no. 854009. New York: International Center for the Disabled.

Hobbs, N. 1975. *The futures of children: Categories, labels, and their consequences.* San Francisco, Calif.: Jossey-Bass.

Johnson, M. 1987. Emotion and pride. *Disability Rag* 8(1): 1, 4–6.

Joseph, G. 1981. The incompatible ménage à trois: Marxism, feminism, and racism. In *Women and revolution: A discussion of the unhappy marriage of Marxism and feminism,* ed., L. Sargent. Boston: South End Press.

Journal of Sociology and Social Welfare. 1981. *Women and disability: The double handicap.* 8(2). Entire issue.

Journal of Visual Impairment and Blindness. 1983. *Being blind, being a woman.* 77(6). Entire issue.

Kirchner, C. 1987. Assessing the effects of vocational rehabilitation on disadvantaged persons: Theoretical perspectives and issues for research. In *Proceedings of the Annual Meeting of the Society for the Study of Chronic Illness, Impairment, and Disability, 1984–1985.* Salem, Ore.: Williamette University Press. (Forthcoming.)

Kutner, N. G. 1985. Gender, social class, and social support to disabled persons. Paper delivered at the Society for the Study of Social Problems, August, American Sociological Association, Washington, D. C.

Kutner, N. G., and H. L. Gray. 1985. Women and chronic renal failure: Some neglected issues. In *Woman and disability: The double handicap,* ed. M. J. Deegan and N. A. Brooks. New Brunswick, NJ: Transaction.

Lakoff, R., and R. L. Scherr. 1984. *Face value: The politics of beauty.* Boston: Routledge and Kegan Paul.

Lorde, A. 1980. *The cancer journals.* Argyle, N. Y.: Spinsters, Ink.

Macklin, R., and W. Gaylin. 1981. *Mental retardation and sterilization: A problem of competency and paternalism.* New York: Plenum.

Matthews, G. F. 1983. *Voices from the shadows: Women with disabilities speak out.* Toronto: Women's Educational Press.

Melling, L. 1984. Wife abuse in the deaf community. *Response to Family Violence and Sexual Assault* 9(1): 1–2, 12.

Miller, A. 1970. Role of physical attractiveness in impression formation. *Psychonomic Science* 19: 241–43.

Mudrick, N. R. 1983. Disabled women. *Society* (March), 51–55.

Nagi, S. 1969. *Disability and rehabilitation.* Columbus, Ohio: Ohio University Press.

National Council on Alcoholism. 1980. *Facts on alcoholism and women.* New York: Affiliate.

New York Times. 1984. Panel details "abusive conditions" in California care facilities. January 16, B11.

New York Times. 1986. Census study reports one in five adults suffers from disability. December 23, B7.

off our backs, 1981. *Women with disabilities.* 11(5) Entire issue.

Omolade, B. 1985 (1981). Black women and feminism. In *The future of difference,* ed. H. Eisenstein and A. Jardine. New Brunswick, N. J.: Rutgers University Press.

Packer, J. 1983. Sex stereotyping in vocational counseling of blind/visually impaired persons: A national study of counselor choices. *Journal of Visual Impairment and Blindness* 77(6): 261–68.

Person, E. S. 1982. Women working: Fear of failure, deviance, and success. *Journal of the American Academy of Psychoanalysis* 10(1): 67–84.

Rapp, R. 1984. XYLO: A true story. In *Test-tube women: What future for motherhood?* ed. R. Arditti, R. Duelli-Klein, and S. Minden. Boston: Pandora Press.

———. 1987. Chromosomes and communication: The discourse of genetic counseling. *Medical Anthropology Quarterly* (forthcoming).

Rehab Group. 1979. *Digest of data on persons with disabilities.* Falls Church, Va.: May.

Rich, A. 1980. Compulsory heterosexuality and lesbian existence. *Signs* 5(4): 631–60.

Rose, P. 1984. Hers. *New York Times,* April 5, C2.

Roskies, E. 1972. *Abnormality and normality: The mothering of thalidomide children.* Ithaca, N. Y.: Cornell University Press.

Roth, W. 1981. *The handicapped speak.* Jefferson, N. C.: McFarland and Co.

———. 1983. Handicap as a social construct. *Society* (March—April), 56–61.

Rothman, B. K. 1986. On the question of Baby Doe. *Health/PAC Bulletin* 16(6): 7, 11–13.

Rousso, H. 1984. Fostering healthy self-esteem. *The Exceptional Parent* (December), 9–14.

———. 1987. Positive images for disabled women. Conference Presentation at Moving

Up and Out Together: Women and Disability, April 11, Southern Connecticut State University, New Haven, Conn.

Ruddick, S. 1980. Maternal thinking. *Feminist Studies* 6(3): 343–67.

Safilios-Rothschild, C. 1977. Discrimination against disabled women. *International Rehabilitation Review* (February), 4.

Sargent, L. 1981. *Women and revolution: A discussion of the unhappy marriage of Marxism and feminism.* Boston: South End Press.

Saxton, M. 1984. Born and unborn: The implications of reproductive technologies for people with disabilities. In *test-tube women: What future for motherhood?* ed. R. Arditti, R. Duelli-Klein, and S. Minden. Boston: Pandora.

Scotch, R. K. 1984. *From good will to civil rights: Transforming federal disability policy.* Philadelphia: Temple University Press.

Sheehy, L. 1984. *Women and disability.* Unpublished thesis for LL. M., Columbia University Law School, October 2.

Siller, J., L. Ferguson, D. H. Vann, and B. Holland. 1976. *Structure of attitudes toward the physically disabled.* New York: New York University School of Education.

Snitow, A., C. E. Stansell, and S. Thompson. 1983. *Powers of desire: The politics of sexuality.* New York: Monthly Review Press.

Stone, D. 1986. Policy case: Selecting clients for rehabilitation. Paper presented at the Hastings Center for Society, Ethics, and the Life Sciences, Hastings-On-Hudson, New York, May.

Titley, R., and W. Viney. 1969. Expression of aggression toward the physically handicapped. *Perceptual and Motor Skills* 29: 51–56.

Unger, R. 1985. Personal appearance and social control. In *Women's World: A new scholarship,* ed. M. Safire, M. Mednick, D. Izraeli, J. Bernard. New York: Praeger.

Unger, R., M. Hilderbrand, and T. Mardor. 1982. Physical attractiveness and assumptions about social deviance: Some sex-by-sex comparison. *Personality and Social Psychology Bulletin* 8: 293–301.

U. S. Census Bureau. 1983. *Labor force status and other characteristics of persons with a work disability: 1982.* Current Population Reports, Series P-23, no. 127. Washington, D. C.: GPO.

U. S. Commission on Civil Rights. 1983. *Accommodating the spectrum of individual abilities.* Washington, D. C.: GPO.

U. S. Department of Education. 1987. *Ninth annual report to Congress on the implementation of the Education of the Handicapped Act.* Washington, D. C.: U. S. Department of Health.

U. S. Department of Health, Education, and Welfare. 1975. *Report of a comprehensive service needs study.* Contract no. 100–74–03–09. Washington, D. C.: GPO.

U. S. Department of Labor, Employment Standards Administration. 1982. *A study of accommodations provided to handicapped employees by federal contractors.* Washington, D. C.: GPO.

Vash, C. 1982. Employment issues for women with disabilities. *Rehabilitation Literature* 43(7–8): 198–207.

Weinberg, N. 1976. The effect of physical disability on self-perception. *Rehabilitation Counseling Bulletin* (September), 15–20.

Women and Disability Awareness Project. 1984. *Building community: A manual exploring issues of women and disability.* New York: Educational Equity Concepts.

Wright, B. A. 1960. *Physical disability: A psychological approach.* New York: Harper and Row.

———. 1983. *Physical disability: A psycho-social approach.* New York: Harper and Row.

14

Toward a Feminist Theory of Disability

SUSAN WENDELL

We need a feminist theory of disability, both because 16 percent of women are disabled, and because the oppression of disabled people is closely linked to the cultural oppression of the body. Disability is not a biological given; like gender, it is socially constructed from biological reality. Our culture idealizes the body and demands that we control it. Thus, although most people will be disabled at some time in their lives, the disabled are made "the other," who symbolize failure of control and the threat of pain, limitation, dependency, and death. If disabled people and their knowledge were fully integrated into society, everyone's relation to her/his real body would be liberated.

In 1985, I fell ill overnight with what turned out to be a disabling chronic disease. In the long struggle to come to terms with it, I had to learn to live with a body that felt entirely different to me—weak, tired, painful, nauseated, dizzy, unpredictable. I learned at first by listening to other people with chronic illness or disabilities; suddenly able-bodied people seem to me profoundly ignorant of everything I most needed to know. Although doctors told me there was a good chance I would eventually recover completely, I realized after a year that waiting to get well, hoping to recovery my healthy body, was a dangerous strategy. I began slowly to identify with my new, disabled body and to learn to work with it. As I moved back into the world, I also began to experience the world as structure for people who have no weaknesses.[1] The process of encountering the able-bodied world led me gradually to identify myself as a disabled person, and to reflect on the nature of disability.

Some time ago, I decided to delve into what I assumed would be a substantial philosophical literature in medical ethics on the nature and experience of disability. I consulted *The Philosopher's Index*, looking under "Disability," "Handicap," "Illness," and "Disease." This was a depressing experience. At least 90 percent of philosophical articles on these topics are concerned with two questions: Under what conditions is it morally permissible/right to kill/let die a disabled person and how potentially disabled does a fetus have to be before it is permissible/right to prevent its being born? Thus, what I have to say here about disability is not a response to philosophical literature on the subject. Instead, it reflects what I have learned from the writings of other disabled people (especially disabled women), from talking with disabled people who have shared their insights and experiences with me, and from my own experience of disability. It also reflects my commitment to feminist theory, which offers perspectives and categories of analysis that help to illuminate the personal and social realities of disability, and which would, in turn, be enriched by a greater understanding of disability.

We need a theory of disability. It should be a social and political theory, because disability is largely socially constructed, but it has to be more than that; any deep understanding of disability must include thinking about the ethical, psychological and epistemic issues of living with disability. This theory should be feminist, because more than half of disabled people are women and approximately 16 percent of women are disabled (Fine and Asch 1988), and because feminist thinkers have raised the most radical issues bout cultural attitudes to the body. Some of the same attitudes about the body which contribute to women's oppression generally also contribute to the social and psychological disablement of people who have physical disabilities. In addition, feminists are grappling with issues that disabled people also face in a different context: Whether to stress sameness or difference in relation to the dominant group and in relation to each other; whether to place great value on independence from the help of other people, as the dominant culture does, or to question a value-system which distrusts and devalues dependence on other people and vulnerability in general; whether to take full integration into male dominated/able-bodied society as the goal, seeking equal power with men/able-bodied people in that society, or whether to preserve some degree of separate culture, in which the abilities, knowledge and values of women/the disabled are specifically honoured and developed.[2]

Disabled women struggle with both the oppressions of being women in male-dominated societies and the oppressions of being disabled in societies dominated by the able-bodied. They are bringing the knowledge and concerns of women with disabilities into feminism and feminist perspectives into the disability rights movement. To build a feminist theory of disability that takes adequate account of our differences, we will need to know how experiences of disability and the social oppression of the disabled interact with sexism, racism and class oppression. Michelle Fine and Adrienne Asch and the contributors to their 1988 volume, *Women and Disabilities*, have made a major contribution to our understanding of the complex interactions of gender and disability. Barbara Hillyer Davis has written in depth about the issue of dependency/independence as it relates to disability and feminism (Davis 1984). Other important contributions to theory are scattered throughout the extensive, primarily experiential, writing by disabled women;[3] this work offers vital insights into the nature of embodiment and the experience of oppression

Unfortunately, feminist perspectives on disability are not yet widely discussed in feminist theory, nor have the insights offered by women writing about disability been integrated into feminist theorizing about the body. My purpose in writing this essay is to persuade feminist theorists, especially feminist philoso-

phers, to turn more attention to constructing a theory of disability and to integrating the experiences and knowledge of disabled people into feminist theory
as a whole. Toward this end I will discuss physical disability[4] from a theoretical
perspective, including: some problems of defining it (here I will criticize the most
widely used definitions—those of the United Nations); the social construction
of disability from biological reality on analogy with the social construction of
gender; cultural attitudes toward the body which oppress disabled people while
also alienating the able-bodied from their own experiences of embodiment; the
"otherness" of disabled people; the knowledge that disabled people could contribute to culture from our diverse experiences and some of the ways this knowledge is silenced and invalidated. Along the way, I will describe briefly three issues
discussed in disability theory that have been taken up in different contexts by
feminist theory: sameness vs. difference, independence vs. dependency and
integration vs. separatism.

I do not presume to speak for disabled women. Like everyone who is disabled,
I have a particular standpoint determined in part by both my physical condition
and my social situation. My own disability may be temporary; it could get better
or worse. My disability is usually invisible (except when I use a walking stick).
I am a white university professor who has adequate medical and long-term disability insurance; that makes me very privileged among the disabled. I write what
I can see from my standpoint. Because I do not want simply to describe my own
experience but to understand it in a much larger context, I must venture beyond
what I know first-hand. I rely on others to correct my mistakes and fill in those
parts of the picture I cannot see.

WHO IS PHYSICALLY DISABLED?

The United Nations offers the following definitions of and distinctions among
impairment, disability and handicap:

> "*Impairment:* Any loss or abnormality of psychological, physiological, or anatom-
> ical structure or function. *Disability:* Any restriction or lack (resulting from an
> impairment) of ability to perform an activity in the manner or within the range
> considered normal for a human being. *Handicap:* A disadvantage for a given indi-
> vidual, resulting from an impairment or disability, that limits or prevents the ful-
> fillment of a role that is normal, depending on age, sex, social and cultural factors,
> for that individual."
>
> Handicap is therefore a function of the relationship between disabled persons
> and their environment. It occurs when they encounter cultural, physical or social
> barriers which prevent their access to the various systems of society that are avail-
> able to other citizens. Thus, handicap is the loss or limitation of opportunities to
> take part in the life of the community on an equal level with others. (U. N.
> 1983: 1.c. 6–7)

These definitions may be good enough for the political purposes of the U. N.
They have two advantages: First, they clearly include many conditions that are

not always recognized by the general public as disabling, for example, debilitating chronic illnesses that limit people's facilities but do not necessarily cause any visible disability, such as Crohn's Disease. Second, the definition of "handicap" explicitly recognizes the possibility that the primary cause of a disabled person's inability to do certain things may be social—denial of opportunities, lack of accessibility, lack of services, poverty, discrimination—which it often is.

However, by trying to define "impairment" and "disability" in physical terms and "handicap" in cultural, physical and social terms, the U.N. document appears to be making a shaky distinction between the physical and the social aspects of disability. Not only the "normal" roles for one's age, sex, society, and culture, but also "normal" structure and function, and "normal" ability to perform an activity, depend on the society in which the standards of normality are generated. Paradigms of health and ideas about appropriate kinds and levels of performance are culturally dependent. In addition, within each society there is much variation from the norm of any ability; at what point does this variation become disability? The answer depends on such factors as what activities a society values and how it distributes labour and resources. The idea that there is some universal, perhaps biologically or medically describable paradigm of human physical ability is an illusion. Therefore, I prefer to use a single term, "disability," and to emphasize that disability is socially constructed from biological reality.

Another object I have to the U.N. definitions is that they imply that women can be disabled, but not handicapped, by being unable to do things which are not considered part of the normal role for their sex. For example, if a society does not consider it essential to a woman's normal role that she be able to read, then a blind woman who is not provided with education in Braille is not handicapped, according to these definitions.

In addition, these definitions suggest that we can be disabled, but not handicapped, by the normal process of aging, since although we may lose some ability, we are not handicapped unless we cannot fulfill roles that are normal *for our age*. Yet a society which provides few resources to allow disabled people to participate in it will be likely to marginalize *all* the disabled, including the old, and to define the appropriate roles of old people as very limited, thus handicapping them. Aging is disabling. Recognizing this helps us to see that disabled people are not "other," that they are really "us." Unless we die suddenly, we are all disabled eventually. Most of us will live part of our lives with bodies that hurt, that move with difficulty or not at all, that deprive us of activities we once took for granted or that others take for granted, bodies that make daily life a physical struggle. We need an understanding of disability that does not support a paradigm of humanity as young and healthy. Encouraging everyone to acknowledge, accommodate and identify with a wide range of physical conditions is ultimately the road to self-acceptance as well as the road to liberating those who are disabled now.

Ultimately, we might eliminate the category of "the disabled" altogether, and simply talk about individuals' physical abilities in their social context. For the present, although "the disabled" is a category of "the other" to the able-bodied, and for that very reason it is also a politically useful and socially meaningful category to those who are in it. Disabled people share forms of social oppression, and the most important measures to relieve that oppression have been initiated by disabled people themselves. Social oppression may be the only thing the disabled have in common;[5] our struggles with our bodies are extremely diverse.

Finally, in thinking about disability we have to keep in mind that a society's labels do not always fit the people to whom they are applied. Thus, some people are perceived as disabled who do not experience themselves as disabled. Although they have physical conditions that disable other people, because of their opportunities and the context of their lives, they do not feel significantly limited in their activities (see Sacks 1988); these people may be surprised or resentful that they are considered disabled. On the other hand, many people whose bodies cause them great physical, psychological and economic struggles are not considered disabled because the public and/or the medical profession do not recognize their disabling conditions. These people often long to be perceived as disabled, because society stubbornly continues to expect them to perform as healthy people when they cannot and refuses to acknowledge and support their struggles.[6] Of course, no one wants the social stigma associated with disability, but social recognition of disability determines the practical help a person receives from doctors, government agencies, insurance companies, charity organizations, and often from family and friends. Thus, how a society defines disability and whom it recognizes as disabled are of enormous psychological, economic and social importance, both to people who are experiencing themselves as disabled and to those who are not but are nevertheless given the label.

There is no definitive answer to the question: Who is physically disabled? Disability has social, experiential and biological components, present and recognized in different measures for different people. Whether a particular physical condition is disabling changes with time and place, depending on such factors as social expectations, the state of technology and its availability to people in that condition, the educational system, architecture, attitudes towards physical appearance, and the pace of life. (If, for example, the pace of life increases without changes in other factors, more people become disabled simply because fewer people can keep up the "normal" pace.)

THE SOCIAL CONSTRUCTION OF DISABILITY

If we ask the questions: Why are so many disabled people unemployed or underemployed, impoverished, lonely, isolated; why do so many find it difficult or impossible to get an education (Davis and Marshall 1987; Fine and Asch 1988, 10–11); why are they victims of violence and coercion; why do able-bodied people ridicule, avoid, pity, stereotype and patronize them?, we may be tempted to see the disabled as victims of nature or accident. Feminists should be, and many are, profoundly suspicious of this answer. We are used to countering claims that insofar as women are oppressed they are oppressed by nature, which puts them at a disadvantage in the competition for power and resources. We know that if being biologically female is a disadvantage, it is because a social context makes it a disadvantage. From the standpoint of a disabled person, one can see how society could minimize the disadvantages of most disabilities, and, in some instances, turn them into advantages.

Consider an extreme case: the situation of physicist Stephen Hawking, who has had Amyotrophic Lateral Sclerosis (Lou Gehrig's Disease) for more than 26 years. Professor Hawking can no longer speak and is capable of only the smallest muscle movements. Yet, in his context of social and technological support, he is able to function as a professor of physics at Cambridge University; indeed he says his disability has given him the *advantage* of having more time to think, and he is one of the foremost theoretical physicists of our time. He is a courageous and talented man, but he is able to live the creative life he has only because of the help of his family, three nurses, a graduate student who travels with him to maintain his computer-communications systems, and the fact that his talent had been developed and recognized before he fell seriously ill (*Newsweek* 1988).

Many people consider providing resources for disabled people a form of charity, superogatory in part because the disabled are perceived as unproductive members of society. Yet most disabled people are placed in a double-bind: they have access to inadequate resources because they are unemployed or underemployed, and they are unemployed or underemployed because they lack the resources that would enable them to make their full contribution to society (Matthews 1983; Hannaford 1985). Often governments and charity organizations will spend far more money to keep disabled people in institutions where they have no chance to be productive than they will spend to enable the same people to live independently and productively. In addition, many of the "special" resources the disabled need merely compensate for bad social planning that is based on the illusion that everyone is young, strong, healthy (and, often, male).

Disability is also frequently regarded as a personal or family problem rather than a matter for social responsibility. Disabled people are often expected to overcome obstacles to participation by their own extraordinary efforts, or their families are expected to provide what they need (sometimes at great personal sacrifice). Helping in personal or family matters is seen as superogatory for people who are not members of the family.

Many factors contribute to determining whether providing a particular resource is regarded as a social or a personal (or family) responsibility.[7] One such factor is whether the majority can identify with people who need the resource. Most North Americans feel that society should be organized to provide short-term medical care made necessary by illness or accident, I think because they can imagine themselves needing it. Relatively few people can identify with those who cannot be "repaired" by medical intervention. Sue Halpern makes the following observation:

> Physical health is contingent and often short-lived. But this truth eludes us as long as we are able to walk by simply putting one foot in front of the other. As a consequence, empathy for the disabled is unavailable to most able-bodied persons. Sympathy, yes, empathy, no, for every attempt to project oneself into that condi-

tion, to feel what it is like not to be ambulatory, for instance, is mediated by an ability to walk (Halpern 1988, 3).

If the able-bodied saw the disabled as potentially themselves or as their future selves, they would be more inclined to feel that society should be organized to provide the resources that would make disabled people fully integrated and contributing members. They would feel that "charity" is as inappropriate a way of thinking about resources for disabled people as it is about emergency medical care or education.

Careful study of the lives of disabled people will reveal how artificial the line is that we draw between the biological and the social. Feminists have already challenged this line in part by showing how processes such as childbirth, menstruation and menopause, which may be presented, treated, and therefore experienced as illnesses or disabilities, are socially constructed from biological reality (Rich 1976; Ehrenreich and English 1979). Disabled people's relations to our bodies involve elements of struggle which perhaps cannot be eliminated, perhaps not even mitigated, by social arrangements. *But* much of what is *disabling* about our physical conditions is also a consequence of social arrangements (Finger 1983; Fine and Asch 1988) which could, but do not, either compensate for our physical conditions, or accommodate them so that we can participate fully, or support our struggles and integrate us into the community *and our struggles into the cultural concept of life as it is ordinarily lived.*

Feminists have shown that the world has been designed for men. In North America at least, life and work have been structured as though no one of any importance in the public world, and certainly no one who works outside the home for wages, has to breast-feed a baby or look after a sick child. Common colds can be acknowledged publicly, and allowances made for them, but menstruation cannot. Much of the world is also structured as though everyone is physically strong, as though all bodies are "ideally shaped," as though everyone can walk, hear and see well, as though everyone can work and play at a pace that is not compatible with any kind of illness or pain, as though no one is ever dizzy or incontinent or simply needs to sit or lie down. (For instance, where could you sit down in a supermarket if you needed to?) Not only the architecture, but the entire physical and social organization of life, assumes that we are either strong and healthy and able to do what the average able-bodied person can do, or that we are completely disabled, unable to participate in life.

In the split between the public and the private worlds, women (and children) have been relegated to the private, and so have the disabled, the sick and the old (and mostly women take care of them). The public world is the world of strength, the positive (valued) body, performance and production, the able-bodied and youth. Weakness, illness, rest and recovery, pain, death and the negative (de-valued) body are private, generally hidden, and often neglected. Coming into the public world with illness, pain or a de-valued body, we encounter resistance to mixing the two worlds; the split is vividly revealed. Much of our experience goes underground, because there is no socially acceptable way of expressing it and having our physical and psychological experience acknowledged and shared. A few close friends may share it, but there is a strong impulse to protect them from it too, because it seems so private, so unacceptable. I found that, after a couple of years of illness, even answering the question, "How are you?" became a difficult, conflict-ridden business. I don't want to alienate my friends from my experience, but I don't want to risk their discomfort and rejection by telling them what they don't want to know.[8]

Disabled people learn that many, perhaps most, able-bodied people do not want to know about suffering caused by the body. Visibly disabled women report that curiosity about medical diagnoses, physical appearance and the sexual and other intimate aspects of disability is more common than willingness to listen and try to understand the experience of disability (Matthews 1983). It is not unusual for people with invisible disabilities to keep them entirely secret from everyone but their closest friends.

Contrary to what Sue Halpern says, it is not simply because they are in able bodies that the able-bodied fail to identify with the disabled. Able-bodied people can often make the imaginative leap into the skins of people physically unlike themselves; women can identify with a male protagonist in a story, for example, and adults can identify with children or with people much older than themselves. Something more powerful than being in a different body is at work. Suffering caused by the body, and the inability to control the body, are despised, pitied, and above all, feared. This fear, experienced individually, is also deeply embedded in our culture.

THE OPPRESSION OF DISABLED PEOPLE
IS THE OPPRESSION OF EVERYONE'S REAL BODY

Our real human bodies are exceedingly diverse—in size, shape, colour, texture, structure, function, range and habits of movements, and development—and they are constantly changing. Yet we do not absorb or reflect this simple fact in our culture. Instead, we idealize the human body. Our physical ideals change from time to time, but we always have ideals. These ideals are not just about appearance; they are also ideals of strength and energy and proper control of the body. We are perpetually bombarded with images of these ideals, demands for them, and offers of consumer products and services to help us achieve them.[9] Idealizing the body prevents everyone, able-bodied and disabled, from identifying with and loving her/his real body. Some people can have the illusion of acceptance that comes from believing that their bodies are "close enough" to the ideal, but this illusion only draws them deeper into identifying with the ideal and into the endless task of reconciling the reality with it. Sooner or later they must fail.

Before I became disabled, I was one of those people who felt "close enough" to cultural ideals to be reasonably accepting of my body. Like most feminists I know, I was aware of some alienation from it, and I worked at liking my body better. Nevertheless, I knew in my heart that too much of my liking still depended on being "close enough." When I was disabled by illness, I experienced a much more profound alienation from my body. After a year spent mostly in bed,

I could barely identify my body as my own. I felt that "it" was torturing "me," trapping me in exhaustion, pain and inability to do many of the simplest things I did when I was healthy. The shock of this experience and the effort to identify with a new, disabled body, made me realize I had been living a luxury of the able-bodied. The able-bodied can postpone the luxury of identifying with their *real* bodies. The disabled don't have the luxury of demanding that their bodies fit the physical ideals of their culture. As Barbara Hillyer Davis says: "For all of us the difficult work of finding (one's) self includes the body, but people who live with disability in a society that glorifies fitness and physical conformity are forced to understand more fully what bodily integrity means" (Davis 1984, 3).

In a society which idealizes the body, the physically disabled are marginalized. People learn to identify with their own strengths (by cultural standards) and to hate, fear and neglect their own weaknesses. The disabled are not only de-valued for their de-valued bodies (Hannaford 1985), they are constant reminders to the able-bodied of the negative body—of what the able-bodied are trying to avoid, forget and ignore (Lessing 1981). For example, if someone tells me she is in pain, she reminds me of the existence of pain, the imperfection and fragility of the body, the possibility of my own pain, the *inevitability* of it. The less willing I am to accept all these, the less I want to know about her pain; if I cannot avoid it in her presence, I will avoid her. I may even blame her for it. I may tell myself that she *could have* avoided it, in order to go on believing that I *can* avoid it. I want to believe I am not like her; I cling to the differences. Gradually, I make her "other" because I don't want to confront my real body, which I fear and cannot accept.[10]

Disabled people can participate in marginalizing ourselves. We can wish for bodies we do not have, with frustration, shame, self-hatred. We can feel trapped in the negative body; it is our internalized oppression to feel this. Every (visibly or invisibly) disabled person I have talked to or read has felt this; some never stop feeling it. In addition, disabled women suffer more than disabled men from the demand that people have "ideal" bodies, because in patriarchal culture people judge women more by their bodies than they do men. Disabled women often do not feel seen (because they are often not seen) by others as whole people, especially not as sexual people (Campling 1981; Matthews 1983; Hannaford 1985; Fine and Asch 1988). Thus, part of their struggle against oppression is a much harder version of the struggle able-bodied women have for a realistic *and positive* self-image (Bogle and Shaul 1981). On the other hand, disabled people who cannot hope to meet the physical ideals of a culture can help reveal that those ideals are not "natural" or "normal" but artificial social creations that oppress everyone.

Feminist theorists have probed the causes of our patriarchal culture's desire for control of the body—fear of death, fear of the strong impulses and feelings the body give us, fear of nature, fear and resentment of the mother's power over the infant (de Beauvoir 1949; Dinnerstein 1976; Griffin 1981). Idealizing the body and wanting to control it go hand-in-hand; it is impossible to say whether one causes the other. A physical ideal gives us the goal of our efforts to control the body, and the myth that total control is possible deceives us into striving for the ideal. The consequences for women have been widely discussed in the literature of feminism. The consequences for disabled people are less often recognized. In a culture which loves the idea that the body can be controlled, those who cannot control their bodies are seen (and may see themselves) as failures.

When you listen to this culture in a disabled body, you hear how often health and physical vigour are talked about as if they were moral virtues. People constantly praise others for their "energy," their stamina, their ability to work long hours. Of course, acting on behalf of one's health can be a virtue, and undermining one's health can be a vice, but "success" at being healthy, like beauty, is always partly a matter of luck and therefore beyond our control. When health is spoken of as a virtue, people who lack it are made to feel inadequate. I am not suggesting that it is always wrong to praise people's physical strength or accomplishments, any more than it is always wrong to praise their physical beauty. But just as treating cultural standards of beauty as essential virtues for women harms most women, treating health and vigour as moral virtues for everyone harms people with disabilities and illnesses.

The myth that the body can be controlled is not easily dispelled, because it is not very vulnerable to evidence against it. When I became ill, several people wanted to discuss with me what I thought I had done to "make myself" ill or "allow myself" to become sick. At first I fell in with this, generating theories about what I had done wrong; even though I had always taken good care of my health, I was able to find some (rather far-fetched) accounts of my responsibility for my illness. When a few close friends offered hypotheses as to how *they* might be responsible for my being ill, I began to suspect that something was wrong. Gradually, I realized that we were all trying to believe that nothing this important is beyond our control.

Of course, there are sometimes controllable social and psychological forces at work in creating ill health and disability (Kleinman 1988). Nevertheless our cultural insistence on controlling the body blames the victims of disability for failing and burdens them with self-doubt and self-blame. The search for psychological, moral and spiritual causes of illness, accident and disability is often a harmful expression of this insistence on control (see Sontag 1977).

Modern Western medicine plays into and conforms to our cultural myth that the body can be controlled. Collectively, doctors and medical researchers exhibit very little modesty about their knowledge. They focus their (and our) attention on cures and imminent cures, on successful medical interventions. Research, funding and medical care are more directed toward life-threatening conditions than toward chronic illnesses and disabilities. Even pain was relatively neglected as a medical problem until the second half of this century. Surgery and saving lives bolster the illusion of control much better than does the long, patient process of rehabilitation or the management of long-term illness. These latter, less visible functions of medicine tend to be performed by nurses, physiotherapists and other low-prestige members of the profession. Doctors are trained to do something to control the body, to "make it better" (Kleinman 1988); they are the heroes of medicine. They may like being in the role of hero, but we also like them in that role and try to keep them there, because *we* want to believe that someone can always "make it better."[11] As long as we cling to this belief, the patients who cannot be "repaired"—the chronically ill, the disabled and the dying—will symbolize the failure of medicine and more, the failure of the Western scientific project to control nature. They will carry this stigma in medicine and in the culture as a whole.

When philosophers of medical ethics confine themselves to discussing life-and-death issues of medicine, they help perpetuate the idea that the main purpose of medicine is to control the body. Life-and-death interventions are the ultimate exercise of control. If medical ethicists looked more closely at who needs and who receives medical help, they would discover a host of issues concerning how medicine and society understand, mediate, assist with and integrate experiences of illness, injury and disability.

Because of the heroic approach to medicine, and because disabled people's experience is not integrated into the culture, most people know little or nothing about how to live with long-term or life-threatening illness, how to communicate with doctors and nurses and medical bureaucrats about these matters, how to live with limitation, uncertainty, pain, nausea, and other symptoms when doctors cannot make them go away. Recently, patients' support groups have arisen to fill this gap for people with nearly every type of illness and disability. They are vitally important sources of knowledge and encouragement for many of us, but they do not fill the cultural gulf between the able-bodied and the disabled. The problems of living with a disability are not private problems, separable from the rest of life and the rest of society. They are problems which can and should be shared throughout the culture as much as we share the problems of love, work and family life.

Consider the example of pain. It is difficult for most people who have not lived with prolonged or recurring pain to understand the benefits of accepting it. Yet some people who live with chronic pain speak of "making friends" with it as the road to feeling better and enjoying life. How do they picture their pain and think about it; what kind of attention do they give it and when; how do they live around and through it, and what do they learn from it? We all need to know this as part of our education. Some of the fear of experiencing pain is a consequence of ignorance and lack of guidance. The effort to avoid pain contributes to such widespread problems as drug and alcohol addiction, eating disorders, and sedentary lives. People with painful disabilities can teach us about pain, because they *can't* avoid it and have had to learn how to face it and live with it. The pernicious myth that it is possible to avoid almost all pain by controlling the body gives the fear of pain greater power than it should have and blames the victims of unavoidable pain. The fear of pain is also expressed or displaced as a fear of people in pain, which often isolates those with painful disabilities. All this is unnecessary. People *in* pain and knowledge *of* pain could be fully integrated into our culture, to everyone's benefit.

If we knew more about pain, about physical limitation, about loss of abilities, about what it is like to be "too far" from the cultural ideal of the body, perhaps we would have less fear of the negative body, less fear of our own weaknesses and "imperfections," of our inevitable deterioration and death. Perhaps we could give up our idealizations and relax our desire for control of the body; until we do, we maintain them at the expense of disabled people and at the expense of our ability to accept and love our own real bodies.

DISABLED PEOPLE AS "OTHER"

When we make people "other," we group them together as the objects of *our* experience instead of regarding them as fellow *subjects* of experience with whom we might identify. If you are "other" to me, I see you primarily as symbolic of something else—usually, but not always, something I reject and fear and that I project onto you. We can all do this to each other, but very often the process is not symmetrical, because one group of people may have more power to call itself the paradigm of humanity and to make the world suit its own needs and validate its own experiences.[12] Disabled people are "other" to able-bodied people, and (as I have tried to show) the consequences are socially, economically and psychologically oppressive to the disabled and psychologically oppressive to the able-bodied. Able-bodied people may be "other" to disabled people, but the consequences of this for the able-bodied are minor (most able-bodied people can afford not to notice it). There are, however, several political and philosophical issues that being "other" to a more powerful group raises for disabled people.

I have said that for the able-bodied, the disabled often symbolize failure to control the body and the failure of science and medicine to protect us all. However, some disabled people also become symbols of heroic control against all odds; these are the "disabled heroes," who are comforting to the able-bodied because they reaffirm the possibility of overcoming the body. Disabled heroes are people with visible disabilities who receive public attention because they accomplish things that are unusual even for the able-bodied. It is revealing that, with few exceptions (Helen Keller and, very recently, Stephen Hawking are among them), disabled heroes are recognized for performing feats of physical strength and endurance. While disabled heroes can be inspiring and heartening to the disabled, they may give the able-bodied the false impression that anyone can "overcome" a disability. Disabled heroes usually have extraordinary social, economic and physical resources that are not available to most people with those disabilities. In addition, many disabled people are not capable of performing physical heroics, because many (perhaps most) disabilities reduce or consume the energy and stamina of people who have them and do not just limit them in some particular kind of physical activity. Amputee and wheelchair athletes are exceptional, not because of their ambition, discipline and hard work, but because they are in better health than most disabled people can be. Arthritis, Parkinsonism and stroke cause severe disability in far more people than do spinal cord injuries and amputations (Bury 1979). The image of the disabled hero may reduce the "otherness" of a few disabled people, but because it creates an ideal which most disabled people cannot meet, it *increases* the "otherness" of the majority of disabled people.

One recent attempt to reduce the "otherness" of disabled people is the introduction of the term, "differently-abled." I assume the point of using this term is to suggest that there is nothing *wrong* with being the way we are, just different. Yet to call someone "differently-abled" is much like calling her "differently-coloured" or "differently-gendered." It says: "This person is not the norm or paradigm of humanity." If anything, it increases the "otherness" of disabled people, because it reinforces the paradigm of humanity as young, strong and healthy, with all body parts working "perfectly," from which this person is "different." Using the term "differently-abled" also suggests a (polite? patronizing? protective? self-protective?) disregard of the special difficulties, struggles and suffering disabled people face. We are *dis-abled*. We live with particular social and physical struggles that are partly consequences of the conditions of our bodies and partly consequences of the structures and expectations of our societies, but they are struggles which only people with bodies like ours experience.

The positive side of the term "differently-abled" is that it might remind the able bodied that to be disabled in some respects is not to be disabled in all respects. It also suggests that a disabled person may have abilities that the able-bodied lack in virtue of being able-bodied. Nevertheless, on the whole, the term "differently-abled" should be abandoned, because it reinforces the able-bodied paradigm of humanity and fails to acknowledge the struggles disabled people face.

The problems of being "the other" to a dominant group are always politically complex. Our solution is to emphasize similarities to the dominant group in the hope that they will identify with the oppressed, recognize their rights, gradually give them equal opportunities, and eventually assimilate them. Many disabled people are tired of being symbols to the able-bodied, visible only or primarily for their disabilities, and they want nothing more than to be seen as individuals rather than as members of the group, "the disabled." Emphasizing similarities to the able-bodied, making their disabilities unnoticeable in comparison to their other human qualities may bring about assimilation one-by-one. It does not directly challenge the able-bodied paradigm of humanity, just as women moving into traditionally male arenas of both may produce a gradual change in the paradigms. In addition, assimilation may be very difficult for the disabled to achieve. Although the able-bodied like disabled tokens who do not seem very different from themselves, they may *need* someone to carry the burden of the negative body as long as they continue to idealize and try to control the body. They may therefore resist the assimilation of most disabled people.

The reasons in favour of the alternative solution to "otherness"—*emphasizing differences* from the able-bodied—are also reasons for emphasizing similarities among the disabled, especially social and political similarities. Disabled people share positions of social oppression that separate us from the able-bodied, and we share physical, psychological and social experiences of disability. Emphasizing differences from the able-bodied demands that those differences be acknowledged and respected and fosters solidarity among the disabled. It challenges the able-bodied paradigm of humanity and creates the possibility of a deeper challenge to the idealization of the body and the demand for its control. Invisibly disabled people tend to be drawn to solutions that emphasize difference, because our need to have our struggles acknowledged is great, and we have far less experience than those who are visibly disabled of being symbolic to the able-bodied.

Whether one wants to emphasize sameness or difference in dealing with the problem of being "the other" depends in part on how radically one wants to challenge the value-structure of the dominant group. A very important issue in this category for both women and disabled people is the value of independence from the help of others, so highly esteemed in our patriarchal culture and now being questioned in feminist ethics (see, for example, Sherwin 1984, 1987; Kittay and Meyers 1987) and discussed in the writings of disabled women (see, for example, Fisher and Galler 1981; Davis 1984; Frank 1988). Many disabled people who can see the possibility of living as independently as any able-bodied person, or who have achieved this goal after long struggle, value their independence above everything. Dependence on the help of others is humiliating in a society which prizes independence. In addition, this issue holds special complications for disabled women; reading the stories of women who became disabled as adults, I was struck by their struggle with shame and loss of self-esteem at being transformed from people who took physical care of others (husbands and children) to people who were physically dependent. All this suggests that disabled people need every bit of independence we can get. Yet there are disabled people who will always need a lot of help from other individuals just to survive (those who have very little control of movement, for example), and to the extent that everyone considers independence necessary to respect and self-esteem, those people will be condemned to be de-valued. In addition, some disabled people spend tremendous energy being independent in ways that might be considered trivial in a culture less insistent on self-reliance; if our culture valued *interdependence* more highly, they could use that energy for more satisfying activities.

In her excellent discussion of the issue of dependency and independence, Barbara Hillyer Davis argues that women with disabilities and those who care for them can work out a model of *reciprocity* for all of us, if we are willing to learn from them. "Reciprocity involves the difficulty of recognizing each other's needs, relying on the other, asking and receiving help, delegating responsibility, giving and receiving empathy, respecting boundaries" (Davis 1984, 4). I hope that disabled and able-bodied feminists will join in questioning our cultural obsession with independence and ultimately replacing it with such a model of reciprocity. If *all* the disabled are to be fully integrated into society without symbolizing failure, then we have to change social values to recognize the value of depending on other and being depended upon. This would also reduce the fear and shame associated with dependency in old age—a condition most of us will reach.

Whether one wants to emphasize sameness or difference in dealing with the problems of being "other" is also related to whether one sees anything valuable to be preserved by maintaining, either temporarily or in the long-run, some separateness of the oppressed group. Is there a special culture of the oppressed group or the seeds of a special culture which could be developed in a supportive context of solidarity? Do members of the oppressed group have accumulated knowledge or ways of knowing which might be lost if assimilation takes place without the dominant culture being transformed?

It would be hard to claim that disabled people as a whole have an alternative culture or even the seeds of one. One sub-group, the deaf, has a separate culture from the hearing, and they are fighting for its recognition and preservation, as well as for their right to continue making their own culture (Sacks 1988). Disabled people do have both knowledge and ways of knowing that are not available to the able-bodied. Although ultimately I hope that disabled people's knowledge will be integrated into the culture as a whole, I suspect that a culture which fears and denigrates the real body would rather silence this knowledge than make the changes necessary to absorb it. It may have to be nurtured and cultivated separately while the able-bodied culture is transformed enough to receive and integrate it.

THE KNOWLEDGE OF DISABLED PEOPLE AND HOW IT IS SILENCED

In my second year of illness, I was reading an article about the psychological and philosophical relationship of mind to body. When the author painted a rosy picture of the experience of being embodied, I was outraged at the presumption of the writer to speak for everyone from a healthy body. I decided I didn't want to hear *anything* about the body from anyone who was not physically disabled. Before that moment, it had not occurred to me that there was a world of experience from which I was shut out while I was able-bodied.

Not only do physically disabled people have experiences which are not available to the able-bodied, they are in a better position to transcend cultural mythologies about the body, because they *cannot* do things that the able-bodied fell they *must* do in order to be happy, "normal" and sane. For example, paraplegics and quadriplegics have revolutionary things to teach about the possibilities of sexuality which contradict patriarchal culture's obsession with the genitals (Bullard and Knight 1981). Some people can have orgasms in any part of their bodies where they feel touch. One man said he never knew how good sex could be until he lost the feeling in his genitals. Few able-bodied people know these things, and, to my knowledge, no one has explored their implications for the able-bodied.

If disabled people were truly heard, an explosion of knowledge of the human body and psyche would take place. We have access to realms of experience that our culture has not tapped (even for medical science, which takes relatively little interest in people's *experience* of their bodies). Like women's particular knowledge, which comes from access to experiences most men do not have, disabled people's knowledge is dismissed as trivial, complaining, mundane (or bizarre), *less than* that of the dominant group.

The cognitive authority (Addelson 1983) of medicine plays an important role in distorting and silencing the knowledge of the disabled. Medical professionals have been given the power to describe and validate everyone's experience of the body. If you go to doctors with symptoms they cannot observe directly or verify independently of what you tell them, such as pain or weakness or numbness or dizziness or difficulty concentrating, and if they cannot find an objectively observable cause of those symptoms, you are likely to be told that there is "nothing wrong with you," no matter how you feel. Unless you are very lucky in your doctors, no matter how trustworthy and responsible you were considered to be *before* you started saying you were ill, your experience will be invalidated.[13] *Other* people are the authorities on the reality of the experiences of your body.

When you are very ill, you desperately need medical validation of your experience, not only for economic reasons (insurance claims, pensions, welfare and disability benefits all depend upon official diagnosis), but also for social and psychological reasons. People with unrecognized illnesses are often abandoned by their friends and families.[14] Because almost everyone accepts the cognitive authority of medicine, the person whose bodily experience is radically different from medical descriptions of her/his condition is invalidated as a knower. Either you decide to hide your experience, or you are socially isolated with it by being labelled mentally ill[15] or dishonest. In both cases you are silenced.

Even when your experience is recognized by medicine, it is often re-described in ways that are inaccurate from your standpoint. The objectively observable condition of your body may be used to determine the severity of your pain, for instance, regardless of your own reports of it. For example, until recently, relatively few doctors were willing to acknowledge that severe phantom limb pain can persist for months or even years after an amputation. The accumulated experience of doctors who were themselves amputees has begun to legitimize the other patients' reports (Madruga 1979).

When you are forced to realize that other people have more social authority than you do to describe your experience of your own body, your confidence in yourself and your relationship to reality is radically undermined. What can you know if you cannot know that you are experiencing suffering or joy; what can you communicate to people who don't believe you know even this?[16] Most people will censor what they tell or say nothing rather than expose themselves repeatedly to such deeply felt invalidation. They are silenced by fear and confusion. The process is familiar from our understanding of how women are silenced in and by patriarchal culture.

One final caution: As with women's "special knowledge," there is a danger of sentimentalizing disabled people's knowledge and abilities and keeping us "other" by doing so. We need to bring this knowledge into the culture and to transform the culture and society so that everyone can receive and make use of it, so that it can be fully integrated, along with disabled people, into a shared social life.

CONCLUSION

I have tried to introduce the reader to the rich variety of intellectual and political issues that are raised by experiences of physical disability. Confronting these issues has increased my appreciation of the insights that feminist theory already offers into cultural attitudes about the body and the many form of social oppression. Feminists have been challenging medicine's authority for many years now, but not, I think, as radically as we would if we knew what disabled people have to tell. I look forward to the development of a full feminist theory of disability.[17] We need a theory of disability for the liberation of both disabled and able-bodied people, since the theory of disability is also the theory of the oppression of the body by a society and its culture.

NOTES

Many thanks to Kathy Gose, Joyce Frazee, Mary Barnes, Barbara Beach, Elliot Gose and Gordon Renwick for helping me to think about these questions, and to Maureen Ashfield for helping me to research them. Thanks also to the editors of the issue of *Hypatia* in which this article was originally published, Virginia Warren, and two anonymous reviewers for their work on editing an earlier version of the paper.

1. Itzhak Perlman, when asked in a recent CBC interview about the problems of the disabled, said disabled people have two problems: the fact that the world is not made for people with any weaknesses but for supermen and the attitudes of able-bodied people.

2. An excellent description of this last issue as it confronts the deaf is found in Sacks 1988.

3. See Matthews 1983; Hannaford 1985; Rooney and Israel (eds.) 1985, esp. the articles by Jill Weiss, Charlynn Toews, Myra Rosenfield, and Susan Russell; and, for a doctor's theories, Kleinman 1988.

4. We also need a feminist theory of mental disability, but I will not be discussing mental disability in this essay.

5. In a recent article in *Signs*, Linda Alcoff argues that we should define "woman" thus: "woman is a position from which a feminist politics can emerge rather than a set of attributes that are 'objectively identifiable.'" (Alcoff 1988, 435). I think a similar approach may be the best one for defining "disability."

6. For example, Pelvic Inflammatory Disease causes severe prolonged disability in some women. These women often have to endure medical diagnoses of psychological illness and the skepticism of family and friends, in addition to having to live with chronic severe pain. See Moore 1985.

7. Feminism has challenged the distribution of responsibility for providing such resources as childcare and protection from family violence. Increasingly many people who once thought of these as family or personal concerns now think of them as social responsibilities.

8. Some people save me that trouble by *telling me* I am fine and walking away. Of course, people also encounter difficulties with answering "How are you?" during and after crises, such as separation from a partner, death of a loved one, or a nervous breakdown. There is a temporary alienation from what is considered ordinary shared experience. In disability, the alienation lasts longer, often for a lifetime, and, in my experience, is more profound.

9. The idealization of the body is clearly related in complex ways to the economic processes of a consumer society. Since it pre-dated capitalism, we know that capitalism did not cause it, but it is undeniable that idealization now generates tremendous profits and that the quest for profit demands the reinforcement of idealization and the constant development of new ideals.

10. Susan Griffin, in a characteristically honest and insightful passage, describes an encounter with the fear that makes it hard to identify with disabled people. See Griffin 1982, 648–649.

11. Thanks to Joyce Frazee for pointing this out to me.

12. When Simone de Beauvoir uses this term to elucidate men's view of women (and women's view of ourselves), she emphasizes that Man is considered essential, Woman inessential; Man is the Subject, Woman the Other (de Beauvoir 1952, xvi). Susan Griffin expands upon this idea by showing how we project rejected aspects of ourselves onto groups of people who are designated the Other (Griffin 1981).

13. Many women with M. S. have lived through this nightmare in the early stages of their illness. Although this happens to men too, women's experience of the body, like women's experience generally, is more likely to be invalidated (Hannaford 1985).

14. Accounts of the experience of relatively unknown, newly discovered, or hard-to-

diagnose diseases and conditions confirm this. See, for example, Jeffreys 1982, for the story of an experience of Chronic Fatigue Syndrome, which is more common in women than in men.

15. Frequently people with undiagnosed illnesses are sent by their doctors to psychiatrists, who cannot help and may send them back to their doctors saying they must be physically ill. This can leave patients in a dangerous medical and social limbo. Sometimes they commit suicide because of it (Ramsay 1986). Psychiatrists who know enough about living with physical illness or disability to help someone cope with it are rare.

16. For more discussion of his subject, see Zaner 1983 and Rawlinson 1983.

17. At this stage of the disability rights movement, it is impossible to anticipate everything that a full feminist theory will include, just as it would have been impossible to predict in 1970 the present state of feminist theory of mothering. Nevertheless, we can see that besides dealing more fully with the issues I have raised here, an adequate feminist theory of disability will examine all the ways in which disability is socially constructed; it will explain the interaction of disability with gender, race and class position; it will examine every aspect of the cognitive authority of medicine and science over our experiences of our bodies; it will discuss the relationship of technology to disability; it will question the belief that disabled lives are not worth living or preserving when it is implied in our theorizing about abortion and euthanasia; it will give us a detailed vision of the full integration of disabled people in society, and it will propose practical political strategies for the liberation of disabled people and the liberation of the able-bodied from the social oppression of their bodies.

REFERENCES

Addelson, Kathryn P. 1983. The man of professional wisdom. In *Discovering reality*. Sandra Harding and Merrill B. Hintikka, eds. Boston: D. Reidel.

Alcoff, Linda. 1988. Cultural feminism versus poststructuralism: The identity crisis in feminist theory. *Signs: Journal of Women in Culture and Society* 13(3): 405–436.

Bullard, David G. and Susan E. Knight, eds. 1981. *Sexuality and physical disability*. St. Louis: C. V. Mosby.

Bury, M. R. 1979. Disablement in society: Towards an integrated perspective. *International Journal of Rehabilitation Research* 2(1): 33–40.

Beauvoir, Simone de. 1952. *The second sex*. New York: Alfred A. Knopf.

Campling, Jo, ed. 1981. *Images of ourselves—women with disabilities talking*. London: Routledge and Kegan Paul.

Davis, Barbara Hillyer. 1984. Women, disability and feminism: Notes toward a new theory. *Frontiers: A Journal of Women Studies* VIII(1): 1–5.

Davis, Melanie and Catherine Marshall. 1987. Female and disabled: Challenged women in education. *National Women's Studies Association Perspectives* 5: 39–41.

Dinnerstein, Dorothy. 1976. *The mermaid and the minotaur: Sexual arrangements and human malaise*. New York: Harper and Row.

Ehrenreich, Barbara and Dierdre English. 1979. *For her own good: 150 years of the experts' advice to women*. New York: Anchor.

Fine, Michelle and Adrienne Asch, eds. 1988. *Women with disabilities: Essays in psychology, culture and politics*. Philadelphia: Temple University Press.

Finger, Anne. 1983. Disability and reproductive rights. *off our backs* 13(9): 18–19.

Fisher, Bernice and Robert Galler. 1981. Conversation between two friends about feminism and disability. *off our backs* 11(5): 14–15.

Frank, Gelya. 1988. On embodiment: A case study of congenital limb deficiency in American culture. In *Women with disabilities*. Michelle Fine and Adrienne Asch, eds. Philadelphia: Temple University Press.

Griffin, Susan. 1981. *Pornography and silence: Culture's revenge against nature*. New York: Harper and Row.

Halpern, Sue M. 1988. Portrait of the artist. Review of *Under the eye of the clock* by Christopher Nolan. *The New York Times Review of Books*, June 30: 3–4.

Hannaford, Susan. 1985. *Living outside inside. A disabled woman's experience. Towards a social and political perspective*. Berkeley: Canterbury Press.

Jeffreys, Toni. 1982. *The mile-high staircase*. Sydney: Hodder and Stoughton Ltd.

Kittay, Eva Feder and Diana T. Meyers, eds. 1987. *Women and moral theory*. Totowa, NJ: Rowman and Littlefield.

Kleinman, Arthur. 1988. *The illness narratives: Suffering, healing, and the human condition*. New York: Basic Books.

Lessing, Jill. 1981. Denial and disability. *off our backs* 11(5): 21.

Madruga, Lenor. 1979. One *step at a time*. Toronto: McGraw-Hill.

Matthews, Gwyneth Ferguson. 1983. *Voices from the shadows: Women with disabilities speak out*. Toronto: Women's Educational Press.

Moore, Maureen. 1985. Coping with pelvic inflammatory disease. In *Women and Disability*. Frances Rooney and Pat Israel, eds. *Resources for Feminist Research* 14(1).

Newsweek. 1988. Reading God's mind. June 13. 56–59.

Ramsay, A. Melvin. 1986. *Postviral fatigue syndrome, the saga of Royal Free disease*. London: Gower Medical Publishing.

Rawlinson, Mary. 1983. The facticity of illness and the appropriation of health. In *Phenomenology in a pluralistic context*. William L. McBride and Calvin O. Schrag, eds. Albany: SUNY Press.

Rich, Adrienne. 1976. Of woman born: *Motherhood as experience and institution*. New York: W. W. Norton.

Rooney, Frances and Pat Israel, eds. 1985. *Women and disability. Resources for Feminist Research* 14(1).

Sacks, Oliver. 1988. The revolution of the deaf. *The New York Review of Books*, June 2, 23–28.

Shaul, Susan L. and Jane Elder Bogle. 1981. Body image and the woman with a disability. In *Sexuality and physical disability*. David G. Bullard and Susan E. Knight, eds. St. Louis: C. V. Mosby.

Sherwin. Susan. 1984–85. A feminist approach to ethics. *Dalhousie Review* 64(4): 704–713.

Sherwin, Susan. 1987. Feminist ethics and in vitro fertilization. In *Science, morality and feminist theory*. Marsha Hanen and Kai Nielsen, eds. Calgary: The University of Calgary Press.

Sontag, Susan. 1977. *Illness as metaphor*. New York: Random House.

U.N. Decade of Disabled Persons 1983–1992. 1983. *World programme of action concerning disabled persons*. New York: United Nations.

Whitbeck, Caroline. Afterword to the maternal instinct. In *Mothering: Essays in feminist theory*. Joyce Trebilcot, ed. Totowa: Rowman and Allanheld.

Zaner, Richard M. 1983. Flirtations or engagement? Prolegomenon to a philosophy of medicine. In *Phenomenology in a pluralistic context*. Wilharn L. McBride and Calvin O. Schrag, eds. Albany: SUNY Press.

15

Feminist Theory, the Body, and the Disabled Figure

ROSEMARIE GARLAND THOMSON

THE FEMALE BODY AND THE DISABLED BODY

Many parallels exist between the social meanings attributed to female bodies and those assigned to disabled bodies. Both the female and the disabled body are cast within cultural discourse as deviant and inferior; both are excluded from full participation in public as well as economic life; both are defined in opposition to a valued norm which is assumed to possess natural corporeal superiority. Indeed, the discursive equation of femaleness with disability is common, sometimes in the service of denigrating women and sometimes with the goal of defending them. Examples abound, from Freud's understanding femaleness in terms of castration to late nineteenth-century physicians' defining menstruation as a disabling and restricting "eternal wound" to Thorstein Veblen's describing women in 1900 as literally disabled by feminine roles and costuming. Feminists today even often invoke negative images of disability to describe the oppression of women, as does Jane Flax—to cite a common example—in her assertion that women are "mutilated and deformed" by sexist ideology and practices.[1]

Perhaps, however, the founding association of femaleness with disability occurs in the fourth book of *Generation of Animals*, Aristotle's inaugural discourse of the normal and the abnormal in which he refines the Platonic concept of antinomies so that bodily variety translates into the hierarchies of the typical and the aberrant. "[A]nyone who does not take after his parents," Aristotle asserts, "is really in a way a monstrosity, since in these cases Nature has in a way strayed from the generic type. The first beginning of this deviation is when a female is formed instead of a male." Here the philosopher whom we might consider the founding father of Western taxonomy projects idealism onto corporeality to produce a definitive, seemingly neutral "generic type" along with its particularized antithesis, the "monstrosity," whose departure from such a "type" constitutes a profound "deviation." In this narrative of embodiment, Aristotle employs a spatial metaphor which places a certain corporeal figure who is deemed the "generic type" at the normative center of his system. On the outer margin is the "monstrosity," the corporeal consequence of Nature's having "strayed" from a central paradigm along a path of deviance, the first stop along which is the female body. Aristotle's choreography of bodies thus conjoins the "monstrosity"—whom we would today term "congenitally disabled"—and the female on a course leading away from the definitive norm. In Book Two, Aristotle also affirms his connection of disabled and female bodies by stating that "the female is as it were a deformed male"or—as it appears in other translations—"a mutilated male."[2]

More significant than his simple conflation of disability and femaleness is that Aristotle reveals here the source from which all otherness arises: the concept of a normative, "generic type" against which all corporeal variation is measured and found to be different, derivative, inferior, and insufficient. Not only does this definition of the female as a "mutilated male" inform later versions of woman as a diminished man, but it arranges somatic diversity into a hierarchy of value that assigns plenitude to some bodies and lack to others based on their configurations. Furthermore, by focusing on defining femaleness as deviant rather than the maleness he assumes to be essential, Aristotle also initiates the discursive practice of marking what is deemed aberrant while concealing the position of privilege by asserting its normativeness Thus we witness perhaps the originary operation of the logic which has become so familiar in discussions of gender, race, or disability: male, white, or able-bodied superiority is naturalized, remaining undisputed and obscured by the ostensible problem of female, black, or disabled deviance. What this passage makes clearest, however, is that without the monstrous body to demarcate the borders of the generic, without the female body to distinguish the shape of the male, and without the pathological to give form to the normal, these taxonomies of bodily value that underwrite political, social, and economic arrangements would collapse.[3]

Considering this persistent intertwining of disability with femaleness in Western discourse provides a fruitful context for explorations of social identity and the body. As Aristotle's pronouncement suggests, the social category of disability turns upon the significance accorded bodily functioning and configuration, just as the social category woman does. Placing disability studies in a feminist context allows feminist theory's recent inquiries into gender as a category, the body's role in identity and selfhood, and the complexity of social power relations to be brought to bear on an analysis of disability. Moreover, applying feminist theory to disability analyses infuses it with feminism's politicized insistence on the relationship between the meanings attributed to bodies by cultural representations and the consequences of those meanings in the world. In viewing disability through a feminist lens, I hope at the same time to suggest how the category of disability might be inserted into feminist theory so that the bodily configurations and functioning we call "disability" will be included in all feminist examinations of culture and representation. This brief exploration aims then at beginning the work of altering the terms of both feminist and disability discourses.

FEMINIST THEORY AND DISABILITY DISCOURSE

Contemporary feminist theory has proved to be porous, diffuse, and—perhaps most significant—self-critical. Thus, we speak now of "feminisms," "conflicts in feminism," "hyphenated feminisms," and even "postfeminism." Historically, academic feminism can be seen as a convergence of the highly political civil rights and accompanying identity politics impulses of the 1960s and '70s with the theoretical critique of liberal humanism's faith in knowledge, truth, and identity mounted by poststructuralism, nuanced by an insistence on historicizing gleaned from Marxist thought. The focus of feminist dialogue has shifted from early debates between liberal and radical feminisms which focused on achieving equality to later formulations of cultural and gynocentric feminisms which fore-grounded and rehabilitated female differences. Most recently, the debate between viewing gender in terms of minimizing differences in order to achieve equality and elaborating difference in order to valorize the feminine has been complicated by an interrogation of gender construction itself and the recognition of multiple axes of identity, both of which profoundly challenge the very notion of "woman" as any kind of unified identity category.[5] Such simultaneous insistence on a politics of location, coupled with the relentless questioning of identity and subjectivity as cultural constructs, along with the maintenance of a resolutely political critique comprise the theoretical milieu in which I want to place disability.

Thus, the strands of feminist thought coinciding most harmoniously with disability concerns are those which go beyond a narrow focus on gender alone and avoid the exclusion of other forms of social inflection; they undertake a broad sociopolitical critique of systemic, inequitable power relations based on binary social categories grounded in the body. In its largest sense, feminism becomes a theoretical perspective and methodology that examines gender as a discursive, ideological, and material category that interacts with but does not subordinate either other social identities or the particularities of embodiment, history, and location that inform subjectivity. Briefly put, feminism's often conflicting and always complex dual aims of politicizing the materiality of bodies while rewriting the category of woman are exactly the kinds of interrogations that should be brought to bear upon disability.[6]

I want to extend in a fresh juxtaposition, then, the association of disability and femaleness with which I began this essay. Rather than simply conflating the disabled body with the female body, however, I want to theorize disability in the ways that feminism has theorized gender. Both feminism and the interrogation of disability I am undertaking challenge existing social relations; both resist interpretations of certain bodily configurations and functioning as deviant; both question the ways that particularity or difference is invested with meaning; both examine the enforcement of universalizing norms; both interrogate the politics of appearance; both explore the politics of naming; both participate in positive identity politics. Nevertheless, feminism has formulated the terms and probed the logic of these concerns much more thoroughly than has disability studies, at this point.[7]

Eve Sedgwick's distinction, for example, between a "minoritizing" and a "universalizing" view of difference can be applied usefully to disability discourse. One minoritizes difference, according to Sedgwick's hybrid of feminist and queer theory, by imagining its significance and concerns as limited to a narrow, specific, relatively fixed population or arena of inquiry. In contrast, a universalizing view sees issues surrounding a particularized form of difference as having "continuing, determinative importance in the lives of people across the spectrum of [identities]."[8] I would advocate for disability studies to be seen as a universalizing discourse in the way that Sedgwick imagines universalizing gay studies and feminism. Such a conceptualization makes possible, among other things, recognizing that disability (or gender or homosexuality) is a category that structures a wide range of thought, language, and perception not explicitly articulated as "disability" (or gender or homosexuality). Universalizing, then, names the impulse behind the attempt here to show how the unarticulated concept of disability informs such national ideologies as American liberal individualism and sentimentalism, as well as explorations of African-American and lesbian identities. Such semantics emerging from feminist theory can be enlisted to dislodge the persistent assumption that disability is a self-evident condition of bodily inadequacy and private misfortune whose politics concern only a limited minority—just as femaleness so easily seemed before feminism.

A universalizing disability discourse which draws on feminism's confrontation with the gender system requires asserting the body as a cultural text which is interpreted, inscribed with meaning, indeed *made*, within social relations of power. Such a perspective advocates political equality by denaturalizing disability's assumed inferiority, casting its configurations and functions as difference rather than lack. But while this broad constructionist perspective does the vital cultural work of destigmatizing gender or racial differences as well as the corporeal traits we call disability, it also threatens to obscure the material and historical effects of those differences and to destablize the very social categories we analyze and, in many cases, claim as significant in our own and others' lives. Thus, the poststructuralist logic that destabilizes identity potentially frees marginalized people from the narrative of essential inadequacy, but at the same time it risks denying the particularity of their embodied experience.[9] The theoretical bind is that deconstructing oppressive oppositional categories can neutralize the political aspects of material differences.

A disability politics cannot at this moment, however, afford to banish the category of disability according to the poststructualist critique of identity and in the way that some feminists have argued for abandoning the concept of woman as hopelessly imprisoning and abstract.[10] The kind of legally mandated access to public spaces and institutions which began for women in the nineteenth century and has accelerated since the 1960s was only fully launched for disabled people by the Americans with Disabilities Act of 1990, a broad civil rights bill that is only beginning to be implemented. And while race and gender are accepted generally as differences rather than deviances in the political moves toward equality, disability is still most often seen as bodily inadequacy or misfortune to be compensated for through a pity, rather than a civil rights, model. So, on the one hand, it is important to employ the constructionist argument to denaturalize the assumption that disability is bodily insufficiency and to assert instead than disability arises from the interaction of embodied differences with an unaccommodating physical and social environment. But, on the other hand, the particular, historical materiality of the disabled body that demands both accommodation and recognition must be preserved as well. Consequently, the embodied difference that using a wheelchair or being deaf makes should be claimed, but without casting that difference as lack.[11]

Both constructionism and essentialism, then, become theoretical strategies—framings of the body—invoked when useful to achieve specific ends in the political arena, to liberate psychologically subjects whose bodies have been narrated to them as defective, or to facilitate imagined communities from which a positive identity politics can emerge. Thus, a strategic constructionism destigmatizes the disabled body, locates difference relationally, denaturalizes normalcy, and challenges appearance hierarchies. A strategic essentialism, by contrast, validates experience and consciousness, imagines community, authorizes history, and facilitates self-naming. The identity "disabled" operates, then, as a pragmatic narrative, what Susan Bordo calls "a life-enhancing fiction," grounded in the materiality of a particular embodiment and perspective embedded in specific social and historical contexts.[12]

IMAGINING FEMINIST DISABILITY DISCOURSE

But if the category "disabled" is a useful fiction, the disabled body set in a world structured for the normative, privileged body is not. Disability, perhaps more than other forms of alterity, demands a reckoning with the messiness of bodily variegation, with literal individuation run amok. Because the embodiment we think of as disability exists not so much as a set of observable predictable traits—like racialized or gendered physical features—but rather as *any* departure from an unstated corporeal norm, disability foregrounds embodiment's specificity. In other words, the concept of disability unites a highly marked, heterogeneous collection of embodiments whose only commonality is being considered abnormal. As a departure from a norm made neutral by an environment created to accommodate it, disability becomes intense, extravagant, and problematic embodiment. It is the unorthodox made flesh. Occupying the province of the extraordinary, disability refuses to be normalized, neutralized, or homogenized. More important yet, in an era governed by the abstract principle of universal equality, disability signals the body that cannot be universalized. Unified only by exclusion, disability confounds any notion of a generalizable, constant corporeal subject by flaunting the vagaries of an embodiment shaped by history, defined by particularity, and at odds with its environment. The cripple before the stairs, the blind before the printed page, the deaf before the radio, the amputee before the typewriter, and the dwarf before the counter—all testify with their particular bodies to the fact that the myriad structures and practices of material, daily life enforce the cultural expectation of a certain standard, universal subject before whom all others appear inferior.

Indeed, the identity category of disability can pressure feminist theory to acknowledge bodily particularity and history. Perhaps feminism's most useful concept for doing so is standpoint theory, which recognizes the local and complex quality of embodiment. Emphasizing the multiplicity of all women's identities, history, and embodiment, this theory of positionality recognizes that individual material situations structure the subjectivity from which particular women can speak and perceive with authority. In incorporating postmodernism's challenge of the unsituated, objective Enlightenment viewpoint, feminist standpoint theory has reformulated a monologic notion of gender identity into a more complex conception of identity as a dynamic matrix of interrelated, often contradictory, experiences, strategies, styles, and attributions mediated by culture and one's specific history, forming a network that cannot be separated meaningfully into discrete entities or ordered into a hierarchy. Acknowledging identity's particular and complex nature allows inflections other than the usual trinity of race, class, and gender to emerge. Standpoint theory and the feminist practice of explicitly situating oneself when speaking make way for complicating inflections such as disabilities or, more broadly, the category of corporeal configuration—as in such attributions as fat, disfigured, abnormal, ugly, or deformed—to be inserted into our considerations of identity and subjectivity. Such a dismantling of the unitary category woman has enabled feminist theory to encompass—although not without contention—such feminist differentiations as Patricia Hill Collins's "black feminist thought," for instance, or my own explorations of a "feminist disability studies."[14] So while feminist theory can bring to disability discourse strategies for destabilizing the meanings of embodied differences and identifying sites where those meanings seep into other discourses, it provides for articulating the particularity of identity and its materiality as well.

I am suggesting, then, that a feminist political praxis for women with disabilities needs strategically to focus at times on the specificity and perhaps the ineluctability of the flesh and to find clarity in the identity it occasions. For example, in one of the inaugural explorations of the politics of self-naming, Nancy Mairs claims the appellation "cripple" because it demands that others acknowledge the singularity of her embodiment. "People . . . wince at the word 'cripple,'" Mairs contends. Even though she retains what has been a derogatory term, she insists on determining its significance herself: "Perhaps I want them to wince. I want them to see me as a tough customer, one to whom the fates/ gods/viruses have not been kind, but who can face the brutal truth of her existence squarely. As a cripple, I swagger." Here Mairs is not so much rehabilitating the term of otherness as a celebration or as an attempt to reverse its contemptuous connotation; rather, she wants to call attention less to her oppression and more to the material reality of her crippledness, to her bodily difference her experience of it. For Mairs, the social constructionist argument risks neutralizing the difference of her pain and her struggle with an environment built for a body other than hers.[15]

The confrontation with bodily difference that disability provokes also places some disabled women at odds with several mainstream feminist assumptions that do not take into account disabled women's material situations. For example, while feminism quite legitimately decries the sexual objectification of women, disabled women often encounter what Harlan Hahn has called "asexual objectification," the assumption that sexuality is inappropriate in disabled people. One woman who uses a wheelchair and is at the same time quite beautiful reports, for example, that people often respond to her as if this combination of traits were a remarkable and lamentable contradiction. The judgment that the disabled woman's body is asexual and unfeminine creates what Michelle Fine and Adrienne Asch term "rolelessness," a kind of social invisibility and cancellation of femininity which sometimes prompts disabled women to claim an essential femininity which the culture denies them. For example, Cheryl Marie Wade insists upon a harmony between her disability and her womanly sexuality in a poem characterizing herself as "The Woman With Juice."[16] As Mairs's exploration of self-naming and Wade's assertion of sexuality suggest, a feminist disability politics would uphold the right for women to define their corporeal differences and their relationship to womanhood for themselves rather than acceding to received interpretations of their embodiment.

Wade's poem of self-definition echoes Mairs by maintaining firmly that she is "not one of the physically challenged," but rather she claims, "I'm the Gimp/I'm the Cripple/I'm the Crazy Lady." Affirming her body as at once sexual and different, she asserts, " I'm a French kiss with cleft tongue." Resisting the cultural tendency to erase not only her sexuality but the depreciated materiality of her embodiment, she characterizes herself as "a sock in the eye with gnarled fist." This image of the disabled body as a visual assault, as a shocking spectacle to the normative eye, captures a defining aspect of disabled experience. Whereas feminists claim that women are objects of the male gaze which demarcates their subjectivity, Wade's image of her body as "a sock in the eye" subtly reminds us that the disabled body is the object not of the appropriating gaze but of the stare. If the male gaze informs the normative female self as a sexual spectacle, then the stare sculpts the disabled subject as a grotesque spectacle. The stare is the gaze intensified, framing her body as an icon of deviance. Indeed, as Wade's poem suggests, the stare is the material gesture that creates disability as an oppressive social relationship. And as every person with a visible disability knows intimately, managing, deflecting, resisting, or renouncing that stare is the daily business of life.

In addition to having to prove their sexuality, disabled women must sometimes defend as well against the assessment that their bodies are unfit for motherhood or that they are the infantilized objects upon which others exercise their virtue. Whereas motherhood is often seen as compulsory for women, disabled women are often denied access or discouraged from entrance to the arena of reproduction that some feminist thinkers have found oppressive. The controversial feminist ethic of care also has been criticized by feminist disability scholars as potentially threatening to symmetrical, reciprocal relations among disabled and nondisabled women as well as for suggesting that care is the sole responsibility of women. Philosopher Anita Silvers claims, for example, that "far from vanquishing patriarchal systems, substituting the ethics of caring for the ethics of equality threatens an even more oppressive paternalism."[17]

Perhaps more problematic yet, feminist abortion rationale seldom questions the prejudicial assumption that "defective" fetuses destined to become disabled people should be eliminated. The concerns of older women, who are often disabled, tend also to be ignored by younger feminists, as well.[18] One of the most pervasive feminist assumptions that undermines some disabled women's struggle is the ideology of autonomy and independence emanating from liberal feminism and the broader impulse toward female empowerment. By tacitly incorporating the liberal premise that levels individual particularities and differences in order to posit an abstract, disembodied subject of democracy, feminist practice often leaves no space for the needs and accommodations that disabled women's bodies require.[19] The angry and disappointed words prominent disability rights activist Judy Heumann spoke to me reflect an alienation not unlike that between some black women and some white feminists: "When I come into a room full of feminists, all they see is a wheelchair."[20] These conflicts testify that feminists, like everyone else, including disabled people themselves, have been acculturated to stigmatize those whose bodies are deemed aberrant.

FEMININITY AND DISABILITY

So while I want to insist on disabled women's particularity and identity even while questioning its sources and its production, I also want to suggest nevertheless that a firm boundary between "disabled" and "nondisabled" women cannot be meaningfully drawn—just as any absolute distinction between sex and gender must be problematized. Femininity and disability are inextricably entangled in Western culture, as Aristotle's equation of women and disabled men illustrates. Not only has the female body been represented as deviant, but historically the practices of femininity have configured female bodies in ways that duplicate the parameters of disability. Feminizing conventions such as Chinese foot binding, African scarification, clitoridectomy, and Euroamerican corseting were (and are) socially accepted, encouraged, even compulsory, forms of female disablement that ironically constitute feminine social enablement, increasing a woman's value and status as a woman at a given moment in a particular society. Similarly, such conditions as anorexia, hysteria, and agoraphobia are in a sense standard feminine scripts writ large enough to become disabling conditions, blurring the line between normal feminine behavior and pathology.[21]

Feminine beauty's disciplinary regime often obscures the seemingly self-evident categories of the "normal" and the "pathological" as well. For example, the nineteenth-century Euroamerican prescription for upper-class feminine beauty precisely paralleled the symptoms of tuberculosis just as the cult of thinness promoted by the fashion industry approaches the appearance of disease.[22] In another instance, the iconography and language of contemporary cosmetic surgery presented in women's magazines persistently casts the unreconstructed female body as having "abnormalities" that can be "corrected" by surgical procedures which "improve" one's appearance by producing "natural looking" noses, thighs, breasts, chins, and so on.[23] This discourse casts women's unmodified bodies as unnatural and abnormal while the surgically altered bodies become normal and natural. Although cosmetic surgery is in one sense only the logical extension of beauty practices such as make-up, perms, relaxers, skin lighteners, and hair removal, it differs profoundly from these basically decorative forms of self-reconstruction because, like clitoridectomies and scarification, it involves mutilation, pain, and wounding that is definitive of many disabilities.

While all of these practices cannot, of course, be equated, each nevertheless transforms an infinitely plastic body in ways similar to the ways disability alters the body. The difference is that these changes are imagined to be choices that will sculpt the female body so it conforms to a feminine ideal. Disabilities, despite their affinities with beautifiction procedures, are imagined, in contrast, to be random transformations that move the body away from ideal forms. Within the visual economy in which appearance has come to be the primary index of value for women, feminizing practices normalize the female body, while disabilities abnormalize it. Feminization prompts the gaze, while disability prompts the stare. Feminization alterations increase a woman's cultural capital, while disabilities reduce it.[24]

But as Aristotle's equation of femaleness with mutilated males suggests, the normalized female body is abnormal in reference to the universally human male body. The normative female body—the figure of the beautiful woman—is a narrowly prescribed version of what the ideal male figure is not. If he is to be strong, active, hirsute, hard, and so on, then she must be his opposite—weak, passive, hairless, soft, and so on. The normative female body, then, occupies a dual and paradoxical cultural role: it is the negative term opposing the male body, but it is also simultaneously the privileged term in reference to the abnormalized female body.

For example, the nineteenth-century obsession with scientific quantification actually produced a detailed description of absolute beauty, laid out by Havelock Ellis, which posited a Darwinian ranking of beauty, determined entirely by corporeal characteristics and ranging from the "beautiful" European woman to what was considered to be her grotesque opposite, the African woman.[25] Moreover, scientific discourse conceived this anatomical scale of beauty as simultaneously one of pathology. The further a female body departed from absolute beauty, the more "abnormal" it became as a female body. The markers of this indubitable pathology were traits such as dark skin and physical disability, or behaviors like prostitution, which were often linked to bodily characteristics. Within this scheme, all women are seen as deviant in their femaleness, but some women are imagined as doubly deviant. So the simple dichotomy of objectified feminine body and masculine subject is complicated, then, by other sets of binary oppositions that further clarify the original terms. Indeed, the unfeminine, unbeautiful body mutually constitutes the very shape of the feminine body. This other figure of woman has been identified variously in history and discourse as black, fat, lesbian, sexually appetitive, disabled, ugly, and so on. What is important for this study, however, is that her deviance and subsequent devaluation are always attributed to some visible bodily characteristic—a mark that can operate as an emblem of her difference—just as beauty has always been located in the body of the feminine woman. As one manifestation of the unbeautiful woman, the third term that disrupts a tidy pair of antinomies, the figure of the disabled woman tends to complicate discourses announcing themselves as trafficking in oppositional paradigms.

As this discussion of normalized and abnormalized female bodies suggests, it is the cultural figure of the disabled woman, rather than the actual woman with a disability, that this essay focuses upon. Within the politics of representation I have explored here, the figure of the disabled woman is best apprehended as a product of a conceptual triangulation. She is a cultural third term, a figure constituted by the originary binary pair of the masculine figure and the feminine figure. Thus, the disabled female figure occupies an intragender position; that is, she is not only defined against the masculine figure, but she is imagined as the antithesis of the normative woman as well. But because representation structures reality, the cultural figures that haunt the days of the living often must, like Virginia Woolf's Angel of the House, be wrestled to the floor before even modest self-definition, let alone political action, can proceed.

NOTES

1. See page 7 in Patricia Vertinsky, "Excercise, Physical Capability, and the Eternally Wounded Woman in Late Nineteenth-Century North America," *Journal of Sport History* 14, 1 (1987): 7–27, p. 7; Thorstein Veblen, *The Theory of the Leisure Class* (Boston: Houghton Mifflin, 1973); *Jane Flax, Thinking Fragments: Psychoanalysis, Feminism, and Postmodernism in the Contemporary West* (Berkeley: University of California Press, 1990), *p. 136.*

2. Aristotle, *Generation of Animals*, trans. A. L. Peck, (Cambridge: Harvard University Press, 1944) Book IV, 401 and Book II, 175. For discussions of Aristotle's conflation of femaleness with monstrosity and deformity, see Maryanne Cline Horowitz," aristotle and Women" *Journal of the History of Biology* 9 (1976): 183–213; Nancy Tuana, *The Less Noble Sex: Scientific, Religious, and Philosophical Conceptions of Woman's Nature* (Bloomington: Indiana University Press, 1993); and Marie-Helene Huet, *Monstrous Imagination* (Cambridge, MA: Harvard University Press, 1993). Edwin Schur examines the assignment of deviance to women in *Labeling Women Deviant: Gender, Stigma, and Social Control* (Philadelphia: Temple University Press, 1983).

3. For discussions of the notion of woman as an inferior version of man, see Thomas Laquer, *Making Sex*, and Nancy Tuana, *The Less Noble Sex*. Feminist studies has informed masculine studies in this arena and black studies has given rise recently to an examination of whiteness. For a discussion of whiteness, see David Roediger, *The Wages of Whiteness* (New York: Verso, 1991) and Richard Dyer, *the Matter of Images: Essays on Representation* (New York: Routledge, 1993). For a seminal discussion of the mutual constitution of the normal by the pathological, see Georges Canguilhem, *The Normal and the Pathological*, trans. Carolyn R. Fawcett with Robert S. Cohen (New York: Zone Books, 1989).

4. Examples are Diane Price Herndl and Robyn Warhol, *Feminisms* (New Brunswick: Rutgers University Press, 1991); Marianne Hirsch and Evelyn Fox Keller, eds., *Conflicts in Feminism* (New York: Routledge, 1990); "hyphenated feminism" is used

by Judith Grant, *Fundamental Feminism: Contesting the Core Concepts of Feminist Theory* (New York: Routledge, 1993), 3; Brigitta Boucht, et al., *Postfeminism* (Esbo, Finland: Draken, 1991).

5. A good overview of this history of academic feminist theory is Elizabeth Weed, "Introduction: Terms of Reference," in Elizabeth Weed, ed., *Coming to Terms: Feminism, Theory, Politics* (New York: Routledge, 1989), ix–xxxi. For discussion of these debates and bifurcations in feminism, see Linda Alcoff, "Cultural Feminism Versus Post-Structuralist Feminism: The Identity Crisis in Feminist Theory"*Signs* 13, 3 (1988): 405–36; Hester Eisenstein, *Contemporary Feminist Thought* (Boston: G. K. Hall, 1983); and Josephine Donovan, *Feminist Theory* (New York: Continuum, 1992). Early complications of gender identity include Elizabeth Spelman, *Inessential Woman: Problems of Exclusion in Feminist Thought* (Boston: Beacon, 1988) and Monique Wittig, "The Straight Mind,"*Feminist Issues* Summer 1980: 101–10. Diana Fuss, *Essentially Speaking: Feminism, Nature, and Difference* (New York: Routledge, 1989) deconstructs the opposition between essentialism, often associated with cultural feminism, and constructionism, often associated with radical feminism. Judith Butler's *Gender Trouble: Feminism and the Subversion of Identity* (New York: Routledge, 1990) and *Bodies That Matter: On the Discursive Limits of "Sex"* (New York: Routledge, 1993) most complexly articulate the constructionist approach to gender.

6. Feminist texts that announce themselves as postmodernist and materialist often take the positions I am outlining here; some examples of studies that rigorously maintain this version of feminism are Susan Bordo, *Unbearable Weight: Feminism, Western Culture, and the Body* (Berkeley: University of California Press, 1993); Rosemary Hennessy, *Materialist Feminism and the Politics of Discourse* (New York: Routledge, 1993); Jennifer Wicke, "Celebrity Material: Materialist Feminism and the Culture of Celebrity" *South Atlantic Quarterly* 93, 4 (Fall 1994): 751–78; Judith Grant, *Fundamental Feminism*; Linda Nicholson, ed., *Feminism/Postmodernism* (New York: Routledge, 1990).

7. Most theorists of disability either naturalize disability while protesting exclusion and oppression of disabled people or they adopt a strict social constructionist perspective in order to claim equality, while asserting difference for the purposes of establishing identity. For an example of the former, see the collection of essays by Harold E. Yuker, ed., *Attitudes Toward Persons with Disabilities* (New York: Springer, 1988); an example of the latter can be found in Harlan Hahn, "Can Disability Be Beautiful?," *Social Policy* (Fall 1988): 26–31.

8. Eve Kosofsky Sedgwick, *Epistemology of the Closet* (Berkeley: University of California Press, 1990), p. 1.

9. For discussions of this problem, see Susan Bordo,"Feminism, Postmodernism, and Gender Skepticism," in *Unbearable Weight*, 215–43; Judith Butler, *Bodies That Matter*; and Betsy Erkkila, "Ethnicity, Literary Theory, and the Grounds of Resistance," *American Quarterly* 47, 4 (Dec. 1995): 563–94.

10. For example, see Monique Wittig, "The Straight Mind."

11. For histories of civil rights legislation for people with disabilities, see Joseph Shapiro, *No Pity: People with Disabilities Forging a New Civil Rights Movement* (New York: Times Books/Random House, 1993); Claire Liachowitz, *Disability as a Social Construct*; and Richard Scotch, *From Good Will to Civil Rights*. An anecdote illustrates that physical access is only now being gained for people with disabilities. On September 6, 1995, the Modern Language Association headquarters in New York completed the building of a wheelchair ramp minutes before the arrival of a dele-

gation of MLA members who had been invited to discuss disability issues with the MLA's Executive Director. Although the MLA is a very progressive institution, eager for inclusion and willing to recognize disability issues, apparently the fundamental issue of accessibility had never been addressed before.

For more discussions of disability as a civil rights rather than a pity issue, see Joseph Shapiro, *No Pity*, and Paul Longmore, "Conspicuous Contribution and American Cultural Dilemmas: Telethons, Virtue, and Community," forthcoming in David Mitchell, and Sharon Snyder eds., *Storylines and Lifelines: Narratives of Disability in the Humanities*.

The problem of how to accommodate difference with equity is addressed in many arenas of feminist theory. Most often it appears as a critique of liberalism not unlike the one I undertake later in this chapter. For a concise discussion of this problem, see the introduction and conclusion to Carole Pateman and Elizabeth Gross, eds., *Feminist Challenges: Social and Political Theory* (Boston: Northeastern University Press, 1986); also see, for example, Carole Pateman, *The Sexual Contract* (Stanford: Stanford University Press, 1988); Jean Bethke Elsthain, *Public Man, Private Woman: Women in Social and Political Thought* (Princeton: Princeton University Press, 1981); Iris Marion Young, *Justice and the Politics of Difference* (Princeton: Princeton University Press, 1990); and Martha Minow, *Making All the Difference*.

12. Diana Fuss in *Essentially Speaking* examines this tension between constructionist and essentialist conceptions of identity, concluding that to deconstruct identity is not to deny categories, but rather to expose the fictionality of them even while claiming them for political purposes and to establish community and affinity. Benedict Anderson's concept of "imagined communities" is useful here to suggest the strategic aspect of such communities for political and psychological purposes; see *Imagined Communities: Reflections on the Origin and Spread of Nationalism* (New York: Verso, 1991). I support here as well Judith Butler's subtle but significant point in *Bodies That Matter* that the social construction of the body must not be seen as simply overlaying meaning on a body that is prior to culture, but that culture actually constitutes that body. Also see Susan Bordo, *Unbearable Weight*, quotation on p. 229.

13. This questioning of identity and focusing on difference has been theorized by way of the feminist epistemological modes variously called perspectivism by Ellen Messer-Davidow, "The Philosophical Bases of Feminist Literary Criticism," *New Literary History: A Journal of Theory and Interpretation* 19, no. 1 (Autumn 1987): 65–103; standpoint theory by Patricia Hill Collins, *Black Feminist Thought: Knowledge, Consciousness, and the Politics of Empowerment* (Boston: Unwin Hyman, 1990); and Bettina Aptheker, *Tapestries of Life: Women's Work, Women's Consciousness, and the Meaning of Daily Experience* (Amherst: University of Massachusetts Press, 1989); and positionality by Linda Alcoff, *Signs*. Standpoint theory has been recently criticized, however, by Judith Grant in *Fundamental Feminism* as fragmenting the feminist communal project and risking a degeneration of feminism into individualism. Elizabeth Fox-Genovese also implicitly assails this tendency in recent feminist thought to atomize individuals at the expense of recognizing commonality and utilizing the beneficial aspects of received, shared culture in *Feminism Without Illusions* (Chapel Hill: University of North Carolina Press, 1991).

14. See Collins, *Black Feminist Thought*, and Rosemarie Garland Thomson, "Redrawing the Boundaries of Feminist Disability Studies," *Feminist Studies* 20 (Fall 1994): 583–95.

15. Nancy Mairs, "On Being a Cripple," *Plaintext: Essays* (Tucson: University of Ari-

zona Press, 1986), quotation on p. 90. For a discussion of my own concerns about focusing on pain and dysfunction in disability discourse, see Thomson, "Redrawing the Boundaries of Feminist Disability Studies," in which I reflect upon Mairs's elaboration of the critical subgenre she calls "The Literature of Catastrophe."

16. Hahn's comment is quoted from a personal conversation. The anecdote about the wheel chair user is drawn from Fred Davis, "Deviance Disavowal," 124. Michelle Fine and Adrienne Asch, "Disabled Women: Sexism without the Pedestal," *Women and Disability: the Double Handicap*, eds., Mary Jo Deegan and Nancy A. Brooks (New Brunswick, NJ: Transaction Books, 1985), 6–22, 12. Cheryl Marie Wade, *MS* II (3): 57.

17. Anita Silvers, "Reconciling Equality to Difference: Caring (f)or Justice for People with Disabilities," *Hypatia* (forthcoming); for a critique of the feminization of caregiving for people with disabilities, see Barbara Hillyer, *Feminism and Disability* (Norman, OK: university of Oklahoma Press, 1993); for discussions of the ethic of care, see Nel Noddings, *Caring: A Feminine Approach to Ethics and Moral Education* (Berkeley: University of California Press, 1984) and Eva Feder Kittay and Diana T. Meyers, *Women and Moral Theory* (Totowa, NJ: Rowman and Littlefield, 1987).

Although cultural feminism tends to view motherhood as less of an oppression than do early liberal feminists such as Shulamith Firestone, for instance (*The Dialectic of Sex: The Case for Feminist Revolution* (New York: Morrow, 1970)), motherhood nevertheless is most often cast as a choice to be evaluated and sometimes, but seldom as a bodily experience, denied to some women on the basis of cultural prejudices; see Michelle Fine and Adrienne Asch, eds., *Women with Disabilities: Essays in Psychology, Culture, and Politics* (Philadelphia: Temple University Press, 1988), 12–23.

18. Regarding the feminist position on "defective" fetuses, a recent example which supports my point is the new Maryland abortion legislation, hailed in the March 4, 1991, issue of *Time* magazine as a "feminist victory," which permits unconditional abortion until fetal viability, but only allows abortion after that if a woman's health is endangered or if the fetus is "deformed" (p. 53). I am not suggesting abortion restrictions here; rather, I am questioning the myth of "free choice" regarding the bearing of congenitally disabled infants in a society in which the received attitudes about disabled people tend to be negative, oppressive, and unexamined. Disabled people simply need advocates who will examine the cultural ideology inherent in these rationales and policies. For discussions of the issue of disability in relation to abortion and reproductive rights, see Ruth Hubbard, "Who Should and Should Not Inhabit the World," in this anthropology and in Ruth Hubbard, ed., *The Politics of Women's Biology* (New Brunswick, NJ: Rutgers University Press, 1990); Marsha Saxton, "Born and Unborn: The Implications of Reproductive Technologies for People with Disabilities," in Rita Arditti, Renate Duell Klein, and Shelley Minden, eds., *Test-Tube Women: What Future for Motherhood?* (Boston: Pandora, 1984), 298–312; and Anne Finger, "Claiming All of Our Bodies: Reproductive Rights and Disability," in Arditti et al., ed., *Test-Tube Women*, pp.281–96; Fine and Asch, eds., *Women with Disabilities*, esp. ch. 12 and 13; and Deborah Kaplan, "Disabled Women," in Alison Jaggar, ed., *Living with Contradictions: Controversies in Feminist Social Ethics* (Boulder: Westview Press, 1994).

For discussions of ageism in feminism, see Shulamit Reinharz, "Friends or Foes: Gerontological and Feminist Theory" *Women's Studies International Forum* 9, 5 (1986): 503–14; and Barbara McDonald with Cynthia Rich, *Look Me in the Eye: Old Women, Aging, and Ageism* (San Francisco: Spinsters, Ink, 1983).

19. Susan Bordo argues in a similar vein that the feminist search for equality has caused a flight from gender and, hence, from the body, that often masquerades as "professionalism." Disabled women's inability to erase the claims of their bodies or to be able to fit the standardized image of the "professional" often alienates them from feminists who enter the workplace on such terms. See Bordo, *Unbearable Weight*, 229–33, for a discussion of this point; also see Fine and Asch, eds., *Women with Disabilities*, 26–31.

20. Personal conversation, Society for Disability Studies Annual Meeting, June, 1991, Denver, CO.

21. The philosopher Iris Marion Young argues for the construction of femininity as disability, for example, by asserting that the cultural objectification of women is manifest in their tendency to be inhibited in using their bodies as unselfconscious agents of physical capability. "Women in a sexist society are physically handicapped," concludes Young in the essay that focuses on the phenomenon of "Throwing Like a Girl" (*Throwing Like a Girl*, 153). For discussions of foot binding, scarification, clitoridectomy, and corseting, see Mary Daly, *Gyn/ecology: The Metaethics of Radical Feminism* (Boston: Beacon, 1978) and Barbara Ehrenreich and Deirdre English, *For Her Own Good: 150 Years of the Experts' Advice to Women* (Garden City, NY: Anchor Books, 1979). For discussions of anorexia, hysteria, and agoraphobia, see Susan Bordo, *Unbearable Weight*; Kim Chernin, *The Hungry Self: Women, Eating, and Identity* (New York: Times Books, 1985) and *The Obsession: Reflections on the Tyranny of Slenderness* (New York: Harper & Row, 1981); and Susie Orbach, *Fat Is a Feminist Issue: The Anti-Diet Guide to Permanent Weight Loss* (New York: Paddington Press, 1978) and *Hunger Strike: The Anorectic's Struggle as a Metaphor for Our Age* (New York: Norton, 1986).

22. Susan Sontag, *Illness as Metaphor* (New York: Farrar, Straus & Giroux, 1977). For cultural critiques of beauty, see Lois W. Banner, *American Beauty* (New York: Knopf, 1983); Robin Tolmach Lakoff and Raquel L. Scherr, *Face Value: The Politics of Beauty* (Boston; Routledge and Kegan Paul, 1984); Naomi Wolf, *The Beauty Myth: How Images of Beauty are Used Against Women* (New York: Morrow, 1991); Sharon Romm, *The Changing Face of Beauty* (St. Louis: Mosby-Year Book, 1992); Rita Jackaway Freedman, *Beauty Bound* (City? Publisher? Year); Susan Bordo, *Unbearable Weight*, esp. Part II; and Susan Faludi, *Backlash: The Undeclared War Against American Women* (New York: Crown, 1991).

23. This language comes from advertising for cosmetic surgery in *Newsweek* magazine, although it can be found in almost any of the many ads and articles in women's magazines. One is reminded here of Foucault's "docile bodies" described in *Discipline and Punish: The Birth of the Prison*, trans. Alan Sheridan (New York: Vintage, 1979), 135–69. For discussions of cosmetic surgery, see Kathryn Pauly Morgan, "Women and the Knife: Cosmetic Surgery and the Colonization of Women's Bodies," *Hypatia* 6, 3 (Fall 1991): 25–53; and Anne Balsamo, " On the Cutting Edge: Cosmetic Surgery and the Technological Production of the Gendered Body," *Camera Obscura* 28 (Jan. 1992): 207–36; and Kathy Davis, *Shaping Female Bodies*.

24. Mary Russo's *The Female Grotesque: Risk, Excess, and Modernity* (New York: Routledge, 1994) observes what she calls "the normalization of feminism" which involves "strategies of reassurance" that encourage feminists to focus on standard forms of femininity and avoid the female sites she calls "the grotesque," which I might term the "abnormal."

25. Gilman, *Difference and Pathology*, p. 90.

part five

Disability and Education

16

Integrating Disability Studies into the Existing Curriculum

The Example of "Women and Literature" at Howard University

ROSEMARIE GARLAND THOMSON

As a white woman with a quite visible physical disability who is a professor at a historically black university, I envision my role to be introducing complexities into my students' tendency to see race as the primary, if not exclusive, focus of individual and group identity. The centrality of racial history, issues, identity, and community to many of the humanities and social science courses at Howard, as well as the predominant black presence, foster a strong sense of black solidarity among our students. Yet, at the same time, Howard's almost exclusively black student and majority black faculty population also afford the kind of safe atmosphere where distinctions among the black community can be examined without the kind of recourse to minimizing differences in order to establish black solidarity that sometimes prevails at predominantly white institutions. My job at Howard is to invite students to consider how gender, class, and disability bisect racial groupings and to interrogate the very process of social categorization according to physiological or psychological characteristics. While many of my colleagues balance race with gender and class analyses, introducing disability as a category of social analysis is rare. Disability studies is simply not a part of the general educational currency at Howard or at most other institutions. The salience of race as an analytical category at my university seems to me to be both obscure and invite an examination of disability as a parallel yet distinct social identity based in corporeal or mental differences. The hyper-awareness of racial considerations often overshadows or minimizes other forms of what I call socially constructed "corporeal otherness" even while it serves as a model for examining those same forms of cultural marginalization. What I intend to discuss here is how I attempt to introduce disability studies—disability consciousness, if you will—in the context of a sustained focus on racial difference and to a lesser extent on gender distinctions.

In the broadest sense, my aim in teaching disability studies is to complicate the received "we" and "they" conception that implies both a victim/perpetrator and a normal/abnormal relationship between the disabled and the nondisabled. To do so, I probe the categories of "disabled" and "nondisabled," questioning their interpretation as mutually exclusive groups who are sorted according to bodily or mental traits. I emphasize the social aspect of disability, its relativity to a standard that is culturally determined, rather than its physical aspect, precisely because our traditional account of disability casts it as a problem located in bodies rather than a problem located in the interaction between bodies and the environment in which they are situated. In short, this pedagogical goal requires removing disability from its traditional medical model interpretation and placing it into a minority role model understanding. It means not describing disability in the language of inherent physical inferiority or medical rehabilitation but instead adopting the politicized language of minority discourse, civil rights, and equal opportunity so as to invoke such historical precedents as the Black Civil Rights Movement and the Women's Movement. In other words, by focusing on the social construction of disability, by framing disability as a cultural reading of the body that has political and social consequences, and by invoking a politics of positive identity, I hope to facilitate understanding and identification across identity groups rather than guilt and resentment. Such an approach is intended to relativize and politicize both the categories of "disabled" and "able-bodied" while casting a critical eye on the cultural processes that produce such distinctions.

Yet, the kind of curricular refashioning that enables me to teach courses in disability studies is not easily accomplished. It is often not feasible or timely to convince institutions to offer new courses whose titles include the term "disability" because it is difficult to classify them. Administrations wish to know where they fit in the traditional scheme of the disciplines and categories: does disability belong to the humanities, to sociology, to special education, to health or science? More problematic yet, how broad an appeal might such courses have? Disability sometimes seems at first glance like a tangential or narrow field of inquiry, one that would attract only a special population. Although I would argue that disability studies should be a humanities course which, most appropriately, satisfies a diversity requirement, it can be arduous to reframe institutionally what might have been previously perceived as a health course so that it can be understood as minority studies or cultural studies. To diffuse this logic and its accompanying resistance, I propose that we teach disability studies as an integrated part of all the courses we design, just as many of us have begun to consider race, gender, and class issues as fundamental aspects of all disciplines and subjects of inquiry. Indeed, as the disciplines of women's studies and ethnic studies have learned, such categories sometimes foster the assumption that these are the only arenas where racial or gender concerns are appropriately addressed. One of the goals of disability studies should be, then, to knit disability as a category of analysis into all of the courses in which we examine the workings of culture, especially courses that address issues of representation, identity, subjectivity, or the political implications of ideology.

In such a spirit, I integrate disability issues into all the courses I teach as an English professor. By way of example, I will discuss here how I infuse disability studies into a particular undergraduate humanities course called "Women in Literature" that I teach regularly at Howard. I intend to show here, first, examples of material from various disciplines that are not explicitly labeled "disability studies" but which can nevertheless be marshaled to elucidate the way that disability, along with other stigmatized identities, operates in Western culture. Second, I will suggest how literary and cultural analysis might be enlisted to reveal the ways that social relations produce the cultural distinctions of disability, race, gender, as well as class. Third, I will reflect on student responses to the material and the approach.

In all my teaching, rather than focusing exclusively on disability as the sole form of social otherness under consideration, I simultaneously investigate the bodily based social identities of race, ethnicity, gender, and sexual orientation as parallel but distinctive social categories whose function is, among other things, both to differentiate and in some cases to stigmatize individuals on the basis of corporeal differences. By intertwining analyses of a range of identities culturally constructed from bodily traits and behaviors, I encourage students to draw comparisons among them as well as mobilize their own varied experiences of different types of social marginalization or oppression. Thus, my aim is not to privilege disability identity, but rather to prove the sociopolitical and psychological aspects involved in a matrix of often overlapping forms of social identity which rest on a premise of irreducible corporeal difference.

Even though the course I am assigned to teach at Howard is entitled "Women in Literature," I subtitle it "Human Variation and the Politics of Appearance" with the intention of linking political subordination to the cultural valuing and devaluing of bodies on the basis of their appearance. Centering our inquiry on appearance enables us to discuss not only the system of standards upon which social discrimination draws, but to consider how appearance norms contribute not only to racism but to other forms of social oppression as well. In order to scrutinize simultaneously race, gender, class, and disability, the course undertakes as its primary subject a critical examination of feminine beauty. Since the politics of appearance along with its value system, "beauty," encompass multiple forms of social marginalization, all students can identity with the issues in one way or another. Thus, ableism becomes one variation of a general form of social discrimination rather than an issue that the nondisabled students might think has nothing to do with them.

By focusing on beauty as an oppressive cultural ideology perpetuated and enforced by a wide range of institutions and received traditions, we are able at the outset to diffuse any simple split between those who could slip into the normative position in regard to our topic and those who are outside of it. There is no "we" and "they" when it comes to issues of appearance and beauty. It is quickly apparent that feminine beauty is a personal issue for all the students, even the men. Because the course fulfills a university humanities requirement, it draws from a range of ages, and the students who enroll represent a wide variety of academic interests and experiences. The majority of students are women, some of whom are sympathetic to and familiar with feminism, some of whom are resistant to assertions of any cultural or historical gender differences, and most of whom are curious about investigating an academic subject that seems so close to lived experience. Men usually comprise ten to fifteen percent of the class. Some of the men are feminists themselves or quite interested in women's issues, while often a handful of the men seem vociferously hostile to the course's persistent focus on the female position. Most students are from middle-class or black elite backgrounds, while some are from the inner-city and are working class or from the working poor. Although virtually all the students are black, they represent a rich diversity of cultural backgrounds—African-American, African, Caribbean, Southern rural, Northern urban, Western U.S., mixed race and nationality—as well as a wide range of notions of what it means to be black. The only confident generalization I can make about black students is that they are black, a social identity which signifies diversely for them.

All the students seem quite eager to discuss and examine beauty standards, body-image issues, women's changing social position, questions of identity and community, and especially relations between men and women (a point I will return to later). Indeed, the course's greatest challenge is managing coherent, focused discussions which draw on personal stories yet retain an analytical edge. I nevertheless explicitly introduce the feminist assertion that the personal is political so as to encourage sharing personal observations and experiences both in class as well as in the daily reading response journals students are required to keep. What critically and personally scrutinizing beauty eventually allows us to explore is the ways in which cultures saturate bodies with meanings, an essential concept for understanding the disabled category. Along with illuminating how bodies are interpreted within societies, interrogating beauty also encourages students to flush out the value systems and the power dynamics that underpin those interpretations.

At the beginning of the course almost all students rather uncritically assume that beauty is a somewhat fixed property of the female body. Although many students recognize the historical and cultural relativity of appearance standards, they tend to see beauty as an absolute physical quality free from political implications or relations of power. Many students are willing to challenge impossible beauty norms, but few have taken their critiques beyond the arena of personal adequacy or inadequacy. Beauty, they often feel, is something corporeal that one has or does not have—just like a disability. But whereas having a disability seems a disadvantage, having beauty seems an advantage. Few students have considered the disadvantages of beauty. Thus, we probe the operation of beauty and disability to see the parallels and to uncover the social relations that govern enforcement of bodily norms. What I try to develop is a global critique of appearance norms which at once transcends and draws from students' individual relationships with their bodies and their personal negotiations with beauty demands.

One successful way to do this, I have found, is to shift our attention to beauty's mutually constituting opposite, "ugly," which under scrutiny yields up the recognition that while beauty may not initially seem oppressive, the attribution of its flip side, ugliness, is indeed disempowering—a point I will return to later. Introducing ugliness makes it easier to denaturalize beauty, to show that it is a series of practices and positions that one takes in order to avoid the stigmatization of ugliness. I accomplish this by introducing and juxtaposing two historical figures to the class, Marilyn Monroe, and another woman who epitomized beauty's opposite—not just ugliness, but freakdom. She is Saartje Bartmann, the nineteenth-century African woman known as "The Hottentot Venus," whose body, which was normal in her own culture, differed so much from the European standard that she was recruited into English and French freak shows. By recognizing how constructed Marilyn's beauty was—the hair dye and makeup, the photo techniques, the cosmetic surgery, the name change—and how vulnerable it made her to its transience as well as its exploitation, the students see that beauty is not only a set of practices but that its empowerment is quite limited if not actually detrimental, as Marilyn's biography illustrates so well. What Marilyn and Saartje have in common is that their bodies were displayed for profit before audiences in ways that were not necessarily beneficial to them but that were dictated by the culture's need to articulate formally its standards for the female form.

While the students' response to Saartje Bartmann's display as an exoticized, sexualized freak is uniform disgust and outrage, their responses to Marilyn Monroe are usually more varied and complex. Juxtaposing the exploitative display of a white woman and a black woman invites, of course, a consideration of race and its accompanying power dynamics. The students who reveal great hostility toward Marilyn as the figure of perfect white beauty that has been held up to them as forever unattainable are generally softened and their judgment is legitimated by Gloria Steinem's analysis of the star's miserable life. Other students clearly admiringly identify with Marilyn, expressing sympathy that her life was not the fairy tale that they imagined beauty would confer. Regardless of whether they adore or despise her, students generally find shocking the pathology and liability of Marilyn's beauty. For the most part, they are unaware of the ways that beauty is mediated by cultural presentation: they assume that what they see is the natural, unreconstructed woman and that beauty delivers fulfillment. Most students are also astonished that white women try to reconfigure their bodies because they depart from beauty norms. They are very aware of the disparity between female bodies of African heritage and the stylized contemporary white beauty standard, but many do not realize that European female bodies usually cannot conform to the impossible ideal either. For example, students frequently express interest and surprise when I reveal my own conviction about the inadequacies of my hair, which is straight and limp. This sometimes creates a complex dynamic in which students identify across race with white women on the basis of shared gender experience even as they recognize white women's relative privilege within beauty culture's hierarchy of bodies. What they witness is an affirmation of what they already know but which cultural pressures mute: that a satisfying life is not so simply linked to looking right. This, of course, lays the groundwork for examining the body's social context and suggesting that the disabled body does not necessarily produce misery.

In order to denaturalize and politicize beauty culture, at the outset of the course we critically view a number of advertisements to catalogue the qualities of beauty which are so hyperbolically and relentlessly choreographed in the pages of women's magazines. With a little guidance, students adeptly and zealously read the images, compiling a stunningly uniform and narrow profile of acceptable body traits for women which include—among others—hairlessness, odorlessness, a prepubescent slimness and youth, softness, whiteness, thick wavy hair, as well as psychological characteristics such as passivity and self-consciousness. While the students are keenly aware of the racist implications in the ads' celebration of European physical features and of thinness, they have not usually thought through the role of women's bodies as spectacles in a consumer society that accords males the role of spectator and actor—a relationship that is writ large, if subtly, in advertising. Analyzing the images and reading theoretical critiques—such as John Berger's *Ways of Seeing*, an exploration of the social relation between the male spectator and the female spectacle in European oil painting—reveals for students a dynamic, in this case gendered and racialized, in which one role is to look, judge, and act while the other role is to be gazed upon, measured, and passive. They begin to understand here that the usually disembodied, usually male figure who has the power to define and to valuate is seldom pictured in these ads, but that the woman presenting herself before the gaze is displayed for his approval and explication. Such critiques provide the students with explanatory vocabularies which they tend to wield in their journals and essays as they discuss their lives. Often they write authoritatively of spectators and spectacles, of gender and racial systems, and of social constructions.

While the class is certainly a feminist analysis of how beauty operates as sexism, it at the same time illustrates the more general process of how the body is the arena where asymmetrical power relations are acted out. This sets us up for discussing how the categories of normal and abnormal so fundamental to disability oppression are products of a social relationship in which one kind of person has the power to judge and to assume normativeness, while another must submit to judgment. The overwhelmingly female class is thus able to make a leap of identification between themselves as women, particularly black women and people who have disabilities: they come to understand that the process of objectification that is a part of the ideology of feminine beauty is related to the process of objectification that is a part of being considered disabled. Just such a dynamic between the defining subject and the defined object produces the traditional interpretation of physical disability as abnormality or inferiority. Examining this relationship allows us to uncover the power relations involved in the gaze not only in terms of gender and race, but also to relate that concept to "the stare" that is a specific form of social oppression for people with disabilities. The evaluating gaze of the male upon the female can be seen as parallel to the evaluating gaze of the "ablebodied" upon the disabled. One of the students' favorite readings, Alice Walker's autobiographical essay "Beauty" When the Other Dancer is the Self," specifically links disability to the politics of appearance as well as to the matrix of race, class, and gender. This essay interrelates Walker's becoming blind with her loss of femininity and worth and then chronicles how she regained a valued self image. Like the Marilyn Monroe story, this particularized narrative is popular with students because it manifests in an individual life the points that the cultural analyses explicate.

The course also highlights several cultural sites where ambiguity exists between beauty and disability to suggest that the coercive valuing of certain body types over others is what lies at the heart of both disability and beauty oppression. The first of these intersections is the nexus where prescriptions for beauty result in bodily transformations that amount to "disabilities." Discussing such historically and culturally varied practices as corseting, foot binding, clitorectomies, anorexia, and cosmetic surgery reveals to us the cultural relativity of the concept of disability, for such practices are understood in one context as the achievement of beauty or social acceptability and in another context as precisely the kind of bodily transformation that is taken to be a "disability." We particularly focus on cosmetic surgery because it is the practice for normalizing the (usually female) body that seems the least exotic, distanced, or pathological to modern American sensibilities. Indeed, many of the students accept the confessional mode I invite with the reading response journals to reveal anoretic or bulimic tendencies or admit to having considered cosmetic surgery to "improve" their looks or to "correct" what beauty has told them are their deficiencies. Because studies indicate that black women are generally more comfortable with their bodies than white women and generally suffer less frequently from eating disorders, I am surprised that many of my students disclose how inadequate they—often secretly—imagine their bodies to be, how tormented they are by these convictions, and how willing they would be to alter painfully their bodies to fit the standards. My suspicion is that the studies are measuring class differences more than race differences and that my students are responding to middle-class pressures to conform to beauty norms that underclass women, who are perhaps more alienated from mainstream requisites, might be spared.

Through framing cosmetic surgery as part of the beauty industry and ideology, students can recognize that the surgical normalization of the female body to meet cultural standards of beauty is parallel to the coercive "corrective" procedures that disabled people are often subjected to in order to reform their bodies to meet norms that they defy. Some of the images and discourses we examine are found in articles and ads on cosmetic surgery that are featured in women's magazines. Critically studying this marketing language enables students to understand how uniform the appearance standard is and how constructed it is even as it masquerades as natural and effortless. Perhaps most interesting is that with both disability and beauty the naturally occurring body is mutilated in order to conform to a standard that is presented to us as "regular" or "normal." Just as rhinoplasty and liposuction sculpt the "ugly" nose or the "fat" hips to the standard contours beauty dictates, surgeons "reconstruct" the disabled body and fit it with myriad prosthetics—often only to police life's physical variations, ones that are apparently so intolerable within contemporary American culture. It is this tyrannical concept of "normal," serving as it does capitalism, white supremacy, and patriarchy, that I want the students to come to question.

Mounting such a comprehensive cultural critique creates some pedagogical dilemmas I am not sure I successfully negotiate. By attacking beauty standards, even if I let the material speak for me, I risk implying that the students are complicit in their own oppression. What floats palpably in the classroom—coming from many sources—is the accusation of false consciousness, the suggestion that the students themselves are being castigated for their participation in beauty practices. More problematic yet is the logic inherent in the critique that caring about men is consorting with enemy. I try to address this problem directly by discussing the concept that there is no place outside acculturation for anyone to be, that we all want to be attentive to our appearance even as we try to avoid being in thrall to it. We talk much about placing ourselves in relation to beauty norms in ways that we can live with. Nevertheless, indictments erupt in class discussions that I try at once to defuse and to play out. The intense hair debate, provoked predictably by Alice Walker's witty and highly politicized essay about "oppressed hair," always provides a forum which at least exposes this dynamic even if we never resolve it. The discussion about what it means and whether or not a black woman should straighten her hair is highly charged with defensiveness, accusations, and humor, serving as a conduit to examining identity politics, the racism inherent in beauty standards, and the politicization of personal practices. The ever inconclusive hair question perhaps best illustrates the complexity of these issues.

Another dynamic that requires scrutiny is what I call coercive agreement. Most students' response to the concept of disability as a site of oppression is that they have never thought about it before. Many quickly and profoundly make the connections I hope to establish with race and gender, while some seem unreflectively to adopt an overly sympathetic attitude that I suspect may be in deference to me because I have a disability and am the teacher. This coercive agreement is one of the hazards of advocating in the classroom for a group to which you belong. Such a situation is one reason I prefer invoking as many manifestations of corporeally justified oppressive social relations as I can to analyze the larger processes at work.

One of the liveliest and most polarized of these instances always occurs around the issue of "fat," which lies in a zone somewhere between ugliness and disability, and is often the conduit through which female students come personally to identify with the social stigmatization that accompanies disabilities. While being overweight can constitute a functional disability, the students are quick to see that the social condemnation attached to being obese is usually far more detrimental than the impairment involved. Furthermore, the students' own struggle with our cultural tyranny of slimness enables them to recognize that bodily aberration is relative to a cultural and historically specific standard that serves particular interests, such as the cosmetic or fashion industries, for example. Again, autobiographical essays—Roberta Galler's about being disabled and Carol Munter's about being obese—are read together so that students can compare the subjective experiences of both women. As I mentioned before, my students seem to respond with greater understanding and interest to the personalizing mode of the individual life story presented in the subjective voice than they do to theorizing or historical surveys. While each writer concludes that society rather than their bodies needs to change, Munter's movingly account of the denigration of her body because it is fat presents an idea new to most students, who, of course, have internalized the script of blaming the overweight person rather than the impossible standards the culture of beauty demands. Yet, frequently arguments erupt in class when some students frame fat as unhealthy, undisciplined, and inexcusable excess while others fiercely defend themselves or friends and family as victims. Fat—which I point out legally constitutes a disability—is the subject most often mentioned in the reading response journals. It is remarkable how freely some students assail obese people in ways they would never openly denigrate people with disabilities, on the assumption that obesity can be altered by an act of will. The class never reaches consensus on this point or on the lively argument of whether it is appropriate for black women to straighten their hair. Nevertheless, the juxtaposition of disability and fat oppression emphasizes that often the cultural context surrounding and defining our bodies, not our bodies themselves, creates problems for us—and that this context rather than our bodies requires alteration.

To complement the autobiographical accounts and to move the issue of appearance from the individual body into the larger context of social relations and value systems that support power dynamics, we read as well excerpts from historical critiques of those systems such as Naomi Wolf's *The Beauty Myth*, Gerda Lerner's *The Creation of Patriarchy*, Simone de Beauvoir's *The Second Sex*, Elizabeth Spelman's *Inessential Woman*, and bell hooks's *Black Looks: Race and Representation*. Some students find the accounts of the systematic nature of sexist oppression to be a revelation that frees them from a sense of individual failure for their own insecurities as women, while others resist accounts of patriarchy as having so much historical force and precedence. One of the most persistent sentiments among many students—both male and female—is the narrow-minded and rather defensive conviction that women of this generation are fully liberated from the residue of sexism, that the problems are simply gone. It is interesting that students tend to recognize the enduring presence of racism, while insisting that society no longer limits women. Perhaps this is an important enabling progress narrative that should not be questioned; on the other hand, it risks denial and naivety. One of my most difficult challenges is to facilitate a comprehensive critique of systematic racism, sexism, and ableism while still encouraging empowerment and exploring modes of resistance.

So in order to expose the systematic nature of oppression without suggesting that it inevitably overwhelms individual agency, the first part of the course delineates the complex workings of oppression while the second part explores potential strategies of opposition. Because the course "Women in Literature" is offered as an English as well as a humanities course, literary analysis occupies a central place. To this end, we read two novels which place at the center of their social critiques the institution of feminine beauty as it is inflected with racial, class, and gender considerations. First is Toni Morrison's *The Bluest Eye*, a powerful novel which presents how the inextricable, institutionalized forces of racism, sexism, and classism combine to enact the tragic destruction of a young, black girl, abetted by the often unwitting complicity of the very community that might have saved her. The second is Alice Walker's novel *The Color Purple*, which provides a prescription for combatting the complex matrix of forces which attribute "ugly" to certain female bodies. While Morrison's is a descriptive account of the tragic political and personal consequences precipitated by what I am calling "the ideology of beauty," Walker's account offers students an optimistic paradigm for resistance and transformation. Morrison's novel is a tragedy which demonstrates the complexity and relentlessness of oppression and Walker's novel is a comedy (not a funny story but a painful tale with a happy ending) which details the triumphs of a woman over those same crushing forces. Taken together, the two novels constitute the dual aspect of cultural critique: a complex articulation of the problem in its multiple material manifestations and a speculative strategy for resistance.

As preparation for reading the assigned novels and autobiographical writings, we thoroughly discuss the issue of representation, stressing the ways that representation shapes the reality that it supposedly reflects. We examine the political and ethical consequences of literary representation by reading Susan Sontag's study *Illness as Metaphor*, which elaborates the metaphorical uses of tuberculosis in the nineteenth century and cancer in the twentieth century in order to suggest the negative consequences that these modes of cultural representation hold for people who have the diseases. Sontag's classic analysis thus allows us to use the representation of disability as a vehicle to understand the representation of race in Morrison's novel.

The juxtaposition of *The Bluest Eye* and *The Color Purple* form the center of the course. Around each novel are clustered the analytical or historical essays and the shorter biographical readings (all of which are listed at the end of this essay) so that Morrison's and Walker's narratives act as individualized testimonies to the concepts the course is designed to examine. The particularization of the issues that the novels accomplish gives the students a sense of reality and immediacy about the ways that the politics of appearance functions in the complexity of lived experience. Moreover, their journals, discussions, and essays suggest that the students are able to identify often in profound ways with the two central characters, Pecola and Celie, on the basis of their being judged as "ugly." What Morrison's novel allows the students to understand is that "ugliness" is not located in any objective physical criteria but instead in the ideological systems of denigration that produce "ugliness" as a condition of racism, sexism, and classism, not as a property of a particular body. Yet the students seem to find most compelling the emotional involvement they establish with the characters, the personalization of social and political issues that narrative and identification make available to them. My intention is to devastate them with Morrison and uplift them with Walker, for Celie transforms the sentence of ugliness not through Prince Charming nor cosmetic surgery nor weight loss nor any of the traditional prescriptions for female self-creation. Instead, Walker's Celie transfigures from ugliness not into beauty, but into personal empowerment catalyzed by female community, meaningful work, economic independence, sexual sovereignty, and loving recognition of others. Women in the class respond particularly favorably to *The Color Purple* because, I think, it enables them to imagine themselves escaping social judgments of their bodies.

When the class seems adept at articulating this transformation, I use it as an opportunity to move beyond racism, sexism, and disability by differentiating between what I call the traditional "narrative of overcoming" and another story I term the "narrative of resistance," both of which are common disability narratives. Although both narratives are affirmative and perhaps related, an essential distinction needs to be made. The conventional "narrative of overcoming" suggests that one's body is the recalcitrant object that must be surmounted, often either by some physical or psychological fear of rehabilitation or by a spiritual transcendence of the anomalous body. In contrast, the "narrative of resistance" claims rather than transcends the body, rejecting the traditional pronounce-ments of its inferiority and asserting the right of that body to be as it is. The notion of "resistance" thus locates the disabled or otherwise disapproved body within a cultural environment in which norms create deviance while the con-cept of "overcoming" places the deviance within the body deemed aberrant.

If on the one hand the novels act as touchstones for identification and understanding, on the other hand they also arouse the most profound resistance among students. In both Morrison's and Walker's novels a simplistic reading sug-gests that the women are victims and the men are perpetrators. Although I offer ample textual evidence that no easy polarity between innocent women and guilty men is supported by the texts, the subjects of incest and rape that the novels explore always spark discussions in which some students usually take entrenched positions which pit men against women. The conflict that is some-times fueled is exacerbated by the issue of racial solidarity and is shot through with suggestions of betrayal on both sides. Sometimes in class discussions, a great deal of hostility between men and women emerges that I must try to process sen-sitively and equitably. There are also always resistances to the critique of beauty that follow the logic that to reject beauty standards is to reject men. In every class, I feel that some students leave with the conviction that the course is essen-tially anti-male, no matter how much I attempt to present complexity and draw parallels among racism, sexism and ableism. The journals indicate that a few stu-dents choose to see beauty as innocent and me as a curmudgeon. Most often, some of the men hold this view, perhaps because they are emotionally identified with the male characters in the novels rather than with the women or perhaps because beauty is less anxiety provoking for them.

In conclusion, I need perhaps to offer a caveat concerning the position I have advocated so unequivocally here. It is important to recognize the limitations of the methodology that underlies the course that I am describing. By relating a variety of forms of social stigmatization, one risks failing to make clear the speci-ficity, the distinct character, of each form. In comparing the disability category with race or gender systems, one must be vigilant not to conflate them so as to suggest that racial categorization, for example, is the same thing as disability, but simply in another form. The distinguishing aspects of disability such as physical pain, impairment, onset and origin, social milieu, specific economic concerns, and the like must not be erased by the move toward embracing a minority model. Nor should we fall into the simplistic equation I often hear either that "every-body has a disability of some sort" or that "being a woman (or black) is a dis-ability." Comparing various forms of marginalized identities also risks invoking unproductive attempts to determine a hierarchy of oppression. I try with vary-ing degrees of success to shift discussions of who suffers more than whom into examinations of complexity, interrelatedness, and uniqueness. While it is useful and illuminating to make comparisons and seek out underlying similarities among stigmatizing processes, it is equally important to particularize each iden-tity so as to address precisely how it works in the world and how its attribution affects the persons involved.

COURSE READINGS AND WORKS CITED

Alexander, Elizabeth. "Cuvier." *The Venus Hottentot*. Charlottesville: University of Virginia Press, 1990. 3–7.

Bass, Alison. "When the Mirror Reflects a Distorted Self-Image." *Boston Globe* 21 October 1991: 27–29.

Berger, John. *Ways of Seeing*. London: BBC and Penguin Books, 1972. Chapter 3, 45–64.

Caputi, Jane E. "Beauty Secrets: Tabooing the Ugly Woman." *Forbidden Fruits: Taboos and Tabooism in Culture*. Ed. Ray Browne. Bowling Green: Popular Press, 1984. 36–55.

Clements, Marcelle. "The Mirror Cracked." *New York Times Magazine* 15 September 1991: 71–73.

Davis, Kathy. *Reshaping the Female Body: The Dilemma of Cosmetic Surgery*. New York: Routledge, 1995.

de Beauvoir, Simone. *The Second Sex*. Trans. and ed. H. M. Parshley. New York: Vintage Books, 1952. xv—xxiv.

Galler, Roberta. "The Myth of the Perfect Body." *Pleasure and Danger: Exploring Female Sexuality*. Ed. Carole S. Vance. Boston: Routledge & Kegan Paul, 1984. 165–172.

Gould, Stephen J. "The Hottentot Venus." *The Flamingo's Smile: Reflections in Natural History*. New York: W. W. Norton, 1985. 291–305.

hooks, bell. *Black Looks: Race and Representation*. London: Turnaround, 1992.

Lakoff, Robin. "Beauty and Ethnicity." *Face Value: The Politics of Beauty*. Boston: Routledge & Kegan Paul, 1984. 245–276.

Lerner, Gerda. *The Creation of Patriarchy*. New York: Oxford UP, 1986. 212–243.

Lorde, Audre. *Zami: A New Spelling of My Name*. Freedom, CA: The Crossing Press, 1982.

Morgan, Kathryn Pauly. "Women and the Knife: Cosmetic Surgery and the Colonization of Women's Bodies." *Hypatia* 6.3 (Fall 1991): 25–53.

Morrison, Toni. *The Bluest Eye*. New York: Washington Square Press, 1970.

Munter, Carol. "Fat and the Fantasy of Perfection." *Pleasure and Danger: Exploring Female Sexuality*. Ed. Carole S. Vance. Boston: Routledge & Kegan Paul, 1984. 225–231.

Piercy, Marge. "Hello Up There." *To Be of Use*. New York: Doubleday, 1969. 93.

———. "A Work of Artifice." *To Be of Use*. New York: Doubleday, 1969. 75.

———. "Unlearning Not to Speak." *To Be of Use*. New York: Doubleday, 1969. 97.

Sontag, Susan. *Illness as Metaphor*. New York: Farrar, Straus, and Giroux, 1977.

Steinem, Gloria. "The Body Prison." *Marilyn*. New York: New American Library, 1986. 137–154.

Wade, Cheryl Marie. "I am Not One of the." *Sinister Wisdom* (1987). Reprinted *Radical Teacher*.

Walker, Alice. *The Color Purple*. New York: Washington Square Press, 1982.

———. "Oppressed Hair Puts a Ceiling on the Brain." *Living by the Word: Selected Writings, 1973–1987*. San Diego: Harcourt Brace Jovanovich, 1988. 69–74.

———. "Beauty: When the Other Dancer is the Self." *In Search of Our Mothers' Gardens*. New York: Harcourt Brace Jovanovich, 1983. 384–393.

———. "Finding Celie's Voice." *Ms.* December 1985: 71–96.

Wolf, Naomi. "The Beauty Myth." *The Beauty Myth: How Images of Beauty Are Used Against Women*. New York: William Morrow, 1991. 9–19.

Young, Iris Marion. "Breasted Experience." *Throwing Like a Girl and Other Essays in Feminist Philosophy and Social Theory*. Bloomington: Indiana UP. 190–209.

———. "Women Recovering Our Clothes." *Throwing Like a Girl and Other Essays in Feminist Philosophy and Social Theory*. Bloomington: Indiana UP. 177–187.

17

Silence Is Not Without Voice

Including Deaf Culture within Multicultural Curricula

H. DIRKSEN L. BAUMAN AND JENNIFER DRAKE

At a time when universities work to incorporate multicultural curricula and canon revisions, they still perpetuate the pathologization of Deaf culture, language, and literature.[1] Most universities have yet to realize that Deaf people are not a loosely knit group of audiologically impaired individuals, but are, rather, a linguistic and cultural minority whose complex history, language, and literature warrant sustained recognition. Only a handful of American universities, for example, presently accept American Sign Language for legitimate language credit. As social science and humanities departments do not perceive Deaf studies to fall within their curricular domain, the study of "deafness" becomes relegated to special education departments—discursive straightjackets that confine Deaf culture to pathological constructions.

But what can a predominantly "hearing" university without a Deaf studies department do to rewrite these misunderstandings about the Deaf community? This is a question that we have been asking for different reasons and from different positions. When Dirkson crossed the border into a Deaf cultural space as a dormitory supervisor at the Colorado School for the Deaf and the Blind, he began to redefine his own pathological notions about Deaf persons. The Deaf students and faculty were not isolated and linguistically deprived as he had assumed; rather, they enjoyed a strong sense of community based on an "official" language. He, not the Deaf, became the linguistic outsider. Upon returning to a university setting, Dirksen found that even "progressive" language and literature faculty did not recognize American Sign Language as an "official" language or Deaf identity as a cultural identity.

Over the past few summers Jennifer had been creating the curriculum for "Narratives of Struggle," a writing course exploring the centrality of so-called marginal communities in forging American (multi)culture. When Dirksen became co-instructor for the course, the personal and pedagogical benefits of linking Jennifer's work in multicultural studies with Dirksen's work on Deaf culture became obvious. We hoped that the multicultural context of the course would encourage an engaged reading of Deafness as culture rather than deafness as disability, and that the texts on deafness as disability, and that the texts on

Deaf studies would disrupt hearing teachers' and students' reductive ways of thinking about culture, identity, and community.

We taught "Narratives of Struggle" as part of the 1994 Binghamton Enrichment Program (BEP) at SUNY's Binghamton University. BEP is part of New York State's Educational Opportunity Program (EOP) at Binghamton, which provides academic support to students from educationally and economically disadvantaged backgrounds. As such, students in the Binghamton Enrichment Program come from the working class or working poor; some come from group homes or foster care; many grew up in single-parent families; most are from New York City, though a few live upstate; and the majority are of African, Caribbean, Latino, and/or Asian descent.

Students enrolled in "Narratives of Struggle" also enrolled in "Media (Ill) Literacy and Self-Governance," taught by Kassie Fleisher. While the media studies course taught students to read the media's representations of "truth" in critical and complex ways, our writing course looked at texts that bell hooks would call "critical fixtures"—texts that resist dominant discourses, challenge our expectations of what "literature" is/does, and require the development of engaged reading strategies. Hooks's essay "Narratives of Struggle," in Philomena Mariani's *Critical Fictions: The Politics of Imaginative Writing*, served as the template for the course, providing students with a critical vocabulary—"(de)colonization," "political self-recovery," "resistance," "imagination"—that they could use, and struggle with, throughout the course.

Each week had its own thematic focus, such as "Resisting Silences/Finding Voices," "Hybridity and Cultural Survival," and "(De)Colonization, Coalition Building, and Difference." At the start of each week the class wrestled with the meanings and implications of these titles by brainstorming associations on the chalkboard, unpacking dictionary definitions, returning to hooks's essay, and playing with the critical possibilities suggested by these title phrases.

Discussions of Deaf culture first occurred directly after reading Maxine Hong Kingston's "Song for a Barbarian Reed Pipe" during the "Resisting Silences/Finding Voices" week. This juxtaposition of texts and cultures worked to extend and to complicate the discussions of language and (multi)cultural identity, voice, and silence that we had begun in response to Kingston's work. Student facilitator Vivian Lei began a lively discussion about whether or not silences can work as a strategy of resistance and about how one person's silence is another person's expressiveness—think of Kingston's black paintings "full of possibility," about to reveal "mighty operas." Faced with the difference between Kingston's empowering reading of her own paintings and her teacher's pathologization of them, students began to talk about negotiating two or more languages and cultures. While some students focused on their own and Kingston's struggles to live "inbetween" and the pressure to assimilate, others described the benefits of drawing on two languages and cultural traditions, pointing out that "inbetweenness" might be lived not as culture clash but as a powerful position from which to speak and construct personal and community identities.

These conversations about language, culture, assimilation, and resistance provided a strong transition into discussions of Deaf culture as represented in Mark Medoff's play *Children of a Lesser God* and excerpts from Bernard Bragg's *Lessons in Laughter: The Autobiography of a Deaf Actor*, as signed to Eugene Bergman. Bragg's autobiography raises issues of the role of education as a means to coerce assimilation into "hearing" culture. Student facilitators Silvia Sanchez and Sabrina Lebron led the class through a close reading of Bragg's title scene in which a hearing teacher forces his Deaf students to laugh like "humans," that is, hearing people. Students were appalled that hearing culture could be so coercive and violent in the name of education.

We then moved on to Medoff's play, which also takes up the role of education in disciplining "cultural subjects." In addition, since Medoff is a hearing playwright, the play opens up discussion about "hearing" representations of Deaf persons. These issues of representation become especially pronounced when the written text of the play is juxtaposed with the film version. Silvia and Sabrina, for example, brought in film clips in order to illustrate the film's depoliticization of Deafness in favor of the love story, which, they agreed, was more likely to sell movie tickets. Reading and watching these two textual representations of Deafness as imagined by hearing people encouraged the class to reflect upon our own situation as a hearing classroom talking about Deaf culture. In this situation, hearing students and teachers might think of themselves not as speaking in place of Deaf people—for Deaf people may "speak" through texts and invited lecturers and performers—but rather, as hearing people engage in self-reflective conversation about the audist oppression of the Deaf community.

Student Youlla Pierre chose to write one of her papers about *Children of a Lesser God* in order to explore more fully dominant cultural assumptions about the Deaf community. In the following passage, she articulates the differences between "hearing" and "listening," "silence" and "deafness:"

> Hearing is when you have heard what a person has said and you learn and empathize with that person. . . . Deaf means that due to biological reasons you were born without the ability to hear voices. It could also mean that you are unwilling to hear. The word silence means not speaking with your voice or it could also mean that you, unwillingly or willingly, want to communicate using other methods . . . [The Deaf] have the knowledge to communicate in other ways . . . that may not be known to us . . . Maybe that makes us hearing people the silent ones to them.

Youlla went on to illustrate her ideas by writing about two major characters in the play: Sarah is a strong Deaf woman and James, Sarah's hearing husband and a teacher at the school for the Deaf, tries to teach Sarah to speak. Drawing on Friere's discussion of the "deposits" made in banking education and hooks's discussion of colonized minds, Youlla writes:

> James had a colonized mind . . . James became fearful of Sarah's independence because what would society think of a person who cannot overpower or as they would put it nicely, "help" a "disabled" person? . . . And since society had thrust

upon him the idea that he had to take care of her . . . he thought that society would think less of him because he would not be able to control his "disabled" child. So because of that feeling, James ended up turning a "deaf" ear to Sarah . . . He only thought of himself and his need for her to [talk]. He did not leave himself any room to empathize with Sarah at all.

In her paper, Youlla continued to connect the inability to "hear" with the inability to listen and to empathize in order to argue that the dominant culture is "disabled" by its inability to listen to the "voices" of different communities. By creating the distinction between biological and empathetic deafness, Youlla articulated a convincing argument for depathologizing Deaf identity.

Clearly, discussing Deaf language and culture in a multicultural context encouraged students to consider that American Sign Language is a "real" language and that the Deaf are a "real" cultural community. For example, a paper by Amoy Chambers argued that bell hooks's call for "political self-recovery" requires the use of so-called "minority" languages like American Sign Language. Reading a scene from the film in which Sarah starts dancing with James but ends up dancing with herself and loving it, Amoy suggests that Sarah resists the label "disabled" by claiming an identity based on the powerful expressiveness of her body's movements in dance and sign. Amoy also links the political and cultural struggles of the Deaf community to other resistance movements:

> If sign language is a recognized language, then why is it not implemented in our curriculum as other languages are? So, society is overtly disregarding another culture, as it always does . . . society is not willing to acknowledge subjects/people that are different.

As the course continued, this acknowledgement of Deaf persons as cultural subjects dovetailed with discussions about identity-formation within multiple communities, including educational institutions such as the classroom and the university where our discussions were taking place. Students began to see that the family is not the only site for the transmission of cultural identity and that communities include, and are built from, our differences and multiple allegiances.

Including texts about Deaf culture in a multicultural curriculum demonstrated to students that "culture" cannot be thought of monolithically only in terms of "race." This realization opened the way for strong discussions of essays by Gloria Anzaldúa and Audre Lorde, in which the writers resist bearing allegiance to one community/self at the expense of another. In fact, students began to think about Anzaldúa's and Lorde's lesbianism in terms of "culture" and "community" and so, congruent with our discussions of Deaf culture, began to move away from a reductive pathologization of homosexuality. In later weeks, students continued to talk about the Deaf, gays, lesbians, and virtually all American cultures and subjectivities as hybrid, multicultural identities and so began to link various resistance struggles to their own struggles against racism and classism.

When approached with critical awareness, incorporating Deaf culture into multicultural curricula can bear substantial rewards for both Deaf and hearing communities. For the Deaf, recontextualizing Deaf identity in a cultural framework alongside Latinos, African-Americans, Chinese-Americans, gays and lesbians, and other cultural/racial/ethnic groups represents significant advancement toward the recognition that the Deaf community is a linguistic minority in the United States. In addition, hearing students introduced to the relevant historical, political, and social issues surrounding Deaf culture are encouraged to expand and to challenge their existing notions of multiculturalism, disability, and language. Such expansion of terms becomes a useful means of developing a wider, more inclusive critical consciousness among students and teachers whose notions of multiculturalism tend to over-determine race at the expense of other significant and simultaneous sites of difference. Such reciprocal benefits to the Deaf and hearing communities serve to emancipate both from oppressive misconceptions about disability, language, and cultural identity.

NOTE

We use "Deaf," rather than "deaf," in order to distinguish between Deaf people who identify with Deaf culture and deaf people who do not. This distinction also helps to clarify the differences between Deaf education (bilingual/bicultural education) and deaf education (the historically hearing-dominated forms of education based on the medical view of deafness).

part six

Disability and Culture

18

Toward a Poetics
of Vision, Space, and the Body

Sign Language and Literary Theory[1]

H. DIRKSEN L. BAUMAN

> Suppose that we had no voice or tongue, and wanted to communicate with one another, should we not, like the deaf . . . make signs with the hands and head and the rest of the body?
>
> —Plato *The Cratylus* (212)

An exchange between literary theory and sign languages is long overdue. Centuries overdue: for as early as Plato's *Cratylus*, Western "hearing" intellectuals have been aware of the manual languages of Deaf[2] communities, but twenty-five centuries since Plato, we remain largely ignorant that our concepts of language and literature have evolved within a false dualism of speech and writing. Only as recently as William Stokoe's linguistic research in the 1960s, have we realized that Sign[3] is an "official" human language with the capacity to generate a nearly infinite number of propositions from a vast lexicon. Yet, while linguists have been exploring this revolution in language, literary critics remain largely unaware that Sign is a natural linguistic mode capable of producing a body of literature.[4] This body of literature is, rather, a literature of the body that transforms the linear model of speech and writing into an open linguistic field of vision, time, space, and the body.

As Sign literature emerges in the late twentieth century, we can only wonder how its absence has helped to shape our ideas about language, literature, and the world. We must wonder if Sign's absence has lead to hidden limits and desires in our relationship to language. One could, perhaps, argue that speech and writing have been searching for their visual/spatial counterpart since Simonides of Keos' formulation that "poetry is speaking painting" while "painting is mute poetry," and extending through, among others, Horace's dictum *ut pictura poesis*, centuries of religious "pattern poetry,"[5] Blake's illustrations, Stein's cubism, Pound's ideograms, Olson's hieroglyphics, concrete poetry, performance poetry, ethnopoetics, video-texts, and virtual texts. These experiments have, in their various ways, sought to imbue speech and writing with the visual and spatial dimensions of images and the body. Have these experiments emerged out of a phantom-limb phenomenon where writers have sensed language's severed visual-spatial mode and went groping after it?[6] If the Deaf poet had been mythologized as the blind poet has been, would literature have developed differently? Would the map which draws the historical relation between visual and literary arts have to be redrawn? What sorts of genres would have emerged? Would our metaphysical heritage have been different if we were not only the speaking but also the "signing animal"?

While these questions are beyond the scope of the present essay, they lead toward its general purpose: to show that what many scholars would consider the marginal literary practices (if you can even call them "literary") of "disabled" persons is, on the contrary, of central importance to any one, hearing or Deaf, who is interested in the relations of language and literature to culture, identity, and being. In order to recognize Sign as a medium for literature, we must open an exchange between Sign and theory by exploring ways that theory enhances our understanding of Sign and ways that Sign enhances—and challenges—our understanding of theory and literature. This opening exchange will ask numerous questions that will gesture toward a more in-depth study of Sign literature.

The following dialogue between Sign and theory is more like a conference call between Sign and interconnected and contradictory areas of criticism: deconstruction, cultural studies (at the intersection of feminism/postcolonialism/multiculturalism), semiotics, and phenomenology. Rather than applying a monolithic paradigm, I hope to assemble a collection of perspectives that will offer the best vantage points from which to explore a nonwritten, spatial form of literature. This eclectic approach is especially important as the small body of criticism of Sign literature remains rooted in one-dimensional approaches. The formalist analyses of Clayton Valli and Edward Klima and Ursula Bellugi and the semiotic approaches of Jim Cohn and Heidi Rose are much needed contributions to their field, but are unable to place Sign literature in its proper historical, political, metaphysical perspective—which is the goal of this present study. My intent, though, is ultimately not to feed Sign poems through a convoluted critical machine to produce insightful "readings" or rather, "viewings"; instead, one hopes these concepts and connections will eventually develop dialogically with Sign poetic practices themselves.

DECONSTRUCTION AND DEAFNESS:
PHONOCENTRISM, AUDISM, AND SIGN LANGUAGE

The exchange between theory and Sign should open, appropriately, with Jacques Derrida, for it is he who has brought the importance of nonphonetic linguistic modalities to the forefront of twentieth-century thought by severing the "natural" connection between the voice and language. The voice, Derrida believes, is more than a means of communicating—it is the source for Western ideas of truth, being, and presence. The system of "hearing-oneself-speak," Derrida contends, "has necessarily dominated the history of the world during an entire epoch, and has even produced the idea of the world, the idea of world-origin" (8). This constitutive role of the voice results from the self-presence created by hearing-oneself-speak. One's own voice is completely interior, fully present to the speaker; it is the source of self-identity, of self-presence. Meaning constituted within this full-presence then becomes the standard for notions of identity, precipitating a metaphysics based on the full-presence of self, meaning, and identity. The privileging of the voice, which Derrida calls "phonocentrism," is the linguistic phenomenon that leads toward "logocentrism," the Western metaphysical orientation which perceives meaning to be anchored by the self-presence of identity. Against this tradition, Derrida recognizes that the voice has no natural primacy over nonphonetic forms of language and that the metaphysics of presence is infused with the free-play and undecidability of language. Seeking to deconstruct phonocentric metaphysics, Derrida explores nonphonetic forms of language—hieroglypics, ideograms, algebraic notations, and nonlinear writing. His explorations lead beyond phonocentric linguistics toward "grammatology," a science of writing and textuality.

When seen through deconstructive lenses, Sign dilates its sphere of influence from the sociopolitical site of the Deaf community to the entire history of Western "hearing" metaphysics. With its deconstruction of the voice-centered tradition, grammatology, one might say, initiates a "Deaf philosophy"—if it weren't for the fact that Derrida fails to engage theoretical issues of deafness or signing to any significant degree. The exchange between Sign and deconstruction, then, recognizes the metaphysical implications of Sign while Sign, in turn, extends the project of deconstruction beyond its own limitations drawn by the exclusion of Sign and Deaf history.

The theoretical significance of "deafness," in this sense, takes on new historical and metaphysical importance that pathologized "deafness" cannot. If nonphonetic writing interrupts the primacy of the voice, deafness signifies the consummate moment of disruption. Deafness exiles the voice from the body, from meaning, from being; it sabotages its interiority from within, corrupting the system which has produced the "hearing" idea of the world. Deafness, then, occupies a consummate moment in the deconstruction of Western ontology. Further, deafness does more than disrupt the system of "hearing-oneself-speak"; it creates an embodied linguistic system which, unlike speech, is not fully present to itself. Signers, unless gazing into the mirror, do not fully see themselves signify. While they may see their hands, they cannot see their own face perform much of Sign's grammatical nuances. The eye, unlike the ear in the system of "hearing-oneself-speak," can only partially "see-oneself-sign." There is always a trace of nonpresence in the system of signing.

One wonders, then, if Derrida had engaged the theoretical implications of deafness and Sign further, might he have expanded the term "Sign" as he did "Writing" to signify *differance*, Derrida's neologism that cannot be spoken but only seen, signifying that phonetic writing is not simply a copy of speech. At this point, we can only begin to conjecture what sort of different philosophical resonance would occur by re-reading deconstruction with regards to Sign in the place of—or in addition to—writing.

While Derrida does not engage the theoretical implications of deafness or

Sign in any depth, he does entertain Rousseau's contradictory relation to the language of gesture, which Rousseau attributes to Deaf persons on occasion. Early in the *Essay on the Origin of Human Languages* when Rousseau imagines that a society could develop arts, commerce, government—all without recourse to speech. After all, Rousseau writes, "The mutes of great nobles understand each other and understand everything that is said to them by means of signs, just as well as one can understand anything said in discourse" (*Essay* 9). This observation leads Rousseau to muse that "the art of communicating our ideas depends less upon the organs we use in such communication than it does upon a power proper to man, according to which he uses his organs in this way, and which, if he lacked these, would lead him to use others to the same end" (10). Derrida seizes on this nonphonocentric moment in Rousseau to destablize the primacy of the voice in Western philosophy. "It is once again the power of substituting one organ for another," Derrida writes, "of articulating space and time, sign and voice, hand and spirit, it is this faculty of supplementarity which is the true origin—or nonorigin—of languages" (241). As the condition leading toward the supplement, deafness could be read, ironically, as that which makes the origin of language possible. Deafness summonses up the visual-spatial dimension of language to supplant the voice from within. It sets *differance* in motion.

This inversion of deafness—from linguistic isolation to the precondition of language itself—has political implications for the Deaf community's difficult task of depathologizing Deaf identity within the culture of academia. After considering deafness in relation to deconstruction, one may begin to see the Deaf community—not as a group defined by its pathological relation to language—but rather as an example of a culture flourishing beyond the reaches of logocentrism. The possibility of such a community raises questions. Is resisting phonocentrism tantamount to resisting logocentrism? What are the phenomenological differences between "being-in-the-deaf-world" and "being-in-the-hearing-world"? Are Deaf persons—over ninety percent of whom are born in hearing families— really out of reach of logocentrism? By raising issues surrounding Sign to the metaphysical level, could the argument for a Deaf cultural identity be expanded beyond the anthropological and socio-linguistic identifications of distinctly "Deaf" cultural acts—such as Deaf folklore, jokes, attention getting strategies, and social organizations—to encompass a deeper level: a level that Sign and "not-hearing-oneself-speak" creates outside of hearing-dominated metaphysics?

Given the relevance of these questions to grammatology, it is surprising that Derrida never engages signing and deafness as theoretically and historically significant issues.[7] When he does mention deafness it is through the "voices" of others: Hegel, Leibniz, Rousseau, and Saussure. Making others speak about deafness is a strange ventriloquism which demonstrates that Derrida is aware, obviously, of Sign and Deaf communities. One may link this critical oversight as being symptomatic of not really *seeing* Deaf people, of tacitly acknowledging their absence from being. If this is so, this audist oversight reinscribes the very phonocentrism Derrida sets out to deconstruct. At the very least, one may accuse Derrida's grammatology of suffering from an undertheorized sociopolitical site because he neglects Deaf history. While he considers logocentrism to be "the most original and powerful ethnocentrism," (3) he does not follow this statement to its most severe sociopolitical manifestation: audism.

Audism is the most extreme deployment of phonocentrism ranging from incarcerating Deaf persons in mental institutions, to eugenics movements (one sponsored by Alexander Graham Bell in America, another currently practiced in China), to the oppression of sign language in the education of Deaf persons. Many Deaf adults today tell of their violent experiences growing up in oralist schools—their hands slapped or tied behind their backs if they were caught signing.[8] Further, early Deaf schools offered a collection of subjugated bodies on which doctors could develop the science of otology. Acids, needles, and hammers all violated the ears and skulls of Deaf children so that they could be returned to "normal."[9]

While he could have made many relevant connections between phonocentrism and oralist educational practices, Derrida instead labels the condemnation of Leibniz's desire for a nonphonetic, universal script as "the most energetic eighteenth-century *reaction* organizing the defense of phonologism and of logocentric metaphysics" (99). I propose, instead, that the history of deaf education, as it is marked by violent oppression of sign and the subjugation of Deaf persons, is a more "energetic reaction" to phonocentrism. It is where phonocentrism meets social and educational policy. Indeed, nowhere will one find a more vehement declaration of voice-as-presence than by reading the words of oralist educators. Consider, for example, the following declaration from the father of deaf education in German-speaking lands:

> The breath of life resides in the voice. . . . The voice is a living emanation of that spirit that God breathed into man when he created him a living soul . . . What stupidity we find in most of these unfortunate deaf . . . How little they differ from animals. (Lane, 107)

This all too common association between Deaf persons and animals offers arguably the most vivid illustration of Derrida's central connection between voice and human presence. As Douglas Baynton, Harlan Lane, and others have shown, Deaf identity has been publically constructed through metaphorics of animality, darkness, imprisonment, and isolation, resulting in a relay of hierarchized binary oppositions which divide along the axis of absence and presence: animal/human; prisoner/property owner; foreigner/citizen; darkness/light; normality/ pathology. Just as the Deaf voice is exiled from its own body, Deaf persons have been exiled from the phonocentric body-politic.

One hopes these initial ideas point toward a future critical project of exploring a grammatology of Sign that recognizes Sign's historical and metaphysical context while also documenting phonocentrism's political legacy. Such a project, however, would require a broader theoretical base than grammatology itself offers. If Sign criticism is to be an instrumental means of spreading the recognition of Sign literature and Deaf culture, it needs to articulate itself as an oppositional discourse alongside others which oppose oppression in its various forms. For this reason, Sign criticism would benefit from exploring its relation with feminism, postcolonialism, and multiculturalism, in addition to deconstruction.

FEMINISM/POSTCOLONIALISM/MULTICULTURALISM AND SIGN LITERATURE

Inviting feminism, postcolonialism, and multiculturalism into a dialogue with deconstruction brings together an uneasy alliance. It has become a critical cliche, for example, to accuse deconstruction of decentering the human subject just as disempowered groups were gaining empowered subjectivities. Despite important differences, however, deconstruction may find its greatest alliance with these oppositional discourses in its dismantling of phonocentrism and audism. Instead of exhuming well-documented contentions, therefore, it seems more advantageous to draw together overlapping concerns in order to form a broad textual, social, and political context for the emergence of Deaf/Sign literature.

Forming such a coalition of ideas is based on Audre Lorde's belief that sexism, homophobia, and racism are "particular manifestations of the same disease" (137)—as are ethnocentrism, colonialism, ableism, and audism. "Can any one here," Lorde asks, "still afford to believe that the pursuit of liberation can be the sole and particular province of any one particular race, or sex, or age, or religion, or sexuality, or class?" (140). Indeed, we cannot—nor can we continue to neglect the commonly elided category of "ability" from this "pursuit of liberation."

In clearing a space to talk about Deaf culture and Sign literature, a number of questions arise in the initial dialogue between Deaf studies and each area: feminism, postcolonialism, and multiculturalism; and from those questions, a few overlapping concerns may be identified that will form ways of talking about Sign literature in a political and cultural context. This exchange will, one hopes, begin to build for Deaf studies a strong sociopolitical foundation while Deaf studies, in turn, may expand the "pursuit of liberation" to include ableism and audism which are frequently overlooked by an overdetermination of racism and sexism.

The project of recognizing Deaf identity bears similarities to the feminist project of re-gaining a "body of one's own" through linguistic and literary practices. Sign, in a more graphic way, perhaps, than *l'écriture feminine* is a "writing of/on the body." The relation between Sign and *l'écriture feminine* raises questions that could have interesting implications for feminist performance. Does the anti-phonocentric nature of Sign offer a means of averting the essentializing tendency of *l'écriture feminine* ? Does the four-dimensional space of performance offer ways of deconstructing phallogocentric linear discourse? How does the gender of the signer influence the reading/viewing of the "text" itself? How does the male gaze construct the female body/text? Can gender ever be bracketed out of a reading of a Sign performance?

Many of these feminist issues anticipate those of postcolonial discourse. At first glance, though, one would not think of Deaf persons as being "colonized"—disciplined, yes, but colonized? However, as Harlan Lane shows, audism is homologous with colonialism, including "the physical subjugation of a disempowered people, the imposition of alien language and mores, and the regulation of education in behalf of the colonizer's goals" (32). How accurate is Lane's position? Could one consider medicine's often brutal experimentation on the ears of Deaf children a form of physical subjugation? Could the controversial surgical procedure used to restore hearing—the cochlear implant—be considered a form of colonizing the Deaf body and eradicating a Deaf culture? Is the effort to impose English-only in Deaf residential schools similar, say, to forcing Native Americans to adopt a nationalized language and identity in residential schools? Is the fact that oral-based pedagogies exclude Deaf persons from deaf education a means of securing hearing dominance over the Deaf community? How does a postcolonial writer/signer resist the hegemony of dominant literature while working within the field of literature?

In addition, if Sign literature is to be considered as an "ethnic" literature, it should inquire into its relation to other minority literatures and their ethnic origins. The very claim that Deaf identity is cultural rather than pathological provokes an interrogation of our assumed "natural" categories of cultural identity. How can Deaf persons share a cultural identity if they do not have a common religion, nationality, race, or ethnicity? Do predominantly "Deaf spaces," such as Deaf residential schools and Deaf clubs, constitute a type of national 'homeland'? How does Deaf identity intersect with other simultaneous subject positions— gender, race, nationality, class? Would a Deaf American feel more "at home" with, say, a Deaf Japanese than a hearing American from around the block? Is it possible to acknowledge the strength of Deaf identity but not fall into the trap of hierarchizing identities? Is Deaf culture, as it crosses national, racial, and economic borders, an emblematic postmodern culture? And finally, how does a postmodern theory of Deaf culture influence a theory of Sign literature?

This initial meeting of Deaf studies, Sign literature, and cultural studies helps to identify a few underlying concepts—anti-essentialism, hybridity, and border consciousness—that will be helpful in providing a political context for discussing Sign literature. Because of the relay between logocentrism, phonocentrism, and audism, any critical practice of Sign literature needs to move beyond logocentric ways of looking at identity—that is, basing one's identity on essentialized definitions such as "speech is an *essential* human trait" or "whites are *essentially* more intelligent than other races." Instead, we need to recognize identities as constantly being constructed within a complex network of social, political, and linguistic influences. Such anti-essentialist thinking is important, for, as Edward Said comments, "essentialisms have the power to turn human beings against one another" by allowing us to slide into "an unthinking acceptance of stereotypes, myths, animosities, and traditions encouraged by imperialism" (229). If audism is itself a form of essentialist thinking, then Deaf resistance to it should not be a reinscription of it. We need to recognize, then, that a person cannot be *purely* Deaf apart from the confluence of multiple subject positions—nationality, race, gender, class, disability, sexual preference—just as one cannot be *purely* Female, Mexican, or Asian. Avoiding an essentialist view of Deaf identity would be the equivalent of avoiding what Frantz Fanon calls "the pitfalls of national consciousness" that reinscribes the oppressive essentialism of colonialism.

As opposed to an essentialized "national" or "audist" consciousness, Sign literature might be more effectively approached through a "border consciousness" that recognizes the uniqueness of Deaf culture and Sign literature, but that also acknowledges their social construction. Indeed, the institutional patterns of Deaf cultural transmission offer a particularly postmodern example of the constructed rather than essential nature of identity. Over ninety percent of Deaf persons do not form their cultural identity through their family but through social organizations and institutions. As Carol Padden and Tom Humphries explain, one learns to be Deaf, not through an essential "presence of a common physical condition," but by gaining "access to a certain cultural history, the culture of Deaf people in America" (25). To paraphrase Simone de Beauvoir's famous statement about female identity: one is not born but rather becomes Deaf. Such a perspective of Deaf identity has bearing on the ways we discuss Sign literature; for, as Edward Said reminds us, we need to recognize that all "cultural forms are hybrid, mixed, impure, and the time has come in cultural analysis to reconnect their analysis with their actuality" (14).

In fact, the notion of "Sign literature" is itself a product of hearing/Deaf borderlands. As the term "literature" derives from the Latin *litere*, or "letter," "Sign literature" is oxymoronic in the same sense as "oral literature." Because of the inaccuracy of the label, Heidi Rose has proposed that creative use of American Sign Language be known as "ASL ART" which "should be studied as a distinct phenomenon, not as some sort of hybrid between the written and oral form" ("Critical Methodology," 15). Rose's re-definition raises interesting ontological questions regarding the definition of Sign literature. Yet, rather than establishing a wholesale re-definition, it may be wise to let the question of ASL "literature" remain just that, a question. The desire to define whether creative use of ASL is or is not "literature," I feel, unnecessarily limits the discussion to an essentialized either/or opposition. The issues involved in making such a distinction are far too complex and important to both hearing and Deaf communities to be reduced to such a dichotomy. Rather than offering a totalizing answer, it may be wise to tolerate the ambiguity that ASL "art" both *is* and *is not* "literature," that it is akin to hearing literary practices, but also cannot be contained by those practices.[10]

There are too many political and analytical benefits of discussing creative Sign as literature to banish it from the curricular domain of literature. These benefits have been demonstrated best, perhaps, by Clayton Valli who has defined such techniques as "lines" and "rhymes" in Sign poetry. In his essay, "The Nature of a Line in ASL Poetry," Valli explains how an ASL poet creates signed "lines" through visual rhyme patterns. A signed rhyme is made through a repetition of particular handshapes, movement paths, sign locations, or nonmanual markers such as facial expressions or body postures. For example, in his poem, "Snowflake," Valli employs visual rhyme by repeating the same "five" handshape (palm open, all fingers extended) to sign TREE, then to draw the outline of the leaves on the tree, and then to show the leaves falling to the ground. In addition, Valli and others accept the same genre distinctions for Sign as for hearing literature. Identifying such hearing-centered literary analogues demonstrates that Sign can be explored creatively to produce as linguistically complex "texts" as can speech and writing. That Sign can partake in the literary traditions of the West is an indispensable argument in convincing universities to recognize Sign literature, a move which would continue to depathologize Deaf identity in the minds of hearing persons.

However, uncritically adopting the signifier of "literature" dismisses the fact that "literature has been formed within exclusive practices of spoken and written languages. As the linear model is the structural embodiment of hearing forms of literature, Valli's concept of the "line" places Sign literature directly within a phonocentric/audist tradition. Why even concern ourselves with the discussions of "lines" and "rhymes"? What sort of political, historical, and metaphysical baggage do those terms carry? How well can the terms of an aural/temporal art be applied to a visual-spatial art? In order to discuss Sign as literature, then, one must proceed through the lexicon of hearing criticism and interrogate the terms for their imbedded audist ideologies and their critical accuracy. In some instances, terminology can take on new dimensions when it crosses the inter-semiotic gap to visual/spatial language—or old dimensions, as with "rhythm" which originated, not in the musical arts, but in dance.[11] Within Sign criticism, the concept of rhythm may be restored to its original connection with the movements of the body in time and space.

In fact, there is no reason to confine a lexicon for Sign literature to the literary arts. As a visual performance art, Sign literature may bear more similarity to painting, dance, drama, film, and video than to poetry or fiction. A "line" in Sign poetry, for example, might be more accurately modelled after the concept of the "line" in painting or a choreographed "phrase" in dance. Instead of moving from left to right, the Sign poet draws lines through space in all directions. In addition, given the cinematic nature of ASL,[12] the Sign lexicon must be expanded to include such concepts as "editing," "montage," "panning," "close-up," and "slow-motion." Indeed, why not go so far as to invent a new vocabulary in Sign and then translate that lexicon into written glosses for ASL signs?

This "border theory" asks us to consider ways to avert a reductive either/or response to Sign literature; it asks us how we may refer to it in such a way that always already implies resistance to being called "*literature*"; it asks us to see Sign literature as a hybrid creation, at once unique to Deaf cultural experience, but also crossing over a multitude of national, economic, racial, ethnic, gendered, sexual, linguistic, artistic, and textual borders. Identifying the borders that a particular poem, narrative, or performer crosses over, invites critical dialogue about the relations between minority and dominant literatures, between Deaf and hearing worlds, and between Deaf identity and Sign literature.

One hopes that, as Trinh Minh-ha writes, "this shuttling in-between frontiers is a working out of and an appeal to another sensibility, another consciousness of the condition of marginality: that in which marginality is the condition of the center" (216). The ultimate scope of this project, then, is to recognize the previously marginalized body of Sign literature, and in so doing to expose the false dualism of speech and writing that has helped to structure the hearing "center" of Western civilization.

TOWARD A "POETICS OF SPACE":
FROM SEMIOTICS TO PHENOMENOLOGY

If Sign literature offers a rare opportunity to reconsider what literature is, then Sign criticism needs to amass the critical breadth for such an undertaking. The first step is to move beyond Sign criticism's preoccupation with formalist linguistic analysis. The writings of Clayton Valli, Edward Klima, and Ursula Bellugi offer a useful vocabulary for describing a Sign's physical and linguistic characteristics, but they are unable to explore the wider metaphysical, sociopolitical, and phenomenological dimensions of Sign literature. As linguists, these writers are more concerned with demonstrating ASL's depth and flexibility than with exploring a fundamental rethinking of the way that literature is produced and perceived.

Heidi Rose is one of the first persons to break away from linguistic formalism to discuss Sign literature in the context of a more contemporary criticism—semiotics. In her essay, "A Semiotic Analysis of Artistic American Sign Language and a Performance of Poetry," Rose makes a significant contribution toward a theory of Sign literature by applying C. S. Peirce's semiotics to a reading of a signed poem. According to Peirce, signs (not ASL "signs," but rather anything that produces meaning) can take three different forms: icon (representation by likeness, e.g., portrait, onomatopoeia), index, (representation by relation, e.g., smoke to fire, temperature to fever) and symbol (representation by arbitrary signifiers, e.g., conventional words). Unlike speech and writing, Sign is most often associated with iconic signification. Rose agrees that Sign's unique character is its iconicity, but only after demonstrating that a Sign poem is more complex than a series of manual pictures in the air. During the course of a performance, Rose explains, the hands may sign on the iconic or symbolic levels while the nonmanual markers (i.e., facial expressions) tend to produce indexical meaning. In the end, though, the noniconic elements of the poem "flesh out the manual signs and complete the message with the final effect highlighting the iconic means of communication" (154). The body signifies differently throughout the course of a poem, though its ultimate goal, according to Rose, is to embody iconic images, to move closer to the thing-itself.

Underlying Rose's analysis (and the existing body of Sign criticism), however, is the assumption that iconicity is an inherent and constant element within the text, independent of the viewer's relationship to the poem. This assumption is closely allied with another: that Peirce's semiotic taxonomy is mutually exclusive and stable. Deaf critic Joseph Grigely, however, demonstrates that semiotics cannot, in the end, produce the predictable science of language that it had hoped. "Peirce's taxonomy of signs," Grigely writes, "is essentially an unstable ontology, and that the attribution of sign values—iconicity, indexicality, and arbitrariness—is part of a dynamic process by which a reader circumscribes frames of reference as part of the act of reading" (243). While Grigely discusses but does not focus on Sign poetry, he helps Sign criticism to move beyond its preoccupation with iconicity to engage the larger process of how iconicity is itself produced and received. In "The Implosion of Iconicity," Grigely writes:

> Every time we claim to discover an iconic presence—be it an onomatope like "moo-cow" or in a visual analogue like the ASL sign for TREE—our discovery is actually a hermeneutic act, an interpretation of certain textual relations. . . . An interpretive model of iconicity does not require a factual similarity between a sign and its referent, but merely an impression that similitude of some kind or form exists—whether or not it actually does. (246)

Iconicity, therefore, is less an element of the poem itself than a form of perception, less an absolute value than, as Charles Morris has remarked, "a matter of degree" (quoted in Grigely, 246). Taking into account the role of the reader or viewer in the production of meaning, Grigely moves away from the formalized "text-as-object" toward the "text-as-an-event" that takes place somewhere between the poet and the audience. This move is liberating, especially to oral and sign poetics, for it recognizes the inescapable performative nature of literature.

Once we expand our criticism to accommodate the viewer's active role in creating the poem, we are no longer limited to discussing poems as if they took place in objectifiable, linguistic space, for we do not *perceive* that space. Such linguistic space is based on a Newtonian constancy of spatial relations. The poetic space we perceive, however, is of a different nature. Calculating and recording the positions of the hands in relation to the body, for instance, may help to describe the physical properties of text, but leaves us unable to explain our perceptions of embodied images that appear, dissolve, enlarge, shrink, transform, as they shift from close-up to far-away, wide-angle, slow-motion, fast-forward, and freeze-frame. While these spatio-temporal techniques have their basis in Sign's unique linguistic use of four-dimensions, their effect can only be articulated within a theory that remains rooted in the perceptions of the body. For this reason any linguistic or semiotic analysis is incomplete without considering viewer-oriented phenomenological criticism.

Phenomenology takes as its starting point Edmund Husserl's questioning of the "natural attitude" that objects exist independently from our consciousness of them. Human consciousness, according to Husserl and other phenomenologists, is not formed through a passive reception of the ready-made world, but through active constitution of that world. Phenomenological or "reader-response" criticism, then, inquires into the ways that readers are themselves producers of literary texts. Any "viewer-response" criticism of Sign poetry must begin by taking into account the embodied perception of space, vision, and time, and then by considing these in relation to phenomenologies of language and the literary imagination. This confluence of phenomenologies leads toward what may be called the "poetics of space," intentionally borrowing from Gaston Bachelard's book by the same title.

A starting point for the understanding of the poetics of space is Merleau-Ponty's phenomenology of language which applies to Sign as well as to speaking and writing. "The word and speech," Merleau-Ponty writes,

> must somehow cease to be a way of designating things or thoughts, and become the

presence of that thought in the phenomenal world, and, moreover, not its clothing, but its token or *its body*. . . . [W]e find there, beneath the conceptual meaning
of the words, an existential meaning which is not only rendered by them, but
which inhabits them" (*Phenomenology of Perception*, 182).

In taking on a phenomenal, embodied presence of its own, language is not condemned to the perpetual task of mimesis and referentiality; language is itself the
body, flesh, and bone of meaning. When audiences watch Clayton Valli's poem,
"Dew on Spiderweb," for example, they may witness the linguistic spinning of a
spiderweb as real as any spiderweb seen before. Of course, this is an image of a
spiderweb, but as Gaston Bachelard asks, "why should the actions of the imagination not be as real as those of perception?" (158). Valli's image does not so
much iconically *refer* to a spiderweb "out-there," but rather brings what Merleau-
Ponty has called "a diagram of the life of the actual" ("Eye and Mind," 126) into
being. As witnesses of this poetic incarnation, we inhabit the poem's four-dimensional topography and find ourselves in the intimate physical and phenomenal
presence of image-things.[13]

Such an experience cannot be measured. We do not so much see the text as
an object "out there" as we "see according to, or with it" (Merleau-Ponty, 126).
We do not so much see a stable volume of linguistic space, but rather a much
more volatile volume of poetic space. For "everything, even size, is a human
value," Bachelard writes. Just as "miniature can accumulate size . . . [and become]
vast in its own way," "the dialectics of inside and outside can no longer be taken
in their simple reciprocity" (216). In the poetics of space, the "duality of subject
and object is iridescent, shimmering, unceasingly active in its inversions" (xv).
Indeed, it would even be difficult to say exactly where any given image *is*; in the
"text-as-event," the borders between viewer and text, subject and object, inside
and outside, become porous.

We now enter into a whole new field of questions about the nature of perception, body, space, time, Sign, and literature. A few beginning questions
must be asked, even if there is not time to answer them: How is (or isn't) "poetic
space" different from "everyday" space? How is spatial perception in Sign different from that of speech and writing? Does Sign structure the world differently?
What are the poetic and cultural implications of this different 'structure'? How
would a phenomenology of Sign change the ways we talk about relations
between the viewer and the text, the subject and the object?

In order to demonstrate briefly how the poetics of space may help us to
approach Sign poetry, I return to the notion of the poetic "line." As Valli chooses
the rhymed line break as the exclusive model for the signed line, this analogy
precludes ASL from more contemporary types of line breaks, such as those of free
verse. One wonders why Sign criticism would want to coerce ASL's most unique
quality—its four dimensions—into the one-dimensional model of the line. Not
only is this an inaccurate analogy, it also places ASL literature as a derivative
form of poetry.

Instead of forcing the linear model of oral and written poetics on Sign, it may be more beneficial to inquire into the phenomenological reception of a "line." A viewer does not actually perceive line division rhyme as such—for it is a linguistic analogy. What the viewer sees, rather, is a complex assemblage of lines drawn through space by fingers, hand movements, arm movements, or whole body movements. If the afterimage of all the lines were recorded on video throughout the course of a poem, the visual effect would be more like that of a Susan Howe poem than a sonnet.

Take, for example, the opening of Flying Word Project's "Poetry," where performer Peter Cook gestures shooting a gun. He begins the "line" by tracing the direction of the bullet with the index finger. Cook repeats the motion quickly, conveying the speed of the bullet. This line drawn through space then extends and curves as it transforms into signifying a moon circling a planet.

This radical transformation from human to cosmic scale, from straight to circular, threaded together through the same handshape, moves the reader through vastly different experiences of space. From the intimacy of a mid-range shot to the immensity of the distance shot of a whole planet, the producer/viewer's body not only shifts perspectives, but in so doing, *inhabits a new kind of space*. This perceived "line," in other words, cannot be measured as a constant volume, but only in its ability to generate *poetic volume*.

Seeing the line within the full space and time of the body leads Sign literature away from the phonocentric literary model, and toward concepts more akin to the visual and performative arts. Indeed, at the hands of Sign poets, the poetic line may resemble a Klee more than a Keats; and like the lines in a Klee, Sign is "a matter of freeing the line, of revivifying its constituting power" (Merleau-Ponty, "Eye and Mind," 143). Such a liberation of the prosaic line may provide an example of the margin freeing the center from its own constraints.

Further phenomenological study of Sign poetry will, one hopes, explore other literary concepts in their visual-spatial quality, as opposed to their linguistic quantity. This approach will keep Sign criticism close to the original site of poetic creation: the meeting of body, time, space, and language. In the end, we may arrive at a viewing practice in which Sign poems are not so much "read" or "seen" as they are *lived in* from the inside.

CONCLUSION

Drawing out all the possible connections, contradictions, and ambiguities between deconstruction, cultural studies, semiotics, and phenomenology as they apply to Sign literature will be a major critical task. To begin, a few key critical concepts may be isolated: while Sign literature is a minority cultural practice, it nonetheless has profound implications for the dominant group's understanding of language, literature, and culture. These implications manifest at the metaphysical site (the breaking of the hegemony of speech-writing); the sociopolitical site (the emergence of a postmodern culture outside of phonocentrism); the textual site (the practice of a postmodern bardic tradition recorded only through video-text); and the phenomenological site (the performance of an alternative visual-spatial means of being-in-the-world). Through the performance of a signed text, all these sites operate simultaneously, each within the other. Boundaries give way and become openings. "A narrow gate," Bachelard writes, "opens up an entire world" (185). One hopes the narrow gate of Sign literature and criticism will open up the entire world of experience previously foreclosed by the dominance of speech and writing. If the figure of the blind poet inhabits the origins of poetry, then we may look toward the Deaf poet to explore the future of poetry as it becomes increasingly visual, spatial, and embodied.

NOTES

1. Deaf persons, I believe, are first and foremost members of a cultural and linguistic community, bearing more similarity, say, to Hispanics than to persons with cerebral palsy. My publishing this article in a disability studies reader, however, highlights what I feel may be a coalition formed between Deaf studies and disability studies. This coalition must be aware that Deaf persons form a unique linguistic and cultural group, but that both groups may strive in tandem to resist the pathologization of the body by the abled body-politic. Deaf and disability studies, for example, could collaborate to resist China's present eugenics practice of sterilizing "disabled" persons. Only by joining forces and resources may the Deaf and persons with disabilities gain a larger political voice to denounce China's human rights violations as well as America's policy to China.

2. In keeping with conventions within Deaf studies, I use the capitalized *Deaf* to refer to the cultural group of ASL-users while lower case *deaf* and *deafness* refer to the physical phenomena of not hearing.

3. I refer to sign languages collectively as "Sign." Sign includes all native sign languages—British Sign Language, American Sign Language, French Sign Language, Chinese Sign Language, etc. but does not include manual versions of dominant languages such as Signed Exact English. The distinctions between manual versions of dominant languages and the native languages of Deaf communities presents an interesting field of study which may illuminate the constitutive nature of vision in Sign grammar that is at odds with the logic of spoken languages.

4. Since the advent of video publications, a number of Deaf poets and storytellers have achieved national recognition within the Deaf community: Ella Mae Lentz, Dorothy Miles, Bernard Bragg, Debbie Rennie, Patrick Graybill, Gilbert Eastman, Ben Bahan, Sam Supalla and Flying Words Project (Peter Cook and Kenny Lerner). The most accessible videos are produced by Dawn Sign Press which has published the *Poetry in Motion* series featuring Debbie Rennie, Patrick Graybill, and Clayton Valli, the *ASL Literature* series featuring narratives by Ben Bahan and Sam Supalla, and more recently, Clayton Valli's *Selected Works*. In Motion Press has also published a collection of poems by Ella Mae Lentz entitled *The Treasure*.

5. See Dick Higgins's *Pattern Poetry: Guide to an Unknown Literature*.

6. Indeed, some writers tread so close to the poetics of Sign, that it is only their inability to see through the label of disability (and the oppression of Sign in the early part of this century) that precluded recognition of Sign as a medium for literature. Ernest Fenollosa's *The Chinese Written Character as a Medium for Poetry* might have been more accurate had he written about ASL rather than the Chinese ideogram. In addition, Artaud's *The Theater and its Double* praises sign language without ever connecting the language of gesture to the Deaf community. No doubt, Artaud, Fenollosa, and Pound would have been enthralled with the experimental poetics of avant-garde Deaf poets. More recently, only a scattering of contemporary poets and

critics have recognized Sign poetry. Jerome and Diane Rothenberg include an article on Sign poetry by Edward Klima and Ursula Bellugi in *Symposium of the Whole: A Range of Discourse Toward an Ethnopoetics;* in 1984, Allen Ginsberg visited the National Technical Institute for the Deaf in Rochester, New York where he met with Deaf poets (cf. Cohn's "Visible Poetics" essay.); and in the *MLA Newsletter*, critic W. J. T. Mitchell wrote that "The poetry of the deaf stages for us in the most vivid possible form the basic shift in literary understanding that has been occurring in the last decade: the movement from a "textual" model (based in the narrowly defined circuit of writing and speech) to a "performance" model." (14).

7.   In the thirty years since the publication of *De la Grammatologie*, Derrida continued to overlook deafness and Sign. In those years, Europe and the United States have witnessed the most important years in Deaf history. With the 1988 Gallaudet Revolution, Deaf culture has become recognized in the international media. And yet, Derrida continues to avoid the questions raised by deafness even though he, along with Paul de Man has explored the metaphorics of blindness. Derrida, however, is not the only deconstructionist to miss the metaphysical implications of deafness. In *The Telephone Book*, Avital Ronell is an audist tourist in her brief foray into Deaf culture. In fact, she treats the audist, Alexander Graham Bell, so sympathetically that she fails to see the strong arm of logocentrism reaching through Bell's call for a eugenics movement to eradicate "a deaf variety of the human race." When discussing the work of Bell, Ronell writes, "We are still talking art, and of the poetry diverting a child from the isolation of deafness, saving the child in language, bringing him to the proximity of speech with his father. AGB did this—an act of genuine *poiesis* . . ." (329–30). Is this not, rather, an act of coercing a deaf child into phonocentrism?; is it not a form of violence to deny a child a natural visual language when he cannot hear speech? Would it not be more of an act of genuine *poeisis* to teach the Father to sign? Further, Ronell's worst kind of tourism is evident as she does not bother to understand basic cultural literacy of Deaf persons. She calls the Abbé de l'Epée the "first literate deaf-mute"; the Abbé, however, was a hearing man in his fifties who stumbled upon two deaf women in Paris and subsequently became interested in deaf education.

8.   See Bernard Bragg's *Lessons in Laughter: The Autobiography of a Deaf Actor* as signed to Eugene Bergman. Bragg recounts his childhood experiences being taught how to laugh like hearing persons because his teacher was annoyed that his pupils sounded like animals when they laughed.

9.   See Harlan Lane, *The Mask of Benevolence* for further discussion, especially p. 212–16. Lane is the first to use the work of Michel Foucault as it applies to deafness. As with Derrida, Foucault's work may be enormously beneficial to Deaf Studies, even though he overlooks the question of Deaf Culture. In fact, the discursive "birth of deafness" is so closely allied to the births of the asylum, the clinic and prisons, it is quite surprising to find no mention of deafness in Foucault. The same years that witnessed the rise of Pinel's asylums for the insane also witnessed Pinel's methods of observation and classification deployed by his student, Jean-Marc Itard, within the newly founded "Asylums for the Deaf and the Dumb"; when the medical gaze penetrated the surface of the body in the age of Bichat, otologists probed the workings of the ear; when *écoles normales* produced disciplinary pedagogies, "oralist" teachers (some of whom were also teachers at *écoles normales*) developed pedagogies to discipline the deaf body into normative language practices. In short, the Asylum for the Deaf and Dumb served as a point of convergence of discourses which, as Foucault demonstrates, all work toward the same goal: to

separate the normal from the abnormal, the hearing from the deaf, in order to nor-malize the transgressive Other, to eradicate all differences—while ironically exac-erbating them, perpetuating the subjugation of the abnormal body.

10.   The inability to define ASL literature is not unique to ASL; rather, I believe hear-ing literature itself cannot be defined with any consistency and accuracy. The term *define* originates from the Latin *definare*, meaning to limit; I believe that it is unwise to be overly concerned with limiting the boundaries of creative practices—whether Deaf or hearing.

11.   As J. J. Pollitt notes, "[rhythmos] were originally the "positions" that the human body was to assume in the course of a dance in other words the patterns or *schemata* that the body made. In the course of a dance certain obvious patterns or positions, like the raising or lowering of a foot, were naturally repeated, thus mark-ing intervals in the dance. Since music and singing were synchronized with danc-ing, the recurrent positions taken by the dancer in the course of his movements also marked distinct intervals in the music. . . . This explains why the basic com-ponent of music and poetry was called a . . . foot" (quoted in Mitchell 280–81).

12.   Linguist William Stokoe describes the cinematic properties of ASL, a concept orig-inally developed by Deaf artists Bernard Bragg and Gil Eastman: "In a signed lan-guage . . . narrative is no longer linear and prosaic. Instead, the essence of sign language is to cut from a normal view to a close-up to a distant shot to a close up again, and so on, even including flashback and flash-forward scenes, exactly as a movie editor works. . . . Not only is signing itself arranged more like edited film than like written narration, but also each signer is placed very much as a camera: the field of vision and angle of view are directed but variable. Not only the signer signing but also the signer watching is aware at all times of the signer's visual ori-entation to what is being signed about" (quoted in Sacks, 90).

13.   While this phenomenology of language could lead toward a type of logocentric self-presence, Merleau-Ponty recognizes the ambiguity of absence/presence which underlies all perception. "The perceived thing exists only insofar as I perceive it, and yet its being is never exhausted by the view I have of it. It is this simultane-ous presence and absence that is required for 'something to be perceived at all" (*Logos and Eidos: The Concept in Phenomenology*, 10). For this reason, Merleau-Ponty refers to the realm of language and the imaginary to be "quasi-present."

WORKS CITED

Artaud, Antonin. 1958. *The Theater and Its Double*. Trans. Mary Richards. New York: Grove Press.

ASL Literature Series. 1994. Video with Ben Bahan and Sam Supalla. Pro. Joe Dannis. Dir. James. R. DeBee. Sand Diego: DawnSignPress.

Bachelard, Gaston. 1969. *The Poetics of Space*. Trans. Maria Jolas. Boston: Beacon Press.

Baynton, Douglas. 1992. "'A Silent Exile on This Earth': The Metaphorical Constrcution of Deafness in the Nineteenth Century." *American Quarterly* 44.2 : 216–43.

Cohn, Jim. 1986. "The New Deaf Poetics: Visible Poetry." *Sign Language Studies* 52: 263–77.

Derrida, Jacques. 1976. *Of Grammatology*. Trans. Gayatri Spivak. Baltimore: The Johns Hopkins Press.

Fanon, Frantz. 1968. *The Wretched of the Earth*. Trans. Constance Farrington. New York: Grove Press.

Fenollosa, Ernest. 1968. *The Chinese Written Character as a Medium for Poetry*. Ed. Ezra Pound. San Francisco: City Lights Books.

Graybill, Patrick. 1990. *Patrick Graybill*. Video. Series *Poetry in Motion: Original Works in ASL*. Burtonsvitle, MD: Sign Media.

Grigely, Joseph. 1993. "The Implosion of Iconicity." *Word and Image Interactions A Selection of Papers Given at the Second International Conference on Word and Image*. Ed. Martin Heusser. Wiese Verlag Basel.

Higgins, Dick. 1987. *Pattern Poetry: Guide to an Unknown Literature*. Albany: SUNY Press.

Klima, Edward and Ursula Bellugi. 1983. "Poetry Without Sound." *Symposium of the Whole: A Range of Discourse Toward an Ethnopoetics*. Eds. Jerome and Diane Rothenberg. Berkeley: University of California Press.

Lane, Harlan. 1992. *The Mask of Benevolence*. New York: Alfred Knopf.

Lentz, Ella Mae. 1995. *The Treasure*. Video. In Berkeley, CA: Motion Press.

Lorde, Audre. 1984. "Learning from the 60s." *Sister Outsider*. Freedom, CA: The Crossing Press.

Merleau-Ponty. 1989. *The Phenomenology of Perception*. Trans. Colin Smith. London: Routledge.

———. "Eye and Mind." 1993. *The Merleau-Ponty Aesthetics Reader: Philosophy and Painting*. Ed. Galen Johnson. Evanston, Ill: Northwestern University Press.

Mitchell, W. J. T. 1989. "Gesture, Sign, and Play: ASL Poetry and the Deaf Community." *MLA Newsletter*. Summer (1989): 13–14.

———. 1974. "Spatial Form in Literature: Toward a General Theory." *The Language of Images*. Ed. W. J. T. Mitchell. Chicago: University of Chicago Press.

Padden, Carol and Humphries, Tom. 1988. *Deaf in America: Voices from a Culture*. Cambridge: Harvard University Press.

Plato. 1937. *The Dialogues of Plato*. Vol. 2 Trans. Jowett Benjamin. New York: Random House.

Rennie, Debbie. 1990. *Debbie Rennie*. Video. *Poetry in Motion: Original Works in ASL*. Burtonsvitle, MD: Sign Media.

Ronnell, Avital. 1989. *The Telephone Book: Technology—Schizophrenia—Electric Speech*. Lincoln: University of Nebraska Press.

Rose, Heidi. 1993. "A Critical Methodology for Analzying American Sign Language Literature." Dissertation, Arizona State University.

———. 1992. "A Semiotic Analysis of Artistic American Sign Language and a Performance of Poetry." *Text and Performance Quarterly* 12.2: 146–59.

Rothenberg, Jerome and Rothenberg, Diane, eds. 1983. *Symposium of the Whole: A Range of Discourse Toward an Ethnopoetics*. Berkeley: University of California Press.

Sacks, Oliver. 1990. *Seeing Voices: A Journey into the World of the Deaf*. New York: HarperPerennial.

Said, Edward. 1994. *Culture and Imperialism*. New York: Vintage.

Trinh, Minh-ha. 1995. "No Master Territories." *The Post-Colonial Studies Reader*. Eds. Ashcroft, Bill, Griffiths, Gareth, Tiffin, Helen London: Routledge.

Valli, Clayton. 1995. *ASL Poetry: Selected Works of Clayton Valli*. Video. Pro. Joe Dannis Dir. Clayton Valli. San Diego: DawnSignPress, 1995.

———. 1990. *Clayton Valli*. Video. Series *Poetry in Motion: Original Works in ASL*. Burtonsvitle, MD: Sign Media.

———. 1990. "The Nature of the Line in ASL Poetry." *SLR '87 Papers from The Fourth International Symposium on Sign Language Research*. Eds. W. H. Edmondson and F. Karlsson. Hamburg: Signum Press.

19

The Enfreakment of Photography

DAVID HEVEY

Before reading this chapter, I feel I must contextualise what lies ahead for the reader. In many ways, charity advertising as oppressive imagery appears to be the *bête noire* of disabled people. Unfortunately, oppressive as it is, it represents colours of a social order tied to a specific mast. Those colours and constructions also exist in other areas of photographic representation. This is demonstrated in this chapter. I ask the reader to join me on a journey into oppressive disability imagery. At times, particularly in the examination of the work of Diane Arbus, it can be depressing. However this chapter is here because I feel we have to take the fight against constructed oppression (whether by non-access or by representation) into the camp of the oppressors.

Apart from charity advertising, when did you last see a picture of a disabled person? It almost certainly wasn't in commercial advertising since disabled people are not thought to constitute a body of consumers and therefore do not generally warrant inclusion. It might have been within an "in-house" health service magazine, in which disabled people are positioned to enflesh the theories of their oppressors. The stories might range from the successes of a toxic drugs company to the latest body armour for people with cerebral palsy, and some person with the proverbial "disease" will be shown illustrating the solution and its usefulness. It might have been in an educational magazine, in which a non-disabled "facilitator" will regale in words and text the latest prototype "image-workshop," using disabled people as guinea pigs while developing their "educational" ideas. The text brags about the colonization of disabled people's bodies and identities, while the images show how much "the disabled" enjoyed it. Passive and still and "done to," the images bear a bizarre resemblance to colonial pictures where "the blacks" stand frozen and curious, while "whitey" lounges confident and sure. Whitey knows the purpose of this image, the black people appear not to (or at least, perhaps as employees, have no right to record visual dissent).

The "positive" side of their ultra-minority inclusion, then, is that disabled people are there to demonstrate the successes of their administrators.[1] Apart from the above areas, however, disabled people are almost entirely absent from photographic genres or discussion because they are read as socially dead and as not having a role to play. But although the absence is near absolute, the non-representation of disabled people is not quite total. Taking the structured absence as given, I wanted to discover the terms on which disabled people *were* admitted into photographic representation. As Mary Daly once wrote of feminism, the job entails being a full-time, low-paid researcher of your own destiny.[2]

I visited one of the largest photographic bookshops in London and leafed through the publications. Generally disabled people were absent, but there was a sort of presence. Disabled people are represented but almost exclusively as symbols of "otherness" placed within equations which have no engagement to them and which take their non-integration as a natural by-product of their impairment.

I picked books at random. *The Family of Man*; *Another Way of Telling*; *diane arbus*; *Figments from the Real World*. There were obviously lateral associations but only one, *diane arbus*, I knew to include images of disabled people. In the research for this book, I had begun to uncover sometimes hidden, sometimes open, but always continuous constructions of disabled people as outsiders admitted into culture as symbols of fear or pity. This was particularly true in literature[3] but I wanted to see if it held true in photography, so I picked the books at random. They may have been connected in styles or schools but, as far as I knew, had no connection whatsoever on disability representation. Only Arbus was infamous for having centred disabled people in her work but I felt an uneasy faith that all of them would "use" disabled people somewhere.

The first book examined was entitled *The Family of Man*.[4] The Family of Man exhibition at the Museum of Modern Art, New York, in 1955 is considered the seminal exhibition for humanist-realist photography. It was the photographic height of postwar idealism. It showed the great "positive image" of an unproblematised and noble world—a world from which pain was banished. Where there are images of "working folk," their muscles and their sweat appear to be a part of the great spiritual order of things. Where there are images of black people, the images show poverty; some show harmony, but all are visually poetic. Black life has been harmonised through aesthetics.

However, throughout the catalogue of the show, which contained 503 images show from 68 countries by 273 male and female photographers, there is only one photograph of someone identifiably disabled. This is more than an oversight. Put together ten years after the Second World War, *The Family of Man* was about "positively" forgetting the past and all its misery. Forward into glory, backward into pain! Although this publication and exhibition heralded a brave new world of postwar hope and harmony, on reading it it becomes clear that the inclusion of disabled people—even disabled people tidied up like black people and working people—was not a part of the postwar visual nirvana. Why was this?

The one image of a disabled person appears on the penultimate page of the 192-page publication. It is mixed in among six other images on that page and is part of the final section of the book, which covers children. Children are shown laughing, playing, dancing, crying and so on. Of the thirty-eight images in this section, three buck this trend. The three are all on this penultimate page. In the final section, after five pages of innocent joy, you encounter on the sixth page three that remind you it is not like that always. At the top of these three is a disabled boy who appears to be a below-the-knee amputee. He is racing along the beach with a crutch under his right arm. He is playing and chasing a football. His body tilts to our right as he approaches the ball, while his crutch tilts to our left, to form a shape like an open and upright compass. The ball is situated in the triangle which his left leg and his right-side crutch make on the sand. The triangle shape is completed by a shadow which the boy casts from his right leg to the crutch (and beyond). The ball enters this triangle focusing point but his right leg does not. Its absence is accentuated and impairment here is read as loss. The game he plays is his personal effort to overcome his loss.

The photograph creates a flowing but awkward symmetry and our reading of its flow is continually interrupted by the fact that the triangle's neatness is dependent on the absence of a limb. Two readings occur simultaneously: it is tragic but he is brave. In a book of hope, the disabled person is the symbol of loss. The disabled boy is a reminder that all is not necessarily well in the world but *he* is doing *his* best to sort it out. The image is "positive" in that he is "positively" adjusting to his loss. Because he is "positively" adjusting to his loss, the image is allowed into the exhibition and the catalogue. The image of his disablement has been used not for him but against him. The image's symbolic value is that disability is an issue for the person with an impairment, not an issue for a world being (inaccessibly) reconstructed. In *The Family of Man*, disabled people were almost entirely absented because harmony was seen to rest in the full operation of an idealised working body. The exhibition and catalogue did not admit disabled people (bar one) because it did not see a position for disabled people within the new model army of postwar production or consumption.

Photographically speaking, the decline of this high ground of postwar hope in the "one world, one voice, one leader" humanity was heralded (in historical photographic terms) by an equally influential but far more subversive exhibition, again at the Museum of Modern Art, New York, which was held in 1967. This exhibition was called New Documents and brought into a wide public consciousness reportage portraiture showing the human race as an alienated species bewildered by its existence. New Documents featured the work of Gary Winogrand, Lee Friedlander and Diane Arbus. The importance of these three photographers (and others like Robert Frank)) is that their work heralded the breakdown of the universal humanism of *The Family of Man* into a more fragmented, psychic or surrealistic realism. The appalling reverse of the coin is that they anchored the new forms of a fragmented universe (to a greater or lesser extent) in new, even more oppressive images of disabled people.

What is particularly crucial in terms of the representation of disabled people in this photojournalism is a clear (yet still uncritical) emergence of the portrayal of disabled people as the *symbol* of this new (dis)order. Whereas the tucked-away disabled person in *The Family of Man* had been a hidden blemish on the body of humanity, in a world of the Cold War, the Cuban Missile Crisis and Vietnam, disabled people were represented as the inconcealable birthmark of fear and chaos. Diane Arbus was the second photographer whose work I looked at. The monograph that I had pulled from the shelf is from her posthumous retrospective, held at the Museum of Modern Art, New York, in 1972 and entitled *diane arbus*.[5]

Of all photographers who have included or excluded disabled people, Diane Arbus is the most notorious. She was born into an *arriviste* family of immigrants, whose money was made in the fur trade. She became a photographer through her husband, Allan Arbus, and worked with him in fashion photography. She moved away from that (and him) into work which still dealt with the body and its surrounding hyperbole but from a very different angle. It was on her own and in her own work that she became known, unwittingly according to her, as "the photographer of freaks." Whether she liked it or not, there can be no doubt that this is how her work has been received. The monograph contains 81 black-and-white images, of which eleven are of disabled people. These eleven can be divided into three quite critical periods of her work. The first is demonstrated in two portraits of "dwarfs"; the second with the portrait of the "Jewish giant"; and the third with the imagery shot just before her death, that of the "retardees" (her term for people with Down Syndrome).

In any of the material on Arbus, including this monograph, Patricia Bosworth's biography of her entitled *Diane Arbus, A Biography*, and Susan Sontag's discussion of her work in *On Photography*, the stages of her oppressive representations of disabled people are never discussed. Moreover, the "factual" recording of disabled people as freaks is accepted totally without question by major critics like Sontag, who says, "Her work shows people who are pathetic, pitiable, as well as repulsive, but it does not arouse any compassionate feelings."[6] Later, she rhetorically adds, "Do they see themselves, the viewer wonders, like *that*? Do they know how grotesque they are?" (her italics). Sontag brings to the disability imagery of Arbus a complete faith in Arbus's images as unproblematic truth-tellers. Bosworth also colludes by patronising disabled people, telling us of Arbus's "gentle and patient" way with "them." Neither of these critics, it goes without saying, considered asking the observed what *they* felt about the images in which they figured. Once again, the entire discourse has absented the voice of those at its centre—disabled people.

Since there is only one other book on Arbus's work, and that deals with her magazine work,[7] it is safe to say that Bosworth and Sontag represent key parts of the Arbus industry. In their validations of Arbus's work, they both miss a central point. Although she was profoundly misguided (as I demonstrate further on), there can be no doubt that her work paradoxically had the effect of problematising, or opening up, the issue of the representation of disabled people. Her critics and defenders have built a wall around her work (and any discussion of disability in her work) by "naturalising" the content. In this, the images of disabled people have been lumped into one label, that of "freaks." Perhaps this has been done because her work appears to buck the contradictory trend of "compassion" in the portrayal of disabled "victims" practised by other photographers. Although Arbus's work can never be "reclaimed," it has to be noted that her work, and the use of "enfreakment" as message and metaphor, is far more complicated than either her defenders or critics acknowledge. The process of analysis is not to rehabilitate her or her work but to break it down once and for all.

She was a part of the "snapshot aesthetic" which grew up beyond the New Documents exhibition and exhibitors. This form attempted to overturn the

sophisticated and high-technique processes of the Hollywood fantasy portrait, as
well as rejecting the beautiful toning of much of *The Family of Man*. However,
more than any of her peers, she took this aesthetic nearer to its roots in the
family photograph or album (indeed she intended to shoot a project entitled
Family Album).[8] Arbus had experienced, in her own family, the emotional and
psychological cost of wealth in terms of the painful subjectivity and isolation of
the individual hidden and silenced within the outward signs of bourgeois upward
mobility and success. In terms of disability, however, Arbus read the bodily
impairment of her disabled subject as a sign of disorder, even chaos; that is, as a
physical manifestation of *her* chaos, *her* horror. Despite her relationships with disabled people (often lasting a decade or more) she viewed these not as social and
equal relationships but as encounters with souls from an underworld.

There was nothing new in this pattern of "reading" the visual site of a disabled
person away from a personal value into a symbolic value which then seals the representational fate of the disabled person. However, at least in the first period of
her disability work, Arbus deviated from the Richard III syndrome by reading this
"disorder" as the manifestation of a psychic disorder not in the subject but in society. There is no question of Arbus using her subjects "positively"—it is clear that
she always intended them and their relationships to themselves and others to
symbolise something other than themselves. She saw herself and her "freaks" as
fellow travellers into a living oblivion, a social death. There is a perverse sense
in which she was right—disabled people are expected to inhabit a living death—
but the crucial thing is that she considered her projection to be more important
than their reality. She "normalised" subjects like Morales, *The Mexican Dwarf*,[9]
or *The Russian Midget Friends*[10] by specifically placing them in that great site of
bourgeois culture and consumption, the home. The "horror" of Arbus's work is
not that she has created Frankenstein but that she moved him in next door!
What is more, the freak had brought his family! The "shock" for the hundreds
of thousands of non-disabled viewers was that these portraits revealed a hinter-
land existing in spite of the segregationist non-disabled world view.

For Arbus, the family—her own family—represented an abyss. She saw in the
bourgeois promise to the immigrant family, her own family, a Faustian contract.
Her Mephistopheles, her threat to the bourgeois privilege, was to move a non-
disabled fear that dare not speak its name into the family snap. In a sense, this
first period of her work (a period not of time but of understanding) is her least
oppressive and in some ways complete. The sitters acknowledge her presence and
her camera. They stare out from the picture at the viewer. Far from making
apologies for their presence, they are distinctly proud, they are committed to
their identity. Although the disabled people portrayed existed within subcultures
(such as the circus), they were clearly not segregated and it is this which
shocked the public who flocked to her posthumous retrospective at the Museum
of Modern Art in 1972. It is the *conscious dialogue* between Arbus and the subjects which "horrified" and yet fascinated people more used to compassionate
victim images of disabled people obligingly subhuman and obligingly institu-
tionalised as "tragic but brave." Morales, the Mexican "dwarf" in *diane arbus*, is
pictured naked but for a towel over his crutch. He wears a trilby at a rakish angle

and his elbow leans casually on to the sideboard, resting just in front of a bottle of liquor. It is not clear quite what went on between Arbus and Morales (though Arbus had previously "spent the night" with another disabled subject, Moondance, as part of his agreement to be photographed) but the eroticism of the image cannot be denied. Not only is the so-called "dwarf" distinctly unfreaky in his three-quarters nakedness, he is positively virile! A constant theme of Arbus's work, not just of her disability work, is the relationship between people's bodies and their paraphernalia. While the attire is crisp and clear, the flesh of the subject has been "zombified." This, however, is not the case with her first pictures of "dwarfs." Morales's body is very much alive.

Arbus had attempted to trace the psychic disorder of consumer society back to a primal state of terror within everyday life. That she believed disabled people to be the visual witness of this primal state is clear. That is, she accepted at the level of "common sense" the non-integration of disabled people. However, much of "the Horror, the Horror'[11] with which Arbus's work has been received is in her location of this disabled terror within non-disabled normality. The disabled subjects themselves, at least in this early "freak" work, are treated reverentially. The camera is close. The camera is engaged. The subject has agreed to the session (but agreed in isolation?). The "horror" of the process for non-disabled society is in her placing a disabled normality within a non-disabled normality. The horror is in how she could even think them equivalent. The horror, I repeat, was in Arbus's recording in her constructions of disabled people a double bind of segregation/non-segregation. The "non-segregation," however (and this is where Arbus's crime really lay) did not lead towards integration—the "Russian midgets" were not living down the road as part of an independent living scheme—but towards transgression. It was a spectacle, not a political dialectic (the disability paradox) that Arbus wanted to ensnare. For this she accepted, indeed depended, on the given segregation of disabled people as "common sense."

Things began to disintegrate for Arbus in the second part of her disability work. This is illustrated in the monograph by the image entitled *A Jewish Giant at Home with his Parents in the Bronx, N.Y. 1970*. Again, we see a cosy family setting of a front room with two comfy chairs and a sofa, two elderly and self-respecting pensioners, a lamp by the drawn curtains, a reproduction classic painting in a tasteful frame, and a giant. The "giant" is not given a name in the title but his name was Eddie Carmel.[12] Again, Arbus did not sneak in and sneak out in this shot but got to know and photograph Eddie Carmel over a period of ten years before printing this one which she considered to work. This image of *A Jewish Giant* with its glaring flash-lit room, its portrayal of "the beast" from the womb of the mother, shows less harmony, even a deliberate asymmetry from that of her "dwarf" images. In *A Jewish Giant* she had created an image which took her beyond the reverence in both form and content of her "dwarf" images. Unlike them, Eddie the Jewish "giant" directs his attention away from the presence of the camera, his only acknowledgement that an image is being made is by being on his feet like his parents. His body language appears unclear and unsettled. The flash has cast black halos round the bodies of the subjects and they begin to resemble a Weegee as a found specimen of urban horror. The image of the "giant" as he crouches towards his more formal parents is that of a father over two children. The classic family portrait of parents and child is completely reversed by her use of their size relationship. The body language of the "Jewish giant" is more "out of control" (that is, it diverges more from non-disabled body language signs) than that of the "dwarf." It is all the more "threatening" to the non-disabled family snap because his body is situated with that of his "normal" parents. A clash or a confrontation between styles and discourses is occurring. The alchemy, confrontation and visual disorder of the image bring Arbus closer to avenging the control and repression in her own family. This is the key to her use and manipulation of isolated disabled people. During the ten years of their knowing each other, Eddie Carmel told Arbus about his ambitions, about his job selling insurance, about his acting hopes (and his despair at only being offered "monster" roles), and so on. Arbus dismissed this in her representations. She clearly found his actual day-to-day life irrelevant. Indeed, she appears to have disbelieved him, preferring her own projection of a metaphysical decline. His real tragedy is that he trusted Arbus, and she abused that trust outside of their relationship in an area within her total control, that is, photography.

The visual dialogue within the image between herself and the subject in the "dwarf" works, although decreasing in the imagery of Eddie the "giant," was still prevalent and was important precisely because it created a snapshot family album currency within the imagery. The commonness of this form was a part of its communicative power. As a structure it spoke to millions, while its content, Arbus's enfreakment of disabled people,[13] spoke to the able-bodied fear of millions. Were the subject to disengage, to reject the apparent co-conspiracy (in reality a coercion) or contract between themselves and Arbus, the images would move from the genre of family album currency and understanding of millions, to a reportage subgenre position of one specialist photographer. Arbus's work would then be that of an outsider constructing outsiders which need not be internalised by the viewer. The enfreakment in her disability images was internalised by the non-disabled viewers because the disabled subjects, while chosen for their apparent difference, manifested body language and identity traits recognisable to everyone. Arbus was concerned to show the dichotomy, even the pain, between how people projected themselves and how she thought they "really" were. The projection of this "imagined self" by the subject was through the direct gaze to camera (and therefore direct gaze to viewer). The image of A Jewish Giant, to Arbus, suggested a higher level of fear and chaos than the "dwarf" work. This higher level of discrepancy between order (the setting is still the family at home) and chaos (Eddie outgrowing that which contained him), than that manifested in the "dwarf" work, is also highlighted by the fact that, although the "giant" is on his feet posing with his parents, his dialogue is as much between him and his parents as between him and Arbus/the viewer.

Arbus was reported to have told a journalist at the New Yorker of her excitement over this image, the first one that had worked for her in the ten years of photographing Eddie. "You know how every mother has nightmares when she's pregnant that her baby will be born a monster? I think I got that in the mother's face as she glares up at Eddie, thinking, 'OH MY GOD, NO!'"[14] You could be forgiven for imagining that the mother recoils from her Eddie much like Fay Ray recoiled from the horror of King Kong, but this is not the case. Arbus betrayed in her excited phone call to the journalist what she wished the image to say, rather than what it actual does say (though, of course, meanings shift). Arbus's comment about "every mother's nightmare" speaks of her nightmare relationship with her own body, which I believe she viewed as the sole site of her power. It was this loss of control of the body which she saw disability/impairment as meaning. Arbus once quoted a person who defined horror as the relationship between sex and death. She also claimed that she never refused a person who asked her to sleep with them. Furthermore, Bosworth hints that Arbus may have been confused about her bi-sexuality. In any event, the clues suggest that while she viewed her body and sexuality as key points of her power, her sexuality was not clear to her, and sex itself probably failed to resolve her feelings of aloneness and fragmentation. She sought the answer to this dilemma in locating bodily chaos in all her subjects (to varying degrees) and felt she'd found it in its perfect form in disabled people. (That major institutions of American representation, like the Museum of Modern Art, promoted her work shows their willingness to cooperate with this oppressive construction of disabled people.)

The "OH MY GOD, NO!" which she attributes to the mother in *A Jewish Giant* is in reality an "OH MY GOD, YES!" victory call that Arbus herself felt. She had made her psychic vision physical, or so she felt. Diane Arbus's daughter, Doon Arbus, has written that her mother wanted to photograph not what was evil but what was *forbidden*.[15] She believed she had pictured a return of the forbidden and repressed within her own remembered family. In her construction, the awkwardness of *A Jewish Giant* hints at the unwieldiness of her vision as a long-term solution to her own needs and begins to hint at this vision's ultimate destructiveness—not only, and obviously, to disabled people, but to the psychic well-being of Arbus herself.

It is here that the third period in her work on disabled people begins. She starts to photograph "retardees" (as she labels people with Down Syndrome). She moves from observing her subjects at home to observing them in a home; that is, an institution. These images of people with Down Syndrome were practically the last she shot before killing herself. They are clustered, six of them, at the end of the book. In the previous work with "dwarfs" and *A Jewish Giant* Arbus had maintained that she did not photograph anybody who did not agree to be photographed. This was undoubtedly so (although coercion is probably truer than agreement), but the images show a decline in conscious frontal participation of the subject. This decline was also mirrored in the growing discordance on the technical side of her work. The beautiful tones of Morales, the "dwarf," give way to a harsh flash-light in the "Jewish giant." There is no doubt that Arbus, as an ex-fashion photographer, knew what she was doing in using technical disharmony as an underwriting of the narrative disharmony. When we come into the third period, her work on "retardees," Arbus continues to pursue technical discordance. She still uses flash-and-daylight to pick up the figures from their landscape, but the focus is clearly weaker than that of the previous work. The subjects are now barely engaged with Arbus/the viewer *as themselves*.

Arbus finds them not in a position to conspire with her projection. The visual
dialogue collapses. The dialectic between body and attire which Arbus had pursued is broken. The chaos of their paper and blanket costumes appears, to her,
not to challenge their bodies but to match them. Arbus's order-chaos paradoxical projection has not happened. Instead, Arbus sees zombies in another world.
To her they project no illusions of being neighbours to normality. These people
are not at home but in a home. The institution of the family give sway to the
institution of segregation (in this case, a New Jersey "home" for "retardees").
The people with Down Syndrome are set in a backdrop of large open fields
showing only distant woods. For Arbus, their consciousness and activity is arbitrary. She does not know how to make them perform to her psycho-ventriloquist
needs. In her career-long attempt to pull the psychic underworld into the
physical overworld by manipulating the bodies of disabled people, she has
come to the borders in these images. She had met "the limits of her imagination"; she had not found in these images the catharsis necessary for her to continue. Arbus first loved then hated this last work. She entered a crisis of
identity because these segregated people with Down Syndrome would not perform as an echo of her despair. Because of this, her despair deepened. In the final
image of this series and the final image of her monograph, nine disabled people
pass across the view of the camera. Of the nine, only one turns towards the
camera. His gaze misses the camera; consequently the possibilities that might
have been opened up by a direct gaze are, for Arbus, lost. He joins the rest of
this crowd who come into the frame for no purpose. Arbus's camera became
irrelevant not only for disabled people, but for Arbus herself. This was her last
work before she killed herself.

The next book I looked at was Gary Winogrand's *Figments from the Real
World*.[16] Of the 179 black-and-white plates in *Figments from the Real World*, six
included the portrayal of disabled people on one level or another. Like Arbus,
the inclusion of disabled people, regardless of their role, was that of a significant
minority with their oppression unquestioned and constructed as intact. Unlike
Arbus's work, however, Winogrand did not produce any images (at least not for
public consumption) whose central character was the disabled person or disablement. He did produce bodies of work on women, for example, but where a
disabled person appears in the work, it is as a secondary character to the women.
Nevertheless, within the "underrepresentation" in *Figments from the Real World*,
it becomes clear that, like Arbus and the others from my ersatz list, "the disabled"
had a role to play. Nevertheless, Winogrand consciously or otherwise included
disabled people with the specific intention of enfreaking disability in order to
make available to his visual repertoire a key *destabilising* factor.

With regard to the representation of women by Winogrand, Victor Burgin has
critiqued Winogrand's work and has explored the reading of meaning within his
imagery and the relationship of this meaning to the wider social and political
discourses of his time.[17] Burgin describes and discusses an image of Winogrand
from an exhibition in 1976. The image is of four women advancing towards the
camera down a city street. The group of women, who are varying degrees of

middle age, is the most prominent feature in the right-hand half of the image; equally prominent is a group of huge plastic bags stuffed full of garbage. The introduction to the catalogue of the exhibition makes it clear that this "joke" is intended. The reading of middle-aged women as "old bags" is unavoidable.

Despite the protestations by John Szarkowski in the introduction of *Figments from the Real World* that Winogrand celebrated women (he called the book of this phase of his work, *Women are Beautiful*), it is clear that his construction of women singly or in groups advancing towards the camera from all directions displays an unease, a fear, of what the results of his desire for them might be. Their faces frown by his camera, their eyes bow down to avoid his gaze. Burgin highlighted the dynamics of his "old bag" image. Winogrand's fear at what he reads as a loss of (female) beauty in ageing is registered by his "old bag" image. It is no coincidence that one of the six disability images (and the only one of two showing a wheelchair user) in *Figments from the Real World* involves an almost identical dynamic to that of the "old bags'.

The centre of the image is three young women. They are lit by a sun behind them and their sharp shadows converge towards the camera. They dominate the centre third of the image and they are walking along a ray of light towards the lends. They are dressed in the fashion of the moment. In their movement is recorded an affecting, perhaps transitional beauty. Their symmetry is, however, broken by the gaze of the woman on the right. The symmetry is further challenged by this woman being a step ahead of the other two as she stares down at the presence, in the shadows, of a crouched wheelchair user. The other two women slightly move their heads towards the wheelchair. All of their eyes are tightened and all of their facial expressions "interpret" the presence of the wheelchair user with degrees of controlled horror.

Unlike Winogrand's dumping of middle-aged women into "old bags," he confronts these young women with a warning. He observes them as beautiful but warns them that their beauty and all its "paraphernalia" is all that separates them from the "grotesque" form they are witnessing. Beauty is warned of the beast. Clearly, Winogrand could not assuage his desire for women, whom he spent years photographically accosting on the street. His work harbours a resentment that they do not respond to his aggressive desire and so he implants warnings. The asymmetry of the imagery is anchored in the non-disabled reading (in this instant, Winogrand's) of disabled people as sites of asymmetrical disharmony. The women's body harmony (as Winogrand desires it) is set against the wheelchair user's disharmony (as Winogrand sees it). Winogrand's use of the disabled person, again enfreaked, is to bring out of the underworld and into the shadows a symbol of asymmetry *as fear and decay* which challenges the three women's right to walk "beautifully" down the street.

Like Arbus, Winogrand's use of disability is to warn the "normal" world that their assumptions are fragile. This he does by the use of differentness of many disabled people's bodies as a symbol of the profound asymmetry of consumer society, particularly in the Untied States. Despite the fact that the American President Roosevelt had been disabled, the enfreakment of disabled people in these new practices became the symbol of the alienation of humanity which these new photographers were trying to record.

The Family of Man exhibition had all but excluded disabled people because they did not represent hope in the new order, so the post New Documents practitioners *included* disabled people for precisely the same reasons. The Family of Man and the New Documents exhibitions, constructed within photographic theories as radically separate, are inextricably linked, in that the inclusion of disabled people does not mean progress, but regression. Disabled people increased their presence in the new reportage of these photographers not as a sign of enlightenment and integration, but as a sign of bedlam.

The fourth book picked at random, I realised afterwards, takes us to a European setting. In *Another Way of Telling*,[18] the inevitable inclusion of a disabled subject comes almost at the very beginning. This book deals heavily with photographs of the countryside and the peasantry of various countries and the first photo-text piece sets this agenda. This is a story of Jean Mohr taking photographs of some cows, while the cow owner jokingly chastises him for taking pictures with permission and without payment. This first part very much sets the geographic and political agenda for the whole book, which explores the three-way relationship between the photographer, the photographed and the different meanings and readings taken from the photographs.

In every image or image-sequence, excluding the second one in the book (that of a blind girl in India) the images are more or less openly problematical. That is, the relationship between the image and its apparent informative or communicative value is put to the test. "Only occasionally is an image self-sufficient," says Jean Mohr. From this assertion, Mohr and Berger explore the image-making processes and what can be taken on or used within the process of photography that might work for both the photographer and the subject. The genesis of the book is to question meaning and use-value of imagery from all points, not just that of the photographer.

In Mohr's eighty-page first part, he illuminates different contexts of his own image-making, from shooting running children from a passing train, to shooting and reshooting working people and directing his work according to their expressed wishes. The theme which pervades the whole book is that of the working process. Moreover, the working process that they have chosen to explore visually is that of people working on the land and their lives and communities. The image-sequences, whether of cow-herders or of wood-cutters, begin with labour and its dignity. Clearly, unlike many "concerned" social realist photographers, Mohr is attempting to inhabit the process from the inside, not just to observe it externally. His method is through the voice, feedback and acknowledgement of the person photographed in their work. Their work is the anchor, the base, from which the story unfolds.

At one point and in one sequence, Mohr turns the camera on himself. He puts himself in the picture. He talks about the fear, the anxiety, even the panic which assails many people when they are the subject of the camera. Am I too fat? Am I too skinny? Is my nose too large? He tells us that he finds the process of putting himself in the picture difficult and talks about how he attempts to lose his image through technical disguises, like deliberately moving the camera during an exposure so as to blur the image, and so on. He anchors this process of putting himself in the picture on the quite valid and narcissistic idea that he used to imagine that he looked like Samuel Beckett. After bringing the story home by saying that he was finally forced to view his own image by being the subject matter of *other* people's lens, rather than his own, he finally finishes it by telling us that a student who photographed him felt that he did indeed resemble Beckett.

His work on other people's images and stories and his work on his own image and self are linked because, in grappling with the process of representation of his self or of others, he tells us and attempts to show us that the meaning of images is rooted in the process and context in which they were made. This is an important assertion but not unique. This book was published in 1982 and came at a time when other photographers and theorists, like Victor Burgin, Allan Sekula, Photography Workshop (Jo Spence/Terry Dennett) *et al.*, were questioning and problematising and naturalist truth-telling assumptions underpinning the left's use of social realist photography. *Another Way of Telling*, then, was a part of this "movement."

However, *Another Way of Telling*, and Jean Mohr's opening piece in particular, is clearly anchored in finding another way of using naturalist reportage, not abandoning it altogether. Mohr explains the use-value of the naturalist image to the subject. He tells stories of how this or that peasant wanted the image to show the whole body—of the person, of the cow, of the tree-cutting process—rather than be "unnaturally" cropped. Naturalism, then, to him, has a purpose *in context.*

Here, we begin to get close to the *purpose* of the blind girl pictures within Jean Mohr's piece and the book as a whole. The realist (time/place) agenda is set in the first image, that of the cowman, but the *underlying agenda of "simple" naturalism* (that is to say, Mohr and Berger's belief in its ability to tell a simple story) is anchored in the hypersimplicity of the blind girls' pleasure. These pictures of a disabled person—a blind Asian girl—form the apex of the book's naturalist thesis that the value of naturalism is in its portrayal of unconscious innocence.

The story is called "The Stranger who Imitated Animals." The "stranger" in question is Jean Mohr. In the 250-odd words which accompany the five images, he tells us of visiting his sister in the university town of Aligarh in India and of his sister's "warning" of the blind girl who comes round and likes to know what is happening. He awakes the next morning unclear of where he is when

> The young blind girl said Good Morning. The sun had been up for hours. Without reasoning why I replied to her by yapping like a dog. Her face froze for a moment. Then I imitated a cat caterwauling. And the expression on her face behind the netting changed to one of recognition and complicity in my play-acting. I went on to a peacock's cry, a horse whinnying, a large animal growling—like a circus. With each act and according to our mood, her expression changed. Her face was so beautiful that, without stopping our game, I picked up my camera and took some pictures of her. She will never see these photographs. For her I shall simply remain the invisible stranger who imitated animals.[19]

Clearly, despite his simplification of his response ('without reasoning why'), he responded with impersonations precisely because he had observed that she was blind. He objectified her, his first impulse on waking up to see a blind person was to play games with the blindness. Underlying this was the assumption that blind people (whatever the level of visual impairment)have no idea of quantifiable physical reality and would, of course, think that the sound really was of a yapping dog waking up in bed. His joke reveals his disability (un-) consciousness, not hers.

But she responds to this with laughter, she joins in. So, he further objectifies her by again distancing himself. While she laughs along with his imitations, he secretly photographs her, because her laughing but blind face was "so beautiful." Clearly, because she is laughing in his pictures, he presumably continued his imitations while he photographed her. The game for two turned into manipulation by one. The pictures show her leaning against the dark wooden surround of the door. She is framed by this and leans into this frame by pressing her ears to his mimicry. She is kept at a distance and keeps her responses on that surface of the mosquito net which fits into the wooden frame. This framing of her by the door is copied in his framing of her in the camera. Out of the five pictures in the sequence, four clearly show her eyes. Technically, these have been deliberately whitened in the printing to highlight the blindness.

As labour is the anchor in the other series, and as narcissism is the anchor in his self-image series, shooting the whites of her eyes is the anchor in this series. Her blindness is the symbol of innocence and nobility. Her blindness is the anchor of her simplicity. Her blindness is the object of his voyeurism. He has taken and symbolised this disabled person's image, which he says "she will never see" (he obviously didn't consider aural description), as the anchor and beauty of naturalism. The text which accompanies this series of images doesn't quite have the once-upon-a-time-ness of some of the other photo-essays, but it still serves to push the imagery into the magical or metaphysical. The always-to-be natural images of the blind girl are the only set that have no significant time element to them. His work with the cowman spans days, his work with the wood-cutter is over a period of time (enough for the wood-cutter to give an opinion of the finished prints), but the work with the blind girl of beauty and innocence needs saying once, because it is forever. Again, like The Family of Man, like Arbus and Winogrand, Mohr has chosen to absent both the three-dimensional disabled person and their social story because it is incongruous to their own disability (un)consciousness. Their images tell us nothing about the actual lives of disabled people, but they add to the history of oppressive representation.

I have just analysed a random selection of four major photographic books, only one of which I knew to have been involved in disability representation. In the event, all four were. In the final analysis, these books which include disabled people in their field of photographic reference do so on the condition that disabled people are, to use Sontag's term for Diane Arbus's work, "borderline" cases. Sontag meant this term in its common reference to psychic or spiritual disorder. However, disabled people in the representations which I have discussed in this and the previous chapters share a commonality in that they live in different camps beyond the border. Whether beauty or the beast, they are outsiders. The basis for this border in society is real. It is physical and it is called segregation. The social absence of disabled people creates a vacuum in which the visual meanings attributable (symbolically, metaphorically, psychically, etc.) to impairment and disablement appear free-floating and devoid of any actual people. In the absence of disabled people, the meaning in the disabled person and their body is made by those who survey. They attempt to shift the disablement on to the impairment, and the impairment into a flaw. The very absence of disabled people in positions of power and representation deepens the use of this "flaw" in their images. The repression of disabled people makes it more likely that the symbolic use of disablement by non-disabled people is a sinister or mythologist one. Disablement re-enters the social world through photographic representation, but in the re-entry its meaning is tied not by the observed, disabled people, but by the non-disabled observers.

It is here that all the work, picked at random, is linked. Disabled people, in these photographic representations, are positioned either as meaningful or meaningless bodies. They are meaningful only as polarised anchors of naturalist humility or psychic terror. Brave but tragic: two sides of the segregated coin? Disabled people are taken into the themes pursued by Arbus, Winogrand, Mohr, and so on, to illustrate the truth of their respective grand narratives. The role of the body of the disabled person is to enflesh the thesis or theme of the photographer's work, despite the fact that most of the photographers had taken no conscious decision to work "on" disability. It is as if the spirit of the photographer's mission can be summed up in their manipulation of a disabled person's image. "The disabled" emerge, like a lost tribe, to fulfil a role for these photographers but not for themselves.

Disabled people appeared either as one image at a time per book or one role per book. The use of disabled people is the anchor of the weird, that is, the fear within. They are used as the symbol of enfreakment or the surrealism of all society. "Reactionary" users of this notion hunt the "crips" down to validate chaos within their own environment (Arbus); "progressive" users of this notion hunt them down within their own environment to find an essential romantic humanity in their own lives (but no question of access). The US "crip" symbol denotes alienation. The impaired body is the site and symbol of all alienation. It is psychic alienation made physical. The "contorted" body is the final process and statement of a painful mind.

While this symbol functions as a "property" of disabled people as viewed by these photographers, it does not function as *the* property of those disabled people observed. Its purpose was not as a role model, or as references for observed people, but as the voyeuristic property of the non-disabled gaze. Moreover, the impairment of the disabled person became the mark, the target for a disavowal, a ridding, of the existential fears and fantasies of non-disabled people. This "symbolic" use of disablement knows no classic political lines, indeed it may be said to become more oppressive the further left you move.[20] The point is clear. If the disability paradox, the disability dialectic, is between impaired people and disabling social conditions, then the photographers we have just examined represent the construction of an "official" history of blame from the disabling society towards disabled people.

The works were selected at random and I fear their randomness proves my point. Wherever I drilled, I would have found the same substance. Were I to continue through modern photographic publications, I have no doubt that the pattern I am describing would continue; the only variation being that some would use disabled people for the purposes described, while others would absent disabled people altogether. A cursory widening of the list, to glance at photographers who have come after those named above, people like Joel-Peter Witkin,[21] Gene Lambert,[22] Bernard F. Stehle,[23] Nicholas Nixon,[24] and others who have all "dealt with" disablement, shows photographers who continued a manipulation of the disability/impairment image but have done so in a manner which depressingly makes the work by, say, Arbus and Mohr (I don't suppose they ever felt they'd be mentioned in the same breath!) seem positively timid! The work of many of the "post New Documentaries" has shifted the ground on the representation of disabled people by making "them" an even more separate category. While the volume of representation is higher, the categorisation, control and manipulation have become deeper. In this sense, the photographic observation of disablement has increasingly become the art of categorisation and surveillance. Also, from a psychological viewpoint, those that appear to have transgressed this commodification of disabled people have only transgressed their own fears of their constructions. The oppression remains the same. The segregated are not being integrated, they are being broken into! The photographic construction of disabled people continues through the use of disabled people in imagery as the site of fear, loss or pity. Those who are prevented by their liberal instincts from "coming out" in their cripple-as-freak, freak-as-warning-of-chaos, circumvent it by attempting to tell the unreconstructed "natural" story of oblivion. Either way, it is a no-win victim position for disabled people within those forms of representation. My intention in this essay is to suggest new forms.

A final note of hope. Diane Arbus was "extremely upset" when she received a reply from "The Little People's Convention" to her request to photograph them. They wrote that, "We have our own little person to photograph us.'[25] In terms of disabled people's empowerment, this is the single most important statement in all of the work considered.

NOTES

1. Vic Finkelstein has argued that the "administrative model" of disablement has replaced the "medical model" to the extent that it is now the dominant oppressive one. This model, according to Finkelstein, suggests that the move away from the large "phase-two" institutions (which mirrored heavy industrial production) towards the dispersal of "care in the community" has meant that disablement has shifted from a predominantly cure-or-care issue to an administrative one. There is no doubt in my mind that this shift is being echoed in the production of "positive" images within the UK local authorities. They are similar to the functionalist images of the charities third-stage imagery in their portrayal of the administration of service provision to (grinning) disabled people.

2. *GYN/ecology* (1981), by Mary Daly, London: Women's Press.

3. *Images of the Disabled, Disabling Images* (1987), ed. Alan Gartner and Tom Joe, New York: Praeger.

4. *The Family of Man*, exhibition and publication by the Museum of Modern Art, New York, 1955. (Reprinted 1983.)

5. *diane arbus* (1990), London: Bloomsbury Press.

6. *On Photography* (1979), by Susan Sontag, London: Penguin.

7. "Arbus revisited: a review of the monograph," by Paul Wombell, *Portfolio* magazine, no. 10, Spring 1991.

8. Ibid., p. 33.

9. *diane arbus*, op. cit., p. 23. The full title of the photograph is *Mexican Dwarf in his Hotel Room in N.Y.C. 1970.*

10. *diane arbus*, op. cit., p. 16. The full title for this photograph is: *Russian Midget Friends in a Living Room on 100th St. N.Y.C. 1963.*

11. The death cry of Kurtz on discovering the unpronounceable, in Conrad's *Heart of Darkness.*

12. *Diane Arbus: A Biography* (1984), by Patricia Bosworth, New York: Avon Books, p. 226.

13. It is important to remember that the ability of naturalist photographic practice to "enfreak" its subject is not peculiar to the oppressive portrayal of disabled people. For example, the same process of fragmenting and reconstructing oppressed people into the projection of the photographer is particularly marked in the projection of the working classes. See *British Photography from the Thatcher Years* (book and exhibition) by Susan Kismaric, Museum of Modern Art, New York, 1990.

14. *Diane Arbus: A Biography*, op. cit., p. 227.

15. Ibid., p. 153.

16. Gary Winogrand (1988), *Figments from the Real World*, ed. John Szarkowski, New York: Museum of Modern Art.

17. *The End of Art Theory: Criticism and Post-Modernity* (1986), by Victor Burgin, London: Macmillan, p. 63.

18. *Another Way of Telling* (1982), by John Berger and Jean Mohr, London: Writers and Readers.

19. Ibid., p. 11.

20. For the "left" use of disability/impairment as the site of a defense of the welfare state, see "Bath time at St. Lawrence" by Raissa Page in *Ten-8*, nos. 7/8, 1982. Alternatively, for a cross-section of the inclusion of disability imagery within magazines servicing the welfare state, see the King's Fund Centre reference library, London. Finally, see the impairment charity house journals and read the photo credits, i.e., the Spastics Society's *Disability Now*. Network, Format, Report and other left photo agencies regularly supply uncritical impairment imagery.

21. *Masterpieces of Medical Photography: Selections from the Burns Archive* (1987), ed. Joel-Peter Witkin, California: Twelve-tree Press.

22. *Work from a Darkroom* (1985), by Gene Lambert (exhibition and publication), Dublin: Douglas Hyde Gallery.

23. *Incurably Romantic* (1985), by Bernard F. Stehle, Philadelphia: Temple University Press.

24. *Pictures of People* (1988), by Nicholas Nixon, New York: Museum of Modern Art.

25. *Diane Arbus: A Biography* (1984), by Patricia Bosworth, New York: Avon Books, p. 365.

20

Modernist Freaks
and Postmodern Geeks

DAVID MITCHELL

In general, literature projects cultural assumptions about physical or cognitive difference into its presentations of disability even as it situates the creative act itself as the compensatory value of writing. This essay seeks to explore the opportunistic collusion between literature, metaphor, artistic aesthetic, and disability in order to demonstrate that the literary grotesque—those physical and cognitive anomalies, malformations and deformities placed in the service of symbolic social and artistic meanings[1]—is an artistic fantasy that invokes physical aberrancy as a visible symptom of social disorganization and collapse. Vexed by the titillating and often apolitical nature of this interest, scholars of disability in the humanities share a general suspicion that the grotesque turns disability into a shorthand method of characterization that simplistically reveals the intangible secrets of a psyche in conflict.[2] Even as the literary grotesque is interpreted as denoting a host of social "outcasts" made allegorical and apparent through their physical "deviance," traditional interpretations of the grotesque in literature end up reinscribing biology, rather than social institutions, as the causal agent of physical aberrancy.

By contrasting two novels, Sherwood Anderson's American classic, *Winesburg, Ohio*, and Katherine Dunn's contemporary cult novel, *Geek Love*, we can assess the ways in which the deployment of the grotesque in literature continues to serve as "matter" for the writer's grist mill.[3] On the one hand, my argument here is that while modernism endeavored to unmoor the static languages of Victorianism from their "sterile" and more "puritanical" sources in the nineteenth century, writers of the period nonetheless reified categories such as the grotesque in their association with pathological cultural models. On the other hand, postmodernist writers have tended to take up inherited tropes such as the grotesque from their predecessors and interrogate the very nature of their historical and artistic allure. Rather than touting *Geek Love* as a "redemptive" site of postmodernist revision, I want to argue that the novel serves as a caricature of the artistic desire to yoke physical aberrancy to metaphors of denigration and perversity.[4] Instead of seeking to transcend an abject matter explicitly associated with the body, postmodernist texts investigate the site of metaphorical operations themselves. In this sense, Dunn's novel provides a useful case study of the contradictions embedded in modernist deployments of the grotesque while steeping itself in the very "art" and language of the grotesque itself.

Whereas a general readership of reviewers and scholars have tended to read the novel as an allegory of the perversions of capitalism,[5] this paper seeks to attend to Dunn's overt grappling with issues of bodily "norms." Through her work, we can begin to define constitutive features of a subjectivity of disability—one that longs for a seamless integration into normative ideals in the midst of occupying a body of irreducible differences. Such a definition of disability, one predicated less upon a traditional narrative of romantic transcendence and more upon variations of incapacity that structure and define bodies, supplies a credible version of disabled subjectivity itself.

Scholars in disability studies understandably express uncertainty about imaginative works such as Dunn's that exploitatively replicate disability as "freakishness" and commodified horror. This essay identifies and analyzes the role of history and aesthetics in literary constructions of physical differences as "disabilities" and "liabilities." Such an approach establishes the utility of adding a definitively postmodern subjectivity to an expanding repertoire of disability studies models for representing physical difference as a cultural process rather than a static biological condition.

THE MODERNIST FREAK

Sherwood Anderson's *Winesburg, Ohio*, begins with an enigmatic dream sequence wherein the protagonist, a writer who is physically infirm, old and has a white mustache, conjures up a "curious procession of figures" (Anderson, 22). "The Book of the Grotesque" acts as a kind of myth of origins that theorizes an important connection between the moment of creative inspiration for the writer and the "grotesque" products of his imagination. Instead of being terrifed by this vision and its nightmarish associations, he is moved to leave his bed and write stories about these "grotesques" that "represented all the men and women he had ever known":

> In the bed the writer had a dream that was not a dream. As he grew somewhat sleepy but was still conscious, figures began to appear before his eyes. He imagined the young indescribable thing within himself was driving a long procession of figures before his eyes.
>
> You see the interest in all this lies in the figures that went before the eyes of the writer. They were all grotesques. All of the men and women the writer had ever known had become grotesques. (Anderson, 22)

To posit the curious equation of creativity—"the young indescribable thing within himself"—with this curious freak show of imagination makes a critical link between literature's exploitation of constructed deviancy and the world of physical being. For the reader such a scenario proffers access to a "mysterious process": the moment of invention that compels the writer to leave the comfort of his bed and record a vision. Creativity relies upon a process of making the familar abhorent and strange. In other words, the writer writes only when he or she recognizes the formula of a subject matter worth writing about, and *because* that material inevitably surfaces out of one's experience, the unfamiliar "distortion" of the dream of the grotesque announces the arrival of a "full-fledged" story.

Significantly, it is in this dreamlike state that the protagonist first encounters this "figural" world, and connects it to a physical form(ula) of the grotesque. Like the superficial facade of small town life that Anderson suggests harbors an array of perversities, violences, and abnormalities, the grotesque acts as a symptomatic visage that connects the deformities of a secreted internal life with various distortions of the physical landscape. The writer's "dream" provides him with a necessary fantastical transmutation of what he categorizes as the banal and familiar. The shadowy substance of character barely discernible on the surface, is suddenly "revealed" to the writer in the physical landscape of the body; the "everyday" metamorphoses into the literary "matter" of the grotesque.

In essence, Anderson's introduction illustrates that art, in this case literature, makes physicality mediate between the visible exterior world and the invisible interior life of the subject. As the narrative of the writer's dream continues and the "rationale" for the appearance of these grotesque figures emerges, Anderson yokes this unnatural visage with an analysis of individual pathology. As we discover in the second-to-last paragraph, what "made the people grotesques" were not physical properties but a more ephemeral "truth."

> It was the truths that made the people grotesques. The old man had quite an elaborate theory concerning the matter. It was his notion that the moment one of the people took one of the truths to himself, called it his truth, and tried to live his life by it, he became a grotesque and the truth he embraced became a falsehood. (Anderson, 24)

By objectifying truth in this manner, in making an abstract concept into material that can be snatched up like a valise or pocketed as a possession, the grotesque is constructed through a process of sublimation. To move from the nebulous world of possibility and multiplicity to the "falsehood" of solidity entails a kind of moral error in Anderson's fictional world. The writer's characters moor their identity to an absolute and unchanging definition of self, and the consequence is a perversion of the dynamics of Being itself. No longer are these once human subjects capable of change, they contort an inner reality into a restrictive mold that imprisons them within the corrupt world of an inelastic identity. The "evidence" of this fatal fixity for Anderson's narrator is "embodied" in his own physical caricatures.

Consequently, Anderson exposes an artistic formula of the grotesque that gestures toward an inaccessible interior landscape "deformed" by an unnatural desire for stasis. In doing so, the artist/writer supplies the physical realm as the evidence of this distortionary process. The figures of the dream-world "parade" before his mind's eye as people who have been "drawn out of shape" and there are even those whose deformities "hurt the old man with their grotesqueness." In *Winesburg*, abberant physicality commands interest in that it supplies both the fascination of a horrific distortion *and* evidence of the artist's own perverse methodology. As evidence of creativity's repulsion/attraction to the formula of the grotesque, the introduction ends with a crucial distinction. While the writer's fascination with the grotesque threatens to overcome him and make him in effect a victim of his own grotesque landscape, he is saved from such a fate. "The young thing inside him" that previously served as the wellspring of creative vision preserves his own sense of physical and psychological integrity. Anderson's writer resists falling prey to his own distortionary system by virtue of his mastery over the artistic or creative mechanism itself.

The exoneration of the artist from implication in the artistic contrivance that the town of Winesburg represents establishes an important moment in our understanding of literary modernism. Because canonical modernism openly embraced definitions of twentieth century culture as inherently alienated and fragmented, its narrative method forthrightly sought out working symbols of this degraded malaise. Yeats's "rough beast" in "The Second Coming" announced the arrival of a moment that would find its most powerful expression in the perversion and contortion of physical and literary form themselves. Such an attempt to couple physical and literary form developed as a result modernism's self-styled proclamation that language could act upon the Real and metamorphose its seemingly static and stable properties. In *The Modern Tradition*, Ellmann and Fieldelson describe this impulse to reorganize the reigning paradigms of social and individual perception as an inherently symbolist endeavor.

Ironically, the radicality of modernist experimentation left the symbolic order reeling while further reifying a tendency to pathologize cultural institutions through metaphorical perversions of the body itself. One strain in the modern tradition that developed out of an imperative to use language in order to orchestrate a revolution of consciousness imagined itself as a transcendence of a degraded and de-romanticized nature. Instead of the artist striving to provide a mirror of perfect nature as in Romanticism, modernism began to characterize the artist as an actor who surpassed a now largely defoliated, alien, and imperfect world:

> . . . many symbolists look at nature askance in all these senses, as a kind of brutal, massive, and crude encroachment of the non-human and sub-human. Their rebellion against it leads to Wilde's paradox that art holds no mirror up to nature, but is rather man's protest against nature's ineptitudes, his substitution of perfect imaginative forms for rudimentary natural ones. (Ellmann, 7–8)

Through this artistic ideology the physical world would come to stand for the perverse and inept productions of a degraded physical landscape. The symbolists would defiantly posit imagination as an aesthetic combat of symbols seeking to shore up and revise the monstrosities of nature.[6] To nail down this point, modernist poets, painters and novelists would consistently deploy the visible world as twisted and unidentifiable —a symbolic wreckage of Romanticist repression.

The implementation of the symbolic order into a visage of environmental dis-array strategically perverted audience expectations from a variety of perspectives. Social codes, morality, aesthetic form, plot, and so on, all served as mediums for communicating a distinct upheaval in the times.

THE POSTMODERN GEEK

In the concluding chapter of *Freaks: Myths and Images of the Secret Self*, Leslie Fiedler argues that the literature of the freak has been transformed from the seductive peep of the prohibited to the lurid intimacy of "kinky sex and com-pulsory candor" (Fiedler, 335). Within such a model, contemporary desires give way to a new kind of exploitation that thrives upon a once-taboo intimacy:

> Unreal, surreal to the point of making the whole tale seem more parable than his-tory, that improbable juncture also opens up possibilities for the grossest scatolog-ical and sexual humor. . . [I]t is precisely such revelations about Freaks that we demand of those who reimagine them. What do they do on the stool? in bed? in all those private moments once considered out of bounds to public curiosity? There have always been some who suspected that the appeal of the Freak show was not unlike that of pornography, and in the age of the explicit, the secret is out. (Fiedler, 335)

Fiedler's idea of "pornographic" intimacy helps to explain the narrative method of *Geek Love* which hinges upon an exposé of what Fiedler terms the "private self." While Fiedler first critiques the exploitative voyeurism of nineteenth-cen-tury forms such as the freak show, he finds even less solace in the invasive con-ventions of contemporary literature.[7] Not only does he find the freak show alive and well in current literary metaphors, he argues that the artistic thirst for the freakish and grotesque now openly revels in that which the former century con-cealed and dissimulated. With bodily aberration on display in *Geek Love*, the most intimate details of a life lived under the auspices of disability come into full view.

While *Winesburg, Ohio* endeavors to "rescue" its characters from the horror and distance of the grotesque, *Geek Love* embraces the very material that Ander-son's novel establishes and then eschews. Like Anderson, Dunn provides us with access to the "gnarled" interior lives of her characters, but *Geek Love* explicitly structures those lives as determined by the bodily experience of the "freak." Dunn's strategy is to present the body as definitively involved in the formation of subjectivity, and in doing so *Geek Love* uses its portrait of sideshow life as a way of allegorizing what Elizabeth Grosz has called the relationship between "*embod-ied subjectivity*[and] *psychical corporeality*" (Grosz, 22).[8] Dunn positions the sub-jectivities of her "freakish" characters as existing on the cusp between biological and psychological worlds in order to establish a more adequate model that avoids reducing subjectivity to a strictly psychic affair.

Dunn's novel also begins with the fabricated "grotesque" as its own inspira-tional metaphor for the creative act. After being introduced to the key actors in the "Binewski's Carnival Fabulon," *Geek Love* offers up its own parable for the originary moment of its freakish "conception":

> My father's name was Aloysius Binewski. He was raised in a traveling carnival owned by his father and called "Binewski's Fabulon." Papa was twenty-four years old when Grandpa died and the carnival fell into his hands. Al carefully bolted the silver urn containing his father's ashes to the hood of the generator truck that powered the midway. The old man had wandered with the show for so long that his dust would have been miserable left behind in some stationary vault.
>
> Times were hard and, through no fault of young Al's, business began to decline. Five years after Grandpa died, the once flourishing carnival was fading. . . . Al was a standard-issue Yankee, set on self-determination and independence, but in that crisis his core of genius revealed itself. He decided to breed his own freak show. (Dunn, 7)

Thus, in one stroke the novel makes a parallel between the social systems of patriarchy and carnival as naturalized foundations of ideological interpollation and systemic logic.[9] Aloysius Binewski finds himself unexpectedly in possession of an economic enterprise subject to the whims of historical, cultural, and individual fate. Because the younger Binewski was "raised in a traveling carnival," he never questions the morality or redemptive value of the freak show itself. Instead he accepts the "carnival" as a natural outgrowth of coincidence and patrilineal determinism, a legacy neither to be disputed nor refused by the rightful beneficiary.

By bolting his father's ashes to the hood of the generator truck, Aloysius provides the novel with an ironic symbol of its own artistic legacy. Rather than distance itself from the legacy of "the grotesque" by leaving its progenitor's ashes to suffer the misery of "a stationary vault," *Geek Love* flaunts the ashes of past literary traditions as the engine of its own narrative structure. In doing so, the family dependency upon the freak show as an exploitative source of capital and personal survival establishes a parallel with the writer's own metaphorical opportunism. By beginning with an open commentary on the artificiality of the grotesque, the novel simultaneously embraces its own sordid literary origins and announces the object of its critique. When the father declares his decision to "breed his own freak show" as a means of revitalizing the failing business, the story unveils the artificiality of its own artistic method in order candidly to pursue the economic and cultural forces that drive its desires.

No longer content with the banality of performed behavioral oddities such as Lil's chicken-biting geek act, the carnival couple now searches for ways in which to provide side-show-goers with the tangible fascination of bodily distortion itself. Aloysius' s"brain child" parodies a quintessentially modernist mechanism of "high" literature—the epiphany—by linking it to a debased economic motivation. As he and his now pregnant wife, Lil, experiment with an array of fetus-altering chemicals from the mundane affects of cocaine and amphetamines to the extravagant agents of insecticides and radioisotopes, an explicit connection is drawn between the day-dreaming narrator of *Winesburg, Ohio* and the alchemy of a capitalistic underworld in *Geek Love*. The stated need to reproduce with an eye toward the "freakish" and "bizarre" locates an allegory for literature's dependency upon idiosyncratic and scandalous subject matter. Like the visible medium of the grotesque in Anderson's fantasy sequence, the characters of Dunn's parable formulate an artificial plot for re-establishing the visual evidence of the Fabulon's unique character.

Such an open nod to the material foundations of a past tradition in the grotesque provides a paradigm of the methodology of *Geek Love*. In her essay on postmodern narrative strategies and the only other published analysis of Dunn's novel, "Postmodern Parataxis: Embodied Texts, Weightless Information," N. Katherine Hayles argues that shifts in historical paradigms occur within the metaphorical roots of narratives themselves. As one interpretive system's "metaphoric coherence" begins to dwindle and lose explanatory authority, another arrives to take its place. The interim of such a shift inevitably leaves behind its own historical residue: "In transition areas, where the power of one set of metaphors is not yet exhausted and the ascendancy of others not fully established, the systems interact with each other. The fading metaphors partly determine how the emerging metaphors will be understood, just as the newer metaphors cause the older to be reinterpreted" (Hayles, 396). In *Geek Love*, metaphors of the grotesque signal the reverberations of a prior representational strategy and self-consciously privilege the very process of the category's reinterpretation and revision. The "grotesques" of Dunn's story-line pay lip service to their function as symbols of psychological horror and cultural collapse, while simultaneously "returning" these mythic selves to the realm of a thoroughly "embodied" experience.

While Anderson's narrator establishes a necessary distance between his grotesque vision and his own artistic project, Dunn self-consciously exploits the allure of the grotesque and indicts the dream-work of art itself. Once the economic context of Aloysius's and Lil's re-invention of the freak show is established, the novel immediately introduces the narrative perspective of one of the parents' "freakish" projects: the hunchbacked, albino, Olympia. Unlike Anderson's narrator who views the world from the safety and artificially constructed vantage point of a raised bed (he begins his introductory parable by employing a carpenter to build a platform that will make his bed even with the window to better secure his voyeuristic tendencies), *Geek Love* begins with the perspective of the "grotesque" subject itself. In doing so, the novel effectively collapses the distance between its audience and modernist metaphorics of physical aberrancy.

Dunn parallels the mythic fascination of physical difference that accrues around the "freak" to the more mundane experiences of individuals with disabilities. In dispersed segments, "Notes for Now," Olympia comments upon the meanings of her family's tumultuous past and her own contradictory contemporary moment. As the sole survivor of the conflagration that kills her family and destroys the Fabulon as a viable economic entity, Dunn's narrator tells the story in retrospect from the "knowing" perspective of the second generation. When

Olympia acknowledges that her parents were secretly disappointed in the banality of her physical anomalies, she simultaneously introduces a division between the apocalyptic (and thus, more "valuable") freakish qualities of her brothers and sisters—Arty "the Aqua Boy," Elly and Iphy, sisters joined at the hip, and Chick, the clairvoyant—and her own "less interesting deformities." As categories, "freak" and "disability" interrogate each other; the novel thematizes and disturbs the associational lineage of physicality with metaphors of psychological alienation and moral corruption.

In re-establishing traditions of the literary grotesque as the artistic precursor of *Geek Love*, the narrative ironizes the "genetic material" from which the "grotesque" hails: Olympia and her freakish siblings "embody" the results of a past experiment gone awry. In a direct revision of the gendered thesis of Simone de Beauvoir's *The Second Sex*, Olympia at one points states that ". . . a true freak cannot be made. A true freak must be born" (Dunn 20). Such a sentiment establishes one of the crucial paradoxes of physical disability: while the body serves as host to an array of parasitic social mythologies regarding abnormality and difference, it is also bound to a notion of biology as *inborn essence*. The Binewski children prove capable of adeptly manipulating fantasies of bodily difference in order to carve out a niche in a fethishistic commodity capitalism, yet such a manipulation leaves them ambivalently tethered to a physical fate.[10] Faced with the dictates of a culture that confuses biology with destiny, Olympia embraces a dubious ideal that she and her siblings possess the "originality" of a "true difference," one that cannot be reproduced by any array of imitators to the throne of uniqueness and absolute individuality.

Such paradoxes can be seen throughout the novel as Dunn's characters exploit their physical aberrations for their spectacular perversity while simultaneously contemplating the effects of their willing participation in the "meat market." During one early scene when Olympia models for her daughter who sketches portraits of physical suffering and unique bodily types, the narrator is torn between rewarding her daughter's refusal to denote her as exceptionally disabled and feeling like an object in the service of artistic mimesis:

> Watching her work is comfortable. I feel invisible again, as though she had never spoken to me beyond "Good Morning." She is not interested in my identity. She doesn't notice it. Her eyes flick impatiently at me for a fast fix—a regenerative fusing of the image on her retina, the model she inflicts on the paper. I am merely a utensil, a temporary topic for the eternal discussion between her long eye and her deliberate hand. (Dunn, 30)

The impulses that Olympia believes guide her daughter's art are both medicalized and artistic—as the poser she is simultaneously "a utensil" or "temporary topic" of a conversation from which she is excluded, or an anonymous object in need of "a regenerative fusing." As she goes on to inquire about the origins of her daughter's artistic interests she is quickly corrected with the reply, "No, no. A medical illustrator. For textbooks and manuals . . ." (Dunn, 30). This critical connection that Dunn makes between the creative impulses of art and the cataloguing objectives of medicine situates physical aberrancy as a foundational objective of both worlds. In either scenario Olympia feels her physical being extorted from herself, metamophosed into a mere "model" inflicted on to the paper and her own identity.

Yet, paradoxically, the sketching scene also begins with a mood of tranquility—the narrator finds herself comforted by the anonymous act of being sketched by one who is not "interested in my identity." Such a longing for personal anonymity—to be provided a space where one's identity is not synonymous with the material properties of physical being itself—establishes the key coordinates of Olympia's subjectivity. Torn between an ethics of physical exceptionality championed by her family and her own personal desire for assimilation, Dunn theorizes a psyche of disability that longs for a seamless integration into humanity in the midst of an experience of irreducible difference. As the artist's illustration passes from individual portraiture to the anonymous diagnostic catalogue of the medical textbook, Olympia recognizes the risks of identifying with either the utterly individualized abnormality or the anonymous representative specimen.

Such competing desires mark the disabled subject as multiply split. Unlike the freakish performers of the Fabulon who extract a living by virtue of their own mythic existence as living anomalies, Olympia feels consigned only to the horror of her commonplace freakishness. In the street she is taunted by passersby who register shock over the "affront" that her physical difference poses; in her professional life she is relegated to a disembodied "voice" on the airways of a local radio station; as an unexceptional "freak" she is relegated to the diminished role of barker outside the exhibit of her infamous brother. As one who is denied access to the larger-than-life authority of her circus-show siblings, Olympia is left to contemplate her own diminished standing.

The catalogue of ways in which Olympia is subjected to the cultural coordinates of her physical condition proves integral to Dunn's construction of disability as a less "spectacular" version of what Leslie Fiedler has defined as "the mythic prototype of the freak." More than the uncanny shock of physical difference and the everyday terror of physical debilitation, the freak evokes associations with the monstrous and mythic fabulations of the most primordial kind:

> The true Freak . . . stirs both supernatural terror and natural sympathy, since, unlike the fabulous monsters, he is one of us, the human child of human parents, however altered by forces we do not quite understand into something mythic and mysterious, as no mere cripple ever is. (Fiedler, 34)

This instrumental division between Fiedler's "fabulous monsters" and the "mere cripple" stakes out a terrain that *Geek Love* explicitly invokes. By foregrounding a world of characters who exist in this "no body's land" of physical deviancy, Dunn endeavors to trace out the process by which "cripples" are transformed into "monsters." Rather than reify the traditional distinction that Fiedler invokes in the above passage—a division that, according to Robert Bogdan, "does not stray from the traditional view of 'freak' as a physiological condition" (Bogdan, 7)—Dunn defines the designation *resolutely* as a matter of physical "packaging." As Books I and II delve into the voyeuristic fascination of private lives and theatrical maneuvers that go on "behind the scenes" of a vaudeville of the flesh, Fiedler's mythic monstrosities are unveiled in a myriad of exploitative conventions. Not only does *Geek Love* manage to manipulate successfully the "lowest common denominator" of specular desire, the novel shamelessly refuses to "demystify" the grotesque moorings of its own literary lineage.

While Fiedler will draw a critical dichotomy between the "true Freak" and the "mere cripple," Dunn argues that the freak must be erected and molded from the outside. Constituted through an assortment of theatrical props and technological circuitry, Arturo stages his own public myth for mass consumption. Longing for a vision that can lead them away from the burden and suffering that accompany the excesses of a bodily existence, the Binewski followers absorb Arturo's mythic ambiance with the zeal of the devout. For Norval Sanderson, the family's unofficial biographer and journalist, Arty's character is best defined in terms of the "lacunae" in his knowlege. Cut off from the historical traditions that have gone into the making of Arturo's freakish ambiance, his larger-than-life performance commands the attention of those who unwittingly act upon the culturally encoded "lure" of bodily deviancy. While Sanderson flippantly derides the performance as "[o]bvious horseshit" (Dunn, 190), he fails to recognize that it is bodily difference rather than its technological packaging that ultimately constitutes the "material" of Arty's reign.

Arty understands that the realm of the biological represents the last outpost of material determinism, and consequently he flaunts his freakish physicality as the capital of idiosyncrasy. When Al McGurk, the proficient electrician who later constructs the laser-like light show of Arty's performance, seeks to join forces with the Arturan ranks by virtue of his own disability, Arty distinguishes between the power of the freak and the insufficient model of physical impairment:

> "But I guess you want my credentials," McGurk said . . . He slid his hand up the other trouser leg and both legs lay on the floor with steel shining out of the hollow tops of the knees. He pulled his pants leg up his thighs and showed the steel caps on the stumps. There were a groove, a few grip protrusions, and a number of electrical contact points protruding from each unit. He looked up, calmly waiting. . . . "You figured it wrong. The whole thing," said Arty. He rocked slightly, chuckling. "You've got yourself a little old disability there, so you took pleasure in feeling sorry for me. Well. You figured wrong . . . You're just going along with what *they* want you to do. *They* want those things hidden away, disguised, forgotten, because they know how much power those stumps could have." (Dunn, 169, 170)

Ironically, the scene pivots upon Arty's tactical inversion of McGurk's attempt to flaunt the secrecy of his physical "credentials." While McGurk's prosthesis involves an elaborate contraption made up of grooves, grip protrusions and electrical contacts, the "unveiling" serves to secure his "membership" in the community of the norms through the proof of a nearly seamless bodily apparatus. Like Arty, McGurk also demonstrates the nature of his own "technological" being; yet, while McGurk believes his "achievement" rides upon the success of his assimilation into an ambulatory ideal, Arty diminishes the power of the electrician's gambit by responding, "[y]ou've got yourself a little old disability there." Such masculine sparring exemplifies the key to Arty's deft manipulation of the conventions of disability—rather than cater to fantasies of physical wholeness and the sleight-of-hand that is the promise of prosthesis, he re-wires McGurk's desires into the circuitry of the norms. For Arty, a prosthetic supplement geared toward a seamless integration reveals only a personal capitulation to the "comfort" and "power" of those who determine the standards of bodily aesthetic and physical capacity.

In Arty's worldview, "disability" (the "less" spectacular linguistic cousin of "freak") equates with an attempt to deny the "threat" that physical difference poses to cultural recitations of a wholistic bodily mantra. In lieu of the disguise that even the most "lifelike" prosthesis affords to the contemporary cyborg, Arturo charges McGurk with an act of "re-membering" himself in order to cover up and downplay his own physical difference. Within this model the reconstruction of a body back into anonymity denies the "power" of an overt encounter with cultural perceptions of perversity and deformity that are part of the historical baggage of the tradition of the "freak." Since the body plays host to cultural fantasies about personal capacities and individual prowess, the flaunting of physical aberrancy promises a necessary rebuke to the ideology of biological homogeneity.

One of the centerpieces of Bakhtin's theory of the grotesque crystallizes around his notion of "fusion" where "monstrosity" accumulates an expansive series of references and meanings. Because the grotesque body is an architecture that "is never finished," its peculiar and resourceful functioning comes from the ability to "swallow the world and [be] swallowed by the world" (Bakhtin, 317). Not only do the Arturans submit to radical bodily alteration in order to model themselves upon the mythology of the freak, but the body undergoes all kinds of novelistic permutations in order to further challenge normative definitions of bodily difference. When Olympia tracks down Miss Lick, an independent philanthropist who finances the education of "physically ruined" women, she becomes acquainted with alternatives to the spectacle of physical aberrancy offered by the side show. As she sits in Miss Lick's apartment watching video tapes of "traumatically scarred women" who have gone on to fulfill intellectual and professional careers, Olympia's ideas of femininity as a biologically pathologized condition connect up with her brother's earlier freakish exploits.

> Different girl entirely from what she had been. Old pursuits, interests, wiped out entirely. Friends tried to be polite but she made them nervous. Boys all gone west as far as she was concerned. Interesting to see the change. She seemed to have taken in the situation completely while she was still in the hospital. Turned her head around. She studied. All that old energy of hers turned to books. . . . She's a chemical engineer. (Dunn, 157, 158)

The fact of such a "deforming" accident jettisons Lick's subject from the community of the norms and completely reroutes the traditional feminine story of marriage and children into one of "all brain stuff" (Dunn, 158). Linda's expulsion from a life based upon physical coordinates—"she couldn't rely on being cute and catching a man" (Dunn, 158)—leads Lick to conclude that a more desirable life of the mind understandably results. Rather than follow the modernist linkage of physical deformity and interior pathology, Dunn strategically "deforms" an aesthetic of traditional femininity into a rationale for intellectual pursuit and professional accomplishment. As Lick explains to Olympia, "It's not that surprising when you think about the precedents. . . . Crippled painters and whatnot" (Dunn, 158).

Because the physical surface acts as the evaluative criteria of femininity as it does disability, an alteration in the exterior presentation also redefines avenues of individual opportunity and Bakhtinian "possibility." As "the grotesque" surfaces in the guise of third-degree scarring and Linda (at the prodding of Miss Lick) turns down "numerous cosmetic options" that could provide her with a medical pathway back into the society of the norms, Olympia registers an increasing alarm as she recognizes a disturbing determinism at work in the realm of the biological. While she is uncertain about the openly "deformative" projects of Miss Lick and Dr. Phyllis (who performs the Frankenstein-like surgery for the Arturans), she also understands that the alternative proves to be equally violent and basely ideological. If the "materials" of belief are predominantly bound to physical appearances, and thus the body, then her earlier maxim of "the true freak must be born, not made" may be alarmingly "truthful." Since bodily markers such as femininity and disability seem to "explain" the incapacities of entire populations as well as individuals, the physical surface functions as a guide to the truth of individual potential. In this way, the body serves as a particularly effective metaphor for the operations of cultural belief. Its constitutive compounds are *simultaneously* historically malleable and biologically absolute.

Despite the physical basis of Olympia's own annexation from an ableist culture, she begins more fully to comprehend the nature of sedimented biological mythologies only in the wake of her associations with Dr. Phyllis and Miss Lick. As her associative repertoire of public myths that connect biology and pathology increases—she also links the "deformations" of race and poverty with those of disability and femininity—Olympia acts as a conduit for our readerly alternatives. At one point she realizes that her own life has negotiated a parallel "mobility" in the face of a seemingly "immobilizing" physical condition:

A hunchback is not agile enough for efficient skulking. But my voice can take me anywhere. I can be a manicured silk receptionist, a bureaucrat of impenetrable authority, or an old college chum named Beth. I can be a pollster doing a survey of management techniques or a reporter for the daily paper doing a feature on how employees view their bosses. Anonymous, of course—no real names used and all businesses disguised. (Dunn, 150)

Such a catalogue of professional substitutions provides the narrator with a variety of personas for the taking. In an age where the "voice" can act as the medium of public intercourse, Olympia realizes—like her brother before her—that Being and identity are themselves devices for technological manipulation. As Avital Ronell has argued in her monumental study, *The Telephone Book: Technology, Schizophrenia, Electric Speech*, technology has always grounded its value in the ability to resuscitate and revitalize an imperfect body: "The prosthesis . . . to a certain extent enjoys the status of the fetish, covering a missing or inadequate body part, amplifying the potentiality of a constitutively fragile organ" (Ronell, 88). While Arty recreates his physical inadequacies as the ideal instruments of a new philosophy through various special effects, Olympia seeks to "escape" the social limitations of her physical presence through an electronic "disguise." Rather than electing the hyperbolic and artificially augmented visage of the freak, disability in this guise effaces itself in the more ephemeral simulations of audio equipment.

In posing the oppositions of the mythic freak and prosthetic assimilation Dunn determines her narrator's disabling identity as perpetually oscillating between these two unsatisfactory choices. Caught between the theatrical extravagance available to her siblings and the "annoyance" she represents to the intolerant world of the "norms," Olympia's physical deviancy leaves her alienated from a useable tradition and a communal identification. The narrator's intimacy with the market machinations of the freak show and her own marginal position within the family hierarchy of physical anomalies leaves her to mediate between the conflictual meanings of physical difference in the public and private realms. The inheritor of the sordid family genealogy of the Fabulon, Olympia strategically casts herself as the orphan of a once viable economic tradition now extinct and as the idiosyncratic product of a past genetic experiment gone awry.

The critical quandary for Dunn's narrator is that the physical "fact" of disability inevitably overrides the personal coordinates of the autobiographical subject. Threatened with the usurpation of the unique coordinates of her story, Olympia's predicament alludes to a "transitional moment" in the public meaning of disability. Rather than acting as the vehicle symbolizing cultural collapse and fragmentation as in the modernist tradition, Olympia "naturalizes" the disabled body as the site of its own subjectivity and narrative interest. Once the distance of the third-person perspective of the grotesque is challenged and interrupted by the now-speaking subject of its own metaphor, *Geek Love* establishes its own material metaphorics of the body in cathedral-like fashion as that which houses the incomplete forces of history and species:

> I was full-grown before I ever set foot in a house without wheels. Of course I had been in stores, offices, fuel stations, barns, and warehouses. But I had never walked through the door of a place where people slept and ate and bathed and picked their noses, and, as the saying goes, "lived," unless that place was three times longer than it was wide and came equipped with road shocks and tires.
>
> When I had first stood in such a house I was struck by its terrible solidity. The

thing had concrete tentacles sunk into the earth, and a sprawling inefficiency. . . .
That building wasn't going anywhere despite an itchy sense that it was not entirely
comfortable where it was. (Dunn, 321)

The "itchy sense" to which Dunn refers in this final sentence represents
Olympia's understanding that an absolute "solidity" contains its own terror.
While her own personal history in the travelling Fabulon provides her with a
more fleeting sense of herself and others in time and space, Olympia's sense of
discomfort arrives as she experiences a feeling of "unnatural" concreteness in the
meaning of her physical Being. Given the flaunted and exposed variations on
themes of bodily conditions and appearances in *Geek Love*, this observation by
the narrator involves the formulation of a final, tragic philosophy that under-
pins the entire novel. Because the body "houses" the unique differences that
compose the details of an individual subject, then the "terrible solidity" of an
immovable structure parallels Olympia's experience of her own "grounded"
bodily identity. As the possibilities of her later adult life become increasingly cir-
cumscribed by social attitudes and perceptions of her person as a bald, albino
hunchback, she encounters a terrifying fixity that cannot be undone. Like a
house with its foundation sunk deep into the earth, Olympia's multiple disabilities entrench her in an identity synonymous with her external appearances.

This final project of Dunn's novel crystallizes around her attempt to unmoor
disability from the "terrifying solidity" of its own historical and cultural lineage.
By representing the "crux" of disabled subjectivity as existing in the nexus of the
mythic freak and the isolation of physical difference, Dunn's postmodern gambit
is to flaunt the titillation of her absurdist fiction as a product of the historical
baggage that we all carry.[11] Rather than repress or ostracize the invaluable contents of the literary grotesque, *Geek Love* demonstrates that we still experience
the allure of the grotesque by participating in its perpetual reinvention. In this
sense the novel's "cultish" capital depends upon a readership still bound to the
fabulation and seduction of physical aberrancy as an inexhaustible "resource,"
while also demonstrating that the residue of this fetishistic interest nonetheless
informs our current understanding of disability.

In the final chapter of *Freaks*, Fiedler argues that his own literary moment is
founded upon the writing of a parasitic grouping of writers who are "pretenders"
to the throne of the freak. In fact, despite the visible disappearance of the spectacular dimensions of the freak show there has been a mutation of its carniva-
lesque presence in contemporary literature. To characterize such a literary
"revitalization" and return to the altar of freakshness, Fiedler disdainfully dredges
up the term, "geek," as a way of simultaneously delineating and undermining this
"newly" acquired literary taste for the grotesque. By way of explaining such a
phenomenon he resuscitates the following definition of the "geek" as a historical formula:

The Geek, on the other hand, seems these days to be coming into his own, precisely because he is a fictional Freak, not merely perceived through a preexistent

mythological grid like Giants and Dwarfs and the Lion-faced Man, but invented to satisfy psychic needs bred by infantile traumas or unquiet ancestral memories. . . . What he eats raw [are] . . . repulsive forms of lower animal life, chiefly chickens and rats—biting off their heads before they are dead and slobbering his chin with their fetid blood. (Fiedler, 342)

As an act the Geek played upon its own performative artificiality to seduce and interest audiences. In comparison to the "real" deformities sported by the sideshow's human oddities, the Geek was a "behavior" that paid homage to the physical specimens catalogued just beyond the flap of the circus tent. The "performer" served to whet the appetites of its audience for increasingly more outlandish and "unbelievable" spectacles promised by the freak show itself. The Geek constructed its own status as a "living anomaly" out of the ephemeral and malleable tissue of behavior—biting off the heads of chickens and rats and "animalistically acting out" to amuse and repulse spectators before they imbibed the real thing—and, in doing so, demonstrated that "freakishness" was a state of mind: programmed and packaged to appeal to its audiences' yearning for the unusual and different. The brash "acting out" of artistic perversity in Dunn's postmodern novel endeavors to appeal to an appetite much like that of the geek, and in turn, to self-consciously provide a space within which to interrogate the mythic packaging that designs our desires.[12]

NOTES

1. One of the more influential theorists of literary affect, the Russian formalist critic Mikhail Bahktin, distinguishes the "grotesque" as a pervasive mode in modern, as opposed to antique, literature: "This boundless ocean of grotesque bodily imagery within time and space extends to all languages, all literatures, and the entire system of gesticulation; in the midst of it the bodily canon of art, belles lettres, and polite conversation of modern times is a tiny island. This limited canon never prevailed in antique literature. In the official literature of European peoples it has existed only for the last four hundred years" (Bakhtin, 319). Despite the historical newness of this mode, a "boundless ocean of grotesque bodily imagery" overwhelms the tiny island of alternative, polite discourse. Bakhtin's work importantly identifies the centrality of the grotesque to modern literature itself—making the mode essential to understanding social investments in the literary. Because the emergence of the "modern" occurs simultaneously with a burgeoning literary interest in the grotesque we can discern, through Bakhtin, the mutual dependence of literary productions of the grotesque and the "break" that always attends acclamation of a new "modern" moment.

2. This general understanding of art's role in perpetuating equations between physical disability and symbols of cultural collapse has been demonstrated most persuasively by disability scholars such as Paul Longmore, David Hevey, and Martin Norden. Respectively their works have produced a series of trenchant analyses of the restrictive narrative conventions that undergird disability's protrayal in the visual arts. In Paul Longmore's seminal essay, "Screening Stereotypes: Images of Disabled People in Television and the Media," he argues that characters with disabilities abound in the mainstream media yet we never get stories where commu-

nities set their minds to task of accomodating disabled individuals within an inhibiting social and architectural environment. In David Hevey's book, *The Creatures That Time Forgot*, he provides a significant history of the stereotypical conventions that guide photographic depictions of people with disabilities as pitiful wards of the state, and Martin Norden's work, *The Cinema of Isolation: A History of Physical Disabilities in the Movies*, documents voluminous examples of disability and themes of isolation in film from silent movies to present.

3. While Southern writers in the U. S. such as William Faulkner, Eudora Welty, and Flannery O'Connor would seemed to have monopolized the market on characterizations informed by an aesthetic of the grotesque, disability scholars have argued for the necessity of expanding the categorization itself. If we widen our definition of the grotesque to include any artistic use of cognitive or physical distortion or deformation to represent social ills (as I believe we should), then disability studies can begin to convincingly argue in terms of disability's omnipresent status in literature. Most recently Lennard Davis's *Enforcing Normalcy*, and Rosemarie Thomson's *Constituting the Corporeal*, have helped to futher our understanding of the centrality of disability to works as varied as Mary Shelley's *Frankenstein*, and the novels of contemporary African American women writers. In addition, I am currently co-editing a collection of essays with Sharon Snyder that explore representations of disability from Ancient Greece to contemporary American cinema entitled, *Discourses of Disability: The Body and Physical Difference in the Humanities*.

4. In contradistinction to Dunn's embrace of the literary grotesque as a device of readerly titillation and interest, several writers have recently taken up a critique of the grotesque in their work. Richard Powers' *Operation Wandering Soul* assesses the genocidal legacy of normative physical ideals in history and mythology. In doing so, he creates a ward of children with disabilities who refuse the malignant or tragic narratives traditionally associated with the grotesque. Arthur Frank's psychological study of illness and storytelling entitled *The Wounded Storyteller* argues that disease and disability need to be placed into an explanatory framework and assessed as inseparable from the body. His argument endeavors to distance the disabled body from a traditional history of medical objectification and pathological associations. Also, Michael Ondaatje's Booker prize winning novel, *The English Patient*, engages his characters—one a burn patient and the other a thief whose thumbs have been amputated as a punishment for his crimes—in an extended debate about the body as a site of experience and knowledge. The novel develops an extensive critique of postmodern theory that has excluded any notion of lived bodily experience from our current theorizations of subjectivity formation.

5. Both *The Nation* and *The New York Times Book Review* assessed *Geek Love* as a sprawling and relatively uninspired artistic critique of American capitalism where the Freak show symbolized the degraded packaging of American life as market commodity. N. Katherine Hayles also takes up a similar line in her discussion of "embodied" postmodern fiction. She sees the novel as a descent into the underbelly of an American corporate festishization of the body, where deodorant and facial cosmetics promise to control and restrain the body's excesses and general disorderliness.

6. Many scholars have analyzed the disturbing intersections between early twentieth-century art, literary modernism and the ascendancy of the eugenics movement. See for example, Martin Norden's *The Cinema of Isolation: A History of Physical Disability in the Movies*, Stephen Trombley's *The Right to Reproduce: A History of Coercive Sterilization*, Martin Pernick's *The Black Stork: Eugenics and the Death of the*

'Defective' Babies in American Medicine and Motion Pictures since 1915, and Sander Gilman's *Difference and Pathology*.

7.   Fiedler's grouping of artists wallowing in an age of the "explicit" include John Barth, Brian DePalma, Craig Nova, James Joyce, Ursula LeGuin, Alan Friedmann, Lindsay Gresham, etc.

8.   In *Volatile Bodies: Toward A Corporeal Feminism*, Elizabeth Grosz convincingly critiques philosophy and feminist theory for excluding discussions of a more corporeal subject. According to Grosz, we need theoretical models that "demonstrate some sort of internal or constitutive articulation, or even disarticulation, between the biological and the psychological, between the inside and the outside of the body, while avoiding a reductionism of mind to brain. Any adequate model must include a psychical representation of the subject's lived body as well as of the relations between body gestures, posture, and movement in the constitution of the processes of psychical representations" (Grosz, 23). This call represents one critical area where disability scholars can enter into the current frenzy of theories of the body that adopt too naive and simplistic a social constructivist perspective.

9.   In *Monstrous Imagination* Marie-Helene Huet argues that the mid-nineteenth century charged that "in theories of monstrosity the maternal element repressed the legitimate father. The maternal imagination erased the legitimate father's image from his offspring and thus created a monster" (Huet, 8). Dunn involves herself in an inversion or revision of this paradigm in explaining that Aloysius gives birth to the idea of conceiving his own carnival of birth defects, thus re-establishing the father's hand in the tetratogenic process.

10. Both Robert Bogdan's *Freak Show* and Vicky Ann Lewis' play, PH*R*E*A*K*S, allude to the fact that freak shows historically offered a viable way of making a living for people with disabilities. Rather than denounce the industry as objectifying and exploitative, scholars of disability have ambivalently acknowledged freak shows as one of few examples that consistently supplied employment for people with disabilities. Also, circus and side-show actors orchestrated significant political communities from which to express their critiques of able-bodied ideologies and economic practices.

11. Dunn's strategy of resignifying the denigrated terms of disability parallels that used in the disability arts community itself. The work of Cheryl Marie Wade and Mary Duffy both flaunt the horrific able-bodied associations that accrue around perceptions of bodily deviation. In Wade's one-woman performance entitled *Sassy Girl: Portrait of a Poster Child Gone Awry* she invokes the terror of physical disability with a poem about her "gnarled" hands: "Mine are the hands of your bad dreams, ooga booga, from behind the black curtain. Crinkled, puffy, sweaty, scarred. Claw hands. The Ivory girl's hands, after a decade of roughing it. My hands." In a May, 1995 performance at the University of Michigan, Mary Duffy posed as the Venus de Milo in front of a black screen and poetically unveiled a disturbing history of medical and social stories about thalidamide. In the process, she quotes terms and phrases such as "congenital malformation," "teratogenic," and "monstrosity," in order to designate the deterministic tragedy that consistently informs able-bodied narratives of disability. Versions of both of these performances are included in our recent feature-length documentary video entitled *Vital Signs: Crip Culture Talks Back*.

12. I would like to thank Sharon Snyder for her substantial work on this essay. In addition to helping design the essay's current organization, she also discussed and formulated many of the readings in the paper with me.

WORKS CITED

Anderson, Sherwood. 1982 [1919]. *Winesburg, Ohio*. New York: Penguin Books.

Bakhtin, Mikhail. 1984. *Rabelais and His World*. Indianapolis: Indiana University Press.

Bogdan, Robert. 1988. *Freak Show: Presenting Human Oddities for Amusement and Profit*. Chicago: The University of Chicago Press.

Davis, Lennard. 1995. *Enforcing Normalcy*. London: Verso Press.

Dobyns, Stephen. 1989. Rev. of *Geek Love*, by Katherine Dunn. *The New York Times* 2 Apr.: 11.

Dunn, Katherine. 1989. *Geek Love*. New York: Warner Books.

Ellmann, Richard and Charles Feidelson, Jr., eds. 1965. *The Modern Tradition: Backgrounds of Modern Literature*. New York: Oxford University Press.

Fiedler, Leslie. 1978. *FREAKS: Myths and Images of the Secret Self*. New York: Simon & Schuster.

Frank, Arthur. 1995. *The Wounded Storyteller: Body, Illness, and Ethics*. Chicago: University of Chicago Press.

Gilman, Sander. 1985. *Difference and Pathology*. Ithaca: Cornell University Press.

———. 1991. *The Jew's Body*. New York: Routledge.

Grosz, Elizabeth. 1994. *Volatile Bodies: Toward a Corporeal Feminism*. Bloomington: Indiana University Press.

Hayles, N. Katherine. 1990. "Postmodern Parataxis: Embodied Texts, Weightless Information." *American Literary History* 2. 3: 394—403.

Hevey, David. 1992. *The CreaturesThat Time Forgot: Photography and Disability Imagery*. New York: Routledge.

Huet, Marie-Helene. 1993. *Monstrous Imagination*. Cambridge, MA.: Harvard University Press.

Longmore, Paul. 1985. "Screening Stereotypes: Images of Disabled People in Television and Motion Pictures." *Social Policy*. Summer: 31—48.

Mitchell, David T., and Sharon L. Snyder, eds. 1997. *Discourses of Disability: The Body and Physical Difference in the Humanities*. Ann Arbor: University of Michigan Press.

Mitchell, David T., and Sharon L. Snyder. 1996. *Vital Signs: Crip Culture Talks Back*. Boston: Fanlight Productions and Distribution.

Norden, Martin. 1994. *The Cinema of Isolation: A History of Physical Disability in the Movies*. New Brunswick: Rutgers UP.

Ondaatje, Michael. 1993. *The English Patient*. New York: Vintage.

Pernick, Martin. 1995. *The Black Stork: Eugenics and the Death of 'Defective ' Babies in American Medicine and Motion Pictures since 1915*. New York: Oxford University Press.

Powers, Richard. 1994. *Operation Wandering Soul*. New York: Harper-Collins.

Ronell, Avital. 1990. *The Telephone Book: Technology, Schizophrenia, Electric Speech*. Indianapolis: Indiana University Press.

Smith, Dinitia. 1989. Rev. of *Geek Love*, by Katherine Dunn. *The Nation* 15 May: 673.

Thomson, Rosemarie Garland. 1996. *Extraordinary Bodies: The Figuring of Physical Difference in American Culture and Literature*. New York: Columbia University Press.

Trombley, Stephen. 1988. *The Right to Reproduce: A History of Coercive Sterilization*. London: Weidenfeld and Nicolson.

21

Disability and Postcoloniality in Salman Rushdie's *Midnight's Children* and Third-World Novels

SANJEEV KUMOR UPRETY

Insofar as colonialism involves subjugation and disempowerment of a people, it is not radically different from other forms of oppression, including those rooted in gender, race, class, and ability. It is true that different forms of oppression generate different relations and distributions of power; configurations that are rooted in the specific histories and the political context of those oppressions. However, it seems reasonable to presume that there are certain affiliations and similarities that cut across the diverse forms of oppression. Harlan Lane explores one of these affiliations in his study of the "commonalities between the cultural oppression suffered by the colonized peoples of Africa and that suffered by deaf communities" (32). What one finds particularly striking in Lane's study are the similarities that he discovers between the traits attributed to the Africans in the literature of colonialism, and the traits attributed to deaf people in the professional literature. Both the deaf people and the colonized are described in these representations as aggressive, stubborn, and shrewd on the one hand, and as submissive, shy, and passive on the other; both are described as being "socially, cognitively, behaviourally and emotionally . . . [incompetent]" (Lane, 37).

This essay makes a similar study of the interweaving issues of disability and colonialism, though from a slightly different perspective. Instead of examining the ways in which colonized people are represented in Western metropolitan texts, my primary focus will be upon the ways in which the artists and writers from the third world and previously colonized lands represent themselves. In particular I want to examine those third-world texts that emerge from what Bhabha calls the "in-between space" (7) of cultural hybridity and exchange. In the first part of this essay I will describe what I shall mean by the term "hybridity" within the context of the essay as a whole. Next, I will try to rethink the notion of "in-between space" in terms of the Lacanian theory of castration. In particular, I will examine how the experience of symbolic castration at the site of cultural hybridity leads to a sense of "lack," and to a subsequent feeling of being deformed or deviant. Following this, I shall examine the images of disability/ deformity in some postcolonial cultural texts, with a primary emphasis on Salman Rushdie's *Midnight's Children* and Ben Okri's *Famished Road* and *Songs of Enchantment*. Finally, I will make an attempt to locate these images of disability at the intersections of the political and the psychoanalytical. I will conclude by discussing some of strategies used by postcolonial writers to reconstruct a sense of wholeness and coherence, to "imagine" a body that is not deformed or deviant.

At this point, however, I want to pause for a moment to explain my use of terms "postcolonial" and "third world." The term "postcolonial" is used by various people to speak about a variety of issues, including those of migration, suppression, race, gender, slavery, representation and others. For the purpose of this essay, however, I would accept Ashcroft's and Griffith's contention that all these different manifestations of postcolonial experience are based "in the historical fact of European colonization, and the diverse material effects to which this phenomenon gave rise" (2). I would also follow these theorists in considering the postcolonial as including the neocolonial modes of subjugation and disempowerment—the forms of oppression that are often associated with the emergence of neocolonial elites and institutions within the previously colonized lands. In addition to this, I think, it is necessary to rethink the context of neocolonialism by placing it relation to the contemporary reality of globalization of Western media and television. Conceived in this way, I think, all third-world nations share the neocolonial experience that includes the growth of the often-Western-educated ruling elite, the development of political and economic institutions modelled upon the metropolitan forms, and the proliferation of Western culture through media, movies and satellite television. A nation like Nepal provides a good example of this. Nepal, unlike other nations of the Indian subcontinent was never under colonial rule; yet it displays the same signs of the neocolonial condition as the rest of the subcontinent. It is for this reason that I will be using the terms "postcolonial lands" and "third-world" synonymously in this essay. I am aware of the differences that underlie the categorical distinctions between these terms; what is more important for my purpose, however, is the common neocolonial destiny shared by all third-world nations in the contemporary context, and hence my interchangeable use of the two terms. In addition to this, I think, it is also crucial to understand the differences that are contained within a term like "third world," the "fourth" or the "fifth" worlds that exist within the "third world." I think that there is a tendency within the postcolonial theory to lump all the economically and politically underprivileged nations under the broad rubric that goes by the name of the "third world." However, there are differences within the difference and all the underprivileged nations are not equally underprivileged. Nations, much like the people, occupy different positions of relative privilege or relative deprivation within global and regional circulations of power, and my use of the term "fourth world" is an attempt to address that issue of relativity. I am not so much against the use of the term "third world" as a theoretical category as against an unthinking use of the term that erases the differences that it contains. If used with an awareness of those differences, however, I think the term can still function as a valuable tool in mapping the dislocations and inequalities underlying the global relations of power; and also to understand the emergence of cultural hybridities within the contemporary context.

It is important to understand that the "in-between" space of hybridity is not only an effect of geographical relocation. Hybridity, which is one of the momentous realities of contemporary culture, is not affected as the third-world immigrants try to locate themselves within the Western nations. Each time that a third-world teenager in Madagascar, for example, or in Nepal or Bhutan, sees an Oprah Winfrey show or a David Letterman show, thanks to the technology of satellite communication, he or she needs to come to grips with the issues of cultural mixture. She needs to reorient herself in a cultural space that is traced by the local and global networks of communication, a space animated by multiple forms of writings, texts, and images. Identities that are formed at this site of cultural transformation are necessarily hybrid; they need to assimilate other nations, cultures, texts, and images as they enter into a space traced by multiple symbolic systems.

The issue is one of crossing the borders, of constructing an identity at the moment of rupture, and of dissolving boundaries. The art of Elizam Escobar, the Puerto Rican painter often conveys a sense of a world that appears to be underwater; a world in which various forms and objects constantly merge and dissolve into each other. In his larger paintings, such as *Los Sepultureros*, *La Vegiganta Dormida*, and *Las Oneiras*, forms of people, fish, and guitars dissolve into each other even as they seem to float in a "world that is constantly changing, dissolving, re-forming" (Husband, 109). Salman Rushdie's *Midnight's Children* shows a similar interest in fluid identities and rupturing borders. Rushdie's novel tells the story of one thousand children—the midnight's children that were born within the hour of India' s independence from the British rule. All these children—including the protagonist-narrator Saleem—are born at a moment of a crossover; not only do they cross one of the most important thresholds of life, but also a politico-historical threshold: their birth coincides with the birth of the nation, with the emergence of modern India within a political and historical map. Bodies and identities become transformed in Rushdie's *Midnight's Children* as they enter a hybrid space where the borders are being transgressed and rewritten. The Indian businessmen, including Saleem's father and Rani of Cooch Nahin, are transformed as the color of their skin turns from brown to white; Amina Sinai, Padma, and Durga are altered as they acquire male characteristics—muscular bodies, gruff voices, and a suggestion of hairy growth below their lips; William Methwold, that Englishman with "slicked up hair" becomes transformed as he takes off his wig at the eve of Indian independence to reveal his bald pate. The "in between space" is a locale of transformation where identities and bodies lose their stable boundaries to assume new forms and modes of being. Okri's *Famished Road* shows a similar preoccupation with the interspace; a space within which the world of mythology and spirits mixes with the world of political rallies and elections campaigns for its child narrator Azaro. Azaro, as an *abiku* (spirit-child) is caught up between the two worlds; the world of his spirit companions and the world of the living which is the world of his Mum and Dad.

In the spirit of magic realism, both worlds intersect and shape each other, both competing against each other for their hold upon Azaro. In *Songs of Enchantment* which continues the adventures of Azaro, he finds himself going through a series of transformations as the mythology mixes with history and politics in a collusion of worlds:

> The darkness flowed around them and around me, and I understood the secret of living within the body of the leviathan-spirit of our age. With no choice, resorting to the freedom of the world of spirits, I began to mutate. I turned into a fish: I swam upwards. My scales were of gold. I turned into a butterfly: the air helped me on. I turned into a lizard, and scampered up the body of the night. I fell from the ceiling, hurting my back and landed at dad's feet. (43)

In recent years there has been a tendency in contemporary theoretical formulations to consider hybridity not as a "moral marker of . . . contamination, failure or regression" (Papastergiadis, 9), but a positive concept that signifies the possibility of creative growth and understanding. Taking his cue from Rushdie, Bhabha speaks of the sense of empowerment and "migrant's double vision" (5) in this space of hybridity and transformation, and Braidotti similarly describes the hybrid, "nomadic" state in terms of empowerment and agency. For her the nomadic state does not consist in the literal act of travelling but in "the subversion of set conventions" (5). Identities rooted in a hybrid space do not only occupy a privileged position of understanding at the crossroads of different cultures; their unique position also allows them to subvert and rewrite the cultural codes by using one cultural/symbolic system against another. From their vantage point of "double vision," those with hybrid identities can perceive they can have an understanding of multiple cultures, and they can use that understanding to create now forms of thought, new ways of aesthetic and political expression.

Despite these positive descriptions of the hybridity, however, it seems to me that the in-between space is not only a locale of power and "double vision"; it is also a site of multiple castrations and reiterated pain. Lacan's notion of castration is important here as it allows us to rethink the relationship between the issues of disability, psyche, and power at the site of cultural hybridity. Lacan follows Hegel in believing that the "word is the murderer of the thing"; entering the symbolic, the subject finds himself in a system of absence and difference where the presence of the thing is replaced by its symbol. From then onwards symbols "envelop the life of the man in a network so total . . . that they bring to his birth . . . the shape of his destiny. . . ." (Lacan, 1977, 68). As he enters the system of language the subject acquires his identity through a linguistic marker (his name or the pronoun "I"). However, his ontological being is always in excess of the linguistic marker; the linguistic sign cannot signify the fullness of his being. Thus, the subject "fades away" at the very moment when it articulates itself through language; it is absent in its presentation through language. Rewriting Freud in linguistic terms, Lacan interprets this fading of the subject as a castration; as the subject enters the symbolic order castrated, he must surrender his experience of presymbolic affective fullness (analogous to the preoedipal experience of fullness and unity with the mother's body) to enter a system of absence and lack. This sense of lack leads to the birth of desire and then to a continuous movement through which the subject seeks to fulfill the lack by taking up an infinite chain of signifiers, that is, by making a series of metaphoric and metonymic substitutions to move from one signifier to another. But the sense of lack does not find its fulfillment in any particular signifier, hence the continuous slide along the chain of signifiers. Language thus "chains" the human subject, capturing it irrevocably within the prisonhouse of language.

Once inside this prisonhouse, however, the subject is also subjected to the Law of the symbolic order. Following Freud, Lacan describes this Law as the "Law of the Father." However, the Law here must be understood in the broadest sense possible; it is possible to interpret it not only in biological/ essentialist terms but also in historical/political terms. As the subject enters into language, he/she is subjected to the law of the symbolic—the law that defines him/her as a subject and gives him/her a position not only within the fabric of language, but also a position within the socioeconomic and the cultural space of the society. The law of the symbolic (which also manifests itself through the syntactical and semantic rules of language) is thus not only a biological given that emanates from the transcendental phallus of the father, but also a historical and cultural construct that issues from the scepter of the sovereign. The "Law" has its locus not in any given individual or institution; it derives its power from a virtual sociopolitical and economic center, a node at which various lines and affiliations of power intersect and interrupt each other. Sometimes, especially in the totalitarian regimes, that power center might come close to being identified with a particular person or institution, like for example with the Somali General in Nuruddin Farah's trilogy *Variations on the Themes of an African Dictatorship*. However, such an identification cannot be considered as total. As the dictators and institutions change, and as the configurations of power undergo transformation, the virtual power center is constantly renewed and renegotiated; it is a process rather than a thing, not an actual spatio-temporal location but a virtual one. The "Law" of the symbolic, deriving its justification from that virtual power center, is dispersed throughout the social; it interpellates the subject and gives it a position within the network of social and familial relationships. The biological father may, through a metonymic extension, partake of the power emanating from the virtual sociopolitical, center but cannot be identified with it.

Okri's novels *The Famished Road* and *Songs of Enchantment* can be interpreted as an illustration of the point that we have been discussing. Okri's child narrator is not only caught up between the two worlds, but also between the two fathers: his "Dad" in the real world and the King of the spirit world, "a wonderful personage who sometimes appeared in the form of a great cat" (3). A contest between the two worlds for mastery over Azaro's soul is also a contest between the two fathers. Apart from these two, however, there is yet another father, another guarantor of the political and the economic power; a "father" that finds a symbolic expression in the form of a "gigantic red masquerade, bristling with raffia and rags and nails" (SE 98) that is created by the "party of the rich" to scare away their opponents. The masquerade, which has "long stilts for legs and two twisted horns at the sides of wild jackal's head" (SE 98), however, is more than a symbolic presence. In Azaro's world the masquerade enters as a threatening presence, as an active force of oppression that rides through the street upon a white horse, "swiping the air with its silver machete, the white flag fluttering in its grasp, its jackal mouth slavering, its eyes red" (SE 109). The masquerade is more than a principle of evil; it expands into a kingdom for Azaro as he gets trapped in its' mind and does not know how to get out of it: "The masquerade's head was a mighty house. It was not one mind, but many; a confluence of minds. I wandered in it consciousness and found a labyrinthine kingdom. I saw its pyramids, its cities, its castles, its great palaces, its seas and rivers" (SE 114). As a kingdom the masquerade might stand for the neocolonial Nigeria; a nation facing new forms of oppression perpetrated by the affiliations of ruling elites and the dynamics of consumer capitalism. From another perspective, however, the masquerade can also be understood as a locus of the symbolic "Law"—a law that invents histories and memories, and manufactures both reality and subjectivity:

> I saw the powers of the kingdom, how it manufactures reality, how it produces events which will become history, how it creates memory, and silence, and forgetfulness, how it keeps it supporters perpetually young and vigorous, how it protects them, seals their lives with legality. (SE 115)

The "Law" of the symbolic, thus has its location not in the penis of Azaro's Dad, but in the phallus of the masquerade, the organ that in Azaro' s imagination impregnates Madame Koto, the "ageless matriarch" whom he describes as "the leviathan-spirit of our age" (SE 43). To put it in a simple way, the Dad is not the "father." As the head of his family, he partakes of the power that the patriarchal code of the father's law makes accessible to him; however, he as a supporter of the party of the subaltern and as a leader of the beggars he also fights against that law of social justice. It is this gap between the Dad and the father that calls for a reinterpretation of Lacan's theory of castration. It is at this point that desire and power meet, intersecting at a site where it is possible to develop political implications inherent in Lacan's theory, a direction taken by theorists such as Louis Althusser and Julia Kristeva. It also becomes possible from this perspective to conceive of a third-world identity as a product of multiple castrations, a result of an initiation into the plural "law(s)" of variously colored phalluses. If the human subject is castrated as he/she enters the symbolic order, then the contemporary subject, especially in a third-world context, is castrated many times over. For a subject in a "fourth-world" country like Nepal, for example, identity is not a matter of making a singular entry into a single symbolic system.

In the context of a fourth-world nation like Nepal the multiplicity of economic and political inequalities—regional as well as global—ensure that not one, but many symbolic systems compete against each other within what Lotman describes as the "semiosphere" (123), the space of culture that is traced by multiple symbols, semiotic acts, and texts. There are many symbolic systems and many fathers. There is the local father, the power of whose phallus is guaranteed by what Benedict Anderson calls the "imagined" boundaries of the nation, and by the complex affiliations of class and caste interests. There is the regional father whose shadow looms around New Delhi, the capital of India, the "third"-world country that is in the same position of cultural and economic hegemony vis-à-vis "fourth"-world nations like Nepal, Bhutan, Bangladesh, and Maldives as the first-world countries are with regard to the third world. And there is the global father whose glory is transmitted through the Western media and television. Identity in a third-world context is a matter of multiple and sometimes doubtful parentage. Saleem's case in *Midnight's Children* can be taken in this sense as a metaphor of all third-world identities. The identity of Saleem's father is suspended in the first part of the novel, and the reader, like Padma the fictional narratee, is deliberately left to waddle in confusion. It is only later that we learn that he is an offspring of an illicit relation between William Methwold, the slick-haired Englishman, and Vanita, the wife of a poor Indian entertainer. Saleem is literally a product of a hybrid parentage; born at the same instant as his country—the stroke of midnight on August 15th, 1947—he represents the mixed lineage of India, a nation that inherited its "genes" from both English and local traditions.

Symbolically fathered by many traditions, a third-world subject has to enter multiple symbolic orders; and though each entry brings with it additional benefits, it also affirms his/her lack more acutely, leading to a sense of disability, to a sense of having been deformed or deviant. Saladin Chamcha, one of the protagonists of Rushdie's *Satanic Verses* finds that he is turning into a goat after he falls out of an airplane and crashes into England. After his "fall" he is taken into a sanitorium that is peopled by other deformed creatures like himself. There is a manticore who tries to explain his new environment to Saladin:

> The manticore ground its three rows of teeth in evident frustration. "There's a woman over that way," it said,"who is now mostly water buffalo. There are businessmen from Nigeria who have grown sturdy tails. There is a group of holiday-makers from Senegal who were doing no more than changing planes when they were turned into slippery snakes. I myself am in the rag trade; for some years now I have been a highly paid male model, based in Bombay, wearing a wide range of suitings and shirtings also. But who will employ me now?" he burst into sudden and unexpected tears. (SV 168)

From a psychoanalytical perspective, Saladin Chamcha "falls" literally, into a new symbolic order that castrates him with its linguistic code, and in the process reiterates his original "lack." The experience of lack, symbolically represented by the images of holes, fissures, and ruptures, is a recurring figure in Rushdie's fiction. Aadam Aziz, Saleem's grandfather in *Midnight's Children* is described as having ". . . a hole in him, a vacancy in a vital inner chamber" (12)—a hole that is created at the intersection of multiple symbolic orders. In this he is like the man who is made of holes in *Songs of Enchantment*, a man "with holes in his eyes, holes all over his face, and holes in his neck" (SE 100). Aadam, who learned his craft as a medical doctor in Germany, is perpetually caught between the two worlds, between Western and Hakimi medicine, between his religious faith in "the compassionate, the Merciful Allah" at the one hand, and his anarchist German friends Oskar and Ilse Lubin who "mock his prayers with their anti-ideologies" (13). Both of these worlds come together as he kneels down to pray in the Valley of Kashmir: Aadam is Saleem's grandfather. He (Aadam) kneels down to pray:

> My grandfather bent his forehead towards the earth. Forward he bent, and the earth, prayer-mat-covered, curved up towards him. And now it was the Tussock's time. At one and the same time a rebuke from Ilse-Oskar-Ingrid-Heidelberg as well as valley and God, it smote him upon the point of the nose. Three drops fell. There were rubies and diamonds. And my grandfather, lurching upright, made a resolve. Stood. Rolled cheroot. Stared across the lake. And was knocked forever into that middle place, unable to worship a God whose existence he could not wholly disbelieve. Permanent alternation: a hole" (MC 6)

Aziz speaks of the "hole in the middle of [him] the size of a melon" (MC 23), and his wife dreams of him "walking mournfully up a mountain in Kashmir with a hole in his stomach the size of a fist" (MC 56). Saleem inherits the hole from his grandfather. Like Aadam Aziz and Rushdie, Saleem owes his identity to an "in-between" space of hybridity and exchange. Reiteration of "lack" at the meeting point of multiple symbolic systems creates in him, as in Saladin Chamcha, a sense of having been born deformed. The afflictions of his body , from this perspective, can be interpreted as a metaphorical representation of the experience of "lack":

> I mean quite simply that I have begun to crack all over like an old jug—that my poor body, singular, unlovely, buffeted by too much history, subjected to drainage above and drainage below, mutilated by doors, brained by spittoons, has started to come apart at seams. In Short, I am disintegrating, slowly for the moment, although there are signs of acceleration. (MC 38)

Saleem, like Okri's child-narrator, is caught up between the worlds, and like him he has a body that is different. All of the one thousand and one children born within the hour of Indian independence on August 15th, 1947, are endowed with miraculous faculties "through some freak of biology, or perhaps owing to some preternatural power of the moment, or just conceivably by sheer coincidence" (MC 192). Deviant bodies are formed at the moment of maximum hybridity: at a moment when the collective consciousness of the newly formed nation is still struggling to be free from the categories of experience and thought imposed by an colonial powers; a temporal space that is traced by an interweaving of different symbolic systems. Different symbolic systems—both colonial and local—are overlaid at this moment of hybridity, resulting in new creative possibilities: the miraculous gifts of the midnight's children. This is the positive side of hybridity celebrated by Bhabha and Braidotti. However, there is also an underside of this celebratory moment. The children are castrated by multiple symbolic systems as they cross over the thresholds of life and history; and the reiteration of pain produces marks of deformity upon their bodies, especially upon the much-abused body of Saleem. In the beginning however, they are only aware of the positive aspects of their miraculous gifts. Saleem's gift is that of telepathy; he can move at will into the minds of the teeming millions of India. This leads him to create a grandiloquent fantasy in which he sees the destiny of his country being irrevocably tied to his own personal fate. Others of the "midnight's children" are less ambitious; but all are endowed with one kind of freakish gift or another:

> Midnight's children! . . . From Kerala, a boy who had the ability of stepping into mirrors and re-emerging through any reflective surface in the land . . . a Goanese girl with the gift of multiplying fish . . . and children with powers of transformation: a werewolf from the Nilgiri Hills, and from the great watershed of the Vindhyas, a boy who could increase or reduce his size at will . . . from Kashmir, there was a blue-eyed child whose original sex I was never certain, since by immersing herself in water he (or she) could alter it as she (or he) pleased. . . There was a boy who could eat metal and a girl whose fingers were so green that she could grow prize aubergines in the Thar desert . . . bearded girls, a boy with two bodies dangling off a single head and neck—the head could speak in two voices, one male, one female, and every language and dialect spoken in the subcontinent. . . . [I]n the Gir forest lived a witch-girl with the power of healing by laying-on of hands. . . . [D]hobi's daughter from Madras . . . could fly higher than any bird simply by closing her eyes . . . and Benarasi silversmith's son was given the gift of travelling in time and prophesying the future as well as clarifying the past. . . . (MC 197–98)

Seemingly endowed with miraculous gifts, the midnight's children are, in fact, bearers of the marks of stigma; their gifts are never to meant be displayed, but rather perpetually to be concealed from social gaze. Saleem learns that his parents are not ready to accept his telepathic powers; he alone must carry the burden of having a body that is disabled and different: "In a country where any physical or mental peculiarity in a child is a source of deep family shame, my parents, who had become accustomed to facial birthmarks, cucumber nose and bandy legs, simply refused to see any more embarrassing things in me" (167). His telepathic powers are thus a part of the "peculiarities" that he is born with; they are inextricably linked with the pain of his disabled body. An attempt to tell about his telepathic powers only results in an outraged blow that Saleem receives on the side of his head from his father; a blow that leads to a partial deafness, thus further disabling his body. The body of Saleem—along with the bodies of other midnight's children—is "normalized" towards the end of the novel through "ectomy"; an operation that robs the midnight's children of their gifts: ". . . for all those who had come to the place of the wailing widows with their magical gifts intact, the awakening from anesthesia was cruel indeed, and whispering through the wall came the tale of their undoing, the tormented cry of the children who had lost their magic. . ." (MC 423). The midnight's children are the outcasts, the bearers of stigma who are not well-assimilated in the social order that is organized around the law of the father; they must be castrated by the law and then be assigned a fixed spot within the social system. They are located within a fixed category and a stable subject positions that can be controlled by the panoptic gaze of the father. Magic—"time travelling, transmutation of base metals, possibilities of flights"—makes a mockery of the boundaries and categories imposed by the structure of the panopticon. It is magic then, the Dionysian and the disruptive influence, which must be cured by what Rushdie describes as "ectomy"; an operation that occurs at the meeting point of the psychoanalytical and the political, an operation also which is performed at a hybrid space where the local and the colonial "father(s)" meet.

The ectomy that is performed upon the midnight's children is sanctioned by the local/ national "law," as such it is a fictional representation of the forced vasectomy that was imposed upon the subaltern by police and state power during the emergency period in India in the seventies. However, that act was justified by borrowing the Western notions of progress and family. Saleem also defines his operation by using the terms drawn from the lexicon of Western medicine: "Ectomy (from, I suppose, the Greek): a cutting out. To which medical science adds a number of prefixes: appendectomy tonsillectomy mastectomy tubectomy vasectomy testectomy hysterectomy" (421). Saladin Chamcha's deformity in *Satanic Verses* can be located similarly within the hybrid space of dual symbolic orders and can be seen as a result of the interweaving issues of psyche and power. In "falling" into England not only does Chamcha enter a new symbolic order that is underlined by psychoanalytical necessity, but he also crashes into a social/political order that deforms him with its laws of immigration, and with its legal code of social and political conduct. Both the political and the psychoanalytical merge in supporting the power of the colonial "writing machine" that constructs "aliens" by its powers of description:

> "But how do they do it?" Chamcha wanted to know.
> "They describe us" the other (manticore) whispered solemnly. "That's all. They have the power of description, and we succumb to the pictures they construct."
> (SV 168)

Deformed by the colonial "writing" within a hybrid space, the third-world subject is constructed at an intersection of various impulses, discourses, and interests; a site of multiple affiliations in which the subject "fades away" as it is claimed by a play of numerous voices, texts, and desires. In fact, the same thing can be said of not only the third-world subjects but all other subjects who are formed at a postmodern moment in a postcolonial age. They acquire their identity within a hybrid space of exchange, conflict, and negotiations; from an awareness of the identities rooted in other nations, cultures, ethnicities, races, communities, and people. It is at this site of alterity and hybridity that postcolonialism intersects with poststructuralism and postmodernism. However, there is also a difference. In the case of third-world identities, hybridity is not only a matter of choice, but—more than in any other context—an issue of survival. A third-world subject must memorize the history of other nations, learn other languages, and adopt other fathers if he/she is to acquire a proper place in the social and economic ladder. An inability to learn "other" symbolic codes results in a marginalized position in the social order, and with marginalization comes poverty, unemployment and stigma; one is reduced like other stigmatized people, "from a whole and usual person to a tainted, discounted one" (Goffman 3). One becomes stigmatized if one does not learn the rules of other symbolic systems, and one becomes deformed and doubly castrated—like Saladin Chamcha—as one enters into other languages, into other histories, into the world of other's symbols. Third-world identities are constructed under this double bind that leads to the experience of being deviant and different, to a sense of having a fractured identity that is traced by other identities, cultures, and people.

Ana Mendieta, the immigrant Cuban artist, created self-portraits that resonate with the consciousness of having been wounded, of having been deformed: "Using gunpowder and firecrackers, she would burn signs of herself into sand and soil; using mud and feathers, she would blend herself into the landscape; using blood mixed with tempera, she would metaphorize her pain" (Fusco, 122). The process of being wounded, and that of death are central to Mendieta's art. In some of her performances she would write on walls using blood from her arms, and in others she would soak her body with the blood of white chicken. Camnitzer describes her art as a "search for herself both as a woman and as a cultural entity identified through wounding" (50). Lu Xun, one of the China's greatest writers, often uses the themes of deformity, self-maiming, and cannibalism in his stories. Lu Xun's story "Medicine" tells the story of a dying child who can only be saved by eating steam rolls that are soaked in the blood of a criminal. Briksha, the Nepali poet, has similarly used images of self-mutilation and the wounded body as central themes in his art; and comparable motifs can be found in the novels of modern Indian writers like Amitav Ghosh and Bharati Mukherjee. The chief protagonist of Ghosh's novel The Circle of Reason is Alu—a boy who is deformed with a huge head which is ". . . several times too large for an eight year old, and curiously uneven, bulging all over with knots and bumps" (Ghosh 3). Francis Souza, the Indian artist of Goan origin describes himself as a "blooming maggot in a dung heap" (45). Souza is best known for a male head that appears in many of his works; "a face without a forehead, bearded and pockmarked, eyes bulging from the sides of the skull like a frog's, a mouth full of multiple sets of teeth" (Kapur, 47). Souza' s distorted male heads are often nailed, a motif that also appears in the art of the Peruvian artist Kukuli. This is what Kukuli says about his first experience of sculpting a piece with red clay, the medium often used in his native land:

> When I finished this first piece, I had it standing in front of me, and I still felt that there was no connection between it and me, until I decided to nail it. After I had put a few nails, a friend who was working next to me said "that's enough!" But I

thought,"No, it's not enough", and I put more nails. Once I had finished I felt that I was saying exactly what I wanted to say. it was not the form, the color, or the angle: it was the nails that had the final meaning. (Mills, 97)

A similar theme can also be discerned in Elizam Escobar's art. Escobar's underwater world often contains dissected men and fish, and people with bandaged faces, and horned and grotesque figures known as *"Vejigante,"* figures drawn from the tradition of the Puerto-Rican festival of Santiago Apostle. Escobar has said that he uses the *Vejigante* image because "I want to break something that is mine into pieces, like an autopsy, I want to destroy something that belongs to me" (Husband, 110). It is not my purpose here to try to restrict all these images of deformity to terms of a single explanation; such a reading would indeed be too reductive. Nor is it my intention to explain all third-world texts by using a single interpretive framework. The sheer volume and variety of third-world texts would ensure the failure of such an attempt. However, the overwhelming presence of these images in postcolonial/third-world texts does seem to refer in different ways to the experiences of the third-world/postcolonial subjects who find themselves alienated in the contemporary world order.

Some of the postcolonial texts seem to reveal an attempt to reconstruct wholeness by creating an alternative world; an attempt to overcome the experience of deformity by seeking a "normal" body in the realm of traditional religion, mythology, folklore, dreams, and unconscious. This can be interpreted as a desire to seek an "imaginary" whole in Other worlds; a desire to discover a sense of wholeness that is denied in the contemporary experience of split subjectivity and splintered history. Okri creates a world of spirits, a world that intersects through his child narrator, with the contemporary history of Nigeria:

I didn't want to entirely lose contact with that other world of light and rainbow and possibilities. I had buried my secrets early. I buried them in moonlight, the air alive with white moths. I buried my magic stones, my mirror, my special promises, my golden threads, objects of identity that connected me to the world of spirits. I buried them all in a secret place. . . . (Okri 9)

The alternative world of Okri, however, fails to provide a transcendental locale of imaginary wholeness; it is not free from the hybrid writing of multiple fathers. The Other world of the unconscious (also represented by the fantastic locales of mythology and folktale), as Lacan tells us, is an effect of the repression that follows the subject's entry into the symbolic system. As such, an incursion into the "Other world" of the spirits, instead of providing a locale to imagine normal bodies, reaffirms the sense of lack, deformity, and disjunction:

It seemed as if the whole world was there. I saw people of all shapes and sizes, mountainous women with faces of iroko, midgets with faces of stone, reedy women with twins strapped to their backs, thick-set men with bulging shoulder muscles. . . . I shut my eyes and when I opened them again I saw people who walked backwards, a dwarf who got about on two fingers, men upside-down with baskets of fish on their feet, women who had breasts on their backs, babies strapped to their chests, and beautiful children with three arms. (Okri, 15)

Repression occurs as both a psychological and a political act in Okri's fiction. As a psychological act repression creates the world of dreams, of spirits with "six fingers on each hand" and with "their toes . . . inturned like those of certain animals" (FR 77); a world of monstrous forms and beings that is repressed by the "Law" to ensure the sanity of the social subjects. As a political act, on the other hand, repression banishes the beggars, the disabled, and the subaltern to the margins of the society to ensure the coherence and order of the nation state. The two forms of repression—the psychological and the political—intersect in *The Famished Road*—an act of violence that leaves its visible traces in both the world of the spirits and the world of the subaltern. Both the spirits and the beggars bear various marks of disability and deformity in *The Famished Road* and *Songs of Enchantment*; in the words of Azaro, they all become "a little twisted" (SE 68). Beggars are often described in terms of their deformity; as monstrous people with "missing limbs . . . soft wax legs . . . bulbous goitres . . . [and] monstrous faces. . ." (SE 21). In this they evoke the world of the spirits, strange beings with missing fingers and eyes. The two forms of repression intersect in the figure of Helen, the one-eyed girl who leads the group of the beggars who gather around Azaro's dad. Helen is both a beggar and a spirit, and for Azaro she keeps on crossing over the thresholds of the two worlds; a movement that stresses the interconnection between both the psychoanalytical and the political dimension of repression: "To our terrified astonishment, much as we tramped through the bushes looking for Helen and the beggars, much as we tried, we could not find them. It seemed another realm had swallowed them up. it seemed as if they stepped out of this reality, and into another" (SE 23). Not only are the beggars excluded to the margins of the society, they are also repressed to the other reality of the unconscious. The realm of the unconscious in Okri's fiction is not a ground of transcendental truths; it is rather a repository of everything that is repressed through an act of symbolic castration that is performed by the masquerade-father, the emblem of the party of the rich as well as a procreator of the new nation. It is appropriate, therefore, that the unconscious world of the spirits bears the marks of deformity as a consequence of that psycho-political castration.

Sunderbans, the archetypal magic forest in *Midnight 's Children*, evokes a comparable experience of disability in Saleem and his companions Shaheed, Ayooba and Farooq. The other world of unconscious and mythology is not a locale of transcendence, it a place of deadly hallucinations that drains the life energy of Saleem and his companions and makes them "hollow and translucent as glass" (MC 356). The unconscious is not a place that might offer an enabling vision of a "Buddha" (the enlightened one); it is a place that precipitates insanity, disability, and death, a place that turns one prematurely into a Buddha (an old man):

The mud of the dream forest, which no doubt also contained the concealed translucency of jungle insects and the devilry of bright orange bird droppings, infected the ears of the three boy-soldiers and made them all as deaf as posts; so that although they were spared the singsong accusations of the jungle, they were now obliged to converse in a rudimentary form of sign-language. They seemed, however, to prefer their diseased deafness to the unpalatable secrets which the sundri-leaves had whispered in their ears. (MC 354)

As the traditional sources fail to provide an experience of transcendence outside the postmodern symbolic of multiple writing, postcolonial writers seek new myths of wholeness, new locales to situate the normal body. One of those modern myths is that of the nation. Jameson suggests that we should read third-world texts as "national allegories," texts in which the "the story of a private individual destiny . . . is always an allegory of the embattled situation of the public third world culture and society" (69). One of the motivations that prompts third-world artists to allegorize the nation, however, might be precisely the desire to seek imaginary wholeness. Nation becomes that imagined space where the fractured and alienated third-world subject finds a wholeness of form with which he can identify. Like the child before the mirror in the Lacanian schema, the third-world subject recognizes itself momentarily in the image of the nation. The modern Nigeria is identified with in *The Famished Road* with its narrator Azaro, the *abiku*-child; Azaro's dad describes Nigeria as "an abiku nation, a spirit child nation, one that keeps on being reborn. . ." (FR 494). Rushdie's narrator Saleem, similarly involved in an imaginary capture, tries to swallow the whole of India through his telepathic powers in *Midnight's Children*:

> . . . I hopped down to Madurai's Meenakshi temple and nestled amongst the woolly, mystical perceptions of a chanting priest. I toured Connaught Place in New Delhi in the guise of an auto-rickshaw driver, complaining bitterly to my fares about the rising price of gasoline; in Calcutta I slept rough in a section of drainpipe. . . . I zipped down to Cape Comorin and became a fisherwoman whose sari was as tight as her morals were loose. . . . [S]tanding on red sands washed by three seas, I flirted with Dravidian beachcombers in a language I couldn't understand; then up into the Himalayas, into the neanderthal moss-covered hut of a Goojar temple. . . . [A]t the golden fortress of Jaisalmer I sampled the inner life of a woman making mirrorwork dresses and at Khajuraho I was an adolescent village boy, deeply embarrassed by the erotic, Tantric carvings on the Chandala temples. . . . (MC 171)

Saleem is a "swallower of lives"; he speaks of the teeming millions of India who jostle and shove inside him, and he gulps down Mahatma Gandhi and Jawaharlal Nehru, along with mongoose trainers, magicians, and many-headed monsters to create India in his own image. However, as Benedict Anderson puts it, the modern nation is an "imagined community"; its wholeness and coherence is a historical construct that is imagined by the local elite, an act of imagining that becomes possible by an erasure of the history of subaltern struggle, by a willful forgetting of other histories. The wholeness of the "national body" is also imaginary, and Saleem's self-recognition before the image of India, like that of the infant before the mirror, is no more than a misrecognition; the normal body of India is a imaginary construct that ruptures like the enfeebled frame of Saleem:

> . . . I am alone in the vastness of the numbers, the numbers marching one two
> three, I am being buffeted right and left while rip tear crunch reaches its
> climax. . . . [T]hey throng around me pushing shoving crushing, and the cracks are
> widening, pieces of my body are falling off . . . bones splitting breaking beneath the
> awful pressure of the crowd, bags of bones falling down down. . . . [Y]es, they will
> trample me underfoot, the numbers marching one two three four hundred million
> five hundred six, reducing me to specks of voiceless dust. . . . (MC 445–46).

Rushdie's fiction works within the postmodern space that is suspended
between the serious and the comic, between real history and inventive fantasy.
Suspended between the real and the unreal, it subverts both the "real" history
perpetrated by the colonial powers, and also the equally "true" history invented
by the local elite. Reconfiguring the history of a nation within a postmodern play
of simulacra, Rushdie shows that both versions of history are discursive constructs. On the one hand, thus, the sanitorium scene in *Satanic Verses* can be
considered as a satire aimed at the colonial representations of third-world immigrants. However, the postmodern laughter of Rushdie has a double edge; not only
does it laugh at the colonial gaze that turns third-world identities into "alien"
manticores but it also laughs at the local traditions, at the local fathers, "fathers"
of the modern nation like Jawaharlal Nehru and Mahatma Gandhi. Rushdie's fiction, thus, works from the position of a hybrid double vision; a position of power
from which it is possible to challenge both the colonial and the local structures
of power, the glorious turgidity of both local and colonial phalluses. However,
this power is purchased at a cost; the cost that third-world subjects have to pay
as they enter into the hybrid space of multiple castration and symbolic deformity.
In order to acquire a voice in the contemporary context, they must enter multiple symbolic orders; This act deforms them symbolically, and that deformity
finds expression in the images of the texts that they produce. The power of
rewriting and reinscription must be acquired at the cost of self-erasure and reiterated pain; with double vision comes blindness, as also described by the Filipino
poet Gemino H. Abad:

> As I write I grow blind
> Myself I write down and secrete
> As far down where words cannot go
> And stranded, myself I seek
> Among the ghost of things
> That my words have slain
>   But nowhere I
> With Words More to Speak
>   (Abad 107).

Abad shares the experience of third-world subjects (including artists and writers) who seek to forge an identity for themselves within a hybrid space that is
underlaid by multiple symbols, texts, and semiotic systems. This is especially true

of contemporary third-world subjects who have to form an identity not only within the context of the neocolonialism, but also within the contexts of the postmodern culture that is transmitted through global media and satellite television. The influx of Western media and television has resulted in an increasing hybridization of the sociocultural space within which third-world identities are formed. Various symbols, languages, laws, and fathers are engaged in a perpetual contest within that hybrid space—a contest that often results not in an experience of empowerment and double vision, but in an experience of multiple alienation and disability. It is this experience of disability that is literalized in the works of third-world artists, an experience of losing their voice and vision even as they enter the symbolic networks of the global culture and political economy.

WORKS CITED

Abad, Gemino H. 1985. *The Space Between.* Quezon City: University of Philippines Press.

Ashcroft, Bill, Gareth Griffiths, and Helen Tiffin, eds. 1995. *The Post-colonial Studies Reader.* London: Routledge.

Bhabha, Homi. 1994. *The Location of Culture.* London: Routledge.

Braidotti, Rosi. 1994. *Nomadic Subjects: Embodiment and Sexual Difference in Contemporary Feminist Theory.* New York: Columbia University Press.

Camnitzer, Luis. 1989. "Ana Mendieta." *Third Text* 7 (Summer): 47–52.

Fusco, Coco. 1995. *English is Broken Here: Notes on Cultural Fusion in the Americas.* New York: The New Press.

Ghosh, Amitav. 1986. *The Circle of Reason.* New York: Viking.

Goffman, Erving. 1963. *Stigma: Notes on the Management of Spoiled Identity.* New York: Simon and Schuster.

Husband, Bertha. 1988. "A Deep Sea Diver in the Phantom(ly) Country: Art and Politics of Elizam Escobar." *Third Text* 3/4 (Spring/Summer): 105–17.

Jameson, Frederick. "Third World Literature in the Era of Multinational Capitalism."

Kapur, Geeta. 1989. "Francis Newton Souza: Devil in the Flesh." *Third Text.* 8/9 (Autumn/Winter): 25–64.

Lacan, Jacques. 1977. *Ecrits: A Selection.* Trans. Alan Sheridan. New York: Norton.

Lotman, Yuri. 1991. *Universe of the Mind.* Trans. A. Shukman. London: Tauris.

Lane, Harlan. 1993. *The Mask of Benevolence: Disabling the Deaf Community.* New York: Vintage Books.

Miller, Ivory, ed. 1995. "We, the Colonized Ones: Kukuli Speaks." *Third Text* 32 (Autumn): 95–108.

Okri, Ben. 1992. *The Famished Road.* New York: Doubleday.

Okri, Ben. 1993. *Songs of Enchantment.* New York: Doubleday.

Papastergiadis, Nikos. 1995. "Restless Hybrids." *Third Text* 32, (Autumn) 9–18.

Rushdie, Salman. 1981. *Midnight's Children.* New York: Alfred A. Knopf.

Rushdie, Salman. 1992. *The Satanic Verses.* Dover: Consortium.

Souza, Francis, N. 1992. "Nirvana of a Maggot." *Third Text* 19 (Summer) 41–48.

Blindness and Art

NICHOLAS MIRZOEFF

Derrida's philosophical investigation of blindness leaves many questions to be answered by art historians. Blindness was and remains a central metaphor in Western art, representing and permitting insight and understanding for the artist, gendered male, over his "female" subject-matter. Here it now seems to suggest that visual representation is the outcome of an interplay between the metaphor of insight and the physiological structures of sight. Following Derrida's provocative comments, I shall now re-examine the canon of the blind and blindness from Poussin via David, Ingres and Delacroix to Paul Strand and Robert Morris. Given the force attached by Merleau-Ponty and Derrida to the physiology of seeing, I shall consider blindness not just as a metaphor but as a condition. For Derrida himself stands within a historical construction of blindness as insight, which is not natural but is less than two hundred years old now. How did depictions of blindness change in accord with changing notions of sight and blindness? In what ways is the metaphor of blindness affected by these changes? And what becomes of the Classical body that is known not through insight metaphorized as blindness but through insight enabled by blindness?

In France the modern period is held to begin with the reign of Louis XIV (1648–1715). For art history, this period marks the foundation of the Academy of Painting and Sculpture and the beginnings of public debate over the nature and accomplishments of art. One central moment in this history came in 1666 when Louis ordered that the Academy should hold conferences on works of art for the edification of an audience composed of their peers, students and, occasionally, government ministers. The Seventh conference was given by the artist Sébastien Bourdon, who chose a painting by Nicolas Poussin (1593–1665), *Christ Healing the Blind at Jericho* (1651), as the springboard for his discussion of light, for Poussin was regarded as the greatest artist of the French school. He emphasized that Poussin had chosen to represent an early morning scene, which cast a strong blue light from the left side of the canvas. Bourdon elaborated upon the advantages of such morning light, which later became so conventional that only the angled fall of light from the left was retained. Bourdon, however, read Poussin's painting as a treatise on luminosity:

> For though all the Parts retain their true Teints, yet the Shade which passes above them, is as it were a Veil to extinguish their Vivacity, and hinder their having so much strength as to fill the View, and thrust out other Objects more considerable, and on which the Painter has laid greater Stress. But in return, he has not failed to fill those Places with Light where he saw it would not hurt the beauty of the Figures. (Bourdon 1740: 132)

His audience, however, were not satisfied with such subtleties and demanded to know where the multitude of witnesses described in the New Testament had gone in Poussin's painting. Bourdon replied that

> We cannot suppose that all the Multitude who followed Christ could be about him at once, and being some steps from him, they were concealed by the Buildings. That there are Witnesses enough of the Action, since by that person cloathed in Red, who appears surprised, the Painter has represented the Astonishment of the *Jews*; and by him who is looking very near, he shews the desire that Nation had to see Miracles wrought. A greater Number of Figures would only have occasioned Confusion, and hindered those of Christ and the blind Men from being seen so distinctly. (145)

This literal reading of the painting belied what now seem to be the obvious metaphorical connotations of the painting, connecting the blindness of the figures to the light being spread by Christ. Just as the king could heal by his touch, one might argue, so could artists bring vision into being by their brushstrokes. In this view, the royal artists of the Academy could then claim connection to the sacred person of the king and imbibe something of his divine essence from his aura. Bourdon, however, also insisted on a literal interpretation of blindness:

> By the Action of the first blind Man, his Faith and Confidence in him who is touching him is expressed; in the second, the Favour he is asking is likewise shown. It is common for Persons who are deprived of any one of the five Senses to have the rest better and more subtle; because the Spirits which move in them, to make them known what they want, move with greater force having fewer Offices to perform; thus they who have lost their Sight, have a more acute Hearing, and a more sensible Touch. This is what Mr Poussin has intended to express in the last blind Man, and in which he has wonderfully succeeded. For by his Face and his Arms one may know he is all Attention to the Voice of the Saviour, and endeavoring to find him out. This attentive hearkening appears in his Forehead, which is not quite smooth; the Skin and all the other Parts of which are drawn up. He likewise discovers it, by suspending all the Motions of his Countenance, which continue in that Posture to give time to his Ear to listen more attentively, and that he may not be diverted. (164)

Bourdon thus used the new insights of Cartesian science to explain that the blind have sharper hearing than the average person, a myth that has long outlasted the medical theory of the spirits from which it was devised (as the body has a finite number of spirits to enable the senses, the loss of one sense leaves more spirits available for the others and they are thus enhanced). In fact, the blindness which is on the verge of being cured in Poussin's image calls attention, then, not to insight but to the human voice. Bourdon read the rhetoric of Poussin's painting through physical blindness and found it the key to the expression of the "Voice of the Saviour." He envisaged blindness as a means of intensifying the tactile and auditory response to the painting, rather than as a signifier of incapacity. Light had to be arranged by the painter in such a way as to prevent illegibility, creating a balanced visual economy, which Bourdon described as "a fine Oeconomy of Colours and Lights . . . which makes an agreeable Concert and Charming Sweetness that never cloys the Sight" (170).

The mute painter's achievement was like that of the blind in calling a sensible world into being, while deprived of certain sensory tools. For just as there is a moment of blindness inherent in the act of visual representation, the resulting image was inevitably silent. Throughout the *ancien régime*, artists turned to the gestural sign language of the deaf as a means of overcoming this deficiency for, as the French writer du Fresnoy put it:

> Mutes have no other way of speaking (or expressing their thoughts) but only by their gesture and their actions, 'tis certain that they do it in a manner more expressive than those who have the use of Speech, for which reason the Picture, which is mute ought to imitate them, so as to make itself understood. (Dryden 1695 [1648]: 129)

The mute picture required the assistance of the deaf in order to signify. For in the early modern period, the simple binary opposition between the able-bodied and the disabled did not exist. Instead, the human body was perceived as inevitably imperfect, each person having certain skills that others might not possess. Even Louis XIV had regular bleedings and purgatives before any unusual or tiring activity to purify his body. If the sacred body of the Sun King could be considered imperfect, then his subjects were even more vulnerable. The artists of the period were quick to figure blindness and deafness as complex metaphors in their work, in ways which have been insufficiently recognized.

In the eighteenth century, the sensualist philosophy of the Enlightenment continued this relativist concept of the body, but gave it a moral connotation. Sensualism held that the mind was formed directly from sensory experience and that those with differing senses had different minds. In his *Letter on the Blind*, the philosopher and critic Denis Diderot (1713–1784) reflected at length on the distinctions between the blind and the sighted, pursuing his conviction that: "I doubt that anything at all can be explained without the body" (Josephs 1969: 50). He first mused on the morality of the blind, which he found wanting:

> I suspect them of inhumanity. What difference would there be for a blind man between a man who urinates and a man who, without complaining, was spilling

blood? . . . All our virtues depend upon our manner of sensing, and the degree to which things affect us! Ah! Madame, how different the morality of the blind is from our own. How that of a deaf man would differ again from that of the blind, and how a being which had one sense more than us would find our morality imperfect, to say the least. (Diderot 1975–; vol. 4 (1978): 27)

Diderot found the blind different to the sighted but did not pretend that the sighted were perfect. Indeed, he went on to reflect on ways in which the lack of sight could even be an advantage. He argued that the blind have a tactile memory in the same way that the sighted have a visual memory. The sensation of a mouth on the hand of a blind man and the drawing of it amounted to the same thing, as both were secondary representations of the original. But the blind person had an advantage when it came to abstract thought: "The person born blind perceives things in a far more abstract manner than us, and in questions of pure speculation, he is perhaps less subject to making mistakes" (32). Diderot's example was the blind English mathematician Nicholas Saunderson:

Those who have written about his life say that he was prolific in fortunate expressions . . . But what do you mean by fortunate expressions, you may perhaps ask? I would reply, Madame, that they are those which are proper to a sense, to touch for example, and which are metaphorical at the same time to another sense, like sight; there was thus a double light for those who spoke to him, the true and direct light of the expression, and the reflected light of the metaphor. (Diderot 1978: 41)

Paradoxically, therefore, the sighted person gained a greater illumination by discussing a topic with a blind person.

The paradox was a central concept in Diderot's thought. In the *Paradox on the Actor* (1773–8). Diderot examined this question at length. Discussing the actress Mlle Clairon, he observed:

If you were with her while she studied her part, how many times would you cry out: "That is just right!" and how many times would she answer: "You are wrong!" Just so a friend of Le Quesnot's once cried catching him by the arm: "Stop! you will make it worse by bettering it—you will spoil the whole thing!" "What I have done," replied the artist, panting with exertion, "you have seen; what I have got hold of and what I mean to carry out to the end you cannot see." (Lacoue-Labarthe 1989: 262)

The artist's vision was doubled, like that of the *philosopher* conversing with the blind man, seeing what is present, what is implied and what is yet to come. The true blindness was not that of the visually impaired but of those who believed they could see like the artist but could not. Diderot disliked the "false mimetician or abortive genius who simply *mimes the mimetician.*" The paradox in question stemmed from Diderot's notion that actors "are fit to play all characters because they have none." In the process, actors step outside their characters: "He must have in himself an unmoved and disinterested onlooker. He must have, consequently, penetration and no sensibility, the art of imitating everything, or, which comes to the same thing, the same aptitude for every sort of character and part" (257). For actors to accurately represent the widest range of emotions, it was essential that they themselves have no emotions. Actors constantly observed their work in order to make it appear natural and unforced. For this reason, the British artist John Opie (1761–1807) refused to paint actors at all. Acting was to be no one in order to be everyone, just as it is the blind spot which permits seeing.

In Jacques-Louis David's *Bélisaire, reconnu par un soldat qui avait servi sous lui au moment qu'une femme lui fait aumône* (Lille: Musée Wicar, 1781), blindness was again used by the artist to express a sense of paradox. Belisarius was a Roman general who, after many successes, lost the confidence of the Emperor Justinian and was blinded by him. David (1748–1825) showed the now blind general begging for alms, at a moment when he is recognized by one of his former soldiers. Belisarius' blindness thus comes to have a metaphorical meaning, suggestive of his indifferent not merely to his fate but to the potential spectator. This painting of the blinded Roman general has recently been hailed by art historian Michael Fried as the first truly modern painting, in which David can be seen "reinventing the art of painting" (Fried 1983: 160). Fried in effect proposes that the picture itself postulates a certain blindness in that it is constructed without the needs of a spectator in mind. He argues that David followed Diderot's remark in his *Salon of 1767*: "A scene represented on a canvas or on stage does not suppose witnesses" (Fried 1983: 97). Fried discerns a central distinction between such absorption, which is praised, and vulgar theatricality, which is to be condemned. He argues that David constructed an image which refused theatricality, and instead opted to create a pictorial space in which the characters are wholly absorbed and unaware of the possibility of spectatorship.

Such analyses run counter to the notion of the paradox, developed above, and indeed Fried noted that the late publication of the *Paradox* renders it less relevant for eighteenth-century art history. However, this argument cannot apply to the central example of the *Belisarius*, which was exhibited in the Salon of 1781. Fried applies Diderot's comments of 1762 to David's work:

> If, when one makes a painting, one supposes beholders, everything is lost. The painter leaves his canvas, just as the actor who speaks to the audience [*parterre*] steps down from the stage. In supposing hat there is no-one else in the world except the personnages of the painting, Van Dyck's painting is sublime. (Fried 1983: 149)

Certainly the actor addressing the audience destroys the illusion of the performance but the paradox remains that they know the audience is there. Diderot was not afraid that the actor might communicate with the audience in general but that he might speak to the *parterre*, the popular audience standing in front of the stage. This group was never envisaged in the eighteenth century as being equivalent to the entire audience, as Fried translates it, but were disparaged as a rowdy, disruptive group of pleasure seekers. In the eighteenth century the *parterre* were able to disrupt plays to such an extent that one new production by the Comédie Française had to be cut from five acts to only one and a half. It was a cliché of eighteenth-century French aesthetics that, while the public could form accurate judgments of artistic works, the *parterre* and its socially mixed clientele could not be equated with that public.[1]

Fried's analysis of David's painting concentrates upon the use of architecture to create a sense of space, focusing on the plane created by the Arch of Triumph, which makes it plain that the *Belisarius* was "a painting not made to be beheld" (158). Although this architecture did not appear in the Van Dyck print upon which Fried considers it "virtually certain" that David modelled his work, it was not an original motif. The Arch was in fact borrowed from the illustrations to Jean-François Marmontel's wildly successful novel *Belisarius* (1767) (Boime 1987: 175). Many of the other details of David's painting were taken directly from Gravelot's engravings, including the horrified Roman officer, the block of stone upon which Belisarius' cane rests, and the general's outstretched gesture. The original features of David's work were, then, the woman giving alms and the use of an inscription. The inscription reads "Date obolum Belisario" (Give an obol to Belisarius). In the first version of the painting, it is slightly obscured by Belisarius' staff, but it is prominent in the later copy now in the Louvre. This tag does not feature in Marmontel's text, or any of the other painted versions of the Belisarius story before and after David's work. In itself, it requires a beholder, for only a spectator of the image would be in a position to read it. Furthermore, only an outside beholder would need such an inscription for all the figures painted by David are only too aware of the identity of the general. It would be stretching credulity to suggest that the wandering, blind general carved the sign himself to attract alms. The inscription is an interpellation by David which addresses the outside spectator and calls attention to the political message of the painting. In English political satire, Belisarius had been a symbol of government ingratitude and incompetence since 1710, when a pamphlet compared the then disgraced Duke of Marlborough to the Roman general.[2] Ever since, plays and pamphlets had hearkened to Belisarius as a metaphor for the failings of government.[3] In 1768, the leading radical journal the *Political Register*, published a print decrying the "tyrannical" British policy towards the American colonies, in which the dis-membered figure of Britannia is captions "Date obolum Belisario" (Wilson 1995). The *Political Register* was well known in Paris and ties between British and French radicals were sufficiently close in the period for Jean-Paul Marat, the future revolutionary leader, to campaign in Newcastle and publish his first book—*The Chains of Slavery* (1774)—in English translation. The caption places David's work as one of his first political statements, and it was no coincidence that he made it more legible in the later version.[4]

David did not simply add a political label to an illustration in Marmontel's novel, but changed the dynamics of the scene with the addition of the woman giving alms. Her presence allows the soldier to drop back and recognize his former leader from a safe distance, but more importantly it gives a gendered dynamic to the painting. Gender roles were similarly important in the British print, contrasting Britannia's virtue with the effeminacy of the British political elite. The horror of the soldier is caused as much by the reduced circumstances of the general, indicated by the woman's act of charity, as by his blindness. The paradox of the *Belisarius* is precisely this opposition of gender roles. In the *Paradox*, Diderot advised his readers to "[t]hink of women, again. They are miles beyond us in sensibility; there is no sort of comparison between their passion and ours. But as much as we are below them in action, so much are they below us in imitation" (Lacoue-Labarthe 1989: 263). The unknown woman who acts out of pity for the fallen general is the counterpoint to the masculine sensibility of the soldier. She is also the inspiration for David's exercise in artistic imitation and it is inspiration that, for Diderot, sets the true artist apart from the crowd. "The beauty of inspiration" was what the artist Le Quesnoy could see and his visitor could not. It is what gives a work its force and enthusiasm. But that moment must be contained and controlled in conscious reflection, the masculine quality which women are held to lack. This paradox is contained in the epigram Diderot wrote for the *Belisarius*: "Every day I see it, and always I believe I am seeing it for the first time." The doubled insight of the witness to the blind is given force and freshness by the differing reactions of the spectators within the frame, according to their gender stereotypes. Only the spectator outside, whether it was the artist observing himself, the Salon spectator or the critic, could fully appreciate and meditate upon these different reactions and insights.

Blindness in *ancien régime* art, then, called attention to the relativism and vulnerability of human sensory perception, and the paradoxical nature of artistic creation. The blind were not used as metaphors beyond the specific limitations of their condition, but constituted an important point of reference for sensualist philosophy, as it strove to understand understanding itself. As Ménuret de Chambaud, a principal contributor to the great *Encyclopedia* of Diderot and d'Alembert, opined: "Perhaps it is true that in order to be a good moralist, one must be an excellent doctor" (Rey 1993: 25). However, not long after these words were written, philosophy took a turn away from sensualism to the more abstracted pursuit of epistemology, and medicine became inseparable from morality. In the second half of the eighteenth century, medical science began to rely on a distinction between the normal states of the body and its pathology, that is, its diseases and abnormalities. Disease, abnormality and immorality became linked in a powerful trinity which is still in force today. Georges Canguilhem has analyzed the spread of a distinction between the normal and the pathological from the first appearance of the terms in the mid-eighteenth century to their widespread acceptance in the nineteenth century:

> In the course of the nineteenth century, the real identity of normal and pathological vital phenomena, apparently so different, and given opposing values by human experience, became a kind of scientifically guaranteed dogma, whose extension

into the realms of philosophy and psychology appeared to be dictated by the authority biologists and physicians granted it. (Canguilhem 1991 [1966]: 43)

Sensualist philosophy, which depended upon the authority of sense impressions, was among the first areas to be so affected.

Blindness was at once categorized as a pathological state of the body, in distinction to the normal condition of sight. During the French Revolution the state appropriated the wealth of the Quinze-Vingts, the charitable hospital for the blind in Paris, due to the tradition that patients said prayers for the Church and the King. Moreover, those blind persons who had formerly been in the nobility or clergy received a higher pension than others and there were suspicions of immoral conduct in the hospital. In its place, the revolutionaries proposed to create a national network of "residential assistance for all the blind, public asylums for those who have neither habitation to shelter them, nor family to care for them" (*Observations* An II: 37). In place of royal charity, the Revolution hoped to construct a national, moral and egalitarian system of assistance for the blind, which did not entail any change in the medical care of the blind.

Although there was a seemingly absolute distinction between the pathological blind and the normal sighted, it was soon blurred by further classification among the ranks of the pathological. As the nineteenth century progressed, it became clear that, despite the physical limitations of blindness, it was regarded as less morally debilitating than other sensory loss. In particular, the blind came to be seen as superior to the deaf—in the minds of the hearing and seeing—and to be endowed with special moral qualities. The blind and deaf pupils of the state were initially housed together during the French Revolution, until political discord among their educators forced a separation in 1793. At this time, both the deaf and the blind were seen as pre-civilized beings who required the assistance of the state to render them human. In a pamphlet published in 1783, Perier, a deputy administrator at the Institute for the Deaf, adamantly insisted on the need for such an institution: "The Deaf-Mute is always a savage, always close to ferocity, and always on the point of becoming a monster." Even after birth, the "savage" Deaf could mutate into monstrous forms without the restraining hand of the disciplinary Institute. The language used to describe the deaf was also applied to the blind, as here by one administrator of the blind school in 1817: "The moral world does not exist for this child of nature; most of our ideas are without reality for him: he lives as if he was alone; he relates everything to himself" (Paulson 1987: 95). The initial breakthrough in the education of the blind was the invention of a raised typeface by Valentin Haüy, condensed by Louis Braille (1809–1852) into the code of dots with which we are familiar. As discussions of the old chestnut regarding the preferability of blindness or deafness continued, the issue was decisively resolved (by those who could see and hear) in favour of blindness. For the loss of hearing was held to entail the loss of voice and hence of thought. When the blind read Braille, they converted the dots into the pure medium of sound, which more than compensated for its non-alphabetic character, whereas the deaf used sign language, and thought without sound. By late century, official French government manuals on the care of the abnormal advised that Braille was "an intermediary system between the manuscript and the printed text," but in sign language, "all spiritual ideas will be unhappily materialized" (Couètoux and de Fougeray 1886: 131 and 19). Thomas Arnold (1823–1900), who founded a small school for the deaf in Northampton in 1868, believed that the blind: "mentally, morally and spiritually [are] in a more advantageous condition than the deaf." If the blind could create "a mental language of vibrations and motions" from touch, the deaf were restricted to "a language of mimic gestures . . . which is destitute of all that phonetic language provides of antecedent progress in thought and knowledge" (Arnold 1894: 9–15). In 1840, Braille was considered arbitrary and deaf sign language had won a certain acceptance, but by 1890 it was Braille that had become acceptable and the deaf were considered pre-civilized. Nothing essential had changed in the nature of sign language and Braille in the intervening fifty years. In Arnold's widely accepted viewpoint, the decisive factor in this change of opinion was the blind's ability to hear. Sight was "much inferior in providing us with available mental images and an organ of expression," indicating that hearing alone was now considered a "pure" sense. Arnold's privileged point of reference was the French neurologist Jean-Martin Charcot (1825–1893), as the "abnormal" became the province of what was termed medico-psychology. By way of contrast, French officials considered that deafness rendered even the sense of sight pathological: "[the deaf person] knows that what he does not see does not exist for him; he does not look, he *devours*" (Denis 1895: 23–6). Medico-psychology thus considered the loss of sight to be far less grievous a blow than deafness. This sense that the blind are more "human" than the deaf has persisted to the present and accounts for the greater sympathy and funding that is available for the blind.

The rise of this perceived morality of blindness from the nineteenth to the early twentieth century can also be traced in the cultural representation of blindness. In Paul De Man's famous essay, "The Rhetoric of Blindness," he advances the case that a writer only gains a certain insight because of his or her blindness to other aspects of the problem.

> Insight could only be gained because the critics were in the grip of this peculiar blindness: their language could grope toward a certain degree of insight only because their method remained oblivious to the perception of this insight. The insight exists only for a reader in the privileged position of being able to observe the blindness as a phenomenon in its own right—the question of his own blindness being one which he is by definition incompetent to ask—and so being able to distinguish between statement and meaning. (De Man 1983: 106)

De Man's argument is central to the modern canon of blindness as outlined in this essay. In the pursuit of clarity, insight and self-expression, successive modernist artists have deployed blindness as a key figure for their work. De Man does not, however, clarify that this relationship of blindness and insight is both historically specific—as opposed to a universal truth about criticism—and gendered.

The gendered dimension of the Dibutade myth and David's *Belisarius* came to be transferred to this critical relationship valorizing insight as inevitably and uniquely masculine.

In both Romantic and Neo-Classical painting, blindness was used as a figure for insight and morality. Jean-Auguste-Dominique Ingres (1780–1867) was the leader of the French Neo-Classical school from the collapse of Napoleon's Empire in 1815 until his death. Ingres created a series of painted manifestos, setting out the influences and beliefs of a Neo-Classicism which sought to reclaim the French Classical tradition, stemming from Poussin, while bypassing the images of the French Revolution. As a leading student of David, Ingres was well placed to carry out this artistic revision of history painting, in accord with the wider rewriting of history during the Restoration (1816–30). In his vast ceiling painting, *The Apotheosis of Homer*, Ingres reinvented French Neo-Classicism after the Revolution. This painting, installed in the Louvre in 1827, literally put the lid on what can be called the French cultural revolution (Bianchi 1982). It is a history painting, the most important genre of painting in the period, which became the precondition of all French history painting, depicting the appropriate sources and inspirations for this art. At the centre of the painting is the figure of Homer being crowned by the Muses, surrounded by those who have followed in his wake. Ingres depicted an artistic lineage which passed from the ancient Greek artists Apelles and Zeuxis, via the Renaissance masters Raphael and Poussin, ending by inference with Ingres himself. At the heart of this artistic pedigree sits the blind poet Homer, author if the *Iliad* and the *Odyssey*. Blindness was thus for Ingres quite literally the origin of representation. Clearly, Homer's blindness cannot be understood in the relativizing sensory tradition of the Enlightenment, for Ingres sought to deify Homer, not to place his work in relation to that of others. His blindness, symbolized by his closed eyes, is metaphorical and suggests instead that, in order to achieve the degree of insight attained by Homer, some sacrifice is necessary. Despite his success, Ingres believed that he too had suffered in his artistic career. His *Jupiter and Thetis* had been a dramatic failure at the Salon of 1811 and after his *Saint Symphorien* suffered a similar fate in 1834, Ingres refused to show his work at the Salon. It is hard not to take the metaphor of blindness a little farther. Ingres excluded his own master David and the other leading French Neo-Classicists, such as Gros, Gérard and Girodet from his vision of painting. Homer's blindness was matched by Ingres' own metaphorical blind spot concerning his own artistic formation in the Neo-Classical school of David, overlooked in his painting in favour of the eternal verities of Homer.

Ingres was haunted by the symbolism of blindness. In 1816, he completed the first of many versions of the theme *Oedipus and the Sphinx*, in which Oedipus is shown answering the Sphinx's riddle. His successful response ensured that the second part of his oracle would be enacted, for having already unwittingly killed his father, Oedipus was not to marry his mother. Oedipus is finally the agent of his own destruction, when he seeks to uncover the causes of a plague and discovers the truth of his own actions. By way of self-punishment, Oedipus blinds himself. The Freudian overtones of this story are only too apparent. For Freud, the Oedipus myth was a representation of the most fundamental masculine desires to kill the father and sleep with the mother, as well as of its most potent fear, namely Oedipus' blindness, equated to the fear of castration. It is in fact arguable that without the nineteenth century construct of blindness as moral sacrifice, Freud would not have been able to use the Oedipus myth as he did. Blindness appears at the centre of Ingres' history paintings precisely because of these new resonances it acquired in the period. The meanings conveyed by blindness as metaphor were, however, complex and irreducible to a single message. It was a short step from the moral insight of Homer to the castrated gaze of Oedipus. Blindness became a complex figure in Ingres' work, standing for representation, for morality and for the construction of the masculine ego itself, always haunted by the fear of castration, itself envisaged as blindness.[5]

For Ingres' depiction of history painting is a striking example of what Donna Harraway has called the patriline. His *Homer* is a homosocial world in which women appear only in non-human form as Muses. The transmission and reproduction of cultural value was envisaged as a purely masculine affair, eliminating the fear of castration and the blind(ed) gaze. A central theme of eighteenth-century painting had been the "fallen father," to use Carol Duncan's insightful phrase. History and genre painting had sought to construct an authoritative father figure in a society widely believed to be unusually susceptible to feminine influence. For many revolutionary leaders, this feminizing of the French state was to blame for the political weaknesses and corruption of the *ancien régime*. Even avowed supporters of the monarchy agreed that, in the words of the painter Elizabeth Vigée Lebrun, "the women reigned then. The Revolution dethroned them" (Vigée Lebrun 1989: 49). Rather than return to this charged political controversy, Ingres elided it by creating an idea of culture as the exclusive province of the white male. From its foundation in 1648, the French Academy of Painting had permitted women to become members in theory, although few in practice were able to gain the necessary training. But in 1776, it was felt to be necessary to limit the number of potential women members to four. Even then, the admission of Vigée Lebrun in 1783 required considerable politicking to evade the censure of the leading Academician Pierre (Vigée Lebrun 1989: 34–5). The reformed nineteenth-century Academy excluded women altogether. In Ingres' representation of civilization, there was no place for women.

Eugène Delacroix (1798–1863), the leader of the Romantic school of painting, also represented blindness as the origin of representation, even though he is usually considered as being directly opposed to Ingres' Neo-Classicism. Delacroix chose as a subject *The Poet Milton Dictating to His Daughters* (1826). For the Romantics, the blind poet Milton occupied the same position of authority as Homer for the Neo-Classicists. The subject had been treated by Henry Fuseli in 1799, but he was so anxious to represent Milton's blindness that the poet has ashen skin and sunken eyes, looking more like Boris Karloff's Frankenstein than an inspired poet. Delacroix represented the scene in quieter but altogether more effective fashion. Just as David used the woman giving alms to give meaning to his *Belisarius*, so did Delacroix highlight the contrast between the active women and their passive father. Milton becomes the supreme embodiment of the superiority of the voice and hearing over sight, as his powers of creativity are contrasted with the women, who although sighted, are fit only to copy down their father's words. The poet's insight is such that it overcomes his physical blindness. Milton retains his patriarchal authority, despite having suffered the loss of his sight, and his potency is doubly attested to by the presence of his daughters. Delacroix's confident embrace of blindness as a gendered metaphor for creativity and morality was to gain ascendancy over Ingres' homosocial vision. While the Neo-Classical Ingres saw blindness as both the origin and the potential annihilation of representation, the modern Romantics bestowed creativity on the individual male and were unconcerned to construct secure artistic genealogies. Indeed the Oedipal gesture of revolt becomes *de rigueur* for any aspiring young artist.

The high point of this moralizing trajectory came with Paul Strand's (1890–1976) photograph *Blind Woman* (1916). Taken as a manifesto for Strand's departure from the gradated tones of the Photo-Secession movement, his representation of blindness thus embodied revolt and coming of age. The photograph has long been hailed as a modernist masterpiece:

> The portrait conveys *qualities*: endurance, isolation, the curious alertness of the blind or nearly blind, and a surprising beauty in the strong, possible Slavic, head. The whole concept of blindness is aimed like a weapon at those whose privilege of sight permits them to experience the picture, much like the "dramatic irony" in which an all-knowing audience observes a doomed protagonist onstage. Although he excluded bystanders from the picture, Strand included everyone who sees it. This extraordinary device gives the photograph its particular edge, adding new meaning to a simple portrait. (Haworth-Booth 1987: 5)

In this view, Strand's photograph of the blind woman functions as an abstract, moral discourse on perception. The weapon of blindness belonged not to the blind woman but to the photographer. It was no coincidence that Strand photographed a blind woman. In so doing, he collapsed the moral exchange created by David and Delacroix between the blind man and the sighted woman into one figure. Strand's deployment of gender constituted the originality of his work, for photographers had long considered the blind as an intriguing subject. As early as 1858, the photographic journal *La Lumière* reported the placard of a Parisian male beggar: 'Give to the poor blind man, he will not see you (*La Lumière* 1858: 99). In Strand's work, the woman represents the modernist quandary as to the nature of perception, but it is the photographer who has the key to representation rather than the figure within the image. In his quest to deny the woman any specificity, Strand erased her name and any details about her in order to make blindness a more effective symbol. If blindness is to be fully effective as a moral lesson, it cannot be dogged by such trivial details. None the less, the history of the blind, as opposed to the abstract idea of blindness, is present in this photograph. The blind woman wears a brass badge, bearing the legend "Licensed Peddler. New York. 2622." The badge, together with the crudely painted sign reading BLIND, attests to the state's intervention in controlling the "degenerate" population. In order to sell items on the street, the woman has to be registered and classified, involving tests to ensure that she is "really" blind and not simply "idle." These policies were the culmination of over a century of designating the blind as pathological and hence a problem for the body politic. Strand's abstract moral lesson was enabled and given meaning by the classification and labeling of the blind by that nexus of medical and political authority which Michel Foucault has named bio-power. As a meditation on representation, the photograph takes blindness to be the origin of representation, but denies the woman any participation in this process, except as its object.

This interpretation of the role of blindness in representation received ironic confirmation when the American Minimalist artist Robert Morris (b. 1931) set about his series called *Blind Time* in 1973. Morris had pursued a critique of the prevalent modes of art practice, criticism and display in a variety of media since the early 1960s. Now, seeking to move on from his site-specific earth pieces of the early 1970s, Morris undertook a series of works in which he was unable to see. He assigned himself a specific task and a length of time in which to complete it, drawing on paper with his fingers. By so doing, Morris sought to disrupt the modernist obsession with sight and its representation, as Maurice Berger has noted:

> Like being lost in a labyrinth, such drawing processes radically altered the artist's sense of control of his own actions. By undoing the compositional claims of the artist over his work, the *Blind Time* series distanced the artists from the modernist conceits of ego and temperament. Because the artist's masterful control of his process was not rendered irrelevant, such works travestied the obsession of formalist abstraction with compositional balance and harmony. (Berger 1989: 151)

Morris soon decided to take this process one step farther. In 1976, he commenced the series *Blind Time II*, in which he used a woman who had been blind from birth as what he termed as "assistant." The woman, known only as A. A., was recruited from the American Association for the Blind and was asked to carry out similar tasks to those Morris himself had previously performed. The experience was not a success. A. A. quickly became skeptical of the project and confused as to its intentions. Here, for example, Morris commented:

> She had no idea of illusionistic drawing. I described perspective to her and she thought that was absolutely ridiculous, that things got smaller in the distance. She had no conception of that. She kept asking me about criteria, got very involved in what is the right kind of criteria for a thing. And there was no way that she could find any and finally that sort of conflict became very dramatic. She was operating

in a way that she wouldn't have to invoke [these criteria]. And at the same time she was aghast that she was not able to. (Berger 1989: 153)

This scene, far from constituting a radical experiment, was a re-enactment of the modernist legend connecting blindness to the origin of representation, as if Morris had tried to find his own Dibutade and recreate the origin of drawing in a woman whom he believed had no concept of visual representation. Like Dibutade, A. A. could not record her own work, but relied on the intercession of the male authority figure for her claim to a place in art history. Whereas Paul Strand had used blindness as a weapon, Morris went one further and used the blind woman as a form of tool. He denied her the chance to formulate her own concepts of art practice and refused to let her establish any rules in her work. In 1856, Théophile Gautier had made this distinction central to his "programme of the modern school" of art for arts sake.

The artist much search for his alphabet in the visible world, which supplies him with conventional signs . . .; but if the idea of the beautiful pre-exists within us, would it pre-exist in a man born blind, for example? What image of the beautiful in art could a pensioner of the Quinze Vingts make for himself? (Gautier 1856: 157)

The relativistic notions of perception which had so fascinated Enlightenment critics no longer applied. Sight was essential not just for art, as might seem obvious, but for the very notions of art and beauty. The very initials A. A. by which the blind woman is known are indicative of Morris's sense that she was at the origin of art and could have no rules. Soon becoming dissatisfied with her work, Morris discontinued the project, finding it "[s]parer and less controlled than the artist's own blind drawings, they are more about her impressions and feelings" (Fry 1986: 34). Morris withdrew all 52 works created in the Blind Time II series from circulation. Modernism had so far abstracted blindness and gender from the body that Morris's encounter with an actual blind woman was bound to end in failure.

When he resumed Blind Time in 1985, Morris undertook the works himself. In his version of the project, he added philosophical commentaries on the images produced and the ideas that lay behind them. For example, in one 1985 piece, Morris set about constructing a grid in a seven-minute experiment. As Rosalind Krauss has argued, the grid has been one of the defining motifs of modernism and Morris attached considerable weight to the procedure in his inscription: "Searching for a metaphor for the occupation of that moment between lapsed time and the possibilities spent on the one hand and an imagined but unoccupiable future on the other, both of which issue from that tightly woven nexus of language, tradition and culture which constructs our narrative of time" (Fry 1986: 37). Although Blind Time III makes considerable reference to contemporary physics, citing such figures as Einstein, Bohr and Feynman, this passage seems closer to Marcel Proust and his search for lost time. These literary and philosophical comments could hardly be further removed from the excerpts of conversation between the artist and A. A., which accompanied the previous version of the series. The male artist feels able to explore the metaphorical dimensions and wider implications of his "blindness," precisely the avenues he had blocked for the anonymous blind woman. Morris's modernism denied the blind any possibility of participating in visual representation. While this exclusion might seem natural, it did not seem so to early modern blind sculptors or indeed to A. A. Within this metaphorical framework, blindness-as-lack-of-sight affects only women, whereas blindness-as-insight is a particularly male phenomenon. The radical feminist art collective, the Guerilla Girls, would no doubt wish to note that in Derrida's exhibition at the Louvre, for which he was given access to their entire collection of prints and drawings, the philosopher selected no women artists.[6]

Blindness—or more exactly, the interplay between the insightful artist and the blind woman—is only one metaphor for modernism and is not equivalent to it. But the nexus of race, gender and disability created by the triumph of the Dibutade myth of the origin of painting in the mid-eighteenth century forms a crucial point of investigation for the modern representation of the body, which was caught between two difficult alternatives. The Dibutade myth was itself determined by a wider revision of European intellectual history which excluded African and Semitic influences in favour of a pure Aryan model for ancient Greek history. However, the alternative modernist reading of the body, which privileges the fragmentary and dispersed body and argues that culture oscillates between the poles of blindness and insight, is constructed around a notion of originary gender difference. Both readings of the body thus depend upon essential differences of race or gender, which are both necessarily exclusive and ahistorical. It would be equally disingenuous simply to call for an end to the metaphorization of the body, still more so for an end to the representation of the body—even a Minimalist sculpture can be read as a denial of the body. For it is not enough to reveal yet again that cultural products are social constructions, as Michael Taussig has recently argued: "What do we do with this old insight? If life is constructed, how come it appears so immutable? How come culture appears so natural?" (Taussig 1993a: xvi). Rather than concluding by producing the white rabbit of cultural construction from the intellectual's top hat, it is my point of departure that these contradictions produce a necessary and productive dis-ease concerning the bodyscape.

However, this constructed understanding of the modern body does not make it any less real, nor does it allow the modern subject to bypass the limits of body in a quest for identity. The body cannot be known or understood without visual representation, yet both the body itself and its image seem inevitably flawed. An indication of this problem is that there is no way to describe the body as imperfect (disabled, incomplete, virtual, etc.) which does not logically and linguistically imply the existence of a perfect body. In order to extend our understanding, it is therefore necessary to examine the persistence and cultural function of notions of the perfect body.

NOTES

1. In Britain, by contrast, the pit was held to be the most important venue for determining public opinion in the theatre.

2. See Anon, *Belisarius and Zariana: A Dialogue* (London, 1709) and the play *Belisarius* by William Philips (London, T. Woodward, 1724), dedicated to General Webb, reprinted in 1758.

3. Plays included: *Belisarius* ascribed to John Phillip Kemble (1778) and *Belisarius* by Hugh Downman (Exeter, 1786); a scene concerning Belisarius was published in *The Oracle* (17 October 1795). Many thanks to Kathleen Wilson for these references.

4. Thomas Crow has suggested that the exile referred to was the minister Turgot, an identification made all the more likely by the English parallel.

5. The polysemicity of blindness in the modern period does not undermine Derrida's interpretation, but rather reinforces it. Derrida has often emphasized that the keywords in his readings, such as deconstruction, glyph, hymen, différance, *pharmakon*, and so on, are not to be individually privileged as the key to the Western metaphysic, but are different points of entry to that discourse.

6. In fact, when Derrida discusses sexuality it is male sexuality that is in question, via an examination of representations of the blinding of Samson, read as castration.

WORKS CITED

Arnold, Thomas. 1894. *The Language of the Senses with Special Reference to the Education of the Deaf, Blind, Deaf & Blind*. Margate, England: *Keble's Gazette*.

Berger, Maurice. 1989. *Labyrinths: Robert Morris, Minimalism, and the 1960s*. New York. Harper and Row.

Bourdon, Sébastien. 1740. "Seventh Conference." In [Anon.] 1740 *Seven Conference Held in the King of France's Cabinet of Paintings*. London: T. Cooper.

Canguilhem, Georges. 1991 [1966]. *The Normal and the Pathological*. Trans. Caroyn R. Fawcettt. New York. Zone.

Couétoux, L. and Hamon de Fougeray. 1886. *Manuel pratique des méthodes d'enseignement spéciales aux enfants anormaux (sourds-muets, aveugles, idiots, bégues, etc.)*. Paris: Félix Alcan.

Denis, Théophile. 1895. "Les Artistes sourds-muets au Salon de 1886." In *Etudes variées concernant les sourds-muets. Histoire—Biographie—Beaux-arts*. Paris: Imprimérie de la Revue Francaise de l'Enseignement de Sourds-muets.

De Man, Paul. 1983. *Blindness and Insight*. Minneapolis: University of Minnesota Press.

Derrida, Jacques. 1993. *Memoirs of the Blind: The Self Portrait and Other Ruins*. Trans. Pascale-Anne Brault and Michael Naas. Chicago. Chicago University Press.

Diderot, Denis. 1975–. *Oeuvres complètes*. Paris: Hermann. 25 vols.

Dryden, John. 1695. *De Arte Graphica: The Art of Painting by C. A. du Fresnoy*. London. J. Hepinstall.

Fried, Michael. 1983. *Absorption and Theatricality*. Chicago: Chicago University Press.

Fry, Edward F. with Donald P. Kuspit. 1986. *Robert Morris: Works of the Eighties*. Chicago. Museum of Contemporary Art.

Gautier, Théophile. 1856. "Du Beau dans l'Art." In *L'Art moderne*. Paris: Michel Levy.

Haworth-Booth, Mark. 1987. *Paul Strand*. New York: Aperture.

Josephs, Herbert. 1969. *Diderot's Dialogue of Language and Gesture: Le Neveu de Rameau*. Columbus: Ohio University Press.

Lacoue-Labarthe, Phillipe. 1989. *Typography*. Cambridge, MA: Harvard University Press.

La Lumière Observations. An II. Anon. *Observations pour les aveugles de l'Hopital des Quinze-Vingts sur le project décret du comité de secours de la Convention Nationale pour la suppression de cet hopital*, Paris: J. Grand.

Paulson, William R. 1987. *Enlightenment, Romanticism and the Blind in France*. Princeton: Princeton University Press.

Taussig, Michael. 1993a. *Mimesis and Alterity: A Particular History of the Senses*. New York: Routledge.

Vigée Lebrun, Elizabeth. 1989. *Memoirs of Madame Vigée Lebrun*. New York: George Braziller [1903].

part seven

Fiction and Poetry

Helen and Frida

ANNE FINGER

I'm lying on the couch downstairs in the TV room in the house where I grew up, a farmhouse with sloping floors in upstate New York. I'm nine years old. I've had surgery, and I'm home, my leg in a plaster cast. Everyone else is off at work or school. My mother recovered this couch by hemming a piece of fabric that she bought from a bin at the Woolworth's in Utica ("Bargains! Bargains! Bargains! Remnants Priced as Marked") and laying it over the torn upholstery. Autumn leaves—carrot, jaundice, brick—drift sluggishly across a liver-brown background. I'm watching *The Million Dollar Movie* on our black-and-white television: today it's *Singing in the Rain*. These movies always make me think of the world that my mother lived in before I was born, a world where women wore hats and gloves and had cinched-waist suits with padded shoulders as if they were in the army. My mother told me that in *The Little Colonel*, Shirley Temple had pointed her finger and said, "As red as those roses over there," and then the roses had turned red and everything in the movie was in color after that. I thought that was how it had been when I was born, everything in the world becoming both more vivid and more ordinary, and the black-and-white world, the world of magic and shadows, disappearing forever in my wake.

Now it's the scene where the men in blue-jean coveralls are wheeling props and sweeping the stage, carpenters shouldering boards, moving behind Gene Kelley as Don Lockwood and Donald O'Connor as Cosmo. Cosmo is about to pull his hat down over his forehead and sing, "Make 'em laugh . . ." and hoof across the stage, pulling open doors that open onto brick walls, careening up what appears to be a lengthy marble-floored corridor but is in fact a painted backdrop.

Suddenly, all the color drains from the room: not just from the mottled sofa I'm lying on, but also from the orange wallpaper that looked so good on the shelf at Streeter's (and was only $1.29 a roll), the chipped blue-willow plate: everything's black and silver now. I'm on a movie set, sitting in the director's chair. I'm grown-up suddenly, eighteen or thirty-five.

Places, please!

Quiet on the set!

Speed, the soundman calls, and I point my index finger at the camera, the clapper claps the board and I see that the movie we are making is called "Helen and Frida." I slice my finger quickly through the air, and the camera rolls slowly forward towards Helen Keller and Frida Kahlo, standing on a veranda, with balustrades that appear to be made of carved stone, but are in fact made of plaster.

The part of Helen Keller isn't played by Patty Duke this time; there's no *Miracle Worker* wild child to spunky rebel in under 100 minutes, no grainy film stock, none of that Alabama sun that bleaches out every soft shadow, leaving only harshness, glare. This time Helen is played by Jean Harlow.

Don't laugh: set pictures of the two of them side by side and you'll see that it's all there, the fair hair lying in looping curls against both faces, the same broad-cheeked bone structure. Imagine that Helen's eyebrows are plucked into a thin arch and penciled, lashes mascaraed top and bottom, lips cloisonned ver-million. Put Helen in pale peach mousseline-de-soie, hand her a white gardenia, bleach her hair from its original honey blonde to platinum, like Harlow's was, recline her on a *Bombshell* chaise with a white swan gliding in front, a palm fan being waved overhead, while an ardent lover presses sweet nothings into her hand.

I play the part of Frida Kahlo.

It isn't so hard to imagine that the two of them might meet. They moved after all, in not so different circles, fashionable and radical: Helen Keller meeting Charlie Chaplin and Mary Pickford, joining the Wobblies, writing in *The New York Times*, "I love the red flag . . . and if I could I should gladly march it past the offices of the *Times* and let all the reporters and photographers make the most of the spectacle . . ."; Frida, friend of Henry Ford and Sergei Eisenstein, paint-ing a hammer and sickle on her body cast, leaving her bed in 1954, a few weeks before her death, to march in her wheelchair with a babushka tied under her chin, protesting the overthrow of the Arbenz regime in Guatemala.

Of course, the years are all wrong. But that's the thing about *The Million Dollar Movie*. During Frank Sinatra Week, on Monday Frank would be young and hand-some in *It Happened in Brooklyn*, on Tuesday he'd have grey temples and crow's feet, be older than my father, on Wednesday, be even younger than he had been on Monday. You could pour the different decades in a bowl together and give them a single quick fold with the smooth edge of a spatula, the way my mother did when she made black and white marble cake from two Betty Crocker mixes. It would be 1912, and Big Bill Haywood would be waving the check Helen had sent over his head at a rally for the Little Falls strikers, and you, Frida, would be in the crowd, not as a five-year-old child, before the polio, before the bus acci-dent, but as a grown woman, cheering along with the strikers. Half an inch away, it would be August 31, 1932, and both of you would be standing on the roof of the Detroit Institute of the Arts, along with Diego, Frida looking up through smoked glass at the eclipse of the sun, Helen's face turned upwards to feel the chill of night descending, to hear the birds greeting the midday dusk.

Let's get one thing straight right away. This isn't going to be one of those movies where they put their words into our mouths. This isn't *Magnificent Obsession*, blind Jane Wyman isn't going to blink back a tear when the doctors tell her they can't cure her after all, saying, "and I thought I was going to be able to get rid of these," gesturing with her ridiculous rhinestone-studded, catseye dark glasses (and we think, "*Really*, Jane,"); she's not going to tell Rock Hudson she can't marry him: "I won't have you pitied because of me. I love you too much," and "I could only be a burden," and then disappear until the last scene when, lingering on the border between death and cure (the only two acceptable states), Rock saves her life and her sight and they live happily ever after. It's not going to be *A Patch of Blue*: when the sterling young Negro hands us the dark glasses and, in answer to our question: "But what are they for?" says "Never mind, put them on," we're not going to grab them, hide our stone Medusa gaze, grateful for the magic that's made us a pretty girl. This isn't *Johnny Belinda*, we're not sweetly mute, surrounded by an aura of silence. No, in this movie the blind women have milky eyes that make the sighted uncomfortable. The deaf women drag metal against metal, oblivious to the jarring sound, make odd cries of delight at the sight of the ocean, squawk when we are angry.

So now the two female icons of disability have met: Helen, who is nothing but, who swells to fill up the category, sweet Helen with her drooping dresses covering drooping bosom, who is Blind and Deaf, her vocation; and Frida, who lifts her skirt to reveal the gaping, cunt-like wound on her leg, who rips her body open to reveal her back, a broken column, her back corset with its white canvas straps framing her beautiful breasts, her body stuck with nails: but she can't be Disabled, she's Sexual.

Here stands Frida, who this afternoon, in the midst of a row with Diego, cropped off her jet-black hair ("Now see what you've made me do!"), and has schlepped herself to the ball in one of his suits. Nothing Dietrichish and coy about this drag: Diego won't get to parade his beautiful wife. Now she's snatched up Helen and walked with her out here onto the veranda.

In the other room, drunken Diego lurches, his body rolling forward before his feet manage to shuffle themselves ahead on the marble floor, giving himself more than ever the appearance of being one of those children's toys, bottom-weighted with sand, that when punched, roll back and then forward, an eternal red grin painted on their rubber faces. His huge belly shakes with laughter, his laughter a gale that blows above the smoke curling up towards the distant, gilded ceiling, gusting above the knots of men in tuxedos and women with marcelled hair, the black of their satin dresses setting off the glitter of their diamonds.

But the noises of the party, Diego's drunken roar, will be added later by the Foley artists.

Helen's thirty-six. She's just come back from Montgomery. Her mother had dragged her down there after she and Peter Fagan took out a marriage license, and the Boston papers got hold of the story. For so many years, men had been telling her that she was beautiful, that they worshipped her, that when Peter declared himself in the parlor at Wrentham, she had at first thought this was just more palaver about his pure love for her soul. But no, this was the real thing: carnal and thrilling and forbidden. How could you, her mother said. How people will laugh at you! The shame, the shame. Her mother whisked her off to

Montgomery, Peter trailing after the two of them. There her brother-in-law chased Peter off the porch with a good old Southern shotgun. Helen's written her poem:

> What earthly consolation is there for one like me
> Whom fate has denied a husband and the joy of motherhood? . . .
> I shall have confidence as always,
> That my unfilled longings will be gloriously satisfied
> In a world where eyes never grow dim, nor ears dull.

Poor Helen, waiting, waiting to get fucked in heaven.

But not Frida. She's so narcissistic. What a relief to Helen! None of those interrogations passing for conversation she usually has to endure. (After the standard pile of praise is heaped upon her—I've read your book five, ten, twenty times, I've admired you ever since . . . come the questions: Do you mind if I ask you: Is everything black? Is Mrs. Macy always with you?): no, Frida launches right into the tale of Diego's betrayal " . . . of course, I have my fun, too, but one doesn't want to have one's nose rubbed in the shit . . ." she signs into Helen's hand.

Helen is delighted and shocked. In her circles, Free Love is believed in, spoken of solemnly, dutifully. Her ardent young circle of socialists want to do away with the sordid marketplace of prostitution, bourgeois marriage, where women barter their hymens and throw in their souls to sweeten the deal; Helen has read Emma, she has read Isadora; she believes in a holy, golden monogamy, an unfettered, eternal meeting of two souls-in-flesh. And here Frida speaks of the act so casually that Helen, like a timid schoolgirl, stutters,

"You really? I mean, the both of you, you . . . ?"

Frida throws her magnificent head back and laughs.

"Yes, really," Frida strokes gently into her hand. "He fucks other women and I fuck other men—and other women."

"F–U–C–K?" Helen asks. "What is this word?"

Frida explains it to her. "Now I've shocked you," Frida says.

"Yes, you have . . . I suppose it's your Latin nature . . ."

I'm not in the director's chair anymore. I'm sitting in the audience of the Castro Theatre in San Francisco watching this unfold. I'm twenty-seven. When I was a kid, I thought being grown up would be like living in the movies, that I'd be Rosalind Russell in Sister Kenny, riding a horse through the Australian outback or that I'd dance every night in a sleek satin gown under paper palms at the Coconut Grove. Now I go out to the movies, two, three, four times a week.

The film cuts from the two figures on the balcony to the night sky. It's technicolor: the pale gold stars against midnight blue. We're close to the equator now: there's the Southern Cross, and the Clouds of Magellan, and you feel the press of the stars, the mocking closeness of the heavens as you can only feel it in the tropics. The veranda on which we are now standing is part of a colonial Spanish palace, built in a clearing in a jungle that daily spreads its roots and tendrils closer, closer. A macaw perches atop a broken Mayan statue and calls, "I am queen/I am queen/I am queen." A few yards into the jungle, a spider monkey shits on the face of a dead god.

Wait a minute. What's going on? Is that someone out in the lobby talking? But it's so loud—

Dolores del Rio strides into the film, shouting, "Latin nature! Who wrote this shit?" She's wearing black silk pants and a white linen blouse; she plants her fists on her hips and demands: "Huh? Who wrote this shit?"

I look to my left, my right, shrug, stand up in the audience and say, "I guess I did."

"Latin nature! And a white woman? Playing Frida? I should be playing Frida." "You?"

"Listen, honey." She's striding down the aisle towards me now. "I know I filmed that Hollywood crap. Six movies in one year: crook reformation romance, romantic Klondike melodrama, California romance, costume bedroom farce, passion in a jungle camp among chicle workers, romantic drama of the Russian revolution. I know David Selznick said: 'I don't care what what story you use so long as we call it *Bird of Paradise* and Del Rio jumps into a flaming volcano at the finish.' They couldn't tell a Hawaiian from a Mexican from a lesbian. But I loved Frida and she loved me. She painted "What the Water Gave Me" for me. At the end of her life, we were fighting, and she threatened to send me her amputated leg on a silver tray. If that's not love, I don't know what is—"

I'm still twenty-seven, but now it's the year 2015. The Castro's still there, the organ still rises up out of the floor with the organist playing "San Francisco, open your Golden Gate. . . ." In the lobby now, alongside the photos of the original opening of the Castro in 1927, are photos in black and white of lounging hustlers and leather queens, circa 1979, a photographic reproduction of the door of the women's room a few years later ("If they can send men to the moon, why don't they?") Underneath, in Braille, Spanish, and English: "In the 1960s, the development of the felt-tip pen, combined with a growing philosophy of personal expression caused an explosion of graffiti . . . sadly unappreciated in its day, this portion of a bathroom stall, believed by many experts to have originated in the women's room right here at the Castro Theater, sold recently at Sotheby's for $5 million. . . ."

Of course, the Castro's now totally accessible, not just integrated wheelchair seating, but every film captioned, a voice loop that interprets the action for blind people, over which now come the words: "As Dolores del Rio argues with the actress playing Frida, Helen Keller waits patiently—"

A woman in the audience stands up and shouts, "Patiently! What the fuck are you talking about, patiently? You can't tell the difference between patience and powerlessness. She's being *ignored*." The stage is stormed by angry women, one of whom leaps into the screen and begins signing to Helen, "Dolores del Rio's just come out and—"

"Enough already!" someone in the audience shouts. "Can't we please just get on with the story!"

Now that Frida is played by Dolores, she's long-haired again, wearing one of her white Tehuana skirts with a deep red shawl. She takes Helen's hand in hers, that hand that has been cradled by so many great men and great women.

"Latin nature?" Frida says, and laughs. "I think perhaps it is rather your cold Yankee nature that causes your reaction. . . ." And before Helen can object to being called a Yankee, Frida says, "But enough about Diego. . . ."

It's the hand that fascinates Frida, in its infinite, unpassive receptivity: she prattles on. When she makes the letters "z" and "j" in sign, she gets to stroke the shape of the letter into Helen's palm. She so likes the sensation that she keeps trying to work words with those letters in them into the conversation. The camera moves in close to Helen's hand as Frida says, "Here on the edge of the Yucatan jungle, one sometimes see jaguars, although never jackals. I understand jackals are sometimes seen in Zanzibar. I have never been there, nor have I been to Zagreb nor Japan nor the Zermatt, nor Java. I have seen the Oaxacan mountain Zempoaltepec. Once in a zoo in Zurich I saw a zebu and a zebra. Afterwards, we sat in a small cafe and ate cherries jubilee and zabaglione, washed down with glasses of zinfandel. Or perhaps my memory is confused: perhaps that day we ate jam on ziewback crusts and drank a juniper tea, while an old Jew played a zither. . . ."

"Oh," says Helen.

Frida falls silent. Frida, you painted those endless self-portraits, but you always looked at yourself level, straight on, in full light. This is different: this time your face is tilted, played over by shadows. In all those self-portraits, you are simultaneously artist and subject, lover and beloved, the bride of yourself. Now, here, in the movies, it's different: the camera stands in for the eye of the lover. But you're caught in the unforgiving blank stare of a blind woman.

And now, we cut from that face to the face of Helen. Here I don't put in any soothing music, nothing low and sweet with violins, to make the audience more comfortable as the camera moves in for its close-up. You understand why early audiences were frightened by these looming heads. In all the movies with blind women in them—or, let's be real, sighted women playing the role of blind woman—Jane Wyman and Merle Oberon in the different versions of *Magnificent Obsession*, Audrey Hepburn in *Wait Until Dark*, Uma Thurman in *Jennifer 8*, we've never seen a blind woman shot this way before: never seen the camera come in and linger lovingly on her face the way it does here. We gaze at their faces only when bracketed by others, or in moments of terror when beautiful young blind women are being stalked. We've never seen before this frightening blank inward turning of passion, a face that has never seen itself in the mirror, that does not arrange itself for consumption.

Lack = inferiority? Try it right now. Finish reading this paragraph and then close your eyes, push the flaps of your ears shut, and sit. Not just for a minute: give it five or ten. Not in that meditative state, designed to take you out of your mind, your body. Just the opposite. Feel the press of hand crossed over hand: without any distraction, you feel your body with the same distinctness as a lover's touch makes you feel yourself. You fold into yourself, you know the rhythm of your breathing, the beating of your heart, the odd independent twitch of a muscle: now in a shoulder, now in a thigh. Your cunt, in all its patient hunger.

We cut back to Frida in close up. But now Helen's fingers enter the frame, travel across that face, stroking the downy moustache above Frida's upper lip, the fleshy nose, the thick-lobed ears.

Now, it's Frida's turn to be shocked: shocked at the hunger of these hands, at the almost-feral sniff, at the freedom with which Helen blurs the line between knowing and needing.

"May I kiss you?" Helen asks.

"Yes," Frida says.

Helen's hands cup themselves around Frida's face.

I'm not at the Castro anymore. I'm back home on the fold-out sofa in the slapped-together TV room, watching grainy images flickering on the tiny screen set in the wooden console. I'm nine years old again, used to Hays-office kisses, two mouths with teeth clenched, lips held rigid, pressing stonily against each other. I'm not ready for the way that Helen's tongue probes into Frida's mouth, the tongue that seems to be not so much interested in giving pleasure as in finding an answer in the emptiness of her mouth.

I shout, "Cut," but the two of them keep right on. Now we see Helen's face, her wide-open eyes that stare at nothing revealing a passion blank and insatiable, a void into which you could plunge and never, never, never touch bottom. Now she begins to make noises, animal mewlings and cries.

I will the screen to turn to snow, the sound to static. I do not want to watch this, hear this. My leg is in a thick plaster cast, inside of which scars are growing like mushrooms, thick and white in the dark damp. I think that I must be a lesbian, a word I have read once in a book, because I know I am not like the women on television, with their high heels and shapely calves and their firm asses swaying inside of satin dresses waiting, waiting for a man, nor am I like the women I know, the mothers with milky breasts, and what else can there be?

I look at the screen and they are merging into each other, Frida and Helen, the dark-haired and the light, the one who will be disabled and nothing more, the other who will be everything but. I can't yet imagine a world where these two might meet: the face that does not live under the reign of its own reflection with the face that has spent its life looking in the mirror; the woman who turns her rapt face up towards others and the woman who exhibits her scars as talismans, the one who is only, only and the one who is everything but. I will the screen to turn to snow.

24

Poems

CHERYL MARIE WADE

I AM NOT ONE OF THE

I am not one of the physically challenged—

I'm a sock in the eye with a gnarled fist
I'm a French kiss with cleft tongue
I'm orthopedic shoes sewn on a last of your fears

I am not one of the differently abled—

I'm an epitaph for a million imperfect babies left untreated
I'm an ikon carved from bones in a mass grave in Tiergarten, Germany—
I'm withered legs hidden with a blanket

I am not one of the able disabled—

I'm a black panther with green eyes and scars like a picket fence
I'm pink lace panties teasing a stub of milk white thigh
I'm the Evil Eye

I'm the first cell divided
I'm mud that talks
I'm Eve   I'm Kali
I'm The Mountain That Never Moves
I've been forever   I'll be here forever
I'm the Gimp
I'm the Cripple
I'm the Crazy Lady

I'm The Woman With Juice

CRIPPLE LULLABY

I'm trickster coyote in a gnarly-bone suit
I'm a fate worse than death in shit-kickin' boots

I'm the nightmare booga you flirt with in dreams
'Cause I emphatically demonstrate: It ain't what it seems

I'm a whisper, I'm a heartbeat, I'm "that accident," and goodbye
One thing I am not is a reason to die.

I'm homeless in the driveway of your manicured street
I'm Evening Magazine's SuperCrip of the Week

I'm the girl in the doorway with no illusions to spare
I'm a kid dosed on chemo, so who said life is fair

I'm a whisper, I'm a heartbeat, I'm "let's call it suicide," and a sigh
One thing I am not is a reason to die

I'm the poster child with doom-dipped eyes
I'm the ancient remnant set adrift on ice

I'm that Valley girl, you know, dying of thin
I'm all that is left of the Cheshire Cat's grin

I'm the Wheelchair Athlete, I'm every dead Baby Doe
I'm Earth's last volcano, and I am ready to blow

I'm a whisper, I'm a heartbeat, I'm a genocide survivor, and Why?
One thing I am not is a reason to die.

I am not a reason to die.

25

Queen of the Girls

JULIA/DOLPHIN TRAHAN

My mother says I was born masturbating. All mothers embarrass their children by telling of some adorable act or endearing habit. But my mother talks about my inherent sexual narcissism at dinner parties. She tells it to my friends, says it in front of my sister's boyfriend. She even told our real estate agent.

I've asked her to stop. She just giggles, her rolly-polly body bouncing merrily. I have such a cute mom. I love her very much. I figure she can't help herself.

Actually, I don't mind that she publicly talks of what is usually considered a private act. She's making a political statement. My grandmother the Baptist told her people with disabilities—survivors of traumatic accidents and chronic pain—don't have sexualities. My grandmother said, *It's such a shame. She was such a pretty girl.*

My co-worker told me people born with a leg too short don't think about wild fucking in the back of pick-up trucks or chasing a beloved, naked in a field or holding the hand of a lifetime lover, trembling in fear at a scary movie. He says if they think these things, it certainly shouldn't be said out loud. And, he says, desires are disgusting to act upon if you are hideously disfigured. Such as having one leg too short.

All sorts of people think about sexuality. Trust me. They do. Take me, for instance. Hit by a truck at age eleven. Bloody car seat. Bloody Julia. I am no longer me. I am a body tornadoed through time. I do not want to say good-bye.

Hit by a truck at age eleven. Mangled, mutilated by a truck. Lost a lot of things: 20/20 vision, the use of my left side, the ability to speak or swallow. Even lost my life and rose from the dead, just like Jesus Christ. But that good ole, ever-flowing life juice, erotic sexuality never left me for a moment.

Being born masturbating saved me. A girl needs to have control of her body if she wants to survive in this world.

As a toddler, my parents tell me I'd masturbate everywhere: the kitchen, the living room, the park. My favorite story is how, at age two, the evening of Neil Armstrong's moon launch, I snuck champagne sips from grown-up's glasses and put on a show in front of the TV. My parents scooted me into another room saying, "That's a private act."

Older, and less exhibitionistic, I'd rock on my bed at night dreaming elaborate fantasies. The usual theme was, I, Queen of the Girls, and my favorite Knights had been captured by renegade boy trying to conquer our majestic empire. We'd be tied up, spread-eagled, and fucked in every way, in every opening my eight-year-old mind could imagine. All the boys wanted to fuck me 'cause I was Ruler of the Kid World, the fastest runner, the best reader, and the strongest wrestler. Only the boy Kings and Lords dared to fuck me, and I got fucked the most, the longest and the hardest.

When satiated by enough sucking, fucking, and Shakespearean drama, I and my band of merry Knights would easily overthrow the boys. Dancing back to the girl's camp, we'd sing, eat, and make love recklessly in glorious celebration of our divinely female victory. We never took prisoners. Who would want them?

I spent fantastic childhood nights this way. Sometimes, after school, I couldn't wait for dark. I'd sneak down to the basement, rock on my belly next to my sister's waterbed. Reach behind, stretch my lipcheeks open. Imagine Someone behind filling me. I thrust hard into carpet. When I came I was blue-eyed magic and possibilities. Until one day my sister interrupted "What are you doing!?!"

She was in junior high school and masturbation wasn't cool.

After that I took cold showers in the dark. I loved that moment when ice hit skin. My body spasming and squirming in painful euphoria. My heart tangoed. Leaving the world of a spinning, slightly moldy, metal shower stall. Entering a world of brightly lit blackness. Underwater no one lied, and freedom was possible.

This sacrament proved that I was rightfully Queen of the Girls. I was tough. I knew what mattered.

When doctors told my mother across my hospital bed that I wouldn't recover she put her hand in mine,

"I love you, it doesn't matter, just come back."

Possibilities: unable to think, move, breathe or speak. Dr. Jackson, the neurologist wanted pictures of my brain for a textbook.

"Your daughter will have the prettiest brain in medical history.

My mother said, "No."

She knew they were mistaken. I was her baby, Majesty of the World, Queen of the Girls. I'd escape victoriously when tired of being fucked by boys.

Not wanting to disappoint her, I crafted impeccable twirls and back flips in desperate pursuit of metamorphosis. Guided by my mother's voice. Her hand in mind.

Being born masturbating saved me. Sometimes pain from crushed bones was too much. Orgasmic energy made my body bearable. Waves of electricity washing and soothing my overstimulated burning nerves. My temperature 104 day after day. Only certain thing was, if I didn't die from internal bleeding, time would pass, painfully. Masturbating I'd ward off panic. Pass the time by shooting my psyche into worlds where I valiantly rode blue stallions on untouched oceanshores.

I wasn't aware that I didn't have or wasn't supposed to have a sexuality. . . .

I wanna tell you 'bout my first time. Not the first time I came, but the first time someone touched me, you know, in that way. I was lucky. Some people only have one, but I had three. Three at once. Strong, powerful women who knew what they wanted. They thought I was so pretty, they wanted me. Taught me to be tough. And they were fine looking Black black hair, dark-dark eyes that saw right through me. One wore a little gold cross. And those hands, gentle but demanding. They were always laughing, laughing up a storm. Said they'd fuck me so good, lovin' someone else wouldn't be the same. That I wouldn't want nobody after them. They were right! Every time I came, thought I was dying.

I wasn't aware that I didn't have or wasn't supposed to have a sexuality. The three female nurses that stuck fingers and washcloths up my vagina and anus. Laughing and pinning my dying body still. They knew. The balding urologist who stuck his cock-level fingers and tubes in the same holes, staring lustfully into my little girl eyes. He knew. Even the teenage nurse's aid understood when he rubbed my breasts while I lie immobile, recovering from my thirteenth surgery. These people knew I had a sexuality.

A disposable sexuality, like used snot rags. The user is remotely aware that used tissue are infected with human waste and should be tossed away without remorse. Aware enough to be disgusted.

My hormones didn't slip out on wasted blood. I learned egotistical doctors pay attention and answer questions when flirted with. Comforting nurses and therapists made hot tea, tucking me into bed extra carefully, if I stared adoringly into their eyes.

I never fit in at Rehab. Brat. Punk. My occupational therapist affectionately called me. I beat her at scrabble, asked too many questions, complained that stacking cones bored me, making macrame potholders was God's punishment. Nurses, with ever-shifting faces, tried to stop my wheelchair chariot form flying down the ramp, bucking backwards, twirling from momentum, sharp left turn, down slope into the parking lot. My twelve-year-old deathwish put into action. Only charm saved me from my institutional family's scolding kindness. Terrified, I smiled cheerfully, *"You're the expert. I'm trying my hardest."* After a year or live-in I escaped to become shut-in.

What would've been my sixth-grade class gave me a hero's welcome. Inspired children and adults filled the school playground. Why were they clapping? I just wanted to say "hi." My wheelchair stuck in gravel. I cried. I want to go home.

My good friend, Vickie Smit, the smartest girl in school never came to visit. Neither did friends of the family. I wanted to run down the hill, watch the Little League game. The two-story junior high where brother and sis went grudgingly let me in because my parents threatened a lawsuit. Play runaway gang leader. I hated the required 'special' class. Swim at Little North Fork with Family. Hide in the tilted Oak tree. Violin serenade Scruffy, my howling mutt dog. If teachers thought my wheelchair disruptive I sat against the wall, away from other students. Grandma, the Baptist sued me; 100,000 dollars in accident settlement. A local reporter wrote about my "tragic fate."

Alone, under the covers, I made Captain Caspian, the proud plastic elephant protect the uncorrupted society of camels, tigers, and zebras. His flaming red cape, made from flew gallantly as his scarlet sword delivered justice against snot-colored plastic cowboys. Neither of us understood being attacked while exploring treacherous deserts. Captain's harem massaged and danced. My hand slipped between my legs. My hurting body soon comfortable. Beautiful, brave women kissed my tears, whispering gratitude and admiration. Others spread long hair over my belly and made love to my wetness. Men, women, and children left gifts outside my tent door in homage to my courage. My red iron sword swings in savage wind. Long arms rock me until people act normal again.

I made new friends, a gang too smart to fit properly; streetwise, different colored, slightly criminal. I proudly spoke of my bisexuality. My cigarette buddy, Jolie, tried to rip my shirt off, her knee in my crotch. I punched her, escaped. My wheelchair waiting patiently outside the bathroom stall. Frigid tears pressed the backs of my eyes.

Thirteen years old. Thirteen operations so far. Back in the hospital.

Imagining graceful nurse Felicia straddling my bed-bound body, lifting her freshly pressed skirt. Desire pounding through anesthetized dull. My mouth stoic, determined. Her desires loosen. Someone Someone wanting me. Her juices smothering. I am sacred, proud. Throwing her head back she screams. At last, Wet trickles from my eyes.

Sterile, nurse shift, take your blood, bed bath, time for your test, honey. Busy stranger's inspected my girlish beauty. How delectable I was. My teeth gritted in polite festive child hatred. I never came anymore. Never came. No relief. Alien hands invaded my breasts and crotch daily.

My knee swelled to twelve inches. Arriving home from the hospital Alcoholic Dad catapulted a soup bowl. Hits my ear. He hates me for destroying the family. Ruining his "Leave It to Beaver" life. I was his favorite, and now I'm broken. Bloody Julia. Bloody kitchen floor. Will he hit me for making a mess? I hate him. It's not my fault, Dad. I'm trying my hardest.

Unable to walk, took refuge in my bedroom. Dreamt of fancy cocktail parties. My spread-eagled legs tied open in the doorway. My crotch convenient for amused party goers to clean their shoes. Elegant tuxedoed gentlemen grind my clit with muddy wing-tips. Their ladies, so fine, fucked my hole with five inch heels. My clear come polished their pumps to an I-want-to-die-for-you gleam. I Never screamed. Was rewarded. By ghost cocks pummeling my throat. Phantom long-nailed fingers riping my ass. I shoved hate-filled fingers up my vagina until slow wanting tears slid me to peaceful sleep.

As a teen, when not in the hospital, I went to Catholic high school. Devoutly against Catholicism, and not being Catholic, I felt comfortably alienated. Cindy, red-haired, straight-A cheerleader named my crutch, Mortimer. In her Starsky & Hutch red sports car, I called attention to my bisexuality.

"Why are you telling me this!?"

I joined the Catholics, repressing my shameful sexuality.

Eighteen, grown-up. Freedom!!! Escape to San Francisco. I discover Sister's of Perpetual Indulgence. Fell in AWE with Sister Boom Boom.

A toothless fag chases me through North Beach's adult party stores. demanding to know where a girl got that Marvelously Masculine Masonic red jacket. *"I'm not a Girl, I'm a Drag Queen."* We talked of bodies and gender, life and death. The life-size plastic blow-up dolls listening in. *"What's it like to be in a coma? When you died did you see a bright white light?* I grabbed a ten-inch cock-shaped dildo: *"Let me tell ya 'bout the birds & the bees & the flowers & the trees & The Moon up above & this ting they call LOVE"* Miss Fag kneels, kisses my hand, *"You're the best kind of Queen."*

I had learned to walk and talk and swallow well enough to be considered worth fucking by men. Doesn't take much. I fucked and fucked. Wore men out while living in the Art Institutes spray-paint room. In the ass or them on top. Wanted it all the time. All night long. Fucked their friends when they got sore. Asked for it. Begged for it. Only got raped once. He didn't use weapons, so it doesn't count.

While fucking these men, I thought how good it felt to touch my little girl's body under the blankets, safe, in the dark. Only that touch made my pain go away.

When I touched women it was different. With women I made love and fell in love. Sex was supposed to be like this. Melting into my lover whether she drove a red sports car, dyed my crotch blue with food coloring, or smoked too many menthol cigarettes.

Jane, twice my age, curly blonde hair, serious blue eyes reflecting mine. She liked the way I plunged fearlessly into snow catching a bird's expression on video. I liked the way she sat in back of class, legs outstretched, head held proudly. Obviously, she knew more than the instructor.

Floating on foreign dinners of exotic foods and silly stories of mature lesbians, I didn't understand everything she'd say.

"You're too independent," she sexily accused. I was stepping out of her van into a freezing Minneapolis winter. Thought she meant I was playing hard to get. So I shut the van door and kissed her.

"I'd like to take you home, but I'm uncomfortable with your age and handicap."

"Uncomfortable with my handicap." An honest statement. But what does it mean?

I am more normal looking now. I'M WHITE, Blonde hair, blue eyes, large breasts, fairly tall. But I've grown accustomed to ordinary hideous men and women wanting to jack off. In my cunt.

Falling in love with Natasha, Nadia, Beth, Maritova, and Racael, I've noticed a pattern. It is not just them I love, it is their sweetness, their love of human meekness. Their comforting hands and tender words give me life as I forge ugliness into fiery dreams and watery fantasies.

I hold my lovers, tenderly when they cry, in awe of their tears, grateful they want me to be with them. When my lovers cry I often feel they cry the tears I can't. More flexible, they express pain that I can not bear to see.

Preciously, I kiss my innocence on their faces. The innocence I traded for survival. The innocence murdered in me by those who know only how to jack off.

Twenty-three Maritova and I enter each other three times a day. Waking, we celebrate vigorously. I need my fourteenth operation. She makes chicken soup.

I read in a magazine that one is abused or one is an abuser. How boring.

Twenty-four. Unable to walk. *Hey, where'd everyone go?* In rehab hospital learning to toilet transfer using one leg. *My fabulous friends disappeared.* Nurses insist on watching me pee. One threatens an enema because of bad behavior. Margo, my heroic physical therapist, her hand on my thigh. Me, on my back, legs spread wide.

She whispers, *"I like you in that position."*

Flashes. Memories: Said they'd fuck me so good, lovin' someone else wouldn't be the same!

I learned to walk again. Graduate from Liberal Arts College. Move to the Castro. Blood trickles from holes in my breasts. I rub it warm over my belly, soothing bloody Julia. I hold the knife this time. I am learning to say no. It is not a pretty process.

A man at a bus stop informs me: *"I'm looking for a girl to use."* I stare at his throat, knowing why some days I want to KILL.

I live my mastabatory life for survival. There are those who would jack off on my dead body. I see them. They are predictable. I am no longer frightened.

My mother says I was born masturbating And she should know.

Age 28. I wanna tell you 'bout my first time. . . . I'm grateful if someone takes Time to give Pleasure without Fear. Desire is battery acid in my veins. Each orgasm, hideous beauty that I must remember. Coming everyday. My sweat, cunt juice, tears, breathy moans: Sacraments. So I'll remember this Existence isn't Houses and Haircuts. Not Girlfriends. Not even Identity. With orgasm I lose my body. Discover it on the bed where I left it. In shameful puddles of shit, blood, and vomit. I pick it up, wash it gently. "You are fragile" "Celebrate your mortality. When I come I am the best kind of Queen.

My mother is right. And I am coming and coming and coming and coming.

26

Poems

KENNY FRIES

EXCAVATION

Tonight, when I take off my shoes:
three toes on each twisted foot.

I touch the rough skin. The holes
where the pins were. The scars.

If I touch them long enough will I find
those who never touched me? Or those

who did?   *Freak, midget, three-toed*
bastard. Words I've always heard.

Disabled, crippled, deformed. Words
I was given. But tonight I go back

farther, want more, tear deeper into
my skin. Peeling it back I reveal

the bones at birth I wasn't given—
the place where no one speaks a word.

LOVE POEM

On the narrow bed. Patterns of light
and shadow across your body. I hold

your face in my hands. Tell me, before
I kiss you, what is it like to be

so beautiful? I want to know how other
hands have touched you. What other

eyes, beneath your clothes, imagine.
And how do you imagine me? Do you

feel my calloused skin? See my twisted
bones? When you take off my clothes

will you kiss me all over? Touch me as
if my body were yours. Make me beautiful.

BEAUTY AND ITS VARIATIONS

I want to break your bones. Make them so
they look like mine. Force you to walk on

twisted legs. Then, will your lips still beg
for mine? Or will that disturb the balance

of our desire? Even as it inspires, your body
terrifies. And once again I find your hands

inside me. Why do you touch my scars? You
can't make them beautiful any more than I can

tear your skin apart. Beneath my scars,
between my twisted bones, hides my heart.

Why don't you let me leave my mark? With no
flaws on your skin—how can I find your heart?

27

Sex and the Single Gimp

BILLY GOLFUS

For the sake of good taste, let's call the female person Sarah and her husband Alvin. I'm not a man totally without decorum, and this story has your back street romance, illicit sex, and of course cheating, lots of cheating. As a writer I know that I need to hold your attention.

THE REALITY IS

Let's start with Sarah trying to work something out with Alvin, (you give 'em a name and the game changes, doesn't it?) who is in Illinois or Ohio right now. He had been going with her since before, as they say, and stuck with her through the rough stuff, which is rare, let me tell you. More people than you'd think will split on their main squeeze in the face of disability. Really.

That Alvin stayed with her through her becoming quadriplegic says a lot for that boy in my book. I don't know what else goes on between them, but his sojourn among the gimps is rare and righteous.

The reality is, disability carries lots of getting left at the station and loneliness. Abandonment and isolation is not in the inspirational story of overcoming, but it's there for most of us, under things, around things, on the edge of things. A lot of the time. And what this boy did was help her skate around some of the more disagreeable parts of being a gimp, maybe without even knowing what she missed.

I'd seen her scooting around in her wheelchair for a couple of years, and didn't know a quad could use a manual chair. She's what they call an incomplete quad. Don't you just love the language?

She's this sort of classy looking brunette, with medium length hair that falls straight and curls just above her shoulders. Too-thin lips wearing red lipstick dark enough to make a fire truck look pale. I'd run into her over a couple of years, but we'd never talked. You could say we're at the smiling and nodding stage. Distant smiling and nodding.

If you're a man, this is not a girl you could ignore unless you're a Zen monk who's already crossed into the void. First of all she's knockout beautiful. Alabaster skin, she's got the alabaster skin. Finely chiseled features, she's got your finely chiseled features. The elegant, long, Nefertiti neck, the whole bit. We're talking slick, national book stuff here. Anybody in the Western world except an ideologue could recognize her as ravishing.

Flirting would be the exact way to describe her come-on. But there's this way that some really beautiful women use their looks: "It's not my fault I drive men to their knees. I'm not doing *anything*." It was a look like that probably got Samson a haircut.

Me and Boychick, my partner, are making "When Billy Broke His Head and Other Tales of Wonder," a television documentary about disability, and she's so heart stoppingly beautiful I want her for the show. She blows the sexless stereotype. Machiavellian maybe, but she's just an ingredient in the cake as far as I can see. It's taken me almost ten years to get this documentary to happen, so you don't want to drop the ball now.

Even though she's attractive, I don't really think about her that way partly because the chair makes me not even see her and because after so many years of being disabled you quit thinking about it as an option.

People are always talking about how beautiful she is, but her looks never got to me. Awesome was just something everybody always says about Sarah. You know, I guess she's really attractive. So what?

But I remember one time looking at her and saying to myself, she is very beautiful, and smart. At least you've got to think about it unless you're a toaster or something. I didn't obsess about it.

I don't have any experience with quads, except I know everything probably stops someplace between her neck and the middle of her chest. I know polio folks can feel, but spinal cord injury cuts the telephone line. And if she can't feel, what d'ya do? I'm not looking for conversation lessons.

Everybody knows that the punch line is when Old Faithful goes off. That's the point of chasing them in the first place, isn't it?

If they can't feel, then what d'ya do? Sit around and play old maid, and not think about it?

Look, everybody's been taught that sex is about put tab A in slot B. You were taught that, I was taught that, songs and movies are about that, that's how people think. Tab A in slot B. So what do you do when you can't feel slot B? Forget it? If it's not acrobatic and aerobic, then it's not real sex. How big and how many times is what counts to most people. Then you don't even have to feel much, just keep counting and measuring.

It happened that I started to see these other qualities. Like I say, she's smart and doesn't like the way disabled folks are treated even if some of it comes out like party line, and she's got guts, and, and, and. It was the mountain of conjunctions that let me know I was in trouble. I felt like I was being pulled into something but I didn't have any control. You can't tell me it hasn't crossed your mind to jump when you looked down from a tall building or bridge. Doesn't mean you are going to jump, just those destructive images are in there.

Lookit, nothing happened except I'm looking at her different. I'm looking at the slope of her neck, and these tiny earlobes—I've never stared at a woman's earlobes before—and of course her lips. You couldn't possibly give a soft, sensual kiss with those too-thin lips. Sure they look good with that dramatic dark vamp lipstick, but let's be thinking function here.

I'm starting to segue into a blues, and I'm kicking and screaming trying to get out.

IT'S NOT LOVE

Words would fail me if I tried to describe her
though I know she's not all she should have been
She was the devil with the face of an angel,
she was sweet and cruel, cruel and sweet,
    as homemade sin

          —Percy Mayfield, "Lost Mind"

She hasn't changed, but the way I'm looking at her changed, big time. I didn't even see it happening. Obviously it's not love. I've never spent five minutes alone with her, and a quadriplegic is hardly my idea of a sex object.

What I'm really doing here is torturing myself about how to have a relationship coming from the depths of my being with a woman that's hardly even smiled at me. Where's all this coming from?

If I had a nickel for everyone I've schtupped in my brain-damaged mind, I'd be vacationing on the Riviera. If it was the ones I'd only wanted or worried about, I'd own a summer villa there. I'm thinking a lot about something that's not even happening. Like Edward said to Mary Jo when she told him she might be pregnant, "Let's cross that bridge when we come to it."

I've got a good fantasy going here, and I keep telling myself the same old joke about, "I'm an old Jewish man who's had in my life many problems—90 percent of which never happened." But I've never learned the point of that particular story.

The more interested I get, the more I keep telling myself that it's a foolish idea.

Fantasy or no, she ain't never going to wrap her legs around you. Never! Suck on that for a minute. And you ain't never going to see her in a tight skirt, sheer black stockings, and five-inch stiletto heels doing the Cadillac walk.

Everybody knows the preliminaries, so let's just skip 'em. Over a couple of weeks and events Sarah and I ended up at dinner together, and she tells me that she "might" be breaking up with her husband, and I tell her that I'm attracted to her. When they tell you that they "might" be breaking up, you don't have to keep it to yourself anymore.

Sarah tells me at dinner how she's having some affair with a guy behind Alvin's back, but she explains to me how it's really Alvin's fault. He drove her to it, or he wasn't paying any attention to her or something. It's important to keep track of whose fault it is.

Does it strike you as odd that she'd be talking about this affair to some guy she hardly knows? Maybe she's just trying to unload, but I always think that whenever they talk to you about sex or tell you about their adventures, they're pulling your chain and they know exactly what they're doing.

She tells me she's playing a couple choruses of James Brown's "Sex Machine" with some guy named Dave for a couple of years, hits the coda, and does a little more awakening with a third guy. Meanwhile, the ole man splits the state because he can't stand the pain of Sarah touching another man with lust in her heart.

She's helping this guy, Dave, get his ashes hauled and he's helping her awaken her sexuality, that can't be all bad.

I've been getting all these non-verbals from her, but you don't need a graduate degree to know when somebody's coming on. Only it occurs to me a little later, maybe that's just the way she knows how to talk to men. Heavily seductive, heavy manipulation.

A couple of days later she asked, "What does it mean that you're attracted to me?"

"I want to take your clothes off."

She did this fast loud breathing and said, "I can feel *that*. I can feel that."

She said that it would take her a little while to get used to. Then we talked for about another hour. That seemed like a little while to me.

While we're talking I ask her if she can feel her vagina, and she says no. "Pressure" is what it feels like.

"Well, can you feel your breasts?"

"Pretty much," she says with a smile like she's got a secret. She's tilting her head sideways and the tips of her hair are just touching her right shoulder. The smile is an ember in the warmth of her face, and I'm sitting there looking at her, trying to understand what it means.

THE BIGGEST SEX ORGAN

I ask her, "If you can't feel anything, why were you involved with anybody? I mean, why weren't you buddies or pen pals or something?" She says, "The biggest sex organ is between your ears. Don't you know that? Besides, sex isn't all there is to being married. There's compromise, and going shopping, and paying the bills."

Everything she says seems profound and funny, so I know what's happening to me. I been around the block.

If she's having these affairs, *something's* going on.

Next day, I'm on the horn with Boychick and tell him it isn't just a case of simple lust I'm experiencing, it's complex lust. I'm gone.

He's trying to give me some support and says, "She's the most beautiful girl I've ever seen in a wheelchair."

It takes me about four hours to understand the fish hooks in that supposed compliment.

Ed Roberts is the head of the World Institute on Disability and one of your more famous quadriplegics. He and Mike Boyd are transferring planes at the airport on their way to do a workshop conference, whatever, somewhere in South Dakota which is in the central time zone—forever.

I asked Ed what do you do if she can't feel her, what d'ya call it—vagina. He says, "The back of the neck, shoulders, the inside of the ears are very sensitive." My guts tighten up.

How or why would I want to sniff after this female person that I'm deeply, profoundly, excruciatingly lusting after if she can't feel anything?

But we're putting the cart before the girl. I get up in the middle of the night and start writing her this real Rilke letter about how if we couldn't have sex, we had to make sure that we were honest with each other about our feelings and not hide them from each other. I'm jumping the gun, and at the same time trying to figure out how you have a bottom of your soul, like Rilke says, relationship with a quadriplegic.

Even honesty and communication has limitations. I mean it sounds so inspirational, but it's such bullshit. Remember the scene in "Last Tango in Paris" where Brando says they should try to come mentally.

"Did you come yet?" he wants to know. Maria Schneider says, "No." "Neither did I," says Brando.

I scored a copy of Rilke's *On Love and Other Difficulties* for the girl (and ordered another for myself) and wrote the inscription about being guardians of each other's solitude (from his text). But don't you believe it. Jules Feiffer wrote (did a cartoon?) about how we all want to own our playmates.

Then I left the book on the girl's porch, and got something to eat.

Course she liked the book. Then young Sarah and I talked on the phone until 3:30 A.M. She's having her second affair. In response to my attraction she said, "I don't know what to do. How would you feel about being friends?"

"I'm not sure if that's in my repertoire, but if you hum a few bars, I probably still won't be able to play that tune."

In the morning I wrote her the note (which I'm *not* going to reproduce except to say that it was trés schmaltzy and you could have spread it on with a trowel) and put three—count 'em three—dozen long-stemmed red roses with the schmaltzy note inside her screen door by 10:30 A.M.

Is this the behavior of an adult who's pushing 50?

We're both going to the airport to spend a few hours with Ed and Mike on their return flight this morning before the anti-Jerry Lewis/MDA telethon. She's going to pick me up at 12:45 P.M. But by 1:10 she's not at my crib. All the blood and color drain out of my face from anger. My left arm is spastic and won't respond and my stomach is tight. We're supposed to meet this airplane and she's not here. *Fuck this!*

I leave a note on a clip board with flight number, and arrival and departure times written real large. Then I hang it from a hook on my house by my driveway so she can see it from her van without getting out, and I go to the airport.

FALLING

Ed's still on the plane which has already arrived when I get there. It takes him a millennium to de-plane, as they say, so I'm working within a safety zone. The chair is outside the cabin door and they're getting the sling ready to move him. He's schmoozing with the crew, like he always does, and they're gathered around like a room full of kids listening to Uncle Remus telling about Brer Rabbit. Everybody is looking at him real quiet and respectful.

He's telling about going to the four-story McDonald's in Moscow, telling the ubiquitous, incessant stories about his son Lee. ("Dad, can I have a Honda convertible?" "Isn't that cute?") We get the ventilator, extra parts, tubes, hoses, cords filling a second wheelchair and start moving up the walkway from the plane.

When we roll up into the lobby by the gates, there's Sarah screeching around the corner as fast as a stainless steel ball coming off the bumpers in a pinball machine, bop pop ding ding smack. She catches herself on a pole to keep from tipping over.

She looks at me over this enigmatic smile, straight into my eyes, but I keep my balance. "I couldn't believe all those flowers. I didn't know what to do with them. That's why I'm late."

I thought she and Ed were going to have an affair right there on the spot. She's holding onto his power wheelchair like a trailer and they're shooting through the airport halls so fast I'm betting they're going to get a ticket. We pull into Northwest's lounge for VIPs and grab a table by the window. She's sitting wheelchair to wheelchair, feeding Ed cookies because he has no use of his arms. They're talking about where they grew up, it's part cliché, part each of them telling the other intimate things. She tells him about an abortion; he talks about his divorce. They say things they never thought they'd say.

I'm watching her talk to, and feed, Ed. I mean, she's pretty and all, but just think about the aggravation with her and all her politically correct ideas. Still, I can't stop looking at her, she's so beautiful. Don't I know any better than that?

> Baby, you're so beautiful,
>   you know you got to die someday.
> Baby, you're so beautiful,
>   you know you got to die someday.
> Why don't you give me a little lovin'
>   before you pass away.
> —Jimmy Rushing with the Count

Ed told me that I was staring at her absolutely pie-faced all the time we were at the airport.

It's 4:30 P.M. and time for the plane to go. We wait around the gate for a "thirty minute delay" while they fix some air conditioning on the plane. Then there's another "forty minute delay" before they get on the plane.

Sarah says she's hungry.

I offer to take her someplace nice, but she says we should get something at the airport to save time.

She is one of those strange people who doesn't eat the flesh of dead animals. In a flash of recognition we know that there wasn't going to be a rolled-in-granola-and-brown-rice fast food joint among the Burger King, airport Cheers bar, and Pizza Hut. The only thing to do was to choose from the bounty that God had provided.

A cheese pizza (with meat sauce) is probably as close to food as she's going to get. I had the special: armadillo, grease, and salted spam slices with a pretend beer. Airport Gourmet Magazine had done a two-page fold-out showing a candelabra, the box with grease spots, two slices of the stuff, and a Coke. Elegant airport dining.

AT THE PROTEST

We ate, then went to the anti-Jerry Lewis demonstration at the Burnsville Center. I got stuff for a story. (Security guards said, "You can't use the tape recorder." I used it. "You're not allowed to take pictures." I shot thirty 35mm black and whites, sometimes zone-focusing from the hip.)

A young cowboy with bad breath and a belt full of radios, flashlights, mace, says to me, "Put that camera away. How'd you like to spend the night in jail?"

"Tell you what, either arrest me or sue me, but your instructions are without weight around here."

He walks away to talk to his supervisor. Sarah and a couple of ladies nearby say, "Come and stand by us."

I better hit the freeway. I've got my story, and pictures. I don't think my body can handle jail food, and being deprived of hand cream for my psoriasis, and deprived of esophagus pills. Besides, my bed is on a slant because of reflux. They're not known for making you comfortable in jail. I tell Sarah to meet me at The Sour Pickle Bar and I split.

At the bar I listen to Judy and Bill to Marty Robbins, the ballad of Jed Clampett a la Bob Marley, an Irish fiddle tune, Jimi Hendrix on an amp the size of a pack of cigarettes. Obscure and funny tunes,

> Life is hard but life is harder if you're dumb
> No joie de vivre
> Just endless hours of tedium . . .

For a couple of hours, no Sarah.

I drive the two blocks past her house (that's how men in their late forties behave) and drive twelve more to my house to get her phone number from my Rolodex. While I'm writing it into my pocket calendar, the phone rings. She's at The Sour Pickle.

"I'll be there in five minutes."

I make it in four and a half. She tells me some tall guy with short hair asks if she's waiting for Billy and talks to her for a few minutes and keeps the bikers and drunks off her. She tells me that he was shooting pool.

"That's Spider John Koerner."

"I don't know who he is," she says.

"Famous in beatnik and hippie music circles. Koerner, Ray and Glover were real important in the folk revival of the Sixties. John Lennon waved the "Blues, Rags, and Hollers" album around during one interview in *Melody Maker*. And you could have got his autograph."

The Sour Pickle is narrow with a dark wood bar the length of the room. A single pool table sits right in front of the johns. Sometimes somebody'll open one of the doors too fast and ruin a shot. They pour a lot of beer and peppermint schnapps in here. There are big jars of hard boiled eggs, pickled turkey gizzards, beef jerky, the usual cards with packages of assorted potato chips. Drunks howl inane things during the songs, thinking they're the soul of wit like drunks everywhere.

Sarah and I listened to some music and *schmoozed abissel*. "Alvin doesn't want to talk about my sex with the other guy, but he wants me back."

I keep looking at this face. I can't take my eyes off this face. "You're the most beautiful girl I've ever seen in a wheelchair."

She laughs.

LAST CALL

The bar is closing. Will I walk her to her van? Does the Pope shit in the woods? Is the bear Catholic? She spins her chair and heads for the door. Outside I'm trying to walk alongside her, limping as fast as I can.

"Am I going too fast for you?" she asks.

"Not if you slow down. I'm not a sprint limper."

She's parked right behind me a block down. I unlock my car and put my bag in. You can see she's got something on her mind. "What's up? I can see you've got something to say."

In medias res she says, "It's bad timing. You want something with commitment and I need to explore my sexuality."

I wasn't expecting this. I thought we were going to ride off into the sunset. You don't want to be even a close second in a situation like this, let alone a straggling third. "Explore away *Gasoontarate* [Yiddish for do it in good health]. You're right. It's just bad timing. In another time, at another place, we could have been Ma and Pa Kettle, Mickey and Minnie.

I look at her and I can hear Spalding Gray's voice in "Swimming to Cambodia" when he said, "I wanted to be involved in this project more than any other project I'd almost been involved in."

THE KISS

The cliché is about having your heart ripped out. I can feel the muscle tearing, bleeding, bruising. My chest cage is tight and I'm having trouble breathing. My stomach is rolling like a longboat on the high seas. I can't get any oxygen while my lungs and guts are being spread all over the road. Meanwhile, I'm expected to backchat like Fred Astaire.

"I feel like a fat, middle-aged, crippled guy." I deliver the line with dignity. No pathos, no feeling sorry for myself. I'm just telling her where I'm at. Maybe I should run around the block, take off a couple of pounds.

"No. I'm attracted to you." She says this.

I go back to having trouble breathing. Should I start carrying oxygen?

She drops her lids and looks at her lap. Why do they always look at their fucking laps?

"Would you kiss me?" she asks, giving the illusion that it's a question.

I'm standing with one leg in the street and my left leg must have been on the other side of her on the driver's seat. You forget these details.

I start to give her a peck, but she pulls me toward her. This is the longest, slowest kiss in recorded history. It goes on and on, and on, and on, and on, and on, and on, and on, and on. My right arm is around her and I'm making feather circles around each of her vertebrae with a fingerprint. The cops drive by and flash a strobe light on us and hit the siren for a quick second. But it goes on, and on, and on.

I've given her a complete dental exam with my tongue. We'll dispense with the x-rays this time. I know that she's safe from breast cancer because I've practiced the breast exam until I'm ready to take my boards. I'm ready to open a practice for just this one patient. The underslope of her breast is soft beyond soft. I've touched a breast before but it was never like this. In fact I know they're going to send me to some locked ward treatment center because I can't stop.

I can't stop kissing her. Upper right neck. A millimeter to the right. Above and below, left and right of that. Each of her eyes. I kiss the base of each eyelash and where the lower lip joins the chin, and neck, and shoulders.

No big deal, we're just saying goodbye.

How long have I been standing here? An hour and a half? Two? Two and a half? When did we eat last? Should we take a break for sandwiches? If I never stop kissing her she might drop the final curtain.

Never in my life have I kissed lips whose only purpose is exploration. Touching my lower lip, my tongue, my nose—my God, my nose—with the sensitive flaccid membrane behind those thin lips. Where did this little girl learn this? I'm supposed to be older and experienced. Is this how a bronco feels at that moment when he understands that no way can he throw that rider off him? Am I being tamed? I've never been touched so tentatively, so sensually, so softly, with absolute confidence.

I put my hand behind her neck and kissing her, pull her toward me. I try to stick my head in her mouth, tongue first. My hand as slow as the ice age is moving back and forth on the inside of her thing. Her jeans are fashionably torn and I stick my ring finger inside the threads of the tear. I'm touching her knee as softly as I can. I pull my hand loose and start to stroke the inside of her leg. Her legs are small and beautiful and soft. Her jeans are frayed and torn, made smooth through wear and washing.

Her smell is as lovely as her touch.

I'm touching the back of her neck. The Japanese think the back of the neck is the spot. I watch her bending her head forward to receive. Maybe I am tamed. I only want to give her pleasure.

I'm touching her lips, her cheek, her eyes with my lips that I'm trying to make as gentle as butterfly wings when I realize that she can't feel my hands. Why are we doing this if she can't feel it? She kisses my neck, the inside of my right ear, behind my ear, my neck again, then she takes my hand off the inside of her leg.

"Sarah. What the hell's the difference if you can't feel it anyway?" I take my hand away and kiss her on the bridge of her nose. She kisses me back.

Maybe we should go the two blocks to her house, it would be good for my education. I've never seen a quad with her clothes off.

We have a rabbinical debate and take turns, each taking either side of the question. We should. We shouldn't. We should. We shouldn't.

"Sarah, what are you talking about? I though you wanted to explore your sexuality."

"No. I won't know when to stop."

> *I won't dance, why should I*
> *I won't dance, how could I*
> *I won't dance, merci beaucoup*
> *I know that music leads to way to romance*
> *So if I hold you in my arms, I won't dance*
> —Jerome Kern, Otto Harbach,
> Oscar Hammerstein II

ODYSSEUS

"I've always respected whatever you wanted."

"No, I can't. I know myself."

"OK. Whatever you say. Good night." I get in my car like I was taking off in the Indianapolis 500, pull a U-ey while she's still sitting in hers with the lights and motor off.

I stop my car in the middle of the street across from her. She rolls down her window and sticks her head out. "Are you going to sit there all night?" I ask.

"I'm trying to get myself together."

"How am I going to get myself together," I say, ever the sucker for a corny line.

Driving along the Mississippi River to the bridge the moon flickers on the black water.

Odysseus sailed by the sirens who sat and sang in a meadow heaped with the bones of sailors their beautiful voices had enchanted and drawn to their deaths. Circe told Odysseus the only way he could sail by and hear their songs unharmed was to have his crew bind him to the mast, then plug their own ears with beeswax.

Boychick and I are starting to cut the television documentary that's really about my disability and ten years of my life. Artistically it's what we've both been working for, for a long time. Bringing it to completion takes surgical concentration and the price of even a moment's distraction could be high.

The sea is rough, waves are pounding the hull, I hear the singing and know in my heart that getting bound to the mast just isn't going to be enough.

Bibliography

The Disability Studies Project of Hunter College

In general, books and articles were selected because they are based on a social/cultural/political model of disability. Other references were included which can be used as tools to further the understanding of how disability has been represented in various cultural products. These references were drawn from numerous sources and databases (e.g., social science, humanities, and education indexes).

The April 1995 bibliography will continue to evolve and we welcome your input in developing it further. It is by no means an exhaustive list. Please send references to: The Disability Studies Project, Hunter College, 1016 West, 695 Park Avenue, New York, NY 10021; phone 212–772–4723; fax 212–772–4941.[1]

Ablon, J. (1984). *Little People in America: The Social Dimensions of Dwarfism*. New York: Praeger.

Ablon. J. (1990). "Ambiguity and Difference: Families with Dwarf Children." *Social Science and Medicine*, 30(8), 879–887.

ACEI Publications. (1993). *Common Bonds: Anti-bias Teaching in a Diverse Society*. Wheaton, MD: ACEI Publications.

Ainlay, S., Becker, G., and Coleman, L. M. (Eds.). (1986). *The Dilemma of Difference: A Multidisciplinary View of Stigma*. New York: Plenum Press.

Albrecht, G. L. (1992). *The Disability Business: Political Economy of Rehabilitation in America*. Beverly Hills, CA: Sage Publications.

Albrecht, G. L., and Levy, J. A. (1984). "A Sociological Perspective of Physical Disability." In J. L. Rufini (Ed.), *Advances in Medical Social Science*, (45–106). New York: Gordon and Breach Science Publishers.

Anspach, R. R. (1979). "From Stigma to Identity Politics: Political Activism Among the Physically Disabled and Former Mental Patients." *Social Science and Medicine*, 13A, 765–773.

Armstrong, M. J. (1989). "International Cooperation in Rehabilitation: A Perspective on United States Activity." *Rehabilitation Education*, 3, 337–346.

Asch, A. (1984). "The Experience of Disability." *American Psychologist*, 39(5), 529–536.

Asch, A. (1986). "Will Populism Empower the Disabled?" *Social Policy*, 16(3), 12–18.

Asch, A., and Fine, M. (1988). "Shared Dreams: A Left Perspective on Disability Rights and Reproductive Rights." In M. Fine and A. Asch (Eds.), *Women with Disabilities: Essays in Psychology, Culture and Politics* (297–305). Philadelphia: Temple University Press.

Asch, A., and Sacks, L. H. (1983A). "Lives Without, Lives Within: Autobiographies of Blind Women and Men." *Journal of Visual Impairment and Blindness*, 77(6), 242–247.

Asch, A., and Sacks, L. H. (1983B). "Masking the Social in Educational Knowledge: The Case of Learning Disability Theory." *American Journal of Sociology*, 88, 948–974.

Atkin, K. (1991). "Health, Illness, Disability and Black Minorities: A Speculative Critique of Present Day Discourse." *Disability, Handicap and Society*, 6(1), 37–47.

Baird, J., and Workman, D. (Eds.). (1986). *Toward Solomon's Mountain: The Experience of Disability in Poetry*. Philadelphia: Temple University Press.

Barker, J. C. (1990). "Between Humans and Ghost: The Decrepit Elderly in a Polynesian Society." In J. Sokolovsky (Ed.), *The Cultural Context of Aging*. Westport: Bergin and Garvey.

Barnartt, S. and Christiansen, J. (1985). "The Socio-economic Status of Deaf Workers: A Minority Group Perspective." *Social Science Journal*, 22(4), 19–32.

Barnartt, S. N., and Seelman, K. (1988). "A Comparison of Federal Laws Toward Disabled and Racial/Ethnic Groups in the USA." *Disability, Handicap and Society*, 3(1), 37–48.

Bartoli, J. S. (1990). "On Defining Learning and Disability: Exploring the Ecology." *Journal of Learning Disabilities*, 23(10), 628–631.

Baynton, D. C. (1992). "A Silent Exile on this Earth: The Metaphorical Construction of Deafness in the Nineteenth Century." *American Quarterly*, 44(2), 216–243.

Baynton, D. C. (1996), *Forbidden Signs: American culture and the Campaign Against Sign Language*. Chicago: University of Chicago Press.

Begum, N. (1992). "Disabled Women and the Feminist Agenda." *Feminist Review*, 40, 3–6.

Benedict, R. (Ed.). (1934). "Anthropology and the Abnormal." *Journal of General Psychology*, 10(2).

Berkanovic, E. (1972). "Lay Conceptions of the Sick Role." *Social Forces*, 51, 53–64.

Berkowitz, E. D. (1979). *Disability Policies and Government Programs*. New York: Praeger.

Berkowitz, E. D. (1987). *Disabled Policy: America's Program for the Handicapped*. Cambridge: Cambridge University Press.

Berkowitz, E. D. (1991). *America's Welfare State: From Roosevelt to Reagan*. Baltimore, MD: John Hopkins University Press.

Berkowitz, W. D. (1979). "The American Disability System in Historical Perspective." In E. Berkowitz (Ed.), *Disability Policies and Government Programs*. New York: Praeger.

Berkson, G. (1970). "Defective Infant in a Feral Monkey Group." *Folia Primatology*, 12, 284–289.

Berkson, G. (1973). "Social Responses to Abnormal Infant Monkeys." *American Journal of Physical Anthropology*, 38, 583–586.

Best, E. (1905). "Maori Medical Lore." *Journal of the Polynesian Society*, 15, 3–25.

Best, E. (1906). "The Lore of the Whare Kohunga." *Journal of the Polynesian Society*, 15, 3–25.

Biklen, D. (1986). "Framed: Journalism's Treatment of Disability." *Social Policy*, 16(3), 45–51.

Biklen, D. (1987). "The culture of policy: Disability Images and their Analogues in Public Policy." *Policy Studies Journal*, 15, 515–533.

Biklen, D. (1988). "The Myth of Clinical Judgment." *Journal of Social Issues*, 44(1), 511–521.

Biklen, D. (1992). *Schooling Without Labels: Parents, Educators, and Inclusive Education*. Philadelphia: Temple University Press.

Biklen, D., and Bailey, L. (Eds.). (1981). *Rudely Stamp'd: Imaginal Disability and Prejudice*. Washington, DC: University Press of America.

Biklen, D., and Bogdan, R. (1977). "Media Portrayals of Disabled People: A Study in Stereotypes." *Interracial Books for Children Bulletin*, 8.6 and 7, 4–7.

Birdsell, J. D. (1972). *Human Evolution: An Introduction to the New Physical Anthropology*. Chicago: Rand McNally.

Blaxter, M. (1976). *The Meaning of Disability: A Sociological Study of Impairment*. London: Heinmann.

Bogdan, R. (1987). "The Exhibition of Humans with Differences for Fun and Profit." *Policy Studies Journal*, 15(3), 535–551.

Bogdan, R. (1988). *Freak Show: Presenting Human Oddities for Amusement and Profit*. Chicago: Chicago University Press.

Bodgan, R., Biklen, D., Shapiro, A., and Spelkoman, D. (1982). "The Disabled: Media's Monster." *Social Policy*, 138–141.

Bogdan, R., and Taylor, S. (1987). "Toward a Sociology of Acceptance: The Other Side of the Study of Deviance." *Social Policy*, 34–39.

Borsay, A. (1986). "Personal Trouble or Public Issue? Towards a Model of Policy for People with Physical and Mental Disabilities." *Disability, Handicap and Society*, 1(2), 179–195.

Bosk, C. L. (1992). *All God's Mistakes: Genetic Counseling in a Pediatric Hospital*. Chicago: University of Chicago Press.

Boutte, M. I. (1987). "The Stumbling Disease: A Case Study of Stigma Among Azorean-Portuguese." *Social Science and Medicine*, 24, 204–217.

Bowe, F. (1989). *Changing the Rules*. Silver Spring, MD: TJ Publications.

Boylan, E. R. (1991). *Women and Disability*. London: Zed Books.

Bragg, B. (1989). *Lessons in Laughter: The Autobiography of a Deaf Actor*. Washington, D.C.: Gallaudet University Press.

Braithwaite, D. O. (1990). "From Majority to Minority: An Analysis of Cultural Change from Ablebodied to Disabled." *International Journal of Intercultural Relations*, 14(4), 465–483.

Breslau, N. (1987). "Abortion of Defective Fetuses: Attitudes of Mothers of Congenitally Impaired Children." *Journal of Marriage and the Family*, 49(4), 839–845.

Brodsky, C. M. (1983). "Culture and Disability Behavior." *Western Journal of Medicine*, 139, 892–899.

Brooks, P. (1993). *Body Work: Objects of Desire in Modern Narrative*. Cambridge: Harvard University Press.

Brown, C. (1970). *Down All the Days*. New York: Stein and Day.

Brown, S. F. (1948). "General Semantics and Physical Disability." *Journal of Social Issues*, 4(4) Fall, 95–100.

Browne, S. E., Connors, D., and Stern, N. (Eds.). (1985). *With the Power of Each Breath: A Disabled Women's Anthology*. Pittsburgh, PA: Cleis Press.

Brueggemann, B. (1995). "The Coming Out of Deaf Culture and American Sign Language: An Exploration into Visual Literacy and Rhetoric," *Rhetoric Review* (Spring).

Bryson, L. (1992). *Welfare and the State: Who Benefits?* New York: St. Martin's Press.

Burgdorf, M. P., and Burgdorf, R. (1975). "A History of Treatment: The Qualifications of Handicapped Persons as a Suspect Class Under the Equal Protection Clause." *Santa Clara Lawyer*, 15, 855–910.

Burgdorf, R. L. (1991). "The ADA: Analysis and Implications of a Second Generation Civil Rights Statute." *Civil Liberties Law Review*, 26, 413–522.

Burgan, M. (1995). *Illness, Gender and Writing: The Case of Katherine Mansfield*. Baltimore, MD: Johns Hopkins University Press.

Burleigh, M. (1995). *Death and Deliverance: "Euthanasia in Germany c. 1900–1945*. New York: Cambridge University Press.

Byrd, E. K. (1989). "A Study of the Depiction of Specific Characteristics of Characters with Disability in Film." *Journal of Applied Rehabilitation Counseling*, 20(2), 43–45.

Callahan, J. (1989). *Don't Worry. He Won't Get Far on Foot: The Autobiography of a Dangerous Man*. New York: Vantage Books.

Camping, J. (1981). *Images of Ourselves: Women with Disabilities Talking*. Boston, MA: Routledge and Kegan Paul.

Carlin, M. F., Laughlin, J. L. and Saniga, R. D. (1991). *Understanding Abilities, Disabilities, and Capabilities: A Guide to Children's Literature*. Englewood, CO: Libraries Unlimited.

Carrier, J. G. (1983). "Masking the Social in Educational Knowledge: The Case of Learning Disability Theory." *American Journal of Sociology*, 88, 948–974.

Carrier, J. G. (1986). "Sociology and Special Education: Differentiation and Allocation in Mass Education." *American Journal of Education*, 94(3), 281–312.

Casanave, S. (1991). "A Community of Friends and Classmates." *Equity and Choice*, 8(1), 38–44.

Clement, D. C. (1982). "Samoan Folk Knowledge of Mental Disorders." In A. J. Marsella, and G. M. White (Eds.), *Cultural Conceptions of Mental health and Therapy* (193–213). Boston: Kluwer.

Cleve, J. V., and Crouch, J. (1989). *A Place of Their Own: Creating the Deaf Community in America*. Washington, DC: Gallaudet University Press.

Cloerkes, G., and Neubert, D. (1984). "Cross-cultural and Historical Variations of the Social Reaction Towards Disabled Persons." *International Journal of Rehabilitation Research*, 7(3), 339–340.

Cohen, S. and Taub, N. (Eds.). (1989). *Reproductive Laws for the 1990s*. Clifton, NJ: Humana Press.

Compton, T. (1992). *The Brief History of Disability (or The World Has Always Had Cripples)*. Berkeley: Hillegas.

Conrad, P., and Schneider, J. (1980). *Deviance and Medicalization: From Badness to Sickness.* St. Louis: C. V. Mosby and Company.

Corbett, J. and Barton, L. (1993). *A Struggle for Choice.* New York: Routledge.

Corbett, K. (1987). "The Role of Sexuality and Sex Equity in the Education of Disabled Women." *Peabody Journal of Education*, 64(4), 198–212.

Couser, G. T. (1997). *Recovering Bodies: Illness, Disability, and Lifewriting.* Madison: University of Wisconsin Press.

Crimp, D. (Ed.). (1988). *AIDS: Cultural Analysis, Cultural Activism.* Cambridge: MIT Press.

Cruickshank, W. M. (1948). "The Impact of Physical Disability on Social Adjustment." *Journal of Social Issues*, 4(4), 78–83.

Cumberbatch, G., and Negrine, R. (1991). *Images of Disability on Television.* London: Routledge.

Cunningham, K. (1989). "He Gets Around Pretty Good Once He Gets on a Horse." *Western Folklore*, 48(1), 58–61.

Cutsforth, T. D. (1948). "Personality Crippling Through Physical Disability." *Journal of Social Issues*, 4(4), 62–67.

Davis, F. (1961). "Deviance Disavowal: The Management of Strained Interaction by the Visibly Handicapped." *Social Problems*, 9, 120–132.

Davis, K. (1995). *Reshaping the Female Body: The Dilemma of Cosmetic Surgery.* New York: Routledge.

Davis, L. J. (1992). "The Mask of Benevolence: Disabling the Deaf Community." *The Nation*, (July 6), 25–27.

Davis, L. (1995). *Enforcing Normalcy: Disability, Deafness, and the Body.* London and New York: Verso.

Darling, R. B. (1979). *Families Against Society: A Study of Reactions to Children with Birth Defects.* Beverly Hills: Sage Library of Social Research.

Deegan, M. J. (1985). "Multiple Minority Groups: A Case Study of Physically Disabled Women." In M. J. Deegan and N. A. Brooks (Eds.), *Women and Disability: The Double Handicap.* New Brunswick, NJ: Transaction.

Deegan, M. J., and Brooks, N. A. (Eds.). (1985). *Women and Disability: The Double Handicap.* New Brunswick, NJ: Transaction.

Deegan, M. J. (1987). *Physically Disabled Women and New Directions in Public Policy.* Monticello, IL: Vance.

DeJong, G., and Lifchez, R. (1983). "Physical Disability and Public Policy." *Scientific American*, 248(6), 40–49.

DeJong, G. (1984). "Independent Living: From Social Movement to Analytic Paradigm." In: R. P. Marinelli and A. E. Dell Orto (Eds.), *The Psychological and Social Impact of Physical Disability.* New York: Springer.

Derrida, J. (1993). *Memoirs of the Blind: The Self-portrait and Other Ruins.* Chicago: University of Chicago Press.

De Silva, W. (1983). "Some Cultural and Economic Factors Leading to Abuse and Violence in Respect to Children Within the Family in Sri Lanka." *Child Abuse and Neglect*, 5, 391–405.

Deshen, S. (1982). *Blind People: The Private and Public Life of Sightless Israelis.* Albany: State University of New York Press.

Deutsch, H. (1996). *Resemblance and Disgrace: Alexander Pope and the Deformation of Culture.* Cambridge, MA: Harvard University Press.

Diamond, E. F. (1977). "The Deformed Child's Right to Life." In D. J. Horan and D. Mall (Eds.), *Death, Dying and Euthanasia.* Washington, DC: University Publications of America.

DiCarlo, L. M. (1964). *The Deaf.* Englewood Cliffs: Prentice-Hall.

Di Renzo, A. (1993). *American Gargoyles: Flannery O'Connor and the Medieval Grotesque.* Carbondale, IL: Southern Illinois University Press.

Dorris, M. (1989). *The Broken Cord.* New York: Harper and Row.

D. R. E. D. F. (1982). *No More Stares.* Berkeley: Disability Rights Education and Defense Fund.

Dreikurs, R. (1948). "The Socio-psychological Dynamics of Physical Disability: A Review of the Adlerian Concept." *Journal of Social Issues*, 4(4), 39–54.

Driedger, D. (1989). *The Last Civil Rights Movement: Disabled Peoples' International*. London: Hurst.

Driedger, D., and Gray, S. (1992). *Imprinting Our Image: An International Anthology by Women with Disabilities*. Charlottetown, PEI: Gynergy.

Duckitt, J. (1992). "Psychology and Prejudice: A Historical Analysis and Integrative Framework." *American Psychologist*, 47(10), 1182–1193.

Duff, R. S., and Campbell, A. G. M. (1973). "Moral and Ethical Dilemmas in the Special Care Nursery." *The New England Journal of Medicine*, 289, 890–894.

Durie, M. H. (1988). "A Maori View of Health, Disability, and Rehabilitation." *Rehabilitation in New Zealand*. Palmerston North: Massey University.

Edgerton, R. B. (1970). "Mental Retardation in Non-Western Societies: Toward a Cross-Cultural Perspective on Incompetence." In H. C. Haywood (Ed.), *Socio-cultural Aspects of Mental Retardation*. New York: Appleton-Century-Crafts.

Edgerton, R. B. (1976). *Deviance: A Cross-Cultural Perspective*. Menlo Park: Cummings.

Educational Equity Concepts (1984). *Building Community: A Manual Exploring Issues of Women and Disability*. New York: Educational Equity Concepts.

Eliott, T. R., Byrd, E. K., and Byrd, P. D. (1983). "An Examination of Disability as Depicted on Prime Time Television Programming." *Journal of Rehabilitation*, 49(3), 39–42.

Elks, M. A. (1993). "'The Lethal Chamber': Further Evidence for the Euthanasia Option." *Mental Retardation*, 31(4), 201–207.

Elmore, R. T. (Ed.). (1992). "Curriculum and Cash Notes." *Journal of Policy Analysis and Management*, 11(1), 167–173.

Epstein, J. (1995). *Altered Conditions: Disease, Medicine and Storytelling*. New York: Routledge.

Estroff, S. E. (1981). *Making it Crazy: An Ethnography of Psychiatric Clients in an American Community*. Berkeley: University of California Press.

Fedigan, L. M., and Fedigan, L. (1977). "The Social Development of a Handicapped Infant in a Free-living Troop of Japanese Monkeys." In S. Chevalier-Skolnikoff and F. E. Poirer (Eds.), *Primate Bio-social Development: Biological, Social and Ecological Determinants* (205–222). New York: Garland.

Ferguson, P. M., Ferguson, D. L. and Taylor, S. J. (Eds.). (1992). *Interpreting Disability: Qualitative Reader*. New York: Teachers College Press.

Fernandez, J. (1970). "Persuasions and Performances: Of the Beast in Everybody . . . and the Metaphors of Everyman." *Daedalus*, 101, 39–60.

Ferris, K. (1995). *James Joyce and the Burden of Disease*. UP of Kentucky.

Fiedler, L. (1978). *Freaks*. New York: Simon and Schuster.

Fine, M., and Asch, A. (1981). "Disabled Women: Sexism Without the Pedestal." *Journal of Sociology and Social Welfare*, 8(2), 233–248.

Fine, M., and Asch, A. (1988A). *Women with Disabilities: Essays in Psychology, Culture, and Politics*. Philadelphia: Temple University Press.

Fine, M., and Asch, A. (1988B). "Disability Beyond Stigma: Social Interaction, Discrimination, and Activism. *Journal of Social Issues*, 44(1), 3–21.

Finger, A. (1986). *Basic Skills*. Columbia: University of Missouri Press.

Finger, A. (1990). *Past Due: A Story of Disability, Pregnancy and Birth*. Seattle, WA: The Seal Press.

Finkelstein, V. (1980). *Attitudes and Disabled People: Issues for Discussion*. New York: World Rehabilitation Fund.

Fischlowitz, B. (1980). *I Live Here and I Am Not Handicapped, or Cultural Determinates of Disabilities in Micronesia*. Honolulu: University of Hawaii.

Florian, V. (1982). "Cross-Cultural Differences in Attitudes Towards Disabled Persons: A Study of Jewish and Arab Youth in Israel." *International Journal of Intercultural Relations*, 6, 291–299.

Florian, V., and Katz, S. (1983). "The Impact of Cultural, Ethnic, and National Variables on

Attitudes Towards the Disabled in Israel: A Review." *International Journal of Intercultural Relations*, 7, 167–179.

Florian, V., Weisel, A., Kravetz, S., and Shurka-Zernitsky, E. (1989). "Attitudes in the Kibbutz and City Towards Persons with Disabilities: A Multifactorial Comparison." *Rehabilitation Counseling Bulletin*, 32, 210–218.

Friedberg, J. B. (1985). *Accept Me As I Am.* New York: Bowker.

Friedberg, J. B. (1992). *Portraying Persons with Disabilities: An Annotated Bibliography of Nonfiction for Children and Teenagers* (2nd ed.). New Providence, NJ: R. R. Bowker.

Friedson, E. (1965). "Disability as Deviance." In M. Sussman (Ed.), *Sociology and Rehabilitation.* Washington, DC: American Sociological Association.

Foucault, M. (1975). *The Birth of the Clinic: An Archeology of Medical Perception.* New York: Vintage.

Foucault, M. (1979). *Discipline and Punish: The Birth of the Prison.* New York: Random House.

Foucault, M. (1980). *The History of Sexuality—Volume I: An Introduction.* New York: Vintage.

French-American Foundation (1995). *Parallel Views: Education and Access for Deaf People in France and the United States.* Washington: Gallaudet University Press.

Fulcher, G. (1989). *Disabling Policies: A Comparative Approach to Education, Policy and Disability.* New York: Falmer Press.

Gallagher, H. G. (1985). *FDR's Splendid Deception.* New York: Dodd Mead.

Gallagher, H. G. (1989). *By Trust Betrayed: Patients, Physicians, and the License to Kill in the Third Reich.* New York: Henry Holt.

Galler, R. (1989). "The Myth of the Perfect Body." In C. Vance (Ed.), *Pleasure and Danger.* Boston: Routledge and Kegan Paul.

Gannon, J. (1981). *Deaf Heritage: A Narrative History of Deaf America.* Silver Springs, MD: The National Association of the Deaf.

Gannon, J. (1989). *The Week the World Heard Gallaudet.* Washington, DC: Gallaudet University Press.

Gartner, A., and Lipsky, D. K. (1987). "Beyond Special Education: Toward a Quality System for all Students." *Harvard Educational Review*, 57(4), 367–395.

Gartner, A., and Joe, T. (Eds.). (1987). *Images of the Disabled: Disabling Images.* New York: Praeger.

Gelb, S. A. (1989). "Not Simply Bad and Incorrigible: Science, Morality, and Intellectual Deficiency." *History of Education Quarterly*, 29(3), 357–379.

Gerhardt, U. (1989). *Ideas About Illness: An Intellectual and Political History of Medical Sociology.* New York: New York University Press.

Gibson, D. E. (1984). "Symposium: Hospices." *Mental Retardation*, 22(4), 157–162.

Gill, C. J. (1985). "The Family/Professional Alliance in Rehabilitation Viewed From a Minority Perspective." *American Behavioral Scientist*, 28(3), 424–428.

Gilman, S. L. (1985). *Difference and Pathology: Stereotypes of Sexuality, Race and madness.* Ithaca: Cornell University Press.

Gilman, S. L. (1995). *Picturing Health and Illness: Images of Identity and Difference.* Baltimore: Johns Hopkins University Press.

Gilman, S. L. (1996). *Seeing the Insane.* Lincoln: University of Nebraska.

Gimp Power. (1986, November-December). *Disability Rag.*

Gliedman, J., and Roth, W. (1980). *The Unexpected Minority: Handicapped Children in America.* New York: Harcourt Brace Jovanovich.

Goffman, E. (1961). *Asylums.* Garden City: Anchor Books.

Goffman, E. (1963). *Stigma: Notes on the Management of Spoiled Identity.* Englewood Cliffs, NJ: Prentice-Hall.

Goode, D. (1994). *A World Without Words: The Social Construction of Children Born Deaf and Blind.* Philadelphia: Temple University Press.

Gould, S. J. (1981). *The Mismeasure of Man.* New York: W. W. Norton.

Gould, S. J. (1988, March). "Honorable Men and Women." *Natural History*, 16–20.

Groce, N. (1985). *Everyone Here Spoke Sign Language: Hereditary Deafness on Martha's Vineyard.* Cambridge: Harvard University Press.

Groce, N. (1992). *The U.S. Role in International Disability Activities: A History and Look Towards the Future*. Rehabilitation International, World Institute of Disability, and World Rehabilitation Fund.

Groce, N., and Scheer, J. (1990). "Introduction: Cross-cultural Perspectives on Disability." *Social Science and Medicine*, 30(8), v—vi.

Groddeck, G. (1977). *The Meaning of Illness: Selected Psychoanalytic Writings*. New York: International University Press.

Gwaltney, J. (1983). *Blindness as a Cultural Problem*. Working Papers in Anthropology. New York: Wenner-Gren Foundation.

Hahn, H. (1983). "Paternalism and Public Policy." *Society*, 20(March—April), 36–46.

Hahn, H. (1984). "Reconceptualizing Disability: A Political Science Perspective." *Rehabilitation Literature*, 45(11–12), 362–365, 374.

Hahn, H. (1985A). "Introduction: Disability Policy and the Problem of Discrimination." *American Behavioral Scientist*, 28(3), 293–318.

Hahn, H. (1985B). "Toward a Politics of Disability: Definitions, Disciplines and Policies." *Social Science Journal*, 22(4), 87–105.

Hahn, H. (1987A). "Civil Rights for Disabled Americans: The Foundation of a Political Agenda." In A. Gartner and T. Joe (Eds.). *Images of Disability, Disabling Images*. New York: Praeger.

Hahn, H. (1987B). "Advertising the Acceptably Employable Image: Disability and Capitalism." *Policy Studies Journal*, 15(3), 550–570.

Hahn, H. (1988). "Can Disability Be Beautiful?" *Social Policy*, 18(3), 26–31.

Hahn, H. (1989). "Disability and the Reproduction of Bodily Images: The Dynamics of Human Appearances." In J. Wolch and M. Dear (Eds.), *The Power of Geography: How Territory Shapes Social Life*. Boston: Homan.

Hahn, H. (1991). "Theories and Values: Ethics and Contrasting Perspectives on Disability." In R. P. Marinelli and A. E. Dell Orto (Eds.), *The Psychological and Social Impact of Disability* (3rd ed.). New York: Springer.

Halberstam, J. (1995). *Skin Shows: Gothic Horror and the Technology of Monsters*. Durham, N. C.: Duke University Press.

Haller, M. A. (1963, 1984). *Eugenics: Hereditarian Attitudes in American Thought*. New Brunswick, NJ: Rutgers University Press.

Hanks, J. R., and Hanks, L. M. (1948). "The Physically Handicapped in Certain Non-Occidental Societies." *Journal of Social Issues*, 4(4), 11–20.

Hanna, W. J., and Rogovsky, B. (1991). "Women with Disabilities: Two Handicaps Plus." *Disability, Handicap and Society*. 6(1), 49–63.

Haraway, D. (1989). *Primate Visions: Gender, Race, and Nature in the World of Modern Science*. London and New York: Routledge.

Hardman, M. L., and Drew, C. J. (1978). "Life Management Practices with the Profoundly Retarded: Issues of Euthanasia and Withholding Treatment." *Mental Retardation*, 16, 390–395.

Harris, J. I. (1981). "Ethical Problems in the Management of Some Severely Handicapped Children." *Journal of Medical Ethics*, 7, 117–120.

Heath, J. (1987). *Disability in the Pacific Islands*. Oaklands Park, Australia: McDonald-Heath.

Heineman, A. W. (Ed.). (1993). *Substance Abuse and Physical Disability*. Binghamton, NY: Haworth Press.

Hentig, H. (1948). "Physical Disability, Mental Conflict and Social Crisis." *Journal of Social Issues*, 4(4), 21–27.

Herndl, D. P. (1993). *Invalid Women: Figuring Feminine Illness in American Fiction and Culture 1840–1940*. Chapel Hill: University of North Carolina Press.

Herrera, H. (1983). *Frida: A Biography of Frida Kahlo*. New York: Harper and Row.

Hevey, D. (1992). *The Creatures Time Forgot: Photography and Disability Imagery*. New York: Routledge.

Hey, S. C., Kiger, G., and Seidel, J. (Eds.). (1984). *Social Aspects of Chronic Illness, Impairment and Disability*. Salem: Willamette University Press.

Higgins, P. (1992). *Making Disability: Exploring the Social Transformation of Human Variation.* Springfield: Charles C. Thomas.

Hillyer, B. (1993). *Feminism and Disability.* Norman, OK: University of Oklahoma Press.

Hine, R. V. (1993). *Second Sight.* Berkeley: University of California Press.

Hodge, F., and Edmonds, R. (1988). *Sociocultural Aspects of Disability: A Three Area Survey of Disabled American Indians.* Tucson, AZ: Native American Research and Training Center.

Hodges, D. J. (1984). *Sounds of a Quiet Revolution.* New York: Author.

Hofstakter, R. (1968). *Social Darwinism in American Thought,* (revised edition). Boston: Beacon Press.

Hubbard, R. (1990). *The Politics of Women's Biology.* New Brunswick: Rutgers University Press.

Hubbard, R., and Wald, E. (1993). *Exploding the Gene Myth: How Genetic Information is Produced and Manipulated by Scientists, Physicians, Employers, Insurance Companies, Educators and Law Enforcers.* Boston: Beacon Press.

Huber, J., and Schneider, B. E. (Eds.). (192). *The Social Context of AIDS.* Newbury Park, CA: Sage Publications.

Hudson, R. P. (1987). *Disease and Its Control: The Shaping of Modern Thoughts.* Westport, CO: Greenwood.

Huet, M. (1993). *Monstrous Imagination.* Cambridge: Harvard University Press.

Hughes, J. S. (1987). *The Letters of a Victorian Madman.* Columbia, SC: University of South Carolina Press.

Humphreys, T., and Paden, C. (1988). *Deaf in America: Voices From a Culture.* Cambridge, MA: Harvard University Press.

Huxley, J. (1941, August). "The Vital Importance of Eugenics." *Harper's Monthly,* 163, 324–331.

Ianacone, B. P. (1980). "Historical Overview: From Charity to Rights." In Phillips, W. R. F. and Rosenberg, J. (Eds.), *Changing Patterns of Law: The Courts and the Handicapped.* New York: Arno Press.

Illich, I. (1976). *Medical Nemesis: The Exploration of Health.* New York: Bantam.

Ingstad, B. (1988). "Coping Behavior of Disabled Persons and Their Families: Cross-Cultural Perspectives From Norway and Botswana." *International Journal of Rehabilitation Research,* 11(4), 351–359.

Jagues, M. E., Berleigh, D. L., and Lee, G. (1973). "Reactions to Disabilities in China: A Comparative, Structural and Descriptive Analysis." *Rehabilitation Counseling Bulletin,* 16, 206–217.

Joe, J., and Miller, D. L. (1987). *American Indian Perspectives on Disability.* Tucson, AZ: Native American Research and Training Center.

Johnson, M. (1987). "Emotion and Pride: The Search for a Disability Culture." *Disability Rag,* Jan-Feb, 8, 4–10.

Johnson, M., and Dikins, S. (Eds.). (1989). *Reporting on Disability: Approaches and Issues.* Louisville, KY: Advocado Press.

Johnson, R. A. (1983). "Mobilizing the Disabled." In J. Freeman (Ed.), *Social Movements of the Sixties and Seventies.* New York: Longman.

Johnson, W. G., and Lambrinos, J. (1987). "The Effect of Prejudice on the Wages of Disabled Workers." *Policy Studies Journal,* 15(3), 571–590.

Jones, E., Farina, A., Hastorf, A., Markus, H., Miller, D. and Scott, R. (1984). *Social Stigma: The Psychology of Marked Relationships.* New York: W. H. Freeman.

Jordan, S. (1971). "The Disadvantaged Group: A Concept Applicable to the Physically Handicapped." In E. Sagarin (Ed.), *The Other Minorities: Nonethnic Collectivities Conceptualized and Minority* (262–274). Waltham, MA: Ginn.

Kaplan, D. (1988). "Disability Rights Perspectives on Reproductive Technologies and Public Policy." In S. Cohen and N. Taub (Eds.), *Reproductive Laws for the 1990s* (241–247). Clifton, NJ: Humana Press.

Kassebaum, G., and Baumann, B. (1965). "Dimensions of the Sick Role in Chronic Illness." *Journal of Health and Human Behavior,* 6, 16–25.

Keller, E. F. (1985). *Reflections on Gender and Science*. New Haven: Yale University Press.

Kennedy, J. M. (1993). *Drawing and the Blind: Pictures to Touch*. New Haven: Yale University Press.

Kent, D. (1987). "Disabled Women: Portraits in Fiction and Drama." In A. Gartner and T. Joe (Eds.), *Images of the Disabled, Disabling Images* (47–64). New York: Praeger.

Kent, D. (1988). "In Search of a Heroine: Images of Women with Disabilities in Fiction and Drama." In M. Fine and A. Asch (Eds.), *Women with Disabilities* (90–110). Philadelphia: Temple University Press.

Kevles, D. J. (1985). *In the Name of Eugenics*. Berkeley: University of California Press.

Kevles, D. J., and Hood, L. (Eds.). (1992). *The Code of Codes: Scientific and Social Issues in the Human Genome Project*. Cambridge, MA: Harvard University Press.

Kleck, R., et al. (1966). "The Effect of Physical Deviance Upon Face-to-face Interaction." *Human Relations*, 19, 425–436.

Kleege, G. (1994). "Call It Blindness," *The Yale Review* 84 (2), 46–69.

Kleege, G. (1995). "Here's Looking at You," *The Southwest Review* 80 (22 & 23), 285–96.

Kleege, G. (1996). "Up Close, In Touch," *Raritan*. 16 (1), 54–77.

Kleinfield, S. (1979). *The Hidden Minority: A Profile of Handicapped Americans*. Boston: Little, Brown.

Koblas, L. E. (1988). *Disability Drama in Television and Film*. Jefferson, NC: McFarland.

Komlos, J. (1994). *Stature, Living Standards, and Economic Development: Essays on Anthropometric History*. Chicago: University of Chicago Press.

Kovic, R. (1976). *Born on the Fourth of July*. New York: McGraw Hill.

Krause, E. A. (1976). "The Political Sociology of Rehabilitation." In G. L. Albrecht (Ed.), *The Sociology of Physical Disability and Rehabilitation* (201–221). Pittsburgh: University of Pittsburgh Press.

Kriegel, L. (1964). *The Long Walk Home*. New York: Appleton-Century.

Kriegel, L. (1969). "Uncle Tom and Tiny Tim: Some Reflections on the Cripple as Negro." *The American Scholar*, 38.3, Summer, 412–430.

Kriegel, L. (1982). "The Wolf in the Pit in the Zoo." *Social Policy*, 13(2), 16–23.

Kriegel, L. (1987). "The Cripple in Literature." In A. Gartner and T. Joe (Eds.), *Images of the Disabled, Disabling Images* (31–46). New York: Praeger.

Kushel, R. (1973). "The Silent Inventor: The Creation of a Sign Language by the Only Deaf Mute on the Polynesian Island." *Sign Language*, 3, 1–28.

Lakoff, R. T. (1989). "Women and Disability." *Feminist Studies*, 15(2), 365–375.

Lakoff, R. T., and Scheer, R. L. (1984). *Face Value: The Politics of Beauty*. Boston: Routledge and Kegan Paul.

Lane, H. (1984). *When the Mind Hears: A History of the Deaf*. New York: Random House.

Lane, H. (1992). *The Mask of Benevolence: Disabling the Deaf Community*. New York: Knopf.

Laquer, T. (1990). *Making Sex: Body and Gender from the Greeks to Freud*. Berkeley: University of California Press.

Larson, L. (1983). "The Elephant Man." *Modern Drama*, 26(3), 335–336.

Lawrence, D. H. (1993). *Lady Chatterley's Lover: A Propos of Lady Chatterley's Lover*. Cambridge: Cambridge University Press.

Lazerson, M. (1983). "The Origins of Special Education." In J. G. Chambers and W. T. Hartman (Eds.), *Special Education Politics: Their History, Implementation, and Finance* (15–47). Philadelphia: Temple University Press.

Leder, D. (1990). *The Absent Body*. Chicago: The University of Chicago Press.

Lemert, E. M. (1962). "Stuttering and Social Structure in Two Pacific Societies." *Journal of Speech and Hearing Disorders*, 27, 3–10.

Levin, B. W. (1990). "International Perspectives on Treatment Choice in Neonatal Intensive Care Units." *Social Science and Medicine*, 30(8), 901–912.

Levine, P. L., Bruhn, J. G., and Turner, N. H. (1990). *The Psychosocial Aspects of AIDS: An Annotated Bibliography*. New York: Garland.

Levitin, T. E. (1975). "Deviants As Active Participants in the Labeling Process: The Visibly

Handicapped." *Social Problems*, 22, 548–557.

Lewontin, R. C., et al. (1984). *Not in our Genes: Biology, Ideology and Human Nature*. New York: Pantheon.

Liachowitz, C. H. (1988). *Disability as a Social Construct: Legislative Roots*. Philadelphia: Pennsylvania University Press.

Liggett, H. (1988). "Stars Are Not Born: An Interpretive Approach to the Politics of Disability." *Disability, Handicap and Society*, 3(3), 263–275.

Lifton, R. J. (1986). *The Nazi Doctors: Medical Killing and the Psychology of Genocide*. New York: Basic Books.

Linton, S. (1994). "Reshaping Disability in Teacher Education and Beyond." *Teaching Education*, 6(2), 9–20.

Longmore, P. (1985A). "Screening Stereotypes: Images of Disabled People." *Social Policy*, (Summer), 31–38.

Longmore, P. (1985B). "The Life of Randolph Bourne and the Need for a History of Disabled People." *Reviews in American History*, (December), 581–587.

Longmore, P. (1985C). "A Note on Language and the Social Identity of Disabled People." *American Behavioral Scientist*, 28(3), 419–423.

Longmore, P. (1985D, May 5). "'Mask': A Revealing Portrayal of the Disabled." *The Los Angeles Sunday Calendar*, 20–23.

Longmore, P. (1987A). "Uncovering the Hidden History of People with Disabilities." *Reviews in American History*, (September), 357–364.

Longmore, P. (1987B). "Screening Stereotypes: Images of Disabled People in Television and Motion Pictures." In A. Gartner and T. Joe (Eds.), *Images of the Disabled, Disabling Images* (65–78). New York: Praeger.

Lonsdale, S. (1990). *Women and Disability: The Experience of Physical Disability Among Women*. New York: St. martin's Press.

Lorde, A. (1985). *The Cancer Journals*. San Francisco, CA: Aunt Lute Books.

Lowrey, L. (1987). "Rehabilitation Relevant to Culture and Disability." *Journal of Visual Impairment and Blindness*, 81(4), 162–164.

Loyd, M. (1992). "Does She Boil Eggs? Toward a Feminist Model of Disability." *Disability, Handicap and Society*, 7(3), 207–221.

Luczak, R. (Ed.). (1993). *Eyes of Desire: A Gay and Lesbian Reader*. Boston: Alyson Publications.

MacDonald, M. (1981). *Mystical Bedlam: Madness, Anxiety and Healing in Seventeenth-century England*. Cambridge: Cambridge University Press.

MacKenzie, C. (1993). *Psychiatry for the Rich: A History of Ticehurst Private Asylum, 1792–1917*. New York: Routledge and Kegan Paul.

MacRae, D. G. (1975). "The Body and Social metaphor." In J. Benthall and T. Polhemus (Eds.), *The Body as a Medium of Expression* (57–73). New York: Dutton.

Mairs, N. (1986). "On Being a Cripple." *Plaintext: Essays*, 9–20, Tucson: University of Arizona Press.

Mairs, N. (1989). *Remembering the Bone House*. New York: Harper and Row.

Mairs, N. (1990). *Carnal Acts*. New York: HarperCollins.

Makas, E. (1988). "Positive Attitudes Toward Disabled People: Disabled and Nondisabled Person's Perspectives." *Journal of Social Issues*, 44, 49–61.

Mashow, J. L. (1979). "The Definition of Disability from the Perspective of Administration." In E. Berokowitz (Ed.), *Disability Policies and Government Programs*. New York: Praeger.

Mathews, J. (1992). *A Mother's Touch: The Tiffany Callo Story*. New York: Henry Holt.

Matthews, G. F. (1983). *Voices from the Shadows: Women with Disabilities Speak Out*. Toronto: Women's Educational Press.

Mazumdar, P. (1992). *Eugenics, Human Genetics and Human Failings*. New York: Routledge and Kegan Paul.

McCarthy, A. E. (1984). "Is Handicapped External to the Person and Therefore 'Man Made'?" *British Journal of Mental Subnormality*, 30(1), 3–7.

Messikomer, C. M. (1991). "A Social Anatomy of Disability." *Dissertation Abstracts International: The Humanities and Social Sciences*, 51(10), April, 3523-A—3524-A.

Meyerson, L. (1948). "Experimental Injury: An Approach to the Dynamics of Disability." *The Journal of Social Issues*, 4(4),68–71.

Meyerson, L. (1948). "Physical Disability as a Social Psychological Problem." *Journal of Social Issues*, 4(4), 95–100.

Meyerson, L. (1988). "The Social Psychology of Physical Disability: 1948 and 1988." *The Journal of Social Issues*, 44(1), 173–188.

Mezey, S. G. (1988). *No Longer Disabled: The Federal Courts and the Politics of Social Security Disability*. New York: Greenwood.

Milam, L. W. (1984). *The Cripple Liberation Front Marching Band Blues*. San Diego: Mho and Mho Works.

Miller, J. (Ed.) (1992). *Fluid Exchanges: Artists and Critics in the AIDS Crisis*. Toronto: University of Toronto Press.

Minnich, E. K. (1990). *Transforming Knowledge*. Philadelphia: Temple University Press.

Minnow, M. (1990). *Making All the Difference: Inclusion, Exclusion and American Law*. Ithaca, NY: Cornell University Press.

Mitchell, D. (1997)."Invisible Bodies and Corporeal Difference," *Minnesota Review* (forthcoming).

Mitchell, D and S. Snyder (1997). *Discourses of Disability: The Body and Physical Difference in the Humanities*. Ann Arbor: University of Michigan Press.

Morris, D. B. (1991). *The Culture of Pain*. Berkeley: University of California Press.

Mudrick, N. (1983). "Disabled Women." *Society*, 20(3), 52–55.

Murphy, R. (1987). *The Body Silent*. New York: Henry Holt.

Murphy, R. F., Scheer, J., Murphy, Y., and Mack, R. (1988). "Physical Disability and Social Liminality: A Study in the Rituals of Adversity." *Social Science and Medicine*, 26(2), 235–242.

Nelkin, D., and Tancridi, L. (1990). *Dangerous Diagnostics: The Social Power of Biological Information*. New York: Basic Books.

Nolan, C. (1989). *Under the Eye of the Clock: The Life Story of Christopher Nolan*. New York: Doubleday.

Norden, M. F. (1994). *The Cinema of Isolation: A History of Physical Disability in the Movies*. New Brunswick: Rutgers University Press.

Oliver, M. (1986). "Social Policy and Disability: Some Theoretical Issues." *Disability, Handicap and Society*, 1(1), 5–17.

Oliver, M. (1992). "Changing the Social Relations of Research Production." *Disability, Handicap and Society*, 7, 101–114.

Osius, A. (1991). *Second Ascent: The Story of Hugh Herr*. Harrisburg, PA: Stackpole Books.

O'Toole, C. J., and Bregante, J. L. (1992). "Lesbians with Disabilities." *Sexuality and Disability*, 10, 163–172.

Owen, M. J. (1987). "Welcome to the Post Harris Poll World: The Reality of Emerging Minority Mindset." *Disability Studies Quarterly*, 7(1), 1–3.

Padden, C., and Humphries, T. (1988). *Deaf in America: Voices from a Culture*. Cambridge: Harvard University Press.

Parsons, T. (1951). *The Social System*. New York: The Free Press.

Pastore, J. L. (Ed.). (1993). *Confronting AIDS Through Literature: The Responsibilities of Representation*. Champaign: University of Illinois Press.

Percy, S. L. (1990). *Disability, Civil Rights and Public Policy: The Politics of Implementation*. Tuscaloosa: University of Alabama Press.

Pfeiffer, D. (1991). "The Influence of the Socio-economic Characteristics of Disable People on their Employment Status and Income." *Disability, Handicap and Society*, 6(2), 103–114.

Phillips, M. J. (1985A). "'Try Harder': The Experience of Disability and the Dilemma of Normalization." *Social Science Journal*, 22(4), 45–47.

Phillips, M. J. (1985B). "Disability and Ethnicity in Conflict: A Study in Transformation." In

A. Asch and M. Fine (Eds.), *Disabled Women: Psychology From the Margins.* Philadelphia: Temple University Press.

Phillips, M. J. (1988). "Disability and Conflict: A Study in Transformations." In M. Fine and A. Asch (Eds.), *Women with Disabilities: Essays in Psychology, Culture, and Politics,* (195–214). Philadelphia: Temple University Press.

Phillips, M. J. (1990). "Damaged Goods: Oral narratives of the Experience of Disability in American Culture." *Social Science and Medicine,* 30(8), 849–857.

Phillips, W. R., and Rosenberg, J. (Eds.). (1980). *Changing Patterns of Law: The Courts and the handicapped.* New York: Ayer.

Porter, R. (1987). *Mind-forg'd Manacles: A History of Madness in England from the Restoration to the Regency.* London: The Athlone Press.

Post, J. M., and Robins, R. S. (1990, June). "The Captive King and his Captive Court: The Psychopolitical Dynamics of the Disabled Leader and his Inner Circle." [Annual Conference of the American Political Science Association (1987, Chicago, Illinois)]. *Political Psychology,* 11(2), 331–351.

Post, J. M., and Robins, R. S. (1993). *When Illness Strikes the Leader: The Dilemma of the Captive King.* New Haven: Yale University Press.

Powell, T. H., Aiken, J. M., and Smylie, M. A. (1982). "Treatment or Involuntary Euthanasia for Severely Handicapped Newborns: Issues of Philosophy and Public Policy." *TASH Journal,* 6, 3–10.

Proctor, R. (1988). *Racial Hygiene: Medicine Under the Nazis.* Cambridge: Harvard University Press.

Quart, L., and Auster, A. (1982). "The Wounded Vet in Postwar Film." *Social Policy,* Fall, 24–31.

Quicke, J. C. (1988). "Speaking Out: The Political Career of Helen Keller." *Disability Handicap and Society,* 3(2), 167–171.

Radley, A. (Ed.). (1993). *Worlds of Illness: Biographical and Cultural Perspectives on Health and Disease.* New York: Routledge.

Reilly, P. R. (1991). *The Surgical Solution: A History of Involuntary Sterilization in the United States.* Baltimore, MD: Johns Hopkins University Press.

Reiter, S., Mar'i, S., and Rosenberg, Y. (1986). "Parental Attitudes Towards the Developmentally Disabled Among Arab Communities in Israel: A Cross-cultural Study." *International Journal of Rehabilitation Research,* 9(4), 335–362.

Richardson, S. (1961). "Cultural Uniformity in Reaction to Physical Disabilities." *American Sociology Review,* 26, 241–247.

Ricks, C. (1989). "Wiseman's Witness." *Grand Street,* 8(2), 160–171.

Robertson, J. A. (1978). "Legal Issues in Nontreatment of Defective Newborns." In C. A. Swinard (Ed.), *Decision Making and the Defective Newborn.* Springfield: Charles C. Thomas.

Rosenberg, C. E. (1986). "Disease and Social Order in America." *The Milbank Quarterly,* 64, suppl. I.

Rosenberg, C. E., and Golden, J. (Eds.). (1992). *Framing Disease: Studies in Cultural History.* New Brunswick: Rutgers University Press.

Ross, J. A. (1983). "An Anthropological View of the Change in Attitudes Toward Mental Illnesses and Physical Handicaps." *History and Social Science Teacher,* 18(3), 135–140.

Roth, W. (1983). "Handicap as a Social Construct." *Society,* 20(3), 56–61.

Rothman, D. (1971). *The Discovery of the Asylum: Social Order and Disorder in the New Republic.* Boston: Little, Brown.

Rothman, D., and Rothman, S. (1984). *The Willowbrook Wars: A Decade of Struggle for Social Justice.* New York: HarperCollins.

Rousselot, J. (Ed.). (1966). *Medicine in Art: A Cultural History.* New York: McGraw Hill.

Rousso, H. (Ed.). (1988). *Disabled, Female and Proud! Stories of Ten Women with Disabilities.* Boston: Exceptional Parent Press.

Rubenfeld, P. (1993). "The More Things Change, The More They Stay the Same: A Call for a New Drive to Integrate Students with Disabilities." *Journal of Disability Policy Studies,* 4(1).

Russo, M. (1995). *The Female Grotesque: Risk, Excess and Modernity*. New York: Routledge.

Sacks, O. (1989). *Seeing Voices: A Journey into the World of the Deaf*. Berkeley: University of California Press.

Sacks, O. (1992, May 10). "A Neurologist's Notebook: To See and Not See." *The New Yorker*, 85–94.

Samuelson, D. (1986). "A Letter to My Daughter/myself: On Facing the Collective Fear of Being Different." *Feminist Studies*, 12, 156–168.

Sarason, S. B. (1993). *The Case for Change: Rethinking the Preparation of Educators*. San Francisco: Jossey-Bass.

Saxton, M. (1988). *Prenatal Screening and Discriminatory Attitudes About Disabilities*. New York: Harrington Park Press.

Saxton, M., and Howe, F. (Eds.). (1987). *With Wings: An Anthology of Literature by and About Women with Disabilities*. New York: The Feminist Press at the City University of New York.

Scheff, T. J. (1984). *Being Mentally Ill: A Sociological Theory*. New York: Aldine.

Schein, J. D. (1986). *The Deaf Jew in the Modern World*. Katv Publishing House.

Schein, J. D. (1989). *At Home Among Strangers*. Washington, DC: Gallaudet University Press.

Scheer, J. (1984). "They Act Like It Was Contagious." In S. C. Hey, G. Kiger, and J. Seidel (Eds.), *Social Aspects of Chronic Illness, Impairment and Disability* (62–69). Salem: Willamette University Press.

Scheer, J., and Groce, N. (1988). "Impairment as a Human Constant: Cross-cultural Perspectives on Variation." *Journal of Social Issues*, 44(1), 23–37.

Schlissel, L. (Ed.). (1965). *The World of Randolph Bourne*. New York: Dutton.

Schwartz, D. B. (1992). *Crossing the River: Creating a Conceptual Revolution in Community and Disability*. Brookline Books.

Schuchman, J. (1988). *Hollywood Speaks: Deafness and the Film Entertainment Industry*. Urbana: University of Illinois Press.

Scotch, R. (1984). *From Good Will to Civil Rights: Transforming Federal Disability Policy*. Philadelphia: Temple University Press.

Scotch, R. (1988). "Disability as the Basis for a Social Movement: Advocacy and the Politics of Definition." *Journal of Social Issues*, 44(1), Spring, 159–172.

Scotch, R. (1989). "Politics and Policy in the History of the Disability Rights Movement." *Milbank Quarterly*, 67 (suppl. 1.2 part 2), 380–400.

Scott, R. A. (1979). *The Making of Blind Men: A Study of Adult Socialization*. New York: Russell Sage Foundation.

Searer, A. (1981). *Disability: Whose Handicap?*. Oxford: Blackwell.

Self, P. (Ed.). (1984). *Physical Disability: An Annotated Literature Guide*. New York: Dekker.

Shapiro, J. (1993). *No Pity: People with Disabilities Forging a New Civil Rights Movement*. New York: Times Books/Random House.

Shuman, M. (1980). "The Sounds of Silence in Noyha: A Preliminary Account of Sign Language Use by the Deaf in a Maya Community in Yucatan, Mexico." *Language Sciences*, 2, 144–173.

Sibley, A. (1986). "Altered Images." *Plays and Players*, 397, 8–11.

Silvers, A. (In press). "Reconciling Equality to Difference: Caring (f)or Justice for People with Disabilities." *Hypatia*.

Simon, B. (1988). "Never-married Old Women and Disability: A Majority Experience." In M. Fine and A. Asch (Eds.), *Women with Disabilities: Essays in Psychology, Culture, and Politics* (215–225). Philadelphia: Temple University Press.

Sleeter, C. E. (1986). "Learning Disabilities: The Social Construction of a Special Education Category." *Exceptional Child*, 53(1), 46–54.

Sleeter, C. E., and Grant, C. A. (1987). "An Analysis of Multicultural Education in the United States." *Harvard Educational Review*, 57(4), 421–444.

Sleeter, C. E., and Grant, C. A. (1991). "Race, Class, Gender and Disability in Current Textbooks." In L. K. Christian-Smith (Ed.), *The Politics of the Textbook* (56–77). New York: Routledge, Chapman and Hall.

Sobsey. (1991). *Disability, Sexuality and Abuse: An Annotated Bibliography.* Baltimore, MD: P H. Brooks.

Solecki, R. (1971). *Shanidar: The First Flower People.* New York: Knopf.

Sontag, S. (1978). *Illness as Metaphor.* New York: Farrar, Straus and Giroux.

Sontag, S. (1989). *AIDS and Its Metaphors.* New York: Farrar, Straus and Giroux.

Squires, M. (1983). *The Creation of Lady Chatterley's Lover.* Baltimore, MD: Johns Hopkins University Press.

Stewart, J. (1989). *The Body's Memory.* New York: St. Martin's Press.

Stone, D. A. (1984). *The Disabled State.* Philadelphia: Temple University Press.

Sullivan, E. J. (1975). "Ribera's Clubfooted Boy: Image and Symbol." *Marsyas,* 19, 17–21.

Szasz, T. S. (1974). *The Myth of Mental Illness: Foundations of a Theory of Personal Conduct.* New York: HarperCollins.

Szasz, T. S. (1990). *Insanity: The Idea and Its Consequences.* New York: Wiley.

Szasz, T. (1991). *Ideology and Insanity: Essays on the Psychiatric Dehumanization of Man.* Syracuse, NY: Syracuse University Press.

Tate, D. G., and Weston, N. H. (1982). "Women and Disabilities: An International Perspective." *Rehabilitation Literature,* 43(7–8), 222–227, 272.

Tavris, C. (1992). *Mismeasure of Woman.* New York: Simon and Schuster.

TenBroek, J. (1966). "The Right to Live in the World: The Disabled in the Law of Torts." *California Law Review,* 44, 841–919.

√ Thompson-Hoffman, S., and Storck, I. F. (1990). *Disability in the United States: A Portrait From National Data.* New York: Springer.

Thomson, R. G. (1990). "Speaking About the Unspeakable: The Representation of Disability as Stigma in Toni Morrison's Novels." *Courage and Tools: The Florence Howe Award for Feminist Scholarship 1974–1989.* New York: Modern Language Association.

Thomson, R. G. (1994). "Redrawing the Boundaries of Feminist Disability Studies." *Feminist Studies* 20, Fall, 583–595.

Thomson, R. G. (1996). *Freakery: Cultural Spectacles of the Extraordinary Body.* New York: New York University Press.

Thomson, R. G. (1997). *Extraordinary Bodies: Figuring Disability in American Culture and Literature.* New York: Columbia University Press.

Thurer, S. (1980). "Disability and Monstrosity: A Look at Literary Distortions of Handicapping Conditions." *Rehabilitation Literature,* 41(1–2), 12–15.

Tietze-Contrat, E. (1957). *Dwarfs and Jesters in Art.* London: Phaidon.

Todd, A. D. (1984). "Women and the Disabled in Contemporary Society." *Social Policy,* 14(4), 44–46.

Todd, D. (1995). *Imagining Monsters: Miscreations of the Self in Eighteenth-Century England.* Chicago and London: University of Chicago Press.

Tomlinson, R. (1982). *Disability, Theatre and Education.* Bloomington: Indiana University Press.

Treichler, P. (1988). "AIDS, Homophobia, and Biomedical Discourse: An Epidemic of Signification." In D. Crimp (Ed.), *AIDS: Cultural Analysis/Cultural Activism.* Cambridge, MA: MIT Press.

Trinkhaus, E., and Shipman, P. (1993). *The Neanderthals: Changing the Image of Mankind.* New York: Knopf.

Turner, B. (1984). *The Body and Society.* New York: Blackwell.

Tyor, P. L., and Bell, L. V. (1984). *Caring for the Retarded in America: A History.* Westport, CT: Greenwood Press.

Usborne, C. (1992). *The Politics of the Body in Weimar German: Women's Reproductive Rights and Duties.* Ann Arbor: University of Michigan Press.

Vance, C. S. (1990). *Pleasure and Danger.* Boston: Routledge and Kegan Paul.

Van Cleve, J. V. (1993). *Deaf History Unveiled: Interpretations From the New Scholarship.* Washington, DC: Gallaudet University Press.

Van Cleve, J., and Crouch, B. (1989). *A Place of Their Own: Creating the Deaf Community in America.* Washington, DC: Gallaudet University Press.

Verma, G. K. (1993). *Inequality and Teacher Education: An International Perspective.* New York: Falmer Press.

Vernon, M., and Mackowsky, B. (1969). "Deafness and Minority Group Dynamics." *The Deaf American,* 21, 3–6.

Vice, J. (1993). *From Patients to Persons: They Psychiatric Critiques of Thomas Szasz, Peter Sedgwick, and R. D. Laing.* New York: Peter Lang.

Waxman, B. F. (1991A). "Protecting Reproductive Health and Choice." *Rehabilitation Medicine,* 154, 629.

Waxman, B. F. (1991B). "Hatred: The Unacknowledged Dimension in Violence Against Disabled People." *Sexuality and Disability,* 9(3), 185–199.

Wehman, Paul. (1993). *The ADA Mandate for Social Change.* Baltimore, MD: Paul H. Brookes.

Weinberg, N. (1988). "Another Perspective: Attitudes of People with Disabilities." In H. E. Yuker (Ed.). *Attitudes Towards People with Disabilities,* (141–153). New York: Springer.

Weiner, F. (1986). *No Apologies.* New York: St. Martin's Press.

Weitz, R. (1987). "The Interview as Legacy: A Social Scientist Confronts AIDS." *Hastings Center Report,* 17(3), June, 21–23.

Wendell, S. (1989). "Toward a Feminist Theory of Disability." *Hypatia,* 4(2), Summer, 104–126.

Wertlieb, E. C. (1985). "Minority Group Status of the Disabled." *Human Relations* 38(11), 1047–1063.

West, J. (1991). *The Americans With Disabilities Act: From Policy to Practice.* New York: Milbank Memorial Fund.

Wendell, S. (1996). *The Rejected Body: Feminist Philosophical Reflections on Disability.* New York: Routledge.

Wills, D. (1995). *Prosthesis.* Stanford: Stanford University Press.

Wolfensberger, W. (1972). *The Principle of Normalization in Human Services.* Toronto: National Institute on Mental Retardation.

Wolfensberger, W. (1975A). "Reflection of Foucault's Insights Into the Nature of Deviancy and Our Residential Institutions." *Mental Health,* 23(2), 21–22.

Wolfensberger, W. (1975B). *The Origin and Nature of Our Institutional Models.* Syracuse, NY: Human Policy Press.

Wolfensberger, W. (1981). "The Extermination of Handicapped People in World War II Germany." *Mental Retardation,* 19(1), 15–17.

Wolfensberger, W. (1982). "The Important of Social Imagery in Interpreting Societally Devalued People to the Public." *Rehabilitation Literature,* 43(11–1), 356–358.

Wolfensberger, W. (1984). "Hospice and the New Devaluation of Human Life-reflections." *Mental Retardation,* 22(4), 166–168.

Wright, B. (1988). "Attitudes and the Fundamental Negative Bias: Conditions and Corrections." In H. Yuker (Ed.), *Attitudes Toward Persons with Disabilities* (3–21). New York: Springer.

Young, I. M. (1990). *Justice and the Politics of Difference.* Princeton, NJ: Princeton University Press.

Ziegler, C. R. (1980). *The Image of the Physically handicapped in Children's Literature.* New York: Arno Press.

Zola, I. K. (1982). *Missing Pieces; A Chronicle of Living with a Disability.* Philadelphia: Temple University Press.

Zola, I. K. (1983). "Medicine As an Institution of Social Control." In I. K. Zola (Ed.), *Sociomedical Inquiries* (247–268). Philadelphia: Temple University Press.

Zola, I. K. (1985). "Depictions of Disability: Metaphor, Message, and Medium in the Media: A Research and Political Agenda." *The Social Science Journal,* 22(4), 5–17.

Zola, I. K. (1987). "The Portrayal of Disability in the Crime Mystery Genre." *Social Policy,* 17(4), 34–39.

Zola, I. K. (1991). "Bringing Our Bodies and Ourselves Back In: Reflections on Past, Present and Future Medical Sociology." *Journal of Health and Social Behavior,* 32, 1–16.

Zola, I. K. (1992). "The Politics of Disability." *Disability Studies Quarterly,* 12(3) Summer.

SELECTED JOURNALS WITH ISSUES DEVOTED
TO VARIOUS TOPICS IN DISABILITY STUDIES

Journal of Social Issues, 4(4) 1948
Journal of Social Issues, 44(1) 1988
The Minnesota Review, ns40, Spring/Summer 1993—The Politics of AIDS
Policy Studies Journal, 21(4), 1993—Disability Issues in Public Policy

AND JOURNALS/MAGAZINES WORTH EXAMINING ANYTIME

The Disability Rag and Resource
Disability and Society
Disability Studies Quarterly

NOTE

1. Additions to this bibliography have been made by the editor for *The Disability Studies Reader*.

Contributors

Adrienne Asch is professor of social psychology and reproductive ethics at Wellsley College. She is co-editor of *Women With Disabilities: Essays in Psychology, Culture and Politics*.

Douglas C. Baynton is Visiting Assistant Professor of History and American Sign Language at the University of Iowa. He is the author of *Forbidden Signs: American Culture and the Campaign Against Sign Language* (University of Chicago Press, 1996).

H. Dirksen L. Bauman is an English instructor at the National Technical Institute for the Deaf/ Rochester Institute of Technology. He is currently working on his dissertation on American Sign Language poetry at Binghamton University (State University of New York). He has published various articles and presented papers on ASL literature.

Bradley Berens is currently finishing his dissertation on the relationship between source study and reception theory in Shakespeare; he teaches in the Department of English at the University of California at Berkeley.

Lerita M. Coleman teaches psychology at the University of Michigan.

Lennard Davis teaches disability studies, cultural studies, and literature at Binghamton University (State University of New York). He is a founding member of the Modern Language Association's standing committee on the status of academics with disabilities and disability studies in the humanities, has written about disability for *The Nation* and *The New York Times*, and is the author of *Enforcing Normalcy: Disability, Deafness, and the Body* (Verso) as well as other books on politics and the novel. He is an active member of CODA (Children of Deaf Adults).

Jennifer Drake is a graduate student at Binghamton University (State University of New York) completing her doctoral dissertation on arts activism and multiculturalism.

Martha Edwards is an assistant professor at Northeast Missouri State University where she teaches courses about the ancient world.

Michelle Fine is professor of psychology at the City University of New York, Graduate Center and the Senior Consultant at the Philadelphia Schools Collaborative. Her recent publications include *Chartering Urban School Reform: Reflection on Public High Schools in the Midst of Change* (1994), *Beyond Silenced Voices: Class, Race, and Gender in*

American Schools (1992), *Disruptive Voices: The Transgressive Possibilities of Feminist Research*, and *Framing Dropouts: Notes on the Politics of an Urban High School* (1991) She was awarded the Janet Helms Distinguished Scholar Award 1994.

Anne Finger's most recent book is a novel, *Bone Truth* (Coffee House Press). She teaches creative writing at Wayne State University in Detroit, where she lives with her son Max.

Kenny Fries received the Gregory Kolovakos Award for AIDS Writing for *The Healing Notebooks* (Open Books, 1990). He is the author of *Body Remember: A Memoir* and editor of *Staring Back: An Anthology of Writers with Disabilities*, which are forthcoming from Dutton. *Anesthesia*, a book of poems, is forthcoming from The Avocado Press. He teaches in the MFA in Writing Program at Goddard College and lives with the painter Kevin Wolff in Northampton, Massachusetts.

Erving Goffman (1922–83) was professor of sociology at the University of California at Berkeley and the University of Pennsylvania. Of his many books on social interaction the best known is *Presentation of Self in Everyday Life*.

Billy Golfus is a writer and filmmaker. His recent film "When Billy Broke His Head . . . and other tales of wonder" has received wide acclaim and was broadcast nationally on PBS. He has written for *Mouth*, *The Disability Rag*, *Seventeen*, and other publications.

Harlan Hahn is a professor of political science at the University of Southern California. He is the author of numerous books and articles on disability.

David Hevey is a disabled person and an issue-based photographer. His clients range from the United Nations, to *Time Life* to the Disability Movement. He lives in London.

Ruth Hubbard teaches biology at Harvard University and is the author of *The Politics of Women's Biology*.

Harlan Lane is Distinguished University Professor at Northeastern University,, Research Associate at the Massachusetts Institute of Technology, and Lecturer at Harvard University Medical School. He is the author of numerous articles in professional journals concerning speech, hearing,and deafness, and of several books, among them, *The Wild Boy of Aveyron*, *Foundations of Special Education*, *When the Mind Hears: A History of the Deaf*, and *The Mask of Benevolence: Disabling the Deaf Community*.

David Mitchell is chair of English graduate studies at Northern Michigan University. He has published essays on contemporary American women writers of color and co-directed a feature-length documentary on disability and the arts entitled *Vital Signs: Crip Culture Talks Back*. He is also one of the founders of the Modern Language Association standing committee on the status of academics with disabilities. Currently he is editing a volume of essays tentatively entitled *Storylines and Lifelines: Disability Studies in the Humanities*.

Nicholas Mirzoeff is assistant professor of art history at the University of Wisconsin,

Madison. He is the author of *Bodyscapes* and *Silent Poetry: Deafness, Sign, and Visual Culture in Modern France*.

Jennifer Nelson completed her Ph. D. at the University of California at Berkeley and teaches in the Department of English at Gallaudet University.

Susan Sontag is the author of numerous novels and essays including *Against Interpretation, On Photography, Death Kit* and *The Volcano Lover* as well as the *Illness as Metaphor* and *Aids and Its Metaphors*, from which the excerpt in this anthology was taken.

Rosemarie Garland Thomson is assistant professor of English at Howard University in Washington, D. C. Her essays on disability in literature and culture appear in *American Literature, Feminist Studies*, and *Radical Teacher*. She is the author of *Exceptional Bodies: Figuring Physical Disability in American Literature and Culture* and the editor of *Freakery: Cultural Spectacles of the Extraordinary Body*.

Julia/dolphin Trahan is a crippled, queer Hawaiian haole living in San Francisco. She earned her B. A. in Media Theory at Antioch College in Yellow Springs, Ohio. She manages BUILD, a community-based gallery/performance space and produces theatrical extravaganzas that blur cultural lines of race, class, disability and gender. She is an active member of the Corporation for Disabilities and Telecommunications as well as Wry Crips Disabled Women's Theatre. "Queen of the Girls" was taken from performance script of the same name. Contact Pamela Walker, Booking Agent: tel. (510) 549–2209 or FAX (510) 451–2050. Other writings can be found in *Virgin Territory 2, Queer Looks, Frighten the Horses, Sinister Wisdom,* and *Mouth: the Voice of Disability Rights*.

Sanjeev Kumar Uprety has taught literary theory and criticism at Tribhuvan University, Kathmandu, Nepal. His novel *Potato, Butter, and Coffee* was published in 1993 in Nepal, and he has translated Nepalese short stories into English. He is currently a Fulbright recipient pursuing graduate studies at Brown University.

Cheryl Wade is the recipient of the 1994 National Endowment for the Arts Solo Theater Artist's Fellowship and the CeCe Robinson Award for disability writing and performing. Her latest show, *Sassy Girl: Memoirs of a Poster Child Gone Awry* was featured in the Mark Taper Forum's 1994/95 New Work Festival. She writes a regular feature for *The Disability Rag* called "Culture Rap."

Susan Wendell is associate professor of women's studies at Simon Fraser University. She expanded the ideas in the essay published in this book into *The Rejected Body: Feminist Philosophical Reflections on Disability* (New York: Routledge, 1996). She has lived with Myalgic Encephalomyelitis, also called Chronic Fatigue Immune Dysfunction Syndrome, since 1985.

Margret A. Winzer is associate professor in the faculty of education at the University of Lethbridge, Alberta, Canada.

Index